Political Economy of Stateb

'This is an important book because it focuses on the most critical and, sadly, often-neglected aspect of statebuilding – the political dimension. The high-quality essays in this volume not only illuminate statebuilding cases and practices, they also make a compelling case that shaping political economies and fostering political settlements conducive to reform are foundational and essential to success.'

Brig. H.R. McMaster, US Army

'This book, which contains a magisterial introduction by Mats Berdal and Dominik Zaum, brings together some of the top thinkers in the world of peacebuilding. It takes the commonly expressed idea that "development" is a necessary route to peacebuilding, and shows how neo-liberal interpretations of "development" have often promoted instability, not least by promoting large-scale unemployment.'

David Keen, LSE, UK

'Focusing on the interactions between external "statebuilders" and local power brokers – and how these processes shape post-war developments – Mats Berdal and Dominik Zaum have produced an impressive collection of thematic and country cases that significantly enriches our understanding of the consequences of statebuilding interventions.'

Astri Suhrke, Christian Michelsen Institute, Norway

This volume examines and evaluates the impact of international statebuilding interventions on the political economy of conflict-affected countries over the past 20 years. It focuses on countries that are emerging, or have recently emerged, from periods of war and protracted conflict. The interventions covered fall into three broad categories:

- international administrations and transformative occupations (East Timor, Iraq, and Kosovo);
- complex peace operations (Afghanistan, Burundi, Haiti, and Sudan);
- governance and statebuilding programmes conducted in the context of economic assistance (Georgia and Macedonia).

This book will be of interest to students of statebuilding, humanitarian intervention, post-conflict reconstruction, political economy, international organisations and IR/Security Studies in general.

Mats Berdal is Professor of Security and Development in the Department of War Studies at King's College London. He is Visiting Professor at the Norwegian Defence University College, and author/editor of several books.

Dominik Zaum is a Reader in International Relations at the University of Reading, and a Senior Research Fellow at the Department for International Development (DFID). He is author of several books on state- and peacebuilding.

Routledge Studies in Intervention and Statebuilding
Series Editor: David Chandler

Statebuilding and State-Formation
The political sociology of intervention
Edited by Berit Bliesemann de Guevara

Political Economy of Statebuilding
Power after peace
Edited by Mats Berdal and Dominik Zaum

Political Economy of Statebuilding

Power after peace

Edited by Mats Berdal and Dominik Zaum

LONDON AND NEW YORK

First published 2013
by Routledge
2 Park Square, Milton Park, Abingdon, Oxon OX14 4RN

Simultaneously published in the USA and Canada
by Routledge
711 Third Avenue, New York, NY 10017

Routledge is an imprint of the Taylor & Francis Group, an informa business

British Library Cataloguing in Publication Data
A catalogue record for this book is available from the British Library

Library of Congress Cataloging in Publication Data
Political economy of statebuilding: power after peace/edited by Mats
Berdal and Dominik Zaum.
    p. cm. – (Routledge studies in intervention and statebuilding)
    Includes bibliographical references and index.
    1. Nation-building. 2. Post-war reconstruction. 3. Nation-building–
Case studies. 4. Post-war reconstruction–Case studies. I. Berdal, Mats
R., 1965– II. Zaum, Dominik.
    JZ6300.P65 2012
    327.1–dc23

                                                                      2012013308

ISBN: 978-0-415-60478-9 (hbk)
ISBN: 978-0-415-52157-4 (pbk)
ISBN: 978-0-203-10130-8 (ebk)

Typeset in Baskerville
by Wearset Ltd, Boldon, Tyne and Wear

Contents

Illustrations

Maps

Tables

Contributors

Othon Anastasakis (MA Columbia University and Ph.D. London School of Economics) is the Director of South East European Studies at Oxford (SEESOX), University of Oxford and a Fellow at St Antony's College. His most recent books include *From Crisis to Recovery: Sustainable Growth in South East Europe* (co-edited with Jens Bastian and Max Watson, SEESOX 2011), *In the Shadow of Europe: Greeks and Turks in the era of post-nationalism* (co-edited with Kalypso Nicolaidis and Kerem Oktem, Brill 2009) and *Greece in the Balkans: Memory, Conflict and Exchange* (co-edited with Dimitar Bechev and Nicholas Vrousalis, Cambridge Scholars Press 2009). He is the General Editor of the Palgrave Macmillan St Antony's College series.

Kwesi Aning is the Dean and Director of Academic Affairs and Research Department, of the Kofi Annan International Peacekeeping Training Centre (KAIPTC), Ghana. He is also a non-resident Fellow with the Centre on International Cooperation, New York University. He holds a doctorate from the University of Copenhagen, Denmark. His primary research interests deal with African security issues broadly, comparative politics, terrorism and conflicts. He has published a large number of books and articles on peace and security issues in Africa.

Leanne Bayer is a Senior Social Development Specialist with the World Bank in Burundi. She holds a Master's degree in Social Policy from the London School of Economics and is currently completing her Ph.D. from the same institution. Since 2003 she has been working in the Great Lakes Region of Africa on projects in the DRC, Burundi, Rwanda and Uganda. She holds extensive experience in ex-combatant reintegration and community development programming in post-conflict countries.

Kristof Bender is Deputy Chairman of the European Stability Initiative (ESI), a non-profit research and policy institute created in recognition of the need for independent in-depth analysis of the complex issues involved in promoting stability and prosperity in Europe. Educated in sociology in Vienna and Paris, he has worked in South East Europe in various capacities since 1997, before joining ESI in 2000. He has been living in Bosnia and Herzegovina, Macedonia, Montenegro and Serbia, and is currently based in Vienna. He leads various research projects on Central and South Eastern Europe, in particular related to EU enlargement and European norms.

Thorsten Benner is co-founder and associate director of the Global Public Policy Institute (GPPi) in Berlin. His areas of expertise include international organisations (focusing on the United Nations), global security governance, global energy and the public–private interface of global governance, as well as Europe's global role and EU relations with the US and rising powers. His latest book is *The New World of UN Peace Operations: Learning to Build Peace?* (Oxford University Press 2011).

Mats Berdal is Professor of Security and Development in the Department of War Studies, King's College London. He was formerly Director of Studies at the International Institute for Strategic Studies in London. He is the author of *Whither UN Peacekeeping?* (Brasseys/IISS 1993), *Disarmament and Demobilisation after Civil Wars* (Oxford University Press/IISS 1996), *Building Peace after War* (Routledge/IISS 2009) and is co-editor with Spyros Economides of *United Nations Interventionism 1991–2004* (Cambridge University Press 2007).

Richard Caplan is Professor of International Relations and Fellow of Linacre College at the University of Oxford. He is the author of *Europe and the Recognition of New States in Yugoslavia* (Cambridge University Press 2005) and *International Governance of War-Torn Territories: Rule and Reconstruction* (Oxford University Press 2005). He is the editor of the forthcoming *Exit Strategies and State Building*, to be published by Oxford University Press.

Christine Cheng is the Bennett Boskey Fellow in Politics and International Relations at Exeter College, University of Oxford. She holds a DPhil in politics at the University of Oxford (Nuffield College). Her dissertation is entitled 'Extralegal Groups, Natural Resources, and Statebuilding in Post-Conflict Liberia'. It deals with ex-combatant groups that have taken over natural resource areas in the aftermath of war and the problem that these groups pose for long-term statebuilding. She co-edited the book *Corruption and Post-Conflict Peacebuilding* (Routledge 2011) with Dominik Zaum. Christine has published her work in *International Peacekeeping* and *Political Research Quarterly*.

Hannah Davies has worked in a variety of roles with the UN since 2003 including in the UN Mission in Liberia (UNMIL), the Department of Field Support and in the secretariat of the General Assembly budgetary committee. She is a Ph.D. candidate in the Department of War Studies at King's College London.

Toby Dodge is a Reader in International Relations in the Department of International Relations at the London School of Economics and Political Science. He has carried out research in Iraq both before and after regime change. In 2001 and 2002 he travelled across the country examining the effects of sanctions on Iraq's state, society and economy. In 2003 he was in Baghdad researching the political transition in the aftermath of regime change. In 2007 he spent two months in Iraq researching the country's descent into civil war and returned to Baghdad in 2008 to examine state capacity.

Spyros Economides is Senior Lecturer in International Relations and European Politics at the London School of Economics. He received the Robert Mackenzie Prize for his doctoral thesis on 'The International Implications of the Greek Civil War'. His subsequent work has concentrated on the international affairs of South Eastern Europe and EU external relations. He was a Research Associate of the Centre for Defence Studies at King's College and the IISS, London, and Specialist Adviser to the House of Lords EU Committee. His publications include: *UN Interventionism: 1991–2004* (with Mats Berdal, Cambridge University Press 2007) and *The Economic Factor in International Relations* (with Peter Wilson, I.B. Tauris 2001).

Atta El-Battahani is Professor of Political Science, University of Khartoum; and Senior Advisor for the International Institute for Democracy and Electoral Assistance (International IDEA) in Sudan. He has published widely on issues of governance and conflict in Sudan. His research interests include the politics and dynamics of conflicts, governance, institutions and institutional reform, the political economy of modern Islamic movements, and gender politics. He holds a Ph.D. from the University of Sussex, an MSc and BSc in Political Science and a BA in Philosophy from the University of Khartoum (Sudan).

Antonio Giustozzi is an independent researcher associated with the IDEAS (LSE). He is the author of several articles and papers on Afghanistan, as well as of three books, *War, Politics and Society in Afghanistan, 1978–1992* (Georgetown University Press 2000), *Koran, Kalashnikov and Laptop: The Neo-Taliban Insurgency, 2002–7* (Columbia University Press 2007) and *Empires of Mud: War and Warlords in Afghanistan* (Columbia University Press 2009), as well as a volume on the role of coercion and violence in statebuilding, *The Art of Coercion* (Columbia University Press 2011). He is currently researching issues of governance in Afghanistan, from a wide-ranging perspective which includes understanding the role of army, police, sub-national governance and intelligence system.

Anthony Goldstone has been closely involved with East Timor since the late 1970s when he was the Amnesty International researcher on the country. Between the referendum of 1999 and 2002 he worked as a Political Affairs Officer with successive UN missions in East Timor. In 2003–2005 he was co-editor of the Final Report of the East Timor Truth and Reconciliation Commission, CAVR. Since 2006 he has continued to visit the country as a consultant to the UN and to international NGOs.

Niamatullah Ibrahimi worked for the International Crisis Group in 2003–2005 and for the Crisis States Research Centre in 2005–2010 and authored a number of studies on the politics of Hazarajat. He is about to publish a study of Maoism in Afghanistan. In 2010–2011 he served as co-director of Afghan NGO Afghanistan Watch. He is currently at the Free University in Berlin as a Research Associate.

Verena Knaus has been with the European Stability Initiative (ESI) from its foundation in 1999 until 2010, and was a lead researcher for the Lessons Learned and Analysis Unit in Kosovo from 2001 to 2004. Since July 2010, she has worked as an independent analyst and strategic adviser on EU integration and with UNICEF in Kosovo and Brussels. She is a World Fellow of Yale University, a Young Global Leader of the World Economic Forum and co-author of the *Kosovo Bradt Guide* (Bradt 2010), the first ever English-language guidebook on Kosovo.

S. Neil MacFarlane is Lester B. Pearson Professor of International Relations at Oxford University. He works on the politics and international relations of the Caucasus, and has a general interest in the theory of security.

Robert Muggah is a Fellow at the Instituto de Relações Internacionais, Pontifícia Universidade Católica do Rio de Janeiro. Previously, he was Research Director of the Small Arms Survey. His most recent publications include *The Global Burden of Armed Violence* (Cambridge University Press 2011), *Security and Post-Conflict Reconstruction: Dealing with Fighters in the Aftermath of War* (Routledge 2009) and *Relocation Failures in Sri Lanka: A Short History of Internal Displacement* (Zed 2008). He received his DPhil at Oxford University and his MPhil at the Institute for Development Studies, University of Sussex.

Michael Pugh is Professor of Peace and Conflict Studies, University of Bradford, Leverhulme Emeritus Fellow, Honorary Professor, University of St Andrews and editor of the journal *International Peacekeeping*. He has a special interest in the political economy of Bosnia and Herzegovina, and published numerous refereed articles and book chapters. He has authored/edited six books, including *War Economies in a Regional Context: Challenges of Transformation* (with Neil Cooper, Lynne Rienner 2004) and *Whose Peace? Critical Perspectives on the Political Economy of Peacebuilding* (with Neil Cooper and Mandy Turner, Palgrave 2008).

Benjamin Reilly is Head of the School of Social Sciences and International Studies at the University of New South Wales in Sydney. He was Senior Visiting Professor at the Johns Hopkins University's School of Advanced International Studies in Washington DC, and Professor of Political Science in the Crawford School of Economics and Government at the Australian National University, Canberra. He was previously Director of the Centre for Democratic Institutions and has also worked for the United Nations, the International Institute for Democracy and Electoral Assistance, and the Australian government.

Naila Salihu is a Programme and Research Officer at KAIPTC. She holds a Master of Philosophy Degree in International Affairs from the University of Ghana. Her research interest has been in conflict analysis, peacekeeping, civilian protection, conflict prevention, post-conflict reconstruction and human security in Africa.

Ricardo Soares de Oliveira is Lecturer in Comparative Politics in the Department of Politics and International Relations at Oxford University, Fellow of St Peters College and Fellow of the Global Public Policy Institute, Berlin. He is the author of *Oil and Politics in the Gulf of Guinea* (Hurst and Columbia University Press 2007), co-editor of *China Returns to Africa* (with Daniel Large and Chris Alden, Hurst/Columbia 2008) and *The New Protectorates: International Tutelage and the Making of Liberal States* (with James Mayall, Hurst/Columbia 2011).

Álvaro de Soto is currently a Visiting Professor at PSIA/Sciences Po, in Paris, a Senior Fellow at the Ralph Bunche Institute in New York, an Associate Fellow at the Geneva Centre for Security Policy and a member of the Global Leadership Foundation. In a twenty-five-year UN career spanning the terms of three Secretaries-Generals, de Soto, a Peruvian diplomat, led the 1990–1991 negotiations which resulted in the peace accords ending the war in El Salvador and the 1999–2004 negotiations on the Cyprus problem which concluded with parallel referendums on the 'Annan plan' for a settlement. He was the chief UN envoy for the Arab–Israeli conflict 2005–2007.

Oisín Tansey is Lecturer in International Relations at the University of Reading. His research focuses on the international influences on regime change and regime type, and his previous work has focused in particular on processes of democratisation in the context of international statebuilding. He is the author of *Regime-Building: Democratization and International Administration* (Oxford University Press 2009) and has published articles in journals such as *Journal of Democracy, Democratization, Review of International Studies* and *Survival*.

Stina Torjesen is Associate Professor II at the Centre for Peace Studies, University of Tromsø and Project Manager in the corporate social responsibility consultancy SIGLA. In her academic work she specialises in security, energy, politics and interstate relations in the Caucasus, Central Asia and South Asia. She holds a DPhil in International Relations from the University of Oxford.

Peter Uvin is Academic Dean and Henry J. Leir Professor of International Humanitarian Studies at the Fletcher School of Law and Diplomacy at Tufts University. He is the author of four books and tens of articles dealing with development aid and its relation to human rights and conflict, war in the African Great Lakes region, and hunger and food aid. His best known book is *Aiding Violence: The Development Enterprise in Rwanda* (Kumarian

Press 1998) which received the African Studies Association's Herskowits award for the most outstanding book on Africa in 1998. In 2006, he was awarded a prestigious Guggenheim Fellowship to analyse young people's lives in post-transition Burundi, leading to his latest book *Life after Violence: A People's History of Burundi* (Zed 2008).

Peter Woodward is Emeritus Professor at the University of Reading, UK. He formerly taught at the University of Khartoum, and has been Visiting Lecturer at the University of Natal and the American University in Cairo. He is the author and editor of a number of books on North East Africa, most recently *US Foreign Policy and the Horn of Africa* (Ashgate 2006). He is a former editor of *African Affairs*, the journal of the Royal African Society; and edited *British Documents on Foreign Affairs: Africa, 1914–1956* (University Press of America 1994–2011).

Susan L. Woodward is Professor of Political Science at the Graduate Center of the City University of New York. A specialist on the Balkans, her current research focuses on transitions from war to peace, international security and state failure, and post-war statebuilding. She is a member of the United Nations Committee of Experts on Public Administration, 2010–2014, was a senior fellow at the Brookings Institution in Washington, DC, 1990–1999, and at the Centre for Defence Studies, King's College, London, 1999–2000, head of the Analysis and Assessment Unit for UNPROFOR in 1994, and a Professor of Political Science at Yale University, 1982–1989, Williams College, 1978–82, and Northwestern University, 1972–1977. Her many writings include *Balkan Tragedy: Chaos and Dissolution after the Cold War* (Brookings Press 1995) and *Socialist Unemployment: The Political Economy of Yugoslavia, 1945–1990* (Princeton University Press 1995).

Dominik Zaum is Reader in International Relations at the University of Reading, and a Senior Research Fellow in Conflict and Fragility at the UK's Department for International Development. He is author of *The Sovereignty Paradox: The Norms and Politics of International Statebuilding* (Oxford University Press 2007) and *Selective Security: War and the United Nations Security Council since 1945* (with Adam Roberts, Routledge/IISS 2009). He is co-editor of *The United Nations Security Council and War: The Evolution of Thought and Practice since 1945* (with Vaughan Lowe, Adam Roberts and Jennifer Welsh, Oxford University Press 2008) and of *Corruption and Post-Conflict Peacebuilding: Selling the Peace* (with Christine Cheng, Routledge 2011).

Foreword

Álvaro de Soto

Boutros Boutros Ghali's epiphany came soon after he became the UN's sixth Secretary-General. His first official mission away from UN Headquarters took him to Mexico City for the formal signing, on 16 January 1992, of the Peace Accord which ended the twelve-year conflict in El Salvador. A scholar and a quick study, he returned well versed on the Accord and the challenge ahead.

A fortnight later the Security Council met at the summit for the first time in its history, with the Cold War a thing of the past. At a time when the UN seemed at last poised to play the role for which it was conceived, the leaders asked the new Secretary-General for his analysis and recommendations on ways to strengthen its capacity for preventive diplomacy, peacemaking and peacekeeping. Boutros Ghali set up a Secretariat team to help him prepare these recommendations, which would take the form of a report to the General Assembly and the Security Council.

While travelling with him in Brazil at the end of May, I gave him a late draft of the report, received from New York that morning. As he pored over it, he looked up from the page and asked,

> Where does El Salvador fit here? It isn't preventive diplomacy. It isn't peacemaking – peace has already been made – and it isn't peacekeeping as we know it. It's something else: it's… [he paused, searching for the right words] *post-conflict*, and it's more like peace-*building*, isn't it?

He didn't levitate or show other manifestations of spiritual enlightenment, so I can't honestly know whether Boutros Ghali experienced his insight as an epiphany. But it was certainly an epiphany for me. I could hardly wait to convey to New York his decision to add to the draft report a section, on 'Post-Conflict Peace-Building', on the same footing as the three that the Security Council had asked him to address.

In his report, entitled *An Agenda for Peace*, 'post-conflict peace-building' was defined as *action to identify and support structures which will tend to strengthen and solidify peace in order to avoid a relapse into conflict*. So far so good, but the remainder of the introductory paragraph touched on a miscellaneous list of activities – disarming of warring parties and dealing with their weapons, restoring order, repatriating refugees, providing advisory and training support for security personnel and monitoring elections – of unquestionable importance but more related to stabilisation than to the creation or strengthening of the underpinnings of the state. To get a glimpse of the 'structures' which, according to the definition, would need to be 'strengthened so as to solidify peace in order to avoid a relapse into conflict', the reader had to wait until the last item which referred to 'reforming or strengthening governmental institutions and promoting formal and informal processes of political participation'. The institutions of economic management, budget formulation and resource allocation appeared nowhere.

The text then digressed again by turning, in the following paragraphs, to international conflict, peacebuilding as a form of preventive diplomacy and de-mining, returning to the issue at hand only in the final paragraph of the section, which – at last, warming to the core subject – touched on *the transformation of deficient national structures and capabilities, the strengthening of new democratic institutions, the importance of social peace and the connection between good governance and the consolidation of peace.*

The digressions had the unfortunate effect of blurring Boutros Ghali's vivid original insight. Some of us in the Secretariat were disappointed at what appeared to be a dilution of the concept as originally stated, and made it our business to highlight and flesh it out on our own, unsupported but unopposed.

Think of it, we told sceptical audiences: in 1992 the UN had only just emerged from decades of marginalisation. The last three-and-a-half years in office of Boutros Ghali's predecessor, Javier Pérez de Cuéllar, had seen the most successful flurry of peacemaking in history, either led by the UN or carried out in its framework – the withdrawal of Soviet troops from Afghanistan, the end of the wars between Iran and Iraq, in Cambodia and Mozambique, the removal of foreign military personnel from Angola and the independence of Namibia, the defusing of the 'Contra War' and a comprehensive settlement for the internal conflict in El Salvador.

Yet even at this early stage in the UN's new era, here was the Secretary-General, at the pinnacle of an organisation composed of states, predicting that the UN's groundbreaking role in El Salvador, the first case of the UN mediating the resolution of internal conflict between a government and an insurgent group, was likely to be followed by many more such interventions of a multidisciplinary nature, in which the personnel devoted to institutional reform so as to underpin civil liberties and respect for human rights, enlarge political space and promote inclusion, were at the centre of activity, outlasting the initial stages of demobilisation of the insurgent army and the profound reforms and reduction of the armed forces and their subordination to civilian authority.

These interventions, inherently consensual, were to take the UN in a new, uncharted direction: after interstate conflict, the danger of recurrence of conflict diminishes drastically once armies go home. After internal conflict, fighting forces are doomed to coexist under the same roof, and it cannot be taken for granted that fraternal reconciliation will follow fratricidal confrontation.

To avoid relapse of internal conflict, channels and institutions – to ensure that future such disputes can be peacefully resolved – must be put in place. Helping to bring this about will increase the depth and the duration of the UN's involvement. This was a responsibility that could not be shirked by the Security Council: the UN's primary mission under the Charter is the maintenance of international peace and security, whose stewardship lies on the Council's shoulders. What could be more germane to the discharge of its responsibilities than to make sure that, once the guns are silenced, actions are taken to *identify and support structures which will tend to strengthen and solidify peace in order to avoid a relapse into conflict?*

Boutros Ghali's breakthrough insight provided an opportunity, even a catalyst, for the formulation of cogent policy and unified action by the international community as embodied in the various entities that can play a leading role in statebuilding – the United Nations, UNDP, the IMF and the World Bank, regional organisations and individual states and groups of states.

Alas, despite the universal praise showered on Boutros Ghali's *Agenda*, the opportunity went unseized. Boutros Ghali, it seemed, was content with having pinpointed a challenge and formulated a concept. The locus of responsibility in the UN Secretariat, which would have been the starting point of formulating a common strategy, was perfunctorily assigned but allowed to drift. With UN Headquarters speaking in dissonant voices, there was little hope of building a broader consensus within and beyond the UN. No wonder that some players took the conceptual fuzziness and sprawl as a licence to go about their activities as before. Key multilateral players swaddled themselves in the coat of many colours provided by *post-conflict peacebuilding*, making little or no effort to adjust their priorities or practices so as to synchronise them with the fundamentally political objective that it was meant to enshrine. International intervention in this area was left to the ministrations of multifarious players in a cacophony reminiscent of Pirandello's *Six Characters in Search of an Author*. Far from midwifing cogent policy and strategy, *post-conflict peacebuilding* was orphaned in infancy.

Political Economy of Statebuilding: Power after Peace is a sober and penetrating examination of statebuilding in war-affected countries as it is, not as it should, or could, be. It looks specifically at statebuilding efforts through the examination of 'countries that are emerging, or have recently emerged, from periods of war and violent conflict', focusing on 'contemporary external or exogenous statebuilding efforts'. The editors, Mats Berdal and Dominik Zaum, both noted in their academic fields and well respected by practitioners, have gathered a sterling group of scholars to home in on their subjects with unforgiving seriousness and merciless equanimity.

Berdal and Zaum tell us that their major aim was 'to explore whether statebuilding efforts have succeeded in transforming, and in what ways they have done so, the political economy and power structures that have fuelled conflict and violence in the first place', particularly by examining 'how international statebuilding policies have affected the domestic actors who, at the end of the conflict, exercise political power, dominate state institutions and control and exploit economic assets'. International post-conflict statebuilding intervention, we are told, is of a 'fundamentally political character' – a statement to which I heartily subscribe.

Some of the revelations of the chapter authors are as stark as the conclusions drawn by the editors are sobering. Though a high price is still being paid for the missed opportunity to build on Boutros Ghali's 1992 insight, the picture is not entirely grim: there has been some excellent work in the field by strong, inspired envoys who have understood the challenge, and have rallied the key players to work with them towards the same goal. But it is hard to see what value is added by the much-touted creation, at the 2005 World Summit of the UN Peace-Building Commission. Quite apart from adding intergovernmental and secretariat layers, the failure to even mention, in the PBC's terms of reference, the central goal of preventing recurrence of conflict strikes me as value subtraction.

Under the UN Charter, the members of the UN have conferred on the Security Council 'primary responsibility for the maintenance of international peace and security'. Other than all-out war, it is hard to think of a task more germane to that responsibility than making sure that peace in countries emerging from violent conflict is consolidated. Some may believe that by diluting the Council's role in this area they have struck a blow for the democratisation of international institutions or thwarted a sinister plot to undermine the sovereignty of small and weak countries. The truth is that the Council has shown little enthusiasm about shouldering this responsibility which lies so squarely at its feet. Those who have placed the Council at a further remove from this responsibility have in fact provided it with an alibi; the losers may be those fragile countries in their difficult journey to recovery.

If decision makers are paying attention, there is much in this volume that should prompt action to overcome the disarray that prevails in international action in this field, which is central to ensuring the durability of peace. If they aren't paying attention, they should be doing so. With hindsight, in the early 1990s some of us may have fallen under the spell of Cold War's end hubris, only to see our hopes dashed. *Political Economy of Statebuilding* can help point us back in the correct direction.

Paris, April 2012

Acknowledgements

The idea for this volume emerged from a range of discussions of statebuilding in cafés in the vicinity of King's College London's Strand campus, during which we gradually realised that one of the key questions about statebuilding practices, namely what their impact is on the political economy of conflict-affected countries, had remained woefully underexplored in the existing statebuilding literature. How statebuilding interventions shape the structures and exercise of power in conflict-affected countries is thus the guiding research question of this project, which developed through a range of workshops from 2009 to 2011 at the University of Reading, King's College London, and at Wilton Park under the aegis of the *Power after Peace* project funded by the Carnegie Corporation of New York.

In addition to the authors, who patiently addressed our comments and revised their chapters, we would like to thank Charles Call, Ben Crampton, Carlos dos Santos Cruz, Gwinyayi Dzineza, Alan Doss, Raymond Gilpin, Minna Jarvenpaa, Iain King, Whit Mason, Ken Menkhaus, Engjellushe Morina, Ghia Nodia, 'Funmi Olonisakin and Alan Renwick for presentations at the workshops, or their comments on the different chapters. We also want to thank the three members of the project's advisory board, Álvaro de Soto, Desmond Bowen and Mark Hoffmann, for their continued support throughout the project.

Our work on this project benefitted greatly from two doctoral students at the University of Reading: Ana Omaljev, who provided excellent administrative assistance throughout the project, and from Corinne Heaven, who supported the work on the bibliography and final copy-editing of the book. We would also like to thank Pauline Savage for her excellent copy-editing of some of the chapters.

Finally, we want to express our gratitude to the Carnegie Corporation of New York, and in particular Stephen del Rosso, for the generous financial support for the *Power after Peace* project. Without it, the project and this volume would not have been possible.

M.B. and D.Z., April 2012

Abbreviations

AAC	*Associacão dos Antigos Combatentes de Falintil de 1975*
ACHPR	African Commission on Human and Peoples' Rights
ADFL	Alliance of Democratic Forces for the Liberation of Congo
AfDB	African Development Bank
APRA	Arusha Peace and Reconciliation Agreement
APSA	African Peace and Security Architecture
AREU	Afghanistan Research and Evaluation Unit
ASSN	African Security Sector Network
AU	African Union
BiH	Bosnia and Herzegovina
BINUB	UN Integrated Office in Burundi
CAFAO	Customs and Fiscal Assistance Office
CARERE	Cambodia Area Rehabilitation and Regeneration Project
CCK	Coordination Centre for Kosovo and Metohija
CDD	Community Driven Development
CENI	*Commission Electorale Nationale Indépendente*
CEP	Community Empowerment Programme
CFSP	Common Foreign and Security Policy
CNDD–FDD	*Conseil National de Défense de la Démocratie/Forces de Défense de la Démocratie*
CNPC	Chinese National Petroleum Corporation
CNRM	National Council of Maubere Resistance
CNRT	National Council of Timorese Resistance
CoE	Council of Europe
CPA	Coalition Provisional Authority (in Iraq)
CPA	Comprehensive Peace Agreement (in Sudan)
CPIA	Country Policy and Institutional Assessment
CPLP	Community of Portuguese Speaking Countries
CPP	Cambodian People's Party
CSCE	Conference for Security and Cooperation in Europe
CSP	Comprehensive Status Proposal
DAC	Development Assistance Committee

DDR	Disarmament, Demobilisation, and Reintegration
DFID	Department for International Development
DFSE	*Delegação da Fretilin em Serviço no Exterior*
DIAG	Disarmament of Illegal Armed Groups
DPA	Democratic Party of Albanians
DPKO	Department of Peacekeeping Operations
DRC	Democratic Republic of the Congo
DSSRP	Defence and Security Sector Reform Programme
DUI	Democratic Union for Integration
DUP	Democratic Unionist Party
EAP	Eastern Partnership
EBRD	European Bank for Reconstruction and Development
EC	European Commission
ECOWAS	Economic Community of West African States
ECPF	ECOWAS Conflict Prevention Framework
EITI	Extractive Industries Transparency Initiative
ENP	European Neighbourhood Policy
ESDP	European Security and Defence Policy
ETTA	East Timor Transitional Administration
EU	European Union
EU SSR Guinea-Bissau	EU Security Sector Reform Mission Guinea-Bissau
EUBAM	European Border Assistance Mission
EUFOR RCA	EU Force Central African Republic
EUJUST LEX	EU Integrated Rule of Law Mission Iraq
EULEX	EU Rule of Law Mission
EUMM	EU Monitoring Mission
EUPOL	EU Police Mission Afghanistan
EUSEC RD Congo	EU Security Sector Reform Mission Guinea-Bissau to the DR Congo
EUTM	EU Training Mission in Somalia
FDI	Foreign Direct Investment
F-FDTL	Defence Force of East Timor
FNL	*Forces Nationales de Libération*
FRODEBU	*Front pour la Démocratie au Burundi*
FUNCINPEC	United National Front for an Independent, Neutral, Peaceful and Cooperative Cambodia
G-77	Group of 77
GDP	Gross Domestic Product
GEMAP	Governance and Economic Management Assistance Programme
GNU	Government of National Unity
GoSS	Government of South Sudan
GTEP	Georgia Train and Equip Program
HDI	Human Development Indicators
HIPC	Heavily Indebted Poor Countries
HNP	Haitian National Police

ICG-GB	International Contact Group on Guinea Bissau
ICO	International Civilian Office
ICTY	International Criminal Tribunal for the former Yugoslavia
IDA	International Development Assistance
IDP	Internally Displaced Person
IFIs	International Financial Institutions
IGAD	Inter-Governmental Authority for Development
IGC	Iraqi Governing Council
ILO	International Labour Organisation
IMF	International Monetary Fund
IMPP	Integrated Mission Planning Process
INA	Iraqi National Alliance
IPA	Instrument for Pre-Accession Assistance
ISAF	International Security Assistance Force
ISCI	Islamic Supreme Council of Iraq
ISF	International Stabilisation Force
JAM	Joint Assessment Mission
JMAC	Joint Mission Analysis Cell
JOC	Joint Operation Centre
KFOR	Kosovo Force
KPC	Kosovo Protection Corps
LDK	Democratic League of Kosovo
MDTF	Multi-Donor Trust Fund
MIA	Ministry of Internal Affairs
MICIVIH	*Mission Civile Internationale en Haïti*
MINURCA	UN Mission in the Central African Republic
MINURSO	UN Mission for the Referendum in Western Sahara
MINUSTAH	United Nations Stabilisation Mission in Haiti
MIPONUH	*Mission de Police civile des Nations Unies en Haïti*
MONUC	UN Organisation Mission in the Congo (*Mission des Nations Unies en République démocratique du Congo*)
MONUSCO	UN Organisation Stabilisation Mission in the Democratic Republic of the Congo
NAM	Non-Aligned Movement
NATO	North Atlantic Treaty Organisation
NCP	National Congress Party
NDP	National Development Plan
NEPAD	New Economic Partnership for Africa's Development
NGO	Non-Governmental Organisation
NIF	National Islamic Forum
NLA	National Liberation Army
NPC	National Petroleum Commission
NRDF	National Reconstruction and Development Fund
OAS	Organization of American States
OCHA	Office of the Coordination of Humanitarian Affairs

OCINC	Office of the Commander in Chief
ODA	Official Development Assistance
OECD	Organisation for Economic Cooperation and Development
OED	Operations Evaluation Division
OHCHR	Office of the High Commissioner for Human Rights
OHR	Office of the High Representative
ONUMOZ	UN Operation in Mozambique
ONUB	UN Operation in Burundi (*Opération des Nations Unies au Burundi*)
OSCE	Organization for Security and Co-operation in Europe
PAG	Police Assistance Group
PBC	Peacebuilding Commission
PCCF	Post-Conflict Countries Facility
PCRD	Post-Conflict Reconstruction and Development
PDK	Democratic Party of Kosovo
PDP	Party for Democratic Prosperity
PIU	Project Implementation Unit
PISG	Provisional Institutions of Self-Government
PNTL	Timorese National Police Service
POLRI	*Kepolisian Negara Republik Indonesia* (Indonesian Police Force)
PR	Proportional Representation
PRGF	Poverty Reduction and Growth Facility
PRODERE	Development Programme for Displaced Persons, Refugees and Returnees in Central America
PRSP	Poverty Reduction Strategy Paper
PRT	Provincial Reconstruction Teams
PSC	Peace and Security Council
PWYP	Publish What You Pay
RDTL	Democratic Republic of East Timor
REC	Regional Economic Community
RUF	Revolutionary United Front
SAA	Stabilisation and Association Agreement
SAp	Stabilisation and Association process
SDSM	Social Democratic Union of Macedonia
SEC	Securities and Exchange Commission
SHIK	Kosovo Information Service
SME	Small and Medium Enterprise
SNTV	Single Non-Transferable Vote
SOFA	Status of Forces Agreement
SPLA/SPLM	Sudan Peoples Liberation Army/Movement
SPIC	Sudan Political Islamic Corporate
SSG	Security Sector Governance
SSR	Security Sector Reform

SSRDF	South Sudan Reconstruction and Development Fund
TAL	Transitional Administrative Law
TCC	Troop-Contributing Country
TLPS	Timor Lorosa'e Police Service
TNI	*Tentara Nasional Indonesia* (Indonesian Armed Forces)
UÇK	Kosovo Liberation Army
UN	United Nations
UNAMA	UN Assistance Mission in Afghanistan
UNAMET	UN Assistance Mission to East Timor
UNAMSIL	UN Mission in Sierra Leone
UNCDF	UN Capital Development Fund
UNDP	UN Development Programme
UNDP ANBP	UN Development Programme Afghanistan New Beginnings Programme
UNHCR	UN High Commissioner for Refugees
UNICEF	UN Children's Fund
UNIOGBIS	UN Integrated Peacebuilding Office in Guinea-Bissau
UNIOSIL	UN Integrated Office in Sierra Leone
UNIPSIL	UN Integrated Peacebuilding Office in Sierra Leone
UNITA	National Union for the Total Independence of Angola
UNMIBH	UN Mission in Bosnia and Herzegovina
UNMIH	UN Mission to Haiti
UNMIK	UN Interim Administration Mission in Kosovo
UNMIL	UN Mission in Liberia
UNMIS	UN Mission in Sudan
UNMIT	UN Integrated Mission in East Timor
UNMISET	UN Mission in Support of East Timor
UNMISS	UN Mission in the Republic of South Sudan
UNMIT	UN Integrated Mission in Timor-Leste
UNMOT	UN Mission of Observers in Tajikistan
UNOCI	UN Operation in Côte d'Ivoire
UNOGBIS	UN Peacebuilding Support Office in Guinea Bissau
UNOMIG	UN Observer Mission in Georgia
UNOMSIL	UN Organisation Mission in Sierra Leone
UNOSOM II	UN Operation in Somalia II
UNOTIL	UN Office in Timor Leste
UNPOL	UN Police
UNSMIH	UN Support Mission in Haiti
UNTAC	UN Transitional Administration in Cambodia
UNTAES	UN Transitional Administration for Eastern Slavonia, Baranja and Western Sirmium
UNTAET	UN Transitional Administration in East Timor
UNTAG	UN Transition Assistance Group
UNTMIH	UN Transition Mission in Haiti

UPRONA	*Union pour le Progrès national*
USAID	United States Agency for International Development
VMRO-DPMNE	Internal Macedonian Revolutionary Organisation – Democratic Party for Macedonian Unity
WGI	World Wide Governance Indicators

1 Power after peace

Mats Berdal and Dominik Zaum

The post-Cold War era has witnessed a remarkable growth in international efforts to assist in the rebuilding of states and societies affected by war and violent conflict. Many of these interventions have involved what has become known as statebuilding: "actions undertaken by international and national actors to establish, reform, or strengthen the institutions of the state and their relation to society" (Call 2008a: 5).[1] In a rich variety of settings and circumstances, international organisations and donor states have found themselves involved, to an unprecedented degree, in the creation and reform of representative political institutions, the strengthening of governmental capacity, the promotion of judicial reform and the liberalisation of economies. This book is concerned with one aspect of that experience in particular: the impact of statebuilding interventions on the political economy of war-torn societies. Our understanding of the "political economy of statebuilding" is discussed more fully below, suffice it to say here that an underlying concern throughout is with the impact of outside intervention on the complex relationship, in terms of power and influence, between *formal* and *informal* political and economic actors, groups and networks within war-torn and conflict-affected societies.

While statebuilding today is typically discussed in the context of "peacebuilding" and "stabilisation" operations, the current phase of interest in external interventions to (re)build and strengthen governmental institutions can be traced back to the "good governance" policies of the International Financial Institutions (IFIs) in the early 1990s. These sought political changes and improvements in the quality of governance in countries that were subject to, or were seeking support under, IFI-designed structural adjustment programmes (see Susan Woodward's chapter in this volume). The focus of this book is specifically on statebuilding efforts in *conflict-affected* countries: countries that are emerging, or have recently emerged, from periods of war and violent conflict. Even this limitation, however, leaves a wide range of relevant experiences and statebuilding activities to investigate. The interventions covered in the present volume fall into three broad and overlapping categories: international administrations and transformative occupations (East Timor, Iraq and Kosovo); complex peace operations (Afghanistan, Burundi, Haiti and Sudan); and governance and statebuilding programmes conducted in the context of economic assistance (Georgia and Macedonia). This very range hints at one of the conclusions that emerge in detail from the individual case studies: the experience of the past 20 years is one of great diversity of statebuilding approaches, a reflection in part of the variety of motivations held by external actors engaged in the exercise. We are not, in other words, looking at a coherent or consistent approach to statebuilding by donors and international organisations in the post-Cold War era. This of course should not come as any great surprise. States and international organisations have different national and institutional interests that they pursue when they engage in post-conflict statebuilding. Crucially, they often also have different perspectives on the origins and character of the conflicts that prompted intervention in the first place. These realities all necessarily shape and skew the priorities and approaches of actors to statebuilding.

The growing interest and involvement of external actors in war-torn states through statebuilding is reflected in two developments.

The first of these is the growing number of peace operations in war-torn countries that have, as part of their mandate, engaged in or supported statebuilding activities. Out of a total of 49 UN-led peacekeeping operations established between 1989 and 2011, 29 had some form of statebuilding mandate. The scope and transformative ambition of these operations make them qualitatively different from earlier activities, be it UN peacekeeping operations during the Cold War, or League of Nations activities in the 1920s and 1930s. In some cases, the resources devoted by external actors to a statebuilding project have exceeded the country's GDP, in some cases (i.e. Liberia and Afghanistan) by multiples. While there are major differences between operations – differences in terms of the extent and nature of outside involvement, the resources committed by donors and the political context within which statebuilding is undertaken – they have all typically been characterised, and justified, in terms of their ambition to promote and undertake institutional and societal transformations aimed at eradicating the underlying or "structural" sources of violence.

The second development alluded to above is the identification of "state failure" – rightly or wrongly – as a major threat to both human and national security by many Western countries. A consequence of this has been for statebuilding to be viewed as a policy response to a growing number of international social ills. It has been presented as the "solution" to a very diverse set of threats and challenges:

- strengthening state capacity is considered central to the economic development of poor and conflict-affected countries (World Bank 1997; UN Millennium Project 2005; OECD 2011: 15);
- democratisation, the promotion of justice and economic liberalisation in weak, post-conflict states can reignite violence without strengthened state institutions to support these objectives (Paris 2004);
- weak and fragile states are seen as posing threats to wider regional and international security, and have been associated with international terrorism (White House 2002), drugs trafficking, organised crime and the proliferation of weapons of mass destruction (Fearon and Laitin 2004).[2]

Statebuilding has therefore become one of the central policy tools deployed both by multilateral institutions and by major donor countries to address the diverse challenges faced by developing and, in particular, conflict-affected countries.

Central themes and questions posed

Although international statebuilding efforts can play, and on occasion have played, an important role in helping societies to move out of conflict (i.e. in Burundi or Macedonia, see Uvin and Bayer's, and Bender's chapters in this volume), the overall impact in terms of ensuring stability, promoting development and mitigating violence remains decidedly mixed. Indeed, according to Ken Menkhaus, "few international aid programmes have met with such consistent frustration as state-building" (2010: 173), a conclusion broadly supported by the present volume. By focusing on the political economy of statebuilding in war-torn societies, the present book highlights a number of recurring themes that help explain *why* international statebuilding interventions have tended to fall short of the visions of interveners and local populations alike. These include, perhaps most notably, evidence of important continuities between wartime and "post-conflict" economies and authority structures, which are often consolidated as a consequence of international involvement; tensions arising from what are often the competing interests and values held by different interveners and local actors; and, finally, the continuing salience of economic and political violence in statebuilding processes and war-to-peace transitions.

These themes, that statebuilding outcomes have differed from expectations, and that security and development gains might not only be more fragile, but also of a different character and quality than statebuilders might have expected and desired, is a starting point for the analysis in this book, rather than a conclusion, as they raise a range of important questions that are addressed in the different parts in this book. What are the aims of external statebuilders, and how do they differ between actors and over time? How have these agendas interacted with the interests and agendas of local actors, and with what consequences? How are statebuilding practices mediated through local actors and institutions? What is the character of the states that have been (re)built? Have statebuilding efforts, despite their mixed record, contributed to political stability, justice and economic development in the affected societies? What have been the factors that help us to understand the reasons for the shortcomings of international statebuilding practices? These are the kinds of questions posed by the authors – from the perspective of different practices, countries and organisations – brought together in this volume.

While not a comprehensive account of international statebuilding practices since the end of the Cold War, the book seeks to provide both an accurate overview and evaluation of these efforts, and of how they shape the character of post-conflict states. Before that, though, it is important to revisit and explain some of the assumptions, definitions and concepts that underpin the book, most obviously the concepts of political economy and statebuilding.

A political economy perspective on statebuilding: restating the central research question

The term "political economy" has been employed broadly and with a range of different meanings across time and subjects. Since the mid-twentieth century, it has been used to describe both the close relationship between economics and politics, and the application of the methodology of economics to the inquiry into questions of politics (Weingast and Wittman 2006: 3–4). Robert Gilpin's understanding of the political economy, as a set of questions that are "generated by the interaction of the state and the market as the embodiment of politics and economics in the modern world" (1987: 9), fits into this tradition and provides a useful starting point for conceptualising the political economy of statebuilding. To further develop our understanding of a political economy of statebuilding, however, three additional observations are merited.

First, many statebuilding policies aim to restructure the relationship between the state, society and the market, and affect the capacity of the state to regulate and intervene into the economy. The emphasis on market liberalisation and on the privatisation of state-owned enterprises that have been at the core of the economic development policies of many post-conflict statebuilding operations (i.e. in accordance with the strictures of the so-called the "Washington Consensus"), aim to limit the role of the state in the market (del Castillo 2008; Woods 2006). The World Bank's 1997 *World Development Report: The State in a Changing World*, for example, argued that states' roles should match their capabilities, and that "[w]eak states must tailor their ambitions to their capability" (1997: 41). The key functions on which weak states, including post-conflict states, should focus are those core functions necessary to support free markets (ibid.; see also Susan Woodward's chapter in this volume). Statebuilding efforts therefore have important consequences for the relationship between state and market in post-conflict countries.

Second, to finance the institutions of the state and the public goods that they are expected to provide, a state needs to develop an economic base and the capacity to extract resources – in particular through taxation – to finance its activities. The success of any statebuilding effort is therefore intricately tied up with wider questions about the political economy of post-conflict countries.

Finally, war, and in particular civil war, transforms the relationship between state and market, and creates its own political economy. It gives rise to new structures of political power and authority, new actors controlling economic resources, and new forms of interaction between the political and economic life. While traditionally civil war has been considered as a breakdown of order and "development in reverse" (in particular Collier *et al.* 2003, but also World Bank 2010), scholars such as Christopher Cramer (2006) and David Keen (1998) have convincingly argued that civil war is not simply the collapse of a "normal" peacetime order but also involves the emergence of different, alternative kinds of order, governed by their own political and economic logic. Importantly, such war economies persist into peacetime, and are likely to shape the character of the post-war political economy. Transforming these very political wartime economies is a central challenge for statebuilding operations. As Michael Pugh and his co-authors have observed, "At best, an inability to transform war economies perpetuates corruption, flawed governance, and tensions created by competing patrimonies and ethnic groups … At worst, it can store up long-term problems that can lead to the recurrence of conflict" (2004: 3–4).

These observations suggest that the political economy of post-conflict statebuilding has to go beyond Gilpin's focus on formal rules and institutions, and the interaction of state and markets, but also needs to be concerned with informal political and economic structures, in particular (but not exclusively) those arising from conflict. Thus, for the purpose of this book we understand the political economy of statebuilding to encompass the relationships between formal and informal economic and political structures in post-conflict environments. Our concern is both with formal political and economic structures and with the "alternative systems of power, profit and protection" (Berdal and Keen 1997: 797) rooted in war and conflict but certain to have mutated, adapted and survived into the "post-conflict" phase. Such a perspective brings out not only the fact that those on the receiving end of statebuilding exercises are neither passive nor inert (MacGinty 2011), but also that the international presence *itself* forms an important part of the political economy of post-conflict statebuilding (and that, by extension, the policies and actions of outsiders feed back into and do themselves play a critical role in shaping the character and dynamics of conflict-ridden societies).

Thus, to sum up, the political economy of post-conflict statebuilding being investigated has three dimensions:

- the institutions and structures of the formal state, which are reformed and supported by external statebuilding actors;
- the informal structures and actors which precede and/or emerge during the conflict (such as tribal and clan structures, war lords, and criminal and smuggling networks), and which are often central to the organisation and exercise of power in conflict-affected states, and which both complement and compete with formal institutions;
- the international presence, with its peacekeepers, aid agencies, donors and consultants, who often exercise state functions (such as the provision of security), and who (whether intentionally or not) are participants in the politics and conflicts of post-conflict countries.

With this in mind, we can restate in a slightly different form the major aim of the book: to explore whether statebuilding efforts have succeeded in transforming, and in what ways they have done so, the political economy and power structures that have fuelled conflict and violence in the first place. In particular, it aims to examine how international statebuilding policies have affected the domestic actors who, at the end of the conflict, exercise political power, dominate state institutions, and control and exploit economic assets.

Shortcomings of the existing statebuilding literature

Such a political economy perspective challenges two important strands of the literature on post-conflict statebuilding. First, it challenges what has aptly been described as a "mechanical metaphor" of state failure that has informed both the writings on and the practice of Western-led statebuilding. This is the tendency to treat failed states much "like broken machines, [which] can be repaired by good mechanics" (Ellis 2005: 6). It is a conception of state failure that naturally lends itself to technocratic approaches and solutions. Second, it challenges the literature on "liberal statebuilding" and "liberal peacebuilding", which has been highly critical of these efforts predominantly (but not exclusively) on normative grounds, and which has made some rather brave assumptions about the coherence of the "liberal state-building project" (Richmond 2005), and the extent to which the failures of statebuilding can be attributed to the imputed underlying liberal ideology.

Technocratic approaches to statebuilding

Much of the writing on statebuilding has been technocratic and template driven in nature, proceeding from the assumption that state failure is fundamentally a "function of low capacity". Ken Menkhaus (2010: 176) neatly summarises the policy prescriptions that flow from this view:

> By reducing state failure to a matter of low capacity, this view lends itself to technical solutions … More funding, better trained civil servants, a more professionalised and equipped police force, and a healthy dose of democratisation (where not politically inconvenient) have been the main elements of state-building strategies.

As a consequence, the focus of this literature has mainly been on "inputs" such as time, financial aid, and troops and police on the ground (Dobbins *et al.* 2005a, 2005b), and on the promotion of particular institutional templates – especially democracy (i.e. Rotberg 2004) – rather than actual processes of statebuilding, the dynamics between external and local actors, and their impact on the political economy of societies. Approached in this way, it is hardly surprising that statebuilding practice and much of the writings on it (including key donor documents from the World Bank and OECD/DAC) have tended to focus on (a) how to strengthen state capacity by building formal institutions and/or (b) problems specifically relating to "delivery", including, *inter alia*, lack of donor coordination, bureaucratic turf battles among agencies, poor sequencing and inadequate implementation of otherwise sound plans. These are not unimportant issues, but focusing only on them runs the risk of conceptualising and treating societies subject to statebuilding interventions as passive and static.

A political economy perspective on statebuilding points to two problems with this literature in particular. First, a technocratic approach to statebuilding fails to account for the fundamentally political character of such interventions. It tends to view the statebuilding policies promoted or imposed by external actors as largely unproblematic technical fixes to capacity and collective action problems, taking their local legitimacy for granted (i.e. Ghani and Lockhart 2008; Paris 2004; Rotberg 2004), especially if these interventions are conducted by liberal states or multilateral institutions such as the UN (i.e. Keohane 2003; Dobbins *et al.* 2005a). However, not only do such efforts affect deeply political questions, such as the balance of power between different societal groups and the distribution and access to state resources, but the institutional changes advanced by external actors also interact with local values and interests, and local conceptions of legitimacy, which shape the perceptions of populations affected by statebuilding of both the objectives and the legitimacy of external statebuilding actors and their policies (see also Whalan 2010).

Second, technocratic approaches to statebuilding fail to consider the ways in which international and local actors interact in statebuilding contexts, how local interests and values shape these interactions, and what the implications of this are for statebuilding outcomes. They typically gloss over the interests and motivations of local actors, in particular local elites, and fail to consider that not only might a weak or "failed" state be in the interest of certain local actors, but also that in some cases local elites have actively worked to hollow out the state and its institutions in order to entrench their own power and personal economic interests (Bayart *et al.* 1999; Reno 2011b). Above all, they fail to account for the critical role of informal and traditional authorities and power structures in post-conflict environments, the continued existence of wartime economic and political networks, and the historical and cultural specificities of each case. Understanding these, and the impact of statebuilding efforts on them, is, we contend, also central to an understanding of the particular challenges that a peaceful and stable order faces in different war-torn countries.

In response to criticisms that key donors' statebuilding efforts have not been sensitive to their impact on conflict recidivism (i.e. del Castillo 2008; Paris 2004), to the specific cultures of different statebuilding environments (i.e. MacGinty 2008; Richmond 2011; Zaum 2007) and to the continuities of war economies (i.e. Berdal 2009; Cramer 2006), there has been a marked shift in some of the most recent donor documents on statebuilding practices (if not necessarily their practice). The World Bank's 2011 *World Development Report: Conflict, Security, and Development*, emphasises the importance of "drawing from the beginning on the knowledge of national reformers", and recognises that "institutional changes that could produce greater long-term resilience against violence frequently carry short-term risks" (2011: 2, 8).

Similarly, a recent guidance document by the OECD/DAC on statebuilding affirms that any statebuilding effort requires "an in-depth analysis of the political, historical, cultural, economic, institutional and social context to understand how it is shaping the incentives and interests of local actors, and the opportunities for state-building" (OECD 2011: 46). Whether statebuilding practice will follow this shift in the rhetoric remains to be seen.[3]

The "liberal statebuilding" critique

The second strand of the literature on statebuilding that is challenged by a political economy perspective is the growing literature on "liberal statebuilding" that has been highly critical of the interventionism of liberal states and international organisations since the end of the Cold War in general, and the state- and peacebuilding efforts associated with it in particular.[4] The "liberal statebuilding" label is most commonly attached to interventions that are either conducted by liberal, Western states (liberal agency); or are motivated by liberal objectives such as responding to large-scale human rights violations or under an international responsibility to protect (liberal objectives); or that promote liberal-democratic political institutions, human rights, effective and "good" governance, and economic liberalisation as a means to bring peace and prosperity to war-torn countries (liberal causal beliefs).

At the core of the criticisms of liberal statebuilding have been two claims in particular. The first is that the promotion – or imposition – of liberal institutions in conflict-affected countries by Western states and international organisations is normatively questionable as, like colonial and imperial rule, it denies autonomy to those subject to such statebuilding interventions (Chandler 2010; Bain 2003).The second is that the specifically liberal character of these statebuilding interventions has caused many of the pathologies suffered by the affected countries (Richmond 2011; Jahn 2007). While an assessment of the normative critique of statebuilding is beyond the scope of this book, many of the detailed case studies of the political economy of statebuilding highlight the often detrimental effects that particular aspects of external interventions have had on post-conflict states and that critics of liberal statebuilding emphasise, such as entrenching large-scale unemployment in Kosovo (see Zaum and Knaus's chapter in this volume), the disintegration of the security sector and the return to violence in East Timor (see Goldstone's chapter in this volume) or the re-militarisation of Iraqi society (see Dodge's chapter in this volume). However, a political economy perspective also highlights several rather problematic assumptions at the heart of these critiques of statebuilding.

The first is the assertion of the existence of a coherent liberal statebuilding project. It is assumed that all those participating in the liberal statebuilding project – Western countries, international organisations and Western NGOs – have similar (liberal) normative commitments, shared motivations for their engagement, shared objectives and similar understanding of the impact of liberal institutions. Not only does it assume a degree of coherence and consensus within liberal thought on statebuilding, but also that external statebuilders act for liberal reasons. However, as we have already observed, the diversity of approaches to and reasons for involvement in statebuilding is considerable. As the cases of Burundi or Kosovo highlight,[5] it can be the divisions between different external actors that create opportunities for the resistance to particular external statebuilding prescriptions, for the assertion of local agency and for the "hybrid" outcomes that critics of statebuilding have identified (McGinty 2011; Richmond 2011).

Second, while statebuilding in post-conflict countries during the 1990s was largely justified in cosmopolitan terms, through references to universal human rights and notions of sovereignty as responsibility; the first decade of the twenty-first century witnessed an increased reliance on justifications based on narrower understandings of national and international security – a development particularly pronounced in the aftermath of the 9/11 attacks. George W. Bush's (2005) justification for regime change in Iraq during his 2005 inaugural address was probably the apogee of this securitisation of statebuilding: "[t]he survival of liberty in our land increasingly depends on the success of liberty in other lands. The best hope for peace in our world is the expansion of freedom in all the world." However, over the last decade the statebuilding efforts in Afghanistan, Iraq or Kosovo have frequently been justified by politicians and officials from the intervening states and organisations with references to the threats of terrorism or of organised crime. While earlier interventions as in Cambodia, Bosnia or Sierra Leone were undoubtedly never purely informed by humanitarian motives, this securitisation of statebuilding and the growing emphasis on the contribution of these interventions to the national security of the interveners, introduces distinctly non-liberal motivations into statebuilding discourses.

Third, as Oisín Tansey (2008) and Roland Paris (2010) have noted, some of the most ardent critics define liberalism and also liberal statebuilding so broadly that the concept fails to provide much analytical purchase anymore. As Paris notes, "such definitional stretching is especially unfortunate because it elides critical distinctions between different forms of external intervention" (2010: 351). One problem is that such a broad understanding of the concept effectively makes every statebuilding intervention by a liberal state a form of liberal statebuilding, focusing attention on the identity of the intervenor rather than the characteristics of the intervention, and subsuming under the same label interventions that have otherwise little in common. Furthermore, such conceptual stretching might actually provide some interventions that have an, at best, perfunctory commitment to liberal values with a veneer of legitimacy amongst audiences that might otherwise be more critical of such efforts. In the case of Iraq, for example, the liberal provenance of the motivations for regime change remains fiercely contested, and the statebuilding programme pursued by the Coalition Provisional Authority and the US military was selective at best in its commitment to liberal values. Grouping it together with far less controversial interventions is likely to diffuse much of the criticism of this particular intervention.

A broader understanding of statebuilding

One assumption that the critics of liberal statebuilding share both with the technocratic literature on the topic, as well as with many donors, is a rather narrow understanding of the state and in consequence of statebuilding. As Menkhaus noted above, literature and donor documents have tended to focus on the capacity of state institutions to develop public policy and deliver particular public goods, and the availability of mechanisms to hold state institutions accountable, in particular democratically accountable. The growing emphasis on building state legitimacy in some of the more recent literature and donor documents (i.e. Call 2008a; Ghani and Lockart 2008; OECD/DAC 2008), reflecting the recognition of the importance of state legitimacy for local support for and compliance with its institutions (Zaum 2012b), also builds on these two elements: greater capacity is seen as central to better state performance when delivering key public services, while democratic accountability is seen as increasing the responsiveness of the state to demands from society.

This conception of statebuilding builds on a particular view of the state, its functions and its relationship to society. It views the state as an actor autonomous from society, deriving its authority from an implicit social contract. Strengthening state capacity then not only improves its ability to fulfil its responsibilities under a social contract but also strengthens its infrastructural power and its autonomy from sectional interests (Mann 1984), while the focus on accountability and democratic legitimacy aims to ensure that the state continues to act within the bounds of the social contract. "Statebuilding", in the words of the OECD, therefore "involves the ongoing negotiation of an unwritten contract between state and society" (OECD/DAC 2011: 13). While critics of the liberal peace have argued that the imposition of institutions and of a very limited, neo-liberal conception of a state responsibility towards its population, have undermined the development of a meaningful social contract (i.e. Pugh and Divjak 2011; Richmond 2011); they still conceive of statebuilding as "vertical statebuilding", structuring the relationship between an autonomous state and society.

Associated with this conception of the state and statebuilding is a particular understanding of the origins of the conflicts that have elicited statebuilding interventions, rooting them in the weakness, persistent fragility and even the collapse of state institutions (i.e. Ghani and Lockart 2008; Herbst 1997; Rotberg 2004; Zartmann 1995). Just as economic, "greed" based explanations for civil war have been criticised for failing to consider the important interdependencies between economic motives and opportunities and political grievances and motivations for conflict (Berdal 2009), the focus on state capacity (or lack thereof) and state–society relations has distracted from the relationships between different groups within society, the role of the state in structuring these relationships and the ways in which different groups (rather than society as a whole) relate to the state. It ignores that the ways in which different groups experience the state, and its apparent weakness or failure, differs between various social groups. It ignores that it might not be problems of rule and control (the lack of which is implicit in the state weakness argument), but questions of allocation of resources – of jobs, of state services – by the state to different constituencies that fuel conflict. As this volume highlights, it is often the character of this latter relationship, and the resulting discrimination against and marginalisation of particular groups, that has fuelled conflict in places such as Burundi, Kosovo, Macedonia or Sierra Leone. What Kalevi Holsti has termed the "horizontal legitimacy" of the state – "the attitudes and practices of individuals and groups within the state toward each other and ultimately to the state that encompasses them" (1996: 84) – is as important for understanding the particular challenges to be addressed by statebuilding efforts as are the sources and character of state weakness or failure.

Understanding the impact of statebuilding on the political economy of post-war states and on the sources of continuing violence within them, then, requires a broader understanding of statebuilding beyond the focus on democratic legitimacy and governmental capacity. It also needs to take account of "state design" (Call 2008a: 8–11) and of the ways in which external statebuilding efforts, through the formal and informal institutions they give rise to, structure the relations between different social groups, for example through power sharing agreements, consociational institutions, transitional arrangements or territorial settlements, including, as in the case of Sudan, secession and the creation of a new state.

The present volume was conceived with this broader understanding of statebuilding in mind. Its chief virtue is to bring out and draw attention to the complex ways – direct and indirect, intended or unintended – that external statebuilding efforts have impacted on the distribution of power and influence within conflict-affected societies. As such, it is also a vital requirement for sound policy making. In this respect, the book points to five broad conclusions of wider policy relevance.

First, the narrow understanding of statebuilding that dominates much of the literature and that has tended to shape policy making – and whose focus is on state weakness primarily as a source of conflict – is shown by these essays to be problematic and unsatisfactory. It ignores that the experience of the state, and its apparent weakness or failure, is different for various social groups, and it might not be problems of rule and control (the lack of which is implicit in the state weakness argument), but questions of allocation of resources by the state to different constituencies that fuel conflict. These questions about allocation – of state services, of jobs and other public goods – are at the heart of the conflicts and of the statebuilding efforts in places as diverse as Sudan, Macedonia, Burundi or Kosovo.

Second, informal structures and war economies that have crystallised during periods of protracted violence are resilient, adaptable and difficult to transform by outsiders, especially so if that presence is constrained by finite resources and time, conflicting interests among donors and by a set of statebuilding priorities that privileges formal institutions over the underlying political economy of war and peace. As the contributions in this volume show, clandestine structures that form in times of conflict have remained central to the political economy of places as diverse as East Timor, Kosovo or Afghanistan.

Third, understanding the political economy of any given conflict zone is of particular importance to an understanding of the multiple and overlapping sources of violence in post-war states (and how the actions of outsiders can contribute to that violence). A political economy approach draws attention to how different actors in a post-conflict zone – political and military elites, economic interest groups, external players – can develop an interest and see functional utility in the continuation of violence and conflict. When these interests come together, new social and economic orders, often illiberal and predatory, emerge in the midst of state "collapse" or "failure". Key examples of this include the emergence of "popular organisations" in Haiti, but also the complex role of elites in resisting earlier political settlements in the country (see Robert Muggah's chapter in this volume), and the way in which key wartime leaders able to threaten or exercise violence were able to capture the statebuilding processes for example in Afghanistan and reinforce the political and social order that had emerged during the time of conflict (see Stina Torjesen's chapter in this volume).

Fourth, the continuities from the pre-war and wartime period are often as central to the post-war organisation of power and political economy as are the changes induced by both conflict and statebuilding. In Burundi, the dramatic change of personnel in the governing elite, and international statebuilding efforts aimed at democratising and reforming political and administrative institutions have left the practices and organisation of power largely untouched (as discussed in Uvin and Bayer's chapter in this volume). As Toby Dodge argues in his chapter, US-led statebuilding efforts in Iraq have recreated a highly militarised state that continues to dominate the national economy in terms of employment and its reliance on the oil economy. In Kosovo, the number of people employed in the formal economy, and the dependence of the state on external transfers, has remained largely unchanged since the 1970s – despite a decade of sanctions, conflict and over a decade of international statebuilding efforts.

Finally, none of the above is meant to suggest that the impact of outside statebuilding is either negligible or uniformly negative, only that the effects have sometimes proved perverse and unintended. This is especially clear when we look at one of the central themes that emerges from the contributions to this volume: how state- and peacebuilding policies, including elections and power-sharing deals, can serve to consolidate the power of wartime elites or facilitate their re-emergence or "recycling" after the formal end of hostilities.

Organisation of this book

The remainder of this book is divided into three parts. The first part (Chapters 2 to 7) examines the political economy of statebuilding thematically. Chapter 2 examines the efforts to reshape the institutional framework and the organisation of power in conflict-affected countries through involvement in processes of constitutional design, and argues that existing power structures and domestic political dynamics tend to prevail over international designs. This theme of continuity in the political economy is also reflected in Chapters 4 and 5, which highlight the ability of wartime elites to use statebuilding interventions to entrench their pre-eminence in the post-war order, and the continued importance of informal wartime actors and power structures complementing and at times colonising formal state institutions respectively. Chapter 3 examines the role of elections for post-conflict political development, and argues for the importance of developing programmatic political parties that are not personalistic and rooted in already existing patronage structures. The remaining chapters in this part discuss the focus on anti-corruption in statebuilding operations (Chapter 6) and efforts to regulating the extraction and trade in natural resources that have frequently fuelled conflict and challenged statebuilding efforts (Chapter 7).

The second part of the book (Chapters 8 to 11) examines the approaches to statebuilding taken by different regional and international organisations. Chapter 8 argues that the UN's lack of a coherent approach to statebuilding is shaped both by its intergovernmental character and the fragmentation into a wide array of specialised agencies involved in such efforts, and the deep divisions amongst its members over the organisation's peace- and statebuilding activities. It has no consistent conception of the kind of state that it wants to build, or approach it pursues, in contrast to the World Bank and the IMF. As Susan Woodward argues in Chapter 9, "[the] model of the state in all IFI policies, regardless of country context, is that which is considered necessary for markets and the private sector to function, and no more" (p. 144). Chapters 10 and 11 discuss regional organisations' engagement in statebuilding examining the European Union, and the African Union (AU) and ECOWAS respectively. Both chapters highlight that regional organisations, despite extensive involvement in statebuilding, have to date been unable to play a leading strategic role, either because their limited resources meant that ambitious statebuilding frameworks have yet to be implemented (in case of the AU or ECOWAS), or because they have mostly left the leadership of such operations to other bodies, such as the UN or ad hoc arrangements (in case of the EU).

The book's final part (Chapters 12 to 20) examines a diverse range of case studies, loosely grouped into three categories. The first three cases of Iraq, East Timor and Kosovo (Chapters 12 to 14) are instances where statebuilders assumed comprehensive executive authority for a temporary period. Chapters 15 to 18 examine the complex peace operations in Afghanistan, Burundi, Sudan and Haiti. The final two chapters (19 and 30) assess the impact on the political economy of governance and statebuilding programmes conducted in the context of economic and governance assistance in Georgia and Macedonia.

We have sought to include a wide range both of statebuilding cases and practices, and of contributors to this book. Despite this, the book is neither a complete record of statebuilding, nor can it do justice to the wide variety of opinions on statebuilding as a central practice of contemporary international order. Important practices like security sector reform are not discussed in dedicated chapters, but feature in the discussion of a range of case studies, such as Iraq, East Timor, Haiti and Macedonia. Paradigmatic cases of state-building, such as Bosnia, Cambodia or Sierra Leone, are not discussed in sep-arate chapters, but are examined in the context of some of the thematic chapters. We take full responsibility for these omissions.

Notes

1 Other authors use very similar definitions. David Chandler (2006: 1) defines state-building as "constructing or reconstructing institutions of governance capable of providing citizens with physical and economic security"; while Roland Paris and Timothy Sisk (2009: 1) define it as "the construction or strengthening of legitimate governmental institutions in countries emerging from civil conflict". A conceptually useful distinction is sometimes drawn between "statebuilding" and "state forma-tion". State formation refers to endogenous processes taking place within a longer historical time frame and is not necessarily confined to the creation of formal insti-tutions and state capacity. It may also cover less tangible factors such as the gradual development of a sense of community and emergence of shared civic virtues. While our focus, by contrast, is on contemporary external or exogenous statebuilding efforts, we do recognise, as do many of our authors, the relevance of the insights offered by the literature on state formation (an important theme of which has been the role of organised violence and fiscal extraction in the process) to an under-standing the contemporary statebuilding challenges.
2 For the argument that the threat from weak states is overstated, see Patrick 2011.
3 A closer reading of the 2011 *World Development Report* suggests that it does not con-stitute a significant departure from the Bank's traditional involvement in post-conflict countries. The underlying assumption of state weakness or failure as the main driver of conflict and the key obstacle to peace and development, and the associated conception of the state, its roles and functions, and its relationship with the wider civil society, have remained largely unchanged. Throughout the report, there is little critical reflection on the impact that policies promoted by the Bank have had on post-conflict states, and which are well documented in the literature. While it recognises the importance of the local context, it does not question the suitability of its reform packets for different countries, merely the speed with which they are implemented. For a more detailed discussion, see Zaum 2012a.
4 Much of this literature uses the term *liberal peacebuilding*, rather than *liberal state-building*, but considers statebuilding to be a critical part of the liberal peacebuilding model.
5 See chapters by Uvin and Bayer, and Zaum and Knaus.

Part I

A political economy perspective on selected statebuilding practices

2 Statebuilding and the limits of constitutional design

Oisín Tansey

The political economy of any individual post-conflict or fragile state can be traced to a multitude of antecedent conditions, including the history of conflict within the country, the societal cleavages that exist within the population and the inequality in access to resources enjoyed by different groups. Some of these conditions, such as history and geography, are deeply embedded and difficult if not impossible to change, while others are more amenable to alteration and redirection. One arena in which political actors in all countries see potential for managing and possibly reshaping economic and power relations is that of formal constitutional institutions, which can be used to regulate society and have the added benefit of being relatively easy to amend. Constitutional design is thus a key tool in the armoury of those who wish to modify patterns of political economy in post-conflict settings, even when those figures are external actors not usually associated with constitution writing.

Constitutions can in some ways be seen as the ultimate expression of a state's sovereignty and independence. These documents lay down the fundamental laws of the state and are often the result of extensive deliberation among national politicians and publics about the values and principles upon which a state is founded. Constitutions are often sources of national pride, and in some cases are tightly bound up with a sense of national identity. Yet throughout history many of these quintessentially 'national' institutions have been shaped by international influences, both through the passive diffusion of constitutional politics beyond a state's borders and also through the more direct influence of international involvement in the constitutional drafting process itself. Constitutional ideas spread easily across borders, and constitutional advice is commonly offered by experts in one country to constitutional drafters in another.

In the context of statebuilding, international involvement in constitutional design and development is arguably at its peak, as external officials assume roles in the domestic political system that are usually held by domestic actors and actively seek to influence and reshape the domestic political landscape. In a statebuilder's ideal world, this task is often a relatively simple one of institutional reform. International actors develop a clear vision of the most important political challenges to be addressed, and then identify the optimal institutional arrangements that will help resolve and overcome these challenges. New or reformed institutions are designed to achieve the desired political outcomes, often by revising or replacing existing constitutions, and once they are introduced at the national level they steadily lead to changes in the domestic political environment that improve conditions and lead to peace, democracy and stability.

However, the reality is obviously not so simple. The task of institutional design is profoundly complex, and such ambitious efforts have multiple opportunities for miscalculations, missteps and errors. Even if the design process itself is flawless, the separate challenge of implementation creates a fresh range of opportunities for slippage between international goals and ultimate institutional effects. The focus of this chapter is the inherently limited nature of constitutional design in the context of statebuilding, and the range of obstacles that statebuilders will face in any effort to alter the political economy of post-conflict states. Three separate categories of limits are identified, each of which constrains statebuilders in their efforts to reshape and transform existing political structures. The complexity and unpredictability of institutions themselves, the fundamental differences between domestic and international actors, and the resilience of domestic political structures all combine in ways to ensure that the goals and outcomes of institutional reform rarely coalesce as planned. No matter how much international actors wish to reshape and reform the domestic political economy, it is the primacy of domestic politics that is a major theme of recent statebuilding efforts, as domestic actors and structures have outlasted and at times outmanoeuvred international actors and have ensured that the statebuilding process has been as much a domestic political enterprise as it has an international one.

Statebuilding and institutional design

Political institutions come in myriad forms, and definitions of political institutions are no different. Although informal customs and practices undoubtedly shape political outcomes, in this chapter I focus on formal political institutions that, following Pierson (2004: 104), can be defined as 'the codified rules of political contestation'. Furthermore, I focus in particular (although not exclusively) on constitutional institutions, and address the efforts of international statebuilders to use constitutional reform as a means to alter domestic political structures and outcomes.

There is a long history of foreign intervention in constitutional affairs. Krasner (1999) has shown how state sovereignty has routinely been breached throughout international history, often due to the intention of one state to shape the constitutional arrangements of another. The victorious powers of the First World War intervened to ensure that the successor states of the Ottoman Empire had constitutions and leaders that were deemed acceptable. The aftermath of the Second World War saw similar efforts, as the Allied powers were instrumental in the development of constitutional structures in the defeated powers, with the US involvement in the drafting of Japan's constitution often seen as the paradigmatic instance of constitutional imposition under external occupation. Yet Japan is far from the only case, and a recent study by Elkins *et al.* (2008) has identified 42 constitutions that were developed under conditions of occupation (excluding multilateral statebuilding), with Russia, the US and France the most intrusive states in overseeing new constitutions. These trends can also be seen as part of a wider pattern over several centuries in which international actors have routinely sought to impose their favoured political institutions in other countries (Owen 2002). In the context of recent statebuilding efforts, a central goal of this form of intervention has been a desire to alter and reshape the structures that govern domestic politics, to reshape the domestic political economy. As Chesterman (2005: 947) writes, 'the rationale for international engagement is typically the malevolence or incapacity of existing governance structures: intervention is premised precisely on the need to transform or build those structures, rather than to maintain them.'

One of the central strategies for reshaping these structures is to reform existing institutions or to create new ones. In the context of international statebuilding, international actors are in a position to involve themselves in these reform processes through a number of intrusive mechanisms. International statebuilders are in a position not only to pressurise or persuade local actors into reforming their institutions, but in some settings can also draft and impose their own institutional provisions and thus remove the very need for any action on the part of domestic elites themselves. Particular forms of leverage available to international actors in these settings include:

- *agenda-setting powers*, which can enable statebuilders to influence which issues are subject to discussion;
- *veto powers*, which can include the ability to strike down institutions that are proposed by domestic actors;
- *drafting powers*, where international actors can involve themselves in drafting basic constitutional provisions;
- *imposition authority*, which provides international administrations with the ability to bypass domestic actors entirely and enforce measures they deem necessary.

Given these powers, the need for action on the part of domestic parties can sometimes be removed completely, as international statebuilders effectively replace domestic politicians and officials. Similarly, when domestic actors do make decisions, if they are not compatible with international priorities and interests, they can be overruled and essentially nullified. However, the impact of such measures does not always correspond to the objectives they were designed to achieve. Even when international actors have extensive executive authority at the domestic level, the reality is that the processes of institutional design and reform are characterised by complexity and unpredictability, and international actors are rarely able to implement their plans without constraint. There are several reasons to believe that international actions in the context of statebuilding will not quickly result in the translation of international intentions into domestic-level political outcomes, and the remainder of this chapter will identify three separate considerations that highlight the particular limitations of constitutional design in the context of statebuilding. The next section explores limits on institutional design in general, and highlights how the perspectives of institutional designers and the complexities of institutions themselves create obstacles to the easy translation of goals into outcomes. The subsequent sections highlight limitations that are directly related to the context of statebuilding itself, and show how the distinct identity of international statebuilders and the resilience of pre-existing actors and structures ensure that constitutional design in these settings is a difficult process in which institutional changes do not necessarily lead to changes in pre-existing power structures.

The limits of institutional design

The creation of new constitutions and the reform of existing constitutional institutions are seen as some of the most promising ways of altering the character of politics within a country, and often accompany periods of political transition and change (Elster *et al.* 1998; Reynolds 2002). Yet there are a number of factors that suggest efforts to reshape or rebuild political institutions will not easily lead to intended outcomes. Paul Pierson (2004) has identified a range of limitations to instrumental institutional design that highlight the ways in which the ultimate effects of institutions will often differ from the aims of the institutional designers. Although Pierson writes with reference to national actors in domestic politics, his insights are highly relevant for assessments of international statebuilding, and many of the limitations he identifies can be seen in international efforts to build and reform constitutional institutions in weak or post-conflict states.

First, Pierson writes that institutional designers may have short-term time horizons, and as a result that institutions may reflect immediate rather than long-term considerations. In domestic politics, the electoral cycle is the principal reason for the short time horizons of political actors, but in the context of statebuilding similar limitations may also apply to international actors, who often have financial and political pressures of their own that provide incentives for short-term results. Consequently, institutions may be designed to achieve swift political outcomes, even when the underlying challenges being addressed may require longer-term considerations. For example, the UN mission in East Timor, UNTAET, promoted a relatively short timetable for constitutional design despite some national opposition, in part due to financial pressures facing the mission itself (Tansey 2009; see also Anthony Goldstone's chapter in this volume).

Second, even when institutional designers have clear long- or short-term goals, it is often the case that institutions have unanticipated and unintended consequences. Actors can make mistakes in institutional design, and the nature of politics can mean institutions will have effects in realms they were not intended to influence. Because of the complexity of social and political interaction, it is difficult for institutional designers to anticipate the effects new institutions will have once they are established. Time constraints, scarcity of information and the need for individuals to delegate responsibilities to others means that initially precise institutional designs may be reshaped by the actors who work within and interact with them on a day-to-day basis. Consequently, institutions may have multiple effects, and even when they bring about expected and desired outcomes, they may also lead to distinct and potentially undesirable effects in other areas (Pierson 2004). Provisions of the Bosnian constitution, for example, have been interpreted in ways that were originally unanticipated by its international and Bosnian drafters. In 2000, Bosnia's Constitutional Court ruled that the constitution's commitment to the equality of each of the 'constituent peoples' in Bosnia (the term used in the constitution to designate the Bosniac, Serb and Croat ethnic groups) meant the constitutions of Bosnia's two sub-state entities (the Federation and Republika Srpska) were incompatible with the state constitution and had to be amended. While the Preamble to the state constitution named the Bosniacs, Croats and Serbs as constituent peoples of Bosnia, the entity constitutions seemed to name entity constituent peoples more selectively; for example, in Republika Srpska the entity constitution declared the entity to be 'the state of the Serb people'. The result of the Court's ruling, which itself rested on a five/four majority vote that included the affirmative votes of three international judges, was a prolonged and fraught series of negotiations between the international community and Bosnia's political parties that was ultimately only resolved by the controversial imposition of new legislation by the High Representative. The resulting changes weakened the political grip of the majority communities in each entity and ensured greater political representation for minority interests that had previously been marginalised (ICG 2002).

Finally, there is the problem of 'actor discontinuity'. Institutions are often designed to outlive their creators, and to become part of a permanent political structure. However, there is no guarantee that future generations – what Pierson (2004) calls 'the inheritors' of an institution – will have the same political goals and will wish to use the institution in the same way. Consequently, institutions may only last for as long as their creators are actively engaged in maintaining them before they are removed or altered by the subsequent generation of political actors. This final limitation on institutional design applies to all contexts, but has particular relevance for episodes of statebuilding, when the international authorities by definition represent a temporary presence in domestic politics, and the 'inheritors' of the institutions may not be a distant generation of the political class, but the existing domestic political elites who soon regain full control of domestic authority. In such settings, as will be explored further below, domestic actors may feel no loyalty to constitutional structures that were established in part through international fiat.

Statebuilding and the limits of international design

The limits of institutional design discussed above are not unique to state-building environments, and can be seen in many cases of institutional development in advanced industrial democracies as well as in transitional and post-conflict settings. Yet the nature of statebuilding itself does create a distinct political environment, and some of the characteristics of international statebuilding can also add further limits to the process of institutional design that may not apply in more conventional settings. This is largely due to the particular context of international statebuilding, when international actors are heavily involved in political processes at the domestic level. While these external elites often play roles that in more conventional cases are associated with domestic actors, their status always remains separate from that of their local counterparts, and their distinct identities and interests can have implications for the design process.

As Killick (1998) has highlighted with reference to international aid provision, international and domestic authorities retain separate identities and interests for a number of reasons. First, they have different histories and political origins, which can lead outside actors to apply ahistorical models and templates to distinctive political settings without regard to important historical legacies. Second, the constituencies they need to satisfy are also separate, with domestic actors having to address the demands of local electorates, while international authorities are often accountable to international bodies such as the UN Security Council, which in turn are made up of individual states that have their own domestic electorates to consider. Third, the fact that one party to the relationship (the international authorities) does not bear the full consequences of its actions (for example, does not have to abide by institutional arrangements it recommends or imposes at the domestic level) gives rise to a separate set of attitudes regarding the risk and desirability of political change. Each of these three points of distinction suggests that there are particular limits on institutional design that are specific to contexts of international statebuilding.

First, the differing histories and origins of international and national actors can lead to different understandings about the appropriateness of particular institutions. One of the key themes in assessments of international statebuilding efforts has been the lack of context-specific information on the part of international actors, who often lack expert knowledge of a country's history and political background. As Caplan (2005: 177) has written of statebuilding operations,

> given the profile of the personnel who serve in these missions – many of them consultants or career diplomats on secondment to the mission for a limited period of time – it has usually been very difficult to recruit a sufficient number of individuals with detailed understanding of the region and the history of international engagement in the region, let alone of other regions. As a result, the knowledge base and knowledge accumulation have both been limited.

This lack of local knowledge has at times led to the introduction of institutions that have not been suitable given the particular nature of the existing political environment in which they have been established. For example, UN efforts at political reform in East Timor were criticised for failing to acknowledge and account for traditional patterns of authority that were not fully compatible with the new institutions (Hohe 2004). The distinct histories and origins of international statebuilders can thus lead to particular challenges to institutional design that are not faced when national actors are pursuing similar efforts.

The second distinction between international and domestic actors, that of their separate political constituencies, also has implications for institutional design. The need for national and international actors to satisfy distinct political audiences means that their interests may often diverge. As a result, international actors may have incentives to approach the task of institutional design with a view to satisfying domestic constituencies at home, for example by moving swiftly to create new institutions that will facilitate international withdrawal, rather than satisfying either the interests of local parties or even the interests international actors might wish to pursue in the absence of their own domestic pressures.

For example, the political timetable in Iraq went through many iterations in the early months of the US-led occupation, and the dates in its fluctuating calendar were sometimes the result of domestic US considerations rather than considerations of Iraqi politics. When the chief administrator of the Coalition Provisional Authority, Paul Bremer, announced a seven-step timetable for political transition (including constitution writing) in September 2003, it appeared to suggest a political process that could last up to two years (Dobbins *et al.* 2009). However, it quickly became clear that such a lengthy commitment was unpopular within the Bush administration and the US army (as well as members of Iraq's Governing Council), and the timetable was swiftly revised to give a clear, and expedited, date of 30 June 2004 for the handover of sovereignty. This date did not hold any particular significance within Iraq, and was widely interpreted as a means of achieving a significant reduction in US presence in Iraq before the November US presidential elections. Although there would be no significant drawdown of troops, the removal of Bremer and the CPA was deemed a necessary step by the Bush administration to show progress in time for the domestic elections (Feldman 2004: 117).

The third disjuncture between the identities and interests of international statebuilders and national actors concerns the fact that the former can introduce new institutions that they will ultimately not be bound by, and as a result they may be less concerned with issues of risk and sustainability than their local counterparts. Actors who do not have to be bound by the rules they are drawing up may be freer to be more ambitious and innovative in the institutional designs they develop, without having to worry about risks involved or how the institutions will affect their own positions in a national political system. However, this freedom also means that they may draft rules that will create such concerns for domestic elites, and that may thus be vulnerable to efforts by national elites to reverse or amend the institutional reforms, or may simply not be implemented once introduced.

One area where international standards may be applied but where domestic structures and political will may not be fully supportive is in the areas of human rights and minority protections. A common theme of international involvement in constitutional development in recent years has been a strong emphasis on enshrining international human rights law and ensuring robust (and often intricate) provisions for the protection of minority communities. The recent process leading to the introduction of Kosovo's 2008 constitution entailed international encouragement for the inclusion of robust minority rights protection provisions, described as the most advanced set of minority rights in the world (Weller 2009: 257). However, this has also raised questions about sustainability. As leading Kosovo and minority rights expert Marc Weller (ibid.: 257) has noted,

> it remains to be seen whether such a comprehensive set of obligations can be fully implemented through Kosovo's limited institutional structure ... Implementing the very ambitious set of provisions in full will certainly strain the resources and capacity of Kosovo significantly.

The primacy of domestic politics

The challenges to institutional design raised above relate primarily to the identity and character of the institutional designers, and their role in the design process. A further challenge to institutional design in the context of statebuilding derives from the domestic actors and structures that play a critical role in mediating the activities and influence of international actors, and that are instrumental in determining the ultimate outcome of external statebuilding efforts. In the process of constitutional design, in the efforts to have a constitution ratified and in the process of constitutional implementation, national-level factors will often play a central, if not determinant, role. It can be helpful here to distinguish between two stages of the constitutional process. First, the process by which a constitution comes into being, and is drafted by a range of interested political actors. Second, and subsequently, comes the process by which this new document becomes (or fails to become) implemented in the political system. Both stages are crucially important, and both are heavily shaped by the nature of pre-existing domestic political structures, even when such structures are themselves the target of the institutional reform efforts.

Constitution drafting

International statebuilders are rarely able to work in isolation from their national counterparts. One important category of mediating factors that can limit international design efforts are thus the domestic elites who command political authority at the national level and can directly or indirectly involve themselves in the drafting process. These central actors can comprise national politicians, bureaucrats or other prominent actors such as military, religious or civil society leaders. Together, they help constitute the domestic political landscape, and it is often their patterns of political elite authority that international statebuilders seek to alter and reshape through their constitutional reform efforts. However, even as targets of change, these national elites are often in a position to engage with and constrain international actors, thus limiting their constitutional endeavours and frustrating their efforts at political change.

Involvement of local negotiators

In the realm of constitutional design and development, one of the clearest ways in which national actors can influence the process is through involvement in the design process itself. Although there is an increasing literature on 'imposed constitutionalism' (Chesterman 2005; Feldman 2005), it is rare for important domestic institutions to be fully imposed from outside without any significant domestic input. In all recent cases of international statebuilding, constitutional design efforts have entailed a process of interaction between international and national actors, often through quite formal procedures. As a result, the process of institutional design has involved extensive negotiation and bargaining between these distinct sets of elites, and those seeking to promote change from outside have often found that their *de jure* authority on the ground is worth little when compared to the *de facto* authority of respected and popular national political players.

Several recent instances of constitutional design in the context of statebuilding have seen international constitutional plans significantly modified by the involvement of national elites in the drafting process. In Kosovo, the UNMIK mission quickly established some interim consultative institutions before initiating a process to develop a more comprehensive constitutional structure that would pave the way for a significant transfer of power to elected local authorities. During 2001, Kosovo experienced a critical period of political transition, as international and domestic officials negotiated, and clashed, over this new legal framework. To facilitate the process, UNMIK established a joint working group that would bring international and local officials together to develop the new set of institutions. From the beginning, each side sought to ensure their political priorities were advanced at the expense of the other. The local Kosovo Albanian members sought to ensure the legal framework would closely resemble a conventional constitution, while the international side sought to avoid prejudging the sensitive issue of Kosovo's political status by ensuring that the document did not suggest that Kosovo was an independent state or even on the road to independence. Ultimately, the document fell far short of Kosovar demands for a full constitution that would include provisions allowing for a referendum on independence. The UN mission set down a series of 'red-line' issues and used its extensive authority to ensure they were not crossed.

However, even though the international administration enjoyed full legislative and executive authority under its sweeping UN mandate,[1] it was forced to give way on a number of issues during the negotiation period after sustained Kosovar pressure. The document contained provisions that had not originally been anticipated by the UN negotiators (for example, the provision for a president of Kosovo), and although it fell well short of the standing of a full constitution, it resembled one to a much greater extent than had originally been intended (Tansey 2009: 124–130).

Similarly, in Iraq in 2003, the US-led administration quickly found that its preferences for constitutional design and development could not easily be translated into reality due to the mediating role of national political elites. Some of these elites were not directly involved in the negotiating process (to be discussed further below) while others had a seat at the table and played an integral role in the drafting process. One of the critical stages of institutional development in Iraq concerned the development of the Transitional Administrative Law (TAL) in 2003/4, which was to act as Iraq's interim constitution before a permanent one could be drafted. As with Kosovo, the international administrators in Iraq had some red lines across which they did not want the negotiations on the TAL to cross, and they were able to veto some domestic demands. A key area of concern was the role of Islam in the constitution, and the US negotiators ensured that Islam was referred to as '*a* source' of legislation, rather than *the* source. The US also pushed hard (and succeeded) in inserting a provision for a low parliamentary threshold for the ratification of international treaties (a simple majority rather than a two-thirds majority). This was resisted by the Iraqi negotiators, but the US pressure (based on its interests in being able to sign security treaties with Iraqi authorities) ensured that a provision requiring a two-thirds majority for such treaties was dropped from the draft document (Diamond 2005: 159).

However, the Iraqi negotiators also succeeded in inserting provisions that the international administrators had not anticipated and had argued against. Towards the end of the negotiations over the TAL, Islamist Shiite negotiators gained a concession which forbade the passage of any law that would contradict 'the universally agreed tenets of Islam', which was counter to the original US intentions (Feldman 2004: 88). Similarly, the Kurdish negotiators bargained extensively with their international counterparts, and with Sunni and Shiite representatives, to achieve many of their desired preferences. According to Larry Diamond, one of the CPA's constitutional negotiators, the Kurds were the most effective Iraqi negotiators and achieved many core goals (such as regional autonomy and an effective veto ratification of the constitution) which had been initially opposed by other negotiators including the CPA (Diamond 2005: 174).

Domestic actors outside negotiations

A separate dynamic concerning political elites in this area of constitutional design relates to those influential actors who are not directly involved in the political process, but whose stature in society is such that their views must be taken into account and their influence can be felt even despite their lack of formal political authority. Often these influential elites can be found among tribal or religious leaders in societies where traditional forms of authority are valued more than those associated with the modern state. Statebuilders in Afghanistan, for example, have had to contend with a society where tribal and religious leaders are perceived in some quarters as more legitimate authorities than those representing the central states, and struggled at times to appreciate the extent of their influence (Ponzio 2011). Possibly the clearest example of such indirect influence is the role of Ayatollah Ali Al-Sistani in Iraq. Al-Sistani was a senior Shiite cleric who intervened in the constitutional debate in Iraq in the early stages of the US-led occupation through a series of public statements and the practice of some shrewd and quiet diplomacy. Although he had limited formal political authority, his pronouncements ultimately had considerable effects on the policies of the CPA and the nature of Iraq's transitional constitutional process. In particular, two of Al-Sistani's interventions changed US constitutional plans in significant ways. The first was a fatwa he released in June 2003 that criticised the international administrators for suggesting that Iraq's permanent constitution might be written in an unelected chamber. The CPA's original plan had envisaged an appointed national conference to draft the constitution, and Al-Sistani's fatwa questioned the jurisdiction of the international occupation, asserted that the CPA's constitutional plans were unacceptable and called for an elected chamber to draft a constitution that would then be subject to ratification by public referendum (Feldman 2004: 40). Although the CPA did not initially appreciate the full weight of this fatwa, it ultimately realised that Al-Sistani's authority within Iraq meant that an appointed constitutional body would lack legitimacy in the eyes of the Shiite community and was no longer feasible. However, its alternative suggestion, as outlined in the so-called 15 November agreement of 2003, was for an interim government to serve in power until elections could be held for a Constituent Assembly. These plans also fell foul of Al-Sistani, as the interim government was to be indirectly elected through a complex system of regional caucuses. Once again, Al-Sistani made clear his preference for direct elections, this time for the interim government (Diamond 2005: 58). However, the CPA was adamant that elections could not be held in time for the June 2004 transfer of sovereignty due to a range of considerations including practical concerns about the lack of a capable electoral administration and political concerns about the risk that early elections might bring hardliners to power. As a result, a compromise was reached and the US turned to the UN and requested that it explore the feasibility of elections. A mission led by the senior UN diplomat Lakhdar Brahimi was deployed, and ultimately concluded that elections were not a viable option before June 2004 (United Nations 2004b). Al-Sistani accepted the findings, but while he did not get the direct elections for the interim government that he had sought, the US plan for regional caucuses was dropped and the UN was heavily involved in the appointment of a relatively technocratic interim government. Throughout the period of the CPA's administration of Iraq, Al-Sistani demonstrated the limits of *de jure* international authority and highlighted the capacity of important domestic actors to place significant constraints on the institutional design efforts of international statebuilders.

Implementing constitutional changes

For any constitution or political institution to be successful, it has to be accepted by the political elite and implemented and institutionalised. Even in more conventional settings where international actors do not play any significant role, the process of institutionalisation faces obstacles and is difficult to achieve; constitutional intent is often not matched by constitutional practice. Horowitz (2002) has written of 'the slip between the constitutional cup and the adoptive lip', as constitutional designers do not always choose coherent constitutional models from the menu of available options. A similar 'slip' applies to the institutionalisation of the constitutional provisions that are adopted, as political actors may not ultimately alter their behaviour in order to abide by the new principles and practices enshrined in the legal document. This distance between constitutional provision and day-to-day practice may also increase over time, as those who gain authority from the new constitution may seek to alter it to enhance further their own position. This task is made easier if the institutions are designed in ways that place only limited restrictions on further modifications. To quote Horowitz again, 'the looser the design and the easier the adoption, the easier the alteration as well. Slippage is not complete at the moment of adoption' (ibid.).

As with other limits on constitutional design, these challenges are arguably exacerbated in contexts of international statebuilding, when new institutions are in part drafted by outside actors who differ from those in charge of implementation. Such conditions do not make a conducive environment for the stable and predictable implementation of new institutional features, and international efforts to alter domestic political structures may be frustrated by the very resilience of those domestic political authorities. In particular, domestic actors can create parallel institutions to challenge newly created ones, can alter new institutions from within and can politicise the reform process in ways that make implementation difficult to achieve.

Parallel structures

An important limitation of international efforts to promote new constitutional structures during periods of statebuilding concerns the ability of local actors to work around these new formal institutions by operating through pre-existing informal structures. These structures can vary in their nature, but have in common their role as focal points for political action and organisation by domestic actors in areas that newly created institutions seek to regulate. In certain contexts, such informal structures are rooted in a history of conflict, as opposing sides in a civil war establish quasi-governmental structures to administer the war effort and wield authority in their controlled areas of territory. In these cases, the conduct of war itself promotes the establishment of new institutions. In the history of state formation in Europe, such institutional emergence in the context of war has been identified as a key factor for the development of modern states. As Tilly has famously written, 'War made the state, and the state made war' (1975: 42). However, in the context of civil war, when competing institutions are established by opposing forces within pre-existing state boundaries, the new structures cannot easily co-exist with central state institutions once the war is over. Yet neither do they easily die away. Kosovo and Bosnia both highlight the resilience of such parallel institutions and the ways in which they can undermine newly established constitutions.

While the 1995 Dayton agreement in Bosnia formalised some of the conflict-era parallel state institutions by creating two sub-state entities, the Republika Srpska and the Federation, several important structures remained after 1995 that represented a challenge to Bosnia's new constitutional order. For example, the unofficial Croat Republic of Herceg-Bosna that was established during the Yugoslav conflict continued to exist after the Dayton settlement, and Croat political parties worked to ensure that it endured at the expense of the new constitutional institutions that were to have official jurisdiction. As a result, much of the constitutional structures outlined in Dayton existed only 'on paper' for several years, and these parallel structures governed day-to-day life in Croat-populated areas rather than the newly created central or entity-level institutions (ESI 1999).

In Kosovo, parallel structures dated not only from the conflict in 1998/9, but also from the earlier era of peaceful resistance to Serb rule. During the 1990s, Kosovo Albanians established parallel structures of governance throughout Kosovo, particularly local health and education systems that provided for the Albanian-speaking population (Malcolm 1998). During the 1998/9 conflict the Kosovo Liberation Army (UÇK) also set up a separate range of informal institutions, and when the UN arrived in June 1999 it found that the UÇK's recently declared Provisional Government, led by self-proclaimed 'Prime Minister' Hashim Thaçi, existed in a strong position throughout the province, especially at the local level. These Kosovo Albanian structures were also mirrored by similar parallel institutions in Serb areas within Kosovo, where Belgrade-supported parallel institutions had been established to provide services for the Serb community. These structures have included separate courts and security structures, as well as health and education provision, and have been coupled with prolonged Serb boycotts of Kosovo's principal political institutions (OSCE 2007) While the Albanian institutions were largely incorporated over time into Kosovo's central state institutions, the Serb structures continue to flourish and have hampered efforts to bridge the divide between the two communities (Tansey and Zaum 2009).

Adapting institutions from within

National officials and politicians can also work with newly created political arrangements, but can alter them from within by reshaping their core structures and goals. In Bosnia, for example, the specific arrangements set out in the new constitution that was agreed as part of the Dayton agreement were quickly stretched and reinterpreted as a result of realities on the ground. The constitution, for example, contained provisions for a Council of Ministers that would act as the cabinet of the state-level government. Yet whereas the constitution provided specific power-sharing provisions for many other organs of the new government, the formation of the Council of Ministers was relatively under-specified. The first elections in 1996 were followed by a creative reinterpretation of the Dayton constitution, as deadlock among the newly elected nationalist parties over the composition of the Council led to the introduction of new and ad hoc institutional procedures. The constitutional provision that the Council would have a single Chair was replaced with an arrangement that provided for two Co-Chairs and a Vice-Chair. It was also agreed that the two Chairs would be a Serb and a Bosniac, and that the Vice-Chair position would be held by a Croat politician. The final result was that the positions were carefully distributed among the three communities, so that the first Bosnian government involved a Bosniac Chair of the Presidency, Bosniac and Serb Co-Chairs of the Council of Ministers, a Croat Vice-Chair of the Council of Ministers and a Croat foreign minister. To complicate matters further, the agreement held that the two Co-Chairs would rotate weekly in the role of Chair (Tansey 2009). Very quickly, therefore, the provisions of Bosnia's constitution that had been painstakingly drafted and agreed on at Dayton were amended on an ad hoc basis to fit to realities on the ground, and the structure of the Council of Ministers has continued to be a target of institutional reform in subsequent years.

Politicisation of constitutional institutions

A further way in which the resilience of these underlying divisions manifests itself is through politicisation of the constitution itself. As discussed, internationally mediated constitutions are often designed precisely in order to resolve and move beyond pre-existing conflicts and divisions by altering domestic power structures and relations. However, the new documents themselves can frequently become the newest in a long line of political disputes, and can become the subject of existing political divisions rather than serving to overcome them. In both Bosnia and Iraq the new constitutions, introduced in 1995 and 2005 respectively, quickly became sources of political controversy and disagreement across familiar lines of division. As discussed, as early as 1996 the Bosnian constitution was being amended on an ad hoc basis due to the inability of the main nationalist parties to abide by the terms within it. In recent years, Bosnia's constitution has become a major point of contention between political parties, as international pressure for constitutional reform has been coupled with a revival of nationalist rhetoric and constitutional disputes. Successive rounds of international mediation have failed to achieve substantive reform, and constitutional disagreements have recently been some of the most divisive in Bosnia. A crucial issue concerns the relative weakness of central state institutions compared to the veto-wielding power of lower levels of governance in both entities. Bosniacs wish to see a stronger Bosnian state, while Bosnian Serbs and Croats refuse to give up the veto power they hold through any transfer of authority from entity to state level (Bieber 2010). Furthermore, Bosnian Serbs have regularly asserted the right of Republika Srpska to secede, while Bosniac parties have called for the abolition of Bosnia's two entities even as Croats demand their own third entity (Latal 2010). The constitutional debates were complicated further in 2009 when the European Court of Human Rights ruled that the constitutional provisions for the state-level presidency and House of Peoples violated the European Charter on Human Rights, as they restricted eligibility for these bodies to members of Bosnia's three main communities at the exclusion of the minority 'Others'. There is consensus that the ruling requires constitutional reform, but no consensus on whether that reform should be minimal (the Serb position) or more radical (Sebastián 2011). So while the constitution enshrined in Dayton helped end the Bosnian conflict, it has failed to overcome the underlying divisions that were central to that conflict and has instead become an instrument of those divisions.

Similarly, the permanent constitution drafted in Iraq in 2005 has been subject to dispute since its inception. Drafted largely by Kurdish and Shia negotiators due to a Sunni boycott, the constitution is perceived in some quarters as biased towards Kurdish and Shia interests. Sunni support for the constitution in the 2005 constitutional referendum was only secured at the last minute through a US-brokered deal that provided for an immediate review of the constitution with a view to incorporating amendments within the term of the first legislature (Morrow 2005). Consequently, a Constitution Review Committee was established and tasked with developing a set of amendments that would reflect Sunni concerns while also being acceptable to Kurds and Shias. Unsurprisingly, this mandate proved difficult to achieve, and the Review Committee required several extensions before it could put forward any agreed proposals in late 2009, which have yet to be acted on (Gluck 2009). Constitutional disputes have centred around the federal structure of Iraq, the distribution of oil revenues and the status of oil-rich territories such as Kirkuk. The inability of Iraq's different ethnic groups to agree on constitutional amendments has, as in Bosnia, contributed to divisions in Iraq rather than alleviating them, and the constitution itself has become one more point of disagreement along pre-existing lines of division that it was designed to overcome.

Conclusion

In any context, the process of constitutional design and implementation is a complex one, with numerous opportunities for slippage between designer intent and institutional impact. In the context of international statebuilding, these opportunities are multiplied, as a troubled domestic environment is coupled with the temporary intervention of external actors. In these settings, the central goal of international statebuilders is often to bring about a stable and democratic state by reshaping the nature of domestic politics and altering the balance of authority among domestic actors – in other words, by modifying the political economy of the state in question. However, this gives rise to a dynamic that can be seen as a central tension within the very practice of statebuilding itself, namely that it is precisely these targets of international ambitions that by their very nature can serve to frustrate international objectives. When international statebuilders wish to eliminate the dysfunctional structures of the state by introducing new constitutional provisions, they sometimes have to face the reality that these pre-existing structures can retain a level of local legitimacy and resilience that no legal document or international order can remove. When international statebuilders wish to reorder the political elite landscape and promote moderation and inclusiveness at the expense of hard-line and exclusionary politics, it is often the informal authority and popularity of the most nationalist politicians that can allow them to act as spoilers and frustrate international plans. And when international statebuilders wish to introduce constitutional settlements that will address the underlying sources of societal division and lead to political reconciliation, it is often the case that these new constitutions themselves become a source of tension across the pre-existing divides, and that they lengthen the list of political grievances rather than serve to reduce it.

Consequently, one of the lessons of recent statebuilding is that it is important not to overestimate the extent to which international actors can alter domestic politics in any significant way. There is no question that international statebuilding missions have been influential, but in the constitutional arena it is also clearly the case that their efforts have been constrained by a series of limitations. Some of those limitations derive from the very nature of institutional design itself, and from the nature and identity of international actors. Others, however, derive from the character of domestic politics, and the enduring and resilient authority of the very domestic features that international statebuilders are often seeking to overcome. One of the trends of contemporary statebuilding may thus be that when international actors seek to reshape the political economy of the states in which they intervene, it is often the political economy that ends up reshaping the international efforts. In the interaction between international and national actors and structures, the outcomes have had a tendency to point to the primacy of domestic politics.

Note

1 SC Res. 1244 of 10 June 1999.

3   Elections and post-conflict political development

Benjamin Reilly

Elections are a centrepiece of most international efforts to rebuild states and promote democracy after violent conflict. By enshrining a new political order centered on rule-based competition for office rather than open warfare, it is argued, elections in post-conflict settings can channel the expression of societal conflicts so that they take place within the boundaries of a democratic political system rather than through armed violence. By replacing the rule of the bullet with the ballot, elections directly impact upon the political economy of post-war states. Elections are thus seen as a key step on the road from war to peace. Particularly in high-profile international interventions, elections are also symbolically important, signalling to both domestic and international audiences that the cloak of legitimate government authority has been restored – an essential step in the process of state reconstruction. For all of these reasons, elections are today considered a central part of the process of post-conflict statebuilding. Iraq and Afghanistan are only the latest in a long line of international interventions stretching back at least as far as the United Nations operation in Cambodia in 1993 in which elections have been assigned a dual role in transitions *to* democracy and *from* violent conflict.

In reality, however, there has been a considerable variation in the success of post-conflict elections in meeting these goals (Kumar 1998). One problem is that the goals themselves are often unrealistic. Conflict-zone elections tend to be saddled with multiple and sometimes incompatible objectives, being expected to simultaneously bring an end to armed violence and usher in a new era of democratic peace, while also mobilizing and expressing societal cleavages via a competitive but non-violent political process (Lyons 2005). Similarly, there is a tension between the massive international support lavished upon transitional elections by the United Nations and other international actors, which often build up the capacity of election administrations to unsustainable levels, and the reality that successful election processes can be used as an 'exit strategy' by the international community from situations which have not attracted a commitment to longer-term statebuilding (Reilly 2004, 2008).

This chapter examines the political and developmental impacts of some of the key choices facing both international and domestic actors in regards to post-conflict elections:

- First, there is the question of election timing: should elections be held immediately after a conflict, to take advantage of a peace deal and quickly introduce the new democratic order? Or is it better to wait so as to allow the political routines of peacetime politics to come to prominence? Likewise, is it better to hold national elections before local ones, as some scholars have argued? Or should local-level elections be held in advance of national ones, in the hope of gradually inculcating voters in the rights and responsibilities of democracy?
- Second is the question of the electoral system used, which determines the way votes cast at elections are translated into seats in a representative body such as a parliament, presidency or constituent assembly. The choice of electoral systems is considered by political scientists as a particularly crucial institutional variable because it influences not just who gets represented and who does not, but also shapes the behavioural incentives for campaigning politicians, the relative payoffs for resorting to national versus sectarian appeals and many other aspects of post-conflict political development.
- Finally, there is the often underestimated issue of the effect of post-conflict elections on the development of civil society and political parties. In post-conflict situations, civil society organizations tend to be weak or non-existent, or closely associated with conflict parties (e.g. veterans groups), often through patronage. As a result, politics is typically highly personalized. This makes the aggregative role of political parties particularly important – especially in societies divided by ethnicity, region, tribe or language group. In such cases, the interaction between civil society, political parties and the electoral process can become highly fraught, as demonstrated by recent cases such as Kenya where flawed elections became the catalyst for large-scale ethnic violence.

In all of these issues, there is some evidence of changing approaches and sequential learning over time by both international and domestic actors. Internationally, the 'exit strategy' model of rushed elections which prevailed in the 1990s in cases such as Cambodia, Haiti and Liberia has been modified somewhat by a more sober calculation of longer-term engagement in the post-9/11 era. Domestically, local elites have become more vocal and demanding on issues such as election timing, administration and institutional design. In cases as different as East Timor and Iraq, for instance, local elites effectively demanded elections be held ahead of the prevailing international timetable. And there has also been progress in the scholarly understanding of some issues, such as the best ways to sequence local and national-level elections. Nonetheless, debilitating problems of both strategy and execution continue to dog the field, making elections an increasingly problematic area of post-conflict assistance.

Election timing and sequencing

How soon to hold an election following a period of violent conflict is a recurring dilemma of any international intervention. Because elections play such important substantive and symbolic roles, there is nearly always pressure to hold them as soon as possible following a period of violent conflict. At the same time, it is increasingly accepted in policy circles that early elections held in highly polarized environments often expose deep social cleavages, making the process of post-conflict peacebuilding more difficult.

During the 1990s, the United Nations and other international actors followed a kind of standard operating procedure in interventions in many post-conflict countries. Once a minimum level of peace had been obtained (which did not necessarily mean a full ceasefire agreement), and a basic level of infrastructure was in place, national elections were often the next step – sometimes within a year or so of the start of the mission – followed by a rapid handover to newly elected local authorities, and in some cases an even more rapid departure of international troops and personnel. However, this 'quick exit' approach suffered from multiple problems. Perhaps the most serious was that, if held too early, free and fair elections can actually undermine rather than reinforce the development of a more substantive post-conflict democratic order.

The fate of the transitional 1993 elections conducted by the United Nations Transitional Administration in Cambodia (UNTAC) is a case in point. The UNTAC operation, which began in 1992, was at the time the largest and most ambitious peacekeeping and democratisation mission the UN had ever undertaken. The mission had to disarm 200,000 soldiers and 250,000 militia, repatriate 360,000 refugees and help resettle another 700,000 refugees, as well as register 4.7 million new voters. The culmination of this process was the organization and conduct of Cambodia's first ever democratic elections, held in May 1993, to determine the representative government of a country which had never known one.

After running what was a technically near-faultless election, however, UNTAC ran up against the realities of power politics as soon as election results began to show that the incumbent Cambodian People's Party (CPP) had gained fewer seats than the royalist opposition, FUNCINPEC, effectively leaving no party with a working majority. Amid threats of renewed civil war from the CPP if it was excluded from government, a hastily brokered deal saw a powersharing coalition featuring 'co-prime ministers' from the two parties installed – an arrangement which proved highly unstable in practice and fell apart completely in 1997, when the CPP routed FUNCINPEC to claim power alone. But by then UNTAC had long-since departed, declaring the peaceful holding of elections themselves proof of the success of the mission.

This model was to set the stage for subsequent internationally sponsored elections throughout the 1990s. In some cases, such as Bosnia and Kosovo, international forces did not depart but rather installed themselves as a kind of ongoing quasi-administration. But in most interventions outside Europe, the 'minimal security, quick elections and departure' model was prevalent. This necessitated holding elections relatively early in the post-conflict cycle, giving both domestic and international actors a political and a symbolic marker of progress that could be used as the justification to begin turning power over to local forces.

Local actors also contributed to this pattern. In Iraq, for instance, there was strong international pressure to hold quick elections after the US-led invasion of 2002 for reasons both substantive (the need for a Constituent Assembly to draft a new constitution) and symbolic (the need to demonstrate the validity of the prevailing US policy of transforming Iraq into a bastion of democracy in the Middle East). But there was also significant domestic pressure from local elites such as Grand Ayatollah Ali Al-Sistani to hold a constitutional convention as quickly as possible. This led to nationwide elections being held in early 2005 in the absence of popular security and in the face of a boycott from one of the Iraq's main ethnic groups, the Sunni – a decision which arguably hindered rather than helped the longer-term process of democratization. A similar combination of local and international pressures was evident in East Timor, where UN administrator Sergio Vierra de Mello was under constant pressure from local elites associated with Fretilin, the party of the resistance struggle, to hold elections to a constitutional assembly before other parties could organize to challenge it.

Another difficulty of early elections is the way they tend to entrench conflict actors in their new guise as political parties in central positions of power and authority. One common drawback of post-conflict elections is thus their tendency to become a de facto contest between former warring armies masquerading as political parties, as has been the case in the Balkans. This greatly hampers the development of peacetime politics in deeply divided societies even years after the war has ended – as demonstrated by the regular re-election of hardliners from rival communities at Bosnia's successive elections since 1996, where nationalist parties and elites have not only continued to be elected, but sought to use the democratic process to press for sectarian objectives.

So when should post-conflict elections be held? Ideally, an extended process of consultation and local-level peacebuilding, in which some of the real interests and concerns that provoked the conflict are addressed in a step-by-step fashion *before* national elections are held, may offer better prospects for a peaceful transition in post-conflict societies. In practice, however, most countries do not have the luxury of such an extended period of international tutelage. I have previously suggested that a period of two or three years between the end of a conflict and the holding of elections should be seen as a minimum, based on the examples of both Kosovo and East Timor, where a multi-year period of transitional administration took place before founding elections were held (Reilly 2008). This timeline has recently received support from an innovative large-N study of post-elections, which found that elections held in the first year in new democracies drastically shortens the time till conflict relapse, as do elections held in the second year. Only when new democracies wait till the third year or later of the recovery period to hold their first post-conflict election do these elections help delay relapse into civil conflict.

(Flores and Nooruddin 2009b)

Economists have taken different approaches to this issue, asking 'When can a donor successfully exit from an on-the-ground presence in a post-conflict state?' The answer, based on how soon conflict states can expect to fund their recurrent budgets from tax revenue rather than international donor support, is: not for a very long time. Looking at less high-profile cases of international involvement in Liberia, Mozambique, the Solomon Islands and East Timor, one study found that even the best-case scenario for successful exit requires an international engagement lasting between 15 and 27 years. Such an extended donor presence, it was argued, is essential for the creation, sustenance and maturation of institutions that are finally able to undergird the state from rolling back into renewed failure upon donor exit (Chand and Coffman 2008).

Such an extended open-ended commitment, however, is unrealistic for the vast majority of post-conflict states. Indeed, pressure to hold elections quickly after peace has been restored has been and is likely to remain a recurring theme of international interventions. This is in part due to the symbolic reasons discussed earlier: as the 'signalling' role of elections is particularly important for the news media and other Western policy consumers, the mere holding of elections is usually taken as an indicator of political progress (although highly flawed elections can have the reverse effect, as the disastrous experience of the 2009 presidential elections in Afghanistan shows). At the same time, the substantive value of providing international actors with a legitimate local counterpart remains a central part of any exit process for the international community, as these are the actors to whom authority is handed, and with whom the details of the new political order are negotiated.[1]

There is evidence of genuine learning over time by the UN and other international actors on some of these issues. Today, there appears to be more recognition of the need for sustained international involvement for several years after a conflict rather than a rushed 'in-and-out' approach, and donors have increasingly recognized that 'second elections' in transitional states can be as important as the first. The experience of recent UN operations in Kosovo, East Timor and Afghanistan suggests that pressure to hold 'instant' national elections was resisted to some degree. In both Kosovo and East Timor, for instance, relatively peaceful national elections were held in 2001, some two years after the peak of the conflict. In Afghanistan, the initial presidential elections were held in 2004 and parliamentary elections in 2005, several years after the 2002 *Loya Jirga* which chose the country's transitional administration. In each case, competitive (if hardly trouble-free) second-generation elections have since been held. Although questions remain as to whether even two years is time enough to develop the routines of peacetime politics, there is now a relative consensus in opinion (if not always in practice) on the benefits of this more gradual approach as opposed to the 'instant election' model of earlier years.

A separate but related issue is the coordination of national and sub-national elections. Some scholars argue that in a new democracy, holding national elections before regional ones generates incentives for the creation of national, rather than regional, political parties – and hence that the ideal process of election timing is to start at the national level before holding regional or local polls (Linz and Stepan 1996: 98–107). Others believe that simultaneous national and local elections are the best option, as they

> can facilitate the mutual dependence of regional and national leaders. The more posts that are filled at the regional and local level ... the greater the incentive for regional politicians to coordinate their election activities by developing an integrated party system.
>
> (Diamond 1999: 158)

This was the approach used at Indonesia's transitional 1999 elections following the collapse of the Suharto regime, with identical party-list ballots being presented to voters at simultaneous elections for national, provincial and local assemblies in a calculated effort to strengthen the nascent party system.

While this process of simultaneous elections has real advantages in terms of party building, there are also strong arguments for the opposite sequence: i.e. to start with municipal elections before national ones. Indeed, this seems to increasingly be the approach followed by international actors, in part because local elections can act as a trial run for national elections, but also because local elections bring different issues to the fore and are more likely to be focused on service delivery than the kinds of political disputes which typically strengthen the hand of the wartime parties (Paris 2004). In Kosovo, for instance, local elections were held in 2000, less than one year after the war, and helped weaken the political power of the party associated most closely with the Kosovo Liberation Army and strengthened perceived moderates in Ibrahim Rugova's Democratic League of Kosovo (LDK). Other local consultation processes which preceded national elections, such as the World Bank's Community Empowerment and Local Governance project in East Timor in 2000, also helped to move the political focus on to more nuts-and-bolts issues of development. In sum, election sequencing and timing has a significant independent impact on the political economy of post-conflict states.

The choice of electoral systems

Institutional and constitutional rules, such as the choice of electoral system, are important for all political systems, but their impact is probably magnified during times of tension and uncertainty as prevail during post-conflict periods. In addition to the fundamental question of who will govern, basic issues of political accountability, representation and responsiveness are all directly affected by the electoral system. As a result, electoral systems have a particularly important impact in post-conflict societies, where the rules of the political game are fluid, the players often novices and outcomes inherently uncertain.

Electoral systems are the rules and procedures via which votes cast in an election are translated into seats won in the parliament or some other office (e.g. a presidency). An electoral system is therefore fundamentally a mechanism to translate votes into seats. But electoral systems also act as the conduit through which the people can hold their elected representatives accountable. Different electoral systems give incentives for those competing for power to couch their appeals to the electorate in distinct ways. In divided societies, for example, where language, religion, race or other forms of ethnicity represent a fundamental political cleavage, particular electoral systems can reward candidates and parties who act in a cooperative, accommodatory manner to rival groups; or they can punish these candidates and instead reward those who pursue more exclusive, in-group appeals.

Electoral systems are often categorized according to how proportionately they operate in terms of translating votes into seats won. A typical three-way structure divides such systems into plurality-majority, semi-proportional and proportional representation (PR) systems. Plurality-majority systems typically give primary emphasis to local representation via the use of small, single-member electoral districts than to overall proportionality of outcomes. Amongst such systems are plurality (first-past-the-post), runoff, block and alternative vote systems. By contrast, PR systems – which typically use larger multi-member districts and deliver more balanced outcomes – include 'open' and 'closed' versions of party list PR, as well as mixed-member proportional and single transferable vote systems. Semi-proportional systems offer yet other approaches, as well as various mixtures of plurality and proportional models – such as the 'parallel' mixed-member models by which part of the parliament is elected via PR and part from local districts, a common choice in many new democracies in recent years.[2]

One of the great political science debates of the past decade has concerned which electoral systems are most appropriate for promoting peaceful politics in divided societies. Two schools of thought predominate. The scholarly orthodoxy has long argued that some form of PR is all but essential if democracy is to survive the travails of deep-rooted divisions. The tendency of PR to produce multi-party parliaments and hence coalition governments, in which all significant segments of the population can be represented, is especially important in post-conflict elections, where 'consensual' or 'consociational' solutions are often favoured as a means of promoting power-sharing between former enemies in joint government (Jarstad 2008).

In contrast to this orthodoxy, an alternative approach argues for the use of more 'centripetal' electoral systems which work to break down the political salience of social divisions rather than foster their representation.[3] One way to do this is to require winning candidates to gain a broad spread of votes from across the country in order to claim victory, as is the case for presidential elections in Indonesia, Nigeria and Kenya. Another is to use electoral models like the alternative vote (as in Papua New Guinea) or the single transferable vote (as in Northern Ireland) which permit or require voters to declare not only their first choice of candidate on a ballot, but also their second, third and subsequent choices amongst all candidates standing. A third centripetal approach is to try to ensure that political parties develop along multi-ethnic lines or are organizationally plural, with offices and members spread across the country, as in post-Suharto Indonesia (Reilly 2010).

In contrast to these kinds of domestic reform initiatives, most of which have derived from within third wave democracies themselves, elections conducted under United Nations auspices almost always favour simple models of PR which facilitate minority inclusion but also presents strong incentives for political fragmentation. Indeed, major transitional elections in Namibia (1989), Nicaragua (1990), Cambodia (1993), South Africa (1994), Mozambique (1994), Liberia (1997), Bosnia (1996), Kosovo (2001), East Timor (2001), Iraq (2005) and the Democratic Republic of Congo (2006) were held predominantly or entirely under some form of party-list PR, sometimes with the entire country forming a single electoral district. This has advantages and disadvantages. On the one hand, such systems can play an important role in ensuring inclusion and some sharing of power between different groups. On the other hand, because large-district PR systems allow both minority and majority parties to form and compete freely, they often feature parties which are ethnically based or thinly veiled versions of the former warring armies.

Regardless of these political strengths and weaknesses, in practice the adoption of large-district PR systems for UN-administered elections has frequently been dictated more by technical concerns, such as the need to avoid demarcating individual electoral districts and produce separate ballot papers, than deeper issues of political development. In war-torn environments, national party-list PR systems are sometimes argued to be the only feasible way to hold credible elections. The reasons for this are essentially administrative in nature: national party-list systems enable a uniform national ballot to be used, do not require electoral districts to be demarcated and greatly simplify the process of voter registration, vote counting and the calculation of results. Problems of population displacement and the lack of accurate census data also work in favour of a proportional system with a single national constituency which does not tie voters to specific electoral districts.

Unfortunately, national PR systems also have some real disadvantages. They provide no geographic link between voters and their representatives, and thus create difficulties in terms of political accountability and responsiveness between elected politicians and the electorate. Many new democracies – particularly those in agrarian societies – have much higher demands for constituency service at the local level than they do for representation of all shades of ideological opinion in the legislature (Barkan 1995). In addition, national list PR systems such as those used at Iraq's transitional 2005 election, tend to reward political fragmentation, encouraging political fractionalization rather than aggregation. The result is often an excessive number of parties and a deeply polarized and often unworkably fragmented legislature.

In Iraq, for this reason, international experts initially favoured a system based around provincial boundaries, to ensure greater accountability and representation of local constituencies. However, this would have entailed a lengthy national census. In the interests of time, it was therefore decided to fall back on a single, nationwide district elected by PR in which 1/275th of the vote was sufficient to gain a seat for the 2005 constituent assembly and national parliament elections. While this doubtlessly facilitated the administration of the election itself, it also had the effect of fragmenting the legislature, marginalizing numerically smaller groups like the Sunni and doing nothing to prevent ethnic polarization amongst the electorate. As Toby Dodge observes in his chapter:

> Because of organisational and security concerns, the vote itself was held with one nationwide electoral constituency ... This removed local issues and personalities from the campaign; marshalling many politicians and parties into large coalitions ... most of which played to the lowest common denominator, deploying ethno-sectarian rhetoric.
>
> (p. 200)

For Iraq's most recent elections, in 2010, this system was replaced by a regional PR model along the lines of that initially recommended by external experts. As Dodge highlights, this did correspond to the resurgence of a nominally secular political party. But by then the die had been cast: the party system remained based around ethnic and religious identities, with the Sunni–Shi'ite division the most important political cleavage in Iraqi electoral politics. Indeed, there was a sense that the many predictions made in Washington and elsewhere about the inevitability of ethnic polarization and eventual partition in post-Saddam Iraq have become self-fulfilling.

But this ethnification of the party system was not inevitable. Many other new democracies have eschewed the closed list, national PR model foisted upon Iraq in favour of open list or 'mixed' electoral systems, in which greater emphasis is placed on local accountability. Kosovo, for instance, moved to an open list system for its 2007 elections, against the objections of local elites who feared it would weaken their control over parties. In East Timor, the 2001 constituent assembly was mostly chosen by PR, but there were also separate single-member electorates corresponding to each of the country's 13 districts. Some observers argued that a similar system in Iraq would have guaranteed the Sunni minority a baseline of political representation at the provincial level, thus helping to assuage the problems of marginalization and political alienation (Diamond 2005: 265).

Perhaps the most unusual electoral system choice for a post-conflict election in recent years has been the decision to use the single non-transferable vote (SNTV) for parliamentary elections in Afghanistan. Under SNTV each elector has one vote, there are several seats to be elected in the district and the candidates with the highest number of votes fill these positions. As a result, the number of candidates a party nominates in each district becomes a critical choice: too few, and parties miss out on valuable chances to win additional seats; too many, and they risk splitting their vote too thinly and losing winnable seats. Despite being structurally majoritarian, SNTV can thus advantage smaller parties and deliver relatively proportional election outcomes. However, by forcing candidates from the same party to compete against each other for the same pool of voters, SNTV encourages personalistic attributes to be emphasized over and above those of party identification.

This could also be seen as an example of incumbents choosing a system to suit their needs, given the reality that a weak and fragmented parliament suits President Karzai – a reminder that the interests of incumbent elites are always engaged in electoral system choices. However, in a country like Afghanistan, these pathologies tend to undercut the goal of building a stronger political system and encouraging cohesive national political parties. In an ethnically complex, clan-based society such as Afghanistan's, SNTV makes it much harder for a consolidated party system to develop. Illustrating this, the 2005 Afghan parliamentary elections featured over 5,800 candidates – in Kabul alone the ballot paper displayed over 400 names – resulting in a fractionalized and incoherent parliament which has been unable to coordinate around pressing policy challenges.[4]

It is increasingly apparent that successful transitional elections need to encourage both inclusion but also a significant degree of geographic and personal *accountability* – such as by having members of parliament represent territorially defined districts, or at least by allowing voters to choose between candidates and not just parties. For this reason, 'mixed' systems which deliver both district accountability and minority representation have become increasingly popular in recent years. However, as the experience in 2006 of high-profile conflict-zone elections held under mixed systems in cases as varied as the Democratic Republic of Congo (which resulted in a highly fragmented parliament) and the Palestinian National Authority (in which the system was designed to favour the incumbent Fatah party but instead resulted in a victory for Hammas) indicates, there are no panaceas.

Building programmatic political parties

Political parties perform a number of essential functions in a democracy: they represent political constituencies and interests, recruit and socialize new candidates for office, craft policy alternatives, set policy-making agendas, form governments, and integrate disparate groups and individuals into the democratic process (Diamond 1997: xxiii). These linking, mediating and representational functions mean that parties are one of the primary channels for building accountable and responsive government. Yet in many emerging democracies, especially post-conflict ones, parties instead exhibit a range of pathologies that undercut their ability to deliver the kind of systemic benefits on which representative politics depends. They are frequently poorly institutionalized, with limited membership, weak policy capacity and shifting bases of support. They are often based around narrow personal, regional or ethnic ties, rather than reflecting society as a whole. They are typically organizationally thin, coming to life only at election time. They may have little in the way of a coherent ideology, failing to stand for any particular policy agenda. And they are frequently unable to ensure disciplined collective action in parliament, or stop members shifting between parties.

The fact that so few broad-based, programmatic and institutionalized parties have emerged is one reason that post-conflict governments typically struggle to aggregate social demands and deliver meaningful policy agendas. In the absence of such parties, the easiest way to attract voters in post-conflict societies is often to appeal to the very same insecurities that generated the original conflict. This means that instead of attempting to win support with policy appeals, post-conflict parties have a strong incentive to downplay policy choices and instead mobilize voters along identity lines. While electorally appealing, this can have debilitating consequences. Because parties determine so decisively the extent to which social cleavages are replicated in the organs of representative government, they have a crucial impact on broader prospects of political stability and development. Thus, one common factor amongst the few genuinely stable third world democracies is the presence of broad-based 'bridging' political parties: 'the success of democratic politics in developing societies is strongly associated with the presence of broadly-based, heterogeneous, catch-all parties with no strong links to the cleavage structure of society' (Özbudun 1987: 405).

By contrast, 'bonding' parties – that is, parties which 'focus upon gaining votes from a narrower home-base among particular segmented sectors of the electorate' (Norris 2004: 10) – offer few incentives towards political integration, instead relying on direct appeals to a relatively narrow support base for votes. Rather than supplying public goods, these kinds of parties tend to focus on winning and maintaining voter support by providing private or 'club' goods to their supporters – goods which benefit their own community rather than the broader electorate.

Again, this has direct public policy consequences. Roads, health care, government services and other sorts of public goods will be provided unequally (or not at all). While such distributive politics can be electorally rewarding, diverting state resources towards narrow ethnic constituencies in this way tends to be hugely damaging to broader economic development. Studies by a range of authors (summarized by Phillip Keefer of the World Bank) have therefore increasingly emphasized the importance of programmatic parties for sound policy outcomes, not least because the presence or prospect of such parties in government enables politicians to make credible promises to the electorate.[5]

Given their importance, one would think that international efforts to promote democracy would therefore seek to promote programmatic parties explicitly. Instead, in part because of the emphasis on PR and minority inclusion in the election process described earlier, they tend to do the opposite, rewarding narrow sectarian or splinter parties at the expense of programmatic ones. The 2006 elections in the Democratic Republic of Congo, for instance, which cost the international community half a billion dollars to run and deployed the world's largest UN peacekeeping operation ever, MONUC, resulted in a parliament of over 50 parties and an even larger number of independents, with the largest bloc commanding only 22 per cent of the seats. Elections in the other major international interventions of recent years, Iraq and Afghanistan, have led to similarly fragmented parliaments. Dominik Zaum has detailed a similar process of party fragmentation in Kosovo in his contribution to this volume.

The comparative evidence strongly suggests that this is a recipe for not just political instability, but sub-par economic performance as well. A growing body of research suggests that variations in economic outcomes depend in part on the nature of the party system, with two-party or moderate multiparty systems having stronger growth rates and lower public spending than more fragmented multiparty systems (Persson and Tabellini 2005). Because of their central role in aggregating preferences and mobilizing consent, there are sound theoretical and empirical reasons to believe that political parties and party systems do have a direct impact upon public welfare, and that two-party systems are more likely than multiparty systems to provide collective goods to the median voter.[6]

This is one reason why the choice of electoral systems is so important. Classically, political scientists have believed that majoritarian electoral rules will, over time, weed out minor parties and encourage the development of two large, aggregative parties (Duverger 1954). This reductionist tendency occurs through a combination of 'mechanical' and 'psychological' electoral system effects. Mechanically, because they award seats on the basis of individual 'winner-take-all' contests in single-member districts, majoritarian elections tend to overrepresent large parties and underrepresent small ones, particularly those with a dispersed vote share. This tendency is compounded by the psychological impact of this process on voters, many of whom choose not to 'waste' their vote on a minor party but instead switch their support to one with a reasonable chance of success. The cumulative effect of these mechanical and psychological factors is to systematically advantage large parties and thus increase the prospects for majority rule.

A separate theoretical approach, derived from basic game theory, argues that the presence of two parties competing for office should promote a convergence towards the political centre, thus helping avoid ideological polarization. Downs (1957) famously showed that under plurality electoral rules and a unidimensional (e.g. left–right) policy spectrum, winning strategy should focus on the 'median voter' who has an equal number of fellow voters to both the left and the right. In a two-party system, the most successful parties will therefore be those that command the middle ground. As a consequence, office-seeking candidates in such systems need to adopt moderate policies that appeal to the broadest possible array of interests, avoiding extreme positions and focusing instead on widely shared demands: the need for economic growth, competent bureaucracy, clean government and so on.

Thus, in theory, majoritarian elections should encourage a system of a few large, centrist political parties which, if they are to prosper electorally, must cultivate and maintain support across a range of social groups, and therefore need to provide benefits to society at large in order to maximize their chances of re-election. However, it is clear that these theoretical expectations do not always play out in practice, particularly in ethnically diverse societies where identity rather than policy is the key determinant of voter choice. In such cases, appealing to the median voter can be a fruitless exercise, as elections are not decided on policy grounds but on ethnic allegiance with elections more like an ethnic census than a contest for free-floating, informed voters (Horowitz 1985).

In addition, majoritarian elections in divided societies can have very negative effects on minorities, and can easily see some groups excluded from power altogether. Recognition of the dangers of majoritarianism in ethnically diverse societies, as well as the normative preferences of the United Nations and other donors, have increasingly resulted in the governability and social aggregation functions of parties downplayed in favour of inclusion and minority representation. While understandable, this privileging of representativeness over governability is leading to increasingly perverse outcomes.

Consider, for example, the ongoing constitutional crisis in Nepal. Since 2006, following the collapse of the country's monarchy and a near civil war between Maoist rebels and a discredited government, the United Nations and other international donors have been supporting Nepal's constitutional reform process in the hope that it will lead to a stable democratic republic in what is a very poor, mountainous and diverse country. A key achievement to date has been the election of a 573-member Constitutional Assembly, whose membership is explicitly designed to represent the full diversity of Nepalese society, in contrast to the closed, elite-dominated politics of the past. However, this highly inclusive process has made actually reaching agreement on a new constitution exceptionally slow and difficult, and highlighted the competing interests of elected members and international donors. The country was without a prime minister for most of 2010, and remains without a final constitution. While the Maoists and some of the larger parties represented in the Assembly pushed for a constitution which emphasizes unicameral majority rule and clear authority for the government, these priorities get short shrift from the donors, which instead prioritize demands of regionalism, gender balance, minority representation and the inclusion of civil society.[7]

While these are all important issues of political representation, it could be argued that none are as important for a poor country like Nepal as providing the basis for strong and effective government. Indeed, in different ways, each could be seen as undermining this goal. Regional devolution or federalism can have the effect of fragmenting already weak states. The preoccupation with descriptive representation of women and indigenous groups in the constitutional building process is at odds with the need to aggregate basic social cleavages of gender and ethnicity into effective parties. The prioritizing of civil society could also have the perverse effect of undercutting efforts at party building. Indeed, if donor wishes are followed, Nepal could end up with a system in which sectoral and minority representation is so privileged that it becomes almost impossible to govern.

So what should be done? While studies of this issue are surprisingly limited, in practice a great deal of innovation has occurred in many new democracies seeking to influence the shape of their emerging party systems, ranging from ballot inclusion rules to organizational requirements (Reilly and Nordlund 2008). However, few if any of these devices have been applied directly in post-conflict elections in which the United Nations is involved. Rather, they tend to be introduced by governments, rather than the international community, as a direct response to challenges they see as important for their own democratic development. Third wave Asian democracies have been particularly innovative in this respect, over the past decade introducing a swathe of political reforms aimed at building more stable and effective governments which eschew minority representation in favour of aggregative majority rule (Reilly 2006) – in sharp contrast to cases like Afghanistan, where the party system has become more fragmented and sectarianized over time, in part because of the marked lack of any aggregative incentives.

Conclusion

Because of their central role in aggregating preferences and mobilizing consent, there are sound theoretical and empirical reasons to believe that elections have a direct impact upon public welfare, and that these impacts are probably magnified in cases of post-conflict intervention. In particular, we know from scholarly studies that elections which produce broad-based, aggregative parties with a nationwide scope of governing are most likely to generate public goods and economic development. However, in the kind of fragmented multiparty systems now emerging in Iraq, Afghanistan, the Democratic Republic Congo and numerous other examples of international involvement, this process is reversed: as no party can hope to govern outright, and most need only a small percentage of votes to win public office, there is every incentive for them to focus on providing sectoral benefits to their supporters, rather than public goods to the electorate as a whole.

Turning this around is not easy: there are powerful systemic pressures in post-conflict societies towards atomization and ethnic favouritism that are independent of any electoral system. But these tendencies could be mitigated to some extent by a change in the international community's approach to post-conflict democratization, and in particular by adopting policies which prioritize the delivery of public goods over other worthy but less important objectives such as minority representation. Admittedly, such a shift appears unlikely given the prevailing policy settings of the UN and other major international actors. But there is a clear need for a different model of political development in post-conflict settings, given the failure of current approaches. In particular, understanding and incorporation of the political economy literature and application of its findings in post-conflict environments is long overdue.

Notes

1 My thanks to Dominik Zaum for emphasizing this point.
2 For a detailed discussion which expands on these points see Reynolds, Reilly and Ellis 2005.
3 See Wolff and Cordell (2010) for an empirically grounded overview of this long-running debate.
4 See 'Democracy, sort of', *The Economist*, 24 September 2005: 34.
5 See Keefer 2005 for an overview of this literature.
6 Several studies of democratic transitions have also identified party systems as the key institutional determinant affecting the distributive impacts of economic reform. Haggard and Kaufman (1995: 265), for instance, found that economic reforms 'are more likely to be sustained where elite supporters within the policy and business communities could mobilize broader bases of electoral and interest-group support'. For this reason, they 'placed special emphasis on the way party systems aggregated the preferences of competing economic interests', noting that while moderate catch-all party systems appeared to facilitate preference aggregation, fragmented and polarized party systems constituted a particular barrier to reform.
7 For example, the UNDP's Center for Constitutional Dialogue (www.ccd.org.np/new/index.php), the main think-tank advising the Assembly in Nepal, highlights the following 'special' issues on its webpage:

- Women and the Constitution Building Process;
- Indigenous Peoples and the Constitution Building Process;
- Civil Society Organizations in the Constitution Building Process;
- Transition to a Federal Structure and Implementation of the New Constitution.

4 Transition from war to peace

Stratification, inequality and post-war economic reconstruction[1]

Stina Torjesen

How unequal are war and post-war societies? And does the level of inequality matter for how we evaluate and practise statebuilding? This chapter takes these two questions as its point of departure and argues that it is useful to place stratification processes at the heart of how we conceptualise transitions from war to peace. It stresses that economic and political spheres are tightly bound together in war to peace transition. This connectedness may help to solidify inequality in the post-war period. Interestingly, inequality or, for that matter, the closely bound nature of political and economic spheres, are often overlooked in the statebuilding literature and in policy recommendations issued by multilateral organisations. This chapter seeks to highlight these omissions and, in a preliminary fashion, draw attention to the consequences of a failure to conceptualise and address inequality.

The chapter first presents selected theoretical insights on hierarchies and stratification processes in wartime. Stratification is in this chapter conceptualised as a process that generates inequality within communities and creates layers of privileged and less privileged community members. The chapter then highlights how one particular strand of statebuilding policies, guidelines on economic reconstruction, frames key challenges associated with post-war economic recovery. It pulls out three underlying assumptions present in these guidelines and contrasts each of these with the situation in one particular post-war focus: the province of Balkh in northern Afghanistan after 2001. Clearly, the province of Balkh cannot be taken to represent a typical post-war trajectory. The juxtaposition with guidelines on the one hand and the Balkh pattern on the other may, however, trigger reflection on key facets of statebuilding policies and as such serves a useful purpose. The chapter ends with a discussion of what light the Balkh material sheds on patterns of stratification and offers some concluding thoughts on the impact of external statebuilding interventions.

An underlying argument running through this chapter is that stratification is an important concept in the study of statebuilding, because, by assessing this phenomenon we are able to trace some of the central unintended consequences of external interventions. Moreover, stratification mechanisms are at the centre of many pressing statebuilding difficulties that tend to riddle post-war societies, including poor governance, a narrow range of economic opportunities for the poorest strata, and the political and economic entrenchment of wartime power structures. In light of this, a closer look at how we can best conceptualise stratification in analyses of statebuilding, alongside an assessment of how it plays out in policy and practice, as this chapter provides, is a timely and important exercise.

Theoretical insights: inequality and war

War and upheaval have a tendency to enforce order and hierarchy within communities. Violent conflict, whether internal civil wars or inter-state, brings profound changes to societies: new players, new power techniques and associated practices of compliance emerge (Keen 2000). While the outbreak of conflict brings initial chaos, communities might not necessarily become anarchic as they suffer or respond to these in the short or long term – on the contrary, new forms of order or enhanced stratification are frequently central outcomes of violent upheaval.

Michael Mann's assessment of power and stratification through a range of historical periods lends support to the above assertion. Crucially for Mann:

> In pursuit of their goals, humans enter into cooperative, collective power relations with one another. But in implementing collective goals, social organisation and division of labour are set up. Organisation and division of function carry an inherent tendency to distributive power, deriving from supervision and coordination.
>
> (1986: 6)[2]

Similar to Charles Tilly's (1985) stress on the statebuilding effects of war-making, Mann suggests that threats from nature or hostile forces will spur social organisation, and also enhance stratification. War or conflict is a situation where collective power becomes particularly important. Members of a community will need to cooperate in order to obtain an important common goal: safety vis-à-vis an enemy threat. This leads to new forms of social organisation where some segments or individuals may excel at the expense of others.

If war is an event that increases stratification, then a crucial question for societies entering into a post-war period will be whether the patterns of command, organisation and social stratification forged in the war years by warring parties will continue as the society transits from war to peace. The central actors in the war years, which, as the conflict ends, are at the top of the hierarchy, have excelled in providing 'concentrated coercion' directed primarily towards other external adversaries, but also potentially towards members of their home or host communities. These actors have, using Mann's terminology, accrued 'intensive power' – or the ability to organise tightly and command a high level of mobilisation or commitment from participants (Mann 1986: 7–22). With peace, the potential for coercion will remain highly present, but given the formal end to fighting, the acceptance and legitimacy of coercive threats is likely to decline. At the moment of peace, therefore, the pattern of social stratification in a war-torn society is at a critical juncture: stratification is likely to be especially pervasive but the changing environment also raises the prospect of changes in a community's power structures, and a decline in the social importance of violence.

In such periods of transition it might be particularly helpful to think of stratification as a process rather than as purely a structure denoting rank. For Michael Schwalbe, inequality is created and continuously reproduced by institutionalising imbalanced flows of socially valuable resources. These processes are shaped by the 'rules of the game': laws, policies, procedures and norms that allow some people to accumulate benefits or wealth at the expense of others (Schwalbe 2007: 5–15). A central question for Schwalbe is how, within a community, resources continue to be accumulated differently by different actors, and he argues that one factor shaping the distribution of power and socially valuable resources is whether the 'rules of the game' are fair or rigged. A fair game is one where everyone plays by the same rules and is equally well equipped to compete. A rigged game is one where some people get advantages that others do not, because unfairness is built into the rules themselves, and inequality becomes the automatic result of people following rules, rather than the result of people breaking them, thereby institutionalising and normalising inequality (ibid.: 5–15).

Mann and Schwalbe therefore help us single out a central question when analysing the political economy of post-conflict societies: is the transition from war to peace one where the rigged game of a war economy and war society alters into a new post-war rigged game with similar or more pronounced stratification, or is it the beginning of a new fairer post-war game that helps reduce or alter stratification?

Before embarking on an empirical assessment where these issues are explored, one further theoretical perspective bears noting. Karl Polanyi offers some important insights for this study. Polanyi argued that the belief in the free and self-regulating market is profoundly misplaced. Instead Polanyi, when studying market dynamics in England's industrialisation period, found that markets tended invariably towards oligarchy and monopolisation, unless checked by regulation or other social counter forces (Stiglitz 2001: ix). Polanyi, moreover, assessed how different interest groups dominated the regulatory process and how these ensured that the guiding principles for the market economy served them well (in Polanyi's study this was exemplified through the industrial elite's ability to uphold a laissez-faire labour market).

Finally, Polanyi paid close attention to how the market economy was embedded in larger social processes, or how 'man's economy is submerged in his social relationships' (Polanyi 2001: 48). For Polanyi it was not possible to conceptualise economic activity as autonomous from other human activity. Instead economic activity was subordinate to, or part and parcel of, politics, religion and social relations. This is one of the reasons why Polanyi stressed the rapid speed of change that industrialisation encompassed. Polanyi was concerned that the pace of change associated with the market economy placed a heavy strain on social relations: sometimes the *rate* of change was as stressful for society as the actual *form* of change. Using insights from political theory we should expect that issues of inequality and stratification are central features as societies transition from war to peace. Moreover, if we use Polanyi's insights as a starting point we are alerted to the following: if markets during the war years have been devoid of state regulation it is likely that these will tend towards monopolisation. At the same time, however, a reintroduction of state regulation might not constitute an easy fix either: if regulation is easily subject to undue influence by powerful groups (as was the case with the industrialists in nineteenth century England) it might very well be that the civil-war winners can appropriate and influence the post-war state machinery and associated market regulation. Such a 'state capture' would constitute a stark manifestation of attempts to 'rig the game' and institutionalise wartime inequality.[3] It also offers an important note of caution for statebuilding: the (re-)introduction of government institutions and regulation is presented as vital for post-war recovery to succeed. In the economic sphere much stress is placed on the usefulness of invigorating and relying on market mechanisms, but that the market needs to be duly regulated and institutionalised if it is to yield broader social dividends and stabilisation.[4] Using Polanyi's perspective, however, the politics associated with this institutionalisation could potentially further entrench, rather than alleviate, patterns of inequality.

Policy and guidance on post-conflict economic recovery

To what extent do the policies of multilateral organisations acknowledge and address the challenges outlined above, and to what extent might their policies contribute to them? A full survey of statebuilding policies of multilateral organisations is beyond the scope of this chapter.[5] However, an assessment of one particular strand of policy advice within statebuilding can offer some preliminary insights. This section examines key policy documents on post-conflict economic reconstruction, and explores some of the underlying assumptions associated with these policies. These are contrasted with developments in one particular post-war environment: the province of Balkh in northern Afghanistan after 2001.[6]

In 2009, the United Nations launched a common (UN-wide) policy on post-conflict income generation (United Nations 2009a). Individual agencies, the ILO and UNDP in particular, also issued separate but related reports on specific aspects of post-conflict reconstruction (ILO 2010; UNDP 2008a). These were complemented by guidance notes and recommendations issued by the UK Stabilisation Unit (2008) and by the Office of Economic Growth in USAID (2009). The United Nations Integrated Disarmament, Demobilisation and Reintegration Standards (United Nations 2006a) and its section on social and economic reintegration is an important reference for many of the above reports.

These reports are heavily geared towards assessing what types of economic programmes are most appropriate for the different kinds of recovery phases and, in the UN reports, considerable emphasis is placed on how different UN agencies should work together to tackle reconstruction challenges. Taken together these documents constitute a fairly coherent set of ideas, which reach broadly similar conclusions on how multilateral agencies should promote post-conflict economic recovery. The need to trigger growth and employment opportunities in order to prevent a relapse into conflict forms the main rationale for the policies. The guidance typically outlines both macro and micro economic considerations that must be made, and include discussions on the importance of strengthening government institutions. As a collection, the reports offer a number of important contributions, including a comprehensive stocktaking of typical post-war economic challenges that draw on the lessons from post-conflict reconstruction in key conflict zones in the 1990s and 2000s. Three underlying assumptions shape all these policy documents.

A new era?

The first assumption underpinning the reports is that a radical break with the past can be possible and that it should be a central aim of local and foreign actors seeking to trigger reform. The UNDP report *Post-Conflict Economic Recovery* (UNDP 2008a: 5) exemplifies this stance by noting that

> post-conflict recovery is often not about restoring pre-war economic or institutional arrangements; rather it is about creating a new political economy dispensation. It is not about simply building back, but about building back *differently* and *better*. As such, economic recovery as conceived in this report is essentially transformative, requiring a mix of far-reaching economic, institutional, legal and policy reforms.

How likely is it that large-scale reform is possible in the immediate post-war years? Is the post-war moment one where fundamental change can be initiated or is it one that is largely defined by attempts to preserve the status quo? Arguably, this will depend on a range of factors, including the kind of peace settlement that has been arrived at, the relative strengths of the different warring parties and the extent to which any of the parties have social or economic reform agendas they seek to implement. Post-conflict societies are likely to reside along a spectrum of highly/less likely to be responsive to reform. The situation in Balkh, as indicated below, was clearly one of continuation from the war years. While Balkh certainly cannot be taken as representative of a broader set of cases, the very obvious continuity and entrenchment of wartime practices there contrasts sharply with the multilateral agencies' belief in the desirability and possibility of fundamental reform in the immediate post-war period. The central omission, from the side of the multilateral agencies in this case, is a discussion on the degree of ripeness of societies for reform. Instead, the desirability and possibility of transformation is set forward as an article of faith.

Balkh, by contrast, illustrates the degree of both political and economic continuity that may ensue as conflict areas transition from war to peace. Atta Mohammad Noor and the ethnic Tajik military faction and party *Jamiat-e Islami* re-established control over Balkh province and the major northern city of Mazar-e-Sharif in 2001 after the area had briefly been under Taleban control.[7] The core features of Balkh province's subsequent political consolidation have been comprehensively chronicled by Dipali Mukhopadhyay. She notes that Governor Atta

> remains tied to a number of informal organisations and networks that provide him with a brand power and security that the state does not currently afford. Governor Atta is a 'disguised warlord', in that he officially has given up his identity as a *mujahideen* commander in exchange for a formal governing role on behalf of the state. His real power in Balkh, the northern provinces and vis-à-vis Kabul, derives, however, from his ability to leverage a host of informal connections that can signal to all the strength he still maintains. Like any racketeer, Atta can exercise his informal power to threaten the state, but he can also utilise it in ways that advance the interests of the state and the international community.
>
> (Mukhopadhyay 2009b: 549)

The backbone of Atta's rule in Balkh remains the extensive network of former mid-level commanders that was placed, by Atta, in the majority of the central economic, political or security positions within the province's state institutions.[8] This coincided with a reactivation and bolstering of state structures after 2001, much of which was supported and financed by a range of international donors. Central as well as sub-level administrative structures were enhanced, and new representative bodies such as the provincial council were created.[9] While analysts doubted the efficiency of the new and reformed administrative structures, in the economic sphere the state was making its presence felt (Lister 2005).[10] The relevance of government permits, granting of land rights, tax and, often, expectations of bribes, were recurring messages in my interviews with observers or actors in the business sphere. A key elected representative in Balkh province added in one interview that many government posts were bought and sold. This created a continuous 'demand' or need for office holders to elicit bribes in order to pay back their 'investment' in the post.

While donor documents such as the UNDP guidelines mentioned earlier tend to emphasise the break with past economic structures and practices during reconstruction processes, and call for the creation of 'a new political economy dispensation', the case of Balkh highlights how the political economy from the war years has become institutionalised and entrenched in the post-war years. In this way, even as the economic recovery in Balkh has been considerable and impressive, it is very far from transformative. Indeed, given that the wartime winners are permeating the new institutions, the scope for changing the structure and dynamics of the province's political economy is greatly reduced.

Hierarchies and change within groups in the war period

The second theme in multilateral policies is perhaps not so much an assumption as a failure to identify and recognise a key feature of war-torn societies: namely the full scope of change that war brings about *within* warring parties and associated communities *during* the conflict years. Instead there is a bias towards assessing disparities between the warring factions and pre-war patterns of social exclusion. One report notes typically that 'bridging' social capital (between groups) is often profoundly damaged during war, but asserts that 'bonding' social capital within groups is not necessarily lost (UNDP 2008a: 80). Some of the reports stress that it is paramount that post-war economic assistance is context sensitive and that it factors in patterns of exclusion (USAID 2009: VII). Much emphasis is placed on the need to 'do no harm', and practitioners are instructed to make use of context analysis: it is vital that post-conflict recovery helps remedy the causes of the conflict. However, as part of this, the specific features of the contexts that practitioners are urged to pay attention to are typically pre-war years of social conflict and exclusion (UK Stabilisation Unit 2008: 19), the overall political dynamics of the conflict and economic conditions such as the labour market. The tools recommended for building context aware programming are standard conflict analysis or labour marked assessments (United Nations 2009a: 19–20).

Arguably, none of these approaches is likely be able to trace wartime changes *within* communities, including *intra*-community patterns of exploitation.[11] The situation in Balkh during and after the war, however, highlights precisely these issues. The population in Balkh province is predominantly Uzbek and Tajik and the area was controlled for most of the war years by militia groups hailing from northern Afghanistan. Looking at the causes of the war, or the conflict dynamics between the Taleban and the Tajik or Uzbek militias will therefore not be able to offer insights on potential social exclusion within Balkh.

That is not to say, however, that issues of exclusion and inequality are not central to the politics and the economy in the province. The functioning of Afghanistan's markets offers a powerful illustration of this. The post-war market economy in Afghanistan was distinguished by a key feature: while the markets buzzed with activity from a large number of players, most of these players made very small profit margins on their activity. At the same time, at the foci where high profits were made, a group of politically well-connected players usually dominated, with tendencies towards monopolistic behaviour. The Afghanistan Research and Evaluation Unit (AREU) highlighted this pattern in a comprehensive study of market dynamics in six major economic sectors in Afghanistan. One of these sectors, the market for petroleum fuel, offers some useful insights (Paterson 2005).

Balkh province received most of its fuel supplies from Uzbekistan. The two firms occupying the prime roles of wholesale importers were tightly linked to the Uzbek political network *Junbesh-i-Milli* (where the warlord Dostum hailed support) and the Tajik *Jamiat-e Islami* structure (where Atta had his support base). The firms had vertical business structures that were importing, distributing and also running some petrol stations. At the same time a vast number of smaller players also resold petrol purchased from these wholesalers to customers across the province, in this way providing an additional low-tech and close-to-the-customer alternative to the petrol stations. In interviews, traders operating out of the Afghan–Uzbek border town of Heiraton stressed the modest profit margins and their sense of vulnerability.[12] At the time of these interviews in May 2008, the government was in the process of introducing a new tax on petrol imports. This had triggered significant disapproval from the small traders, including the organisation of a strike over a 15-day period in protest. The strike, however, had had no effect. A number of interviewees pointed out how the introduction of the tax hurt, or even threatened the survival of, the small-scale traders, while the few bigger players had significant buffers and profit margins to tackle the new government tax. Some interviewees, though this was contradicted by others, interpreted the introduction of the tax as a way to get rid of the smaller and independent players in the market (interview Heiraton, 19 May 2008)

The six-part market study undertaken by AREU found similar patterns in other sectors that it assessed, including the markets for pharmaceuticals, raisins and carpets (Paterson 2006). In a synthesis paper Anna Paterson argued that the Afghan markets functioned in ways not dissimilar to Indian ones. Barbara Harris-White has described the logic of market dynamics in India in the following way:

> Market structures that constrain competition are ubiquitous, masked by the appearance of crowding … An oligopolistic elite coexists with petty trade in complex marketing systems littered with brokers and giving the impression of competitiveness … large firms may keep petty ones alive while at the same time preventing them from accumulating by controlling the terms and conditions of their acquisition of information, contacts, credit and storage.
>
> (2003: 50)

These profound inequalities between small-scale 'unconnected' businessmen versus the large-scale 'connected' business actors with close ties to the civil war networks has arguably raised a serious developmental challenge in Balkh province after the war. If post-war economic recovery policies were to 'do no harm' and address social exclusion, these challenges should be factored in. However, since the post-conflict policies and tools promoted are geared towards understanding political conflict dynamics and between-communities exclusion, it is likely that these serious post-war economic patterns may pass 'under the radar' of the architects of post-war reconstruction support packages that draw on the standard guidelines for post-war economic recovery.

Closely linked political and economic spheres

The third assumption associated with the multilateral reports is the notion that political and economic spheres can be conceptualised as two distinct entities. Weak institutions, political tensions and corruption are acknowledged in the reports as key post-war challenges that make economic recovery more difficult. However, the reports downplay the extent to which political and economic actors and activities may be inter-linked or tightly integrated. The extensive *Local Economic Recovery in Post-Conflict: Guidelines* (ILO 2010) exemplify this shortcoming. While providing a detailed description on both political and economic challenges with recommendations for a broad set of economic support initiatives in impressive detail, these challenges are conceptualised through an economic lens and fail to incorporate larger political and social issues. The report's discussion on the virtues of local procurement provides one illustration:

> using local labour and raw material in the construction of a school will enhance the economic impact of the investment that was originally focused on getting children back to school. However, there may be barriers that impede local procurement and encourage outsourcing. Such obstacles include among others: the lack of linkages to local suppliers for selected goods and services, the poor quality and/or high price of services and goods produced by local firms, and the lack of capacity of local entrepreneurs to participate in bidding processes ... targeted support to local providers may improve the quality price and timing of goods and services' delivery, thus enabling them to satisfy the existing demand ... attention should be paid to the possible consequences that local corruption may have on the allocation and use of aid flow.
>
> (ILO 2010: 49)

This is a typical technical discussion of economic support activities to one particular economic sector (construction). The discussion focuses primarily on economic challenges associated with helping to reinvigorate activities in one economic sector. The political challenge of corruption receives a mention but no further deliberation is made as to why and how corruption is a relevant issue. This type of apolitical guidance is similar to discussions of economic reintegration support to former fighters in other reports. Here the stress is placed on identifying training needs and finding the right balance in supporting fighters and host communities. There is little mention of the deeply political nature of allocating benefits to a powerful network of foot soldiers and commanders (UNDP 2008a: 72).

Again, the situation in Balkh provides an interesting contrast to the main thrust of the policy documents. Two examples help to illustrate the interconnectedness between politics and the economy: dynamics in the construction sector and the 'sharik' arrangement among entrepreneurs.

The construction sector has been one of the sectors with the highest growth rates after 2001, and the dynamics in this sector provide a useful illustration of the very political economy that has developed in Balkh. Here, the government has been both a biased regulator and an economic actor in its own right. Land rights and land grabbing has been a key feature of post-2001 politics in Afghanistan. There have been recurring cases where claims surfaced that land allocation decisions were taken in favour of government office holders. Mukhopadya and Giustozzi, among others, have noted how some former commanders have utilised their government position to acquire land at low prices and resell at a considerable profit (Mukhopadhyay 2009b; Giustozzi 2007).

In Balkh and the city of Mazar-e-sharif, this phenomenon has had its own twist. As part of post-war reconstruction efforts, two new, up-market housing projects were initiated in the city's suburbs, one by private investors and another one with the involvement of Governor Atta and the provincial administration. The project initiators committed themselves to provide infrastructure plans and services for the then barren and undeveloped land, while the citizens purchasing the land plots committed themselves to construct houses of a certain standard. Prices for plots exceeded $10,000, and the purchaser of the plot would also need to cover expenses associated with actually building the house. The project affiliated with Governor Atta, Khalid-ibn-Waleed, was administered by one of Atta's central sub-commanders. Many of the key sub-commanders had received plots at discount prices in this area. Other prominent members of the Mazar-e-sharif elite, including respected teachers and prominent journalists, also received offers of plots at heavily discounted prices.[13] In the Khalid-ibn-Waleed project, the government machinery was mobilised for the purposes of a peculiar mix of private and public ends. Moreover, it was a also a case where formal elements of the state took an active part in the market dynamics of the construction sector: the promise of relocating government offices to the area as well as the provision of a paved road enhanced the market value of the project and made it more attractive to potential buyers.

A second illustration of the entangled nature of power and profit in Balkh is provided by the informal institutional arrangement of *sharik*, or 'shareholder'. This arrangement essentially denotes a form of joint venture between business entrepreneurs and violent entrepreneurs, i.e. former civil war mid- or top-level commanders with strong social and political capital. Interviewees noted this was a common arrangement, where the commanders help to ensure an operating environment conducive to business, addressing challenges associated with bribes, security of property and enforcement of contract were mitigated. The arrangement seems to be particularly prevalent in sectors with medium to high profit rates such as energy imports or construction. In some cases, the business partners entered into these arrangements on voluntary terms, each recognising the potential benefits the 'joint ventures' could yield, other times the violent entrepreneurs forced the business entrepreneurs to establish a *sharik* arrangement.

Both examples highlight how political actors, most of whom were closely associated with the wartime militia networks, could both be dominant economic actors in their own right, or play an important role facilitating market exchange. Given the centrality of political actors in mainstream economic activity it seems futile to attempt to describe activities in either the political or the economic sphere without factoring in the other. While the depiction of reconstruction challenges by the multilateral policy guidelines on post-war reconstruction in purely economic terms is not necessarily incorrect, the failure to situate economic activity within a broader political context means that such assessments verge towards reductionism. In the ILO statement on local procurement quoted above, the concerns that were highlighted included lack of available quality material and concerns about local corruption. From the brief discussion of the situation in Balkh province, however, a host of other issues emerges that needs to be understood when agencies try to reignite the local economy through procurement or local development initiatives: who, for example, are likely to be the main counterparts in business ventures, and how will operating in the local economy help to support or undermine particular groups of economic actors? These are central questions for statebuilding actors engaging in reconstruction activities; yet, the policy guidelines do not open up for assessments along these lines.

Message from Balkh: stratification is key in transitions from war to peace

This chapter has highlighted three assumptions underpinning the guidelines in multilateral agencies' policy documents on post-conflict reconstruction. Examining them through the lens of statebuilding and reconstruction in Afghanistan's Balkh province highlights how poorly the developments in this particular post-war environment resonate with the documents' core assumptions.

Beyond the use of the Balkh findings for exposing the narrowness of international guidelines on post-war economic reconstruction, the findings also point to the broader issue of stratification in post-war processes.

The Balkh case demonstrates that the network of power wielders from the war years were able to re-establish central positions in both the political and economic spheres in the post-war years. Indeed, it seems that the civil war network thrived in, and perhaps deliberately contributed to, the tight interconnection between politics and the economy in the post-conflict period. Moreover, the state institutions that were being re-established and bolstered were filled with members of the civil war network. In this way the new state apparatus became an important instrument for the transmission of power, position and prestige for civil war strongmen from the war years into the post-war period.

Indeed, the tools of the strengthened state structures were some of the most important assets that enabled civil war power wielders to 'rig' the economic game in ways that, in the words of Schwalbe, ensured that some people got advantages while others did not. This rigging was evident in the construction of the new town, where the Balkh elite received access to land developed with government and foreign support at favourable terms. It was also evident in the abuse of government permits that pushed the unconnected strata of the population to pay bribes to the insiders in government institutions. Finally, the 'sharik' arrangement outlined above constituted a set of informal rules well known to all economic agents in Balkh. These were rules that clearly had, as Schwalbe would expect, unfairness built into them, and that have further entrenched inequality. While some mid-range profit makers tried to avoid the 'sharik' arrangement, few, if any, questioned the underlying rationale of the practice or sought to challenge its prevalence. Two features of Afghan society helped facilitate the emergence of the 'sharik' arrangement: an absence of rule of law in the market economy created a role and demand for the political and security assets of the former commanders; and the re-emergence of the state allowed former civil war players on the inside of state structures to shape state practices in ways that served both public and private ends, including ensuring that new state regulations were designed in ways that were favourable to the former civil war strongmen.[14]

Implications for statebuilding

The way government institutions, and in some cases government regulations (i.e. the unequal effects of the petrol tax on large- and small-scale distributors) came to serve the civil war winners well, resonates well with Polanyi's expectation that powerful interest groups are able to shape institutions and regulations. This puts the considerable technical and financial assistance offered by the international community to Afghanistan in an interesting perspective. A reinvigoration of the state structures was a central aim of the top Afghan political leadership and the international community supporting Afghanistan after 2001. The findings from Balkh province highlights how, as a by-product of these statebuilding efforts, a framework was created that could be appropriated by the men placed at the top of the hierarchy in the war society and turned into a vehicle that transmitted power from the war years into the peace period. That is not to say that, because of this, the efforts to rebuild state structures after the war in Afghanistan were misguided. It might very well be that the kind of stratification patterns observed both in war and peacetime in Balkh were in any case unavoidable. But it still begs the question as to whether there was an awareness that statebuilding and economic reconstruction were likely to become entwined with broader processes of stratification. It is beyond the scope of this chapter to provide answers to that question, but it is useful to note that other studies also highlight how post-war statebuilding initiatives in Balkh were appropriated and served to entrench the role of the civil war strong men.[15]

If we are to extrapolate from the situation in Balkh it seems unlikely that outside initiatives can 'impose' themselves on post-war societies and autonomously direct the process of transformation from war to peace. Instead, the converse seems true: the implementation and outcomes of statebuilding are shaped and determined by the 'indigenous' elements in a society's transition from war to peace. Indeed, it seems likely that international statebuilding interventions may easily get 'hijacked' by indigenous actors and processes.[16] Moreover, while the international statebuilding agenda may encompass aspirations for transformation and reform in the immediate post-war years, it may very well be that indigenous inclinations towards conservation of hierarchies trumps an outside-led transformative agenda. Following on from that, one of the central questions in studies on statebuilding seems to be how the initiatives associated with an outside-led transformative agenda 'mesh' with ongoing indigenous political process and power struggles.[17] Further empirical studies of the relative importance of external versus local agendas may well establish the pre-eminence of local processes, and outside resources and policies merely feeding into and being appropriated by local actors and agendas. If this is the case, one not only needs to rethink statebuilding, but also the way statebuilding is studied. A shift in focus may be in order away from the international statebuilding circuit and towards the distinct post-war social, political and economic processes in particular foci.

Notes

1 Research for this chapter was undertaken under the auspices of project 'The Political Economy of DDR', financed by the Norwegian Research Council POVPEACE programme (Project no. 178689). I am grateful for the kind encouragement, helpful corrections and constructive comments offered by Dominik Zaum and Mats Berdal on earlier versions of this chapter.
2 Power, or 'social power' for Mann, has two aspects. One is distributive power, where person A has power *over* B and is able to carry out his will despite resistance. Second is the collective aspect of power whereby persons in cooperation can enhance their joint power over third parties or over nature (Mann 1986: 6–7).
3 On the concept of state capture, see also Skocpol 1985.
4 Susan Woodward among others stresses the importance of functioning government institutions if market-based economic recovery is to succeed (Woodward 2002).
5 However, the statebuilding practices of different international and regional organisations are examined in Part III of this book.
6 The insights from Balkh draws on field work undertaken in northern Afghanistan in 2007 and 2008. Tahir Qadiry, a journalist and student at Balkh University at the time, was a skilful facilitator of my field research in Afghanistan. I conducted 42 semi-structured interviews in Mazar-e-Sharif (Balkh province), Meymaneh (Faryab province) and Kabul. Interviewees included former combatants, former sub-level commanders, community leaders, representatives of provincial councils, journalists, owners of small- and medium-sized businesses, law enforcement officers, government officials, human rights activists, Balkh University academics, international

military and civilian staff at the ISAF Regional Command North and the Provincial Reconstruction Teams (PRT) in Mazar-e-Sharif and Meymaneh, UN Mission in Afghanistan (UNAMA) representatives, UN Development Programme Afghanistan New Beginnings Programme (UNDP ANBP) project staff and Kabul-based diplomats.

7 This was in part achieved by pledging loyalty to, and forging an alliance with, the central government in Kabul. Atta was made governor of Balkh province in 2004.

8 In return for their support, these former mid-level commanders, many of whom hold positions in law enforcement agencies such as the border and traffic police, have enjoyed a range of benefits, such as protection from prosecution for wartime crimes, and considerable opportunity to misuse government offices for private benefits (Mukhopadhyay 2009b: 550). This arrangement has contributed to the establishment of an effective political order in Balkh province, which has consistently remained one of the most peaceful and prosperous provinces of Afghanistan. While this order is, as Mukhopadhyay notes, far from the liberal vision set out for Afghanistan's peacebuilding process, it does deliver key assets to the local population (stability and economic growth), the central government (loyalty) and the international community (drugs eradication) (ibid.).

9 The Afghanistan Research and Evaluation Unit (AREU) documented in its extensive research on state institutions after 2001 that a skeleton structure of the state administration existed (Nixon 2008). Many of the central ministries were operational and there was also some, even if limited and uneven, state representation in a large number of administrative districts across Afghanistan.

10 The Uzbekistan–Afghanistan border crossing (Heiraton), where goods destined for Balkh and Mazar-e-Sharif transit, is a good example of this. At a visit in May 2008, there was a heavy presence of customs officers and border guards, and according to the head of the border guards at the crossing, the customs intake at the post had increased over the previous two years from $30 million to $60 million (interview Heiraton, 19 May 2008).

11 While the full scope of change is ignored, it is worth noting that war experiences do receive some mention, though then the emphasis is often (with the UNDP's *Post-Conflict Economic Recovery* report as a notable exception) on the destructive effects of war, both on an individual and societal level. The UN's *Integrated Disarmament, Demobilisation and Reintegration Standards* (United Nations 2006a), for example, portray wartime participation as de-skilling:

> Often ex-combatants do not know how to carry out simple activities that are easily understood by their peers, and do not have the confidence to either ask for assistance or find out for themselves. Making choices is often a new experience for ex-combatants, and even for their dependants, as they are used to command structures and collective lifestyles where they are told what to do by others.
>
> (module 4.3: 21).

12 They noted though that they had to offer bribes regularly to government officials, but no more than a small percentage of the profit. The costs of these bribes were passed on to the customers as the traders adjusted the prices upward to recover any funds lost to corruption.

13 This seems to have been an effective way of encouraging allegiance to Atta: a place in the new suburb would bring status and comfort for the person and families offered a plot, while it is likely that the initiators still earned considerable income even at the discounted rate. There were promises that schools and supermarkets would be built in the new area. Moreover, the provincial government had announced plans to relocate some of its offices to the suburbs. Observers of the project noted that there were already paved roads in parts of the project and it was thought the governor had been able to do this through international donor support (interview Mazar-e-sharif, 17 May 2008).

14 It is important to stress though that not all civil war strongmen were able to make the transition from winners in the war years to winners in the peace years. Interviews with fighters have revealed a number of different trajectories, where some mid-level commanders reported having been excluded from the spoils of victories and had returned disgruntled to life as farmers in remote villages. Many of the foot soldiers, unless they could make use of family or other ties to top-level commanders, have also faced a difficult transition. It remains true though that those fighters and commanders that were sufficiently close to Governor Atta seem to have been favoured with good access to, or positions within, the state, which in turn enabled them to command political leverage in the post-war period.

15 Antonio Giustozzi, for example, has argued that the internationally sponsored demobilisation, disarmament and reintegration process in Afghanistan has entrenched the positions of the civil war commanders (Giustozzi 2008b).

16 For a similar argument related to post-conflict macro-economic assistance, see Nakaya 2009.

17 Michael Barnett and Christoph Zürcher offer one such approach (2009).

5 Private and public interests

Informal actors, informal influence, and economic order after war

Christine Cheng

For countries that have experienced armed conflict, the aftermath of war offers the hope of a new and transformed political and economic order. Given that the end of war is often accompanied by the promise of democratic elections, pledges of reconstruction money from the international community,[1] the arrival of peacekeepers, and the imminent disarming of fighting factions, the months and years that immediately follow the signing of a peace treaty are inevitably full of optimism and potential. A brief, but significant window for substantial institutional change opens, and in that short-lived post-conflict moment, a new equitable political and economic order seems entirely possible. This is the tantalizing vision of the future offered by liberal peacebuilding.

This vision, however short-lived, is not entirely born of naivety. Some societies, like South Africa, have witnessed a wholesale transformation of their political and economic order following the end of conflict. However, for the average citizen, the hopeful discourse generated by these kinds of expectations sits in sharp contrast to the difficulties of actually constructing such a new order. This chapter focuses on a key challenge to building such an equitable post-conflict economic order: the role of informal actors and their efforts to exploit their political influence for private gain.

In the period immediately following the end of war – the post-conflict moment – there is a unique opportunity to set a tone of economic opportunity that privileges public interests and aims for a more equitable distribution of resources. Unfortunately, this is also the same moment where informal actors can establish patterns of behaviour that harm the public interest – chiefly by taking advantage of the state's institutional malleability at this time. Specifically, informal actors leverage three key statebuilding policies in this post-conflict window. First, the process of economic and political liberalization that often follows war gives powerful informal actors a prime opportunity to exploit their political connections for personal gain. Second, international actors' emphasis on maintaining stability at all costs means that informal actors who can credibly incite political violence can threaten to destabilize the country if their economic interests are not looked after. Third, emphasizing capacity building without understanding the linkages between formal and informal actors can actually end up undermining the state institutions being supported.

In essence, some 'statebuilding' policies have the opposite of their intended effect: they actually empower and legitimize forces that are harmful to the public interest. Put starkly: some statebuilding efforts do not weaken informal actors but *actually strengthen them.*[2] Depending on how successfully informal actors leverage their post-conflict gains and institutionalize these patterns of behaviour, the long-term consequences for strengthening the capacity of the central state could be dire. Thus, one important consequence of these statebuilding policies is that they consolidate the power of informal actors and *undermine* genuine reforms that would have led to a more equitable distribution of resources throughout society (see Torjesen's chapter in this volume).

Broadly, this chapter argues that key statebuilding policies actually weaken the state by privileging the influence of informal actors and embedding economic power structures that harm the public interest. The result is entrenched inequality, reinforcing the sense that the economic order is fixed in favour of those who are politically connected. This chapter expands upon this argument by tackling the nebulous issue of informal actors in three sections. The first section interrogates and defines the concept of informal actors and examines the linkages between the formal world and the informal world. The second section introduces the concept of conflict capital and argues that after war, informal actors who have access to conflict capital will use it to shape the rules of the economic game. The third section then examines the impact of international statebuilding policies on informal actors. Specifically, the international community's preference for internal stability, its promotion of economic and political liberalization, and its emphasis on capacity building can unintentionally support informal actors and be counterproductive for statebuilding. This section also highlights how foreign powers use their own informal influence in post-conflict societies to reap economic advantages, before offering some brief conclusions.

Informal actors and informal influence

The concept of an informal actor is inherently woolly. In the context of this examination of post-conflict statebuilding, the term 'informal actor' is most easily defined in relation to what it is not – it is *not* a formal actor. Whereas a formal actor holds official, state-sanctioned political power and has an obligation to act in the state's public interest by virtue of her position, an informal actor uses her formal connections to exert influence over the management of state resources and political processes, but without holding formal office in that state. For the purposes of this discussion, formal actors hold official positions in the post-conflict state. All other actors are treated as informal actors.[3]

In the post-conflict state, the issue of what a new economic order will look like and how economic resources are to be distributed is usually not a matter that is publicly addressed. Instead, the contestation over how economic power will be shared is likely to be decided secretly amongst local elites. Out of these parallel contests for power, an alternative power structure of informal rule can coalesce. This structure of informal actors and networks enables a symbiotic relationship with those who hold formal power: they influence and are influenced by government officials. Yet one of the key problems with informal actors is that their very nature makes it difficult to observe their actions and measure their influence.

In contrast to the relatively open theatre of formal negotiations involving key stakeholders (local and international) who are tasked with negotiating the formal political order as part of a peace process, the ways in which informal actors and networks assert their influence occurs quietly, behind the scenes. In some cases, the scale of the deals that are negotiated unofficially can substantially alter and define the post-conflict political and economic order (as with large procurement contracts or the privatization of major industries).

The fact that influence is wielded informally poses two problems: transparency and accountability. The first concern is the lack of transparency –both in outcomes and process. In effect, there may be a set of formal arrangements that are made public, but what is worrisome is that an alternate informal set of arrangements could override the formal ones in practice and the actual details of these will never be made public. Similarly, there is a concern with transparency of process. The question of exactly how informal actors actually exert their influence (coercion, manipulation of their business networks, quid pro quo benefits, bribes, etc.) is not clear. Further, the involvement of informal actors makes decision-making processes that are already opaque even more impenetrable because formal actors will have strong incentives to obscure the influence of informal actors.

A second concern with informal actors is that they wield significant influence without any form of public accountability. Whereas a formal actor is accountable to the people (even if this accountability only exists on paper) an informal actor wields influence without having to answer to the public for the ways in which she influences government policies and decisions. Indeed, it may not even be possible to identify who these informal actors are – especially since they will seek to conceal their influence. While divisions of formal power are made public – as with decisions over who will control state-owned enterprises or cabinet posts – the identity of informal actors and the ways in which they exercise influence over policy outcomes remain difficult to uncover.

Despite these two concerns, it is not informality that is the problem per se. The concepts of informal actors and informal influence have no normative content in themselves. Informal influence can be used to benefit the public interest as much as to harm it. After all, informal actors also encompass family members and personal friends of public officials – relationships which in themselves do not provide cause for concern. Informal actors also constitute the most important elements of a vibrant civil society. This includes prominent religious leaders – whether they are evangelical Christians in the southern United States or imams in the Middle East – as well as powerful corporate lobbyists and special interest non-governmental organizations. While recognizing that informal actors can positively impact the public interest, the focus of this chapter is on *informal actors who act against the public interest for personal or group gain.*

Although violence is not a defining feature of informal actors, it is critical to note that there is a divide between those who employ violence to achieve their goals and those who do not. For post-conflict societies, the primary concern is that informal actors who are violent will become powerful enough to challenge the state, potentially taking the country back to war. There are also other concerns: that these violent groups may come to dominate specific areas and embed themselves locally as with warlords (Reno 1998; Goodhand 2011) and extralegal groups (Cheng 2011), or that they develop into powerful organized crime groups (Farer 1999; Williams 2009a).

Over time, it is possible that the state cedes control to one or more of these violent groups, leaving politicians beholden to powerful informal actors. Under these circumstances, anyone who does not fall into line can be replaced at whim, or even killed. Even where a regime is democratic, reining in this kind of powerful informal actor may not be possible. The end result is what Bayart *et al.* (1999: 20–21) have termed the criminalization of the state: 'a hidden and collective structure of power which surrounds, and even controls, the official tenants of state power'. One of the post-conflict regions that has exemplified this problem is the Balkans.

Across Bosnia, Serbia, Kosovo, Montenegro, and Macedonia, organized crime groups came to wield tremendous authority in the post-conflict years, and even today, many of them remain powerful (*The Economist* 2011a). In the post-conflict period, the most shocking demonstration of this power occurred when former Serbian Prime Minister Zoran Djindjić was assassinated in 2003, allegedly by members of the Zemun clan, an organized crime group. Djindjić was a political reformer who had aligned himself with the state security forces and organized crime for the purposes of protection and financial support. Shortly before his death, Djindjić had been under intense pressure from the West to take action against his allies in organized crime. Once Milorad Luković and his Zemun clan believed that Prime Minister Djindjić was prepared to act against them, Luković had him killed (Corpora 2004; Gordy 2004). The Serbian government's indictments against the Zemun clan only underscore the power of this informal actor, charging that the group:

> had completely regulated 'connections' with various personalities from state institutions, the police, the judiciary, the prosecutors' office, the Security Information Agency (BIA), with the president of the Serbian Radical Party Vojislav Seselj, and with the entire command of the Unit for Special Operations (JSO) which was, in fact, under their strong influence, that is under their command.[4]

Formal–informal relationships

In theory, there is a clear line that separates formal and informal actors, but in reality there is overlap between these categories and significant movement between them. Thus, it is important to examine the nature of the relationships between the formal and informal worlds, especially where institutions of the informal world play a prominent role. Indeed, in some countries, the informal world of clans, ethnic and family ties, religious affiliation, and even secret societies may be of equal importance to the formal political and economic realms that scholars are more often focused on. It is critical to remember that power, resources, and status may be derived from both the formal and informal worlds, and that influence and resources in one domain can be traded for status in another. These domains operate as part of a comprehensive ecosystem. Concentrating on the formal actors who hold official political and economic power would be the ecological equivalent of describing a forest by counting all the trees and bushes without acknowledging the role of the soil, the water, the animals, the insects, the fungi, or the bacteria that help explain how the system works as a whole. In both cases, critical elements of the system are overlooked because they are less obvious to untrained eyes.

It is understandable that scholars and international policy makers have a tendency to pay little heed to the institutions and networks of the informal world – these can be difficult to penetrate and to understand (Helmke and Levitsky 2004). Often, the nature of this influence can only be grasped if there is an understanding of the history of domestic and local politics. For those international actors engaged in statebuilding, it takes an anthropologist's mindset to imagine how the norm of Pashto hospitality might override economic self-interest or even personal security concerns, or how considerations of status within an African ethnic group or a Somali clan might take precedence over national interest. Yet by focusing on the elements of the system that outsiders consider to be the most important, there is a real danger of misattributing the sources of stability or instability to formal domains of influence simply because they are more easily identifiable by international actors.

For example, in 2004, after the end of the civil war in Angola, key partners of China International Fund (also known as China Sonangol) successfully exploited their personal connections to President Jose Eduardo dos Santos to become the middleman for exporting Angolan oil to China (*The Economist* 2011b). It is estimated that billions of dollars in profit have accrued to China Sonangol. It is also alleged that the son of the Angolan president is a director of China Sonangol. This was a textbook example of how informal actors used their influence for private gain at the expense of the public interest.

In Liberia, a different example of the formal–informal relationship is exemplified by the role of Poro societies. These are secret societies that supervise and regulate 'the sexual, social, and political conduct of all members of the wider society' (Lavenda and Schultz 2007). Many of Liberia's zoes (high priests of the Poro societies) wield considerable informal influence in all domains of public and private life and have been long been used by Liberia's leaders – including Charles Taylor – to cement their influence (Harley 1941; Ellis 1999). And yet the ways in which zoes use their informal influence is poorly understood. For instance, a zo might pose as a supernatural spirit by wearing a ceremonial mask in order to publicly reprimand a local chief who is seen to be abusing his power. As the International Crisis Group (ICG 2004: 21) aptly pointed out in a 2004 report, 'The existence of such an important but unfamiliar element of Liberian life poses further challenges to the UN.'

The impact of informal actors

There are at least three ways in which informal actors can significantly harm the public's economic interests: by altering the economic and political rules of the game, by charging excessive rents at the expense of the public purse, and by skewing the distribution of state resources.

As argued by Hellman *et al.* (2000), one of the most important ways in which informal actors can impact the new economic order is by influencing the rules of the economic game in their own favour. It is important to note that the ability to influence the *setting* of the rules is qualitatively different from obtaining specific exceptions to certain rules or even influencing a one-off change in a single rule. Rather, the ability to determine the rules of the game is about controlling the regulatory framework. Matters such as how commercial disputes are settled, the negotiation of tax rates, the appropriation of local land, or the setting of environmental standards are the types of technical issues that critically impact on the behaviour of corporations. Given the prevalence of corruption in post-conflict states (Johnston 2010; Cheng and Zaum 2011a), the process for setting these types of rules can easily be 'captured' (Hellman *et al.* 2000).

Informal actors may also be in a position to charge large rents, as with non-competitive bidding on concessions contracts. In other cases, informal actors can hinder economic activity by selectively influencing who does or does not get to do business in the country, leading to market monopolies and oligopolies. Those companies that are invited to do business end up paying for this privilege, and the entry 'tax' is passed on to customers in the prices of their goods or services. By controlling entry, prices are higher than they would be in the absence of more competition. Given the desperate financial situation faced by many states emerging from war, these excess rents are significant relative to the government budget, and are important to a state's ability to provide public services.

The impact of informal actors also extends to the suboptimal choices that are made in the distribution of state resources. The influence of informal actors can lead to poor choices in hiring government workers, in determining which districts should receive what services, and even in prioritizing areas for reconstruction and development. All of these decisions will impact the economic order. Selected commercial or group interests will outweigh what is good for society as a whole. Where newly anointed government officials are more loyal to their friends and family members than the wider group of citizens they are supposed to represent, post-conflict statebuilding will prove to be an even greater challenge.

Conflict capital and the persistence of informal actors

The years immediately following the end of war are a time of optimism and momentous change. Government ministries are reorganized; new political parties are often formed and new leaders are elected; new laws are passed; new operational systems are put in place. This post-conflict window can provide a rare opening for political renewal and an opportunity to reimagine patterns of interactions between states and citizens, between public and private, and between religious and ethnic groups. At the same time, many post-conflict states also find that their institutions have been substantially weakened by war.[5] Transitional leaders may be perceived as illegitimate, and the country may be reliant upon external actors like the UN to maintain security. Informal actors can exploit this weakness to strengthen their own position.

During this period of rebuilding and reform, informal actors can consolidate the gains they have made through the course of the war and skew the new rules to their own advantage (see Torjesen's chapter in this volume). Once the patterns of how the state conducts its business are set, it becomes much more difficult to break out of this mould as the political situation stabilizes and the memory of war recedes into the background. As the post-conflict window closes, patterns of interaction become more predictable and the cost of disrupting these actors grows. In this way, the 'post-conflict moment' determines a country's political and economic trajectory.

While governments are often weak in capacity and may lack legitimacy after war, the relative strength of informal actors – especially those who are most likely to undermine the public interest – is often rooted in their wartime activities. Informal actors who are the most likely to exert undue influence are those who did well out of war: leaders of the fighting factions; business leaders who benefited from the war economy and their close connections to the leaders of conflict parties; and local bosses and 'big men' who were able to cement their authority because they allied themselves with the winning side (Mampilly 2011). From their positions of privilege and power, these kinds of informal actors are able to leverage their advantage in the post-conflict moment.

But how exactly do these types of informal actors convert their wartime links into political leverage once the conflict is over? In theory, the period of conflict is imagined to be quite distinct from the post-conflict period, with an invisible line separating them. However, in practice, there is much more continuity than change in how individuals relate to one another in the aftermath of war.

One way to analyse these relationships is using the concept of conflict capital – social capital created under circumstances of violent conflict. Building on the social capital literature of Pierre Bourdieu and his colleagues (Bourdieu 1986; Bourdieu and Wacquant 1992), Robert Putnam *et al.* (1993: 167) define social capital as: 'features of social organization, such as trust, norms, and networks, that can improve the efficiency of society by facilitating coordinated actions'. Similarly, conflict capital is a specific derivative of social capital (Cheng 2011: Ch. 2). Conflict capital refers to these same social features, but is created out of shared experiences of armed conflict. Conceptually, it alludes not only to the intense conditions under which these bonds were formed, but also to a shared violent experience. Conflict capital emphasizes the 'stickiness' of the social bonds created out of war, and the ways in which relationships forged around violence are more likely to persist beyond the end of war. These include the relationships between ex-combatants and their commanders, between political leaders and private militias, or between business leaders and organized crime.

Beyond specific networks of those who commit violent acts during war, conflict capital also refers to the changed ways in which people respond to violence as a result of the war. The implication is that those individuals and communities with larger stores of conflict capital are more likely to respond to conflict by using violence (as compared to those with lower levels of conflict capital) – their threshold for the use of violence is lower. To be more specific, researchers have put forward the theory that emotional desensitization in response to violence stimulates aggressive behaviour (Carnagey *et al.* 2007; Huesmann and Kirwil 2007).

Like social capital, conflict capital can also be thought of as a 'moral resource' whose supply increases with use and decreases with lack of use.[6] Over the course of a war, a society's stock of conflict capital will accumulate; if faction leaders, ex-combatants, local bosses, criminal gangs, and others continue to activate it, the amount of conflict capital will continue to grow with destructive consequences. The skills, contacts, and knowledge created through the experience of war could easily find other uses in the post-civil war economy. The danger, as Jonathan Goodhand (2004) observes, is that a criminalized war economy will transform into a criminalized peace economy.

Through the course of war, many informal actors accumulate large deposits of conflict capital which they can draw on after the war. The accumulated stock of conflict capital can also be activated in a way that undermines state-building, including tacit state approval for participation in prohibited activities (e.g. narco-trafficking, hunting endangered species), abusing the privilege of patronage appointments, or selectively enforcing the law (e.g. prosecuting rivals while protecting allies).

In practice, activating conflict capital means threatening the use of force to achieve the desired ends. In Afghanistan, for example, former commander Atta Mohammed Noor successfully translated his battlefield influence and his ethnic ties into formal political power as the Governor of Balkh province (Mukhopadhyay 2009a; see Torjesen's chapter in this volume). Yet long before he held formal power as governor of Balkh, it was clear that Atta held tremendous informal power One episode that revealed the extent of his power occurred in 2004, before he became governor.

In the spring of 2004, Hamid Karzai was attempting to assert his authority in the north of the country. He fired many of the top officials who were loyal to Atta or to General Dostum (a rival leader) and installed Akram Khakrizwal as police chief and appointed 300 new police officers (Edwards and Watson 2003). When Khakrizwal purportedly began to investigate Atta loyalists' links to the drug industry, Atta's fighters took over Mazar-i-Sharf's police head-quarters and held officers hostage. Within days of this incident, Atta was appointed governor.

Once he became governor, Atta placed many of his former field com-manders into positions of formal power. This coercive element of Atta's power and his informal reach remained highly visible to the local population. As described by Dipali Mukhopadhyay (2009a: 536), Atta was able to use this network to keep a close watch on anyone who might threaten his power. Despite the fact that his fighters participated in an internationally sanctioned Disarmament, Demobilization, and Reintegration programme, their loyalties, identities, and values as part of Atta's militia remained intact (ibid.: 544). They retained obligations to Atta as Atta did to them. Even though he had officially joined the government, Atta also maintained a level of informal power that guaranteed his influence in the region and in Kabul

This example of militia-leader-cum-politician Atta in the Afghan context reveals how formal and informal relationships can be used to unleash local violence, but also how these linkages can be used to successfully keep viol-ence in check. Ultimately, it was the combination of securing formal and informal power through a political bargain that led to a relatively stable and prosperous environment in Balkh.

The impact of statebuilding policies on informal actors

Having examined how informal actors pose a challenge to post-conflict state-building, this section will consider how the international community's state-building policies affect informal actors. It will show that the international community's overriding desire for political stability, its liberalization policies, and its focus on capacity building can bolster the influence of informal actors at the expense of the public interest.

Stability first

In the early post-conflict years, governments remain deeply worried about their ability to maintain internal stability. Donors and other international actors are similarly concerned: their first priority is to restore peace. During this period, violent clashes may still be seen as normal, though they may be less frequent than they were during war. For those societies that successfully transition from war to peace, this expectation of violence diminishes and is gradually replaced by an expectation of peace. However, once violent clashes are no longer the norm, the marginal 'cost' of an episode of mass violence to the country's reputation begins to rise because such an episode signals – inwardly and outwardly – that a conflict has regressed.

From this point onwards, post-conflict governments and the international community will go to great lengths to ensure that episodes of political violence do not recur. In this volume, Anastasakis, Caplan, and Economides suggest that 'the EU often has to sacrifice some of its normative claims for the sake of peace, a balance among the different local actors, and the rule of law' (p. 168). Empirically, we have also seen that the threat of violence is powerful enough to silence international actors, even in the face of extreme corruption (Divjak and Pugh 2011; Kosovar Stability Initiative 2010).

The international community's emphasis on stabilization has important knock-on effects. First, post-conflict governments become reluctant to directly confront informal actors with violent capabilities or significant conflict capital, choosing instead to concede to them or where possible, to co-opt them.[7] Unfortunately, once informal actors come to understand why the state and the international community are reacting to transgressions with restraint, they will also realize that short of inciting political violence and destabilizing the country, they will mostly be left alone. This *lack* of a response from the international community signals to the local population that informal actors (especially those with violent capabilities) remain in control and that the international community is unwilling to take action against them. The emphasis on short-term stabilization has created a space that informal actors have exploited to their advantage. For the most powerful informal actors, there are no consequences to breaking the law – effectively, the law can be sidestepped in order to achieve desired goals. Christopher Corpora has argued that: 'The perceived lack of international will directly affect the way people understand their society, providing illicit actors and alliances with a buffer zone for continued growth and reinforcement' (2004: 63).

In Kosovo, the international community's reticence is reflected in the reluctance of the EU Rule of Law Mission (EULEX) and the EU's International Civilian Office (ICO) to challenge the power of certain informal actors (Cheng and Zaum 2011a; see Anastasakis *et al.*'s chapter in this volume). In these cases and others (Goodhand 2011; Looney 2011), the international community is not a hapless bystander, but consciously chose to placate local elites for fear of provoking a violent response. The long-term effect of mollifying powerful informal actors, however, is that corruption erodes citizen confidence in the legal system and the government itself. Some have suggested that this is what happened in Bosnia, for example (Council of Europe 2003; Cheng and Zaum 2011a).

Economic and political liberalization

For international actors, two of the core statebuilding policies are economic and political liberalization. These two policies form the core of the 'liberal peace'. Scholars of post-conflict statebuilding have long debated the merits of the 'liberal peace' (see discussion on pp. 8–9 in this volume), arguing, for example, that the legacies of war economies have made it particularly difficult for liberal institutions to take root (Cramer 2006; Divjak and Pugh 2011; Le Billon 2011). One reason why these institutions have such difficulty taking root is that informal actors exploit their political connections to manipulate the rules of the game. Ex-combatant leaders, key business owners, organized criminals, and other powerful informal actors combine their political influence to leverage three important advantages: stores of conflict capital, access to insider information, and substantial financial resources. This allows them to benefit disproportionately from the processes of political and economic liberalization that are part and parcel of Western- and UN-led post-conflict statebuilding.

The process of opening up a country's political space and installing democracy (where it has not existed before) manifests itself primarily through the holding of elections. In practice, elections tend to be won by those with the most organizational capacity and the greatest funds. This means that in the aftermath of war, informal actors who accumulated conflict capital through their wartime activities will have a significant organizational advantage, especially because the stickiness of these bonds makes it easier to activate these connections. For example, they can draw on former wartime associates, they can use profits from wartime business ventures on political campaigning, and many of these individuals will already have local, or even national, name recognition. In addition, local crime bosses and ex-combatant leaders will also be backed by coercive force. These dynamics signal to the larger population that in fact, democratization and economic liberalization only serve to solidify the gains made by wartime 'winners' and indeed that the rules of the post-war game have already been fixed.

It is society's most notorious informal actors that benefit most from 'insider information' on land deals, privatization possibilities, lucrative procurement proposals, and all manner of government contracts and opportunities. For example, in Bosnia, nationalist elites successfully gained control of formerly state-owned enterprises in telecommunications and energy and used them to fund nationalist parties (Pugh 2004).

Even in situations where informal actors opt not to run for office themselves, their money, influence, and connections can be used to support their favoured candidates. This support can result in a quid pro quo with informal actors later reaping the rewards of these political connections. In Haiti, former President Aristide was accused of protecting the drug kingpin Beaudoin 'Jacques' Ketant from arrest for six years after he had been indicted by the US on drug charges in 1997. Ketant claimed that Aristide was paid $500,000 each month for landing his drug shipments from Colombia on a highway near Aristide's home (Adams 2004).

As part of the economic liberalization process, privatizing government assets also advantages local 'bosses' and business elites. In a post-conflict environment with weak institutional capacity, privatization creates a mechanism for informal actors to launder and legitimize their ill-gotten wartime wealth.[8] By way of illustration, a 2007 report by the Bosnian chapter of Transparency International referred to the 'crooked' privatization of Sarajevo's Holiday Inn hotel and the Mostar aluminum plant (2007).

In most post-conflict societies, the processes unleashed by economic liberalization and democratization can pose serious problems because the same powerful pre-war and wartime elites wind up controlling a country's political power and economic resources. Under these circumstances, the legitimacy of the new government will automatically be called into question. For example, if the same elders, faction leaders, chiefs, religious leaders, business owners, or local bosses are seen to reap the lion's share of economic benefits in the new dispensation, then the post-conflict political order will be viewed as unchanged.

This perception can be dangerous for a new government. If one of the motivations for going to war in the first place was to remove corrupt elites from power, then a newly installed government that is seen as complicit with the despised regime of the past – indirectly linked through informal actors – could have a destabilizing effect. Those who fought against the elites could ultimately decide to return to war. Under these circumstances, informal actors become a cause for concern not only for the post-conflict country but also for an international community that is deeply concerned about local stability.

Capacity building

Post-conflict governments, policy makers, and scholars have long emphasized the importance of building state capacity for post-conflict countries (Paris 2004; Ghani and Lockhart 2008; Fjelde and De Soysa 2009; but see Hameiri 2009). This literature developed out of a recognition that the international community was hollowing out state capacity by creating a parallel bureaucracy consisting of UN civilian staff, international NGOs, bilateral donors, and, nowadays, private contractors. While this parallel bureaucracy problem still persists, capacity-building proponents have made strengthening government institutions a cornerstone policy for international actors in post-conflict states. For example, in a major policy document, the UN Department of Economic and Social Affairs 'considers the "nuts and bolts" of capacity-building for public service in post-conflict situations to be one of its foremost areas of concern'.[9]

What is missing from this discourse is explicit recognition that not all government institutions are equally worthy of support and, further, that informal actors have an important role to play in the development of the post-war order. For example, Gordy points out that the investigation following the Djinjić killing uncovered that high-ranking officials in law enforcement were deeply connected to organized crime. This included the case of Milan Sarajlić, Serbia's deputy state prosecutor at the time, who admitted to blocking legal proceedings against organized crime bosses and to thwarting criminal investigations against them. He also admitted to accepting €150,000 to reveal the whereabouts of a protected witness. In this case, supporting the judiciary without knowing that the senior government official was actually beholden to a powerful organized crime group would have only strengthened the position of informal actors and entrenched economic power structures that are harmful to the public interest.

If the formal and informal worlds are as deeply intertwined as this chapter argues, then the current emphasis by scholars and policy makers on strengthening formal institutions and formal actors *without due regard for informal politics* is deeply problematic. Without a clear understanding of informal actors and the role that they play in local politics, international actors may be unintentionally entrenching economic and political institutions that are viewed as illegitimate by the local population.

The informal influence of major powers

Finally, it is important to acknowledge that major powers – especially from the West – have exerted their formal and informal influence on post-conflict states in ways that have been detrimental to the public interest of those countries. Even when key Western powers intervene with humanitarian intentions (as with the distribution of aid or the protection of civilians), it would be naive to think that they will not subsequently use their influence to benefit their commercial interests and impose their political values. In both the US-led Iraq invasion of 2003 and the 2011 NATO-led intervention in Libya, a common 'person-on-the-street' perception was that Western countries had chosen to fight these wars because they had set their sights on securing access to key oil supplies. This view of Western intentions was confirmed when UK Defence Secretary Philip Hammond asked British firms to 'pack their suitcases' and head to Libya to secure oil and reconstruction contracts the day after former leader Muammar Gaddafi was killed by the National Transitional Council.[10]

Whether or not oil proved part of the motivating force for intervention in either of these cases is beside the point given the substantial informal influence wielded by those with strong military links to the post-conflict regimes. In Iraq, despite outward appearances of favouring non-American firms for primary contracts, the subcontracting of oil services through the tender process has been overwhelmingly dominated by American companies like Halliburton, Baker Hughes, Weatherford International, and Schlumberger (Kramer 2011). In fact, the most financially profitable part of the Iraqi contracts has arguably been in contracts for oil drilling, well building, and equipment maintenance. As noted by Andrei Kuzyaev, the president of Russian firm Lukoil Overseas, 'For America, the important thing is open access to reserves. And that is what is happening in Iraq' (ibid.).

The controversial awarding of a 25-year concession for a key iron ore mine in Liberia provides another case in point. In 2005, multinational conglomerate Mittal Steel won the right to develop the Mount Nimba mine for an investment of $900 million (Bermúdez-Lugo 2009). However, the process by which Mittal was chosen was fraught with irregularities and accusations of impropriety. In this case, after undertaking an open international bidding process, an Inter-Ministerial Technical Committee assessed the bids and initially awarded the contract to the firm Global Infrastructure Holdings Limited (GIHL). This decision was subsequently overturned by then head-of-state Gyude Bryant on the grounds that 'the Project must be more widely advertised' (Willie 2004). The Technical Committee went through the entire process again. Again, GIHL was chosen. At this point, the Assistant Minister of Labour at the time said:

> the Ministry of Labor's representative was asked by the Committee Chairman, Mr. Mulbah Willie, to change the result in favor of Mittal Steel *because Chairman Bryant and the US Embassy want Mittal Steel to be the successful bidder for the award of a Mineral Development Agreement.*
>
> (Mulbah 2005, emphasis added)

Liberia's iron ore deal reveals the delicate balance that post-conflict governments must maintain. On the face of it, it appears that the public interest has lost out to the influence of foreign interests. Yet there is also a credible case to be made that Liberia's transitional government strategically prioritized its relationship with the US. From this perspective, even though Mittal's bid might not have been the most competitive on economic grounds, it is possible to reasonably conclude that the Liberian government may actually have been acting in the public's best interests. American support was required on too many other fronts to risk jeopardizing this relationship.

In addition to problems with the bidding process, the agreement itself also sparked controversy because the terms of the deal were deemed to heavily favour Mittal (Global Witness 2006; Cook 2007; Bermúdez-Lugo 2009). The contract was later reviewed and renegotiated under the auspices of GEMAP, a programme that, ironically, Western donors themselves had forced on Liberia as a response to its problem of pervasive corruption.[11]

While Mittal won the bid in the end, this process reveals the inherent tensions between the West's purported good governance agenda and its political and corporate interests.[12] On the one hand, Western powers demand that post-conflict governments take decisions offering the greatest public benefit; on the other hand, these same powers will lobby as hard as they can for the commercial and political interests of their own countries. Post-conflict governments are stuck in a Catch-22.

Expecting powerful states to cede the advantage of their informal influence in a post-conflict period is unrealistic. As China, India, Brazil, and other emerging countries wield increasing economic clout and become more actively engaged in post-conflict countries, the pressure on major powers to exploit their informal influence when strategic and political interests are at stake will only intensify. Even where powerful countries consciously avoid pressuring post-conflict governments into giving them preferential treatment, those responsible for a peaceful transition will still feel vulnerable: military or political support could be withdrawn if key powers are unable to secure their economic interests. Given the importance of external support in these conditions, post-conflict governments will struggle to balance the overall long-term public interest of their societies with the short-term imperative of managing relations with powerful international actors.

Conclusion

This chapter has focused on the role of informal actors, defining what they are and establishing why they are critical to the post-conflict period. It describes how the conditions of the post-conflict moment allow informal actors to exploit their political connections for private gain. It then demonstrates how three key statebuilding policies – stability, liberalization, and capacity building – can actually strengthen informal actors and undermine the public interest. In each case, informal actors can leverage their influence to take advantage of these processes in a way that entrenches inequality between those who are politically connected and those who are not.

To the extent that many of these informal actors are also in a position to exploit their conflict capital, their financial capital, and their access to insider information, it is also possible to fix the rules, regulations, and processes entirely in their own favour. The exceptional malleability of a post-conflict government's institutions means that informal actors have an opportunity to shape the political and economic realms in ways that provide substantial private benefit to informal actors, often at the expense of the public interest. These new patterns of interaction will define the future of state–society relations.

Fundamentally, informal actors are not accountable for their actions. It is difficult to hold to account informal actors who wield power and make decisions that affect the public welfare when the identities of these individuals cannot even be confirmed and their actions are not documented. In a post-conflict environment where hearsay and speculation often pass for evidence, one thing that *can* be done by post-conflict societies is to closely monitor key individuals in power and publicly scrutinize all major important decisions. While improved transparency and accountability by themselves are unlikely to directly improve short-term outcomes, forcing these processes open for public inspection and discussion should at least stimulate a debate about acceptable standards of behaviour for formal actors. While eliminating the influence of the most notorious informal actors in a post-conflict environment may be impossible, mitigating their negative impact is well within the reach of post-conflict governments and international actors.

Notes

1 Although the 'international community' is often associated with Western powers, I use it here in the broadest sense, to include those from developed and developing countries who are active in post-conflict situations. The term is intended to encompass state actors, international organizations, regional organizations, bilateral agencies, international NGOs, and foreign businesses. In this chapter, it refers to all external actors.

2 Thanks to Dominik Zaum and Mats Berdal.

3 This delineation poses some problems. For example, diplomats from other countries who are lobbying for their country's interests are categorized as informal actors. Similarly, foreign corporations and international organizations are also considered informal actors in this analysis. This chapter emphasizes how these actors exert their informal influence.

4 Cited in Gordy 2004. The full statement from the Serbian government is online, available at www.srbija.sr.gov.yu/vesti/2003-04/29/335683.html.

5 It is not uniformly true that state institutions emerge out of civil war in a weaker state. For example, see Sri Lanka and Uganda.

6 Albert Hirschman, 'Against Parsimony: Three Easy Ways of Complicating Some Categories of Economic Discourse', *American Economic Review Proceedings* 1984 (74): 93. As cited in Putnam *et al.* 1993: 169.

7 See also Cheng and Zaum 2011a.

8 See for example Donais 2004 for a discussion of this in the context of privatization in Bosnia.

9 UN Department of Economic and Social Affairs (2007), Building Capacities for Public Service in Post-Conflict Countries, UN doc. ST/ESA/PAD/SER.E/121, 4.

10 Jo Adetunji, 'British Firms urged to "Pack Suitcases" in Rush for Libya Business', *Guardian*, 21 October 2011.

11 One of the successes claimed by GEMAP is that the terms of the Mittal deal were successfully renegotiated, increasing the company's investment from $900 million to $1.3 billion.

12 The Liberian transitional government's defence in court claimed that the process for awarding the concession was 'a political process exclusively within the domain of the Executive Branch of Government'. See Global Infrastructure Holding Limited 2005.

6   Statebuilding and corruption

A political economy perspective

Michael Pugh

This analysis is a critical examination of the relationship between statebuilding and corruption in the political economies of post-conflict countries. The central contention is that anti-corruption programmes are an important element of 'good governance' for reducing transaction costs in fostering a neoliberal development. The prevalence of a debate that links corruption/anti-corruption to statebuilding requires an explanation at least partly located in ideas of liberal political economy. A 'neoliberal' paradigm of development is fundamental to what has been termed 'the liberal peace' and its arts of governance (for a summary of the debate, see Cooper *et al.* 2011). A variant of the structural adjustment policies of the 1950s onwards, economic assistance usually comes with conditionalities requiring: the privatization and financialization of public goods, entrepreneurship through micro-finance, support to free market competition, foreign investment, poverty reduction within balanced budgets, 'local participation' within neoliberal parameters, export-led growth, and the integration of societies (many with little comparative advantage), into a global trading system. Aggressive neoliberalism may be in retreat as a consequence of economic crisis, interactions with local agency that produce hybrid or 'multibrid' economic forms, and the consequences of China and South American countries getting involved in development with different economic approaches. However, the emphasis on corruption also becomes a problem for the normative objectives of statebuilders because economic dynamism in developing or war-torn countries derives from sources *other than* reducing interference with 'good governance' and the 'free market', strategies that themselves may contradict drives to contain corruption.

The discussion proceeds in five parts, beginning with cautionary notes about the analysis of corruption, including the relevance of contexts and perceptions. The second part of the chapter explains why corruption has been a focus of statebuilding in terms of 'good governance' and neoliberal rationales. The next part examines the impacts of corruption on recovery. Strategies for dealing with corruption are surveyed in the fourth part, followed by a critical assessment of neoliberal polices that engender corruption. The discussion concludes that without understanding the contradictions in broad economic transformation, corruption is likely to remain locked in a 'cycle of reciprocity'.

Caveats

Four caveats are in order concerning the analysis of corruption: problems of definition; the absence of data; the role of corruption in stability and state-building; and the global prevalence of corruption and its importance in western discourses.

First, corruption is a contested concept and a labelling device. Application of the label 'corrupt' is significant in constructing discourses of power in pursuit of economic transformation. The label can cover rent seeking, clientelism, patronage, discrimination, 'plea bargaining' to avoid legal penalties, nepotism, bribery, money laundering the proceeds of organized crime, and in the context of international interventions it can also extend to the protection from prosecution of internationals associated with illegal activities such as sex trafficking (Bolkovac and Lynn 2011). Restricting the definition to contravention of public office (Rose-Ackerman 2011: 48–50) assumes an easy distinction between public and private. Other definitions refer to 'abuse of public interest by narrow sectional interests' (Le Billon 2011: 75), which allows for corruption by non-governmental authorities, though the concept of 'public interest' is highly subjective. Narrow definitions neglect the extent to which 'public' and 'private' interests are symbiotically related in many societies – and have been in the emergence of the Westphalian state system and its colonial offshoots. Additionally, the Western concept of 'public power' assumes the exercise of authority in relation to a state and its organs (which can be decentralized to elders or chiefs, as in Sierra Leone), whereas in many societies, such as the Pacific islands and Timor Leste, state authority has limited meaning (Boege *et al.* 2009).

Madalene O'Donnell's inclusive definition allows that corruption exists across all sectors, governmental and non-governmental, and among political *and* economic elites (2008: 228). It has the advantage of encompassing interests and practices, from contract 'sweeteners' to tax evasion at which financially sophisticated systems excel (see Hope and Cunningham 2011). It is also worth noting that typologies – distinguishing between 'petty' corruption among poorly paid employees, 'administrative' corruption among bureaucrats, and 'grand' corruption by elites – discount the vertical integration occurring when low-ranking employees have to pass bribes upwards. In the other direction, elite corruption that penalises the working classes can prompt forms of popular resistance to unfairness through tax evasion and petty circumvention of formal exchange.

Second, the extent and impact of corruption is hard to assess because it is camouflaged and there are no accepted baselines for measuring it. Only when cases surface in legal contexts can researchers get an inkling of the global scale of corruption – such as the Madoff fraud case in the United States involving US$50 billion, the Cheney/Halliburton bribery case, and others in Nigeria, involving huge sums to secure contracts. The obscurity problem applies even more acutely to nepotism and transactions that discriminate on the basis of favours and cronyism. In post-conflict countries estimating the extent of unaudited economies of all kinds is exceptionally difficult, though informal economic sectors are generally considered to be highly significant because official sources of income are usually scarce. For example, econometric analysis of the role of the total 'grey' economy in Bosnia and Herzegovina (BiH), suggests that it accounted for over 50 per cent of GDP in the years 2001–2003 (Tomaš 2010: 138).

World Bank and Transparency International indexes have to be constructed from local expert opinions, perception surveys, and by proxies such as the condition of the labour market (Tomaš 2010), household income at given employment levels, and evaluations of anti-corruption enforcement (Wolf 2010: 103). As Morris Szeftel shows, those deciding the 'who' and 'what' of corruption are mainly a northern elite whose expertise contributes to the production of corruption indexes. They are 'the people who manage the globalisation process, who lend money, reschedule debts, and conduct business and diplomatic activities' (2000: 293). Their supportive economists claim objectivity in detecting 'underlying pathologies' of corruption – as if diagnosing a disease (e.g., Rose-Ackerman and Søreide 2012: introduction). Surveys can yield ambiguous results. For example, perceptions of corruption in Kosovo have been high, and some 55 per cent of respondents claim they would either willingly pay a bribe or would pay it if there was no alternative. Yet actual participation rates in forms of corruption were reported at 15 per cent in 2004 and 17 per cent in 2008 (UNDP 2009; Spector *et al.* 2003). Local perceptions of corruption are also influenced by broader social and economic change. Thus in former socialist systems, argues Ivan Krastev, crony corruption or *blat*, in which favours were granted, goods procured, and bureaucracy circumvented, depended on the formation of acquaintanceship networks. But as finance capital invaded and manipulated the social and political spheres, bribery, often unmediated by acquaintance, overlay the more intimate forms of corruption (Krastev 2002).

Third, apart from its other functions, corruption, crime, and violence have historically played a role in statebuilding as representations of contested, emergent power rather than its abuse (Tilly 1985: 161–91). It signifies primitive capital accumulation interlinked at various points with social needs, economic development, and the reform practices of international statebuilding agencies (Cramer 2006; Reno 2011a). But far from being considered by intervening agencies as integral to statebuilding, this conceptualization has been overshadowed by a focus on the transaction, discriminatory, and de-legitimation costs to an idealized Westphalian view of the relationship between state and society.

Fourth, liberal concepts of corruption are not universally valid; the nature of corruption is context specific, reflecting local social norms and economic incentives. What is perceived as corruption in many societies can be the distribution of largesse to followers: 'an extension of reciprocity and exchange of gifts in the traditional context' (Boege *et al.* 2009: 604). Patrimonial and clientelistic social systems may offend neoliberal ideals but represent a continuity of tradition and contribute to power, prestige, and social cohesion that is perhaps more meaningful than the contractarian basis of Westphalian statism and shared conceptions of the rights and duties that go with public office. Consequently, as noted by Christine Cheng and Dominik Zaum (2011b: 7–12), corruption can have stabilizing as well as destabilizing effects. In Afghanistan, complex bargaining patterns between political elites and private entrepreneurs for opium extraction have been more stabilizing than either counter-narcotics programmes or private extraction regimes (Goodhand 2011). Illicit taxation, bribery, and nepotism are sometimes acknowledged locally as integral to political and social cohesion, with power-holders providing rewards for support. Moreover, as Francesco Strazzari (2008: 166) comments with regard to the Balkans, criminality can 'accompany (or guide) the unfolding of market and state structure'. It is evident in market-related corruption that can include pyramid schemes, bogus educational institutions and companies – and also overcharging by foreign companies and defaulting on contractual obligations as in Iraq (Dodge 2005; *Guardian* 2006, 2007; Chandrasekaran 2007; Williams 2009a).

The caveats indicate the importance of understanding several issues: that the values underpinning the label 'corruption' sustain an anti-corruption industry; that unaudited economic activities, including corruption, are divorced neither from statebuilding nor everyday livelihoods; and that although corruption is not conducive to objective metric analysis, it is commonly perceived as widespread and wholly negative in its impacts. Corruption structured by war and statebuilding, from Cambodia to Israel, is regarded as usual. But it also figures in relatively stable authoritarian and deregulated political economies, in so-called 'transitional' states, dynamically developing economies, economically advanced states, and states supported by western governments because of their resources (such as Nigeria) or their geopolitical significance (such as Uzbekistan). Corruption is integral to the networks of capitalism and the demand for resources and markets. Proceeds are often lodged in secret jurisdictions or tax havens (originally devised in the 1930s to launder US 'mob money' in the Caribbean), through which a third of corporate foreign direct investment was routed in 2010 (Shaxson 2011). Thus corruption can only be exaggerated as a core threat to global stability (e.g. Rotberg 2009), if the same attribute applies to capitalism. The discussion now turns to the rationales for focusing on corruption in the context of post-conflict statebuilding.

'Good governance' and statebuilding rationales

Among crusaders for economic integrity the economically regressive, socially corrosive and morally repugnant aspects of corruption certainly colour interpretations of the issue. Moreover entire societies and regions have been inscribed as corrupt (Transparency International 2007; Aziz 2002: 22). Given, therefore, that corruption is a widespread and globally significant problem, why does it merit significant attention in assisting recovery from conflict? Designating it as a critical issue in statebuilding can be partly understood as a reflection of an ideology: the specific requirement to institutionalize liberal governance, or 'good governance', in quasi-peace and post-conflict contexts as being central to restoring trust in government (O'Donnell 2008: 227; UNDP 2008a: 151).

But what is 'good governance' and what is it for? As Branwyn Gruyffed Jones observes (2006: 9) the 'discourse about development – and its most recent agenda of "good governance" – has naturalized the structures of global inequality and exploitation that were the product of European expansion and formal colonialism'. It commonly entails law reform, institutional capacity, transparency in government and bureaucracies, systems of accountability, and whistleblower protection, the purpose being economic recovery and development. Mushtaq Khan (2010) notes that from neoliberal economic theory

> comes a neo-liberal policy agenda that if you want to have economic prosperity you need to achieve not only liberalization, privatization and market promoting strategies, but on top of that you need to have the protection of property rights. You need to have the capacity to protect these property rights, you need to have anti-corruption strategies and you need to have accountability and democratization strategies.

The issue is significant because 'thin corruption' is used by the World Bank and donors as a key indicator of low transaction costs and 'good governance'. But as Khan argues, it is unclear which is 'cause', and which is 'effect'; whether good governance leads to strong development or whether development leads to good governance. Anti-corruption measures alone will hardly guarantee effective development that would underwrite a state's popular legitimacy because

> in terms of 'good governance' scores, the average score of rapidly-growing poor countries is the same as that of the slow-growing developing countries and the dispersion of their governance scores is almost exactly the same … nor is there evidence that improving good governance ensures that poor countries will get rich faster.
>
> (ibid. 2010)

This is not an argument for 'bad governance', and nothing here can be construed as an ethical justification for corrupt practices. But the relationship between statebuilding and corruption is more complex than the prevailing discourse implies, leading to the proposition that corruption and lack of accountability do not seem to hold back economic growth, as evidenced in Nigeria, China, and South Korea (see Chang 2007). That authoritarian governance may also be essential to advance neoliberalism is a different argument that highlights a contradiction between neoliberal economics and economic democracy (see Klein 2007). Nevertheless, it is also contradictory for international administrations to claim immunities regarding their own behaviour while insisting on local accountability to international authorities.

In Palestine the international donors have formed a 'shadow administration' controlling and directing the Palestinian Authority budgets, almost on a daily basis, while sidestepping the economic stresses created by Israel's occupation and while relinquishing responsibility for implementing policies that increase poverty and instability (Turner 2009). Space precludes detailed discussion of the issue here, but as David Chandler (2010) and Oliver Richmond (2009) point out, such environments foster virtual states, with resistance or mere token acceptance by many citizens.

However, the neoliberal ideology of low transaction costs has resonance in statebuilding for several reasons.

First, war patriotism and profiteering are often linked and corruption flourishes in times of violent conflict and in legal interregnums when rules cannot be implemented and new ones have not been devised (Naylor 1999). Corruption is also a feature of war-torn societies because of the new opportunities for local capital accumulation, arising for example from controlling goods in short supply. During a conflict or post-bellum interregnum, social norms are loosened and 'deviations', such as theft of public assets, tolerated or at least immunized on grounds of exceptional circumstance, including uncertainty about which laws apply in those circumstances (Jean and Rufin 1996). Bringing predictability and protection to commercial operations, not least to make environments safe for foreign investors and traders, is a key aspiration of international statebuilders. Corporate interests are not necessarily united on the issue, since anti-corruption activities are also a transaction cost. But without state backing, corporate interests would be both constantly undercut by capital ventures that resorted to fraud and deception, and territories would lack the ability to offer advantages as sites for accumulation in a global system of competition (Cammack 2007: 13–14). Furthermore, corruption can be a trigger for popular unrest and revolt (and was a factor in the Arab 'revolutions' of 2011) because it fosters inequalities (Smith 2006). The impact of corruption on institutional and state legitimacy, as O'Donnell argues (2008: 227), is the belief that corruption is a good governance spoiler that undermines both state effectiveness and legitimacy.

Second, corruption does not exist independently of shared norms and rules. Framing corruption begins with the construction of legislation and exploration of moral boundaries and, as with crime generally, corruption is paradoxically related to rules of public office, commercial law, and property rights. Thus statebuilding shapes corruption because establishing a new rule of law as part of statebuilding creates offences (see Philp 2011: 39–41). It is both an affront to a sense of justice and a product of the law. Accordingly, statebuilding's current purpose is to establish liberal norms, rules, and values signifying integrity and to prevent corruption from spoiling the project of bringing state-led stability to a society through neoliberal economic reforms. Thus normative and legal developments specify the duty of individuals and authorities to desist from corruption and stamp it out.

Third, a chief impetus to curb corruption has come from aid donors, determined to demonstrate the effectiveness of aid and to eliminate waste and diversion into private accumulation. In seeking to promote 'good governance', anti-corruption measures are less likely to be politically objectionable in donor countries than some other kinds of programme. Susan Woodward indicates in her chapter (this volume) that problem-solving criticisms focus on implementation techniques rather than on the relevance of the policies themselves. It would be more difficult perhaps for donor governments to justify programmes that support indigenous productive capacity – through protection, subsidies, and loss-financing – in competition with the donors that already have competitive advantages in world trade (Khan 2010).

Fourth, although linking into local civil societies, the anti-corruption movement is predominantly 'first world' in its leadership, discourse, and practices, and overwhelmingly directed against corruption in the third world where most conflict occurs. Partly perhaps because the impact of anti-corruption cannot be gauged, it is an attractive industry for moral entrepreneurs, such that a global social movement headed by Transparency International, and its offshoot *TIRI*, 'now lead[s] an existence independent of the actual phenomenon of corruption itself, and without apparently reducing it' (see Sampson: 2010: 262–3, 276). The focus on corruption in statebuilding agendas serves to reinforce 'a hierarchical conception of subjectivities premised on the primacy of the … liberal self as against others' (Jabri 2010: 43). This is expressed *inter alia* through 'administration, acquisition and the dispossessions of populations, and the "training" of locals into societies amenable to self-discipline, self-regulation, and ultimately self-government limited to the parameters of the liberal project' (ibid.: 53). Indeed, orthodox statebuilding practices have been prone to inscribe war-torn communities as victimized, incapable of governance, illiberal, unworthy of sovereignty, lacking agency (or having too much of the 'wrong' sort), and corrupt. War-torn societies can therefore be represented as being ripe for change, leveraged through aid, while reinforcing a self-identity of superior virtue and probity.

The impacts of corruption are thus perceived to be highly damaging to economic reform and statebuilding processes.

Impacts of corruption on statebuilding

The academic literature is especially rich on the deleterious impacts of corruption in peace processes and economic recovery (e.g. Reno 1995; Keen 1998; Andreas 2004; Berdal 2009: 77–85; Williams 2009b; Cockayne and Lupel 2011; Cheng and Zaum 2011a). Indeed, proceeds of wartime capital accumulation may be leached into the funding of political extremism, privatized armed protection, and threats to peace, such as the diversion of funds to Radovan Karadžić's post-war party in Republika Srpska (Divjak and Pugh 2011: 104). However, if there is to be a nuanced approach it is essential for statebuilding agencies to understand the functionalism of crime and corruption in post-conflict environments. War entrepreneurship and windfalls from control over scarcities can be legitimized as part of a development agenda.

Ill-gotten rents may be invested in transparent and audited production and servicing, giving a boost to recovery. Furthermore, crime and corruption has its own rules and hierarchies of power, actually safeguarding enterprise by distributing risks to lowest levels in the hierarchy. As well as entrenching inequalities of power, corruption may also express power relations that encompass political resistances available to those who have only their labour or poverty to bargain with. Since the economic policies of interveners, donors, and IFIs have been equivocal towards unemployment, labour market dislocation, and the provision of social welfare, crime and corruption may be a form of resistance by 'subalterns'. As Rajko Tomaš observes, informal economies are a species of social programme in the absence of the state or its inability to resolve development, political, and social issues (2010: 129). Corruption may fulfil demand, can be efficient in circumventing bureaucracy, provides a choice of goods and services, and provides access to income. Moreover social functions may be attached to corrupt markets that facilitate 'conspiratorial' exchange and interaction, often between erstwhile enemies (Jasarević 2006).

Consequently, everyday reliance on corruption gets culturally embedded, and avoiding regulation becomes a resistance norm that may shift only gradually when the injustices of corruption and available alternatives to it lead to the mobilization of grievance that could become violent. And the elements of functionalism in crime and corruption do not signify a just or egalitarian order. In labour markets, for example, unemployment is often very high during and after conflict (estimated at 70 per cent in Sierra Leone in 2007). Trade unions are usually weak or non-existent, and may be corrupt. Entrepreneurs often take advantage of this to build up capital by abusing workers and avoiding levies such as welfare insurance (Pugh 2008). A corrupt labour market and casualization of employment foments exploitation and has a detrimental impact on efficiency that will be more likely resisted in turn when regular, taxable income and mechanisms for the protection of labour rights do become available.

Perhaps the most serious consequence of corruption for statebuilding, however, is to deprive authorities of revenue that curtails the ability of governments to budget or to tackle discrimination in provision. In turn this limits the options for public expenditure, and the state's ability to improve services, infrastructure, and direct economic activity towards production and employment creation. The loss of revenue also means that the tax burden on the formal economy is greater. It has been estimated that in 2010 the public revenue of €5.5 billion in BiH could have been increased by approximately €1 billion if 60 per cent of the 'grey economy' could be harnessed by the formal sector – only part of the grey economy being related to crime and corruption (Tomaš 2010: 143 [author's currency conversion]).

Another adverse consequence is that when the political, security, and justice systems are corrupt, often because of the symbiotic relations between economic activities and governing sectors, there are no incentives to regulate and discipline capital accumulation. Establishing or re-establishing a social contract with the state is hindered, especially as the discriminatory impacts of corruption serve to widen gaps between wealthy elites and the masses.

Productivity and economic efficiency are also debilitated. Cronyism and bribery distort markets and are a direct challenge to the western donor ideology (not necessarily the practice) of 'fair competition'. It adversely affects investment and trade in that the hidden costs of doing business, the expectation of bribes for example, can be detrimental to fair competition and a deterrent to business. For example, procurement costs are increased by the need for pay-offs, and productivity is distorted by protectionism that yields private rather than public gains. Such transaction costs disadvantage local investors who refuse to give in to corruption and those foreign investors complying with the OECD Development Assistance Committee's anti-corruption guidelines, and whose comparative advantages in entrepreneurship and capitalization may be shorn.

From the above rationales and observed impacts of corruption, arises the considerable efforts dedicated to anti-corruption strategies.

Anti-corruption strategies and impacts

Donor agencies, the World Bank, the OECD, corporate interests, and NGOs have all made anti-corruption a lynchpin of aid policy. For statebuilding agencies, anti-corruption has become a morally unassailable imperative to accompany the introduction of stressful economic reforms. James Wolfensohn's 'cancer of corruption' speech in 1996 signalled that the World Bank would now stipulate 'good governance' criteria in its lending policies (Sampson 2010: 275). Agencies involved in statebuilding have tried to establish stable currencies, a commercialized banking sector, commercial legislation, new tax systems, and budgetary discipline. But the assumption that 'good governance' and the 'free market' would alone diminish corruption was unsustainable and had to be bolstered by specific anti-corruption measures.

As proposed in a UNDP-sponsored study, '[i]n order to reduce corruption, countries need to build the capacity to design and enforce anti-corruption statutes and legislation ... to scrutinize government payments and disbursements, and monitor regularly the movement of resources from disbursement to use' (UNDP 2008a: 153). Institutionalization has crowned anti-corruption efforts, from the EU's Customs and Fiscal Assistance Office (CAFAO) in BiH in 1996 to Governance and Economic Management Assistance Programme (GEMAP) in Liberia in 2005. The latter's creation followed the identification of crime and corruption as damaging to a peace economy and is interesting because it has been a leading multilateral effort to address corruption comprehensively and has been held up as an exemplar of best practice (Boucher *et al.* 2007: 45–6). It instituted strict transparency and auditing procedures in government and led to the investigation of finance officials. However, such institutions are only as effective as their political independence, the political elite is committed to it (as in Liberia), or a UN military presence lasts (Reno 2011b). Few commissions have been considered effective (UNDP 2005: 5). But in many African countries anti-corruption campaigns and conditionalities threaten governance and accumulation systems that impede international capital, rather than axiomatically stifling development (Szeftel 2000: 295).

The linkage between neoliberal 'good governance' and anti-corruption is exemplified by Sierra Leone's Poverty Reduction Strategy Paper of 2001, which like GEMAP was directed mainly at securing debt relief rather than tackling poverty, singled out corruption as an obstacle to an equitable distri-bution of resources, and specified the creation of an Anti-Corruption Com-mission, which, however, encountered political interference (Heilbrunn 2011: 212). A similar situation occurred in Kosovo, where the Kosovo Protec-tion Corps (KPC) and Democratic Party (PDK) rackets and insider dealing had become an obstacle to good governance (Sadiku 2001; Pugh 2006). Indeed, after ten years of 'international protectorate' the local elite's alleged involvement in crime and corruption surfaced in a leaked NATO/KFOR report which identified Prime Minister Hashim Thaçi and his close ally, Xhavit Haliti, as being at the head of organized crime, which they deny (*Guardian* 2011). UNMIK had set up a unit in 2003 to counter corruption in budget-funded enterprises – and within UNMIK's own ranks after a UN offi-cial was found guilty of embezzling €4.5 million from the power company (*AF-P* 2003). But a local Anti-Corruption Agency did not become operational until 2006 – and then with a very small staff and little clout. Without an end to the politicization of public enterprises and radical reform of procurement, it is unlikely to score many successes (Kosovar Stability Initiative 2010).

John Heilbrunn (2011: 202) contends that the role of institutionalization has not been to tackle corruption directly but to signal seriousness about the issue as 'part of a lengthy process ... in which the rules of the game adjust to new norms that are intolerant of corruption and impunity'. Yet, as he acknowledges, without political independence, they are unlikely to challenge citizens' expectations that corruption will continue (ibid.).

In a retrospective assessment Paddy Ashdown (2004) refers to:

> the overriding priority – as we have discovered in Bosnia, Kosovo, Afghanistan and now Iraq – of establishing the rule of law as quickly as possible. Crime and corruption follow swiftly in the footsteps of war, like a deadly virus. And if the rule of law is not established very swiftly, it does not take long before criminality infects every corner of its host.

The imprecise concept, rule of law, is treated as an a-political panacea to solve governance problems, but (as in McCarthyite America), the rule of law can itself be destructive of personal and public integrity. Although cadastral surveys, property rights, and commercial law may bring regularity and facili-tate compliance, unless they are seen as 'just', they can facilitate policies that cause harm, as in the use of property law to disperse poor people from prime construction or agricultural land (see Rajagopal 2008; Mani 2002: 126–57).

Allied to rule of law, strategies have stressed the importance of reformed and retrained bureaucrats, police, and customs services with certification systems. Unreformed police and, as in Mozambique, ex-military units, may be cadres for smuggling and trafficking. But corruption cannot be tackled solely by disciplinary controls on producers and distributors. As Sebastian Wolf comments, the narrow focus on legal and institutional methods to achieve compliance have had limited effects in Eastern Europe, and anti-corruption entrepreneurs should focus on other variables such as the demand for illicit goods and domestic economic conditions (Wolf 2010: 114).

Other initiatives have emphasized transparency, accountability, whistle-blowing, complaint processes, and a free investigative media. These can result in legal proceedings, as in cases against Milorad Dodik, Prime Minister of Republika Srpska. Much depends, however, on reform of the judicial system. But overshadowing accountability is the binding of international administrators/advisers and local elites through a reciprocal evasion of responsibility, blaming each other for lack of progress. External actors see 'spoilers' and corrupt or incapable locals, whereas locals sometimes see 'white tourists' denying them ownership of decision making (Richmond 2009). Both groups have a pliant, impoverished population in the economic sphere that could be exploited for loyalty (by the war entrepreneurs) and moulded for modernization (by the externals).

Do anti-corruption measures work? As Steven Sampson notes, there is a paucity of baseline data, agreement on what is to be measured, systems for gathering and coding data, or common understandings of what observations signify (2010: 264). The evidence is mixed, and not simply because measurement is unreliable. There is some evidence that the scope of unaudited post-conflict economies can be curtailed by general development paths that emphasize formal income generation through increased employment prospects, strategic support to agricultural and industrial production, tax reforms, and auditing mechanisms. For example, sales tax reform in BiH, and the establishment of public sector audits and procurement seems to have had some effect on reducing the contribution of unaudited economies to GDP by half (Tomaš 2010: 140). In processes of formalization of economic activity, there are also costs and disincentives associated with remaining in or moving into corruption, which itself may be subject to mergers and 'admission charges'.

But where corruption offers comparative advantages for sections of a population over formal, licit, and audited activities, expert opinion continues to report endemic corruption, notably in the legal, medical, educational, and other professional classes, in utility companies and services. Efforts to eliminate corruption 'contaminants' without flexible and distributive economic development, has been a common practice of external agencies engaged in statebuilding. Structural adjustment and the inherent contradictions of neo-liberalism can expand informal economic activity and create incentive structures that present new opportunities for corruption.

Policies fuelling corruption

The social, political, economic shocks of war are accompanied by market instabilities that open up opportunities for external actors to lay down rules of assistance and transformation. Yet a logical consequence of foreign aid and neoliberal structural adjustment, whether intentional or not, can be to expand corruption in several ways.

First, although donor pledges are usually slow to arrive (Suhrke and Buckmaster 2006), an influx of foreign aid and spending is often poorly monitored and accounted for, and there is an absence of bureaucracy to regulate it (von Billerbeck 2011). Lax regulatory environments allow corruption in companies involved in stabilization and statebuilding operations, as in Iraq (see Chandrasekaran 2007, *Guardian* 2006, 2007). A push for physical reconstruction can stimulate a building boom which wartime entrepreneurs fuel through private construction projects. And such regulation as does exist, through licensing and procurement, for example, offers incentives in this sector for bribery and fraud (Large 2005). Thus corruption involving building permits and the illegal construction of thousands of buildings in Kosovo led to an investigation against local politicians (Islami 2002). One consequence is that local politicians may be bypassed by donors who channel aid through NGOs, thereby thinning state domestic responsibility for recovery.

Indeed, second, statebuilding strategies have emphasized economic liberalization, which has the effect of divorcing power from political accountability because economic liberalization requires what Foucault (2004 [2010]: 29ff.) identifies as 'frugal government' in deference to the market's 'natural laws'. In the neoliberal version, applied since the 'Washington consensus', limited government has two main effects: deregulation and government retreat from economic control; and the marketization of public management, including the subcontracting of government functions. Reliance on the market's regime, rather than a regime of justice, is a process of depoliticization that removes accountability. Liberalization produces *different* incentives and opportunities for corruption that accompany governance divorced from accountability. As Sampson remarks, '[t]his led to a new type of corruption, by which bureaucrats who previously sold direct access to government resources or embezzled aid could now profit by collecting a facilitation fee from private contractors or otherwise influence the procurement process' (2010: 275). Clearly, too, such impacts of liberalization foster a need for anti-corruption strategies, the anti-corruption industry – a conglomeration of actors, institutions, programmes – itself benefitting from 'new public management' (ibid. 276).

Third, western donors have made programmes of privatization of state or socially owned assets the *sine quo non* of assistance. Dismantling state or socially owned property and enterprises has fostered asset stripping, crony capitalism, and fraud. Indeed privatization projects engender a coincidence of interests, as war entrepreneurs and their political protectors are in prime positions to 'capture' state assets and to exploit processes of privatization.

The Privatization Agency of Kosovo has been perceived as one of the most corrupt institutions in the country, along with the courts, government, health service, and electricity company, though its predecessor, the foreign-run Kosovo Trust Agency was so enamoured of accountability that it destroyed its records before handing over to local control (Privatization Agency of Kosovo 2009; Pugh 2006).

Fourth, opening economies for foreign investment and growth through trade presents opportunities for contract sweeteners and trade licensing scams. Although foreign investors are generally more sensitive to corruption than locals it is not an absolute deterrent to FDI (Habib and Zurawicki 2002: 313). Corruption can also be a product of economic shifts, sustained when reforms threaten to undermine privileges.

Fifth, an informal economy provides the milieu in which corruption thrives, but coping and survival strategies (see Goodhand 2004) are exacerbated by the neoliberal drive for self-insurance (Duffield 2007: 19–24), and the failure of authorities to stimulate production, mass employment, and alternative livelihoods. Audited income has a scarcity value that attracts its own corruption: bribery to obtain employment is a common feature of customs services, for example (Ćulafić 2002). The World Bank, donors, and local elites are bent on rent seeking and private wealth creation as the motors for economic change. In the late 1990s a third of EU pre-accession funds for BiH went to support small and medium enterprises, though job losses in this sector outstripped new employment (Pugh 2002). A neoliberal drive to improve and expand service sectors, rather than production, also underpins fiscal trends in corruption. One of the legacies of conflict in the Balkans has been corruption in the hotel and travel industry, including money laundering through garage services (Divjak and Pugh 2011). In Sierra Leone, tourism has been promoted as a solution to economic growth, and the 2001 PRSP was budgeted to receive as much funding as job creation generally. But tourism in developing countries reinforces the subaltern status of the poor, ensuring their vulnerability to a fickle trade and, as in the service sector generally, presenting opportunities for corruption (Forna 2009).

In her ethnographic study of the everyday meaning of crime in post-conflict El Salvador, Ellen Moodie observes that the elevation of gang power defied a dominant liberal narrative of post-war reconstruction. Ascribed to personal motives of greed or revenge, the criminality wave was depoliticized. Whereas the violence of war could be labelled ideological and structural, this unknowable, more sinister, highly personalized experience camouflaged the stresses of transformation in which 'money seemed to spring from invisible sources, from remittances sent by absent migrants' labor elsewhere, from the investments of faceless foreign speculators from rumoured narco-trafficking and endemic corruption' (Moodie 2010: 3). Integral to the triumph of neoliberalism, risk management could be devolved to individuals so that

> [p]arsing violent incidents as individual acts, as unconnected to social relations or political conditions, could help rupture the old revolutionary

and solidary social imaginaries – and could help reconstruct how people envisioned their rights and responsibilities toward each other in a mode of neoliberal rationality that would facilitate transnational free-trade currents.

(ibid.: 15)

Ironically, therefore, neoliberalism intensifies competition for capital and induces pressures for corrupt behaviour (Szeftel 2000). In contrast, a shift may be afoot in rethinking post-conflict recovery. A UNDP-sponsored study recommends recognizing that illegal activities have dynamics that can be diverted into post-conflict recovery through an emphasis on enabling local ingenuity and national leadership to meet livelihood needs (UNDP 2008a). Similarly, José Antonio Ocampo and his colleagues propose a macro-social stability that not only provides fiscal and price stability, but also policies involving state loss-leading infrastructure, technological innovation, and employment policies (Ocampo *et al.* 2008: 1–47).

Conclusion

A review of research on post-conflict corruption (by Boucher *et al.* 2007) concluded that security, political will, and public investment were prerequisites to establishing state institutions and delivery of public services that would reduce it. The review understated the extent to which reform such as 'stimulation of an open market economy' creates new corruption opportunities. Statebuilding processes introduce new tensions in local political economies and attack the functional aspects of unregulated political economy that can nevertheless enable people to get by in situations where new regulatory norms are emerging. Concerns about corruption in war-torn societies are relevant to statebuilding, but also conceivably contribute to deflecting attention from stressful, or harmful, elements of economic development. Confronted by the perceived scale of corruption in war-torn societies, the institutions promoting frugal government and free-market enterprise have paradoxically counselled stricter regulation, oversight and accountability mechanisms, financial disclosure provisions, and the engagement of NGOs and civil society in anti-corruption schemes. Such measures may reduce local resistance to audited exchange and provide 'fair' opportunities to foreign investors. Nevertheless, reducing general acquiescence in corruption and fraud is probably contingent on distributive justice, which could even extend to peripatetic internationals paying local taxes and foregoing huge consultancy fees, and to foreign investors no longer receiving subsidies that disadvantage local enterprise. Refocusing economic recovery policies would conceivably require a new emphasis on a distribution of investment and trade proceeds that is regarded as fair and just rather than simply relying on competition to maximize profit. This may require large-scale job creation (e.g. through infrastructure projects) to widen consumption power and increase tax revenues, and on strategies to foster local production. In the economics of global integration, weak economies have little comparative advantage, except in poverty and unemployment, and as the Cambridge economist Ha-Joon Chang (2007) argues, this means 'that poor countries are supposed to continue with their current engagement in low-productivity activities. But … [this] is exactly what makes them poor'. What can be done differently is to allow war-torn societies to choose to 'buck the market' for long-term strategic development. This may entail, for example, accepting short-term protectionism and subsidies, national marketing boards (rather than requiring their demise as in Sierra Leone), and investment in education, technology, and productive capacity. There is no 'quick fix' in development, and such alternatives would not guarantee the elimination of corruption. But without a population's stake in formal economic activity, corruption is unlikely to be modified into manageable forms.

Statebuilding harbours contradictions – immunities and lack of accountability on the part of interventionists, anti-corruption institution building while promoting frugal government, neoliberal economic policies that widen inequalities and make business rather than income a priority. The limitations of neoliberal economic prescriptions may be increasingly understood by practitioners and scholars. Certainly, superior probity over the un-liberal 'other' is rather more problematic for the credibility of liberal statebuilding than at the height of confidence about transforming societies before the Iraq War (Cooper 2007), and modesty about what can be done in war-torn societies has resonance at a time of global economic crisis, when reports of corruption have daily filled the media in developed states.

7 Statebuilding and the political economy of the extractive industries in post-conflict states

Thorsten Benner and Ricardo Soares de Oliveira

Revenues from natural resources, especially in the extractive sector, so the near-consensus in the literature goes, are said to have enabled conflicts, especially civil wars (regardless of whether 'greed' or 'grievance', or a mix of both, are seen as the main drivers). Comparatively little is known in the literature about the post-conflict political economy in resource-rich countries and international efforts to influence its trajectory. This chapter seeks to present an overview of attempts to deal with resource flows in the context of post-conflict international statebuilding (see also Wennmann 2011). This means three things: preventing a return to war by having 'spoilers' access resources; 'building peace' or even 'statebuilding' by having revenues flow to government coffers and increase state capacity as well as economic growth; and, finally, and perhaps more polemically, having those resources 'build' the right kind of state and society through proper revenue management and pro-poor expenditure. Much of this agenda is the product of broader normative and policy concerns around good governance and transparency mainstreamed by western donors over the past 15 years (both bilateral and via the EU, OECD, the IFIs, and the UN system), applied to the statebuilding enterprise.

Territories where there is a major international statebuilding mission have mostly not been characterized by evidently better management of extractive industries (in terms of the conduct of mining and oil firms and of firm–state relations) or revenue management (in terms of the conduct of governments under the 'influence' of international statebuilders) than territories not undergoing this experience. This can be gauged from a cursory look at corruption indexes and ease of doing business reports. The reasons for this record are various. They include the statebuilders' lack of regulatory capacity vis-à-vis local government and the extractive industries, lack of transparency and bureaucratic predictability on the side of the international mission itself, lack of willingness in all but a few instances of direct administration to meddle with the conduct of domestic politicians and governments, and the widespread donor view that a post-conflict country cannot be too choosy about investors and must accept initially poor deals, especially in terms of fiscal intake, in order to attract FDI and rebuild its reputation. A good example of this is the Democratic Republic of the Congo (DRC), where a decade-long UN and World Bank presence barely left a dent in a predatory culture and practices in the extractive industries. The same experience characterizes the international presence in Afghanistan and Iraq, for instance. The very assumption that international statebuilding places emphasis (in practice as opposed to rhetorically) on these matters needs to be reviewed in this regard. This is not merely a matter of poor outcomes (i.e. not the generic critique of the gap between statebuilding's ambitious claims/goals and poor results). It is very much that this has not been a priority, perhaps because mandates are unclear and people on the ground find that there are more pressing problems to attend to.

The exception to this observation is the Governance and Economic Management Assistance Programme (GEMAP) in Liberia, a case discussed in more detail below. Although the programme has had its critics, and it is still too early to see if it has ensured long-term positive outcomes, there is no doubt that GEMAP has been a highly intrusive international arrangement around revenue-generating and handling agencies, albeit one that, for the reasons we know, gained the support of sections of the Liberian elite and the president herself. However, it is noteworthy that GEMAP has not formed a blueprint for UN involvement elsewhere. Missions in other post-conflict countries have not been interested in these issues or pushing for a consistent international supervisory/regulatory role in the extractive industries. The reasons for GEMAP's exceptionalism may have to do with the size and marginality of Liberia and the disproportionate US role there. In higher profile, larger states with a diversified pool of donors who may not be likeminded, as well as multiple foreign agencies, this degree of intrusiveness is a non-starter.

Ironically, post-war states not undergoing international statebuilding missions have embraced some aspects of a reformist agenda in the extractive industries, including participation in the Extractive Industries Transparency Initiative (EITI). This has been driven in particular by the desire to prevent potential spoilers (such as former rebel forces) from accessing mineral revenues, as well as to increase state capacity. Such reforms may involve better oil sector accounting and the shoring up of previously chaotic extractive industries such as diamond production (Angola is a good example on both accounts). But the results are better seen as efforts at consolidating both the state and regime rather than the implementation of the good governance aspirations of liberal peace- and statebuilders, and the improvements are instrumentalized away from liberal peace outcomes.

The chapter proceeds in five sections: first, it outlines the rise of the 'good resource governance' agenda that has informed policies on the political economy of post-conflict countries, at least at a rhetorical level. The second, third, and fourth sections look at the different approaches to the reform of natural resource management in practice: internationally led soft reformist approaches (as exemplified by initiatives such as the EITI, e.g. in the Congo), much rarer internationally led hard reformist approaches (such as the GEMAP in Liberia), and non-reformist approaches (such as international macro-finance deals and locally led efforts at professionalization of the resource sector post-conflict such as in the case of Angola). The final section draws conclusions on the future agenda on extractive industries in post-conflict settings. This chapter does not deal explicitly with the issue of sanctions on the trade in resources in post-conflict countries. While such regimes have clearly formed an important part of conflict specific, ad-hoc efforts to regulate the trade in conflict commodities, they are often more a mechanism (of uncertain effectiveness) for the marginalization of challengers (former rebels or 'spoilers') than a mechanism for the implementation of a better order.

The rise of the good resource governance agenda and its effects on post-conflict statebuilding policies

From the mid-1990s onwards, the perverse governance outcomes of resource extraction in developing countries came into the policymakers' and the broader public's spotlight – and in turn influenced international policies towards resource-rich post-conflict countries. A number of developments contributed to this.[1]

First, policy research identified 'bad governance' as a driver behind the dismal development outcomes in resource-rich countries. Academics and policy centres (such as the World Bank) conducted further research on the links between natural resource exports and 'development'. This showed an inverse connection between mineral resource endowment and broad-based development. Indeed, the research suggested that oil and mineral-rich states in the developing world were more likely to suffer from heightened political competition, lack of provision of basic public goods, corruption, and recurring civil wars than non-resource-rich states, and were also more likely to be poorer in the long run (Ross 2001; Collier and Hoeffler 2004). In this context, of particular importance was the work of the Extractive Industries Review, an independent commission convened by the World Bank which acknowledged that the extractive industries had failed to alleviate poverty in much of the developing world, and had frequently brought about disruption to the environment and local communities.[2] Often, these important findings were presented under the label 'resource curse'. This is a crude misnomer since the term 'curse' suggests a quasi-automatic correlation between the presence of natural resources and dismal development outcomes. However, the examples of the UK and Norway, both major oil exporters, demonstrate otherwise. Neither country magically or accidentally escaped the spell of the 'resource curse', rather, they had institutions in place and made political decisions on how to use the revenues responsibly. This shows that the resource 'curse' is not an unavoidable fact of life. Nor is it a chiefly economic phenomenon. It is mainly a 'political/institutional phenomenon' (Karl 2007: 257), in other words a question of governance, a realization that has taken a while to sink in with policymakers and the public. A related observation is that the dismal development outcomes are due to a linkage between international and domestic factors (both of which make up global energy governance arrangements). This means that the global 'institutions shaped by multinational oil companies, their host governments, and foreign lenders', the elites and institutions of producer states, and their public and private oil companies are jointly responsible for the perverse development outcomes (ibid.), an 'inconvenient reality' that for a long time was not seriously addressed (ibid.). Once the 'resource curse' was reframed in terms of a political-institutional challenge of moving from 'bad' to 'good' governance (and thereby avoiding the resurgence of war in post-conflict states), this made remedies easier to identify for norm entrepreneurs and policymakers.

Second, the diagnosis of 'bad' resource governance and its links to conflict ties in with the broader good governance agenda that came to put institutions at the heart of development efforts after the disappointment with the narrow development policies of the Washington Consensus. As Moisés Naím suggests:

> Public sector institutions are the black holes of economic reforms. In most countries they absorb efforts and investment that yield obscenely low returns to society, distort labor markets, reduce countries' overall productivity, impair international competitiveness, and easily fall prey to vested interests.
>
> (2000: 99)

Western donors and international financial institutions came to appreciate a link between good governance and economic development (Gillies 2010). This led them to conclude that global governance arrangements and outside actors needed to concern themselves with changing domestic governance practices and arrangements. This is in line with the overall concern with 'behind the border issues' that western powers pushed in the context of recasting sovereignty in terms of responsibility. This was particularly the case in settings where international actors nominally held a lot of sway over local actors in post-conflict settings with a sizeable international community presence.

Third, and related, corruption emerged as a key concern on the global agenda – chiefly a result of pressure by organizations such as Transparency International. Corruption had largely been ignored until the 1990s. Until that time, the US Foreign Corrupt Practices Act of 1977 had been the only law effectively criminalizing bribes abroad: in fact, bribes had been tax deductible in many European countries, which arguably promoted such behaviour by home firms in global markets (Eigen 2007). This started to change with the adoption by the OECD's 36 member states of a 1997 Convention on Combating Bribery of Foreign Public Officials, which was followed by an Inter-American Convention against Corruption (1996) and a UN Convention against Corruption (2004). The fact that World Bank President James Wolfensohn helped to lift the taboo around discussions of corruption at the international financial institutions also facilitated discussions of such matters in the energy arena (Mallaby 2004). Subsequent policy suggestions varied from the voluntary and faintly reformist to the radical call for tough regulation of financial flows, but everywhere business practices across the developing world (and in the energy sector in particular) came under scrutiny. Similar policy shifts happened with regard to human rights and environmental sustainability – both posing profound challenges to the practices of resource extraction in developing countries that traditionally disregarded human rights and environmental concerns.

Fourth, the behaviour of transnational corporations in developing countries re-emerged as a key concern in the globalization debate from the mid-1990s onwards (Benner and Witte 2006). Many in the public see transnational corporations, and oil companies in particular, as economic and political heavyweights. Observers note that the 200 largest corporations account for a quarter of the world's gross domestic product. Many, especially oil companies, were seen as engaging in reckless behaviour in developing countries leading to calls for rules for such global players – calls that multinational corporations themselves could not afford to ignore. Particularly venal events such as the execution of Nigerian activist Ken Saro-Wiwa in 1995 put the public spotlight on the dismal conditions in the Niger Delta and forced Royal Dutch Shell to confront its own role and involvement. This made it increasingly clear that the traditional 'the business of business is business' approach was no longer tenable for brand-sensitive western-based multinational corporations.

Savvy norm entrepreneurs in civil society (in organizations such as Global Witness, Transparency International, Catholic Relief Services, and the Open Society Institute) and a number of progressive government officials (mainly in countries such as Norway and the UK) took advantage of these four trends and framed the debate on good resource governance around the norm of transparency (Gillies 2010). Transparency emerged as the guiding light for the institutional remedies for better energy governance (such as the Publish What You Pay (PWYP) initiative and the EITI). The diagnosis was simple:

> Opacity is the glue holding together the patterns of revenue extraction and distribution that characterize petro-states as well as the entire international petroleum sector. Companies do not publish what they pay to states, and states do not disclose what they earn and spend.
>
> (Karl 2007: 265)

As a consequence, 'huge amounts of money are virtually untraceable and not subject to any oversight' (ibid.: 266). Transparency was thus seen as the necessary and logical antidote to obfuscation and opacity. A 2008 report by Transparency International sums up the core assumptions of the transparency activists:

> Transparent resource governance is a vital ingredient to transform this resource curse into a blessing. To do this, companies and governments need to provide more and better quality information on the scale of revenues derived from the extractive industries and on how these revenues flow from producers to governments. If accompanied by greater civil

society oversight, this improved revenue transparency can make decision-makers more accountable for their actions. With better information on natural resource wealth, citizens can pressure governments to use these revenues for social and infrastructure programs that can boost economic growth and reduce poverty. Transparent resource governance is therefore a shared responsibility.

(2008b: 10)

Another observer notes that the 'most promising initiatives so far are those that seek to put in the hands of citizens more information about how much revenue their governments receive and how they spend it, so they can demand accountability' (Ottaway 2005).

These arguments in regard to issues of corruption and lack of transparency in financial transactions between resource-rich states and western corporations fell on fertile ground. A receptive media and public opinion in the west quickly accepted that this particular aspect of north–south relations played a key role in causing the dismal development outcomes in resource-rich developing countries. That said, transparency around oil and gas extraction never gained the same urgency as the debate on diamonds fuelling conflicts in places such as Sierra Leone and Angola. The campaign on 'blood diamonds' captured the western public's imagination and led to swift action in the Kimberley Process (and it is important to note that the Kimberley Process does not have any good governance component in terms of how the proceeds from diamonds should be used for development). No major NGO has even tried to launch a campaign on 'blood oil' or 'dictatorship gas' – unlike with diamonds, the ultimate luxury goods, average western citizens are implicated daily in the oil and gas business when filling up their cars or turning on the heat in their apartments (Ross 2008). Still, it is a remarkable development that the reformist transparency and good governance agenda that originated in small activist constituencies was elevated to the level of high politics in global energy governance. The recognition of the importance of transparency by the G-8 which (at least until recently) fashioned itself as the world's most exclusive and powerful club is proof to this. Equally importantly, belatedly policymakers in the US, where the government has for the most part been a bystander at best during the Bush presidency, have also translated the 'good resource governance' progressive agenda into the language of foreign policy realists. This includes the reframing of bad resource governance as a threat to US security, economic and foreign policy interests. Republican Senator Richard G. Lugar, for example, noted in 2008 that the resource curse 'exacerbates global poverty which can be a seedbed for terrorism, it dulls the effect of our foreign assistance, it empowers autocrats and dictators, and it can crimp world petroleum supplies by breeding instability'. In 2010, this led to stringent transparency provisions for natural resource extraction to be included in the Dodd-Frank financial reform bill.

While the rhetorical rise of the good resource governance agenda is remarkable, it is important to appreciate the overall conditions that enabled the rise of the reform agenda: a unique window of opportunity of unquestioned western dominance in world affairs and energy markets that lasted from 1990 until roughly 2005 and set the normative tone (if not the substance) for the character of the post-Cold War international system. The rise of China and India, the arguably diminished status of the west and the rise of plurality of global power centres mean that this window for normative tone-setting may have now closed (with the passing of the Dodd-Frank bill in the US perhaps being the last big statement of this agenda).

Before this chapter explores how this has come to pass it is important to disaggregate claims of the wholesale and all-encompassing normative shift and note the holes in the subscription to the agenda even when it seemed to have traction. First, even in committed drivers of the agenda such as the UK, Norway, and Germany not all parts of the government signed on to promote it. In Germany, for example, it was mainly the development cooperation ministry pushing the agenda while the economics ministry largely continued its disregard for good governance concerns.

Second, from the start the progressive agenda of putting the 'good' at the heart of global energy governance had little traction with some of the most important new players of the energy game, namely the new importers in Asia such as China and India and their national oil companies. Their understanding of energy policy has remained firmly rooted in *realpolitik*, and has shown little patience towards the reformist agenda, even in post-conflict settings. These states have also advocated their own alternative policies, such as macro-finance deals with resource-rich post-conflict states. In these deals, long-term commitments to the export of natural resources are traded for loans and investment in critical infrastructure. These deals do not have any good resource governance component.

The rise of the good governance and transparency agenda did result in a number of initiatives on the ground in post-conflict countries. They can be classified as 'soft', largely voluntary reformist approaches and 'hard' reformist approaches with more stringent stipulations. The following sections will look at these approaches in practice and then also briefly illustrate the non-reformist macro-finance and locally led approaches.

Internationally led soft reformist approaches

The key initiative in the transparency arena over the past decade has been the EITI, a policy framework launched by UK Prime Minister Tony Blair in 2002 and subsequently developed in a series of international conferences. The EITI aims to improve the management of public revenues in resource-rich countries of the developing world through the voluntary disclosure by companies and states of payments resulting from the sale of both solid minerals and hydrocarbons (EITI 2011). Its membership is composed of member countries (both implementing and supporting EITI), companies (extractive industries and institutional investors), and civil society. It is directed by a Board supported by an International Secretariat based in Oslo, and financed by a Multi-Donor Trust Fund run by the World Bank.[3] While the EITI has developed a standard methodology to increase revenue transparency, the implementation of its standards are the responsibility of individual member state governments. The initiative has seen remarkable growth, and in 2011 had had 35 member countries working towards the implementation of EITI standards, including 11 EITI compliant countries (Azerbaijan, Central African Republic, Ghana, Kyrgyz Republic, Liberia, Mali, Mongolia, Niger, Nigeria, Norway, Timor-Leste) plus 23 candidate countries including a number of (post-)conflict states such as Afghanistan, Chad, Côte d'Ivoire, the DRC, Iraq, and Sierra Leone. Yemen was listed as 'compliant but suspended'.

The other high profile initiative complementing the EITI has been the Publish What You Pay Campaign, also launched in 2002 as the culmination of a number of civil society activities in preceding years, especially by the NGO Global Witness (Gillies and Dykstra 2011). Global Witness had been active since the mid-1990s in investigating the links between conflict and the exploitation of natural resources. It was the 1999 publication of one of its reports on the Angolan civil war and the involvement of foreign business actors in it that triggered the formation of an NGO alliance that eventually included more than 300 organizations worldwide. While sharing the same normative agenda and goals as EITI, PWYP has pushed for the mandatory, as opposed to voluntary, disclosure of revenue payments by companies to the governments of resource-rich countries, to be achieved in particular by way of revenue disclosure laws in both host and home states. But the crucial pressure for compliance is to come from the key stock markets where major corporations are listed: PWYP aims to have regulators such as the Securities and Exchange Commission (SEC) force oil companies to divulge the payments made to foreign governments.

The PWYP campaign has been influential as an agenda setter and some of its key ideas were picked up by important players, as shown by the passing of disclosure stipulations in the 2010 Dodd-Frank reform bill requiring all energy and mining companies listed with the SEC in the US to reveal how much they pay to foreign countries and the US government for oil, gas, and other minerals. Moreover, the portrayal of a clash of agendas between EITI and PWYP is refuted by cross-fertilization between the two efforts, even if EITI has provided those skeptical of a regulatory approach with a less ambitious initiative.[4] Certainly both efforts shared two basic assumptions. The first is that transparency can help to discourage decisionmakers of energy-rich states from stealing from the national coffers – and use the money to ignite conflict. The second is that, once provided with real information about the (mis-)management of revenues, the civil societies of resource-rich states would act on this knowledge in the direction of more accountable governance solutions. This said, the trend over the past decade is that of a consistent preference of voluntary initiatives over regulatory solutions (with the 2010 Dodd-Frank bill as a remarkable exception). This has taken the form, for companies, of a commitment to philanthropy towards directly affected communities and sometimes vaguely worded codes of conduct; for energy exporters, the often symbolic signing up to schemes such as EITI that are hard to enforce at the best of times; and for northern governments, a number of capacity-building initiatives such as those provided by Norway.

Since the EITI is the dominant of the soft reformist approaches and claims to be able to contribute to reducing the likelihood of conflict, and to the potential use of 'resources for peace' (Le Billon and de Freitas 2011), it is worth looking at the record of this initiative in post-conflict settings. Since conflict-affected countries such as the DRC and Liberia have only been engaging with the EITI for a few years, it is hard to draw any firm conclusion. This difficulty is compounded by the fact that there is little data available on the effects of the EITI. The reports of the national EITI bodies contain very little hard data on uncovering irregularities in payments. This is surprising, since from anecdotal evidence one would expect quite a high degree of corruption in resource-rich post-conflict environments. The resource-rich DRC is a case in point (Global Witness 2009). Research finds that natural resources in the DRC have influenced the duration of the civil wars in the country. When they were exploited or sold by the (weaker) rebels, they increased the duration, while the control over these resources by the Alliance of Democratic Forces for the Liberation of Congo's (ADFL) army decreased the duration because in both cases the controlling side was able to invest in additional weaponry (Ross 2004: 58–59). In 2005, the DRC announced its intention to join EITI. Admitted as a candidate country in 2008, it formed a national EITI committee and published its first report (covering the year 2007) in 2010. The international accounting firm PricewaterhouseCoopers found discrepancies amounting to $75 million in payments in this report – however, details on the discrepancies are not available. In September 2010, the Congo sought to attain 'compliant' status with the EITI board. In December 2010, the EITI board judged Congo to be 'close to compliant', and gave it six months until June 2011 'to complete the remedial actions needed to achieve compliance'. In March 2011, the Congolese government published a document called the 'economic governance matrix', in which it made significant commitments to transparency (Ministère des Finances de la RDC 2011). The advocacy group Global Witness applauded the move to publish a number of major contracts with foreign companies in the extractive sector. However, the full details for example of a US$6 billion agreement with China still remain unpublished. At the time of writing, the DRC was still not deemed fully compliant with the EITI's standards, and the exploitation of natural resources continues to fuel the ongoing conflict in the eastern DRC, despite five years of engagement of the DRC government with the EITI.

The Congo certainly is a tough case for EITI implementation. Despite the formal end of the conflict in 2002, for parts of the country the adjective 'post-conflict' remains a crass misnomer. In addition, there is a deeply entrenched culture of corruption and patrimonial rule. In fact, the peace agreement and the subsequent efforts of the government to enhance its standing seems to be based on deals that co-opt former enemies in exchange for allowing them access to revenue from resource riches. While neo-patrimonial networks remain strong, truly independent civil society organizations with a capacity to hold the powerful to account remain rare. It is hard to expect transparency in the form of the soft reformism of voluntary disclosure to work wonders in this context.

Internationally led hard reformist approaches

The big advantage of voluntary approaches is that they are politically palatable and therefore easier to agree to by the political and economic elites in resource-rich post-conflict states – and the elites in consumer states which tend to put a premium on access to resources rather than the good governance questions associated with their production. It is therefore not surprising that only very rarely have we seen approaches that go beyond the voluntary. One such case is the GEMAP in Liberia. The abundance of natural resources is seen as a factor that sustained the civil war in Liberia, with timber, diamonds, iron ore, and rubber the main sources of income. Unsurprisingly, after the end of the civil war the question of overall financial resource management was key in order to prevent the recurrence of violent conflict. The GEMAP scheme, agreed in September 2005 between the transitional government and the International Contact Group for Liberia, was supposed to lay the ground for a sounder, more sustainable management of the country's finances, after two decades of conflict. The Liberian transitional government was pressed into the scheme by public outrage against wasteful spending, as well as through international pressure. As reported by Ashraf Ghani and Clare Lockhart, 'during [this] transitional government in Liberia, between 2003–06, the accountability systems were in such disarray that both government and donors had to resort to weekly budgeting in order to maintain the most basic controls on costs' (quoted in Hope 2010). The key objectives of GEMAP were: 'Securing Liberia's revenue base, ensuring improved budgeting and expenditure management, improved procurement practices and granting of natural resource concessions, establishing effective processes to control corruption, Support the central institutions of government, Foster cross-cutting capacity building'.[5] Under the GEMAP, co-signatures by the international community were required for all major expenses. This made the scheme much more intrusive than other arrangements. While Liberia's transitional government was not fond of the arrangement, the country's first democratically elected president Ellen Johnson-Sirleaf embraced GEMAP when she assumed power. This gave the programme buy-in from parts of the government. Johnson-Sirleaf (2006) argued in her inaugural address:

> If we are to achieve our development and anti-corruption goals, we must welcome and embrace the Governance and Economic Management Program, which the National Transitional Government of Liberia, working with our international partners, has formulated to deal with the serious economic and financial management deficiencies in our

country.... We accept and enforce the terms of GEMAP, recognizing the important assistance which it is expected to provide during the early years of our Government. More importantly, we will ensure competence and integrity in the management of our own resources and insist on an integrated capacity building dimension initiative so as to render GEMAP non-applicable in a reasonable period of time.

The GEMAP scheme officially ended in September 2009, although for some cases the co-signature requirement was extended. The international community reviewed the experience with GEMAP favourably. USAID even produced a promotional movie on the GEMAP experience.[6] UNDP released an overall positive assessment (Hope 2010). Its positive outcomes include a substantial increase in government revenue (up from $80 million in 2004/5 to $317 million in 2009/10; Reno 2011b: 140); greater transparency in public spending; improved procurement practices; admission to EITI and the Kimberley process on conflict diamonds; and the development of an anti-corruption architecture with the development of an anti-corruption strategy and the establishment of the Liberia Anti-Corruption Commission. For the first time, Liberia's fiscal accounts were actually audited.

The UNDP study also mentions a number of weaknesses of the scheme such as the timing of the end of the programme (too early), and the very limited effects of the capacity-building aspects. Even with such a rather intrusive scheme, the outcomes in terms of the management of financial resources in resource-rich countries are limited. President Johnson-Sirleaf herself has acknowledged the persistence of grave problems with corruption. However, those arguing that the situation without GEMAP would have been worse can make a plausible counterfactual argument. It is hard to imagine though that approaches such as GEMAP will gain traction in many other countries. Local elites usually are able to resist such far-reaching measures – and internationals have a long list of priorities for stabilizing post-conflict countries in which good resource governance does not always feature that prominently if push comes to shove. That explains that no GEMAP-style scheme is envisaged for example for South Sudan, even though the new country has remarkably similar issues with corruption, political divisions, and lack of regulatory capacity.

An undisputed triumph for the 'hard reformist' approach was the passing of the provisions on transparency in the 2010 US Wall Street Reform and Consumer Protection Act (also known as the Dodd-Frank bill). The bill requires oil, gas, and mining companies registered with the SEC to publicly disclose their tax and revenue payments to governments around the world. Industry has been fighting hard against these rules, which is a reliable indicator that they will indeed impose a constraint and burden on an industry not used to too many constraints (Aldonas 2011). The question remains whether and how this disclosure requirement indeed 'will deter the corruption which has brought deep poverty and conflict to many resource-rich countries' as Global Witness has claimed (2010). Some analysts, however, doubt whether the SEC, individual investors serving as private attorneys general, or even NGO watchdogs have the capacity to properly police regulated resource extraction issuers to ensure that they accurately report payments made to foreign governments.... Policing problems can be divided into two categories: public policing carried out by the SEC or other governmental agencies, and *private* policing performed by individual investors or civil society groups.

(Firger 2010: 1081)

A special provision of the Dodd-Frank act targets conflict minerals originating from the DRC. It requires companies using casserite, wolframite, gold, and coltan from the DRC to disclose the sourcing of the minerals to the SEC. Ten million people (16 per cent of the Congolese population) are directly or indirectly dependent on small-scale mining. Critics argue that the provision puts an undue burden on these small-scale miners (Stearns 2011). In a much-discussed article, US journalist David Aronson (2011) pointed to what he sees as the unintended side-effects of the rule:

Meanwhile, the law is benefiting some of the very people it was meant to single out. The chief beneficiary is Gen. Bosco Ntaganda, who is nicknamed The Terminator and is sought by the International Criminal Court.... The Chinese have recently opened a trading post in North Kivu; they make cellphones as well, and don't feel the need to participate in transparency schemes the way Western companies do. And because they know they're the only market in town, they are buying at a steep discount.

In contrast, a Congolese field researcher for the Enough Project, an advocacy NGO, has argued that

I have seen how the law has helped lead the Congolese Army to pull out of several mines, and how lowered exports are threatening commanders' profits. The law accelerates reforms. Governments and industry are starting a minerals tracing and validation initiative, Motorola Solutions is pioneering a pipeline of conflict-free minerals, and army commanders are being arrested for their role in this trade.

(Bafilemba 2011)

This debate will continue, and thorough evaluations of the application of the provisions will hopefully inform any adaptations of the bill that might be necessary. At the same time, the Dodd-Frank act provides a much-needed boost to the 'hard' regulatory approach. That boost came at an unexpected moment after much lobbying by civil society groups. The big open question is whether this was a late-blooming one-off success of the regulatory approach in an otherwise adverse environment or whether this signals a revival of a harder regulatory stance.

Non-reformist approaches

Angola, Africa's second major oil exporter after Nigeria, has been at the fore-front of activist agendas on the bad governance/resource wealth nexus since the mid-1990s. Its long-drawn conflict, which only came to an end in 2002, was often interpreted as resource driven, with the UNITA rebels financing their efforts through the diamond sector, and the government finally tri-umphing through its control of the more valuable oil reserves. In reality, the conflict had deep political roots in the country, and cannot be reduced to either 'greed' or to the role of external actors (the primary explanation in the Cold War years). But there is no doubt that the existence of oil wealth in particular has powerfully shaped Angolan institutions, elite choices, and pat-terns of accumulation. Furthermore, it is clear that this wealth has given deci-sionmakers a considerable degree of autonomy vis-à-vis Angolan society, and that revenue management has not been to the benefit of the vast majority: despite being a middle-income country (the last decade having witnessed a doubling of oil production and tripling of oil revenues), Angola's population is still near the bottom of most human development indicators.

Ten years ago, the Angolan government's reaction to criticism of its man-agement of the oil sector was adversarial and uncompromising. Invoking the language of sovereignty, it did not initially even pay lip service to the new transparency concerns, instead hinting darkly at a conspiracy against Angola levelled by unknown enemies through the likes of Transparency Interna-tional, Global Witness, and Human Rights Watch. Angola's embrace of part-nership with emerging powers such as China, which did not push for transparency and good governance (Alden *et al.* 2008) should have consoli-dated this outright rejection. Very soon, however, the government changed tack and engaged in a piecemeal manner with the reform agenda. It did not go as far as joining efforts such as EITI, which it still sees with suspicion, but on its own terms it has brought in some improvements.

This had two major motivations. The first and simplest is that key techno-crats in the regime realized that many of the technical measures that the IMF and other external critics were suggesting actually would improve the elite's control of the oil sector and maximize its rewards. These measures – many of them complex reforms to payments and audit systems and the running of oil block bidding rounds – were devoid of a progressive normative character and could be embraced without fear of unintended consequences, yet still be pre-sented on the international stage in terms of convergence with the demands of critics.

And this takes us to the second reason why the elite eventually embraced segments of a reformist agenda. It realized, as the decade progressed, that many countries (Azerbaijan and Nigeria, for instance) could register imme-diate improvements in their international standing by merely being seen to move, albeit tentatively, in the direction of greater openness however defined. This illusion of reform was necessary to normalize relations with western governments (and in due course, with the IMF as well): contrary to what was argued at that time, the Angolan goal was to have a diversified pool of international partnerships, and not replace the west by China (Soares de Oliveira 2011).

Starting in 2004, therefore, the government published large amounts of oil sector data, ranging from oil production and export revenues to an external audit of the National Oil Company Sonangol in 2010 (Global Witness 2011). This has assuaged a number of erstwhile critics: many western governments in particular, formerly critical of Angola but now keen on doing business there, have accepted this as sufficient proof that the Angolan government is on a 'reformist trajectory' and watered down, or did away with, any criticism. In reality, as explained in recent reports by Human Rights Watch (2010) and Global Witness (2011), the data published are mostly unreliable, raw, and aggregated data that are highly complex and virtually unusable by civil society. The story of the last decade, despite the apparent adoption of some reforms, is that of continuing patrimonial control of oil revenues and indeed the expansion of rentier opportunities for the elite. The system has been reconfigured: the upstream of the oil business is more transparently governed but this has little impact on popular welfare. Instead, there is a substantial degree of diversification and 'downstreaming' of corrupt opportunities in procurement and budget management, resulting from the many schemes allowed by a cash-intensive process of national reconstruction.

The Angolan experience is also a key example of the so-called macro-finance approach that sees large-scale, long-term commitments of foreign investors as key to achieve long-term growth and thereby stabilization. Berdal and Mousavizadeh (2010) argue that the rise of such macro-finance deals 'presents new options for leaders in the developing world', and hold that

> for those societies able to attract multibilliondollar commitments to infrastructure and agricultural development in return for access to their natural resources, the availability of macro-finance as part of a commercial transaction is compelling as a matter of economics, politics and national dignity.

They draw attention to Asian investors 'willing to pay for natural resources through a mix of financial payments and infrastructure investments' (p. 49), and conclude that research 'needs to address the shift towards foreign state-backed investments where natural resources represent the most promising catalyst for the construction of essential national infrastructure' (p. 53). They also argue that this 'is an opportunity for Western and other investors willing to engage African governments as economic partners with valuable assets to offer in return for long-term sustainable investments'. Here the DRC is also a case – with US$6 billion deal with China.

Conclusion

The analysis of the different approaches suggests that their chances of contributing towards realizing the transformative goals of a liberal and pro-
developmental political economy underpinning peace and stability are
severely limited.

For the macro-finance and the indigenous approach this is because this is
not the goal to begin with. The persistence of a crony post-conflict political
economy, the lack of empowered domestic constituencies pushing for the
'liberal' recomposition of the political economy, the character of elites, and
the importance of path-dependence are all factors that add to a negative trajectory. These are also the factors that the reformist approaches that put a
premium on issues of good governance have to deal with. And despite lauda-
ble goals they fall short on the ground. Reasons for this are western actors'
unwillingness to follow through on the political goals of a liberal political
economy agenda (including revenue transparency), and non-western actors'
unwillingness to even entertain basic elements of a good governance agenda.
Therefore, we should not harbour any illusions about the seriousness in
which transformative goals (transparency/good governance) are pursued in
resource-rich post-conflict states.

The idea that a progressive agenda for the extractive industries has been a
consequential segment of the overarching statebuilding agenda needs to be
revisited, despite its rhetorical prominence. At the mission level, UN and
donor actions have either not prioritized transparency/good governance in
the extractive industries, or made them subsidiary to good relations between
local politicians and international donors (which usually means not pressing
for them at all). In some contexts (e.g. the World Bank in the DRC), foreign
donors have been neglectful of these concerns and were implicated in the
setting up of a weak regulatory environment which either furthered non-
developmental practice or did not meaningfully contribute towards stem-
ming it. There is some good practice in the form of GEMAP, but this degree
of involvement does not seem to be an option in larger states. Finally, a consistent progressive role in the extractive sector by peacebuilding entities may
be beyond their reach in both strict technical/regulatory terms and, more
broadly, their legitimacy to intrude on domestic matters.

Notes

1 The following sections build on Benner and Soares de Oliveira 2010.
2 The six-volume report is available at http://go.worldbank.org/T1VB5JCV61.
3 See www.eiti.org/about.
4 Transparency International is one of the founders of PWYP but Peter Eigen, Transparency International founder, was the chairperson of the EITI Board. Global
Witness is a key force in PWYP but it has a record of collaborative work with EITI.
5 See www.gemap-liberia.org/about_gemap/index.html.
6 See www.gemap-liberia.org/GEMAP_movie.html.

Part II

Approaches to statebuilding

8   The United Nations and international statebuilding after the Cold War

Mats Berdal and Hannah Davies

The United Nations has no armed forces, no readily deployable large civilian corps, no significant stockpile of equipment and only very limited Headquarters staff to manage the Organization's activities for the maintenance of international peace and security … there is as yet no fully developed permanent system of peacekeeping, only an ongoing series of ad hoc operations.[1]

(UN Secretary General 1994)

Over the past two decades the United Nations has evolved into the principal instrument for the management of armed conflict. Notwithstanding the changing nature of conflict … the demand for the United Nations to act continues unabated. In addition, there are increasing requests for the United Nations services in contexts outside peacekeeping operations, particularly for assistance with security sector issues, and a demand for better preventive action.[2]

(Report, Senior Advisory Group (UN) 2011)

The UN is not an institution to which people should look if they want logic, consistency, clarity, and simplicity.

(Roberts 2003: 51)

The involvement of the United Nations (UN) in support of international statebuilding efforts after the Cold War – that is, in the establishment of state institutions designed to provide security, public goods and lasting foundations for sustainable economic recovery and development in countries emerging from war – raises a central and striking paradox.

On the one hand, the UN remains a deeply state centric organisation in which the prerogatives of sovereign statehood are carefully guarded by its member states and continue to exercise a profound influence on their diplomatic and political reflexes within UN fora. This is true, above all, for those members that hail from the developing world, loosely organised under the empirically anachronistic, though within the context of UN intergovernmental politics still significant, groupings of the Non-Aligned Movement (NAM) and the Group of 77 (G-77).[3] To some of their members, the growth in state- and peacebuilding activities over the past two decades has been viewed with deep suspicion; as a potential threat to what they consider a fundamental freedom from interference in their domestic affairs by richer and more powerful states.[4] Put differently, the UN's statebuilding activities have been seen as a challenge to the sanctity of the principle of non-intervention and the idea that "matters essentially within the domestic jurisdiction of states" should remain just that.[5] This instinctive and widely held attachment to the principle of sovereign equality continues to inform, in complex but powerful ways, the day-to-day workings of the organisation, at the headquarters level as well as in the field.

On the other hand, none of this has prevented the UN and its agencies from becoming deeply engaged in a diverse range of statebuilding activities, many of which have veered into politically sensitive areas by addressing core competences of the state, be it the protection of human rights, the management of economic affairs or the radical restructuring of a country's armed forces and security sector. While the UN's involvement has varied greatly in scope and intensity – ranging from the provision of mediators and human rights monitors in Central America to the rebuilding of government ministries in Cambodia and the assumption of fully fledged governmental authority in East Timor and Kosovo – the growth and intrusive character of interventions are, by any historical standard, striking.[6] Thus, while on a theoretical and discursive level sovereignty remains the fundamental organising principle, this has not prevented developing countries from supporting UN involvement on a country-by-country basis, particularly when it comes to questions of ensuring adequate resources for the mission in question and where national contingents are involved.[7] Nor are there any signs – for the time being at any rate – suggesting that the demand for UN services is abating. As of late 2011, the number of uniformed staff and civilian personnel on UN missions remains at an all-time high of nearly 120,000, while the budget for UN peacekeeping in 2011–12 was just over $7 billion, up from $3 billion in 1993.[8] Most of these missions include activities that fall within the definition of statebuilding adopted in this book.

This chapter examines both sides of the paradox. It argues that any assessment of the UN's role and performance in support of international state- and peacebuilding efforts after the Cold War requires an appreciation of the inevitable tensions that flow from it. Specifically, they help explain why the pattern of UN involvement has proved inconsistent, why it has taken the particular form that it has in individual cases, why it has prioritised some issues over others and, last but not least, why its record of effectiveness has been so mixed. To explore each of these issues in detail, the chapter and the arguments it advances proceed in three parts.

The first part focuses on the ways in which the distinctive features of the organisation – especially those that flow from its intergovernmental, functionally fragmented and intensely political character – have affected, and will continue to do so, its role in international statebuilding. It argues that the UN "system" is not a system in the true sense of the word, composed as it is of a myriad of specialised agencies, programmes and funds that operate in a semi-autonomous fashion. This reality carries important implications for the varied roles played by the UN in support of statebuilding projects, as does, inescapably, the bureaucratic and intergovernmental politics of the organisation.

The second part examines one of those roles in greater detail: its ability to confer international legitimacy *both* on the actions of statebuilders themselves *and* on the structures and institutions of government that are being built up. This, potentially, is one of the most significant roles played by the UN in support of exogenous statebuilding projects. The importance of the UN in this regard is closely linked to the near-universal character of the organisation and the custodial role it plays in relation to basic principles and norms of international society. In the context of this chapter, however, there is a further and obvious reason why it merits attention: it is the role in which the UN can, and sometimes has, most directly influenced the political economy of post-war settings, as the act of conferring or withholding legitimacy plays directly into the distribution of power and influence of among local elites and actors.

The third part examines how – notwithstanding the limitations identified elsewhere in the chapter – the capacities, tools and resources available to the UN for statebuilding have evolved since the early 1990s. While these are impressive in many respects, their development and utilisation remain subject to intergovernmental politics and constraints. As a result, management reform initiatives aimed at improving the UN's performance in key areas such as planning, finance, personnel and the creation of meaningful analytical capacity in the Secretariat, have all met with mixed results. The degree to which the political and intergovernmental character of the UN also influences seemingly prosaic or managerial questions related to, for example, budgeting, human resources and procurement is an important but often overlooked point. The fact that the UN's peacekeeping and peacebuilding efforts are paid for (or assessed) by all member states further contributes to the UN's legitimacy, but also requires that member states of the General Assembly – rather than the Security Council – ultimately have the final say on administrative and budgetary questions.

The outcome in terms of the operational efficiency and strategic direction of UN efforts in the field is often messy and frustrating. As such, however, it no more than reflects the political divisions within, and the historical and cultural heterogeneity of, the much-vaunted 'international community' in whose name the UN acts.

The nature of the organisation and its implications for statebuilding

The UN needs to be understood *both* as a grouping of sovereign states *and* as a corporate body constituted by an international secretariat working for and with the sovereign states that make up its membership.[9] The relationship between these "two UNs" is complex but vital to an understanding of the workings of the organisation, including its involvement in state- and peacebuilding (Claude 1996).

As an intergovernmental organisation deriving its authority from governments, the UN consists of nearly 200 nominally equal states. Governed in their relations with one another by the principle of sovereign equality and the rule of non-intervention, member states recognise no overarching authority (including that of the Secretary-General), nor do they see the UN as an embryonic world government. The Security Council, the body that has, in nearly all cases, authorised and overseen the growing involvement of the organisation in statebuilding activities after the Cold War, forms an integral and key part of this intergovernmental edifice. It includes five permanent, veto-wielding members whose special privileges were originally granted in recognition of their Great Power status, though also on the assumption that their elevated status carried with it special responsibilities for the maintenance of international peace and security. The effective working of the organisation was premised on the expectation that they would remain united in carrying out those responsibilities. The degree to which they have remained so when setting political objectives and providing support for UN peace- and statebuilding missions has, unsurprisingly, been an important factor determining the comparative "success" of those missions.

Servicing member states is the UN Secretariat and a myriad of functional agencies, programmes and funds, sometimes, albeit misleadingly, referred to as the "UN system".[10] It is misleading because it does not capture the degree to which the UN agencies and bodies outside the Secretariat proper have always retained a high degree of autonomy in their operations, a function in large part of the fact that they remain beholden to their donors (i.e. member states represented on their governing boards) for funding and political support. This in turn has meant that the political character of the Secretariat has sometimes been obscured when in reality, as Thant Myint-U and Amy Scott have rightly stressed, the Secretariat is also "a political institution, a place where the UN's member states compete for power and influence and attempt to diminish the power and influence of others" (Myint-U and Scott 2007: x).

The intergovernmental, functionally fragmented and political character of the organisation provides an important background to understanding the record of the UN's involvement in state- and peacebuilding in three, necessarily related, ways. The first has to do with the way in which these features of the organisation contribute to shaping the mandate and objectives of individual UN statebuilding missions; the second, with how they impact on the management and coordination of in UN statebuilding efforts; the third concerns, more specifically, the consequences for UN statebuilding efforts of the aforementioned attachment to principle of sovereignty by the membership at large, especially the "global south".

Mandates and objectives of UN statebuilding exercises

Statebuilding mandates drawn up by the Security Council – their internal coherence, the resources deployed in support of them, the degree of detailed attention given to their implementation – all reflect the priorities and interests of the member states involved in the process of mandate formulation, including those of major donors. Ideally, those priorities and interests should cohere around an achievable set of objectives underpinned by a clear political end state, adequate resources and sufficient political staying power to see a mission through. On occasion, though it is very rare, they have. More often than not, Security Council mandates have reflected political divisions among governments about the appropriate aims, scale and scope of a statebuilding intervention, leaving the Secretariat with the task of translating political aspirations and declaratory (and usually under-resourced) commitments into realisable objectives on the ground. Such divisions are often an inevitable consequence of "different understandings of the root causes of the conflict, or of wider interests of external actors" (Zaum and Knaus in this volume, p. 244).

The extent to which permanent members and, more generally, external actors consider their core interests to be affected by the outcome and design of a mission has of course differed from case to case, though it always leaves an imprint. In the case of Kosovo, as Dominik Zaum and Vera Knaus show elsewhere in this volume, fundamental disagreements over its political and legal status have "hampered its statebuilding and integration processes" and explain why its "statehood remains contested internationally and the authority of its state institutions continues to be contested internally" (p. 243). Elsewhere, the political interests engaged in the process of mandate formulation and the level of resources that member states have been prepared to devote to a mission have resulted in mandates, or mission objectives, whose credibility has varied greatly. At one extreme, is the doomed Lomé Peace Accord for Sierra Leone reached in July 1999 between the government of Sierra Leone under President Tejan Kabbah and the Revolutionary United Front (RUF) led by Foday Sankho, many of whose provisions were in theory to be implemented by UNOMSIL. The accord reflected awkward political compromises among local and external actors that soon proved, as many had predicted, untenable in the face of violent challenges and local resistance.[11] By contrast, though still not without its problems, are the 1991 Paris Peace Accords for Cambodia and the arrangements made for their implementation through the deployment of a large-scale UN peacekeeping operation (UNTAC) whose intrusive mandate included civil administration, election organisation and various military functions.[12] In this case, the balance of external influences bearing on the long-running conflict and continuing support by the Security Council and key donors played a vital role in shepherding the country through the initial UN-led phase of statebuilding. In many other cases, however, geo-political developments and priorities have influenced the commitment and political attention span of donors and outside actors in much less helpful ways. The lack of interest in Liberia in 1990 stemmed in part from it being overshadowed by the Gulf War. Likewise, sustained attention to the DRC after 2001 was a casualty of the political and security climate of post-9/11.

The *Brahimi Report on UN Peace Operations* of 2000 maintained, sensibly and logically enough, that mandates lacking in clarity, credibility and achievability, should be rejected by the Secretariat (United Nations 2000). This was the chief lesson drawn by the Brahimi panel from the experience of several high-profile UN operations in the 1990s – notably Somalia, Bosnia and Rwanda – where a combination of inadequate resources, absence of strategic direction and, above all, lack of clarity on political end-state had resulted in disaster. And yet, in practice, for the Secretariat to say "no" is very rarely an option. As result, the UN has all too often, in what U Thant identified as one of the organisation's classic if unarticulated functions, found itself landed with "great problems ... because governments have been unable to think of what to do about them" (1978: 32). The "statebuilding" exercise in the DRC over the past decade falls into that category. The process-oriented focus of UN bodies and programmes has the effect of hiding the degree to which member states are unwilling, unable or both, to confront underlying political challenges and are turning instead to the UN, sometimes as "a last-ditch, last resort affair" (ibid.: 32).

Coordination and strategic direction of UN efforts

The fragmentation of the UN system along functional lines and the very fact that major UN agencies are separately administered make coordination and, especially, the *strategic direction* of statebuilding activities by the UN an inherently difficult if not impossible task. The deeper source of the problem can be traced back to the founding of the organisation:

> Functionally speaking, the UN system was set up as a kind of loose confederation of international agencies ... committed to the concept of the coexistence of a "hub" organisation and a group of autonomous "Specialised Agencies", looking to the United Nations proper for coordination and guidance, but enjoying essential freedom of action in their respective fields. This principle of decentralisation modified by persuasive coordination, but not authoritative control from the center, was neither precisely defined nor exclusively applied in the Charter.
>
> (Claude 1984: 68)

The autonomy thus granted has bred an attachment to institutional independence on the part of agencies which, over time, has come to be reflected in different institutional cultures and, often, in different political priorities. Throughout the organisation's history there have been repeated attempts to address the problem of coherence and unity of effort resulting from the workings of the "principle of decentralisation modified by persuasive coordination". The *Jackson Report* of 1969, specifically concerned with the UN development system, famously noted how UN activities were undertaken with "very little 'brain' to guide it" and that "its absence may well be the greatest constraint on all capacity" (UNDP 1970). The growth of UN peace- and statebuilding activities over the past 20 years has magnified the tensions built into the system. As the High Level Panel on UN "system-wide coherence" candidly concluded in its final report of November 2006, the organisation "has become fragmented and weak … [with] a proliferation of agencies, mandates and offices creating duplication and dulling the focus on outcomes, with moribund entities never discontinued".[13]

The political character of the institution as a whole and the loose confederal structure enshrined at the outset are profound obstacles to addressing some of the dysfunctions that result on the ground in UN statebuilding operations. As the High Level Panel also noted: "operational incoherence between UN funds, programmes and agencies is most evident" at the country level (ibid.) As a result, the organisation, as the Secretary-General repeatedly stresses when reporting on individual operations, is left reiterating its "commitment to the principle of 'Delivering as One'", though that is also an implicit acknowledgement that there are limits to what "persuasive co-ordination" can achieve.[14] The creation of coordinating mechanisms such as the Department of Humanitarian Affairs (later rebranded the Office of Co-ordinator of Humanitarian Affairs) and the commitment to "integrated missions" have produced very mixed results.[15] Even the establishment of the much-vaunted Peacebuilding Commission (PBC) and an associated Peace Support Office in 2005 has not managed to overcome the deeper obstacles to effective coordination and delivery. While that was the original intention behind the creation of the PBC, since 2006 intergovernmental bargaining and negotiations have, in the words of Mark Malloch-Brown, "cut the guts out of it", making it a "pale shadow of what had been proposed" (2011: 177).[16]

The uses of sovereignty

The commitment to sovereignty and the associated concern about any erosion of the rule on non-intervention among member states emphasised at the outset of this chapter, reinforce what is a state-centric and process-oriented approach to the challenges of statebuilding by UN bodies and donors. "State-centric" in this context refers to the predilection for the UN's intergovernmental machinery to engage with *formally* recognised structures and authorities; a "built-in bias", in the words of Bernhard Helander, "to work with state-like mechanisms" (2005: 202). While this bias is partly a function of the diplomatic rules of the game, it complicates the attempt by the UN-as-statebuilder to engage meaningfully with non-state actors, with civil society, with local dimensions of conflict and, crucially, with informal networks and parallel structures where actual power and influence are typically located in post-war settings.[17] It is one of the factors that has limited the ability of a UN statebuilding presence to influence and help renegotiate state–society relations and to transform the political economy of post-war settings, as the elites wielding power *locally* have been able to "use state sovereignty strategically" to advance their agendas and to resist external intrusion in ways that would threaten their privileged position. Thus, while sovereignty may be hollow and largely meaningless in purely factual terms it still "works" in other ways, as Peter Uvin and Leanne Bayer perceptively note in their study of Burundi in this volume (p. 276):

> first, it usually benefits the group of people who control the government of the country concerned – who "manage" the sovereignty at the expense of other social forces – and, second, it pushes politics and decisions underground, removed from the donors' prying eyes and interventionist intentions, thus all but assuring that the way politics is done will continue to build off informal, personal, clientelist mechanisms.

Against this reality, it is hardly surprising that the bias for "state-like mechanisms ... may mean unwittingly strengthening self-appointed and violent gate-keepers at the expense of civil society" (Richards 2005: 202). More generally, it has meant that UN bodies, including now the Peacebuilding Commission, often end up confronting specific statebuilding challenges with a profound sense of unreality, as if one is dealing with properly functioning, rationally bureaucratic institutions rather than public façades behind which informality and neo-patrimonial politics reigns (Berdal 2009: 24–26). No doubt, it has also reinforced the tendency, highlighted by Séverine Autesserre and others, for international peace- and statebuilders to privilege a top-down approach to understanding and tackling the drivers of conflict at the expense of local, "micro-level" or bottom-up sources of violence (Autesserre 2009: 41–83).

The more specific or day-to-day implications of the intergovernmental, functionally fragmented and political character of the UN are addressed more fully in the final section of this chapter, suffice it to say here that, taken together, they help explain why it is impossible to speak of a distinctive, let alone coherent, UN approach to statebuilding; why "success" is uneven and why the circumstances and types of intervention and statebuilding involvement have varied so greatly.

Conferring legitimacy on statebuilding exercises

"How many divisions has he got?" Stalin mockingly asked of the Pope. As the history of communism in Eastern Europe would later show, the answer to that question was much less straightforward than Stalin evidently supposed. The UN does not have any divisions, but it does have another asset that is often hard to pin down though it is no less real or important for that reason. This is the ability of the organisation through its political organs, above all the Security Council, to bestow collective legitimacy on the actions of its member states.[18] It is an explicit political function whose value in the eyes of governments derives from the near-universal character of the organisation, and from the sense that, for all the UN's faults and manifest weaknesses, its political imprimatur nonetheless comes closest to reflecting the will and normative aspirations of international society. Judging from the record of the past two decades, it is a function in which the UN retains an advantage over regional and sub-regional bodies whose impartiality and deeper motives in any given intervention – including peace and statebuilding exercises – often comes to be questioned by member states.[19]

There are two aspects to the UN's role here that need to be distinguished, though they overlap in practice.

In the first place, the UN can confer legitimacy on the statebuilding intervention itself, internationalising the efforts of actors and donors and giving the operation a truly multilateral character, even though in practice the lead has been taken by major powers. There are obvious advantages to giving intrusive and politically delicate statebuilding projects an international seal of approval through the UN. Not only might it serve to broaden the international base of support for an operation, but it can also mitigate local resistance to external intrusion. Such considerations explain why the US and the UK were anxious to obtain a resolution explicitly supporting the resort to force in Iraq in 2003, and why, later, the US administration encouraged moves to re-engage the UN in the country, including through the appointment of Lakhdar Brahimi – the politically astute, respected and experienced mediator and statesmen – as UN Special Envoy to Iraq. Concerns about legitimacy also explains why NATO, although it began its air campaign against Yugoslavia in March 1999 without explicit authority from the Security Council, was anxious for the UN quickly to take the lead in setting up an international civilian administration (UNMIK) to help run the province after the end of the war.[20] The broader the consensus among Council members and donors in support of a UN operation, the greater its legitimacy. In Cambodia and Mozambique, such support played an important part in the comparative success of both missions. Success is also, however, influenced by the manner in which the UN *performs* its statebuilding tasks and while the behaviour of its senior officials, military contingents and civilian staff on the ground cannot carry a statebuilding enterprise on its own, it can strengthen or weaken it. Such performance – or "output legitimacy" – as distinct from "structural" legitimacy, which inheres in the organisation itself – can be critical to a mission, especially in its early stages (Zaum 2011: 283–286). An obvious example in this respect is the credibility of UN-organised elections; properly managed they have played an important role in consolidating initial statebuilding efforts by lending legitimacy to the process and the actors involved. Conversely, poorly managed elections lacking in credibility – Angola's general election in 1992 provides a poignant and tragic example – can undermine efforts to stabilise "post-conflict" environments, be divisive and set the stage for renewed violence.

Second, as "dispenser of politically significant approval and disapproval" (Claude 1966: 367) the UN – through the actions not just of the Security Council but also the decisions of its envoys and the leadership of individual missions – can have a very direct impact on the distribution of power, influence and governance at the local level. The fact that statebuilding projects often involve a struggle for legitimacy among local elites only adds to the importance of securing or denying UN political approval. The UN may dispense its approval formally by recognising and dealing with entities previously shunned by the international community (as with the UÇK in Kosovo, albeit renamed KPC after the war in 1999), or it may be more indirect, for example, by acting as an interlocutor with local parties and in so doing legitimising their status.

As the record of the past two decades makes clear, UN blessing of this kind is not necessarily constructive or helpful to the success of a peace- or state-building project in the long run. Indeed, by entrenching the power of illiberal and rapacious elites, UN political endorsement of local actors and ruling elites can be, and often has been, inimical to the avowed aims of UN engagement in the first place. The legitimacy granted in such cases is really of a spurious kind, for while the decision to recognise and deal with some actors at the expense of others may be considered a necessary concession to political realities on the ground, it is also likely to strengthen the hold of predatory elites, perpetuate violent political economies, inflame grievances and, ultimately, encourage new forms of resistance among those that see themselves as having lost out in the "post-conflict" dispensation of political power and influence. The end result is that the norm- and statebuilding exercise that the UN is ostensibly there to support is undermined.

While the potentially damaging consequences of UN actions are easy enough to identify (especially in retrospect), the multiple constraints under which such actions are taken are often underrated. The fact is that the decision-making environment confronting the UN Secretariat and mission leaderships during transitions from war to peace is inevitably shaped by a complex of political and resource constraints, often compounded by moral ambiguities, which ensure that choices rarely present themselves as simple alternatives between "good" or "evil", "right" or "wrong". A case in point is again provided by the aforementioned Lomé Peace Accord for Sierra Leone in 1999, the UN's endorsement of which involved welcoming Foday Sankoh, the RUF leader, back into the fold with what many would argue were entirely predictable consequences (Alao and Ero 2001: 117–134). The accord, however, though flawed, was also a function of regional and geopolitical realities that could not be wished away by the UN Secretariat. These included the unwillingness of Nigeria to continue to carry the major burden of peacekeeping in Sierra Leone coupled with a strong reluctance on the part of traditional troop contributors to step in and assume greater responsibilities for supporting the implementation of any new peace agreement.

There is a further and important consideration here, however. While it is undoubtedly the case that the UN has frequently been confronted with unpalatable options and messy realities on the ground (complicated by the aforementioned bias for dealing with "state-like mechanisms"), it is also true that its engagement in statebuilding has frequently also been marred by an "ignorance of context" and a resulting tendency to favour prescriptions based on prevailing definitions of "best practice" and the assumption that, as statebuilders, outsiders are dealing with a clean slate (see Goldstone in this volume, p. 210). According to Anthony Goldstone this kind of attitude was one of the "peculiarities of UNTAET as government": an ignorance of the complexities of East Timor, specifically the history and fluidity of political organisation in the country, which "seriously limited its capacity as a state-builder" (ibid.). Unfamiliarity with and neglect of context have not been confined to East Timor; a fact that helps explain why the UN-as-statebuilder has, more often than not, failed to effect deeper transformations of society and, in particular, of the political economy of post-conflict states. Contributing to that outcome, as noted earlier, has also been the ability and skill with which ruling elites have harnessed sovereignty in order to "create a protected space where the international community cannot go", endowing "local rulers with the power to resist, subvert and reappropriate" (Uvin and Bayer in this volume, p. 275). As several of the chapters in the book make clear, ruling elites tend to be recycled, leaving the underlying political economy of post-war states largely unaffected by UN involvement. And when, as in Iraq and Burundi, ruling elites are indeed physically replaced, this has not involved any transformation in the "way of doing politics" and the underlying political economy that supports it. Much the same can be said of Hun Sen's Cambodia in the period since the withdrawal of UNTAC in 1993 (Berdal and Leifer 2007: 49–51).

The UN's capacities and resources for statebuilding

In all of the cases cited above, the UN's role as a political actor has required complex and extensive practical support, ranging from premises in which UN civil servants can operate to secure communication mechanisms to report to New York. As a consequence, the capacities and resources now available to the UN for statebuilding have evolved considerably since the early 1990s. In 1990 there was no Department for Peacekeeping Operations; there was no standing police capacity, electoral affairs division or peacebuilding support office. Specialist capacities such as the mine action service did not exist and the UN had no coordinated logistical capacity to deploy operations. Financial, procurement and personnel procedures for field missions were particularly cumbersome and ineffectual.[21] The majority of staff employed in field missions were either seconded headquarters staff or on separate, specific field contracts, often recruited through informal personal networks. The rapid expansion of peacekeeping in the early 1990s was also accompanied by financial constraints as contributions from key member states failed to keep up with expenditure. In 2011, however, the organisation has readily deployable civilian staff, strategic deployment stocks of equipment and two large dedicated departments in New York – the Department of Field Support created in 2007 and the Department of Peacekeeping Operations – to manage and backstop the UN's field activities related to peace and security, in addition to the capacity of the Department of Political Affairs. While the problem of non-payment remains and there is little the Secretary-General can actively do to address this, the financial situation of the UN is much improved since the hand-to-mouth days of the 1990s.

This progression is evidence of the development of a significant body of practice accompanied by member state commitment over the last 20 years within the UN on how to manage peace- and statebuilding type activities. And yet this is not a straightforward story of progress and improvement. The capacities, tools and resources that the UN has developed both reflect and contribute to the intergovernmental character of the organisation. On the one hand, the UN aspires to flexibility, dynamism and responsiveness in addressing the myriad of challenges presented by statebuilding type activities and yet, on the other, to retain its legitimacy it needs to be inclusive, universal and non-discriminatory.[22] Furthermore, a great deal of work in the UN is necessarily dedicated to managing its own processes both internally and in reporting to member states through a wide range of committees, panels and working groups. Inevitably, process often becomes more prominent than outcomes; technical or administrative problems become both easier to recognise and to solve than more profound political disagreements. And, as noted above, the UN tendency to gravitate towards "state like" structures can exacerbate a parallel administrative unreality, as strategic frameworks and other planning tools become disconnected from the nuances and messy dynamics of the host country. As a result, attempts to improve UN capacity for statebuilding have often ended up privileging the managerial over the substantive with New York intergovernmental politics overriding operational autonomy on the ground. The growth in UN capacities and evidence of institutional learning over the past 20 years suggest that the tendency for intergovernmental politics to assert itself is not an insuperable obstacle to progress and meaningful action. Any attempt to understand how the UN has approached statebuilding – specifically, how the reforms and initiatives aimed at strengthening its capacities and resources in the area have fared – cannot, however, afford to ignore this wider intergovernmental context.

This section examines four key areas: personnel; finance and budgeting; planning and coordination; and analytical capacity. It highlights how they are profoundly linked to the wider bureaucratic politics of the UN and the central paradox of UN involvement in statebuilding outlined at the outset of the chapter.

Personnel

The key tension in the management of personnel within the UN is encapsulated in Article 101 of the Charter whereby the paramount consideration for employing staff is the "highest standards of efficiency, competence and integrity". However, due regard shall also be paid to recruiting on "as wide a geographical basis as possible". These two considerations are in no way incompatible, though the enshrining of geography or national representation in the Charter makes questions of human resources a political concern for member states. As the number of personnel employed by the UN has grown exponentially since the organisation has expanded into statebuilding related activities through its peacekeeping and political missions, the scope and possibility for political interest in personnel questions have become more intense: not only as a result of what it is that UN staff are now expected to do (politically sensitive activities such as security sector reform), but who, or which nationality, is employed and how.

In 1993 there were approximately 10,000 *civilians* employed in peacekeeping.[23] In October 2011 there were just under 20,000 civilian personnel.[24] The UN's online recruitment platform, *Inspira*, introduced in 2010, lists engineers, police officers and legal experts, economists and electoral observers, specialists in civil affairs and gender, as well as experts in information technology and public information as some of the jobs now involved in "peacekeeping". The range and diversity of jobs are themselves a reflection of the UN's growing involvement in statebuilding like activities.

To adapt to this expansion, successive secretaries-general have aimed to reflect the increasingly field-based nature of the UN's work in the management of human resources. This has led to a number of systemic reforms across the UN including contractual changes so that headquarters and field mission staff are on the same series of contracts. There has also been a phased harmonisation of the conditions of service so that UN staff in agencies such as UNICEF are not paid significantly more than a staff member performing a similar function in a UN peacekeeping operation. The main objective of these changes is to improve recruitment and retention in the field and build a professionalised staff that has the experience and incentives to engage in some of the statebuilding type activities that the UN undertakes. There has also been strengthening of the resources and processes at headquarters to manage personnel in the field including online tools and the introduction of rosters: prescreened candidates managed centrally who can be quickly deployed where there is a need. Each of these reforms has been negotiated by the General Assembly's budget committee (Fifth Committee) where questions of national interest and geographical bias are as prominent as efficiency and effectiveness.

Perhaps it is a natural tendency for all governments to think that their nationals have the "highest standards of efficiency and competence". A consequence of the financial power of donor nations who can fund extra budgetary activities is that there is always suspicion that field recruitment can be used as back door for already powerful countries to get more of their nationals into the UN. The use of "gratis personnel" seconded from member states to the UN during the 1990s was fiercely contested for this very reason, and was eventually overturned by G-77 and other states through the negotiation of human resources policy in the Fifth Committee.[25]

The results of these reforms and initiatives are mixed.[26] On the one hand, the Secretariat has to work within the constraints of a highly politicised intergovernmental framework; on the other it is expected to deliver cost savings and efficiency benefits within what is a very far from perfect labour market – in concrete terms, the availability of fluent Arabic and English speaking demobilisation specialists with experience of security sector reform and over ten years of working in an international organisation, is surely limited. The result is often a managerialist tendency. Solutions to the inevitable problems of skills and capacity are approached in terms of centralised "tools" and "packages". While headquarters oversight does address the legitimate need for transparency and inclusivity, the approach is not necessarily appropriate for rapid and specialised recruitment, particularly in smaller political offices with very specialist mandates. There are also considerable tensions between headquarters and the field, where mission leadership responsible on a daily basis for delivering specialist assistance related to, for example, justice and corrections or detailed local political knowledge, struggle to recruit the people they need quickly.

The 2011 High Level Panel on civilian capacity does acknowledge that the range of activities the UN is being asked to do requires new thinking as well as additional resources.[27] Its final report also notes that there is much expertise available in a post-conflict situation from within the host country and that parachuting in international expertise can create some perverse incentives. The report also reflects a move within the UN system towards greater use of national staff, partly as a means of reducing costs, but also as a means of building local capacity. However, using national staff is not in any way a neutral mechanism in a post-conflict society and it has sometimes, as when the mission in Burundi was transitioning from a peacekeeping operation to a smaller peacebuilding mission, involved local staff in protests about terms and conditions.[28] Similarly, in the Democratic Republic of Congo, where the UN is one of the largest employers, conflicts with national staff have had a negative spill over effects on the peacebuilding objectives of the mission.[29]

There are also tensions across the system between the UN Secretariat (including the staff of UN peacekeeping and political missions) and the field staff of the funds and programmes such as UNICEF, UNDP and the World Food Programme. As was noted above, the agencies, funds and programmes of the UN have different governance structures with influence from donors. They also have different processes and policies for recruitment, pay and conditions that have been more flexible. The different terms and conditions translate into different priorities and interests among staff and have been an underlying factor in why coordination or "inter-operability" in the field has been so difficult. These kinds of bureaucratic differences inform how staff in the field actually relate to each other when trying to operationalise "delivering as one" and can create tensions and competition over, for example, who should have primacy in dealing with government counterparts on specific statebuilding type issues such as control over natural resources.

The politics of *uniformed* personnel deployed by the UN are equally, if not more, contentious. In 1992 there were 52,154 uniformed personnel deployed under a UN flag. By October 2011 there were 97,614. While this number has fluctuated over the period with a marked decline in the late 1990s, the overall trend has been one of significant growth. This growth in the number of troops and police deployed has also led to the creation of new structures at headquarters including the creation of the Office of the Rule of Law and Security Institution in 2007 with a dedicated Police Division and a senior Police Advisor, new specialist resources for the Office of Military Affairs in 2008 and, in terms of policy and doctrine, the publication in 2008 of the

UN's "Capstone" doctrine, essentially a codification of the principles and guidelines governing peacekeeping practice.

Uniformed personnel deployed to UN missions serve under the terms and conditions of their national forces so the processes of recruitment are fundamentally different from that of civilians. However, there have been attempts to improve training and support for UN military personnel as well as developments in other areas such as conduct and discipline, welfare and recreation, compensation for death and disability that follow the same logic of increasing professionalisation. These initiatives have mainly been led by the troop contributing countries, the largest of which are also vocal participants in the G-77 and NAM. In this way, the politics of troop contributions are an essential part of the north–south dynamics that structure UN politics. The fact that since 1994 there have only been two ad hoc increases to the rate of reimbursing UN military personnel also adds to the conflict between the main financial contributors (developed countries) who already feel that they are paying too much for peacekeeping and the main troop contributors whose nationals are increasingly being required to carry out more robust and complex mandates. Tensions over this issue reached a pitch in June 2011 delaying approval of all peacekeeping budgets and a Senior Advisory Group was established to make recommendations.[30] The group is quite uniquely hybrid in its structure combining elements of the traditional "expert panel" in the shape of five senior experts appointed by the Secretary-General with member state representatives from regional groups as well as nominations from some of the largest troop and financial contributors and chaired by former Deputy Secretary-General Louise Frechette. The fact that the group was mandated by the General Assembly, as well as the "grounding" of the eminent persons within a context that has to represent member-state interests, could lead potentially to more pragmatic and realistic recommendations for reform.

Finance and budgeting

Underpinning the number of UN staff involved in statebuilding and the tasks they are undertaking has been a steady growth in the cost of UN peace and security activities. In 1993 the budget for peacekeeping was approximately $3 billion.[31] The budget for UN peacekeeping 2011–12 is $7.06 billion. In addition there is approximately $1 billion for political missions, which include the assistance missions in Iraq and Afghanistan as well as a number of peacebuilding and political offices.[32]

As with personnel issues, the UN has adapted processes, rules and regulations to address the challenges involved in more extensive and expensive field operations. These include the introduction of a peacekeeping reserve fund in 1992 to provide resources for the start up of new operations allowing the Secretariat some means of responding rapidly, as well as changes to the budgeting process for peacekeeping operations whereby they are annual rather than limited to the length of the Security Council mandate, allowing for some degree of planning and predictability. Other reforms to attempt to make the financing and budgeting of UN field operations more transparent and effective have been less successful. The proposal for separate peacekeeping budgets of each mission to be consolidated into one account so as to provide more flexibility and to cut down on transaction costs was never seriously considered. Such a mechanism was resisted since, among other things, it would allow those states that did not pay on time to be subsidised by those that did.

The budget process has remained essentially intergovernmental and inevitably headquarters focused. This has created limitations in the field. The annual budget process and the length of time between resource proposals being formulated by a mission and approved by the General Assembly can create a misalignment between operational statebuilding activities and bureaucratic processes. As an example, the approval of temporary positions in the UN Mission in Liberia to assist with the conduct of elections at the end of 2011 was only approved from the beginning of July. Taking into account the length of time to recruit and deploy staff, several of the positions approved remained unfilled until after the elections were concluded.

A number of governments would also like to see political missions, such as peacebuilding offices paid for using the peacekeeping scale of assessment, whereby the permanent Security Council members pay more since they are also mainly mandated by the Council. However any suggestion of such a change has been fiercely resisted by the P5.

A more consolidated approach to reforming how the UN provides logistical support to peace and security field mandates was introduced in 2010. Influenced by the logistical problems presented by the missions in Darfur and Chad, the *Global Field Support Strategy* is an attempt by the Department of Field Support to provide a more global and strategic way of managing resources for field missions. The central idea is to move away from mission by mission management of key support assets such as aircraft to more centralised sharing of resources through regional and global service centres, in Entebbe in Uganda and Brindisi in Italy. The strategy is also designed to lead to efficiency savings in response to increasing constraints on UN budgets in the light of the 2008 financial crisis. To some extent it is an attempt to draw on 20 years of practice to come up with more standardised and predictable approach through, for example, using budget templates and modularised logistics support. The strategy was approved by the General Assembly; however member states' concerns over aspects of the proposals illustrate the same intergovernmental tensions particularly over where power and authority should lie when it comes to decisions over resources. The shift away from headquarters in New York to service centres either in Europe and Africa, for example, led to some member states – particularly the large TCCs – questioning the impact on command and control, and a concern that the military representation in New York would lose access to crucial information about logistical questions related to their troops. Moving resources away from New York to Brindisi, where there is no permanent diplomatic representation, raises concerns that the Secretariat might be usurping the *strategic* role played by member states.

At the end of the day, the budgeting and financing of UN peace and security operations are decided by the General Assembly under Article 17 of the Charter, and there is no managerial shortcut around the Fifth Committee – dominated by the "sovereignty-conscious" G-77 grouping – which jealously guards its responsibility for all administrative issues within the UN.

Planning and coordination

As the UN's efforts in statebuilding related activities have become more diverse and involved greater numbers of actors within and outside the UN system, the need for robust planning and oversight has increased. Undoubtedly, the UN has built up significant practice in this area and considerable resources are now devoted to planning and coordination, including dedicated cells within field missions. There is also a strong declaratory commitment to integration across different parts of the UN system both from member states and from the various secretariats. In practical terms the main tool used by the UN is the integrated mission planning process (IMPP), launched in 2006 and designed to address the challenges in deploying an integrated mission, primarily coordination among and between the different actors such as OHCHR, UNDP or OCHA.

But as the Secretary-General's various reports on the subject of planning and preparedness make clear, planning is conceived of more in terms of *process* than results: coordination is, in itself, seen as an outcome rather than the concrete benefit that UN Country Team coordination created. Attempts at integrated planning and the assignment of lead agencies or departments can exacerbate the bureaucratic tendency to privilege process over outcome and a tick box approach to accountability. In spite of the myriad of coordinating committees and working groups – both at headquarters and in the field – there are still considerable tensions over competence and responsibility for particular activities and actions. The UN's work on rule of law illustrates this very clearly.

A high level Rule of Law Coordination and Resource Group is chaired by the Deputy Secretary-General and includes the UN Departments of Political Affairs and Peacekeeping Operations as well as the Office of Legal Affairs and Office of Coordination of Humanitarian Affairs. In addition UNICEF, UNDP, UNHCR, the UN Office for Drugs and Crime and UN Women are represented. A Rule of Law Unit supports this group and sits in the Office of the Secretary General. Its functions are essentially coordination and "developing" system wide strategies.

In operational terms, each of the different bodies participating in the group is involved in rule of law activities: the Office of Rule of Law and Security Institutions in the Department of Peacekeeping Operations manages UN police deployments and develops guidance and policies for field missions. It also manages the standing police capacity. UNDP and the other agencies work with national authorities to develop capacity, UN Women and UNICEF focus on women and children respectively. Inevitably there is a great deal of overlap and competition. In addition, on the level of UN wide policy, all questions related to the UN's activities in the area of rule of law (one of the key components of statebuilding) must be consulted through each of these offices and departments and requires extensive consultation and co-ordination, all of which exacerbates the bureaucratic tendency to focus on internal processes. It can also lead to a kind of "lowest common denominator" approach to policy in order to reach consensus. From the outside the concentration of resources on coordination also raises questions from member states about effectiveness as well as duplication and coherence.

There are also tensions in the field where, organisationally, rule of law activities are grouped together into one component that should be working together to reach mandated goals. Operationally, there can be a tension between justice and order where, on the one hand, the policing component of a mission leans towards a more robust approach to supporting nascent national police institutions and, on the other, the human rights elements of the mission – through OHCHR – will tend to privilege respect for individual rights. Such tensions exist *within* a UN mission but would also play out in terms of coordination with other UN actors and international NGOs.

While planning on the policy level in the UN can be somewhat abstract, in the field the challenges can be very prosaic and resource based. There is a commitment within field missions to coordination and "One UN" at least in principle, but this can be challenged by the detail of day-to-day planning. So while on a strategic level the different UN actors sign up to integrated processes, they also have to manage very practical planning considerations regarding, for example, sharing of resources and premises. As an example, in Burundi where the mandate of the UN's political office is specifically to coordinate the strategies and programmes of UN agencies, funds and programmes,[33] the UN is attempting to put in place cost-sharing arrangements, specifically in the areas of security, medical services, communications and media. The formula for each service will be different depending on the usage by different agencies, funds and programmes, but the idea is to leverage the resources contributed by each.

These kinds of negotiations among the different agencies over cost-sharing formulae are notoriously difficult and the bureaucracy of planning is influenced by the power dynamics and political interests of the different agencies in these processes. In this way the different approaches to funding, budgeting and human resources within the UN system make coordinated UN action exceedingly difficult. The reality of the processes and tools that the UN uses for planning reveal a great deal about the fragmented, ad hoc and frequently competitive nature of the UN "system". The frameworks for planning are also governed by intergovernmental processes that are inevitably politically motivated. While this can create operational frustrations, it is also an aspect of precisely the kind of legitimacy that the UN can confer.

As well as policy competition within the UN Secretariat departments there is also conflict over where management decisions should be taken regarding resources. There is an ongoing tension between the field focused departments particularly the Department of Field Support and the headquarters focused Department of Management that sees itself as the custodian of all financial and administrative policies and the privileged interlocutor with member states on resource questions.

In an attempt to link resources to outcomes and make the Secretariat more accountable, *results-based budgeting* is used to translate the Security Council mandates into a series of objectives, activities and outcomes. While providing a degree of transparency over resources, the approach is crudely top down with the high level instructions on how to interpret the mandate (the budget instructions) being issued from New York according to an established timetable. There is a time lag between the preparation of the frameworks and their implementation on the ground, which leads to a lack of flexibility and responsiveness. The planned outputs can also reflect the bureaucratic tendency to privilege process as when, for example, the chairing of monthly meetings is seen as an "output" contributing to how the UN supports long-term peace, security and socio-economic development.[34]

In addition, the results frameworks of missions are considered and approved by the General Assembly and this further highlights the political nature of the planning process and the central paradox of the UN and statebuilding. As noted above, it is the UN Secretariat that is tasked with undertaking complex statebuilding tasks in fragile, even hostile, environments. Its performance is measured against budgeted resources, which are sometimes inadequate, not just in financial terms but also in how they are spent and allocated to specific tasks. While the member states of the General Assembly may approve resources to achieve the goal of an environment conducive to human rights, there is a limit to what international staff – both uniformed and civilian – can actually do to ensure that a post-conflict country adopts human rights legislation. The planning process, and the role of the General Assembly in approving the frameworks, further demonstrates the paradox of intergovernmental oversight of activities that are the responsibility of individual governments. A clear illustration of this from 2008 was the budget negotiation on the framework for the political mission charged with implementing Security Council Resolution 1559 (2004) in Lebanon. The negotiation actually led to a request to the Secretary-General to revise the framework "taking into account recent developments", specifically the changing relationship between Syria and Lebanon.[35] The sensitivity of this issue reflects a concern that indicators of achievement such as "Increased Accession by the Government of Lebanon to the right to exercise a monopoly on the use of force throughout its territory",[36] are in fact measuring and judging the *actions of member states* and not those of the special envoys or other Secretariat officials. For that reason, the following agreed paragraph is now regularly reaffirmed in discussions both of peacekeeping and of special political missions and illustrate clearly the preeminence attached to sovereignty by member states:

> Notes that some indicators of achievement reflected in the budgets and budget performance reports appear to measure the performance of

Member States, and requests the Secretary-General to ensure that the purpose of the indicators of achievement is not to assess the performance of Member States but, where possible, to reflect the contributions by ... missions to the expected accomplishments and objectives in keeping with their respective mandates.[37]

Analytical capacity

Planning should, of course, ideally be based on sound analysis and reliable information. Just as the UN has improved its planning, the analytical capacity it has at its disposal, both in reporting to the Council and other stakeholders, has expanded. In 2011 the Secretary-General detailed some of the mechanisms that are in place to provide information including, "systematic briefings before and after technical assessment missions allowing both Council members and troop- and police-contributing countries to be better informed about the evolution of peace" and to develop "a shared understanding between the Secretariat and Member States on the future direction of the operations".[38] The same report also indicates how the UN Secretariat has become more proactive in trying to service the needs of the Security Council by undertaking its own research survey to identify the priority information requirements of the Security Council.

The analytical capacity of the Secretariat, at least in terms of processes for capturing and sharing information and data, has expanded enormously over the past 20 years. Supplementing the political affairs officers ("desk" officers) in both the Department of Political Affairs and Department of Peacekeeping Operations, there are now a number of specialised units and services both at HQ and in the field.

The Department for Peacekeeping Operation manages a Situation Centre, established in 1993 to monitor and report on developments on the ground in missions. The Situation Centre gives thrice weekly briefings to DPKO and DFS (Department of Field Support, UN) senior management as well as reporting to the Executive Office of the Secretary General.

Within missions there are a number of mechanisms designed to share information, both analytical and operational, as well as to report back to headquarters: Joint Mission Analysis Cells (JMACs) and Joint Operations Centres (JOCs). These capacities in missions, combining civilian and military staff, are used to provide situational analysis as well as up-to-date reporting and, when well staffed and utilised by mission leadership, can be crucial for strategic planning.[39] There are also Joint Logistics Operation Centres which coordinate the support elements required within missions and that can also play a significant role in implementing mandated statebuilding tasks such as support for elections or developing national institutions such as the building of security facilities and prisons.

There has been a huge expansion in the information and data about the UN's field activities available through, for example, the creation of a specialist information management unit under the Chief of Staff in the Department of Peacekeeping Operation. While the information certainly exists, the ease of access and knowledge about how to find and use it is less well developed but there has been continuous investment in building "best-practice" capacity, including dedicated Best Practice Officers within missions.

In addition, the dedicated division for policy evaluation and training in DPKO has the objective of developing guidance based on best practice and lessons learned to support field operations. In the Department of Political Affairs, a Policy and Mediation Division was established in 2008, which includes a small analytical policy support unit that also has some analytical capacity to support both missions but also reporting to the Security Council, PBC and General Assembly. Specifically to provide information to inform decision making in the Council, the Security Council Affairs Division (part of the Department of Political Affairs) has a dedicated research capacity that, among other things, manages a database of mandated activities and looks at trends in the kinds of tasks the UN is being required to undertake, which is available to Council members to help inform their decision making regarding precedent and practice.

Not all of these programmes and initiatives are properly coordinated and their effectiveness frequently depends on key individual staff. They also require considerable resources and are, therefore consequently, limited in the support they can provide across the loose confederated "UN system". In addition, the information that exists is rather piecemeal and hard to find unless you know exactly what you are looking for. Complicating this further, as Marrack Goulding observed in 1997, is the fact that UN agencies still, though unsurprisingly, feel "inhibited by the knowledge that many Member States, often including their host countries, consider that the reporting of political information would exceed their mandates".[40] That said, there is a high level commitment to making data more coherent and accessible. For example, financial information, including status of reimbursement to troops, is now provided through a secure website to member states. Much of this has been enabled by advances in technology including in the field, where military staff officers have used Google Earth to coordinate movement of personnel and logistics in support of elections.[41]

However, given the political nature of decision making at the strategic level – the inevitable political compromises referred to in the first section of this chapter – there is a limit to how much independent analytical capacity the UN Secretariat can have. Seconded military staff – whether at headquarters or in the field – are informed by the interests and priorities of their own state. Even with all possible data and top-flight analytical capacity there are limits to how it can be used to inform what the UN is actually allowed to do – limits that are not only political but also increasingly financial. For all these reasons, notwithstanding progress in some areas, the capacity of the UN to collect and analyse information continues to exist, and indeed to a degree is doomed to exist, in a "partial and fragmented form".[42]

Conclusion

The active involvement of the UN in support of exogenous statebuilding in the period since the end of the Cold War – in terms of sponsoring and helping to negotiate peace accords as well as in lending and orchestrating practical assistance with the establishment of governmental institutions – is unprecedented in the history of international organisation. This is true not only with regard to the overall level of resources devoted to the task but also, in many cases, to the sheer scope and intrusiveness of UN activities, from the building of law and order institutions and the restructuring of a country's armed forces to the establishment of institutions and the promulgation of laws and regulations designed to secure economic growth and prosperity in the long run.

At the same, however, and as this chapter has sought to argue, the inter-governmental and functionally fragmented character of the UN have meant that its statebuilding efforts have often been reactive, suffering from a lack of strategic focus and beholden to the agendas, priorities and interests of other statebuilding actors working alongside it, be they those of semi-autonomous agencies within the "UN system" itself, regional organisations or Great Powers. Added to this, member states' continuing concern about sovereignty, manifested *inter alia* in a preference for engaging with "state-like structures" in the field and a tendency to focus on procedure over substance in New York, acts as a further constraint on UN action. Nor has the quality of UN involvement been helped by shortcomings in analytical capacity.

None of this, of course, is to suggest that UN activities have not left an imprint, including of a positive kind, on the societies where statebuilding ac-tivities have taken place. The overall record of achievement, however, remains patchy and uneven. In particular, and for reasons explored above, UN efforts have rarely succeeded in effecting lasting transformations of the underlying political economy of post-war societies.

Appendix: UN missions with a statebuilding mandate, April 1989 to August 2011

This is a chronological list of all UN operations that have had statebuilding efforts as part of their mandate. Statebuilding mandates include assistance with the building of capacity of state institutions (both administrative and security institutions), and/or provide support for the implementation of a political settlement (including the organisation and/or monitoring of elec-tions). Most of these operations are UN peacekeeping operations, while some, listed in italics, are political missions. The description of their man-dates in the table only includes the statebuilding elements of their mandate, not other functions of the particular mission.

Table 8.1 UN missions with a statebuilding mandate, April 1989 to August 2011

Name of the mission	Location	Duration	Statebuilding mandate
UN Transition Assistance Group (UNTAG)	Namibia	April 1989 to March 1990	Support the organisation of free and fair elections and the transition to independence.
UN Observer Mission in El Salvador	El Salvador	July 1991 to April 1995	Verify the implementation of the peace agreement and associated institutional reforms between the government of El Salvador and the *Frente Farabundo Marti parala Liberacion Nacional.*
UN Mission for the Referendum in Western Sahara (MINURSO)	Western Sahara	April 1991–	Monitor ceasefire between the Moroccan government and the Polisario Front, and organise a referendum on independence of Western Sahara. No referendum has been organised to date.
UN Transitional Administration in Cambodia (UNTAC)	Cambodia	February 1992 to September 1993	Assist with the implementation of the Paris Peace Accords, in particular the organisation of elections, civil administration and the maintenance of law and order.
UN Operation in Mozambique (ONUMOZ)	Mozambique	December 1992 to December 1994	Support the implementation of the peace agreement, monitor withdrawal of foreign forces, disarmament and monitoring of elections.
UN Operation in Somalia II (UNOSOM II)	Somalia	March 1993 to March 1995	Mandated to assist with the rehabilitation of Somalia's political institution and its economy to promote reconciliation and a political settlement.
UN Mission in Haiti (UNMIH)	Haiti	September 1993 to June 1996	Support implementation of the Governor's Island Peace Agreement, assist with reform of armed forces and establishment of new police force. Mandate later revised to support democratic institutions, reform of the police and military, and support holding of free elections.

continued

Table 8.1 Continued

Name of the mission	Location	Duration	Statebuilding mandate
UN Mission of Observers in Tajikistan (UNMOT)	Tajikistan	December 1994 to May 2000	Support the implementation of the 1997 peace agreement.
UN Angola Verification Mission III	Angola	February 1995 to June 1997	Mandated to support the implementation of the peace agreement. Failed as UNITA returned to war until it was defeated in 2002.
UN Mission in Bosnia and Herzegovina (UNMIBH)	Bosnia and Herzegovina	December 1995 to December 2002	Mandated to monitor, train and assist Bosnian police force.
UN Transitional Administration for Eastern Slavonia, Baranja and Western Sirmium (UNTAES)	Croatia	January 1996 to January 1998	Transitional administration of Eastern Slavonia and management of return of administered territories to Croatia.
UN Support Mission in Haiti (UNSMIH)	Haiti	July 1996 to July 1997	Assist Haitian government with the professionalisation and training of the police, promote institution building, reconciliation and economic development.
UN Transition Mission in Haiti (UNTMIH)	Haiti	August to November 1997	Mandated to provide further support for training and professionalisation of the police.
UN Mission in the Central African Republic (MINURCA)	Central African Republic	April 1998 to February 2000	Maintenance of security, training of the police, assistance with elections.
UN Peacebuilding Support Office in Guinea Bissau (UNOGBIS)	Guinea Bissau	April 1999 to December 2009	Mandated from 2009 to strengthen the capacity of governmental institutions, and to support implementation of security sector reform
UN Interim Administration Mission in Kosovo (UNMIK)	Kosovo	June 1999–	Provision of interim administration of Kosovo after the 1999 NATO war against Yugoslavia, to build institutions of self-governance and to work towards a resolution of the territory's disputed status. The UN failed to resolve the status question and Kosovo declared independence unilaterally in February 2008. Opposition from Russia and China in particular has prevented the closure of the mission.

Mission	Location	Dates	Mandate
UN Mission in Sierra Leone (UNAMSIL)	Sierra Leone	October 1999 to December 2005	Assist with the implementation of the Lome Peace Accords, and assist the government to expand its authority across the country.
UN Transitional Administration in East Timor (UNTAET)	East Timor	October 1999 to February 2002	Provide interim transitional administration and build institutions of self-governance to assist with transition to independence endorsed in a referendum in September 1999.
UN Organisation Mission in the Congo (MONUC)	Democratic Republic of the Congo (DRC)	November 1999 to June 2010	From 2004, MONUC was mandated, *inter alia*, to support the transitional government, the drafting of the constitution, the electoral process, and the passing and security sector reform.
UN Assistance Mission in Afghanistan (UNAMA)	Afghanistan	March 2002–	Mandated to support the implementation of the Bonn Peace Agreement. Mandate extended to support strengthening of government's capacity in key areas such as governance and security.
UN Mission in Support of East Timor (UNMISET)	East Timor	May 2002 to May 2005	Succeeded UNTAET, and continued assistance to the Timorese government.
UN Mission in Liberia (UNMIL)	Liberia	September 2003–	Mandated to support the reform of the police force and the formation of a restructured military; and to assist the strengthening of governance institutions and the electoral process.
UN Operation in Côte d'Ivoire (UNOCI)	Côte d'Ivoire	February 2004	Assist with the restructuring of armed forces, assist with re-establishment of governmental authority throughout the country and support electoral process.

continued

Table 8.1 Continued

Name of the mission	Location	Duration	Statebuilding mandate
UN Stabilisation Mission in Haiti (MINUSTAH)	Haiti	June 2004–	Mandated to restructure and reform the Haitian police, support constitutional and political process, and support organisation of elections. After the January 2010 earthquake, it was further mandated to support capacity building of rule of law institutions, and support the implementation of the government's resettlement strategy.
UN Operation in Burundi (ONUB)	Burundi	June 2004 to December 2006	Support organisation of elections, assist the transitional government and the Burundian authorities with their institution-building efforts.
UN Mission in Sudan (UNMIS)	Sudan	March 2005 to July 2011	Support the implementation of the comprehensive peace agreement, which culminated in a referendum on independence of South Sudan in February 2011.
UN Office in Timor Leste (UNOTIL)	East Timor	May 2005 to August 2006	Support capacity building of key government institutions.
UN Integrated Office in Sierra Leone (UNIOSIL)	Sierra Leone	January 2006 to August 2008	Support to strengthen governance and government capacity.
UN Integrated Mission in East Timor (UNMIT)	East Timor	August 2006–	Mandated to support and strengthen institutions of government, assist with reform and strengthening of the capacity of the police, and to assist with organisation of elections.
UN Integrated Office in Burundi (BINUB)	Burundi	January 2007–	Strengthen the capacity of governmental institutions and strengthen good governance.
UN Integrated Peacebuilding Office in Sierra Leone (UNIPSIL)	Sierra Leone	August 2008–	Strengthening good governance; assisting with the constitutional review.

UN Integrated Peacebuilding Office in Guinea-Bissau (UNIOGBIS)	Guinea-Bissau	January 2010–	Provide support for the work of the UN Peacebuilding Commission in the country, support strengthening of government institutions, support national reconciliation.
UN Organisation Stabilisation Mission in the Democratic Republic of the Congo (MONUSCO)	Democratic Republic of the Congo	July 2010–	Support for strengthening and reform of security and judicial institutions, support for strengthening and reform of military capacity, support for police reform and support to strengthen administrative institutions of the Congolese state.
UN Mission in the Republic of South Sudan (UNMISS)	South Sudan	July 2011–	Mandated to advise, and support to the government on political transition, governance and establishment of state authority, including formulation of national policies; support strengthening and reform of security sector.

Sources: UN website; Centre for International Cooperation, *Review of Political Missions 2010* (New York: Centre for International Cooperation, 2010).

Notes

1 Report of the Secretary-General on Improving the Capacity of the United Nations for Peacekeeping, 1994 UN Doc. A/48/403-S26450, 14 March 1994, para. 12.
2 Civilian Capacity in the Aftermath of Conflict: Independent Report of the Senior Advisory Group, UN Doc. A/65/747-S/2011/85, August 2011, para. 1.
3 Established in 1964 at the first session of the UN Conference on Trade and Development (UNCTAD) to promote the interests and coordinate the negotiating positions of developing countries, the Group of 77 now consists of 131 members. The NAM, whose first summit meeting was held in Belgrade in 1961, now includes 118 members, though it has neither a formal constitution, nor a permanent secretariat.
4 As Aswini Ray put it with respect to India, it still "shares with many of the less advantaged states of the post-colonial world a paranoid infatuation with the principle of national sovereignty" (Ray 2011: 105).
5 UN Charter, Article 2(7).
6 See Appendix to this chapter, which lists 34 UN missions with a "statebuilding mandate", defined for the purpose of analysis as assistance with the building of state institutions and/or support for the implementation of a political settlement.
7 The role of Brazil in the UN Stabilisation Mission in Haiti (MINUSTHA) established in 2004 is a case in point.
8 UN Peacekeeping fact sheet as of 31 October 2011: see www.un.org/en/peace-keeping/resources/statistics/factsheet.shtml.
9 For a typically incisive analysis highlighting and stressing the importance of the distinction, see Claude 1996.
10 The "UN system" as whole employs about 75,000 staff. Of these, 43,000 are employed in the Secretariat proper including around 23,000 in UN field operations (comprising, according to Article 97 of the Charter, "a Secretary-General and such staff as the organisation may require") at headquarters and duty stations around the world. See the Report of the Secretary-General on the Composition of the Secretariat: staff demographics (UN Doc. A/66/347), 8 September 2011.
11 David Keen and Adekeye Adebajo's verdict on Lomé, while accepting that few alternatives existed once ECOMOG and the UN members states declined to support a more ambitious and credible concept, is particularly scathing: the accord was "basically an effort to appease local warlords by giving them political power in exchange for military peace. [It] was an open invitation for warlords to enjoy the spoils of office in a jumble sale of the national wars" (Keen and Adebajo 2007: 257).
12 Agreement on a Comprehensive Political Settlement of the Cambodia Conflict, 23 October 1991.
13 "Delivering as One – Report of the Secretary-General's High Level Panel on UN System-wide Coherence", 9 November 2006, para. 10.
14 Report of the Secretary-General on Afghanistan, UN Doc. A/65/873-S/2011/381, 23 June 2011.
15 Goulding 1997, pp. 50 and 67–70.
16 See also Berdal 2008.
17 For a recent and illuminating series of essays that focus on the importance of informal networks of power and influence, see Utas 2012.
18 The classic treatment of the UN's role in this regard was set out and analysed in Claude 1966.
19 For an illuminating discussion of statebuilding and legitimacy, drawing conceptually useful distinctions between various dimensions of legitimacy and its sources, see Zaum 2011.
20 SC Res. 1244, 10 June 1999.
21 Goulding 1997, pp. 76–78

22 Thus, for example, while the quickest and most efficient way for the UN to build corrections facilities in a post-conflict situation might be a single-source contract with a big multinational company, the financial rules and regulations demand an inclusive procurement process and special consideration to vendors from developing countries. See UN Procurement Manual, www.un.org/depts/ptd/pdf/pmrev6.pdf.

23 Report of the Joint Inspection Unit on Staffing of the United Nations Peacekeeping and Related Missions (Civilian Component), JIU/REP/93/6: 1993.

24 UN Peacekeeping fact sheet as of 31 October 2011: see www.un.org/en/peacekeeping/resources/statistics/factsheet.shtml.

25 In a revealing passage from his UN memoires, Chinmaya Gharekhan, one-time permanent representative of India to the UN in New York and later special adviser to then Secretary-General Boutros Boutros-Ghali, refers critically to this use of gratis military personnel, "nearly all of them", he stresses, "from Western countries". It was part, he maintains, of "a pernicious practice developed in the 1990s when the peacekeeping operations expanded exponentially. The affluent countries took over the Organisation". Gharekhan 2006: 33–34.

26 There has been a greater professionalisation of peacekeeping/peacebuilding and a more standardised approach to training and recruitment. There has also been an overall decline in vacancy rates although this varies a great deal from one mission to the next and within particular occupational groups (some missions always struggle with retention and vacancies for senior financial staff are always high).

27 Report of the Senior Advisory Group on Civilian Capacity.

28 "Burundi Protesters attack UN Staff Car", *Agence France-Press*, 26 March 2008.

29 "As UN Quietly re-starts Military Help in Congo, says not with Zimulinda", *Innercity Press*, 4 March 2010 (www.innercitypress.com/drc1leo030410.html).

30 GA Res. 65/289 of 30 June 2011, para. 73.

31 See www.unjiu.org/data/reports/1993/EN93-06.PDF.

32 The most expensive UN mission is the hybrid mission in Darfur with the African Union (UNAMID). UNAMID's budget for the fiscal year 2011–12 is just under $1.7 billion. Although not statebuilding in the conventional sense, part of the high cost of the mission comes from the need for the mission to construct significant new facilities and infrastructure just to ensure that the mission itself can operate.

33 SC Res. 1959 of 16 December 2010.

34 See for example the discussion of UNIPSIL in UN Doc. A/65/328/Add.3, 11 October 2010, para. 124.

35 GA Res. 63/263 of 24 December 2008.

36 GA Res. 59/286.Add.1 of 27 May 2005.

37 Ibid.

38 Report of the Secretary-General on strengthening the capacity of the United Nations to manage and sustain peacekeeping operations, UN Doc. A/65/624 of 13 December 2010, para. 38.

39 In some cases, notably where a mission has been able to recruit analytical expertise from the research community, the quality of analysis has been very good. An example of this is the work of MONUC's Joint Mission Analysis Cell under its Chief Johan Peleman in the DRC.

40 Goulding 1997: 14.

41 During the elections in Liberia in October to November 2011, UNMIL used real time geographic information via Google Earth to plan movements.

42 Goulding 1997: 13.

9   The IFIs and post-conflict political economy

Susan L. Woodward

The leading international financial institutions (IFIs) – the International Monetary Fund (IMF) and the World Bank – are prohibited by their Articles of Agreement from any policies or actions that would 'interfere in the political affairs of any member'.[1] Paragraph 10 of the Bank Articles specifies further, 'Only economic considerations shall be relevant to their decisions, and these considerations shall be weighted impartially.' Yet reforms of the political system, laws, and administrative practices of a state have been central to the conditions for membership, credits, and loans of both organizations since the 1970s, and the international focus on statebuilding in countries emerging from war can be said to have first begun with their policies for what the Bank began in 1995–96 to call 'post-conflict reconstruction'.

The effects of these policies in post-conflict conditions have been the subject of a substantial research literature, which argues primarily that the policies work at cross purposes to the political goals of international missions sent to implement peace agreements and have outcomes that undermine the bases of a lasting peace. Their role in peacebuilding operations, however, has only grown since the first field-defining analysis, by Álvaro de Soto and Graciana del Castillo on the case of El Salvador, published in 1994. That same year the World Bank was planning an entire post-conflict recovery and reconstruction programme for Bosnia-Herzegovina, agreeing to administer the multi-donor Johan Jørgen Holst Fund for Start-up and Recurrent Costs created in 1994 for the Palestinian authorities after the Oslo Accord, becoming involved directly in peace negotiations to end the war in Bosnia, in November 1995, and in 1996 in Guatemala, and taking the lead in convening donors' conferences to finance post-war reconstruction everywhere.

Now all donor assistance and credits to countries emerging from war are conditioned on a prior negotiated agreement with the IMF on the country's foreign debt and, since 1999, on the formulation of a Poverty Reduction Strategy Paper (PRSP)[2] that the IMF and the Bank must approve. By the early twenty-first century, the United Nations Development Programme (UNDP) was implementing World Bank policies in the interim after war until IMF membership (and thus World Bank lending) had been reestablished or secured. By September 2005, the two had formed a joint project 'to continue their collaboration in the future development of a conceptual and policy-relevant framework for supporting state-building in crisis and post-conflict contexts'[3] while the heads of the United Nations Department of Peacekeeping Operations (DPKO) and the World Bank were in direct consultations over coordination because IFI influence over peacebuilding outcomes had become so large.[4] A task force on fragile and conflict-affected states chaired jointly by the World Bank and the OECD Development Assistance Committee (DAC), representing most development donors, began in 2005 to work out common frameworks, principles, and aid policies and to promote Bank-donor coordination within conflict countries. By 2009–10, the UN Peacebuilding Commission, Peacebuilding Support Office, and Security Council had identified the IFIs as the key partners in peacebuilding and were seeking multiple ways to institutionalize this partnership.

While the contest between IFI[5] policies and peace continues to inform researchers, if not policy debates, our knowledge of their actual influence on countries' post-war power structures is still sketchy and scattered.[6] Because the newest research demonstrates that the outcomes of IFI policies depend on domestic politics and policy choices (Hartzell and Hoddie 2010; Kang 1999; Nooruddin and Simmons 2006), and certainly the political economy of countries emerging from wartime varies substantially, we can expect that impact to vary as well and in complex and contingent ways. The preponderance of single case studies in the literature on post-conflict interventions, however, makes identifying patterns of variation difficult. An even greater obstacle lies in the lack of transparency in the IFI's standard operating procedures, insisting on confidential, behind-closed-doors negotiation on loan packages and conditions, the terms of which are never made public, particularly by the IMF, but also on how lending decisions are made at the World Bank. Nor do either the Fund or Bank even collect information on the impact of their policies and projects that others could then analyse (e.g. Barron 2010: 29).

Nonetheless, the very purpose of the Bretton Woods institutions since their origins in 1945 – to protect the stability of the international monetary and financial system – and their simultaneous imperative to ensure their very survival as financial institutions together generate a common approach in two aspects: the conception of the state that underlies their lending decisions, and the ways the two interact with borrowing countries, their operative policies, and modalities. While both argue that countries in conflict and emerging from conflict have special characteristics that require flexibility and adaptability, their repeated warnings of the danger of moral hazard when presented with requests or pressures to deviate from a standard script of recommended policies and required conditions for loans make very clear their priorities – their institutional purpose and survival. Their policies are not designed for the particular needs and conditions of countries emerging from war. The importance of empirical research on their influence on countries' post-war distribution of power, moreover, is magnified by the role they play in setting the framework of economic possibilities and constraints within which all bilateral, regional, and international actors which declare state-building essential to a sustainable peace agree to operate. In its near absence, this chapter will lay out its parameters – the IFIs' approach to statebuilding and the modalities of its translation in practice – and suggest what such research might demonstrate based on the case-study evidence we do have.

The approach to statebuilding of the IMF and World Bank

Although the term statebuilding is not used until 2002, it begins with the World Bank in 1991 – and unrelated to conflict. Called 'good governance', as a compromise with Bank lawyers who interpreted the term 'democracy' in the 1989 report on Africa as appearing to cross the political line prohibited in its Articles of Agreement, the shift in focus was a continuation of efforts of the IMF and the Bank to resolve the debt crisis of 1979–81. The debt resched-ulings and 'adjustment' approach in the 1980s had actually only worsened the debt problem,[7] but in searching for a new approach, it remained crucial to continue to treat the 'primary cause' of the debt crisis, despite massive evidence to the contrary, as 'internal rather than external to each country' (Woods 2006: 143). As Gordon Crawford (2006: 117–118) writes,

> in the context of poor results from structural adjustment programmes in Africa ... in the 1980s ... it was inconceivable that the set of policy pre-scriptions were wrong, therefore it had to be their *implementation* that was at fault.... Therefore, whereas implementation had previously been regarded as simply a matter of political will (for instance, in the Berg Report), attention now shifted [in 1989] to the nature of government ... to ensure that economic adjustment programmes were fully imple-mented, with reduced 'slippag,' it was necessary that the state acted in a more predictable, rule-based and transparent manner.

By the mid-1990s, as Ngaire Woods writes, 'it was clear that the financial cred-ibility of the IMF and the World Bank could be threatened by members' failure to repay' (Woods 2006: 165). The problem of debt arrears, according to a staff analysis at the World Bank, was most acute in a sub-category of countries – a majority of the most indebted; in fact, those affected by violent conflict. By the fall of 1995, the new Bank president arriving that January, James Wolfensohn, had appointed a 'Task Force on Failed States' to make recommendations for a new operational policy for 'post-conflict reconstruc-tion', on the argument that Bank lending to such countries (18 were identi-fied in the 1998 Operations Evaluation Division [OED] study to follow up on the Task Force recommendations) should no longer be ad hoc and based, as then practised, on the need for emergency funding for 'reconstruction after natural disasters'.[8] Instead, Bank policy should recognize the systematic and distinct problems of 'societies rebuilding after conflict'. As the Bank's Committee on Development Effectiveness wrote in response to the 1997 OED study recommendations, the key condition of those distinct problems confronting Bank policy was 'the often weak government capacity in post-conflict countries' (World Bank 1998: 95). With far less fanfare, the IMF also began at the same time to distinguish the financing needs of post-conflict countries from its general emergency assistance portfolio.

This decision at both IFIs to distinguish and develop separate policies for post-conflict countries did not include a change in either goal or approach. The purpose remained finding a solution to the debt crisis, not to conflict or post-conflict, and as Gordon Crawford writes, the policy package of liberalization, privatization, and priority on macroeconomic stabilization (what John Williamson labelled the 'Washington Consensus' in 1991) remained the same as well. Rather, the change was operational, above all to allow staff greater flexibility and speed in reacting to the needs of assistance and thus greater involvement through decentralized operations to the field where staff could be more 'hands-on' with local authorities. Yet the fact that these countries were characterized as lacking the conditions seen by 1989–91 to be necessary for adopting and successfully implementing these policies, the IFIs' particular conception of 'effective state institutions' and 'good governance', gave at least implicit permission to these field staff to become involved in statebuilding as well.

The public shift by the IFIs to the characteristics of governance in indebted countries, most visible in the topic chosen for the 1997 World Development Report (WDR themes are usually chosen two years in advance), *The State in a Changing World*, generated a scholars' debate about whether this reflected a profound change in the IFIs' neoliberal campaign against the state since the 1978 election of Margaret Thatcher in the UK and of Ronald Reagan in the US in 1980 and, perhaps, even an admission that they had gone too far with their concept of a minimal state. Reinforcing that assessment, research within the Bank in the mid-1990s by David Dollar and Craig Burnside focused on demonstrating that government and government policy (together labelled 'institutions') were decisive in explaining variations in economic growth (a large critical literature since then demonstrates otherwise, however),[9] and, in 1996, Bank researchers Daniel Kaufmann and Aart Kraay began to develop indicators to measure 'good governance' standards, which they called the World Wide Governance Indicators (WGI),[10] combining voice and accountability, rule of law, regulatory quality, political stability, control of corruption, and government effectiveness. The last is based on the country policy and institutional assessment (CPIA), an in-house staff measure for lending decisions that only became public in 2005 under prolonged external pressure for transparency, at which time it was said to 'assess the quality of a country's present policy and institutional framework … [for] fostering poverty reduction, sustainable growth and the effective use of development assistance'. That framework singles out property rights and rule-based governance, quality of budgetary and financial management, efficiency of revenue mobilization, and quality of public administration (Knack 2002). On closer examination of these criteria of 'good governance', however, as Anne Orford and Jennifer Beard (1998) argue, this public focus on the state did not reflect any substantive change in their normative model of the state since that global political shift to neoliberal growth theory in 1979–81. As Marcelo Selowsky, chief economist for Europe and Central Asia at the Bank, retorted against critics in 1998, 'we did not neglect institutional development'.

This model of the state in all IFI policies, regardless of country context, is that which is considered necessary for markets and the private sector to function, and no more. In the 1997 Report, this model is functional – five 'core activities' or 'fundamental tasks' necessary for markets to work: (1) establish a foundation of law, providing security for business and above all protecting property rights; (2) maintain a 'nondistortionary' economic policy that fosters macroeconomic stability; (3) provide basic services and infrastructure while privatizing as much of public utilities and state enterprises as possible; (4) protect the most vulnerable citizens, while utilizing 'business, labor, households, and community [NGO] groups' for most social services so as to reduce costs; and (5) protect the natural environment through 'flexible incentives and meaningful regulatory frameworks' (1997: 5). The overall goal of this functional list is to 'narrow the growing gap between the demands on states and their capability to meet those demands' (ibid.). More conceptually, the state should be 'agencies of restraint', that is, make credible a government's continuing commitment to economic (neoliberal) reform (such as by independent central banks and membership in regional trade pacts), deter or punish public corruption (police and criminal courts), and enforce commercial contracts (the civil legal system and audit professionals) (Collier 1996: 282–283). In other words, their understanding of the state was one that, in theory at least, would achieve the policies they considered necessary to protect the stability of the international monetary and financial system, namely, for the IMF, to restore liquidity to a country's balance of payments and to service their debt, and for the World Bank, to support a neoliberal, open economy approach to economic growth.

Although their economic theory of the state remained consistent as did their explanation, that the goal was a more 'realistic' state by narrowing expectations and scope, the operational effect was the opposite: an increasing willingness to 'restructure' a borrowing country's state institutions and a list of relevant aspects that became over the subsequent 15 years ever more extensive and wide-ranging, from public sector financial institutions and private sector (commercial) banking systems to the 'rule-of-law', civil service, and local (community) assemblies. Merilee Grindle's plea for a 'more realistic goal' of 'good enough governance' was based on her count of the 'characteristics of good governance and the institutions, laws, policies, services, and strategies that are needed to achieve it' for all developing countries in the *World Development Reports* from 1997 to 2002/03 (Grindle 2004). The list in the 1997 report covers 45 items; by 2002, it reached 116. The list and scope of intervention is far greater in those countries considered most in need of reform, those emerging from war. The ability to finance these reforms has also increased over time as both institutions have responded to criticisms of the consequences, not by changing the substance of these 'good governance' and economic policies but by adding and refining the financial facilities designed for these countries, for example, the IMF's Enhanced Structural Adjustment Facility (renamed the Poverty Reduction and Growth Facility [PRGF] in 1999) that increased the concessional component and the length of time allowed for adjustment.[11]

Although such 'economic reform', as it is generally labelled, might be applicable to some countries emerging from war, the rhetoric of statebuilding and the aspirations recorded in IFI documents tend more often to connote starting from scratch: that the ground is a *tabula rasa* and that such market- and private-sector-friendly governments need to be created, not only reformed. Moreover, unlike the usual bargaining between a country and the IMF over an agreement for settling its debt arrears and renewed lending, negotiations over the terms of IMF membership itself (with all its vital consequences) are not constrained by the principles of member consent in its Articles of Agreement. Nor do most countries in these conditions have much or any of the bargaining leverage shown to be influential on the terms agreed in normal negotiations (Kang 1999; Brown 2009). Indeed, as Boon shows, the legal basis of engagement by both the IMF and the World Bank prior to membership has become a Chapter VII mandate (a threat to regional or international peace and security) by the UN Security Council. The 'Security Council has become an institutional enabler' for the growing role of the IFIs in constructing the post-war state which 'can border on the legislative' (Boon 2007: 515). Post-war environments, according to official Bank documents and speeches, are viewed as rare and golden opportunities for their aid and advice to win wholesale political and economic (and thus also social) transformation.

Policies and 'modalities'

The influence of this IFI approach to statebuilding on the political economy of post-war societies actually occurs through a vast array of specific policies and instruments of advice, assistance, and requirements, on the one hand, and the extent to which (and ways) local authorities actually adopt and implement these policies, on the other.

From the side of the IFIs, these policies and assistance fall roughly into three types and stages of post-war transition:

- institutional design of the post-war state negotiated in the peace agreement;
- design of a financial and economic framework for the new country through a post-war recovery and reconstruction strategy and a national development strategy;
- ongoing institution-building through drafting legislation, advising national and international actors on the choice of policies and institutions, and influencing the appointment of key government actors.

Explicit influence can be said to begin during peace negotiations ever since the World Bank decided in the case of the November 1995 Dayton negotiations for Bosnia-Herzegovina and the UN phase of negotiations in 1996 in Guatemala that they should be present to advise parties on the fiscal implications of their design for a post-war government. Although their stated goal is to prevent fiscally irresponsible and unsustainable institutions, the opportunity to press for institutional choices they favour, such as decentralization and a currency board for its central bank in the case of Bosnia or tax reform in Guatemala, is great. As third-party negotiators tend to defer to the presumed expertise of IFI representatives and such outside mediators have become increasingly defining and intrusive in general, this influence has also increased, but we have little evidence about the content of these negotiations or of warring parties' preferences or disagreements on these issues.

The role of the IFIs in post-war state formation and political economy is even more assertive in the first years after a signed peace agreement, but the methods are more conventional and autonomous, providing financial and technical assistance in support of the institutional and policy choices they approve. Because the IFIs require a Security Council mandate to request their assistance to countries that do not yet meet their conditions of membership, the political framework of that mandate has some influence on their activities, but they in turn set the financial and economic framework for the country and its bilateral donors. This occurs in many ways.

Close on the heels of a peace agreement, the IMF begins the process of obtaining agreement on the terms for settling the country's debt arrears. This process is increasingly institutionalized as a result of the Heavily Indebted Poor Countries (HIPC) Initiative, launched in 1996 and enhanced in 1999 (Woods 2006: 166–175). Unless an interested donor provides finance to reduce the proportion of new loans that go to settle past debts and allow looser fiscal policy in the agreed deficit targets, such as the role played by the Netherlands for Bosnia-Herzegovina, or to persuade creditors even to cancel a large portion or all of a country's debts, as the United States did for Iraq in 2003, these negotiations may take two years or more, as in the successful case of Liberia. Taking office in January 2006, the first post-war president and her finance minister reached the 'decision point' of an enhanced HIPC qualifying it for debt relief in March 2008 and were nearing the HIPC 'completion point' when Liberia could begin borrowing in late January 2010. In addition to the specific terms of the IMF agreement, that agreement in turn establishes a framework within which donors and other banks choose, in practice, to work. This establishes a 'culture of conditionality' that early on sets the degree of flexibility and long-term prospects for funding the peace in that country – even though, as Alvarez-Plata and Brück (2007: 267) demonstrate, current debt relief strategies 'fail to take account of the special circumstances of post-conflict economies'.[12] Even when they do not agree with the IMF's terms, as records show, for example, in Mozambique, the World Bank, active regional banks such as the European, Asian, African, and Inter-American Development Banks, and the bilateral donors even accept the specifics, such as targets on wage and price inflation, credit, and the budget deficit that limit monetary and fiscal policy, as unchallengeable constraints.

A country's economic and financial framework is also defined by the national development strategy – its PRSP – it must write according to World Bank guidelines (*Source Book for Poverty Reduction Strategies*) and technical advisers, and approved by the Bank and the IMF, as a precondition since 1999 for all recipients of debt relief (HIPC) or concessional loans (IDA and PRGF). Beginning with an interim PRSP in conflict-affected countries, this strategy paper is supposed to be the product of wide consultation (often called 'participation') with donors, international organizations, civil society groups, and NGOs. Donors agree to 'align' their assistance with it as well, according to the 2005 Paris Declaration on Aid Effectiveness of the OECD DAC. Until the PRSP is ready, the Bank will have prepared a Transitional Support Strategy 'as soon as a resolution is in sight' (World Bank 1998: 6), followed by a needs assessment mission – now commonly done jointly (a joint assessment mission, or JAM) with UNDP and occasionally others – to establish the basis for a Country Assistance Strategy and a multi-donor programme of post-war assistance.

Third, the World Bank always takes the lead in designing this programme, which it labels 'reconstruction', and then in convening the first of many donors' conferences to obtain pledges of financial support to it. Donors defer to Bank leadership because of its very size, sheer technical capacity, experience, and, for some such as the US and UK, its ability to use policy conditionality, its status as a bank that, therefore, does not operate on budgetary assessments, and its special lending instrument for the poorest countries, its IDA window. The Bank becomes the lead economic agency in the field as well, responsible usually for donor coordination because of its size, economic weight, and US preference, and also for managing the primary trust fund for budgetary support and recurrent costs of the post-war government, a tool first used in Palestine but regularly practised once the need for such support (e.g. to pay civil servants' salaries in the first post-war years) gained acceptance with the Kosovo mission in 1999.[13] Typically the reconstruction programme will contain two types of projects, both designed by Bank staff – large physical infrastructure, which usually comprises at least 60 per cent of the programme,[14] and projects labelled community empowerment (CEP) or 'community driven development' (CDD) which aim to decentralize aid decisions and accountability. First tried in post-conflict countries in 1999 in East Timor, based on a programme in Kecamatan, Indonesia, Bank staff convene assemblies in localities to participate in choosing the priority aid project to be funded for their community.[15]

The primary goal of the IFIs, to create a government suited to the global monetary and trading system, occurs through the third path: ongoing policy advice, technical assistance,[16] actual drafting of laws and regulations, influence over the choice of significant government ministers and staff (especially finance), salaries for expatriate professionals to take up such ministerial positions initially, and conditionality. The IMF, for example, will insist on an independent central bank, write the central bank law, and help to build it, build the finance ministry, choose a country's currency (despite its immense national symbolism), establish a payments system, design the tax system, write legislation for public expenditure management, customs, the commercial banking sector, and commercial policy, and advise on budget preparation. The World Bank will advise on social policy such as health, education, and social assistance; design and manage an anti-corruption programme; insist on land privatization; in some cases, beginning in Uganda in 1994, fund and manage the demobilization, demilitarization, and reintegration programme for ex-combatants; and provide, as in Bosnia-Herzegovina in 1996, a political risk guarantee facility to encourage foreign investors. In East Timor, Boon illustrates, the Bank 'assisted in reforming "laws governing land ownership, conflict resolution, investment, business transactions, and commercial arbitration as well as civil and criminal laws"' (Boon 2007: 528).

To the extent that peacebuilding missions in general follow a universal template of transformation called 'liberal internationalism', as many argue, its core is surely the economic liberalism of the IFIs' policies and approach to governmental institutions and the state to implement them. Assessing the effect of this economic ideology on the post-war political economy and state, as the ongoing debate in that literature on the 'liberal peace' would require, is extremely difficult, however, for at least three reasons. First, the components of statebuilding done by other actors, such as the rule of law and human rights focus of UN peacebuilding missions, the security sector reform conceptualized and promoted by the UK, the militarized concept of stabilization operations by the US and its approach to security and to post-war recovery, and the tendency of diplomats to negotiate peace agreements based on power-sharing constitutional arrangements, are not a product of this economic ideology and are also occurring within the country. How to separate out the effects of IFI policies is not easy, although their tendency to insist on a leading actor role even when they are engaged in forums for coordination and their clear functional differentiation of roles and responsibilities make this more possible than would be the case with some other actors.

Second, in defence against criticism of their universal, ideological template and, especially in the case of the IMF, that its systemic mandate even *requires* it to apply the same standards and conditions so as to protect against moral hazard, both organizations insist that their very methods of operating through country teams and negotiations with governments result in context-specific policies. Yet because the institutional mandate then reinforces their reasons for closed-door negotiations, secrecy, and general lack of transparency, there is little access to the information necessary to assess this claim of context-specificity. Moreover, neither is a unitary actor. Any such assessment thus confronts a two-level game where information about, for example, debates among members of their executive boards on particular cases, debates among staff and the relative weight of different camps in their organization's power structure, such as between the social accountability approach to performance management and measurement of the Bank's

Social Development Group, which emphasizes the impact on specific social groups, and the new public management approach of the more powerful Public Sector Management Group with its emphasis on aggregate efficiency (Radin 2007), and above all, disagreements between headquarters and country representatives in the field, is rarely available.[17]

Third, unlike a UN peacekeeping or peacebuilding mission and perhaps even development donors, the IMF and the World Bank will have been influencing governmental institutions, laws, regulatory frameworks, and policies before the war as well, not only shaping the pre-war political economy and state but contributing, in some cases, to the conflict itself (Andersen 2000; Hartzell and Hoddie 2010; Storey 2001; Williams 2004; Uvin 1998). Although there are exceptions, such as their withdrawal from Cambodia in the 1970s and return only with the peace agreement signed at Paris in 1991, they usually continue to operate during wartime as well, either because their leverage over countries (e.g. by threatening to withhold a loan) is useful for members of their executive boards or because they may be the only source of finance accessible to countries at war. Although all international actors are endogenous to the processes of political-economic and governmental change in post-conflict countries, the IFIs are probably the most endogenous in terms of statebuilding – at least for all those countries with multiple structural adjustment loans and programmes and repeated IMF agreements beginning in the early 1980s.

Consequences

Research on the effect of these IMF and World Bank policies and modalities on the post-war political economy has focused primarily on the harm done to the conditions necessary for a sustainable peace, such as the recessionary effect of the IMF priority on orthodox policies of macroeconomic stability without regard for the political priorities of peacebuilding (del Castillo 2008) or their 'insensitivity to the burden adjustment places on the poor and most vulnerable in society' (Nooruddin and Simmons 2006: 1001) due to imposed cuts in public expenditures and rapid liberalization and privatization in both IMF and World Bank requirements for structural adjustment to repay debt and, ostensibly, generate economic growth. But neither the IMF nor the World Bank seek to build peace. Their goal is to transform the structure of pre-war and wartime economic and political power to create a state that facilitates private-sector, market-led growth, particularly its capacity to service its foreign debt while lowering public expectations to that which a country can afford. Such 'good governance' would include transforming patronage-based and rent-seeking politics into non-corrupt, transparent, and efficient management of public finances. What evidence do we have that these statebuilding and developmental transformations occur?

Three characteristics of this political process make it very difficult to answer that question. First, despite the great variation among countries emerging from war – in the nature of their economies, wartime transformation, relative balance of power and organization among social groups at the time of the peace negotiations, economic and political interests of local actors and their ability to influence the content of IFI policies – the evidence is quite overwhelming of the minimal influence of all post-conflict governments in shaping their own development policies. This is due in part to their perceived dependence on external aid and the gate-keeping role of the IFIs on external financing (the fact that most civil wars occur in poor countries surely reinforces this perception) and in part to the many methods used by the IMF and the World Bank to ensure that their policies are chosen, going so far as to veto alterations proposed by the government and/or civil society organizations for their PRSP. Stewart and Wang (2006) find a remarkable similarity across 30 PRSPs, reflecting Bank preferences despite their ostensible goal of 'poverty reduction' and one's expectation that the causes and manifestation of, and thus solutions to, poverty would vary substantially among countries. Yet more specific aspects of aid negotiations and programmes such as public sector reform, which the World Bank admits it does not do well, or the pace of privatization, as of state enterprises in Kosovo or land in Mozambique, do reveal variation in local capacities for independent negotiation and popular action.[18]

The second characteristic is the non-transparency of these negotiating relationships. Even if there were information, according to the study by Whitfield and colleagues on 11 African countries' relations with donors in general through the 1980s and 1990s, the weak bargaining position of most countries emerging from war in these relations with the IFIs leads, most commonly, to a negotiating strategy of 'non-implementation', by which they gain 'some control over what aspects of the donor-driven agenda get implemented and when' (2009: 21).

Third, the incentive structure for IFI staff, particularly at the World Bank, is based on a 'disbursement culture' (Woods 2006: 39) in which their pay and promotion depend on 'moving the money' (Sogge 2002: 89), not on results. Neither organization collects information on the impact of their policies and projects, while the system of competitive tenders and renewable contracting in the market for aid for implementing international NGOs that implement projects deters honest reporting of project results (Cooley and Ron 2002). Officials within these countries face similar incentives. As Isaline Bergamaschi (2009) shows in her study of the production of a 'PRSP implementation joint-assessment matrix' in Mali, both sides of this negotiating relationship benefit by agreeing to confusing, opaque frameworks that need constant renegotiation. The result, 'an unlikely patchwork of stupid indicators' which are irrelevant, 'difficult to measure or can be formally reached without real policy change', nonetheless 'has a function for the actors involved', she concludes, by creating 'a state of permanent negotiations and re-assessment' that gives the Malian government tactical autonomy, additional labour for civil servants responsible for implementation, and donor retention of 'their discretionary power over disbursement decisions'.

Nonetheless, research does provide striking evidence of a consistent effect of IFI policies and modalities on the post-war state, regardless of the variation one might expect. Everywhere, case studies elaborate in graphic detail, the IMF and World Bank insistence on working with the executive branch, above all the minister of finance, on closed-door negotiations, and on stability of economic over political processes (as one Bank staffer characterized it, 'as long as they are keeping the airport and port open and clear of violence, we are happy') strengthens the domestic political position of the existing authorities and especially the executive branch against parliament and political and civil society. These structures of power tend already to be conservative oligarchies, but if they are not, they will be created by IFI pressure for rapid privatization, which also provides substantial opportunities for corruption alongside the executive-focused aid inflow, and to be neopatrimonial because the required cuts in public expenditures reinforce the political imperatives of clientelistic practices (Curtis 2005, 2007; Harborne personal communication; Kahler 2008: 7; Nakaya 2008; van de Walle 2001).

At the same time, IMF limits on public expenditures force retrenchment in the civil service, even when political commitments made in the peace agreement require its expansion.[19] Bank insistence on a trust fund for donor monies because it does not trust the new government also creates a dual public sector, one local and one managed by the World Bank (Ghani *et al.* 2007; Goodhand and Sedra 2010; Rubin 2005). Its methods of aid disbursement and project implementation also create entirely parallel budgetary and administrative structures, de facto outside the control of government – the Project Implementation Units (PIUs) led by a technocratic World Bank task manager 'sitting atop a massive project infrastructure of project manuals, procurement guidelines, organograms, supervision missions, and Key Performance Indicators' (Moxham 2005: 524), with far better salaries and equipment than local counterparts, and de facto control, therefore, over the country's investment budget as well.

Although the World Bank insists on a participatory process to formulate the PRSP and to allocate aid locally (the CDD approach), their concept of participation in practice is actually exclusionary, corporatist consultation. As Woods demonstrates, 'who participates and why in IMF and World Bank consultations' is 'very selective', privileging some groups over others and even 'excludes or marginalizes existing political institutions such as political parties and parliaments' (2006: 171). Stewart and Wang (2006: 297–300) found substantial variation in the extent of participation – the governments of Uganda, Rwanda, and Viet Nam gaining praise from civil society actors – but everywhere certain 'key categories of participants' were 'consistently' excluded: parliamentarians, trade unions, women, and marginalized groups. The singular focus of the IMF and the Bank on financial management and bias against spending ministries and social policy is an additional mechanism for disempowering parliament and, thus, political parties and the voting public as well.

Locally, the CDD projects directly aim 'to change local power structures', but the result in Timor-Leste, according to Hanjan (2002), was that the village councils under the Community Economic Empowerment and Local Governance Project (CEP) reproduced the existing structure of power and economic and social status. Comparing two Timorese districts, he found that the community that had been fully integrated into modern Indonesian organizational culture and village administration benefited far more than the one where the resistance movement had been strong and only 20 per cent of the population had the administrative experience necessary to implement Bank procedures. There the traditional local authorities also resisted the councils' developmental and participatory principles as 'coercive' and captured the microcredits for their own businesses. Rules on equal representation in village councils, including of women, also resulted in the exclusion of village chiefs and traditional leaders from the councils and thus generated an entirely new source of political conflict after the war (Hohe 2005: 65, 68). In Afghanistan, although 'women's meaningful participation' was stressed in the CDD-based National Solidarity Programme, in 'most of the 9,000' councils formed in 29 villages in five provinces, only the men participated and 'most of the projects are male-selected with little or no input from women' (Zakhilwal and Thomas 2008).

Evidence on the effect of IFI policies on the structure of the economy is also, against expectations, remarkably consistent across countries. The primary effect is to shift the balance in favour of foreign-owned firms and to weaken, if not destroy altogether, local firms because liberalization of the exchange rate together with the huge aid inflow in the first years after war have an inflationary result that pushes up the exchange rate and makes local businesses uncompetitive with foreign companies. Not only local firms but also the small- and medium-enterprise (SME) sector so stressed in Bank rhetoric as a solution to job creation are priced out of the market by unaffordable credit due to the effect on interest rates of orthodox stabilization policies, IMF insistence on an independent central bank prioritizing price stability, and the replacement, required by both institutions, of development banks and public investment with private, commercial banks and foreign investors.

In Uganda, according to the Bank's own internal evaluation, the Bank's insistence on raising tax revenues 'had a chilling effect on private investment, driving economic activity into subsistence' because it ignored the legacy of predatory taxation during the conflict years (World Bank 1998: 34). Participating in the 'pervasive bias against local suppliers' among donors and international organizations (Carnahan *et al.* 2006: 6) are the World Bank trust funds and their decisions on production and contracting, even on items as easily produced locally as school chairs and desks. As Emilia Pires underscores, 'It was galling for the Timorese to learn that many contracts for items their people could have produced were given instead to firms in Indonesia' (Pires and Francino 2007: 152, n.21). The IFI policy emphasis, in loans and the PRSP, on the country's long-term ability to service its foreign debt also focuses on export-oriented production over domestic production, including special incentives, privileges, and risk facilities for foreign investors. Particularly at risk from IFI policies is the agricultural sector; even where countries before and during the war were self-sufficient in food, cheaper imported foodstuffs destroy that capacity, as the case of Haiti demonstrates so dramatically.

The Bank solution to post-war livelihoods is decentralization and participation (often called democratization) – the CDD approach. Anecdotal evidence from Afghanistan of their positive effects on local perceptions of improved security[20] and results from a randomized field experiment of such projects in Liberia that they strongly increased communities' ability to act collectively and trust in community leaders (Fearon *et al.* 2009: 32–34) contrast sharply with their uniformly negligible or negative economic outcomes.[21] In Liberia, there was some improved access to education, but not to any other public goods such as water or health, and no improvement at all in household livelihoods, employment, or asset holdings. In Afghanistan, one village replaced the village well, the centre of women's socializing, with individual household wells, and another village chose to build a road so they could transport their perishable goods to market, only to find that no one was building any of the necessary connecting roads (Zakhilwal and Thomas 2008). In Timor-Leste, 54 per cent of the funding for the Bank's CEP project went to microcredit loans for kiosks to be run by older women, and the resulting oversupply, particularly in the context of sky-rocketing prices for wholesale goods due to the inflationary pressures of international assistance,[22] had the consequence, according to a World Bank researcher, that 70 per cent of those widows 'wouldn't make enough money to pay back the original loan' (Moxham 2005: 522–523). Although the Timorese village councils chose education and health 'as the top priorities during broad community consultations' in the CEP, moreover, the remaining 46 per cent went to the 'Bank's preference for infrastructure geared at nurturing the market' (524).

The nearly universal outcome of these policies and their effects is seriously high unemployment, growing rather than receding after war. The reduction in the scope of government, dismantling social safety nets, downsizing the civil service, and steep cuts in public expenditures add further to unemployment and also increase wage and income inequality. Land privatization expels sharecroppers, those without formal title to their land, squatters, and smallholding farmers, adding to the agrarian exodus typical of wartime, and swelling urban slums. The political consequences of inequality and unemployment then reinforce these outcomes over time because they undermine the power resources and bases of political organization of workers, peasants, and the poor without which governments anywhere do not choose redistributive and welfare policies. Nooruddin and Simmons find in a study of social spending in 1980–2000, 'strong and robust evidence' that government cuts in social expenditures under an IMF programme are made most in those sectors that matter most 'to the lower classes', such as education and health, and this effect is much stronger in democracies than authoritarian regimes because governments have 'some leverage over the content and implementation of IMF programs' and democracies make choices in terms of organized interests, cutting those 'relatively less-organized' (2006: 1027). Although rhetorically committed to social safety nets, the World Bank designs post-war reconstruction programmes without any mention at all of social policy (on Bosnia-Herzegovina, see Stubbs 2001), a bias which is then reproduced for the long run in the PRSP, which nowhere pays any attention to conflict or the particular circumstances of post-war countries (Fukuda Parr *et al.* 2008; Obwona and Guloba 2009). Stewart and Wang (2006: 315) also find no coherence between the macro policies required by the IMF under its PRGFs and the Bank's poverty goals, including the content of the country's PRSP.

Finally, and contrary to their goals, perhaps the most significant consequence for the structure of post-war power is the simultaneous shrinking of the formal sector of the economy and increase of the informal sector as the unemployed and displaced seek means of survival in whatever way they can, from smuggling (on Algeria, see Hill 2009: 52–3) to theft and burglary (leading often to a rise in levels of violence such as homicides after the war, as Call and Stanley [2002] first identified in El Salvador and Guatemala), and large, transnational trafficking in organs, illicit drugs, and people as in Kosovo. The informal sector in Bosnia-Herzegovina after 15 years of privileged levels of external assistance to its Bank-led 'post-conflict reconstruction' was, according to official sources including the World Bank, 25–30 per cent of the economy (Woodward 2011); the percentage is far higher (but less precisely calculated) in Kosovo.[23] The IFIs' focus on public financial management by definition focuses only on monetized activities and ignores the entire panoply of non-monetized relations that characterize poor countries, increase during wartime when financial institutions, wage payments, and budgetary transfers tend to stop functioning, and characterize much of any informal economic sector. Their narrow focus on the formal sector alone, to the total exclusion of the informal economy, also occurs in the political sphere. IMF and World Bank programme documents are silent on areas of contested authority and conflict within countries, such as Transnistria in Moldova, as if they do not even exist.

Conclusion

The literature on transitions from intrastate war to a sustainable peace emphasizes the perversities of war economies, their warlords, looting of natural resources such as diamonds and timber, and general criminalization, and then how to overcome them in order to build peace. Those who focus on 'root causes' of civil war emphasize neopatrimonial regimes, horizontal inequalities, and high unemployment, particularly among youth. Yet all of these characteristics, causes, and maladies appear to be reinforced (in some aspects, even created) by the policies of the IMF and the World Bank in post-conflict reconstruction. While they operate in a dense organizational environment and one of their primary contributions is to facilitate others' financing of external assistance to post-conflict countries, their defining role on the strategy for post-conflict reconstruction, the framework for donors, and their conditionality-imposed concept of the state make their role particularly consequential, even if regression analysis would be hard-pressed to distinguish their contribution precisely. In a critical mode, one might argue that the primary problem with the Bretton Woods institutions is their continuing application of policies and conditionalities designed for other circumstances, against all evidence and criticism, both internal and external, about the perverse outcomes in terms of a sustainable peace. This ignores, some counter, the many positive changes since 1995 with new financing facilities for post-conflict countries and capacities at the country level for greater adaptation. There is little evidence in the countries themselves, however, that these innovations have changed in any way their goals, priorities, and concept of the state, or the consequences for the structure of post-war power and statebuilding described in this chapter. As this chapter would lead one to expect, these changes are aimed at improving their own capacity to act in post-conflict countries to achieve the same aims within the same institutional imperatives, not to respond to evidence of their counterproductive effects on the transformation they say they seek or to adopt policies more appropriate to the particular needs and characteristics of post-conflict countries and peace. Their continuing lack of transparency and exclusiveness reinforces the importance of systematic empirical research to test the patterns identified here and the precise role of the IFIs in these outcomes.

Notes

1 Art. IV, §10, of the World Bank's Articles, cited in Boon 2007: 521, who adds that the IMF prohibition is milder, that 'all members of the IMF must consent to surveillance', although it must 'respect the domestic social and political policies of members', and 'no such restriction applies to IMF conditional lending' (note 21).
2 Post-conflict countries are required to formulate an Interim PRSP first.
3 According to the Terms of Reference for a UNDP and World Bank joint project proposal of 2 July 2006 on file with the author.
4 Madalene O'Donnell (2005) was 'contracted by the Peacekeeping Best Practices Section' of DPKO in 2005 to do a study of the relations between World Bank and UN senior managers in the field, while senior DPKO officials in New York held multiple consultations in Washington the same year and following.
5 There are other international financial institutions than the IMF and World Bank, such as the regional multilateral banks in Asia and Europe and the World Trade Organization, but this chapter will follow conventional usage and use the acronym, IFI, for these two largest, most global, and most influential. The approach to statebuilding varies among them all, however. The European Bank for Reconstruction and Development (EBRD), reflecting its origins as a vehicle for the market transitions in eastern Europe after 1989 and the requirement of the Bush administration for its contribution to EBRD capitalization that at least 60 per cent of EBRD loans be to the private sector, for example, can also only lend to liberal (multiparty and pluralistic) democracies.
6 A baseline might be helpful here. In 1997, when I was asked to write the chapter on the IFIs and peace implementation for the CISAC-IPA project that became *Ending Civil Wars*, edited by Stedman, Rothchild, and Cousens (2002), as was the case of all those writing topical chapters, the project directors tasked the case-study authors to answer a series of questions on each topic. I received not a single

answer or piece of information on the role of the IFIs from more than 15 case study authors or their studies. That would no longer be the case.

7 'The debt stock of most ESAF-supported countries had doubled between 1985 and 1995' (Woods 2006: 162), for example. The number of borrowers overdue in loan repayments to the IMF in April 1984 were three by more than six months, and eight more by at least six weeks; by 1990, the number 'in protracted arrears', i.e. six months or more, had grown to 11, 'to the tune of nearly 14 percent of outstanding Fund credits'; in 1984, only one country was in 'nonaccrual status' with the Bank, whereas by 1989, there were nine 'comprising 4 percent of the bank's portfolio' and by the end of December 1998, the number was 40 countries in arrears amounting to $746 million (Woods 2006: 164–165). For an extremely careful and informative discussion of the reasons, see Woods' section (pp. 153–159), 'Was the Prescription Wrong?'

8 As defined by 1984 guidelines, a 1989 Operational Directive 8.50, 'Emergency Recovery Assistance', and its August 1995 Operational Policy 8.5 (OP 8.5).

9 The primary criticism is methodological, that the Burnside-Dollar results are shown to be extremely vulnerable to the specification of the econometric model, including definitions of aid and policy and the dataset used.

10 See www.worldbank.org/wbi/governance/.

11 Bird and Mosely (2006) analyse the results of PRGF lending, finding some successes where governments used the 'streamlined conditionality' to make choices on public expenditure cuts so as to balance social and political stability with austerity, such as Uganda, but many more which did not.

12 I am indebted to Arna Hartmann for explaining this.

13 The United Nations will also manage a Trust Fund, but some donors such as the US criticize its overhead costs and prefer the World Bank where they might have greater say on policy. For Sudan in 2010, for example, there were five separate multi-donor trust funds – one managed by the World Bank, three by the UN, and one by a bilateral donor (3C Conference Report 2009: 44).

14 In the five-year, $5.1 billion Priority Recovery and Reconstruction Programme for Bosnia-Herzegovina, for example, one-tenth of 1 per cent went to social assistance, 20 per cent to fiscal support, 20 per cent to restart productive activity, and more than half to infrastructure.

15 This approach was developed much earlier by the UN Capital Development Fund (UNCDF), beginning with CARERE, 1993–1995, in Cambodia and PRODERE in Central America, but its strategy of linkages to the central government is very different from the free-standing World Bank approach.

16 One-third of all aid to Mozambique was technical assistance to expatriate professionals, according to the World Bank country director, Roberto Chavez, at a Peace Implementation Network Forum on 'Public-Sector Finance in Post-Conflict Situations' held in Washington, DC, in August 1999.

17 Specific examples are available in the case study literature, however. See Boyce (2002: 40–47) for the contradictory messages given to Guatemala by the IMF's Managing Director and IMF staff.

18 Whitfield and Fraser (2009: 20) find that the most successful negotiators were those with favourable structural (political, economic, ideological, and institutional) conditions, but their three examples – Ethiopia, Botswana, and Rwanda – also had 'confidence to translate a country's conditions into negotiating capital and deploying it effectively in aid negotiations'; the sources of confidence varied – ideology of the government, background of the ruling political party and political leaders, and the government's degree of popular legitimacy.

19 The 1998 OED evaluation of Bank policies wrote:

> the Cambodia case study finds that the Bank has continued to push for downsizing the civil service when the political coalition arrangement under the

peace accords was based in part on raising the size of the civil service to absorb large numbers of the incoming parties' functionaries. The Bank's position was not politically realistic from the start.

(World Bank 1998: xvi)

In the case of Sierra Leone, rapid cuts in pay and personnel to the army created 8000 newly unemployed soldiers who defected to the guerrillas and went back to war. Although the Bank now accepts this OED criticism, it has not changed this policy.

20 Personal communication from Minna Jarvenpaa, London, 28 May 2010.
21 Flores and Nooruddin (2009a) find no effect on economic growth of World Bank post-conflict assistance programmes, once one takes selection bias into account.
22 In East Timor, the inflationary mechanism was the high salaries of consultants paid by the donor community and the US dollar economy created by the UN mission, but this phenomenon occurs in all peacebuilding missions as demonstrated by Carnahan *et al.* 2006.
23 On other economic mechanisms that discourage the formal economy and increase the informal, see Bojičić-Dželilović (2002) and Pugh *et al.* (2008).

10 Regional approaches to statebuilding I

The European Union

Othon Anastasakis, Richard Caplan and Spyros Economides

The role of the European Union (EU) in international post-conflict statebuilding is characterised by a curious anomaly. The EU is the largest provider of overseas development assistance, with much of that assistance, since the end of the Cold War, being used in support of post-conflict reconstruction and development initiatives around the globe. The EU also participates in more post-conflict statebuilding operations worldwide than any other regional organisation. And, yet, despite the magnitude of these efforts, the EU does not play a leading strategic role in international post-conflict statebuilding. There are a number of reasons for this.

To begin with, the EU does not normally engage in post-conflict statebuilding operations on its own but, rather, in partnership – and often as the junior member of the partnership – with other international actors. As a junior partner, moreover, the EU's contributions to statebuilding are generally sector specific – concentrating on the reconstruction and/or reform of specific practices and institutions of governance. Also, unlike other international actors – notably the United Nations (UN), the World Bank and the International Monetary Fund (IMF) – the EU has not adopted a distinctive approach to post-conflict statebuilding: for the most part it works within the dominant models of the state and statebuilding that other actors employ, although it is fair to say that the EU, or more accurately some of its leading member states, often exerts considerable influence on the formulation and articulation of these models.

One notable exception to the foregoing pattern is EU statebuilding efforts in the Western Balkans – Croatia, Bosnia-Herzegovina, Serbia, Montenegro, Macedonia, Kosovo, and Albania – which were wracked by violent conflict and upheaval beginning in the early 1990s until the early 2000s. Here the EU has had greater influence ultimately than any other external actor on post-conflict statebuilding for the simple reason that these states are all prospective members of the EU and it is European standards to which they must conform in order to accede to the EU. The prospect of enlargement, in other words, has allowed the EU to demand the most radical change and transformation in every aspect of the Western Balkan states in their political, economic, justice, and security sectors. Yet even then it has often not been until the later stages of post-conflict statebuilding efforts that the EU has assumed the dominant role: leadership in the Western Balkans initially has been assumed by the UN, the North Atlantic Treaty Organization (NATO), or ad hoc bodies such as the Office of the High Representative (OHR) in Bosnia-Herzegovina.

This chapter offers an analysis of EU post-conflict statebuilding. It provides a categorisation of the EU's efforts based on the regional body's objectives and the instruments developed to achieve them; it highlights differences between the EU's efforts and those of other international organisations and institutions; and it examines the political economy effects within post-conflict states of these policies, concentrating primarily on the effects of EU conditionality in the Western Balkans, where the EU's post-conflict statebuilding efforts have been the most far-reaching if not always the most successful. The Western Balkans is a particularly useful case study because it shows the potential as well as the limits of the EU's statebuilding capacity.

Categorising EU post-conflict statebuilding

Any useful categorisation of EU post-conflict statebuilding has to take into account the goals of the policy, the instruments used in attempting to achieve the goals and the geographical spread of these actions. In this section these three variables will be defined and justified, with the aim of creating a framework within which the EU's post-conflict statebuilding activities can be compared to those of other international organisations and their effects on domestic politico-economic structures can be measured.

Goals

Generally speaking, the EU pursues three goals in post-conflict statebuilding: reconstruction, stabilisation and transformation. In other words, the EU's policies are aimed at restoring material and economic infrastructure, stabilising socio-political imbalances while maintaining an absence of violence and in the longer term creating the conditions for peace and prosperity. These goals are firmly located in the framework of general interests and values guiding the EU's foreign policy. It is often the case that these objectives are pursued concomitantly; that is, they overlap in time and practice. However, the means available to the EU in executing its foreign policy and the geographical location of the target state are key determinants in formulating the precise policy of the EU in each post-conflict case. Thus European post-conflict states, such as Bosnia-Herzegovina, Kosovo and Macedonia are treated very differently from more distant cases in the Caucasus, Africa or Asia.

Over time the EU has developed an array of missions that vary by location and by the means available to affect change (which have helped set the objectives for each case). In the European context, especially in the context of South Eastern Europe and the Western Balkans more specifically, the path dependency of Europe's policy is usually set from a starting point of economic and physical reconstruction through to stabilisation, democratisation and institution-building, and culminating with a transformation that allows for potential membership of the EU. Here the key ingredients of this path, which is not as smooth or unilinear as the above progression might suggest, are the proximity of the post-conflict states (to the EU), which generates a greater degree of urgency and awareness, and the fact that indeed the 'targeted' states have a European future. This means that the end goal is not merely a generic condition of 'stability', or 'democracy' or 'peace' but rather a very specific form entailing all three of the above, enabling a transformative process that will create EU member states out of these post-conflict societies.

The biggest investment on the part of the EU, in terms of effort and finances, in this regard (and that is examined below in greater detail) is the case of the Western Balkans. Since the mid-1990s – and perhaps more specifically with the introduction of the Regional Approach of 1997 – the EU's Balkan policy has been geared towards: first, mending the economic and social damage caused by the decline of the communist regimes in the region and the wars of Yugoslavia's collapse (reconstruction); second, providing the politico-economic and institutional framework to stabilise a region seemingly prone to discord and conflict as perceived through the example of the above wars (stabilisation); and third, providing further institutional and financial incentives to promote the reforms and restructuring needed to achieve democracy, welfare and prosperity (transformation). These goals have been reflected in the policies pursued under the Stability Pact for South Eastern Europe, in which the EU was the lead but not sole actor, and which had as its main goal the reconstruction of the region, as well as in the stabilisation policies (including policing, peacekeeping and disarmament missions), and the heavily conditional policies embodied in the Stabilisation and Association process, which aspires to continue to provide the context for the pursuit of reconstruction and stabilisation but emphasises its transformative agenda (Fakiolas and Tzifakis 2008).

This is the most ambitious example of the EU's objectives in post-conflict statebuilding. More often than not, the goals are much more limited or specific, concentrating on the core objective of humanitarian assistance, stabilisation or peacebuilding. The EU mission in Chad for instance (EUFOR Tchad/RCA), which lasted 18 months between 2008 and 2009, was a humanitarian mission centred on protecting displaced peoples and refugees (Mattalaer 2010). EU monitoring missions such as those in Aceh, Indonesia (Aceh Monitoring Mission) and Georgia (EUMM Georgia) aim to assist in the maintenance and implementation of specific peace agreements in the short term rather than build capacity and institutions for longer-term transformation. Similarly, the EU has become increasingly proactive in developing and deploying missions aimed at enhancing stability and peace through security sector reforms. EUSEC RD Congo, the EU's mission to the Democratic Republic of Congo launched in 2005, is a security-sector reform mission aimed at assisting in the transformation of the Congolese Armed Forces, thus contributing to peace and the rule of law. A similar mission, EU SSR Guinea Bissau, was deployed between 2008 and 2010 to assist in the transformation of local police, military/defence and legal/judicial structures. While some of these operations have statebuilding objectives as part of their mandate, it is not their primary objective but rather seen as instrumental to the promotion of stability, and these missions have more generally been characterised as 'peace operations' in the literature (Korski and Gowan 2009).

The EU's statebuilding efforts have been advanced primarily through advisory missions, including the more extensive operations promoting the rule of law and democratisation. The latter have been deployed by the EU to support post-conflict statebuilding through processes of reform in the civilian/political sector, through institution- and capacity-building, and the provision of interim administration (on a limited basis). The most extensive of these cases are those of Bosnia-Herzegovina and Kosovo. In the case of Kosovo, the deployment of the EULEX mission – established in 2008 after nine years of UN administration of the territory – in addition to EU support of the International Civilian Office (ICO) there, shows the scope and potency of these types of missions (Economides and Ker-Lindsay 2010). A rule of law mission has also been deployed by the EU in Iraq since 2005 (EUJUST LEX), and is set to run until 2012, with its aim to 'strengthen the rule of law and promote a culture of respect for human rights in Iraq' (European Council 2005). What is noteworthy about these rule of law missions is not only the aims of the missions themselves, but more importantly that they are EU missions deployed in support of existing efforts by either other international organisations/institutions or individual or groups of states. The broader point that ought to be made here is that the EU rarely pursues independent missions, of whatever type as indicated above, but is more likely to engage in deployments that reinforce existing operations or assist in funding such missions or providing technical advice and support.

What this sub-section has sketched out is the multiplicity of goals of EU statebuilding missions. They stretch from economic assistance to the alleviation of humanitarian suffering; the promotion of economic reconstruction and the creation of the basis for economic development; the provision of civilian/military assistance in the stabilisation and control of violence by monitoring and reforming; political and democratic capacity-building and restructuring through to military security missions. It is a broad range that spans the whole economic, political and military spectrum. But it is fundamentally linked to the idea that has emerged that the EU's multiplicity of foreign policy goals translates into a framework guided by reconstruction, stabilisation and transformation. The type of mission that is launched is partly determined by the values and goals of the EU's foreign policy, but also, as we shall see in the next sections, by the means at the EU's disposal and by the location of the post-conflict state. As a result, the more normative goal of transformation is often compromised by either geographic or instrumental circumstances. Nevertheless, the other elements in the tripartite framework – reconstruction and stabilisation – are still deemed important enough in the short term to be pursued.

Means

The actions of the EU as a statebuilder are partly a function of the means at its disposal. In turn, the means at its disposal have been determined by a combination of value-driven tenets of EU foreign policy, the reality of what instruments the EU can and cannot deploy, and the types of conflicts evident in a post-Cold War international system that may have forced the EU into defining the need for and developing new capabilities. On one level, the EU's statebuilding activities have been determined by the basic premises of its broader foreign policy as enshrined in the 'Copenhagen criteria' (European Council 1993). The heavily normative bases of these premises have, for a long period, set the tone and delimited the instruments that the EU would use in fulfilling its foreign policy ambitions. Hence, the EU developed a long-term dependence on the use of economic instruments of foreign policy to enhance its traditional diplomacy based on declaratory policy and political dialogue. This has been transposed onto the EU's statebuilding capabilities in two significant ways. First, the EU – as mentioned in the previous section – pursues economic assistance programmes for reconstruction as well as for developmental/growth purposes. Second, and more importantly, the EU uses political conditionality as the mainstay of its statebuilding (and broader foreign) policy. These conditionalities, now the hallmark of EU policy, are often aimed at 'macro-processes' of democratisation and economic growth but are key elements of more technocratic and immediate policies of capacity- and institution-building that provide the essentials for the success of the macro-processes. Importantly, until the 1990s, the EU was tied to economic instruments by default. While the normative dimension of the foreign policy to many provided the guiding light for the use of non-coercive, civilian means to achieve goals, there was also no real alternative. Declaratory policy was important but of limited value; enlargement – the most potent of state-building policies – was limited to European states; and military instruments were yet to be developed. Therefore, the EU's statebuilding actions have often been limited both by value-based concerns as well as by a lack of alternative instruments of foreign engagement.

More recently, the EU has also become increasingly active in specific assistance missions that have more immediate and shorter-term goals, as well as missions with an executive mandate, as in Kosovo. Here, the EU still relies on inducements and conditionalities but is also increasingly willing to move into more 'coercive' approaches, relying on a combination of civilian and military/policing activities and instruments. This illustrates two tendencies in the EU's statebuilding approach. On the one hand the EU is straying from its normative self-constraint into the use of instruments that go beyond the 'civilian power Europe' model. On the other hand, the EU, more often than not, pursues policies that rely on overlapping instruments, further blurring the distinction between different types of missions.

The emergence of a common European Security and Defence Policy (ESDP) as the military adjunct to Common Foreign and Security Policy

(CFSP) has developed the EU's capacity to use coercive power. In terms of statebuilding this has led to an increased ability and desire to project military and policing capabilities in support of and/or in conjunction with civilian missions. EUFOR/Althea in Bosnia-Herzegovina and Artemis in the DRC are examples of EU military operations launched under ESDP, which play a clear role in the EU's statebuilding actions within those post-conflict states. What this indicates is not only the willingness of the EU to deploy military missions as part of a statebuilding policy but also how the availability of a military capability is increasingly defining the EU's statebuilding actions: it is no longer bound by limited instruments, which in turn has a definitive effect on what it is attempting to achieve and how. There has been an increase in the means spectrum, from commerce through conditionality and to coercion, which has radically changed the EU's goals in statebuilding missions (Giegerich 2008). The desire for 'global security' and 'building a better world', as outlined in the European Security Strategy of 2003 (European Council 2003), has become an equal goal to the normative aspirations as set out above in the EU's statebuilding missions.

Location

The EU's statebuilding action is also a function of the location of the post-conflict states. A parsimonious categorisation defines the EU's missions according to whether the target is in 'the region', in 'the neighbourhood' or in the wider concentric circle beyond that. In other words, the EU's willingness and ability to act is determined by whether the state in question is a European state, in Europe's near abroad, or located elsewhere on the global map.

Why is this important? Within the 'European' region, the prospect of membership allows the EU to deploy its deepest and most transformative statebuilding capacities, as the target state is eligible and/or in clear pursuit of accession to the EU. Thus, the EU can unleash its full panoply of statebuilding capacities, demanding the most radical change and transformation in every aspect of the post-conflict state's political, economic, judicial and military make up. Based on the heaviest possible conditionality, and often supported by rule-of-law or mixed civilian-military missions, accession- or member- statebuilding in post-conflict countries has a very specific goal: the creation of an EU member state. Currently, the Western Balkans provide the clearest and most extensive set of examples of this type of statebuilding. Even though not all Balkan states have achieved candidate status, and thus have not all begun accession talks yet, the range and depth of the EU statebuilding activities throughout the region is driven by the fact that these states are both deemed to be European and eligible for EU membership. The regional conflicts of the not-so-distant past point to the need for security-based missions as well as those primarily concentrating on civilian-economic dimensions. Restoration, stabilisation and transformation are all on the statebuilding agenda for the Western Balkans. The case of Macedonia as an example of post-conflict statebuilding, driven to a great extent by the proximity of the state to the EU and hence its status in relation to the EU, is a prime one (see Kristof Bender's chapter in this volume). But this argument is equally persuasive in the cases of Bosnia-Herzegovina and Kosovo (see Dominik Zaum and Verena Knaus's chapter in this volume).

In Europe's near abroad, as delimited by the European Neighbourhood Policy (ENP), the objectives are not driven by the same ambition or urgency as those seen in the region. Security concerns are of paramount importance, as are democratisation and economic development. But as accession is not realistic or applicable, the statebuilding agenda is markedly different from that developed to meet the 'European' challenge. Therefore, stability rather than transformation is often the goal. Democratisation and economic development are desired but will not be treated with as radical remedies as those seen in the enlargement context. Thus involvement in Georgia, Moldova or Ukraine (through EUBAM, the EU Border Assistance Mission) are best described as security-based support for statebuilding actions and are on a much more modest scale than those to which potential members of the EU are exposed.

What emerges is a pattern in which the further away (geographically) one moves from Europe's core, the more the EU's statebuilding actions and missions are driven by security interests as defined in the European Security Strategy rather than the more normative concerns as elucidated in the Copenhagen criteria. This does not mean that normative concerns vanish: they are ever present but ever diminishing as a policy driver. Whether it is the EUPOL mission in Afghanistan or the EU Training Mission in Somalia (EUTM), these missions indicate the security concerns of the EU taking precedence over narrower normative concerns and often conducted in support of or in conjunction with another regional or international actor (such as the UN). Nor does it mean that the EU does not attempt to use a wide array of instruments ranging from commercial inducements to coercive measures. Essentially, distance from the EU implies a dominance of security imperatives over normative or transformative aspirations.

Therefore, the EU's statebuilding ambitions are driven by three primary factors: the function of the mission, the instruments available to the EU in each mission and the location of the state or territory in question. In the next section we develop a comparison between the EU and other multilateral organisations involved in statebuilding – with which in many instances they operate in tandem – highlighting both similarities and differences.

The EU in relation to other statebuilding actors

The EU is only one of a large number of multilateral organisations engaged in statebuilding efforts in war-torn states, together with the UN, the World Bank, the IMF and a host of other regional and sub-regional organisations, to name but the most prominent external actors. Within Europe alone, the EU has undertaken initiatives in support of post-conflict statebuilding alongside the Council of Europe (CoE), the North Atlantic Treaty Organization (NATO), the Organization for Security and Cooperation in Europe (OSCE), and the

European Bank for Reconstruction and Development (EBRD), as well as various ad hoc organisations, such as the Office of the High Representative (OHR) in Bosnia-Herzegovina and the International Civilian Office (ICO) in Kosovo.

At a glance, the EU would appear to be one of the most significant international statebuilding actors. The EU is the single largest provider of official development assistance (ODA) worldwide – $81.5 billion in 2009[1] – much of which is deployed in support of post-conflict statebuilding, including infrastructure rehabilitation, security sector reform, the promotion of human rights and the rule of law, political institution-building, macro-financial assistance and numerous other post-war reconstruction and development projects (OECD 2010b). Not only is the EU the single largest donor but, after the UN and the World Bank, it has been engaged in post-conflict peacebuilding and statebuilding in the largest number of countries worldwide.

Despite the magnitude of its efforts, the EU's approaches to post-conflict statebuilding do not constitute a distinctive model in comparison with that of the major statebuilding actors, notably the UN and the World Bank (see chapters by Mats Berdal and Susan Woodward in this volume). The reason for this is that the EU, for the most part, rarely leads or commands major multilateral statebuilding efforts; it is more typically a supporting actor of other agents' efforts. Moreover, its contributions to statebuilding tend to be partial and sectorally oriented rather than comprehensive. So, for instance, in Afghanistan (EUPOL Afghanistan), the EU's chief responsibility has been to provide training to the Afghan National Police, and in Iraq (EUJUST LEX), the EU's primary responsibility has been to provide training to judges, investigating magistrates, and senior police and penitentiary officers. The particular model or models that inform post-conflict statebuilding in these and most other cases do not bear a specifically 'Brussels' imprint.

The singular exception to this pattern is with regard to EU's 'member-state' building efforts in the war-torn territories of the Western Balkans (ESI 2005). As mentioned in the previous section, candidate countries for EU membership in the region – currently Croatia and Macedonia – as well as potential candidate countries – Bosnia-Herzegovina, Serbia, Montenegro, Albania and Kosovo – all benefit from EU financial aid and technical assistance to promote specific economic, political and institutional reforms that the EU regards as necessary to bring these countries into line with European standards. Since 1999 (and earlier under similar schemes), both candidate and potential candidate countries have been receiving EU funding as part of the Stabilisation and Association process (SAp). Total pre-accession funding for these countries has been quite substantial: for the period 2007–13 it amounts to €11.5 billion.[2] The financial assistance is used to support a wide range of root-and-branch reforms that aim to effect the transformation of former communist or authoritarian regimes into consolidated market democracies, and additionally (depending on the country) of war-torn societies into stable and peaceful ones. And yet, despite the EU's extensive engagement in post-conflict statebuilding in its own backyard, it has not had principal responsibility for the administration of war-torn territories there. That responsibility has been entrusted to other multilateral organisations – the OHR in Bosnia-Herzegovina or the UN in Eastern Slavonia (Croatia) and Kosovo.

What is distinctive about the EU's approach to post-war statebuilding efforts in the Western Balkans, in contrast to that of the other multilateral organisations operating there, is that the goals it pursues are overtly normative ones (Tocci 2008). The World Bank, the IMF and the United Nations all operate under formal and informal constraints on normative engagement. The World Bank's Articles of Agreement place strictures on activities that may be construed as political in nature:

> The Bank and its officers shall not interfere in the political affairs of any member; nor shall they be influenced in their decisions by the political character of the member or members concerned. Only economic considerations shall be relevant to their decisions.
>
> (World Bank 1989: Art. 4, §10)

The IMF operates under similar constraints. And while the United Nations supports democracy and promotes democratisation, it takes the view, as then UN Secretary-General Boutros Boutros-Ghali explained, that 'it is not for the United Nations to offer a model of democratization or democracy.... [T]he United Nations does not aim to persuade democratizing States to apply external models or borrow extraneous forms of government' (United Nations 1996: §10–11). Although in many respects these constraints are more nominal than real, the EU is not subject to them at all in its own backyard. To the contrary, because the EU sees itself as 'a community of values', it feels it is entirely appropriate, indeed imperative, to promote these values among the candidate and potential candidate countries in the context of its post-war statebuilding efforts.

Although increasingly nominal, these constraints on other statebuilding actors have in the past had a bearing on the nature of their engagement. When in 1997, for instance, the EU made its offer of post-war assistance to the divided Bosnian city of Mostar conditional on cooperation between Mostar's Croats and Bosniacs (Muslims), the World Bank – ill-disposed towards political conditionality for the reasons noted above – ignored the EU's efforts at integration and offered the Bosniac authorities assistance for the reconstruction of their own separate hydroelectric plant, prompting the EU to abandon its policy (ESI 2000: 45). While donor coordination today remains problematic, donor indifference to the political consequences of their actions is much less common. It is reasonable, therefore, to speak about a broad harmony of approaches between the EU, on the one hand, and other statebuilding actors, on the other hand. There are certainly no major differences among external actors with regard to broad post-conflict statebuilding objectives, which envision the establishment of stable, liberal democratic and market-based states.

It follows from this normative orientation that the EU's approach to member statebuilding, post-conflict or otherwise, is also highly prescriptive in comparison with that of other multilateral organisations: there is little or no scope for negotiating the terms of EU accession on the part of candidate countries. While in practice this is also true of other approaches – notably the World Bank's Poverty Reduction Strategies Papers (PRSPs), which are often the cornerstone of multilateral peacebuilding and statebuilding efforts – in principle these are meant to be participatory processes involving domestic stakeholders as well as the external parties. The fact that the ends of EU member statebuilding are, in effect, non-negotiable (the process culminates in a state's wholesale adoption of the EU's *acquis communautaire*), means that participation is necessarily limited. One implication of this limitation is that it inhibits political debate within candidate countries, leading critics to argue that the accession process is highly undemocratic or even anti-democratic because it also favours elite control over the process. As Ivan Krastev, chairman of the Centre for Liberal Strategies in Sofia, observed in 2007:

> The accession of the Central European countries to the EU virtually institutionalized elite hegemony over the democratic process. Parliament lost its function as a place where major political debates take place and was reduced to an institution preoccupied with adopting the EU's *acquis communautaire*. Ordinary citizens experienced transitional democracies as regimes where voters could change governments but could not change policies.
>
> (Krastev 2007: 58–59)

While this is the case largely with regard to states aspiring to EU membership, the adoption and internalisation of the EU's prescriptions in post-conflict environments – where the political elites are polarised and the political institutions are often challenged and not fully recognised – can be even more intrusive and interventionist. The EU, in post-conflict environments, ceases to be purely prescriptive and external; it becomes a part of the domestic governance process. Conditionality becomes central in post-conflict states and it appears more in the form of stick than carrot, aiming at establishing central, functional and viable states, which otherwise run the risk of falling apart and reverting to conflict. In all of the post-conflict contexts, the EU aims at establishing central authorities who will represent as much as possible the interests of the different sides and will gradually gain legitimacy. This is a Herculean task given the propensity of many local actors to bypass central authorities and create (or maintain) parallel structures in order to preserve their own interests. These problems are all too visible in the Western Balkan post-conflict states, as will be discussed in the following section.

The impact of EU statebuilding in the Western Balkans

The Western Balkans is one of the geographic areas where EU engagement has been more extensive and more influential than elsewhere. The EU has had at its disposal a considerable array of tools – through its Stabilisation and Association process, and its CFSP/ESDP missions – to attempt to mould the post-war political and economic structures of these societies. The results have been mixed and they vary from case to case: there are some countries that perform better than others, and there are some sectors that are more amenable to reform and others where local resistance is hard to overcome.

We can examine the impact of the EU's statebuilding efforts in the Western Balkans in relation to two variables: first, by looking at the nature of local compliance with EU conditionality aiming at building central and functional state institutions. Here an initial expectation would lead us to believe that EU conditionality is overall problematic in the post-conflict settings, where elites and state structures are so divided that there is neither the will nor the capacity to comply. A closer cross-sectoral look, however, tells us that in the post-conflict settings there are some areas of statebuilding where there is some degree of compliance and others where local positions are very resistant to change. Second, we assess progress in the politics and economies of these states. In other words, we assess whether the statebuilding results in building democratic institutions and whether it is able to provide the right environment for an economy that is growing and developing its public and private resources. Here an initial expectation would lead us to think that the polities are far from democratic, that they are hopelessly divided along ethnic lines and parallel local structures, and that the economies are weak as a result of widespread corruption, high unemployment and underdevelopment. A closer look, however, tells us that there is some degree of normalisation of procedural democratic politics and that, in the economic domain, all of these post-conflict (and post-communist) states have accepted the rules and conditions of market economies. These achievements notwithstanding, there are fundamental problems with respect to the quality of democratic governance and the robustness of the economies.

Local compliance with EU conditionality

EU statebuilding processes in the Western Balkans are closely linked to the use of conditionality, the impact and effectiveness of which is often very difficult to assess. While EU conditionality allows the EU to impinge on state sovereignty, the process of conditionality in post-conflict countries has a different dynamic from that of other EU candidate countries and entails a different give and take than with other sovereign states. One can discern three distinctive features of the process of EU conditionality in post-conflict settings. First, the negotiation is taking place between the EU, on the one hand, and a contested and not fully legitimate national authority, on the other. Second, the EU often has to sacrifice some of its normative claims for the sake of peace, a balance among the different local actors and the rule of law. Third, more than in any other normal sovereign context, the way conditionality is perceived and understood by the post-conflict elites goes well beyond the mainstream rationalist explanations whereby divided domestic elites choose to comply – fully, partly or not at all – according to their own complementary or conflicting interests, but also according to the way they perceive the fairness of the criteria

In the Western Balkans, statebuilding is based on the EU's normative and functionalist agenda, which manifests itself in calls for common state structures, respect for the rule of law, reform in the areas of justice and home affairs, the fight against corruption and organised crime, cooperation with the International Criminal Tribunal for the former Yugoslavia (ICTY), justice for the victims of war crimes, the return of refugees and good neighbourly relations. Yet what is 'normal' for the EU is not always perceived as normal and appropriate by post-conflict societies, where such notions can be affected by irreconcilable perceptions and misperceptions. As a rule, most parties see themselves as victims of the injustices of the other ethnic group or external actors, and the allegations are totally different depending on which side claims them. In addition, statebuilding conditionality aims principally at convergence and political transformation from a functional and practical perspective, through the adoption of rules and procedures and/or the creation of institutions and public administrations that are capable of addressing the local political concerns and conforming to the *acquis communautaire*. The functional agenda refers to what is 'common', 'sustainable' and 'viable' for the states in question, with the aim of suppressing conflictual, clientelistic, particularistic and dysfunctional mentalities, practices and rules. Yet, as with 'normal' and 'appropriate', what is functional for the EU is not always perceived as functional by the post-conflict elites. More often than not it is difficult to convince them that a change of policy or a change of institution is a preferable option.

The functionalist approach is evident in the EU's effort to create common state structures in Bosnia-Herzegovina. One of the foremost arguments regarding the dysfunctional nature of the Dayton political structure in Bosnia-Herzegovina makes reference to the existence of 14 governments (at the state, entity and cantonal levels) and the numerous bureaucracies for a population of just 3.8 million people. This has been criticized not only as ethnically divisive but also as utterly inefficient and financially non-viable. The signing of the EU Stabilisation and Association Agreement (SAA) with Bosnia-Herzegovina in June 2008 was conditional on the creation of central state structures in the military, tax system and the police, among others. This conditionality aimed not only at reconciliation, ethnic co-existence, normalcy and respect but also at a more efficient state able to provide public goods to all of its citizens (beyond advancing the interests of particular ethnic and social groups). But, again, what the EU considers normal and functional does not coincide with institutional normalcy and functionality from the local actors' points of view, who are themselves divided on these issues. Bosnian politicians, for instance, have different views on how and whether to revise the Dayton constitution and what the nature of a new constitution should be. The leaders of the Bosniac (Muslim) community favour a constitutional structure that would do away with the two entities, while the ethnic Serbs and

Croats advocate a federal structure along ethnic lines. The ability to advance reforms of different sectors of the Bosnian state has also varied. Bosnia-Herzegovina has been more receptive to the reform of its military and the creation of a common military force, with the help of cross conditionality coming from NATO, and less successful in the vexing matter of police reform, where the EU explicitly called for the unification of the police forces as a prerequisite for progress in the association process but eventually had to water down its strict conditionality in the face of strong opposition from Bosnian Serbs. Similarly in Macedonia, local compliance with EU conditions has varied from sector to sector and has been more consistent in the field of decentralisation, with the strengthening of local structures based on the EU's principle of subsidiarity, and less so in the fields of language and education, which remain highly contested issues that divide the country ethnically.

Political and economic realities

The first priority of the EU in the Western Balkans is to keep the post-conflict states and societies together and to avoid any further territorial disintegration and internal ethnic conflict. Bosnia-Herzegovina, Kosovo and Macedonia are all internally divided along ethnic and territorial lines, and their legitimacy is under constant challenge – by the Albanians in Macedonia, the Serbs and Croats in Bosnia-Herzegovina and the Serbs in Kosovo. To address this challenge the EU tries to strike the right balance between creating stronger and more efficient central states while maintaining a degree of decentralisation, so that localised interests are represented and the concerns of the minorities addressed. For their part, the Serbs in northern Kosovo and Republika Srpska in Bosnia-Herzegovina, and the Albanians in western Macedonia are walking a fine line between grudging acceptance of central authority, on the one hand, and the preservation and strengthening of their own local autonomy, which often results in parallel state structures (in northern Kosovo and Bosnia-Herzegovina) and occasionally some violence, on the other. The current reality in Bosnia-Herzegovina is therefore one of a dysfunctional central state that is hostage to the overlapping and unclear competencies of the lesser administrative units, while Kosovo lacks control of its northern territory, where its authority is undermined by Serbia.

The international community and the EU in particular emphasized from the start the necessity of free, fair and regular elections and the safeguarding of basic democratic principles, such as the protection of human and minority rights, freedom of expression and the media, and civil society development. At present, all three states conduct elections that are, by and large, acceptable by international standards. However, party politics continue to be ethnically divided and there are territorial delimitations in all three areas. Corruption remains a big issue in the three post-conflict states despite EU action plans and the formation of institutions and agencies to fight corruption. While all three countries have ratified human rights conventions, the enforcement of rulings on human rights and minority protection is limited.

And while there is nominal freedom of expression and freedom of media, there is a lot of political pressure on and ethnic bias in the media. Overall, in all three post-conflict states there is a gap between procedural and substantive democracy.

Beyond the deepening of democracy, one of the foremost priorities of the EU is the strengthening of the rule of law in order to fight informal and illegal activities, corruption and organised crime, which are rife in these three states. While all have introduced changes to their judicial systems, the implementation of these reforms remains incomplete, with cases of long delays of trials and political interference in the judiciary, notably in the reappointment process of judges and prosecutors. Moreover, there is often talk of corrupt practices by local politicians and allegations of links with organised crime – legacies of the recent conflicts. In Kosovo, for instance, wartime networks associated with the Kosovo Liberation Army (KLA) continue to wield substantial power that undermines the authority of elected officials and the courts, giving the impression that some people are beyond the reach of law. The EU mission in Kosovo (EULEX), which comprises close to 2000 personnel, is trying, more often without much success, to handle many cases of corruption and organised crime. Compounding this difficulty, there are three sets of 'applicable' laws in Kosovo: the regulations of the UN mission (UNMIK), the laws introduced and promulgated by the new government of Kosovo, and the Serbian laws in the areas north of Mitrovica.

Looking at the economies, all three post-conflict areas are past their reconstruction phase and the focus is more on economic development. All three states have adopted the tenets of economic liberalisation, including privatisation and the opening of their economies to international trade and investment. Due to the post-conflict state and the small size of their economies, their development relies mostly on financial assistance from abroad, on regional and European trade, on foreign direct investment and on economic advice from the EU and financial institutions. As a result, the economies of these countries are vulnerable to the EU's ups and downs and to global economic turns.

Economically, Kosovo remains Europe's poorest region, with more than one-half of its people living in poverty, and with the fastest growing population in Europe, youth unemployment is at more than 60 per cent. The economy of Kosovo functions almost entirely as a consumer society, based on relatively small-scale trade and small family businesses, and is principally sustained by remittances from abroad and by international funding. Bosnia-Herzegovina is an internally divided economy, with unemployment at around 25 per cent. The country has a single market on paper, with the free circulation of goods and equal rates of customs and value-added tax. Yet there are many socio-economic disparities in the country: living standards are higher in the Brčko district, which has a population of some 40,000 people and enjoys considerable autonomy; and doing business in Republika Srpska is faster and easier in terms of procedures than in many parts of the Federation. In Macedonia, finally, reform efforts have in recent years triggered considerable injections of foreign direct investment and the country saw a period of growth. But because the country relies heavily on foreign investment, it was severely exposed during the 2008 financial crisis. Its biggest problem is unemployment, which in 2009 climbed to 33 per cent (Wunch and Rappold 2010).

The economic impact of the EU statebuilding efforts is twofold: the EU gives direct financial assistance through its Instrument for Pre-Accession Assistance (IPA) towards specific targeted sectors in need; moreover, association with the EU exists as an anchor and attraction for foreign direct investment from other financial sources. The high degree of external dependency on funds and trade from Europe, on the one hand, and the insufficient degree of political and economic integration with the EU, on the other, make these countries more vulnerable to any delays in the enlargement process or problems with the eurozone. The involvement of the IMF in the Western Balkans following the 2008 financial crisis testifies to the EU's need for coordination with other IFIs to bring stabilisation and growth to the region. Any financial support, however, whether from the IMF or the EU, is attached to strict conditionality (in the area of budget consolidation and administrative reform), which is already demanding, uneven and highly problematic for the weak structures and the unwilling local actors of these post-conflict states.

Conclusion

What this chapter has shown is that there is no singular 'regional approach' or distinctive model to post-conflict statebuilding in the case of the European Union. Apart from being the world's largest provider of development aid, what distinguishes the EU from other organisations and agencies in the area of statebuilding is the purported transformative power of its enlargement policy. Consequently, while the EU may have regional and global statebuilding policies and goals, its approach is not 'one size fits all', and its effectiveness varies across the cases.

We have argued that in practice, the EU's post-conflict statebuilding policies are primarily driven by three factors: location, function and means. Arguably, geographical proximity to the EU is a decisive factor in determining the nature and function of the EU's statebuilding approach. 'Closer to home' implies a much more normative approach to statebuilding, which becomes more security based the farther away from the EU core the post-conflict state is located. The function of the statebuilding mission is the second of the three determining factors outlined in this chapter and perhaps the broadest in that it incorporates a wide range of goals from meeting humanitarian concerns through to security-based stabilisation programmes and on to democratising and transformative ends. Indeed, what we can say about function is related to the location factor, in that the EU has normative and security concerns that drive its post-conflict statebuilding policies and while these are not mutually exclusive categories, we have shown how and why one or the other concern usually prevails in each specific case. Lastly, with respect to the driving defining factors of the EU's post-conflict state-building policies, we have considered the importance of the instruments at the disposal of the EU in achieving its goals and how these have been partly determined by the underlying values of EU foreign policy in general but also constrained by the type of instruments states wish to deploy. Under this factor, of course, special emphasis has to be put on the policy of conditionality, which underpins much of the EU's statebuilding approach.

If there is one geographic area in which the EU does have a distinctive approach to post-conflict statebuilding, this has been in the Western Balkans. As a result, the chapter has demonstrated the importance of the EU's experiences in the Western Balkans to its statebuilding capacities, highlighting the policy of conditionality in this context. In the case of the Western Balkans what has distinguished the EU's approach from that of other international and multilateral statebuilding actors has been its normative content. Unlike the UN and some of its specialised agencies, for example, the EU has promoted an overtly normative approach to statebuilding in the region based on a value-driven foreign policy. While this is accompanied by constant security-based concerns, the statebuilding policies towards the Western Balkans are firmly rooted in the belief of the power of democratisation and transformation of post-conflict societies into strong states with EU membership potential. The normative agenda is also informed by a functionalist logic with the aim of creating competent and legitimate central authorities that are able to provide for their citizens and can respond to the exigencies of the enlargement *acquis*. With this in mind, the chapter has also taken a close look at the political economy impact of EU statebuilding policies in the Western Balkan region with special emphasis on the factors of local compliance and the obvious political-economic developments arising from statebuilding policies, especially in terms of the normalisation of political activity and the growth in economic activity.

To conclude, the EU has become increasingly active in the area of statebuilding as a result of both its own normative outlook and also because of the significant challenges thrown up by the post-Cold War international system. While the EU has not developed a distinctive approach to statebuilding in comparison with that of other multilateral statebuilders, there are unique features in its approach that are driven by geography, instruments and goals. Ultimately, the experience of statebuilding in the Western Balkans has been central in defining the EU's approach, and many subsequent policies are based on this experience.

Notes

1 Figure reflects the ODA of all DAC EU countries together with the European Commission.
2 Figure includes assistance to Turkey.

11 Regional approaches to statebuilding II

The African Union and ECOWAS

Kwesi Aning and Naila Salihu

This chapter discusses statebuilding within the context of post-conflict reconstruction and development in Africa. It outlines the policies and practices of, first, the African Union (AU) and then the Economic Community of West African States (ECOWAS), and explores how these are implemented in fields of political governance, security sector reform, economic reform, and social justice. These areas are crucial to any effective or comprehensive statebuilding process; if they are not adequately addressed, there is a risk of the country concerned reverting to conflict. Both the AU and ECOWAS can be commended for putting in place policy frameworks for promoting statebuilding in the aftermath of conflicts on the continent. The critical issue to examine is the responsiveness and effectiveness of the AU's approach, using these four fields as our focus. We can then compare the performance of ECOWAS in the same areas.

We argue that the process of statebuilding in the aftermath of conflicts is not limited to external international actors alone: regional organisations such as the AU and ECOWAS can and do play essential roles. Even though the practical involvements of AU and ECOWAS are limited at the moment, these bodies have, through their policies and frameworks, managed to influence the activities of external actors in rebuilding post-conflict African states. We share in the view that regional approaches ensure that statebuilding is led by those parties that have both a deeper understanding of the particular crisis dynamics and an interest in a neighbouring state (Aning and Lartey 2010). Regional organisations also have comparative advantages to ensure the best possible results in promoting and consolidating peace (United Nations Office of the Special Adviser on Africa 2007). In our conclusion we summarize the general challenges confronting the AU/ECOWAS in their policy interventions to rebuild post-conflict member states and offer some recommendations as to how these organisations could improve their statebuilding policies and practices.

The AU's approach to statebuilding

There is an emerging consensus that statebuilding is a critical component in the transition from war to peace. However, it is argued that externally driven statebuilding approaches have not been entirely successful in the developing world in general, and in Africa in particular. Moreover, international support for providing a security framework for post-conflict recovery has been much less resolute in Africa than in other parts of the world (for example, the Balkans, the Middle East, and Afghanistan). As a result, the situation in Africa's post-conflict countries is more fragile, and donors are less inclined to finance recovery efforts (Michailof *et al.* 2002: 7). It has therefore become imperative for African institutions to adopt strategies that respond to the needs of the African terrain. Due to their close proximity, regional actors usually have a more intimate understanding of the country in crisis and greater knowledge of local conflict dynamics, context, and actors. They also have deeper awareness of cultural sensitivities and culturally acceptable and effective ways of managing crises both in conflict situations and in the post-conflict phase.

Post-conflict reconstruction, which refers to the medium- to long-term process of rebuilding war-affected communities, has been central to state-building practices in many conflict-affected African states (Lund 2001). It addresses the root causes of the conflicts, rebuilds the security sector, promotes social and economic justice, and establishes political structures of governance and rule of law. Under the slogan 'African solutions to African problems', the AU has put in place mechanisms to address the challenges to statebuilding on the continent, especially in the area of post-conflict reconstruction and development. The role of benevolent regional hegemons in designing and finding solutions to some of Africa's security challenges has contributed significantly to AU as well as ECOWAS peace initiatives: both Nigeria and South Africa have played key roles in peacebuilding and peace-making in countries in crisis, although they are somewhat constrained by domestic democratic processes (Aning 2007). More importantly, the AU's evolving African Peace and Security Architecture (APSA), specifically the Peace and Security Council (PSC), seeks to 'promote and implement peacebuilding and post-conflict reconstruction activities to consolidate peace and prevent the resurgence of violence' (African Union 2002). In furtherance of this aim and after broad consultative processes, the AU and the New Partnership for Africa's Development (NEPAD) adopted a framework for Post-Conflict Reconstruction and Development (PCRD) in July 2006 at the AU Summit in Banjul, Gambia. This sets out a wide range of policies, activities, and benchmarks in the areas of security, humanitarian/emergency assistance, political governance and transition, socio-economic reconstruction and development, human rights, justice and reconciliation, and women and gender. In addition, the framework seeks to articulate a policy that would coordinate and guide the AU Commission, the NEPAD Secretariat, Regional Economic Communities (RECs) such as ECOWAS, civil society, the private sector, and other internal and external partners in the process of rebuilding war-affected countries. The AU's PCRD policy also endeavours to complement the UN Peacebuilding Commission's work in identifying states that are at risk of failure, by providing timely help to reduce the rate at which war-torn countries may relapse into conflict.

AU and political governance

The lack of effective and transparent governance often creates conditions for political violence, military coups, and destructive intra-state conflicts in Africa (Aning and Bah 2009: 3). In their efforts to address this challenge the international community, specifically the international development institutions, claim that a post-conflict reconstruction agenda that incorporates democratisation alongside liberalised markets is one that is likely to address the fundamental causes of civil war or political instability. However, this approach has produced mixed results in Africa's post-conflict countries; nations such as Guinea Bissau continue to sit on time bombs, in spite of the restoration of a semblance of democratic rule.

Good governance and inclusive political participation are the cardinal elements of the AU's statebuilding policies. These are the pillars of a post-conflict reconstruction system that recognises the importance of an appropriate response to complex emergencies, social and political transitions following conflict, and long-term development. Specifically, this involves the development of legitimate and effective political and administrative institutions, ensuring participatory processes, and supporting political transition. In post-conflict situations, one of the roles of the PSC is to assist in the restoration of the rule of law, the establishment and development of democratic institutions, and the preparation, organisation, and supervision of elections in the member state concerned (African Union 2007: Art. 14). The policy framework seeks to promote programmes that strengthen public sector management and administration. It also aims to establish a representative process, revive local governance, strengthen the legislature, broaden the participation of civil society in the decision-making process, and build the capacity of political parties and civil society for effective governance.

Elections in particular, one of the central tenets of democracy, have not necessarily delivered the dividends of peace in Africa. In some African states, elections have fallen abysmally short of being free and fair, and thus often unleash conflict and tensions, especially if not constructively managed. In post-conflict situations, political transitions through elections are considered crucial to the consolidation of fragile peace. For this and other reasons, elections in African states in general, and post-conflict ones in particular, attract intense attention and support from the AU, as well as from the sub-regional organisations and the international community, in order to ensure the integrity of the processes and to avert violent aftermaths. The AU has focused extensively on monitoring and observing elections. However, the dilemma has been on whether it should simply prepare a calendar of forthcoming elections in a particular year and make plans to observe such polls, or wait until an individual member state invites it to observe elections (African Union 2009). The AU has various organs and structures, such as the Panel of the Wise, whose mandate includes the prevention, management, and resolution of conflicts (including election-related disputes). Special missions have been deployed to various countries to mediate and negotiate a peaceful settlement of post-election conflicts. Within the PCRD, the AU deploys, in an ad hoc manner, multidisciplinary expert missions to assess levels of institution-building and peace consolidation in post-conflict states, and to make short- to medium-term recommendations for consideration by the PSC. For instance, between January and February 2010, missions were deployed to the Democratic Republic of Congo (DRC) and Burundi to assess the dynamics in the peace process, the promotion of development, and regional cooperation (African Union 2010).

The role of civil society

The policy framework acknowledges that civil society can make a significant difference to post-conflict reconstruction and identifies several areas where its contributions are essential: early warning, research, policy development, and capacity-building through training and education. However, since the framework does not clearly indicate how it could collaborate with the AU/NEPAD, civil society does not have a clear, institutionalised interface, beyond discussing the issue at various forums. The AU (and, in particular, the PSC) is charged with leading peacebuilding efforts, while relying heavily on formal state institutions for the implementation of policies to support them. Non-state actors or civil society are accorded important roles, but these remain firmly within the ambit of state-based efforts, whether at the continental, regional, national, or local level. However, it is important to note that while the state arguably remains the principal actor, with the prime responsibility of protecting its citizens and promoting their welfare and well-being, post-conflict governments are extremely weak and often lack the ability to perform their basic functions, such as building the necessary institutional capacity to fulfil their obligations.

In view of the essential contributions that civil society organisations could make to the peace and security endeavour, it is incumbent upon the AU, as well other RECs, to foster effective collaborations. The lack of in-depth analyses of conflicts to provide a sound basis for taking decisions on interventions has been one of the key weaknesses of AU performance (Aning and Birikorang 2010). The AU could therefore harness expert groupings in the areas of conceptual and analytical works in practical peacebuilding activities. This could equally impact on the operationalisation of the AU peace and security architecture in general, and on statebuilding policies in particular.

AU and Security Sector Reform

Security Sector Reform (SSR), although a relatively new concept, has gained greater prominence within the development–security–justice discourse in recent years. This is driven by the understanding that an unreformed security sector is a major obstacle to the promotion of sustainable development, democracy, and peace. As a result, previously separate discourses on security policy, promotion of peace and democracy, and development assistance have now merged (Bryden *et al.* 2005: 8). The absence of effective, democratic governance of the security sector has been a significant factor in many cases of state fragility and civil war in most parts of Africa (Sherman 2009: 2). Furthermore, the ability of state security services to remain neutral in internal political processes has often been a contentious issue (Aning and Bah 2009: 6–7). In most African countries, the security sector has played a dual role in attempting to maintain state stability, while at the same time being itself a major destabilising force. Accordingly, ensuring the democratic governance and improving the performance and overseeing of the security sector (including the military, police, intelligence services, judiciary, and the penal system) can be considered as key to the process of statebuilding. Besides, a security sector that is subject to democratic control and is both effective and efficient could help to reduce the risk of conflict, thereby creating an enabling environment for sustainable development (Tadesse 2010: 20).

In view of this, the Assembly of the African Union charged the AU Commission in February 2008 'to develop a comprehensive AU Policy Framework on SSR, within the context of the Policy Framework on PCRD' (African Union 2008). The policy would, among other objectives, 'assist African states to address the national security imbalance created by not-so-well planned SSR initiatives' (Lamamra 2009). Such a policy on SSR is yet to be formally adopted. However, the PCRD policy framework the AU has tried to incorporate SSR issues in reconstruction processes. SSR is addressed on a case-by-case basis through a three-pronged approach (African Union 2007: Art. 21). First, the broader objective of the policy is to

> create a secure and safe environment for the post-conflict state and its population, through the establishment of the architecture of the state, including the elements of judicial statehood, defined and controlled territory, accountable state control over the means of coercion, and a population whose safety is guaranteed.

Second, the policy touches on the issue of gender, acknowledging the gender sensitive nature of SSR, as well as the issues of political governance. Third, it addresses the main targets of the reform processes and actors or stakeholders.

While the AU's policy framework provision on SSR is encouraging, there are shortcomings in terms of actual practices. Africa is the largest recipient of externally funded SSR-related programmes. However, African ownership and, for that matter, the role of the AU remains limited. Civil society actors and international donors have unabatedly been at the forefront of research, advocacy, and training initiatives in SSR, even before it gained prominence on the continent. On top of this, there has been an extensive focus on normative frameworks at the expense of actual practices in Africa. As mentioned earlier, some of these frameworks are in the formative stage, particularly the AU SSR policy, which could enhance the involvement of the AU, as well as a closer collaboration with other international actors to push for a more broad-based continental buy-in of the SSR agenda. Civil society networks, notably the African Security Sector Network (ASSN), have been facilitating the process by providing technical assistance to the AU. The draft policy document and implementation strategy is subject to deliberation by the PSC and subsequent adoption by the Authority of Heads and States and Governments, before the process of implementation can be kick-started. When this policy, together with the existing framework on PCRD, is fully implemented by the AU, it could promote comprehensive practice of SSR across the continent where the terrain for it is currently very uneven.

AU and economic reform

In all post-conflict countries the challenge of economic recovery is immense and requires a combination of financial resources, policy reforms, and technical assistance, which often has to be provided by external donors. Economic reform is essential to post-conflict statebuilding in Africa because many of the conflict risk factors can be related to the continent's relative economic deprivation. The socio-economic arena is therefore important for dealing with the problems of transforming war economies to sustainable peace economies (Broodryk and Solomon 2010: 17). However, this process remains a serious challenge. In an attempt to address this challenge, the AU policy framework recognises that there is a natural relationship between peace, security, and development, and therefore emphasises the nexus between political stability and economic efficiency. The socio-economic dimension of the AU policy on PCRD covers the recovery, rehabilitation, and reconstruction of basic social and economic services, as well as the return, resettlement, reintegration, and rehabilitation of refugees and internally displaced persons.

One of the cornerstones of AU policy in post-conflict reconstruction is the issue of local ownership and participation. It is widely recognised that externally driven post-conflict peacebuilding and reconstruction activities are not sustainable (United States Institute for Peace 2009: 13). In spite of the lip service paid to the issue of local ownership, external actors are often driven by the need to satisfy their own national interests to the detriment of those of the local population. Post-conflict reconstruction activities should therefore be needs based, and the priorities, sequencing, and pace of delivery need to be informed by the dynamics of the conflict system, through local ownership and meaningful internal/external coordination (De Coning 2008: 101). It is essential to adopt strategies that emphasise the direct transfer of management skills in all affairs to the local citizenry in the shortest possible time. In this regard, there is a need for greater collaboration between the AU/NEPAD and regional economic communities, as well as with the external actors themselves, to map out exit strategies and timetables for international bodies when missions are being planned.

In practice, the AU just like other sub-regional organisations in Africa has yet to deliver concrete measures in promoting sustainable economic reform in both post-conflict and stable countries in Africa. This stems partly from the fact that the AU is itself dependent on external development partners for most of its funding. However, it is worth noting that other agencies, such as the African Development Bank (AfDB), do give practical support to PCRD, and especially economic recovery, in Africa. For example, the Bank helps with both the domestic debt and the heavy burdens owed to the external creditors and other international financial institutions (African Development Bank 2008: 62–4). In 2004 it established the Post-Conflict Countries Facility (PCCF), which helps eligible countries clear their arrears. This is closely co-ordinated with support from the World Bank and the IMF. In June 2004, the AfDB adopted the *Bank Group Post-conflict Assistance Policy Guidelines.* Through this framework, it has worked in close partnership with other donors and international financial institutions to support reconstruction efforts in Liberia, Sierra Leone, Guinea Bissau, and Senegal (Cassamance).

AU and social justice

Addressing social justice ought to be part and parcel of any effort at state-building in post-conflict states, but for Africa it has particular resonance: the issue of fairness or otherwise in the distribution of societal rewards and burdens has been a primary motivation for violent conflict. Even though the Constitutive Act of the AU does not expressly provide for a role in transitional justice on the continent, the AU has become increasingly involved both in negotiating transition in states emerging from conflict and also in fashioning approaches to addressing past human rights atrocities. Accordingly, the AU policy on PCRD identifies the promotion of social justice as essential to the achievement of sustainable post-conflict reconstruction and development in Africa. The policy framework seeks to improve timeliness, effectiveness, and the coordination of activities and to lay the foundation for social justice and sustainable peace, in line with Africa's vision for renewal and growth. Moreover, among its cardinal principles are inclusiveness, equity, and non-discrimination; one of the elements of the policy frameworks encompasses the protection of human and peoples' rights and the respect for their dignity as well as the achievement of justice and reconciliation. However, the framework does not explicitly address the issue of impunity for crimes and atrocities committed during civil conflicts.

It is argued that post-conflict reconstruction cannot be consolidated if there is no transitional healing process or genuine effort at promoting social and economic justice. Nonetheless, the involvement of the AU in addressing past injustices is often ad hoc and focuses on political settlements rather than holistic interventions to achieve lasting peace. Its participation is also contingent upon state invitation or the particular political circumstances in a member state. In most instances, finding the balance between the demands for justice and the many political constraints – especially the maintenance of peace and stability – has been a major challenge (Huyse 2008). The AU is always wary of the retributive effects of such processes. A classic example is its controversial decision not to comply with the warrant issued by the International Criminal Court for the arrest of Omar al-Beshir of Sudan for crimes against humanity in Darfur. The reason proffered by the AU was that, given the fragility of the peace in Sudan, any judicial or criminal accountability process against the leadership might disturb or derail the political situation, in particular the long-term peace process.

Some organs and special institutions of the AU, such as the Pan-African Parliament, the African Court of Justice, the Economic, Social and Cultural Council, African Commission on Human and Peoples' Rights (ACHPR), and the African Court on Human and Peoples' Rights, contribute in various significant roles to fostering social justice in post-conflict and stable states alike. However, not all their efforts have been entirely successful. For instance, the effectiveness of ACHPR is constrained by the fact that it can only issue non-binding resolutions and recommendations to member states.

The issue of gender is one that cuts across all areas of post-conflict reconstruction, but most especially in the promotion of social justice. Considering the adverse effects of conflicts on the grassroots populace, particularly women and children, a policy framework on PCRD that ignores the roles and needs of more than half of the population cannot provide an effective basis for achieving the goals of statebuilding (Murithi 2006). For that reason, it is praiseworthy that the AU policy framework includes women and gender relations as one of its key elements. Nonetheless, the framework has not clearly articulated a commitment to gender mainstreaming, and does not differ significantly from the dominant tendency among international donors to define a limited set of strategic priorities for their engagement in fragile states. These tend to include areas such as the establishment of minimum conditions for security and standards for the delivery of basic services, while issues of gender are generally seen as luxury to be left aside until the supposedly 'gender-neutral' objectives in the domains of security and governance have been achieved (Steven and Smits 2010). This has significant implications for the effectiveness of the statebuilding agenda. Even where there is a commitment to integrate gender into statebuilding programmes, the difficulty lies in transforming this commitment into pragmatic gender-responsive strategies.

The complementary role of ECOWAS in the AU's statebuilding processes

ECOWAS is perhaps the leading sub-regional organisation that has been instrumental in dealing with peace and security issues in Africa. It has made remarkable strides in these areas due to the relatively unstable nature of the West African sub-region and the need to respond to such challenges. The intermittent interventions undertaken by ECOWAS have provided it with a wealth of experience in managing conflicts, and its role and programmes supplement the AU's newly stated continental ambitions in the fields of peace and security (Bach 2006: 7). Sub-regional institutions are considered part and parcel of the overall APSA though the AU has the primary responsibility for promoting peace, security, and stability in Africa. The Peace and Security and chairperson of the AU commission are tasked to make conscious efforts to harmonise and coordinate the activities of Regional Mechanisms in the fields of peace, security, and stability to ensure that these activities are consistent with the objectives and principles of the AU (African Union 2002: Art. 16).

Although ECOWAS is a subsidiary of the AU, its comparative advantage in West Africa and proactive stance on conflicts, as well as its internal organisation and institutional capacity, mean it is often ahead of similar processes within the AU (Musah 2009: 14–15). As noted earlier, Nigeria has committed enormous resources over the years to conflict prevention, management, and resolution, as well as to post-conflict statebuilding in the region. Following its success in restoring peace in Liberia and to some extent in Sierra Leone, ECOWAS has established several comprehensive legal and normative instruments for confronting new threats to both human and regional security on a more permanent and predictable basis (ibid.: 17). Most notable are protocols relating to the Mechanism for Conflict Prevention, Management, Resolution, Peacekeeping and Security of 1999, and the ECOWAS Conflict Prevention Framework (ECPF) of 2008. Unlike the AU, ECOWAS has yet to develop a holistic policy framework on post-conflict reconstruction and development, even if most of its peace and security instruments reiterate the commitment of ECOWAS to democratic governance as key to statebuilding. It therefore has to be said that the involvement of ECOWAS in overall peacebuilding in the region has been comparatively weak and less systematic (Olonisakin 2011). ECOWAS statebuilding practices, especially in the areas of political governance, economic reform, SSR, and social justice, do not differ significantly from those of the AU.

ECOWAS and political governance

Since the 1991 adoption of its *Declaration of Principles of Freedom, People's Rights and Democratisation,* ECOWAS has spearheaded the process of 're-democratisation' as a critical component of its peacebuilding agenda. The declaration consolidates the political ideas that had been evolving in the sub-region and seeks to 'promote and encourage the full enjoyment by all West African people their fundamental human rights, especially their political, economic, social, cultural and other rights inherent in the dignity of the human person and essential to free and progressive development' (ECOWAS 1991). ECOWAS member states are also committed to encouraging political pluralism in their countries and 'those representative institutions and guarantees for personal safety and freedom under the law that are our common heritage'. The Revised ECOWAS Treaty of 1993 emphasises the importance of democracy and the rule of law. This was followed by the Protocol relating to the Mechanism for Conflict Prevention, Management, Resolution, Peacekeeping and Security of 1999, which reaffirms the recognition by ECOWAS and its members of the convergence of socio-economic development and security of peoples and states (ECOWAS 2001: Art. 2(a)). Moreover, the Protocol on Democracy and Good Governance of 2001, as a supplement to the Mechanism, established the guiding principles that would help to foster participatory democracy, good governance and the rule of law, respect for human rights, and a balanced and equitable distribution of resources. This protocol is considered the most elaborate and candid in terms of its linkage of peace, security, and good governance (besides NEPAD) (Bryden *et al.* 2005: 3). It therefore gives ECOWAS the supranational authority for intervention in member states in relation to the issues of governance, democratic development, human rights and respect for constitutionalism, rule of law, and peace and security. However, issues have been raised with regards to the efficacy of the protocol. For instance, it does not have a graduated response mechanism to deal with the manner in which political incumbency is abused and how that contributes to violence in societies (Aning and Bah 2009: 4).

In addition to the above, ECOWAS specifically placed governance-related issues at the core of the ECOWAS Conflict Prevention Framework (ECPF) adopted in 2008, in recognition of the correlation between governance challenges and conflicts in West Africa. ECOWAS also seeks to 'extend opportunities for conflict prevention to post-conflict environments through targeted restructuring of political governance, conflict-sensitive reconstruction and development, as well as humanitarian crisis prevention and preparedness, and related peace-building initiatives' (2008).

In terms of actual practice, some attempts have been made by ECOWAS to promote good political governance, including the observation and monitoring of elections. Over the years, it has also sanctioned some member states for flouting its protocols, thereby compelling some states like Togo, Guinea, and Niger to adopt constitutional rule. ECOWAS took some steps, together with the AU, to wean post-conflict Guinea Bissau off its militarised politics and criminality, and to push for wide-ranging economic and security sector reforms (Musah 2009: 9–10). After adopting the 1999 protocol on the Mechanism and 2001 supplementary protocol on Democracy and Good Governance, ECOWAS became active once again in Guinea Bissau in 2004, especially after the 6 October mutiny (Yabi 2010: 21). It provided a grant of US$500,000 to pay part of the salary arrears to soldiers; it also established a permanent presence in Guinea Bissau by nominating a Special Representative of the Executive Secretary to collaborate with national authorities and the international community in order to promote peace and stability in the country (United Nations 2004a). Together with the UN, AU, and other Portuguese-speaking countries, ECOWAS was instrumental in easing the tensions linked to the controversial candidatures of Nino Vieira and Kumba Yala in the run-up to the presidential elections held in June and July 2005. After the elections, which brought about the restoration of constitutional order, the Executive Secretary of ECOWAS, within his mandate under the 1999 protocol, again deployed a fact-finding mission on the situation of the country in the areas of security, social, humanitarian, and political developments.

The assassinations of the Chief of Defence Staff General Batista Tagme Na Wai and President Joao Bernando 'Nino' Vieira in March 2009 plunged the country into deep insecurity. Various preventive diplomatic initiatives were undertaken by ECOWAS to help find a lasting solution to the political crisis. It subsequently supported the conduct of presidential elections in June and July 2009. Afterwards, an AU/ECOWAS Joint Assessment Mission was deployed between 30 October and 10 November 2009 to assess ways to assist the new government of President Malam Bacai Sanha in the reform of the defence and security sectors, post-conflict reconstruction and development, and the fight against drug trafficking (ECOWAS 2009).

ECOWAS and security sector reform

The ECPF identified security sector governance as one of its key areas of focus. However, the critical issue worth considering at this point is the actual role that ECOWAS has played in SSR in the sub-region. ECOWAS is in the process of implementation of the Defence and Security Sector Reform Programme (DSSRP), considered as a crucial factor in the process of socio-political stabilisation of Guinea Bissau (ECOWAS Commission 2010) and it has allocated $63 million from the community funds to cover the priority activities of the programme. These include: launching of the pension fund and initial demobilisation, reintegration, and socio-economic reintegration operations; deployment of a technical assistance team to strengthen and train national units in charge of protecting institutions and officials; and contributing to protecting the National Inquiry Commission and setting up of a witness protection programme (ECOWAS Commission 2011).

Despite the growing recognition that regional insecurity negatively affects national level security, and that SSR deficits have serious implications for regional security, ECOWAS is yet to implement the Security Sector Governance (SSG) component of the ECPF. A key benchmark in the existence of an operational ECOWAS Security Governance Framework to guide the practice in West Africa is yet to be fully developed (Tadesse 2010). However, there are ongoing processes within ECOWAS towards the development of an SSR concept and action plan. It is obvious that the problems with implementing the ECPF in general, and the SSR component especially, have arisen from a lack of coherence and coordination within ECOWAS, between ECOWAS and the member states, and with donor partners (Lar 2009). There are gaps in coherence and coordination between the ECOWAS Commission, which is expected to facilitate the SSG, and the member states that implement it. In addition, there are internal problems with coherence and coordination within the structures responsible for SSG particularly the Security Division of the Commission for Political Affairs, Peace Keeping and Regional Security.

ECOWAS and economic reform

Although the primary objective for the formation of ECOWAS was to promote economic development through sub-regional integration, its role in achieving this aim, especially in post-conflict countries in West Africa, has been very minimal. The protocols and frameworks we have used as reference points for ECOWAS' statebuilding practice include economic development as a critical element for rebuilding post-conflict countries. For instance, Article 44 of the Mechanism, which deals with peacebuilding at the end of hostilities, reiterates the commitment of ECOWAS to assist member states that have been adversely affected by violent conflicts, aiming to do so through a number of activities, which include 'the establishment of conditions for the political, social and economic reconstruction of the society and governmental institutions'.

ECOWAS, just like other sub-regional organisations in Africa, and even the continental body the AU, has not done much to promote economic reforms in post-conflict countries. This is due to the fact that financially constrained African regional institutions often rely on external international development institutions such as the UN, the World Bank and the IMF, the EU, and bilateral donors for most of their funds. Most importantly, the individual African states that are members of these institutions are themselves recipients of external economic assistance. Usually, these external institutions are instrumental in funding and implementing programmes aimed at promoting economic recovery in post-conflict states. However, most often, such initiatives are undertaken in partnership with regional institutions. For example, a string of external actors, including ECOWAS, the AU, European Commission, IMF, World Bank, United States, Ghana, and Nigeria, came together to introduce the idea of the Governance and Economic Management Assistance Program (GEMAP) for Liberia in September 2005.

In addition, ECOWAS has extended some financial assistance to Guinea Bissau and has been instrumental in engaging the international community, particularly the UN, EU, and the Community of Portuguese Speaking Countries, (*Comunidade dos Países de Língua Portuguesa*, CPLP), to support recovery efforts in Guinea Bissau. ECOWAS spearheaded the creation of an International Contact Group on Guinea Bissau (ICG-GB) to serve as a platform for coordinating and harmonising the intervention of the country's partners with the dual objective of achieving political stability and economic recovery (United Nations 2006a). The ICG-GB made it possible for ECOWAS and other member states represented in this group to carry out advocacy among donor countries and multilateral institutions on the need to consider the peculiar fragility of Guinea Bissau on the one hand, and the relationship between economic stabilisation of the country and enhancing security of the state and that of the whole west African sub-region on the other. Again during the same period, ECOWAS and its most powerful member state, Nigeria, came to the aid of the government of Guinea Bissau, which was besieged with challenges in performing its basic functions, such as the payment of public sector salaries. Nigeria provided emergency financial assistance of $2.5 million, while ECOWAS contributed 1.5 million dollars (ibid.).

ECOWAS and social justice

One of the primary motivations behind regional economic integration is the development of the people of the region concerned. The issue of social justice, especially human rights, has been part and parcel of the ECOWAS statebuilding agenda. The 1991 ECOWAS Declaration of Political Principles is often considered the lynchpin commitment of the sub-regional body to ensure social justice in West Africa. Moreover, the Revised Treaty (which elaborates on it) provides the context for the enhancement of the protection and promotion of human rights. In spite of the elaborate mechanisms for ensuring social justice in general, and promoting and protecting human rights in post-conflict states in West Africa in particular, the greatest challenge has to do with the enforcement through judicial as well as non-judicial mechanisms of the norms. For instance, the Community Court of Justice was established by Article 25 of the Revised Treaty to adjudicate in matters of human rights abuses brought before it by member states and ECOWAS citizens. The jurisdiction of the court has been limited to inter-state matters rather than issues affecting citizens of the community. Although its judgements are binding on all member states, community institutions, individuals, and corporate bodies, the effectiveness of its decisions has been called into question and some member states have not always abided by its decisions. ECOWAS therefore needs to adopt more practical measures to prevent the authority of the Court from being undermined and adopt punitive measures for those who ignore its judgements.

Conclusion

It hardly needs stating that state fragility has significant implications for regional and international peace and security – conflict is a cause or consequence of state weakness or failure. Therefore the building of more secure post-conflict societies is an important ingredient in making war unattractive to armed groups. To this end, post-conflict statebuilding should be based on case-specific policies and strategies that aim at facilitating the transition to sustainable peace, and at the same time addressing the long-term human security needs of conflict afflicted countries and its people. Given the diversity of approaches to statebuilding by various international actors and their differing motives and strategies, regional bodies are important actors because they have a nuanced understanding of conflict dynamics and needs of the post-conflict country concerned and are able to formulate responsive strategies to address them.

There is a wide gulf between the frameworks established by the AU and ECOWAS for regionally sensitive post-conflict reconstruction and development and the actual practice. For example, while the AU has set up a

Post-Conflict Reconstruction and Development Unit within the Conflict Management Division of the Peace and Security Department in 2007, this unit has yet to be operationalised. In addition, a ministerial committee on post-conflict reconstruction and development has still to be established to provide political support and resource mobilisation for implementation of the policy framework. Some steps towards concrete action have indeed been made. These include the establishment of the Post-Conflict Reconstruction Committee on the Sudan. Similarly, ECOWAS has also set up elaborate structures aimed at making the Mechanism operational through a coherent, strategic approach. Nevertheless, operationalising these policies and this framework remains a work in progress.

Several reasons account for the lack of practical activity on the ground, some of which have been discussed in earlier sections, but it worth drawing together some common threads. The slow pace of implementation of their policy frameworks has been a general trend for both organisations and stems from numerous factors. One such is lack of political will and commitment on the part of the member states. Regional and sub-regional organisations in Africa are known for being quick at adopting various instruments aimed at addressing the different challenges confronting the continent. However, when it comes to backing their signatures with actions, these organisations and their member states often do not act with the same sense of urgency and commitment. Besides, they are often driven by and preoccupied with crisis response, rather than forestalling crisis through effective post-conflict reconstruction and development policies and activities.

Regional bodies in Africa in general, and specifically the AU and ECOWAS, are faced with several serious challenges. Both the AU and ECOWAS are severely understaffed and overstretched due to the limited number of personnel available with the requisite technical expertise. Financial constraints further limit the ability of regional bodies to effectively carry out their activities or policies. Over the years, their funding has increased significantly, yet their ambitions continue to outstrip their capacity and resources. ECOWAS is funded to a large extent by internal means, but its activities in the areas of peace and security are significantly dependent on external assistance (United Nations Office of the Special Advisor on Africa 2007: 29). This is a similar scenario for the AU, 95 per cent of whose staff (and to a lesser extent its programmes) are funded directly or indirectly by partners. While external assistance helps regional organisations to increase their role and effectiveness, it also means that they are also left to the mercy of the changing funding patterns of donors. Not only that, but regional organisations face difficulties in utilising the funds received in a timely manner. This challenge coupled with complex financial procedures and reporting requirements, often leads to low levels of absorption of external assistance, a factor that further undermines the effectiveness of the organisations concerned.

In conclusion, we can say that the actual practices of AU and ECOWAS in statebuilding have been minimal. At best they have tried to influence the statebuilding policies and practices of external actors on the continent. Both bilateral as well as multilateral partners are required, such as the UN (particularly the Peacebuilding Commission), the EU, and the World Bank, which has the greater financial and technical resources to partner and strengthen regional institutions as platforms for action in response to state weakness or failure in Africa. There is a need for concerted and coherent efforts aimed at translating these policies into actions that address the social, economic, and political and security needs of the post-conflict countries. The AU and ECOWAS should concentrate on improving state–society relations, effective disarmament, demobilisation and reintegration processes, transitional justice, building strong apolitical state institutions, security sector reform, and rebuilding social infrastructure. Above all, they should try to develop a strong oversight of their policies and programmes aimed at promoting post-conflict statebuilding in Africa.

Part III

Case studies

12 Back to the future

The failure to reform the post-war political economy of Iraq

Toby Dodge

On 27 November 2008, the Iraqi parliament voted to accept a new set of treaties marking the effective end of the American occupation and indeed its post-war ambitions for Iraq. The Status of Forces Agreement (SOFA) sets an unambiguous timetable for all US troops to be out of the country. With a date set for the formal end of the occupation, the scale of the United States' ambitions to transform Iraq, and its failure, have now become fully apparent. US war aims in Iraq involved nothing less than a complete revolution in the country's political economy. The removal of Saddam Hussein's regime was the first and most straightforward part of that plan. However, from Washington's point of view, for regime change to be sustainable, a second stage of the process would be the complete removal of the old Iraqi ruling elite from the commanding heights of the state. They needed to be replaced by politicians who were much less economically and politically autonomous. This would involve removing any political role for former members of the old regime and minimizing their influence in the coercive and administrative structures of the state. The US occupation also needed to identify and marginalize other indigenous political forces that might destabilize a pro-US agenda.

In conjunction with removing the old ruling elite and marginalizing the room for spoilers, the US wanted to reduce the power and capacity of the state's armed forces so it could no longer dominate its population or destabilize the region. By 2011 it was clear that the US had successfully managed the almost complete removal of the old civilian elite and their replacement by the new formally exiled politicians who now dominate politics in Baghdad. But the Iraqi military, in size, role, and political control, had grown to resemble not only comparable security forces across the Middle East but the old armed forces the invasion had targeted for destruction.

Beyond changing the personnel of the state, the occupation set out to completely reform the economy along unabashedly neo-liberal lines, freeing the Iraqi population to interact with global markets, thus minimizing the space for the state to constrain their lives. This, the fourth stage of the US agenda in Iraq, has also singularly failed to produce the desired results.

Finally, in recognition of the ideological justification for regime change, the new governing elite transported back into Iraq by the US would also need to garner for itself a degree of electoral legitimacy.

Attempts at transforming Iraq's post-invasion political economy have resulted in three prime ministers, three sets of national elections, and a new constitution anointed by national referendum. Iraq's new ruling elite, chosen by Washington and put in power by the force of American arms, appeared to be solidly entrenched, capable of coercively and economically sustaining itself after the departure of US troops in 2011. Beyond the ruling elite, however, the political economy of Iraq, the state's relations with the economy and its population, remain remarkably similar to those that structured pre-regime change relations.

The cost of the United States' ambitious reform agenda, not only in terms of American blood and treasure but in the lives and suffering of the 'liberated' Iraqis, is difficult to exaggerate. Three overlapping conflicts, all originating from US attempts at transforming the country's political economy, are conservatively estimated to have killed between 98,691 and 107,708 in the period from 2003 to 2010.[1] The first conflict was caused by the invasion itself and the continued presence of US troops. The second conflict was caused by the insurgency that erupted in the summer of 2003. This saw numerous disparate and localized groups fighting to drive US forces from Iraq and reverse the central tenets of their transformative agenda. The third conflict, the civil war that engulfed Iraq in 2005 and raged until at least 2008, has been the most destructive. In the case of all three conflicts, the agenda and the actions of the US-led coalition either directly caused the rising violence, or policy decisions they imposed contributed to its escalation.

The political dispensation that has emerged from the invasion and civil war may well be sustainable and in broad alignment with the US but it has been achieved at a cost that would have prohibited the initial decision to invade if known at the time. However, the basis to Iraq's political economy, a rentier state fuelled by oil revenue striving to coercively dominate society, remains largely unchanged by the invasion and its aftermath. Invasion, regime change, and civil war have certainly removed the old ruling elite, which has been replaced with a group of formerly exiled politicians loosely tied to Washington. However, as this new ruling elite slowly solidified and tightened its grip on the levers of power given to them by the US, it has set about ruling Iraq in a broadly similar way to the Ba'athist regime it replaced, using oil funded patronage and coercion to guarantee its own survival. The cost of this extended exercise in socio-political engineering and its modest results raise profound questions about the aims and means of interventions into counties about which the putative socio-political engineers know so little.

The changing political economy of Iraq before 2003

The decision makers that drove the US to invade and their top administrator who ran the first year of the occupation were unambiguous that the target of the war and its aftermath was the political economy of Iraq. This political economy, they argued, was broadly similar across the region as a whole.

It had facilitated Saddam Hussein's continued defiance and led to the Middle East being the least 'liberalized' area in the developing world (Dodge 2006). To quote Donald Rumsfeld, the Secretary of Defense during the second National Security Council meeting of the Bush administration's first term: 'Imagine what the region would look like without Saddam and with a regime that's aligned with US interests ... It would change everything in the region and beyond it. It would demonstrate what US policy is all about' (Suskind 2004: 72 and 85). To a large degree, the political economy of Iraq after the Ba'ath Party seized power in 1968 was typical of the post-colonial republican states of the *mashreq*. As these regimes strove to consolidate their power they faced indigenous economic classes who lacked the financial power or social coherence to effectively challenge state dominance (Anderson 1987: 11). The radical nationalists who seized the state after independence were comparatively unrestrained by domestic economic interest groups as they attempted to transform society by unleashing a state driven 'revolution from above'. The post-colonial army officers and bureaucrats who seized control aimed to 'modernize' their economies and societies without mobilizing a mass political movement that could threaten their newly obtained political power (Trimberger 1978: 3–4).

Although there were different levels of autonomy across the region, the state driven development strategies pursued throughout the Middle East from the 1950s onwards were directly and indirectly sheltered from the dynamics of the global economy by increasing oil wealth and its associated inter-Arab aid and worker remittances.[2] From the 1950s until 1973, the oil producing states of the region managed to gain increasing control over the oil extracted from their territory, gradually increasing their autonomy from their own populations and within the international economy. This process increased dramatically with the oil price rises of 1973/4. Oil-rich states could in effect temporarily demobilize the political aspirations of their societies with generous welfare payments and lavish spending on the coercive instruments of repression (Luciani 1990; Beblawi 1990).

This dynamic of oil driven state autonomy reached its regional peak under the Ba'athist state of President Hasan al-Bakr after 1968 and was consolidated under Saddam Hussein after he seized power in 1979. With estimates putting the proportion of the Iraqi GDP that was dependent upon the export of oil at anything between 60 and 75 per cent, the oil price shock of the mid-1970s transformed the political economy of the country. This influx of resources allowed the regime to build a powerful set of state institutions through the 1970s and early 1980s. These shaped Iraqi society, breaking organized resistance to Ba'athist rule and effectively atomizing the population. This change in the political economy of Iraq in the 1970s delivered massive and unprecedented power to the small ruling elite who controlled the state. By 1990, 21 per cent of the active workforce and 40 per cent of Iraqi households were directly reliant on government payouts (al-Khafaji 2000: 68). The state funnelled a proportion of its new resources into a social security system, new housing projects, and investments in health and education. By the 1970s, the

Iraqi population were increasingly and self-consciously linked directly to the largesse of state institutions funded by oil wealth. By deploying coercion, infrastructural power, and patronage in hitherto unheard-of quantities, the Ba'athist regime destroyed any organizational capacity within society that could have been mobilized to threaten it.

In conjunction with building powerfully intrusive state institutions, the first Ba'athist president of Iraq, Hasan al-Bakr and his successor Saddam Hussein, built an equally powerful and invasive patronage network, in effect a shadow state. This flexible network of patronage and control was estimated to have a million people in its pay in exchange for personal loyalty to the upper echelons of the ruling elite (Tripp 2002: 17; Tripp 2002–2003: 23–27; Baram 1998: 13).

Iraq's invasion of Kuwait in 1990 should have seen a dramatic transformation of Iraq's political economy. The United Nations (UN) placed Iraq within the harshest and most intrusive sanctions regime in diplomatic history. This was overtly designed to stop the ruling elite's access to export revenues, forcing it either to conform to the demands of the Security Council or be removed from power through a popular uprising. In 1990 UN Security Council resolutions froze Iraq's worldwide assets and banned all imports and exports. In April 1991, after the successful war to liberate Kuwait, Security Council Resolution 687 stated that sanctions would only be lifted if Iraq conformed to a series of demands that covered not only disarmament and war reparations but also how it ruled its population (Dodge 2010b).

The subsequent effects of sanctions upon Iraq's ruling elite were not what the Security Council had expected in 1991. The extended use of sanctions saw a shift in 'the balance between civil society and the state, weakening civil society and emphasizing state power' (Niblock 2001: 186). In effect, 'given the regime's social structure, the main impact of sanctions was to empower the already powerful and impoverish the victims and opponents of the regime' (al-Khafaji 2000: 80).

In 1990 the Iraqi government did initially move to limit the damage that sanctions were causing the population. It quickly set up a rationing system that delivered basic food parcels to the population in government controlled territory. Every citizen had a ration card and food was distributed through a network of 45,864 government controlled shops (Niblock 2001: 139). Beyond partially meeting the nutritional needs of the population, the rationing system became one of the most coherent institutions of state power under sanctions. In order to receive their meagre monthly basket of staples, households had to supply detailed information to the representative of the state in their neighbourhood. This allowed the state to compile a great deal of information in return for the food distributed. In addition, individuals could not claim their rations outside their designated area thus restricting population movement (Niblock 2001: 186; Graham-Brown 1999: 169–170). Overall, the rationing system tied an increasingly impoverished population to the state, exacerbating their dependence on the ruling elite that sanctions were meant to coerce and societal pressure reform.

One very noticeable effect of sanctions was the retreat from society of the official institutions of the state beyond the rationing system. This was especially pronounced in the areas of welfare, health, and education. Using the excuse of 'self-financing', state agencies from hospitals to schools were hollowed out, starved of funding, and encouraged to extract what resources they could from the wider population (al-Khafaji 2000: 82).

Sanctions, in effect, taught the regime where it had to concentrate its resources in order to guarantee its survival. The shadow state became the major recipient of what resources the ruling elite could access. It gave the regime a comparatively loyal and stable base within society, linking them directly to the small group surrounding Saddam Hussein through personal chains of patronage that by-passed impoverished public institutions. In addition, smuggling and embargo running created 'an emerging class of nouveaux riche, an economic and social "mafia"', who through their ties to the ruling elite managed to prosper and break sanctions (Marr 2000: 90).

The direct effect of sanctions on the ruling elite also had unintended consequences. In the aftermath of the Gulf war, as sanctions made themselves felt, the composition of the elite narrowed. Saddam Hussein, when faced with an extended economic siege, switched his reliance from the people of knowledge, *Ahl al-Kheber*, the technocrats, and party apparatchiks who had largely staffed the middle to higher ranks of the state, to the *Ahl al-Thiaqa*, the people of trust, his family, clansmen, and close associates (Baran 2003). In the first three months after the war, 14 senior army commanders were removed. Saddam's long serving deputy and brother-in-law, Izzat Ibrahim al Duri, was given the job of Deputy Commander-in-Chief, while his paternal cousin, Ali Hassan al-Majid was appointed Minister of Interior. His son-in-law and cousin, Hussein Kamil Hassan al-Majid became Minister of Defence. As the 1990s dragged on, his three half-brothers, Barzan, Wathban, and Sib'awi all came to occupy key posts in the intelligence networks with his youngest son Qusai promoted to become the de facto president-in-waiting (Freedman and Karsh 1993: 419). Below immediate family, members of Saddam's clan, the Beijat, and his tribal grouping the Albu Nasir came to occupy increasing numbers of senior military, intelligence, and government posts (Tripp 2000: 193, 198; Jabar 2003: 85).

On the eve of the US invasion in 2003, the political economy built by the Ba'athist regime had proven to be both robust and remarkably flexible. It had kept the regime in power through the gruelling eight year war with Iran and had been transformed by 13 years of the harshest sanctions ever imposed on a state. However, through diverting resources from the formal public institutions of state power to the covert and flexible networks of patronage, the ruling elite shrank but survived. It was this political economy, which gave the regime such a high degree of autonomy from society, which was the central target of the US invasion. After Saddam Hussein's removal, Iraq was subjected to neo-liberal shock therapy.

US transformational goals for the political economy of Iraq: structural adjustment led by the Marine Corps and Air Force

The American agenda for reforming the post-war political economy of Iraq had three targets; the ruling elite, the coercive capacity of the state, and the state's presence within the economy. This agenda had its heritage in 20 years of neo-liberal policy prescriptions for the post-colonial world. This approach was born of the 'Washington Consensus' developed in the 1980s, which saw the International Monetary Fund and the World Bank applying the 'wisdom of market reliance' to developing countries in economic difficulty. Regime change in Baghdad was to be structural adjustment led by the Marine Corps and enforced by the US Air Force but with transformatory ambitions that outstripped even the wildest dreams of the IMF and World Bank.

Purging the old ruling elite

It was the power of Iraqi state institutions, forged in the 1970s and 1980s, which the US assumed they would inherit once they reached Baghdad. In February 2003, Douglas Feith, Under Secretary for Policy at the Pentagon, told the Senate Foreign Relations Committee 'that Iraq's governmental structures would be salvageable. After eliminating Ba'athists implicated in atrocities, the major institutions and ministries would remain in place and continue to perform essential functions just as before' (Phillips 2005: 125). Condoleezza Rice, the National Security Advisor agreed, 'The concept was that we would defeat the army, but the institutions would hold, everything from ministries to police forces' (Gordon 2004). The plan was for a small and speedy US force, backed by overwhelming air power and 'battlefield dominance' to race to Baghdad. They would then seize the state. Once this initial victory had been achieved the first policy objective was to purge the higher echelons of the state by removing the old Ba'athist ruling elite. After this was done, the US would then move to make sure the state would never again dominate society with such force or pose such a threat to regional stability. This would involve shrinking the state's coercive apparatus. Finally, an overt neo-liberal agenda would be realized by pushing state institutions out of the economy, allowing privatization, 'market reliance', and foreign direct investment to rejuvenate Iraq. Ironically, the head on clash between a neo-liberal policy agenda and Iraqi realities meant that only stage one of this ambitious agenda was ever realized.

It was Paul Bremer, as head of the Coalition Provisional Authority (CPA) from 12 May 2003 to 28 April 2004, who was charged with implementing this plan. On 16 May 2003, after only four days in the country, Bremer issued Coalition Provisional Authority General Order No. 1, 'The De-Ba'athification of Iraqi Society'.[3] This mandated the sacking of all Ba'ath Party members in government employment who had held the top four most senior party ranks. The de-Ba'athification order purged government ministries of their top layer of management, at a time when restoring government services was the most important way to win over sceptical Iraqi public opinion. The administrational capacity of the state had been destroyed by over a decade of sanctions, three wars in 20 years, and then the three weeks of uncontrolled looting triggered by the arrival of American troops in Baghdad. Bremer's decision to pursue de-Ba'athification, in effect, removed what was left of the state: its institutional memory and a large section of its skilled personnel.

For the US the aim of the order was to clear out the old ruling elite from the apparatuses of state power along with the highest echelons of the old technocratic elite. To ensure the thorough reform of Iraq's political economy, the negative influences of the old Iraqi state had to be totally purged. De-Ba'athification would do this, reducing the capacity of the state, pushing its institutions out of areas of the economy and society it should never have entered. This would allow space for the market to flourish, bringing with it the disciplinary effects of capitalism, forcing Iraqis to be free. However, Bremer's desire to reform the state's relations with the market was so great that he did not or could not consider the negative consequences of his actions. Such a brutal attack on an already feeble state far from forcing freedom on Iraqis drove them into open revolt.

Breaking the coercive power of the state

The second decision Bremer took during his first fortnight in Baghdad was equally controversial and far more damaging to the US presence in Iraq: the disbanding of the Iraqi army.[4]

Like General Order No. 1, the disbanding of the army by Bremer so quickly after his arrival in Baghdad shows the determination with which he set about attempting to reform Iraq's political economy but also his almost complete lack of detailed knowledge about the country he was supposed to be reforming. Bremer was well aware that the US occupation faced profound shortages of ground troops. He witnessed the nature and extent of the disorder Baghdad was facing as he flew over the city when he first arrived.[5] However, even after acknowledging the lack of coercive manpower and the violent disorder the CPA faced, he still pushed on with disbanding the Iraqi armed forces. Beyond sheer bloody minded stupidity, the only plausible explanation is the reformist agenda that guided him. Bremer's distrust of Iraqi state power was such that he brushed aside doubts about the consequences of his actions and pushed on with disbanding the army, and initially refused to pay the pensions of sacked and retired soldiers. Following the US government's National Security Strategy, Iraqis were now free to choose 'political and economic liberty' and 'free market democracy' (United States Government 2002). Instead the economic and political space created by Bremer's de-Ba'athification order and the disbanding of the army was predictably filled by a number of hastily organized groups free to deploy violence for their own political ends. Or, as Rumsfeld succinctly put it when confronted with the looting of Baghdad, 'Freedom's untidy, and free people are free to make mistakes ... They're also free to live their lives and do wonderful things. And that's what's going to happen here.'[6]

Implementing neo-liberal economic reform

In June 2003, Bremer listed his third policy objective, neo-liberal economic reform, as his 'top priority'. He wanted to 'corporatize and privatize state-owned enterprises,... to wean people from the idea the state supports everything'. Bremer realized this was 'going to be a very wrenching, painful process, as it was in Eastern Europe after the fall of the Berlin Wall'. However, economic transformation was placed at the very centre of the occupation's policy agenda, 'If we don't get their economy right, no matter how fancy our political transformation, it won't work' (Bremer in Chandrasekaran 2007: 68).

The mechanics of this transformation were announced in September 2003, when Bremer promulgated CPA General Order 39.[7] This threw the Iraqi economy open to foreign capital. It removed any restrictions on foreign investment, allowed for 100 per cent repatriation of profits, and legislated for foreign firms to be treated as equal to Iraqi investors. General Order 39 also slated 192 public sector firms for privatization and allowed for 100 per cent foreign ownership of Iraqi companies that were not involved in banking, insurance, or 'the primary extraction of natural resources'.[8] General Order 37 imposed 'a flat tax that provides for a marginal income tax rate of 15 percent for both corporations and individuals' (Juhasz 2004).

Bremer's radical ambitions were breathtaking. The flat tax, the 100 per cent foreign repatriation of profits, a 5 per cent tax on most imports, and 'national treatment' for foreign firms meant that Iraq in 2003 was to be subject to the most thoroughgoing and extreme form of neo-liberal shock treatment of any country in the world. The flat tax had long been a dream of American right wing politicians and business people like Steve Forbes, Jack Kemp, and Phil Gramm (Juhasz 2004). The certainty with which Bremer imposed his economic reform programme on Iraq indicated both the scale of his ambition and his profound lack of imagination in predicting its effects. He also indicated that given the chance he would dismantle the rationing system set up under Saddam Hussein, seeing it as a 'dangerous socialist anachronism' despite it having saved the population from famine during the 13 years of sanctions (Goldberg 2003).

The indigenous results of exogenous reform: Iraq's contemporary political economy

In the aftermath of invasion, the US occupation focused its ambitious attempt at reforming Iraq's political economy on three targets: the ruling elite, the coercive capacity of the state, and the state's presence in the economy. Since 2003, power has indeed been given to and remains with a new, handpicked ruling elite, which has gone through three sets of national and two provincial elections. This elite's commitment to democracy is open to question. From 2007 to 2010 political power has been increasingly concentrated in the hands of one individual, the Prime Minister Nuri al-Maliki. The

Iraqi armed forces were disbanded in 2003. However, in the face of a rising tide of political violence that drove Iraq from an insurgency into a civil war, a new military was quickly rebuilt and today is broadly similar in size and role to the armed forces before regime change. The armed forces then became increasingly politicized in a way very familiar to those students of post-colonial Middle Eastern history. Finally, neo-liberal economic reform, the radical restructuring and reduction of the state's role in the economy, has been an almost complete failure.

Installing Iraq's new ruling elite

By pushing through de-Ba'athification, the US occupation purged the state of the top four most senior ranks of a party with a total membership of two million people. This had disastrous effects on the administrative coherence of the Iraqi state and its ability to deliver services to its population. However, it did clear a space at the top of the state for a new ruling elite to be installed, allowing America's long nurtured allies to acquire positions of power.

The legacy of 35 years of Ba'athist rule greatly complicated US attempts at building a new ruling elite. The power of the Ba'athist regime was such that those who did not flee into exile found it difficult to avoid co-option into its governing structures. On the other hand, those who did flee and later returned with US forces were greeted with suspicion, damned for collaborating with the Americans, or living in the comparative comfort of exile. The division between those who stayed and those who fled was exacerbated by the politicized and opportunist use of accusations of 'Ba'athism', frequently deployed by returning politicians against those who disagreed with them or stood in their way. To quote the Iraqi author and journalist Zuhair al-Jezairy, 'The returnees looked on the insiders in general like they were the whores of the previous regime. Intellectuals in particular they considered the apologists of the maximum leaders and the marketers of his wars' (al-Jezairy 2009: 160). The extent to which power was transferred from the existing indigenous elite to a new set of formerly exiled politicians is indicated by the work of Phebe Marr. Marr's research in Baghdad suggests that only 26.8 per cent of the post-regime change political elite are 'insiders', those who stayed in Iraq under Ba'athist rule (2006: 8). The rest, the vast majority of those now ruling Iraq, returned to Baghdad in the aftermath of regime change to take control of a country about which they knew little.

This exile-dominated structure of government first gained influence with the formation of the Iraqi Governing Council (IGC) in July 2003. Sergio Viera de Mello, the UN Secretary-General's first post-war envoy, became increasingly concerned that Iraq under occupation had no receptacle for its abrogated sovereignty (Steele 2003). He persuaded Paul Bremer to set up the IGC as both an advisory body and a government-in-waiting. The CPA promoted the IGC as 'the most representative body in Iraq's history'. The representative nature of the IGC did not come from the undemocratic and non-transparent method of its formation: extended negotiations between the

CPA, Vierira de Mello, and the seven dominant, formerly exiled parties (ICG 2003: 14). Instead, the CPA focused on the supposedly 'balanced' nature of its membership. The politicians it chose were believed to represent the ethnic and religious make-up of Iraq: 13 Shias, five Sunnis, five Kurds, a Turkoman, and a Christian. The forced and rather bizarre nature of this arrangement was highlighted by the inclusion of Hamid Majid Mousa, the Iraqi Communist Party's representative, in the 'Shia bloc' of 13. Such sectarian mathematics were also used to expand the number of cabinet portfolios to 25, so that offices (and more importantly the resources that came with them) could be divided up in a similar fashion.

With the encouragement of the formerly exiled parties and the Kurdish parties of northern Iraq, both Vierira de Mello and Bremer had been persuaded to primordialize Iraq, to organize its politics along ethnic and religious lines. For the Iraqi political parties advocating this policy, specifically the Kurdistan Democratic Party, the Patriotic Union of Kurdistan, and the Islamic Supreme Council of Iraq, this primordial approach had the advantage of dividing the Iraqi polity in a way that delivered votes along ethnic and religious lines, conveniently marginalizing other mobilizing dynamics such as insider/outsider, or pro- and anti-occupation. However, for the wider Iraqi population, the introduction of an overtly sectarian discourse into politics was a worrying and destabilizing dynamic.

The handover of sovereign power to the formerly exiled politicians on the IGC accelerated through the autumn and winter of 2003, as violence escalated and the start of George Bush's re-election campaign came closer. In November 2003 the Bush administration set 30 June 2004 as the deadline for transferring sovereignty back to Iraqis. The task now facing both the US and Iraq's new ruling elite was to find a way to anoint this new political dispensation with democratic legitimacy.

The democratic process was inaugurated by the elections of 30 January 2005. Because of organizational and security concerns, the vote itself was held with one nationwide electoral constituency (Turner 2004). This removed local issues and personalities from the campaign; marshalling many politicians and parties into large coalitions (Dawisha and Diamond 2006: 93), most of which played to the lowest common denominator, deploying ethnosectarian rhetoric (see also Ben Reilly's chapter in this volume). The advantage of such a campaign for the political parties was that it forced voters to cast aside their suspicions about the recently retuned politicians and their resentment at the continuing US presence and instead cast their ballots along sectarian lines.

This process to legitimize the new ruling elite in the face of increasing popular alienation and violence reached its peak with a second nationwide ballot for a full-term government on 15 December 2005. Following on from the legacy of the first elections, this poll was again dominated by three multi-party coalitions, attempting to maximize their electoral power by deploying ethno-sectarian ideologies. Voter turnout reached 76 per cent, with the United Iraqi Alliance, the coalition formed to maximize the Shia vote, taking

46.5 per cent of the vote and delivering 128 candidates to parliament. The Kurdish Alliance won 19.27 per cent of the vote and took 53 seats. Increased voter turnout indicated that the Sunni section of the electorate had also been mobilized in terms of identity politics. The coalition gaining the majority of the Sunni vote was the Accord Front, with 16 per cent of the vote and 44 seats. A more radical grouping, the Iraqi Dialogue Front, took 4 per cent and 11 seats (Diamond 2006: 12).

Iraq's new electoral system favoured these large multi-party coalitions. Whilst the president was given a largely ceremonial role, the Office of the Prime Minister became the main vehicle for delivering governmental coherence. Constitutionally and electorally the Office of the Prime Minister was specifically designed to be weak. Real political power was meant to rest with the parties who fought the elections. For them electoral success within larger coalitions was rewarded by dividing up the spoils of government: cabinet portfolios and the jobs and resources they brought.

The politics of patronage still dominated Iraqi politics but rewards for corruption were now spread across all members of the cabinet. At the centre of this system, the prime minister was not meant to dominate the cabinet as first among equals. Instead, his role was that of broker, facilitating negotiations within his own coalition and between it, the American ambassador, and the other coalitions. The prime minister's decisions were based, at least until 2008, on the comparative power of the parties and coalitions he was negotiating with, not his own political vision or agenda for rebuilding the Iraqi state along indigenous lines.

The rise to political dominance of Nuri al-Maliki

It was Nuri al-Maliki, Iraq's third post-war prime minister, who was given the job of making this system work for its first full-term parliament. He was chosen as premier in April 2006 after 156 days of increasingly fractious negotiations between the parties that dominate government. By then the US had succeeded in marginalizing the power of the old ruling elite. It had created a system that empowered competing parties and invested decision-making in a fractious cabinet.

Ironically, however, this muscular political re-engineering does not appear to have purged the system of the centralizing tendencies that came to the fore during the 35 years of Ba'ath Party rule. Initially after his appointment in 2006, there was constant speculation about al-Maliki's motives, competency, and his ability to stay in power.[9] Throughout 2006 and 2007 Baghdad was awash with conspiracies to unseat him. By 2008, however, discussions amongst Iraq's ruling elite were dominated by fears that al-Maliki had become too powerful and that the Office of the Prime Minister was now a threat to Iraq's nascent democracy (Pollack 2009).

This remarkable turn-around for Nuri al-Maliki had its roots in his apparently rash decision at the end of March 2008 to send the Iraqi army into the country's second city Basra to seize it from the control of the *Jaish al Mahdi* militia (Mohammed 2008; Seattle Times News Services 2008). Al-Maliki believed at that time he faced a coordinated plot to unseat him. An upsurge in militia-fermented violence in Basra would be used as a pretext to push a vote of no confidence through the parliament in Baghdad and unseat al-Maliki as prime minister.[10] To outflank this plot al-Maliki sent four division of the Iraqi army into Basra to seize control of the city back from the militias that were threatening his rule. The resulting military campaign almost ended in disaster and defeat was only avoided by the extended intervention of US troops and air support. However, al-Maliki used this eventual victory to stamp his authority on the Iraqi government and the armed forces. To quote the then Commander of US forces in Iraq, General David Petraeus,

> it was a hugely significant moment ... and it re-established his credibility with the Iraqi people of all sects and ethnic groups, because he was taking on his own, in a sense, he was a Shia leader of a predominantly Shia country, taking on a Shia militia.[11]

From April 2008 onwards, the Iraqi prime minister quickly developed both the formal and informal means to centralize power in his own hands. He took over the Sons of Iraq initiative, the so called 'tribal awakening' deployed by General Petraeus and his successor General Odierno to battle against the insurgency in Anbar Province and then across the whole of south and central Iraq. He then removed its most powerful leaders, demobilized the majority of its men under arms, and remoulded what remained into 'Tribal Support Councils' that the Prime Minister's Office then used as informal networks to distribute patronage in return for loyalty (Ashton 2008).

On the campaign trail al-Maliki stressed the success of the military campaigns in Basra and his decision to send troops in the Sadr City area of Baghdad. He also emphasized his role in challenging the Kurdish Regional Government's attempts to gain control over areas along its boundary with the rest of Iraq. In a key campaign speech he set himself against the decentralized federal agenda of his main rivals for the Shia vote, the Islamic Supreme Council of Iraq and their partners within the coalition government, the Kurdistan Democratic Party, and the Patriotic Union of Kurdistan (ICG 2009a: fn. 96).

The extent of al-Maliki's success can be judged by the poor performance in the 2009 elections of his main rival for the Shia vote, the Islamic Supreme Council of Iraq, which tried to repeat the success that an overtly religious approach had given it in 2005. This approach badly misjudged the mood of a country that had only recently emerged from extensive violence justified in the name of sectarian appeals to religious and ethnic identity. In Baghdad, the Supreme Council took just 5.4 per cent of the vote, compared to 39 per cent in 2005. In the Shia religious cities of Najaf and Karbala its share was 14.8 per cent and 6.4 per cent, down from 45 per cent and 35 per cent in 2005 (Visser 2009). In contrast Maliki's coalition won the largest slice of the popular vote in nine out of the 14 participating provinces (International Institute for Strategic Studies, 2009b).

Al-Maliki attempted to reproduce this vote winning formula in the March 2010 national elections. He hoped to capitalize once again on his popularity across the south and centre of the country and on his claim to have been responsible for the drop in inter-communal violence since 2007. However, when the coalition was finally announced in October 2009, it transpired that al-Maliki's hubris in the wake of his provisional election success had hampered his ability to build a broader electoral base. He had failed to make the meaningful concessions needed to build a wider coalition. In addition, al-Maliki refused to rebuild the overtly Shia multi-party coalition that had proved so successful in 2005. This left the two other major Shia parties, the Islamic Supreme Council of Iraq (ISCI) and the Sadrist Current, to form the Iraqi National Alliance (INA), the second major electoral coalition.

The third major electoral coalition, Iraqiyya, was assembled by the former interim prime minister, Iyad Allawi. He brought together geographically disparate parties and united them around a common commitment to Iraqi nationalism and secularism. This left the two dominant Kurdish parties, the Patriotic Union of Kurdistan and the Kurdistan Democratic Party, to form an alliance to maximize the Kurdish vote and hence the influence of the Kurdish Regional Government in Baghdad.

In the event Iyad Allawi's Iraqiyya coalition, took 2,851,823 of the votes and 91 seats in the new parliament. Al-Maliki's State of Law coalition came second with 2,797,624 votes and 89 seats (Fadel and DeYoung 2010). With 163 seats needed for an overall majority neither of the two winning groups gained enough votes for an outright victory. That left the INA, which came third with 70 seats, and the Kurdish alliance with 43 seats, holding the balance of power.

Al-Maliki's attitude to the rule of law was highlighted when faced with electoral defeat. 'No way we will accept the results', he bluntly stated, demanding a recount in order to prevent a 'return to violence' (Parker and Ahmed 2010). The fact that al-Maliki issued this statement as head of the country's armed forces heightened its sinister undertone. Al-Maliki demanded a manual recount of votes in Baghdad. However in mid-May 2010 the electoral commission, backed by the United Nations, announced that it had found no evidence of fraud and the vote and seat allocation remained unchanged (Gatehouse 2010).

A deep legacy of bitterness and mistrust across Iraq's ruling elite was left by the legal wrangling over the vote. This, combined with the fragmented result itself, meant that building a coalition turned out to be a very lengthy exercise. The election result itself appeared to set up a straightforward contest between Allawi and al-Maliki for the premiership.

The negotiations that stretched from March to November 2010 were shaped by two opposing fears: on one hand, that al-Maliki's growing power could lead to dictatorship; but on the other, that an increase in the influence of the Sunni population in an Allawi government could lead to the unravelling of the political settlement that was reached in the years after the 2003 invasion.

The final breakthrough came on 11 November 2010, 249 days after the election itself. Al-Maliki managed to use the threat of Allawi and his Sunni voters to impose a rough and ready unity of the Kurdish and Shia parties who had a great deal to lose from an Allawi premiership (Dodge 2010b). The 11 November announcement put al-Maliki at the head of a government of national unity but gave Iraqiyya very little for their election victory

Overall, when faced with a divided and politically fractured ruling elite, a rapidly rebuilt army, and a country slowly emerging from civil war, Prime Minister al-Maliki successfully concentrated power in his own hands and those of a small number of advisers in his personal office. In his campaign to retain power he returned to an overtly sectarian rhetoric in an attempt to solidify his core vote. During the 2010 election campaign and in its aftermath, he combined the blatant abuse of governmental institutions with overt threats to use state-sponsored violence if he did not get his way. This process looks very familiar to students not only of Middle East history but Iraqi politics itself before regime change. The whole process is far from complete but al-Maliki could well be on his way to cementing his grip over Iraqi politics for the next generation. This would involve building something akin to an elected dictatorship controlling a strong state delivering much longed for stability that uses oil rents to bind the population to its leader.

Rebuilding the coercive power of the state

After disbanding the armed forces in 2003, the US vision for the new post-Ba'athist Iraqi military was focused on all-volunteer force, with no tanks or artillery, whose role would be to guard Iraq's borders (Chandrasekaran 2007: 85). The reality of post-Ba'athist Iraq soon put paid to this idealistic approach. Faced with insurgency and then civil war, the US and Iraqi governments raced to re-militarize the state's relations with society. By 2005, the Iraqi security forces were identified by the Bush administration as the main vehicle through which US military commitment to the country could be speedily reduced whilst avoiding the spectre of defeat. To quote President Bush's oft repeated slogan, 'As the Iraqis stand up, we will stand down.'[12]

From April 2003 onwards, the US spent $19 billion – matched by $16.6 billion from the Iraqi government – in an attempt to train, equip, and pay the new Iraqi armed forces and deliver American ambitions as quickly as possible (International Institute for Strategic Studies 2009a). The Iraqi Ministry of Defence's budget rose by a yearly average of 28 per cent from 2005 to 2009 (SIGIR 2010: 34). As of May 2009, Iraq's security forces employed a total of 645,000 personnel, equivalent to 8 per cent of the total workforce, spread between the Ministry of Interior, Ministry of Defence, and the Iraqi National Counter-Terrorism Force (Department of Defense 2009; Cordesman 2010: 314). This level of expenditure on its armed forces puts Iraq fourth in terms of the world rankings for per capita military spending, with all the counties above it also being in the Middle East (Central Intelligence Agency 2010). So to all intents and purposes, when faced with a rising tide of violence, the US occupation reconstituted an Iraqi military which is broadly comparable to the armed forces across the region.

The US government sought to reassure people about the rapid remilitarization of Iraq by stressing the 'democratic oversight' which would be used to constrain the use of state sanctioned coercion. Officially, the command and control of the Iraqi security forces is centred on the Iraqi Joint Forces Command, which is subservient to the National Operations Centre in Baghdad and overseen by the Minister of Defence. However, Prime Minister al-Maliki has, since 2006, subverted the formal chain of command, tying senior army commanders, paramilitary units, and the intelligence services to him personally. He has in effect both 'coup proofed' the security forces but politicized and personalized its chain of command.

He did this first through the Office of the Commander in Chief (OCINC), using this platform to appoint and promote senior officers who were loyal to him (Dodge 2008). Second, as the security for each province was handed from US to Iraqi control, the prime minister set up a number of operational commands to bring both the army and the police force together under one regional organization. These consolidated, under a single commanding officer, the management of all the security services operating in unstable provinces. These officers are appointed and managed from a central office in Baghdad which al-Maliki controls. Through the use of joint operation commands al-Maliki has by-passed his security ministers and their senior commanders, securing control over the operational level of Iraq's armed forces. To date command centres have been created in Anbar, Baghdad, Basra, Diyala, Karbala, Kirkuk, the mid-Euphraties, Ninawa, and Samarra, allowing the prime minister direct control over the security forces in half of Iraq's 18 provinces (Elliott 2010).

In addition, in April 2007, as control of Iraq's Special Forces was handed from the US to the Iraqi government, a Counter-Terrorism Bureau was set up to manage Special Forces at ministerial level. This effectively placed control of Iraqi Special Forces, with 6,000 men in its ranks, under the direct control of the prime minister, well away from legislative control or parliamentary oversight. This force operates its own detention centres and intelligence gathering and has surveillance cells in every governorate across the country (Cordesman 2010). Since the force was removed from the formal chain of command and from legal oversight, it has become known as the 'Fedayeen al Maliki', a reference to their reputation as the Prime Minster's tool for covert action against his rivals as well as an ironic comparison to Saddam's own militia (Rosen 2010; Bauer 2009).

Finally, al-Maliki has moved to bring Iraq's intelligence services under his direct personal control. This became apparent in the increasingly public conflict between Mohammed al-Shahwani who was the head of the National Intelligence Service and Sherwan al-Waeli, who was appointed by al-Mailki in 2006 to be the Minister of State for National Security Affairs. The National Intelligence Service was set up by the CIA, and al-Shahwani enjoyed a long and close working relationship with Washington over many years. Al-Waeli, conversely, is considered very much to be the prime minister's man (ICG 2010a: 11). Things came to a head in August 2009 after a series of major bombs in the centre of Baghdad. Al-Shahwani argued in the Iraqi press that there was clear evidence linking the attacks to Iran. In the subsequent fallout surrounding the incident al-Shahwani was forced to resign (Ignatius 2009) thus delivering Iraq's security services fully into al-Maliki's grasp.

The rapid remilitarization of the Iraqi state's relations with its own society was pushed through by the US in an attempt to limit its own casualties and hence reduce the domestic political cost of occupying Iraq. However, the speed with which it was done and the massive investment channelled into Iraq's security forces leaves the country, once again, dominated by a huge military machine. After 2006, this machine was targeted by Nuri al-Maliki with the sole aim of guaranteeing his control over it. Iraq now has a set of over-developed coercive institutions increasingly placed at the service of one man, its prime minister. The direct danger this poses to Iraq's democracy is obvious.

Failing to reform the new Iraqi economy

Paul Bremer, on leaving Iraq in June 2004 after his year in control, was asked what he thought his greatest successes were. Amongst his biggest achievements he answered were 'the lowering of Iraq's tax rate, the liberalisation of foreign investment laws, and the reduction of import duties' (Chandrasekaran 2007: 322). Given the instability and violence that dominated Iraq on his departure it is perhaps understandable that Bremer should single out his economic agenda as his central success. However, the primacy of the economic over the political was not just expediency on his part but springs from his own deep commitment to a neo-liberal ideology. However, seven years after his departure evidence of a sustained impact on the Iraqi economy of US imposed reform is very hard to find. In March 2009, the Iraqi government still earned 94 per cent of its revenues from the export of oil (Fifield and England 2009). This means its spending power and beyond that the stability of the Iraqi economy is directly linked to the fluctuating price of oil on the international markets. Bremer's plans to sell off state-owned industries also did not come to fruition. Politically it is still considered too damaging to the country's stability to abolish or 'monetize' the rationing system set up by Saddam Hussein that Bremer was so keen to end.

Beyond subsidies, the most important indicator of the state's relationship with the wider economy is the size of its own payroll. Statistics suggest that since 2005, the number of people employed by the state has risen from 1.2 million to 2.3 million. In 2006, the statistics agency of the Iraqi Ministry of Planning estimated that the state employed 31 per cent of Iraq's labour force and estimated this would rise to 35 per cent by 2008. This would put state employment just 5 per cent lower than the CIA's estimates for 2003 (Robertson 2008).

Running in parallel to the state's dominance of the economy is a post-war explosion in corruption. In both 2007 and 2008, Transparency International rated Iraq as the 178th most corrupt country, with only Myanmar and Somalia warranting a worse score (Transparency International 2008a). This is partly due to the way in which cabinet seats and their accompanying ministries are divided amongst the parties as rewards for their success at the ballot box. With each new government, payrolls are rapidly expanded and ministry budgets asset-stripped as state resources are redeployed to fund party political patronage. In addition, there is also sustained evidence that the highest levels of the Iraqi state are deliberately shielding corrupt practices because of the political benefits it delivers. A 1971 law, still on the statute books, allows ministers to give immunity to those they employ who have been accused of corruption. In 2008, '1,552 corruption cases involving 2,772 officials were dismissed as a result of the amnesty' (Dagher 2009). Beyond this as Prime Minister al-Maliki's power and confidence increased he deliberately and overtly attacked the anti-corruption measures put in place by the CPA in its final days (Glanz and Mohammed 2008). The result of this politically driven and shielded corruption means that an estimated 10 per cent of the central government's revenues are lost through corruption (Reilly 2009).

Conclusions

With an end date for the removal of all American troops from Iraq set, it is now possible to assess whether the US government achieved any of its goals in attempting to reform Iraq's political economy; ridding the Iraqi ruling elite from the hub of state power, reducing the state's ability to coerce Iraqi society, and pushing the state's institutions from the centre of its economy.

This ambitious attempt at reforming a whole state's relations with its economy marked the high watermark of liberal intervention, after the apparent successes of the Balkans and Sierra Leone. However, the cost of such an agenda was extremely high. A total of 4,430 American troops have died in Iraq since the invasion began. In addition, the United States is estimated to have spent $53 billion on reconstruction in Iraq over and above the much larger sum spent on fighting the insurgency and ending the civil war (Williams 2009b).

Despite of the vast sums of blood and treasure expended over seven years and the greater amount of suffering endured by Iraqis, the outcome still remains ambiguous. The invasion and occupation did rid the Iraqi state of its Ba'athist leadership and replace it with a more socially diverse and, to date, regularly elected leadership. However, the electoral process has directly contributed to the endemic corruption that now dominates the state. At the end of the first full term for an elected government, the incumbent prime minister, Nuri al-Maliki, showed clear signs of developing the dictatorial tendencies of his pre-war counterparts. America, after disbanding the old Iraqi security forces and seeking to create a more modest force, then embarked on a crash course of rearming and expanding the Iraqi army, thus remilitarizing Iraqi society to levels comparable to before regime change. This force looks similar, both in its politicization and dominance of society, to the army it replaced. Finally, Paul Bremer's neo-liberal agenda for reforming the Iraqi economy has been an abject failure.

The results of the most violent and ambitious attempt to reform the political economy of a state leaves a larger more difficult issue to be dealt with, the ability of the international community to deliver successfully on the huge tasks involved in interventionism. Here the final word is best left to Amitai Etzioni, 'advocates of nation-building would greatly benefit from following the Alcoholics Anonymous prayer: 'God, grant me the serenity to accept the things I cannot change; the courage to change the things I can; and the wisdom to know the difference' (2004: 17).

Notes

I would like to thank Mats Berdal and Dominik Zaum for inviting me to write the chapter, Kristof Bender and Susan Woodward for encouraging me to widen the historical focus, and Claire Day for her comments on our earlier draft.

1 See Iraq Body Count: www.iraqbodycount.org/, 16 November 2010.
2 Although there are clearly different degrees of economic autonomy across the Middle East, 'Virtually no state in the region relies solely on its domestic production for resources' (Anderson 1987: 14).
3 See www.cpa-iraq.org/regulations/20030516_CPAORD_1_De-Ba_athification_of_Iraqi_Society_.pdf.
4 See www.cpa-iraq.org/regulations/20030823_CPAORD_2_Dissolution_of_Entities_with_Annex_A.pdf.
5 Bremer commented after flying over Baghdad on his arrival, 'nobody had given me a sense of how utterly *broken* this country was' (2006: 18).
6 Quoted by Sean Loughlin, 'Rumsfeld on Looting in Iraq: "Stuff Happens". Administration asking Countries for Help with Security', *CNN*, 12 April 2003.
7 Coalition Provisional Authority Order Number 39 (CPA/ORD/19 September 2003/39).
8 See CPA Order Number 39, and McCarthy (2003), Beattie (2003), Woods (2003).
9 See for example the memo that the then National Security Advisor, Steven Hadley, wrote about Maliki upon returning from Baghdad: 'Text of U.S. Security Adviser's Iraq Memo', *New York Times*, 29 November 2006.
10 See US Brigadier-General H.R. McMaster quoted in *Secret Iraq*, Part 2, BBC 2, 6 October 2010: www.bbc.co.uk/iplayer/episode/b00v8t2t/Secret_Iraq_Awakening/.
11 US General David Petraeus, Commander of Multi-National Forces-Iraq, January 2007 to September 2008. Quoted in *Secret Iraq*, ibid.
12 See 'President Addresses Nation, Discusses Iraq, War on Terror', 28 June 2005, Fort Bragg, North Carolina: www.whitehouse.gov/news/releases/2005/06/20050628-7.html.

13 Building a state and 'statebuilding'

East Timor and the UN, 1999–2012

Anthony Goldstone

This chapter seeks to describe the state that has emerged in East Timor since independence and to assess whether, how, and how deeply international statebuilders, primarily the UN, its missions, and its agencies, influenced the new state's shape. It argues, first, that UN missions influenced the shape of the state that has emerged in East Timor since independence, but in unexpected, unintended, and perverse ways. It will also argue that an autonomous East Timorese state has come into existence that resembles only superficially the donor-prescribed models, and whose defining characteristic has been its ability to cater to groups which see it as the focal point for their demands for various forms of recognition (material, political, and symbolic) to which they feel entitled as compensation for losses sustained or services rendered during the struggle for independence and since.

UN-led statebuilding efforts started in East Timor in October 1999, following the UN-organized referendum in favour of independence, and the final vengeful wave of violence by withdrawing Indonesian troops that followed the vote. The character of the UN's involvement, and its relationship with the Timorese leadership continuously evolved over the following decade, with an increasingly faint international footprint irrespective of the weight implied in the mandates establishing them, and growing Timorese impatience with imported statebuilding doctrines. Until independence in May 2002, the UN Transitional Administration in East Timor (UNTAET) had been empowered by the UN Security Council to act as a transitional government. It was followed by successive missions mandated to continue to provide assistance to the new Timorese state, the UN Mission in Support of East Timor (UNMISET, 2002–2005), and the smaller UN Office in Timor Leste (UNOTIL, 2005–2006). A political crisis and the outbreak of violence in 2006 led to the deployment of a UN Integrated Mission in Timor-Leste (UNMIT) to support the government and restore stability.

The deployment of UNMIT, with a remit almost as broad as UNTAET, appeared to reverse the declining external involvement in East Timor. UNMIT, however, never managed to insert itself into the day-to-day business of government in East Timor. This was not only because of its limited formal powers. UNMIT's leverage was also limited in a sovereign East Timor that was financially self-sufficient due to the massive increases in revenues from gas in the Timor Sea. This arguably transformed the relationship more completely than did the momentous fact of independent nationhood. However, it was also clear that the near-collapse of the statebuilding enterprise in 2006 damaged the UN's credibility as a statebuilder, and thereby also altered the relationship.

In 1999, East Timor had been seen as an 'easy' case for UN-led peace- and statebuilding efforts, based on the perception that the withdrawal of Indonesian forces and their most committed Timorese collaborators had ended the conflict, and had left behind a population united in its support for independence and the statebuilding project. It is true that the 24-year conflict that ran from the Indonesian invasion of December 1975 to the final withdrawal of the occupier in October 1999 was fundamentally a conflict between the Indonesian invaders and the Timorese majority who never accepted them, and was rooted in the contingencies of Portuguese politics and the post-Vietnam fears which united the US and its allies with Suharto's Indonesia. However, even then, local factors – in particular long-standing social cleavages and the new, inflamed party politics which reflected them – were integral to the dynamics of the conflict. They continued to be so in increasingly complex ways in the ensuing years of Indonesian occupation, UN Transitional Administration, and independence. The notion that in East Timor the UN would be working on a blank canvas was mistaken.

Despite the absence of its own statehood, East Timor had in fact developed a rich organizational life, which historically had often operated in parallel with or in opposition to the state structures of Portuguese colonialism and the Indonesian occupiers. Under the latter in particular, political organization attained a new level of complexity and fluidity, although by the time of the Indonesian withdrawal in 1999, it was defined by two main poles, represented by the figures of the resistance hero, Xanana Gusmão, and the Secretary-General of Fretilin, Mari Alkatiri. Among the several peculiarities of UNTAET as government and statebuilder was that, as an outsider, it was unfamiliar with these complexities. This, along with its transitional nature and confused lines of accountability, seriously limited its capacity as a statebuilder, highlighted by its roles in the process of drafting a constitution during the transition to independence and in the development of the 'security sector', both of which were directly linked to the 2006 crisis. Since 2006, in the interplay between a new government buoyed by massive inflows of petroleum revenues, and a new UN mission with a highly ambitious mandate, a state with a distinctively East Timorese cast has emerged and in which the UN has had difficulty in inserting itself.

Legacies of colonialism and Indonesian occupation

Until 1999, the East Timorese experience of the state was almost entirely negative as a result of subjection to Portuguese colonial administration and Indonesian occupation. Both regimes unintentionally strengthened existing indigenous structures and fostered new ones that cohabited uneasily, and often in direct opposition to the state. The Indonesian occupation spawned a proliferation of groupings exhibiting stances that ranged from outright collaboration through more qualified forms of accommodation to armed resistance, whose legacies are reflected in complex post-independence politics.

Statehood for the 'state averse'

The East Timorese have shared with much of South-East Asia an historical inclination to 'state aversion', preferring other ways than the state to 'shape coherences' (Reid 2010: 19, 115). Considering what the state represented under Portuguese colonialism and Indonesian occupation, 'state revulsion' is perhaps more apt in the case of East Timor. From the early twentieth century, starved of human and material resources by the metropole, the Portuguese colonial administration in East Timor exercised an extreme form of indirect rule that contrived to combine minimal direct Portuguese contact with the village with the remorseless extraction of taxes, crops, labour, and military service from its inhabitants. This could be achieved only by heavy reliance on traditional power holders. This in turn entailed the Portuguese offering incentives and sanctions to traditional power holders aimed at aligning the interests of the two. It also meant that the units of social life below the village (*suco*) – the *aldeia* (hamlet) and the 'houses' (*uma*) that comprised the *aldeia* – were more or less untouched (Hicks 1983).

The brief hiatus of Fretilin administration between the end of Portuguese colonial rule in August 1975 and the Indonesian invasion in December of that year (including the declaration of independence of the Democratic Republic of East Timor (RDTL)) was too short and pressured to count as an exercise in statebuilding, and the effectiveness of this administration remains disputed even amongst those who formed part of it (CAVR 2005: Part 3, 49–51, 54). Within four years the Indonesian military had brought under control the Timorese population, and destroyed the barebones administration that had continued in Fretilin-controlled areas. In the early 1980s the question of the continuity of the RDTL was one of several issues that divided the dominant internal faction of the resistance, by then under Xanana Gusmão's direction, and the dominant voice of the resistance in the diaspora, the *Delegação da Fretilin em Serviço no Exterior* (DFSE). Gusmão's repudiation of the RDTL was part of wider strategy for building support internally and internationally (Gusmão 1988: 95–98), and also corresponded to the domestic reality. For the bottom-up, piecemeal recovery of the internal resistance from the massive defeats of 1979–80, the basic constituent of village life, the *uma*, and the prototypical villager, the *Maubere*, were more salient than the state.[1] Under the Indonesians, the *uma* survived in the face of an occupier far more intrusive and harsher than the Portuguese had been. It became the basic unit around which the resistance was structured and a prime reason that it was able to endure. Remarkably it proved resistant not just to the penetrative state imposed by the Indonesian occupiers, but also to the socially subversive forms of state violence that they perpetrated, including systematic sexual violence and repeated displacements (CAVR 2005: Part 4, 37–38). This resilience was probably connected to the fact that its cellular structure and its esoteric forms of communication made it the natural building block of a clandestine movement. The *uma* became a constitutive element of Timorese nationalism and, for the Indonesians, a target of both counter-insurgency operations and of symbolic appropriation (MacWilliam 2005).

The notion of *Mauberes*, clustered in interlocking *uma*, forming clandestine networks that supported and protected the guerrillas was not just rhetorical, but it did greatly oversimplify the rich array of often overlapping clan, political, administrative, educational, economic, religious, and security networks, which might work in opposition to, in parallel with, or inside the state structures established by the Indonesians. Many of these networks continued to operate during the Transitional Administration and after the new state of East Timor came into being. They ranged from traditional non-state village institutions, formalized resistance structures, and the Church and civil society, to more marginal groupings that included gangs, criminal networks, martial arts groups, and cults.

The poles of Timorese politics

The two main poles around which these groupings tended to gravitate after 1999 were represented by two figures: the hero of the internal resistance, Xanana Gusmão, and the Secretary-General of Fretilin, Mari Alkatiri. At the beginning of the 1980s, Gusmão was one of a handful of members of the Fretilin Central Committee still alive and actively resisting the occupation in Timor. During the next decade, he came to be recognized by all parties – in Timor, in Indonesia, and internationally – as the indispensable personality (*personagem incontornável*), however the question of East Timor was going to be resolved.

In 1987, after further setbacks and a lengthy strategic rethink, Gusmão announced an ideological turnaround. He committed the resistance to a national unity strategy, designed to unite the widest possible spectrum of Timorese society, and resigned from Fretilin. Henceforth, he retained the position of Commander in Chief of the armed wing of the resistance, Falintil (also separated from Fretilin, to become a politically neutral, embryonic national army), and president of the newly formed resistance umbrella group, the *Conselho Nacional da Resistência Maubere*, (CNRM, National Council of Maubere Resistance), which eventually became the more inclusive *Conselho Nacional da Resistência Timorense* (CNRT, National Council of Timorese Resistance). After his capture and trial by the Indonesians in 1992, and his subsequent transfer to prison in Jakarta, he continued to be the ultimate leader of the resistance to the Indonesian occupation.

In 1999 Mari Alkatiri was the Secretary-General of Fretilin, the only East Timorese political party to have consistently advocated independence over the 25 years between 1974 and the end of Indonesian rule. On the eve of the Indonesian invasion he was one of a small group of senior Fretilin figures who were sent abroad to muster international support for the recently declared RDTL. He remained in exile for the next 24 years, based for most of that time in Mozambique.

The tensions between the two were real and reflected the differences over strategy and leadership that had emerged in the 1980s, and never been truly resolved. Inside East Timor, these differences had all but ended by the mid-1980s with Gusmão's clear ascendancy. However, the relationship between the armed wing of the resistance in Timor and the Fretilin wing of the Timor-ese diaspora remained uneasy as the DFSE fought a protracted rear-guard action against the new line, and the loss of Fretilin's primacy that it was taken to entail (Mattoso 2005: 120–122, 136–139, 159–161, 178–183; Niner 2009: 114, 118–119; Barbedo de Magalhães 2006: 47–51). Gusmão was able to trump his opponents repeatedly on the strength of the sheer credibility he derived from his presence in East Timor leading the resistance, and of the support of José Ramos-Horta, whose own indispensability as by far the most energetic and most effective advocate of the Timorese cause abroad, even his political opponents in the DFSE had to recognize.

These political realities were more or less hidden from the UN, to whom Xanana Gusmão appeared by the time of its intervention in 1999 to be the obvious choice as chief Timorese interlocutor. There were many reasons for this belief, which a more 'context-sensitive' approach would not necessarily have altered. In the context of a war for independence, the real divide was between the supporters of independence and pro-Indonesian 'integration-ists'. The tensions within the resistance were not widely canvassed, and indeed had seemingly been overcome by the creation in 1998 of the new umbrella group, the CNRT, incorporating Fretilin and non-Fretilin elements under the overall leadership of Xanana Gusmão. Because the CNRT had been preceded by a tortuous process of policy and organizational conver-gence, it looked like something more than window dressing designed to con-vince outsiders that the notorious fractiousness of Timorese politics had finally been overcome. The ability of pro-independence forces to mobilize the vast majority of Timorese to vote for independence in August 1999 under the umbrella of the CNRT in a campaign run by Xanana Gusmão from house arrest in Jakarta seemed to offer conclusive evidence that the national unity policy had worked.

Against this background, in 1999, it was not immediately apparent to Freti-lin leaders returning to East Timor from the diaspora how their party fitted into the internal Timorese political landscape. At a party conference held in Sydney shortly after the formation of the CNRT, Fretilin had approved a political programme that envisaged that in its first five years of independ-ence, East Timor would have a government of national unity with a political base that might be as broad as the CNRT itself (Fretilin 1998). However, by May 2000 Mari Alkatiri and the diaspora politicians who immediately on their return had established dominance over the party had concluded that Fretilin had sufficient grassroots support to justify going it alone, and three months later they withdrew Fretilin from the CNRT (Fretilin 2000).

As a result of the Constituent Assembly elections, held in August 2001, in which Fretilin won 55 of the 88 seats, just short of a two-thirds majority, Mari Alkatiri became Chief Minister of the second transitional government, during the last months of the UN Transitional Administration, and prime minister in May 2002 once Timor became independent and the Constituent Assembly, having completed its work, became the National Parliament. Meanwhile a presidential election, held in April 2002, had given Xanana Gusmão the presidency with an 80 per cent majority, but had elevated this hugely popular figure to a post whose powers were conventionally described as almost entirely ceremonial. This understanding of the powers of the office was shared by Gusmão and Alkatiri (Shoesmith 2003: 244; Fretilin Central Committee 2006). During the first four years of independence, the mismatch in formal power between the executive and the presidency was amplified by the heavy concentration of donor assistance on the executive (NORAD 2007: 53, 65–67). However, when in 2006 the two came into open confrontation, the outcome was not determined by their financial clout or their formal powers.

UN statebuilding and the transition to statehood

Implanted from outside in an unfamiliar setting in response to an emergency for which little planning had been done, and at least as beholden to outsiders as to its nominal Timorese 'client', UNTAET lacked the attributes of a fully fledged government despite being formally endowed with the powers of one. Instead, its transitional nature and confused lines of accountability proved to be a recipe for perverse outcomes.

UNTAET's peculiarities as statebuilder

UNTAET approached its statebuilding mandate in East Timor from the perspective that it was dealing with a 'blank slate'. This perspective was fuelled by the desolation left by the withdrawing Indonesians and their Timorese allies, who had systematically destroyed infrastructure and public buildings as they withdrew. Bereft of funding and almost its entire senior and middle-ranking staff also gone, the machinery of government had ground to a halt. Massive numbers of the population had been displaced from their homes during the course of the year but particularly during the final spasm of Indonesian-instigated violence that followed the August referendum, when about two-fifths of the population was forcibly evacuated to Indonesian West Timor and most of those who remained had fled their homes for remote parts of the country. All of these factors contributed to the seizing up of the economy (the official estimate, that GDP fell by 38 per cent in 1999, is almost certainly an underestimate). It was unknown whether there were still forces in Indonesia – and in particular in Indonesian West Timor – that were not reconciled to the loss of the country's '27th province', requiring that the UN Peacekeeping Force be able to secure East Timor's borders against the possibility of attack by militia and the TNI.

UNTAET arrived in East Timor with reasonably clear statebuilding objectives – to prepare the territory for independence, and to develop administrative and other capacities – but without a blueprint for achieving them. This lack of specificity necessarily entailed improvisation and ad hoc solutions. 'This mandate did not come with an instruction manual', the Transitional Administrator, Sergio Vieira de Mello, noted (de Mello 2002). Moreover, the theory of the blank slate proved remarkably tenacious, even though very few members of the Timorese political elite subscribed to it.[2] Ignorance of context meant that the prescriptions that tended to prevail were those that reflected the definition of 'best practice' as 'methods that have been applied successfully elsewhere' (Ottaway 2002). With regard to the judicial system, for example, de Mello believed that the institutions created by UNTAET were filling a vacuum that needed to be filled and as such their attractiveness would be obvious:

> What cultural change is there to attempt? UNTAET is not trying to implement cultural change. What we are trying to achieve through the creation of the courts, the Serious Crimes Unit and the truth commission is to bring institutions and process back into tune with what the Timorese people expect. We are trying to restore what they lost or never had.
>
> (Bull 2008: 218–219)

While the UN Security Council had given UNTAET unprecedented governmental authority,[3] for three reasons UNTAET never became the fully functioning government envisaged in its mandate. The first reason was financial: the limited resources available to UNTAET to perform its governmental (as distinct from mission) functions meant that the transitional government was dependent on, and sometimes beholden to, the multilateral and bilateral donors. UN administrative practices, in such areas as recruitment and procurement, also meant that basic government functions could not be performed.[4]

Second, UNTAET's answerability to 'New York' – the UN Secretariat, member states, and the Security Council – had consequences in East Timor. There were tensions between the mission (to which it was self-evident that it was necessary to adjust to changing political circumstances on the ground) and New York over readings of the mandate and administrative procedures. As a result, UNTAET was not able to exercise an exclusive 'fiduciary duty' on behalf of its East Timorese client (Morrow and White 2002: 29).

Third, UNTAET's transitional status meant that it would not take decisions in contentious areas that would best be decided by a fully legitimate elected government, and in what might be regarded as crucial elements in any statebuilding agenda – areas as diverse as the choice of official language, laws on land and property, the structure of the civil service, and the relationship between central government and the districts – decisions were put on hold. Thus, UNTAET interpreted its capacity-building mandate as primarily geared to developing the most basic, generic skills so as not to pre-empt the priorities and structures which would have to be decided by the government of independent East Timor (United Nations Country Team 2001: 98). However, as will be discussed further below, its decisions could have seriously damaging unintended consequences – and ultimately contributed to collapse of public order and outbreak of violence in 2006.

On the other hand, other parts of the statebuilding agenda were pursued even in the teeth of strong local or external opposition. When in early 2001 UNTAET dissolved the guerrilla force, Falintil, and created the Defence Force of East Timor (F-FDTL), both the fact and the manner of its establishment were contested (Rees 2004). UNTAET's highly consequential decision to renegotiate the terms of the agreement between Indonesia and Australia on the exploitation of oil and gas in the Timor Sea was an instance of an initiative that aroused external opposition. UNTAET's involvement was strenuously opposed by the Australian government, whose argument that UNTAET's role made the UN partisan against one of its member states also found some sympathetic ears at the UN Secretariat in New York (Cleary 2007: 52–53; Morrow and White 2002: 26; Power 2008: 335–336).

The timing of decisions to create institutions was often dictated by the fact that they were an improvised response to local political circumstances. To the extent that they were politically driven, they stood as early refutations of the theory of the blank slate. The decision to create what became the Timor Lorosa'e Police Service (TLPS – later renamed the PNTL) owed much to the slow deployment of the UN police, but was also prompted by the need to create a counterweight to the CNRT's security wing. The creation of the F-FDTL was almost entirely dictated by the growing danger of confrontation between the Transitional Administration, on the one hand, and the cantoned Falintil guerrillas and their commander and UNTAET's chief interlocutor, Xanana Gusmão, on the other. In the case of the justice system, the rush to fill the nascent judiciary with local appointees was at least in part prompted by the absence of personnel from other sources, although it was justified in terms of 'best practice', which seemed to sanction the application of the untested Kosovo model to the very different circumstances of East Timor.

The political transition: UNTAET and the constitution

The drafting of the constitution and democratic elections were key benchmarks for the transition from UNTAET to Timorese independence. However, the influence of UNTAET on the substance of East Timor's constitution was limited. During the drafting process following the election of the Constituent Assembly in August 2001, the Transitional Administration abided by its undertaking to give the East Timorese the final say on matters of substance. This was easily done because the supposed dilemma between giving the East Timorese the final say and holding firm to some basic human rights and democratic principles did not prove to be a real one. The reason was simple: the normative gloss that the UN might have had to apply had already been applied in the only draft that was given serious consideration by the Assembly.

This draft was the creation of Fretilin, which had gained a comfortable majority in elections for a Constituent Assembly. It was a modified version of a document produced by the leadership of Fretilin in exile in 1998, modelled on the amended Portuguese constitution of 1976, and incorporating many of the latter's institutional arrangements, including its semi-presidentialism. The document approved by the Constituent Assembly was, however, a Fretilin constitution not only in the sense that the party had drafted and sponsored it. Its preamble gave prominence to Fretilin's role in the struggle for independence and the national symbols explicitly provided for in the constitution, the national anthem and the flag, were those devised at the time of Fretilin's declaration of independence in November 1975, which the preamble stated, was 'recognised internationally on 20 May 2002'.

UNTAET did, however, have considerable influence on the process by which the constitution was drafted. Here it found itself in an alliance of convenience with the single best-organized party, Fretilin, and at odds with civil society and, eventually, the leadership of the CNRT. In a speech to the CNRT congress in August 2000, de Mello outlined two possible processes. The first was modelled on the CNRT's proposal for a constitutional commission to produce a draft constitution following an extensive consultative process, which would then be debated, amended, and approved by the Constituent Assembly. The second envisaged an elected Constituent Assembly to draft and approve a constitution following a nationwide consultation process. While de Mello originally seemed to favour the first option,[5] by September the UN had unequivocally come out in favour of the second option, which was compatible with its publicly announced benchmarks and exit strategy. Sergio Vieira de Mello told the Security Council that month that 'our plan' was to hold national elections for a Constituent Assembly, which would have the task of drafting the constitution and, having completed that task, would become the Parliament of an independent East Timor.[6] A constitution would thus be in place at the time of independence.

While the CNRT leadership publicly endorsed UNTAET's preferred plan and the accelerated timetable towards independence that it entailed, at hearings on the political transition organized by the National Council, the expanded consultative body appointed by UNTAET in an effort to 'Timorise' government institutions, the spokespeople for civil society, including the Church, and politicians, including José Ramos-Horta, advocated a slower transition. Many feared that the accelerated process and the reduced opportunities for consultation that it entailed would reduce the legitimacy of the constitution. Several argued for an interim constitution, to be fleshed out, if necessary over a period of years, after independence.

UNTAET made no bones about its preference that the lead in drafting the constitution be taken by an elected Constituent Assembly, arguing somewhat disingenuously that it was the more democratic option, particularly if as UNTAET proposed, there was provision for consultation through district-level constitutional commissions (Galbraith 2001; UNTAET 2001). Whatever the true merit of the case, from UNTAET's point of view there were some clear practical advantages to be derived from it, particularly ones related to timing: the supposed legitimacy of the elected Constitutional Assembly would partly offset the limited public consultation allowed under the timetable; the conversion of the Constituent Assembly into the Parliament once the constitution had been drafted would obviate the need for separate elections to these two bodies; and a constitution would be in place at independence. All of these considerations had a bearing on when the Transitional Administration could be wound up and on UNTAET's claim to have a well-defined exit strategy.

The suspicion that UNTAET was subordinating Timorese interests to its own, externally set timetable was aired at the time (Fonseca 2001). Surprisingly, however, in the public debates, it was not explicitly stated that the proposed timetable would also suit Fretilin well, for two reasons in particular. First, after withdrawing from the CNRT in August 2000, Fretilin was no longer bound by the consensus reached among the parties belonging to the CNRT that for now they would abstain from political activity below the district level, giving it a clear advantage over the parties with which it would be competing in the few months left before the scheduled elections. Second, Fretilin had a draft constitution ready for presentation to the Constituent Assembly that it had every prospect of dominating.

The input of UNTAET, indeed input from any quarter, during the actual drafting process was quite limited (Morrow and White 2002: 40–43; Assembleia Constituinte 2001). Some changes were made at the suggestion of UNTAET, but not the most important ones and there were occasions when UNTAET's advice was ignored. The most important change made after the Constituent Assembly had convened, requiring that Timor-Leste should incorporate the main body of international human rights and humanitarian law into its legal system, was added at the prompting of José Ramos-Horta, in fulfilment of an undertaking given by him on behalf of a future independent Timor-Leste in his Nobel Peace Prize speech in Oslo in 1996 (Ramos-Horta 1996). More comprehensive changes were ruled out by the large Fretilin majority and the limited time available to the Assembly.

Politically the most momentous changes to the 1998 Fretilin draft had already been made before the Constituent Assembly met. They diluted the powers of the president, vis-à-vis the government and Parliament, and specifically his powers to appoint and dismiss the prime minister and the government and to dissolve Parliament. It thus provided for a weaker president than had the constitutions of Portugal and Lusophone Africa (Amorim Neto and Costa Lobo 2010). It seems plausible that these changes were made with the express purpose of consolidating the political dominance of the constitution's Fretilin framers, who were in effect the Government in waiting since they would dominate the first parliament.

The constitution-making process exacerbated the political tensions which had led to Fretilin's withdrawal from the CNRT in August 2000. It thus marked an important moment in the descent into confrontational politics that led to the crisis of 2006. While the discussion of the political timetable was still going on in the National Council, Xanana Gusmão was already distancing himself from the plan he had himself presented to the Council, and in subsequent weeks he effectively disavowed it (Gusmão 2000; CNRT 2001). In March 2001, he resigned as president of the National Council in protest at the Council's endorsement of an UNTAET regulation providing for the most cursory public consultation. The bitterness carried over into the Constituent Assembly elections of August 2001 and the presidential elections of April 2002, and set the political tone for Timor's first years of independence.

The arrangements embodied in the constitution gave institutional legitimacy but unequal formal powers to the two dominant figures in Timorese politics, Gusmão and Alkatiri. In the years after independence, as tensions between the prime minister and the president rose and finally boiled over in 2006, debate on the constitution focused on the institutional arrangements embodied in the particular form of semi-presidentialism that East Timor had adopted (Shoesmith 2003; Feijó 2006). The underlying assumption of this debate was that formal institutional arrangements mattered politically.

However, it seems doubtful that provision in the constitution for a stronger legislature would have actually created a parliament capable of checking the ambitions of the two contending political colossi; or that a fully presidential system would have settled the question of where power lies. Defenders of the semi-presidential system maintained that, given the reality that pitted a hegemonic party, Fretilin, against the massively popular figure of Gusmão, the semi-presidential system should have had the virtue of containing (in both senses of the word) these two contending forces (Feijó 2006: 115–116, 130–140).

Ultimately, the institutional arrangements set out in the constitution were not able to accommodate existing political divisions, rendering constitutional design largely irrelevant. When President Gusmão ousted Prime Minister Alkatiri during the 2006 crisis, he did this not by virtue of his constitutional powers, but through a power play in which he relied on the personal prestige and support networks that he had built up during the resistance period. These pre-existing structures had far greater weight than the new formal institutional arrangements into which they were supposed to fit. This was true not just of Gusmão and the presidency he occupied, but also of the relationship between the guerrilla Falintil and the new defence force, the F-FDTL. Both the president in his dealings with the prime minister, and the F-FDTL in its rivalry with the PNTL were able to overcome the institutional disadvantages of weak legal underpinnings and inadequate resource flows. Weakly institutionalized constitutional norms were in both cases ultimately subverted by guerrilla politics.

Legacies of UN-led statebuilding

Configuring a 'security sector'

A commitment to create security institutions that would concentrate the means of violence in the hands of the state was implicit in the mandate of the

UN transitional administration without being spelled out in detail. The ensuing improvised approach to building a national 'security sector' had the effect of scattering the means of violence among factionalized and antagonistic state security institutions and their non-state allies with near fatal consequences.

The peculiar constraints under which the transitional administration worked were at play in shaping East Timor's security institutions. The development of the armed forces, the F-FDTL, and the police, the PNTL, both came to be related to the departure of their international counterparts, the peacekeeping force, and the UN police. Outside pressures for the exit of the international forces influenced assessments of the capabilities of the two forces and the security threats that East Timor faced. The different rates of development of the PNTL and the F-FDTL were conditioned by the contrast between the clear mandate that UNTAET had to create a Timorese police force and the uncertainty surrounding UNTAET's authority to create armed forces, given its lack of a clear mandate to do so, and the standing UN ban on forming or supporting national armies.

Recruitment of an embryo police force began very early in UNTAET. Recruitment of Timorese for policing functions was seen as operationally necessary and politically advisable, as well as uncontroversial in mandate terms. The slow deployment of UN police, the unfamiliarity with local conditions of those who were deployed, and the desire to downgrade the CNRT's security arm, the *seguransa sivil*, led to the creation in February 2000 of a Police Assistance Group (PAG), recruited largely from Timorese who had served in the Indonesian police (POLRI), based on the belief that their 'previous policing experience' would be an unalloyed asset (UNTAET 2000). This, and the eventual promotion of many of them to senior positions in the PNTL, was the source of easily exploitable resentment among the large number of people excluded by the recruitment process. The latter included members of the motley assortment of 'security groups' that existed in East Timor in 2000. They ranged from those who had served in the formal resistance structures, Falintil and the CNRT, to members of gangs, martial arts groups, and cult and millennial groups, many of whom had also contributed to the resistance in various ways.[7] The sheer number of applicants to the force (with over 12,000 applications to fill the first 350 positions (CSDG 2003: para. 88)) gives some indication of how many people thought they were qualified to join it, and of the level of resentment that was likely to result from the exclusion that the overwhelming majority of applicants faced as a result of the criteria used for recruitment and the relatively small intake.[8]

The way that the F-FDTL came into being made it in many ways a mirror image of the PNTL. It was almost one year into the mission before UNTAET took the highly political and controversial decision to create the force. Fretilin, among others, regarded the disbandment of Falintil and the creation of the F-FDTL as having been forced on UNTAET belatedly by growing signs of discontent among the guerrillas who were supported in their grievances by their commander-in-chief, UNTAET's chief interlocutor, Xanana Gusmão.

Whereas former Indonesian police officers were recycled into senior positions in the PNTL, it was mainly Falintil commanders of the armed resistance, esteemed for having waged 24 years of continuous armed Timorese resistance to Indonesia, who became officers in the F-FDTL. Thus, unlike the PNTL, at its inception the F-FDTL appeared to be a relatively homogeneous body that enjoyed widespread respect. The recruitment from late 2001 of a second battalion, however, with the explicit aim of correcting the regional bias towards Falintil fighters from the east of the first, had the effect of creating an inner core, roughly corresponding to the first battalion, and an outer core, roughly coterminous with the second battalion, separated by generational and regional divisions that were noticeable well before the 2006 crisis (RDTL 2006c). Like the PNTL, from the beginning the F-FDTL excluded large numbers of Timorese who believed that their service in Falintil gave them a rightful claim to membership of the new force.

In the months immediately before and after independence, the voices of excluded veterans demanding a place in either the PNTL or the F-FDTL reached a serious pitch. By far the most vocal (and most threatening) veterans group, the *Associacão dos Antigos Combatentes de Falintil de 1975* (AAC), was closely associated with Rogério Lobato, the first commander of Falintil and Minister of Defence in 1975, and whose base among the veterans aided his elevation into the first post-independence cabinet as Minister of the Interior, with responsibility for the police. Lobato's political rise brought few benefits to the veterans on whose support it had been built. A small number of veterans were recruited into the PNTL in late 2002, but within a year they had formed a faction within the police in opposition to Lobato, whom they accused of reneging on promises on recruitment and promotion. Instead Lobato consolidated his hold over the police by cultivating a small group of officers, mainly ex-POLRI, who were placed in headquarters command positions and at the head of three heavily armed special units that had been created by or (after independence) with the agreement of the UN missions.

Other factors militated against action which might have averted the dangers inherent in these unpromising beginnings. The UN formally retained executive authority over policing for two years after independence, but the gradual handover to the PNTL that began in June 2002 and was completed in January 2004 blurred lines of authority as became evident at times when clarity was most needed, such as when serious demonstrations broke out in Dili in December 2002, or when Lobato sought to build up the PNTL special units. The unclear delineation of responsibilities and the mismatch of reputation and resources between the PNTL and the F-FDTL fuelled the antagonisms between them, and weak parliamentary and ministerial oversight and the slow and politicized development of the machinery designed to allow for consultation and coordination between the branches of the security apparatus meant that there were no institutional checks on this emerging rivalry. Though the potential dangers of breakdown and conflict were recognized both domestically and internationally well before 2006 (CSDG 2003: 231–241; Rees 2004; Hood 2006), the urgency of dealing with them was overridden by the wider political stalemate and wishful thinking among internationals with a timeline to meet. In the meantime factionalism was growing in both forces, defined in the case of the PNTL by relationships to the central figure of Rogério Lobato and increasingly in the case of the F-FDTL in terms of 'east–west' divisions.

The crisis of 2006 began in the armed forces, but quickly threatened wider institutional and societal breakdown. In January, 159 members of the F-FDTL presented a petition to the president complaining about mismanagement and discrimination within the force. The 'petitioners', their numbers swelled by then to about 40 per cent of total F-FDTL strength, were dismissed in March. In April a petitioners-led protest in Dili escalated into serious violence which over the next few days embroiled the PNTL, the F-FDTL, and non-state armed groups allied to both forces (including ones allegedly armed by Rogério Lobato – United Nations 2006b: paras 88–92, 119–120, 133), as well as much of the population of Dili, as participants or targets, causing massive population displacement. The antagonisms within the security apparatus were encapsulated in a toxified form of the long-standing, ill-defined, and hitherto largely innocent, regional stereotypes of easterners (*firaku*) and westerners (*kaladi*), and found resonance in anti-government and anti-Fretilin sentiment in several 'western' districts and more enduringly in the neighbourhoods of Dili. It also brought to a head the conflict between the president and the prime minister.

The crisis triggered the return of a peacekeeping force, the ISF, and of executive policing by the UN. By 2011 both the F-FDTL and the PNTL had in a sense been reconstituted and the relationship between the two more clearly defined, but hardly in ways that had been envisaged under the mandate given to the new mission, UNMIT, by the UN Secretary-General and the Security Council in August 2006.[9]

The economy and the politics of recognition

During the UN transitional administration, there were many hands competing for control of the levers of economic management. The primary division of labour was between the UNTAET, which had budgetary responsibility for government current spending through the Consolidated Fund for East Timor, and the World Bank, which had oversight of the Trust Fund for East Timor, comprising donor funds for reconstruction (Cliffe 2000: 239). Aside from the two trust funds, in the early days of the mission, a humanitarian consolidated appeal, the UNTAET mission funded by member states' assessed contributions, UN agency reconstruction programmes, and bilateral development assistance channelled through NGOs and contractors also funded economic reconstruction, development, and management.

In practice, even the division of labour between UNTAET and the World Bank was neither clear-cut nor uncontested. UNTAET's mandate had included economic development, and its mission and governmental structures were both supposed to perform economic functions. In his regular reports on East Timor to the Security Council, the Secretary-General gave the impression that as a result of UNTAET initiatives, 'significant progress' was being made on the economy. As designer and coordinator of the Joint Assessment Mission (JAM), which started in October 1999 under UNAMET auspices, before the arrival of UNTAET, with the objective of defining East Timor's short-term reconstruction needs and medium-term development goals, the World Bank had defined the JAM's remit to include not just the indisputably economic (infrastructure, health and education, and agriculture) but also core government functions (macroeconomic management, public administration, and community development) (UNDGO/WB 2006: 8). As in the political sphere, in designing the JAM, political differences amongst the Timorese were thought to have been subsumed under the umbrella of the CNRT, which was asked to nominate Timorese participants in the JAM.

The JAM adopted the World Bank discourse of lean government and market-oriented economic policies, and was an eager advocate of the comprehensive dismantling of the economic legacies of the Indonesian state. Faced with a situation of near total destruction of infrastructure and an institutional vacuum, the World Bank saw East Timor as a place where it might introduce economic policy in uncontaminated conditions. One of the chief policies advocated by the JAM was a civil service far leaner than the one the Indonesians had established in Timor, which was seen as having been oversized, corrupt, and ineffective. In this context, the JAM concluded that 'the decimation of the civil service [due to the flight to Indonesia of thousands of its employees] also presents an opportunity for reform' (East Timor Joint Assessment Mission 1999a: paras 15–16).

The World Bank's approach to statebuilding also shaped East Timor's National Development Plan (NDP), adopted at the eve of independence. The elements of the plan – a 'lean, efficient, effective, accountable and transparent civil service', decentralized administration that would be 'closer to the people', good governance rather than big government, the private sector as the engine of growth, for which government would provide an enabling environment, effective property rights, and macro-economic stability – had been foreshadowed in the JAM (Planning Commission 2002: 21–22, 29). The NDP, however, had little bearing on economic policy or the economy's development over the following years: though regularly dusted off and invoked at donors' meetings, the NDP quickly was one among a confusing welter of planning initiatives and action plans, whose relationship to each other was unclear.[10]

The economic reality, however, was that between 2002, the year of independence and the withdrawal of a sizeable chunk of the UN presence together with its substantial spending power, and 2007, even excluding the UN's contribution to the economy (which fell even more sharply), GDP per head fell by almost 10 per cent, and the percentage of the population below the poverty line increased from 36.3 per cent (2001) to 49.9 per cent (2007) (IMF 2008; IMF 2011a; World Bank 2008). The private sector showed none of the resilience expected of it in the NDP. In the four years leading up to the crisis year of 2006, both private and public investment declined, and the number of people employed in the private sector (excluding subsistence agriculture) fell (RDTL 2006b: 22). Agriculture, employing about 80 per cent of the working population, grew more slowly than the rest of the economy.

One result was that migrants from the rural areas continued to swell the population of the main urban centre, Dili, which grew by over 70 per cent between 1999 and 2004. However, few of these migrants managed to find employment in the formal sector. By 2010, 22 per cent of the population of the whole country was living in the capital compared with 11 per cent in 1998 (Neupert and Lopes 2006: 26; National Statistical Directorate 2005: 28; National Statistical Directorate 2010: 9). The pressures and tensions that this population growth generated were expressed in competition for residential land and for space in public markets, and in mounting violence between gangs and martial arts groups that recruited their memberships from the city's youth, among whom unemployment remained staggeringly high.

By 2007 the economy's prospects were on the way to being transformed by huge increases in oil and gas revenues, whose value rose from 14 per cent of non-oil GDP in 2002/03 to a peak of 481 per cent of non-oil GDP in 2008. These revenues permitted the amount allocated to government spending to increase tenfold from FY2002/03 ($68.5 million) to 2009 ($687.1 million); and more than doubled again by 2011 ($1.5 billion).[11] In 2008, against the trend of global recession, official figures put non-oil GDP growth at more than 12 per cent.[12]

The UN played decisive roles in both the downturn of 2002–06 and the upturn that followed. The former was largely attributable to the withdrawal of UN personnel from the urban economy which owed much of its short-lived buoyancy to their spending,[13] while the upturn rested on oil and gas money, whose volume was in large part the result of UNTAET's contested decision to lead the negotiations with Australia that brought East Timor's share of production and revenues into line with normal prevailing terms.[14] While the UN's downsizing and its role in negotiating a new regime for oil and gas exploration in the Timor Sea both had an impact on the course the Timorese economy followed after 2002, the influence of the UN in the area of policy was modest[15] – as has that of the multilateral organizations and bilateral donors. In the first years after independence, this reality was masked by a convergence of views between the Fretilin government and the international agencies on economic management that was reinforced by the small tax base and a correspondingly greater dependence on donor finance. Balanced budgets, centralized procurement, and the establishment of a Norwegian-style Petroleum Fund aimed at fending off the potential ill effects of the resource curse were readily endorsed by the Fretilin government, which in some respects was more assiduous than the Bretton Woods institutions in its embrace of economic orthodoxy.[16]

Timor's economic development after 2007 owed nothing to the tenets of the JAM or the NDP; instead, the government's development policy after

2007 replicated many of the economic structures and dynamics that the JAM had deplored. This was the picture the JAM gave of the economy of East Timor in the latest years of Indonesian rule for which data were available (1994–96): 'The largest contributors to real growth were construction, public administration, and other services ... All of these activities were highly dependent on central government transfers, and benefited primarily the urban population.' (East Timor Joint Assessment Mission 1999b: 11) This is also a more or less accurate picture of East Timor's non-oil economy in the years since 2007, when government spending became by far the largest contributor to expenditure-based GDP growth. The public service, which at the end of the Indonesian occupation had employed an estimated 28,000, had grown to approximately the same size ten years later after having stood at less than 11,000 at the time of independence in 2002 (East Timor Joint Assessment Mission 1999c: 1; Planning Commission 2002: 29). But, while structurally, growth may have been coming from the same sources as in the past, the sheer amount of funds available to the AMP (*Aliansa Maioria Parlamentar*) government that replaced Fretilin in 2007, the abandon with which it deployed them, and the directions in which it channelled them, created a different type of economy.

As soon as it came to power, the AMP government signalled that it would be taking a different approach to economic development, and in its programme announced that it would be drawing up a Strategic Development Plan to supersede the NDP, aiming at 'radically improving the living conditions of the population' (RDTL 2007: 15). The new approach was presented as a different route to sustainability, an alternative to the prudence exemplified by the tightly managed Petroleum Fund, to be achieved through rapidly boosting rates of investment in infrastructure and human resources and thus preparing the way for broad-based development that would eventually be driven by the private sector rather than government spending fuelled by revenues derived from the country's finite oil and gas reserves.

The government's continued advocacy of this approach has rested heavily on it being able to point to economic indicators suggesting that a virtuous circle of success building on success is underway. Already by April 2009, Xanana Gusmão was telling the annual donors' meeting that 'the foundations are in place for Timor-Leste to make a qualitative leap to reach a new stage, the stage of sustainable development' (RDTL 2009: 5). GDP growth and budget execution rates have been the main indicators of choice, and, according to the official figures, both have risen spectacularly since 2007 – to levels that seemed barely credible to some.[17] The government has also made much of claimed improvements in social indicators (SoSCM 2011a, 2011b). As presented to the donors, the new model has a long pedigree – as the theory of the 'big push' needed to lift countries out of the 'poverty trap' – which has been undergoing a revival as the guiding ideology of the UN's Millennium Project Development Goals.[18]

Whatever East Timor's long-term economic prospects, for now government spending is most plainly addressed to the overlapping issues of 'recognition' and 'buying peace', perhaps the defining features of politics under the AMP government and the main short- to medium-term driver of its economic policies. Since independence but particularly since the change of government in 2007, groupings of various kinds, such as veterans of the armed and clandestine resistance, victims of human rights abuses, and the Church, have pressed for recognition from the state in the form of a livelihood and symbolic honours (veterans), reparations (victims of human rights abuses), and favourable policies (the Church).[19] 'Buying peace' has been the acknowledged goal of grants to groups such as the IDPs and the petitioners, but it has become the common currency of political debate, using to describe a whole approach to economic policy (*Lusa* 2009a, 2009b; *Timor Post* 2010; *Fretilin.Media* 2010; Xanana Gusmão 2011).

Since 2007 the most dramatic increases in government spending have been in public servants' wages and salaries, and transfers to selected groups in the form of benefit payments and grants. The main target groups for transfers have been veterans, the elderly, those who were displaced from their homes during the 2006 crisis and its aftermath, the 'petitioners', youth, school children, former office holders, war victims and the disabled, as well as religious organizations and civil society organizations (RDTL 2007: 20, 27).

The superficially more productive categories of government spending – 'goods and services' and 'capital expenditure' – have also often been instruments for distributing patronage, and government procurement has fuelled the overnight emergence of a very mixed ability business class. Attaining the ostensible purposes of these categories of spending – service delivery, and long-term investment in transport, power, and other infrastructure – has proved elusive,[20] and one of the consequences of the huge increases in budget spending and rapid disbursement has been waste and corruption, despite the development of an elaborate anti-corruption architecture.

These politics of recognition have also had two limitations in particular. First, not everybody who feels they should be is recognized. Kent (2010: 194) notes that 'the politics of recognition is within a broader context of identity politics, in which the government ... has its own priorities for conferring recognition'. There are many with claims to recognition who for political reasons do not receive it, and some groups such as the Church, or groups that pose potential threats, such as the 'petitioners', are better placed to gain recognition than others, such as victims of Indonesian (and Timorese) abuses, 'the last resistance generation', and ordinary villagers.

Second, the impact of these policies on reducing poverty appears to have been limited. The poverty rate may have fallen between 2007 and 2009, as the World Bank estimates, but, although the Bank attributes some of this improvement to rising agricultural output, the reversal was largely based on rises in ownership of consumer durables driven by government transfers, and hardly at all on improved social indicators associated with improved delivery of services. (World Bank 2009a: Table 1). This suggests that despite the improvements since 2007, the poverty rate was still higher in 2009 than it was in 2001. Moreover, funds have tended to flow to areas where 'buying peace' is most urgent, the capital, Dili, above all. The resulting distortion in the distribution of wealth between Dili and the rest of the country is striking. According to the Timor-Leste Demographic and Health Survey 2009 10, Dili stood out as the only district whose population belonged overwhelmingly (71 per cent) in the highest wealth quintile while the rest of its population fell in progressively lower numbers into the lower quintiles, with only 0.4 per cent of them belonging in the poorest quintile. Exactly the reverse pattern prevailed in the rural areas where the largest percentage of the population belonged in the lowest wealth quintile (24.6 per cent) and the smallest in the highest quintile (8.7 per cent) (National Statistics Directorate 2010b: 27–28).

Conclusion

At the donors meeting in April 2010, Prime Minister Gusmão noted a 'certain disconnection' between the government and the donors, and reminded the donors that many of them – citing Australia, the USA, and the UK by name – had concluded long ago that Timor was not economically viable and should be absorbed by Indonesia. In contrast, donors (at least publicly) did not waver from their long-established script for these occasions, praising the progress made in all areas of the UN operation's (in this case UNMIT's) mandate, and the need for further consolidation (Haq 2010). What was clear, however, was that the ritual of the donors meeting had been broken, and the statebuilding mystique that the participants had for many years chosen to attach to them (da Silva 2008) had been lost.

Another difficult relationship where 'interfacing' had given way to something close to a face-off, was between UNMIT and Timor-Leste's 'security sector', in whose reform UNMIT had been mandated to assist. In August 2009 the Secretary of State for Defence, Júlio Tomás Pinto, published a 4,000-word newspaper article on all that was wrong in the relationship between the two sides, in the hope, he said, that it would 'encourage a reflection on the approach taken by foreign personalities, agencies or countries in Timor-Leste regarding the reform of the security sector' (Pinto 2009). He said that the government was conducting its own programme of reform, with bilateral assistance of its choosing, and contrasted it with the UN's unsought contribution, which he characterized as more intrusive than helpful.

Other rituals of statebuilding have also broken down. The phased handing over of executive policing from the UNPOL to the PNTL, which had been proceeding since late 2008 on the basis of the rather loose application of a set of criteria for handover, was brought to a rapid end when the prime minister told the UN Security Council that the process should be complete by 27 March 2011, the date of the PNTL's eleventh anniversary. As a result, despite recognized shortcomings in several of the district commands and special units, not to mention headquarters, the criteria for handover were practically suspended and authority was handed over to the PNTL. The vetting process designed to weed out officers with 'disciplinary issues' was effectively abandoned (ICG 2010b: 2–3 and 6).

Accused of forming and arming groups whose mission was to eliminate his opponents, former Minister of the Interior Rogério Lobato was tried and sentenced to seven years' imprisonment on charges of murder, peculation, and illegally importing arms – and then released on medical grounds. A bow to legality was involved in the declaration of crises and states of exception in 2006 and 2008. Elections have fallen short of some important international benchmarks, but have allowed a change of government. The 'presidential drift' (*deriva presidencialista*) that has been a feature of semi-presidential systems in Lusophone Africa has been absent in East Timor: in the 2007 elections, Gusmão, having stood down from the presidency, won the premiership.

There is a tendency to see these phenomena as hybridities, footprints of the international community, and either to dismiss them as evanescent or to grasp them as evidence of a 'good-enough success'. But it is clear that the East Timorese state has its own dynamic. This state has the capacity not just to create but also to resolve crises, as it did after the assassination attempts on Prime Minister Gusmão and President Ramos-Horta in February 2008. In a strategy intended to overcome crisis and establish its own primacy by co-option, absorbing 'informal' institutions into the state, by granting them recognition, material and symbolic, the Timorese state has strayed from the paths of 'good governance', to UN bafflement and consternation (Khare 2009).

Notes

1 On the centrality of the *uma* and its multiple functions, see MacWilliam (2005); on the Maubere as the defining figure of the resistance to Indonesian rule, see Niner (2000: 85–126).

2 A rare exception was the Fretilin Secretary-General and future prime minister, Mari Alkatiri, a Muslim by religion but politically a secularist, who was critical of the post-occupation revival of customary practice (*Suara Timor Lorosa'e* 2007) and of compulsory Catholic religious instruction in schools (da Silva 2007).

3 SC Res. 1272 of 25 October 1999.

4 The 'baseline study' produced by the UN agencies in November 2000, one year after the UN had arrived in Dili, noted that ETTA had yet to establish an overall development planning framework, reliable data were still lacking, and the agencies themselves were still in the early stages of setting up their operations (United Nations Country Team 2001: 6).

5 UN doc. S/PV.4165 of 27 June 2000: 6.

6 UN doc. S/2000/738 of 26 July 2000: 5.

7 In the view of one senior CivPol officer, one of the merits of recruiting former POLRI members was that it would ensure the exclusion of former Falintil and persons associated with the CNRT, and would thus prevent the politicization of the new force (CSDG 2003: 313 fn. 117).

8 Resentment over recruitment played an important role in the violent protests in Baucau in November 2002 and was a contributory factor in the even more serious violence in Dili in December 2002.

9 UN Doc. S/2006/628 of 8 August 2006, paras 56–70; SC Res. 1704 of 25 August 2006.

10 In 2006, at his last appearance as prime minister at a Development Partners Meeting, Mari Alkatiri described the NDP as 'our bible' and claimed that 'our policies have been abiding in full with the dispositions of the [NDP]' (RDTL 2006a).

11 Since 2008 the fiscal year has been based on the calendar year; previously the fiscal year had run from June to July, the last full fiscal year before 2008 being 2006/07 (1 July 2006 to 30 June 2007).

12 GDP data must be regarded as indicative at best. A full national accounts system is still not in place.

13 Carnahan *et al.* (2006) estimated that only about 5 per cent of funds allocated to UNTAET entered the local economy (only two of the nine UN missions that they investigated contributed smaller percentages of their budgets to the local economies). However, because of the small size of Timor-Leste's economy, they also estimated that the impact of this spending was the highest among the nine missions studied, equivalent to more than 10 per cent of GDP.

14 Indonesia had been willing to settle for less favourable terms in the Timor Sea than it accepted in other parts of the archipelago, presumably because of the benefits that it thought it would derive from Australian *de jure* recognition implicit in the ratification of a treaty between the two countries.

15 It is at least arguable that its influence has been negative, particularly in the area of regulation where UNTAET's legacy included legislation on business registration (UNTAET Regulation 2002/4) that partly accounts for East Timor's very low rating in the World Bank's Doing Business rankings.

16 Thus, they resisted suggestions from the World Bank that they borrow internationally even on concessional terms.

17 Even though their budgets were far smaller than the AMP's, the Fretilin governments never managed execution rates above 50 per cent (cash basis). By contrast, according to official figures the AMP spent 61 per cent of its budget in 2008, 89 per cent in 2009, and 91 per cent in 2010. The AMP government attributed the striking improvement to the change from a highly centralized procurement system under Fretilin to a more decentralized one. Official figures suggest that to attain high execution rates an enormous splurge in spending takes place in the final weeks of the fiscal year, raising questions both of the reliability of reporting and the quality of spending.

18 Rhetorically, Gusmão's strategy has strong echoes of the UN Millennium Project, involving 'a big push of basic investments ... in public administration, human capital (nutrition, health, education), and key infrastructure' (Millennium Project 2005: 19.) It has the public support of Jeffrey Sachs, former director of the Millennium Project, who on visits to East Timor in 2010 and 2011 stated that the country could eliminate extreme poverty by 2020 if it used its petroleum revenues more boldly (United Nations News Centre 2010; *Diario Nacional* 2011).

19 Others have addressed the theme of recognition, from the perspective of those seeking reparation for abuses of human rights (Kent 2010); of villagers (the Maubere) who bore the heaviest price of war and occupation (Traube 2007); of the Church (da Silva 2007); and of 'the last resistance generation' (Sousa-Santos 2009).

20 Spending on health and education remains well below the levels thought suitable for countries at Timor-Leste's level of development. For comparative data on spending on health and education, see UNDP 2011: 122.

14 The political economy of statebuilding in Kosovo

Dominik Zaum with Verena Knaus

On 17 February 2008, Kosovo declared its independence from Serbia. Amidst vociferous opposition from Serbia and Russia in particular, the declaration failed to resolve Kosovo's political and legal status, which had been contested since Kosovo was placed under international administration by the UN Security Council in the aftermath of NATO's 1999 war against Serbia.[1] While its statehood was recognised by 75 countries by March 2011, including the US, 22 EU member states, and by all of its neighbours except Serbia, the territory formally remains under UN administration as Russian opposition in particular has prevented the closure of the UN Interim Administration Mission in Kosovo (UNMIK) and has made UN membership, the collective recognition of statehood, a remote prospect. The non-recognition by five EU member states[2] has complicated the EU's engagement with Kosovo, and has hampered the application of its statebuilding and integration processes successfully applied to neighbouring countries such as Macedonia (see Kristof Bender's chapter in this volume).

While the question of Kosovo's status has received extensive attention in recent years (Caplan 2010; Orakhelashvili 2008; Woodward 2007), the focus of this chapter is on the impact of the UN-led statebuilding efforts on internal aspects of Kosovo's statehood, more particularly on its political economy. Undoubtedly, the status question has been inextricably woven into the international perceptions of the character of the Kosovo problem, and into the local political dynamics. It has influenced international approaches to statebuilding in Kosovo, shaped the relationship between Belgrade and Prishtina, and between Serbs and Albanians within the territory, and has affected the dynamics between local elites and the international community. The status question provided substantial leverage over Kosovo Albanian elites and enabled UNMIK to push a substantial transformative agenda, and at the same time proved distractive, directing attention away from important structural political and economic problems. It has been a unique feature of statebuilding in Kosovo, and needs to be considered when comparing the case of Kosovo with other statebuilding interventions.

The international involvement in Kosovo, led by UNMIK until 2008 and by the EU since then, has been driven by an ambitious transformative agenda, aimed at building a multiethnic and democratic political order, and transforming the economic structures shaped by the Yugoslav socialist economy and an informal coping economy that developed under the influence of almost a decade of economic sanctions in the 1990s into a market economy. To that end, UNMIK was not only given extensive powers, acting originally as the supreme executive, legislative, and judicial authority, but also substantial resources: the annual budget of UNMIK and its pillars alone (excluding ODA and expenditure on the NATO-led KFOR peacekeeping force) was between *ca.* $450 million in 2000/1 and *ca.* $220 million in 2007/8.[3]

As this chapter shows, while elements of Kosovo's political economy have been substantially transformed, in particular the institutional apparatus of the state, in other areas political and economic structures have been more resilient. As the formal state institutions in Kosovo mostly vanished as the presence of the Serbian state either withdrew from Kosovo (i.e. the army, special police forces, and paramilitary groups) or dissolved as Serb officials fled the territory (i.e. the judiciary and civil administration); and as the building of a new institutional architecture was a central part of UNMIK's mandate to which it devoted substantial resources, the former is not surprising. Similarly, given that Albanians had been mostly excluded from the institutions of Kosovo's political, social and economic life after 1989, and that the Serb elite fled the country a decade later after the end of the war, a transformation of the political and administrative elite was all but inevitable, independent of external statebuilding efforts.

However, a closer look at the emerging elite also points to the underlying continuities in the political economy, highlighting the important position of the leadership of the Kosovo Albanian paramilitary and civilian structures that resisted Serb rule in the 1990s, in particular the Kosovo Liberation Army (UÇK). Thus, four of the five prime ministers of Kosovo from 2001 until 2011 have been members of the UÇK, three of them senior commanders.[4] Similar continuities can be observed in Kosovo's economic structure, in particular the continued central role of financial transfers into the economy, the small size of the formal (taxed) labour market, and the role of informal employment in particular in subsistence agriculture.

This chapter advances three related points. First, it argues that statebuilding efforts in Kosovo have been shaped by three overlapping perspectives on the challenge posed by Kosovo: first, that it is an ethnic conflict, second, that it is a rule of law problem, and, third, that renewed instability and violence would challenge the international statebuilding efforts and the legitimacy and credibility of the international statebuilding actors. Each perspective is associated with specific political and institutional choices in the statebuilding process, and has shaped the terms on which major Western states have supported Kosovo's independence. Second, it highlights how these perspectives have affected donor priorities; and, third, examines the implications this has had for the character of the Kosovar state that has emerged since the declaration of independence, focussing on three key consequences of statebuilding efforts for Kosovo's political economy: the creation of an executive-dominated state, the limited horizontal integration of Serbs into the state, and the neglect of economic development especially in rural areas, where the majority of the territory's population lives. It highlights that in the midst of substantial change in Kosovo, important aspects of its political economy have persisted, and at times have even been reinforced by international statebuilding policies.

International perspectives on statebuilding in Kosovo

External actors have had three dominant perspectives on the kind of challenge the situation in Kosovo poses to international order, seeing Kosovo as an ethnic conflict, as a rule of law problem, and a challenge to the credibility of international and regional security institutions. These three perspectives have strongly shaped the statebuilding activities of the major external actors.

Kosovo as an ethnic conflict

The dominant perspective on Kosovo after 1999 has viewed the situation as an ethnic conflict that has its immediate cause in the revocation of the province's autonomy by Slobodan Milošević's Serbian government in 1989, and the subsequent systematic exclusion of most Kosovo Albanians from public life (Clark 2000; Judah 2002; Malcolm 1998). This ethnic conflict has two dimensions: first, as a conflict between the Belgrade government and Kosovo Albanians; and, second, a conflict between the Albanian majority and the Serbian minority inside Kosovo. While the first was invoked to justify NATO's military intervention in 1999, the second has been invoked to justify the continued international presence in the territory after 1999, and the 'supervised sovereignty' arrangements of the Ahtisaari status proposal, to protect Kosovo's ethnic minorities.

The ethnic conflict perspective has been most closely associated with the UN more generally, and UNMIK in particular. UNMIK's mandate aimed to address both dimensions of ethnic conflict: resolving the conflict between Belgrade and Prishtina by working towards the resolution of the status question, and managing relations between Albanians and Serbs in Kosovo by establishing inclusive local governance institutions. UNMIK and the wider international community did little to advance the resolution of the status question in the first four years after the war, and focused on the establishment of governmental institutions and their democratic legitimation through a set of elections in 2000 (for municipal assemblies) and 2001 (for the Kosovo Assembly). While UNMIK transferred governmental authority to them, it maintained certain 'reserved powers' in areas such as the rule of law, foreign relations, and the security services, where handing over power would have prejudiced the resolution of the status question, or where it was feared that the full handover to Kosovo institutions would have detrimental human rights implications especially for minorities (Zaum 2007: 131–44). Only in 2003 the two parts of its mandate became conceptually linked through the

'Standards before Status' policy, making status resolution conditional upon the attainment of a set of governance benchmarks (UNMIK 2003; King and Mason 2006).

From this ethnic conflict perspective, statebuilding in Kosovo is pursued to contribute to wider peacebuilding efforts, by creating and strengthening institutions and mechanisms by which a polity can manage and resolve rival claims to power and resources, and address societal conflicts (Cousens *et al.* 2000: 12; Call 2008b). It is clearly reflected in many of the key statebuilding policies pursued by UNMIK between 1999 and 2008:

- the guaranteed representation of ethnic minorities in the legislative and executive Provisional Institutions of Self-Government (PISG);
- the internationalisation of the judiciary in 2000, in particular to try cases involving ethnic crimes or war crimes, following concerns about ethnic bias in the judiciary and the intimidation of judges;
- the appointment of Serb mayors in majority-Serb municipalities such as Srtpce and Zubin Potok after the Serb boycott of local elections in 2007 led to the election of Albanian mayors in these municipalities;
- UN efforts to facilitate a 'Belgrade-Pristina Dialogue' in late 2003, on cooperation on a range of governance issues.[5]

The ethnic conflict perspective is also at the heart of the UN's 2007 Comprehensive Status Proposal (CSP), better known as the Ahtisaari Plan (United Nations 2007). While the proposal was rejected by Serbia and never adopted by the UN Security Council, Kosovo committed itself in its post-independence constitution to the fulfilment of its provisions, and it has been central to statebuilding efforts in Kosovo since 2008. The CSP entails strong protections for Serbian cultural heritage in Kosovo (including protection zones and privileged tax and customs status); and provisions for decentralisation, granting substantial autonomy to minority municipalities, and devolving responsibility for primary and secondary education, healthcare, planning, and an enhanced role in policing to them.

Kosovo as rule of law problem

The second perspective on Kosovo sees it as a rule of law problem. The rule of law has become a prominent feature of statebuilding discourses (Call 2007; Jones *et al.* 2005) and has been increasingly institutionalised within the UN, its peace operations, and donor institutions (Tolbert with Solomon 2006). What Thomas Carothers has termed the 'rule of law revival', elevating the rule of law to a panacea for most social ills (2006: 3), has fuelled the perception that its absence or weakness in Kosovo has exacerbated political instability, weak political and administrative institutions, corruption, and a lack of economic development (European Commission 2004: 38, ICG 2010c: i).

In the absence of an agreed political settlement for Kosovo after the 1999 war, the emphasis on the supposedly technical issue of strengthening the rule of law by external actors is unsurprising, and as William O'Neill (2002) has shown, the rule of law perspective shaped the understanding of the challenge posed by Kosovo to international peace security from early on in the international statebuilding process, leading to the establishment of a dedicated rule of law 'pillar' as part of UNMIK in May 2001. It became the dominant perspective on the situation in Kosovo with the growing role of the EU in the statebuilding process, reflected in particular in the deployment of a dedicated European Union Rule of Law Mission, EULEX, after the declaration of independence.

The EULEX mandate in particular reveals the relatively narrow understanding of the rule of law held by the principal international statebuilding actors, focussing on strengthening the police, border control, and the judiciary, and fighting corruption. This narrow law and order approach is not just limited to EULEX. In the words of the European Commission, the biggest donor in Kosovo, amongst its key objectives in Kosovo is the consolidation of the rule of law 'through strengthening the wider judicial system, police reform, supporting the fight against corruption – in close cooperation with the ... ESDP mission to ensure a well coordinated and mutually reinforcing approach' (European Commission 2007a: 14). While the promotion of the rule of law is pursued to strengthen Kosovo's state institutions, it is also seen as aiding in the pursuit of internal European security policies (Justice and Home Affairs (JHA) issues), such as migration, drugs, and crime – fuelled by the perception that Kosovo is a 'black hole' in the centre of Europe, a haven for organised crime, and a major hub for drug and people trafficking (Kosovar Stability Initiative 2008). The EU has explicitly linked the promotion of its internal security with its CFSP – especially the promotion of the rule of law (Council of the European Union 2005).

Prioritisation of stability

The third perspective is not focussed on the character of the conflict, but rather on the consequence of renewed violence for the reputation of different international actors involved in Kosovo. Key international actors have had an overriding interest in minimising organised violence and the impression of renewed violent conflict in Kosovo, and have thus prioritised the absence of violence over substantive institutional and social change. This has been driven not least by concerns that violent challenges to the presence of UNMIK, NATO, or the EU (as occurred in March 2004) would threaten the credibility of these organisations, and undermine the legitimacy of their presence vis-á-vis the domestic audiences of key member states. In the case of the EU, the perceived failure of its EULEX 'flagship mission' would seriously challenge the feasibility of its Common Foreign and Security policy. This focus on stability was reflected in the sudden policy shift towards status resolution in response to the violence in March 2004, for fear that otherwise the international presence might lose control over the process (Eide 2005; King and Mason 2006; Weller 2008). Similarly, it has made external actors reluctant to take actions against individuals with close links to the government alleged to be involved in organized crime and corruption, or against the leadership of the parallel Serb institutions in the North.

This narrow focus on stability has been exacerbated by the inherent weakness of the two key missions tasked with statebuilding in Kosovo since the declaration of independence, EULEX and the International Civilian Office (ICO). While on paper both EULEX and the ICO have strong mandates with far-reaching executive powers, the international divisions over Kosovo's independence have strongly limited their exercise.[6] At the time of writing (March 2011), the ICO has never made use of its executive powers. For over ten months after its deployment, EULEX lacked a presence in the predominantly Serbian North of Kosovo, while the ICO's presence in the North has remained limited to a small office in Mitrovica. The very limited presence of the ICO and EULEX in the North has underlined the effective division of Kosovo's territory.

This emphasis on stability has had two important consequences for the political economy of post-war Kosovo. On the one hand, it has reinforced the narrowing of the international presence's understanding of the rule of law as essentially law and order, even at the expense of upholding human rights in Kosovo. This has both shaped the missions' own behaviour (as over the arrest and widely criticised trial of the leader of the pro-independence movement *Vetevendosje*, Albin Kurti),[7] and its support for local institutions. With regard to institution building, it has resulted in extensive assistance (both financial and technical) to certain law and order institutions (in particular the police and customs), but little comparable assistance for wider accountability institutions such as the ombudsperson, the media commissioner, or even the Kosovo Assembly.

On the other hand, the preference for stability has made the international presence unwilling to challenge potentially violent spoilers, instead it sought ways of co-opting them. When after the 1999 war most municipalities in Kosovo were effectively controlled by the UÇK, UNMIK co-opted its leadership into the newly established administrative structures, rather than taking them on directly (Zaum 2007: 135–6). Since 1999, first UNMIK and later the ICO and EULEX have mostly been unwilling to openly confront and dismantle the illegal parallel structures established by Serbs (and financed by Belgrade), which have cemented the de-facto division between the predominantly Serb-populated three northern Municipalities and the predominantly Albanian South of Kosovo.

Impact on donor and government priorities

Donor aid to Kosovo, both during the time of the UN administration and since the declaration of independence, has been shaped by these three perspectives, affecting statebuilding priorities and outcomes. Assistance has been focussed in particular on the establishment of political and power sharing institutions, and on the promotion of security and the rule of law. While both government and donor statements have emphasised that programmes should be government-led (Government of Kosovo 2008: 35–7), the importance of harmonising Kosovo's laws with European legislation and the central political role that key donors such as the US continue to play in Kosovo has meant that their priorities are strongly reflected in government policies. In the Kosovo government's key economic and statebuilding planning document for the major donor conference convened in the wake of the declaration of independence in 2008, there is a clear focus on security and the rule of law (ibid.). Agriculture on the other hand, central to economic development in a country where the majority of the population lives in the countryside and engages in subsistence farming, has ended up as one of the ministries with the lowest budgets in Kosovo – with donor priorities reinforcing the pre-existing priorities and prejudices of the Kosovo Albanian political elite, who for years left the Ministry of Agriculture to a Serb minister, highlighting the low priority they attached to it.

From 1999 to 2007, Kosovo received over €2.7 billion in donor aid (excluding humanitarian aid and donor support for UNMIK).[8] Much of this aid was targeted at strengthening political institutions and the coercive capacity of the state – the justice system, police, and customs in particular. More than 21 per cent of the donor aid, €754 million, was spent on institution-building measures, encompassing rule of law reforms (European Commission and World Bank 2008a: 5). Amongst the lowest priorities for donors were education, healthcare, and agriculture (with less than 5 per cent each of donor aid), despite their central importance for the country's development potential (ibid.). In 2005, out of €238 million in ODA committed by donors to Kosovo, over 26 per cent (€63.6 million) were committed to rule of law related issues and less than 3 per cent each to education, health, and agriculture (Narten 2009: table 4). From 2006 to 2008, the EU's three main programmes for Kosovo – CARDS, IPA, and IfS[9] – allocated more than €62.4 million to the rule of law sector (DFID 2008: 13).

A brief look at the programming of the two main donors (EU and USAID) shows that this has changed little since independence.[10] From 2008–10, out of a total IPA budget of €358 million, approximately €66 million were devoted to rule of law related activities, compared to €14.5 million for education, and €18.22 million for agriculture related projects.[11] USAID, the other major donor in Kosovo, allocated $202 million in ODA to Kosovo in 2009 and 2010,[12] of which $19.4 million went on rule of law programmes, $16 million towards education, and $4.6 million towards agriculture – compared with $45 million for the development of the private sector and macroeconomic institutions.[13]

These figures, however, understate the prominence of rule of law and security related expenditure, as they only include direct aid to Kosovo and not resources devoted to particular statebuilding activities by the international presence out of their own budgets. The total cost of NATO's KFOR peacekeeping mission has been estimated to have been €15–17 billion from 2000–4, therefore probably exceeding €20 billion by 2011 (Kramer and

Dzihic 2005: 125–6). In addition, support for the judiciary, customs, and police was provided through a dedicated police and justice 'pillar' of UNMIK, and in the case of customs through the EU pillar, at the cost of €70 140 million per year until the declaration of independence.[14] Since then the EU has committed another €265 million to its dedicated rule of law mission, EULEX, from 2008–10,[15] which has a dual executive and capacity-building mandate. Approximately 20 per cent, or €53 million, of EULEX's budget are devoted to rule of law capacity building.[16] Its support is predominantly geared towards strengthening executive institutions, in particular the Ministry of Internal Affairs (MIA). Thus, in 2009 EULEX had a 16-strong monitoring group in the MIA, advising on policing, border management, and migration, and assisting with the establishment of a civil registry unit. By comparison, there was no monitoring team in the other 'Rule of Law ministry', the Ministry of Justice, only a single EULEX adviser,[17] and no comparable international presence in ministries such as Agriculture, Health, or Education.

Impact on the political economy in Kosovo

Through their impact on statebuilding policy choices and aid, the three perspectives on Kosovo have shaped the priorities of international statebuilding efforts, and have affected the character of the state that has developed since 1999. There have been some obvious successes in particular in the field of democratisation and institution building, which would not have been possible without the substantial resources devoted to this by external actors. The political institutions established by UNMIK enjoy support and have not been challenged by the majority population and the non-Serb minorities; UNMIK has created a police service that reflects the composition of Kosovar society reasonably well, and which is the public institution the public (with the partial exception of Kosovo Serbs) is most satisfied with (UNDP 2010a). Despite occasional violence motivated by ethnic divisions or organised crime, personal physical security in Kosovo is high, with murder and violence rates below that of most Western European countries.

The perspectives taken by the international community on the situation in Kosovo have had three consequences for the political economy of statebuilding in particular: first, they have led to policies strengthening the executive over other parts of the state, and have laid the seeds of authoritarian government weakly balanced by accountability institutions; second, international statebuilding efforts have legitimised Serb parallel structures and have cemented the effective division of Kosovo after independence; and, finally, the focus on security and economic liberalisation has exacerbated the economic development challenge that Kosovo faces, in particular the problem of rural underdevelopment. In the following, these three issues are examined in more detail.

An imbalanced state – the primacy of the executive

International statebuilding efforts in Kosovo have contributed to the emergence of an increasingly imbalanced state, characterised by a comparatively strong state-level executive dominating weak legislative and judicial institutions, and a small and weak civil society. As a consequence, the executive cannot be effectively held accountable by any national institutions, and is ultimately held to account politically and financially mainly by the international presence.

The focus of international assistance on executive institutions, whose capacity has been strengthened at the expense of institutions of deliberation and accountability, such as the Assembly, the judiciary, the Ombudsperson, or the Anti-Corruption Agency, has strongly contributed to this imbalance. While the European Commission's progress reports regularly bemoan the weakness of the Assembly with regard to its capacity to monitor the executive (for example European Commission 2009: 7; European Commission 2010b: 8), committees have received only limited assistance to improve their capacity both to engage effectively in the legislative process and to monitor government activities. Within the central government, assistance has focussed in particular on key ministries in the rule of law and security sector, and on the Prime Minister's office. This has been exacerbated by the demands of the CSP to quickly pass legislation in the wake of independence, which meant that important laws, such as those governing the security services (including laws establishing the security force and the intelligence services), were pushed through the Assembly under special procedures with little opportunity for debate. The importance of harmonising Kosovo's laws and institutions with those of the EU in the context of the pre-accession process has centralised power in the offices of the Prime Minister and the Deputy Prime Minister responsible for this process. While they have received substantial support to draft legislation in accordance with EU standards, there has been little comparable assistance to the relevant Assembly committees expected to participate in the legislative process and the scrutiny of legislation.

This executive dominance has been further compounded by the weakness of the judiciary, rooted in the exclusion of Albanians from the judiciary throughout the 1990s, poor legal education, the destruction of infrastructure and documents in 1999, under-resourcing and staffing of courts and prosecutors, the vulnerability to political pressures and threats of violence, and corruption (EULEX 2009: 83–94; O'Neill 2002; OSCE 2009). Threats to the judiciary have emanated in particular from the persistence of informal UÇK networks, with close links to substantial parts of the political elite (both in government and the opposition) that have their roots in the UÇK. In particular the officially disbanded UÇK intelligence service, SHIK, whose former head has remained a close confidant of Prime Minister Hashim Thaci, has been widely considered not only to wield substantial influence across the government, but also to ensure the compliance of other Kosovar institutions with government wishes (Phillips 2010; ICG 2008), including through threats of violence and the assassination of political opponents (Marzouk 2009).

In a society with little open political dissent until independence in 2008, the government has become increasingly thin-skinned about media and opposition criticism. It has strengthened its editorial control over the state broadcaster RTK, reportedly used its financial muscle as the main advertiser in Kosovo to encourage more pro-government coverage, and put pressure on the largest cable provider in Kosovo to take a channel critical of the government off its airwaves (*The Economist* 2009a). Journalists have been intimidated, at times openly, such as the journalist Jeta Xharra, who was threatened in an editorial in the PDK newspaper *Infopress* that her reporting on a prominent PDK mayor and former UÇK fighter had shortened her own life (Xharra 2009).

Both the focus of international statebuilding assistance and the unwillingness to effectively deal with the persistent informal UÇK structures after 1999 have shaped important aspects of the political economy of post-war Kosovo. The influence of these informal networks is not limited to state institutions: an investigation in 2010 into corruption in road construction highlighted the economic importance of wartime networks linked to the then Minister of Transport, a prominent UÇK commander (Marzouk and Collaku 2010). Importantly, UNMIK, KFOR, and now EULEX and the ICO have been reluctant to challenge these structures and political leaders associated with them, for fear that this might spark unrest and violence.

Statebuilding and the Serb minority

One of the key challenges to statebuilding has been the integration of the Serb minority into the political, economic, and administrative structures of Kosovo. Of a Serb population of approximately 190,000 during the 1990s, 65,000–70,000 were displaced following the 1999 war (ESI 2004: 7), and returns have been very low.[18] Security concerns have undoubtedly limited returns, as has the overall economic underdevelopment of Kosovo, which has driven the emigration of the Serb population from Kosovo since the 1960s (Malcolm 1998: 329–30).

While Kosovo's state-level political institutions guarantee minorities participation in the government and an over-representation in the Assembly,[19] their actual influence on government policy has been very limited – not least because Kosovo's institutions offer no vetoes to different ethnic groups in the way that the Dayton institutions in Bosnia do, even if they require power sharing. Serb politicians have not held any of the key offices in the government, and the Serbs that have been willing to take ministerial posts have normally come from small parties with limited support amongst the Serb community. The integration of Serbs into the polity and state of Kosovo has also been actively discouraged by the Serbian government in Belgrade. Between 1999 and 2008, the unresolved status question made Belgrade reluctant to support the participation of Kosovo Serbs in the evolving institutions of self-government in Kosovo, as it feared that substantive Serb participation would further legitimise these institutions – both internationally and towards Serbs living in Kosovo – and could strengthen the Albanian case for an independent Kosovo. Only between 2000 and 2004, and again since 2010 did substantial numbers of Kosovo Serbs participate in the elections and the Kosovo-wide institutions.

To discourage the interaction of Serbs with Kosovo's institutions, Belgrade has financed a complex web of parallel institutions (OSCE 2003, 2007). While under UNMIK these were limited to the provision of healthcare, education, the establishment of parallel courts and the (publicly denied) presence of Serbian police in Serb municipalities, after independence Belgrade also established parallel political institutions in Kosovo's Serb municipalities. Through high salaries, and the threat of withdrawing financial support to anyone taking up employment with Kosovo's institutions, it aimed to entice Serbs to disengage from the wider political and social life in Kosovo and its institutions – a strategy that was broadly successful in the northern Serb-populated municipalities bordering 'Serbia proper'. The two-thirds of the Kosovo Serb population living mostly in small enclaves in the South of Kosovo, however, generally developed more pragmatic interactions with Kosovo's institutions (ICG 2009b), as for them the cost of disengagement outweighs the benefits provided by the parallel institutions.

The key instrument to channel funding from Belgrade into Kosovo has been the Coordination Centre for Kosovo and Metohija (CCK), a body established by the Serbian government without a formal association with any of the political institutions established by UNMIK in Kosovo. The CCK has been an essential part of the informal power structures and patronage system that developed in the Serb municipalities in Kosovo (for example through the university and the hospital in Mitrovica), in particular in the North. While the parallel system has provided Serb communities with tangible benefits such as employment, healthcare, and education, it has also been characterised by corruption and patronage, and has focussed its largesse predominantly on the northern municipalities, where many of the CCK's more influential members have originated from, at the expense of Serbs living in the Southern enclaves (ibid.).

Importantly though, the CCK became one of the key channels through which the international community in general, and UNMIK in particular, have engaged with the Serb community, and it has been the main Serb interlocutor for many international actors. When after independence Serbs in the North effectively ceased all connections with Kosovo's institutions, the international presence continued to engage with the parallel institutions (many of whose members are allegedly involved in crime and smuggling) to maintain stability. Unless violently challenged by them, EULEX and KFOR have made no efforts to dismantle these structures, threatening to embed informality and crime further into the developing political structures. Through that policy, the international community has tacitly accepted the division of the country along the Ibar river, as a price worth paying for the fragile stability that has endured. The depth of this division is vividly illustrated by the participation rates of Serbs in the Kosovo Assembly elections in December 2010: according to the Central Election Commission, between 43 and 50 per cent of Serbs voted in Serb municipalities in the South (such as Gracanica or Nvo Brdo), while in the North less than 1 per cent of Serbs voted – in the Serb municipality of Leposavić, for example, only three votes went to Serb parties.

The missing perspective: Kosovo as a development problem

The price for the focus of statebuilders on managing ethnic conflict and promoting stability and law and order has been the limited attention to a key aspect of Kosovo's political economy: its economic development. While donors have focussed on some important structural reforms – such as clarifying property rights and promoting privatisation, and establishing certainty for investors – several major structural challenges have remained largely unaddressed. As a consequence, the structural similarities between Kosovo's economy in the 1970s and 1980s, and in 2010 are striking. Despite more than a decade of international assistance, it has remained an economy suffering from very high unemployment, an economy that relies heavily on external fiscal transfers for investment, and one that is dominated by subsistence agriculture.

Until the late 1960s, Kosovo had been a largely pre-industrial economy, characterised by subsistence agriculture and some mining-related industries. While a growing number of socially owned industrial enterprises were established from the mid-1960s onwards, these investments were largely dependent on external funding, either from industrial conglomerates from other parts of Yugoslavia, or in particular from the Yugoslav Federal Development Fund. That fund had been established in 1965 to transfer money from wealthier to less developed republics of Yugoslavia, with the aim of stimulating economic growth in the latter (Mihaljek 1993; Treisman 1999: 151–5). The majority of these socially owned enterprises established in Kosovo never were economically viable, and relied for their continued operation on a steady flow of fiscal transfers especially from the Federal Development Fund (Palairet 1992: 898–900), and on loans from the politicised banking system (ESI 2002: 6–7). The size of these fiscal transfers was very substantial – in 1986 they made up approximately a quarter of Kosovo's GSP (Treisman 1999: 153; Palairet 1992: 899). Still, these investments never managed to generate sufficient employment to keep up with Kosovo's growing population: in 1981, the public sector only employed 178,000 people, out of a population of *ca.* 1.5 million (Malcolm 1998: 337). The limited employment generated by the substantial investments into Kosovo's industrialisation has been attributed in particular to the focus of investments on capital- rather than labour-intensive industries, and a lack of attention to agricultural development (Antic 1981).

Unsurprisingly, Kosovo's industrial economy suffered badly from the triple blow of the breakup of Yugoslavia (and the markets for its products) and the concomitant end of fiscal transfers, of a decade of sanctions against the Federal Republic of Yugoslavia, and international administration after 1999.

Most of its socially owned enterprises ceased operating in the 1990s, and Kosovo underwent a process of de-industrialisation accompanied by both a return of industrial workers to subsistence agriculture, and the establishment of a small but vibrant private sector, mostly engaging in trade (ESI 2002: 8). Some of the key Kosovar Albanians who invested in newly privatised enterprises after 2003 were successful traders (and at times sanctions busters) in the 1990s.

However, a decade of international administration and external statebuilding efforts has not contributed to the development of an economy that can provide employment for what is Europe's youngest and fastest growing population. Despite a plethora of programmes to support the development of small and medium sized enterprises (SMEs) and encourage private sector growth, total formal employment in 2010 was approximately 182,000 – roughly the same total as it was in 1981 (see Table 14.1), while during the same time Kosovo's population grew by a quarter to an estimated 2.18 million.[20] Only the composition of employment has changed, with over 40 per cent of employment now in the private sector – in particular in small trade. Most private enterprises are very small, employing on average only two people (Statistical Office of Kosovo 2009).

A consequence of the weakness of the private sector in Kosovo is the continued reliance on external financial transfers, in particular donor assistance and remittances. Together, they accounted for over 20 per cent of Kosovo's GDP in 2008 (IMF 2009a) – a similar figure to the share of fiscal transfers in Kosovo's economy in the 1970s and 1980s. Just as then, financial transfers

Table 14.1 Kosovo: employment in 2010[1]

Labour force	*Ca.* 1,200,000	
Registered and taxed employment	*Ca.* 181,728	
Budget sector (central government and municipalities)		76,867
POEs[2]		*Ca.* 20,000
SOEs[3]		*Ca.* 5,000
International agencies, embassies, and NGOs		*Ca.* 3,000
Private sector		76,861
Agriculture	*Ca.*180,000	
TOTAL	*Ca.* 361,728	

Note
1 Figures for budget sector employment come from the 2010 Kosovo budget. Figures for private sector employment come from the Statistical Office of Kosovo (2009). The figures for POE and SOE employment, and employment for international agencies are estimates based on field interviews. In 2003, POEs employed *ca.* 17,000 people, while SOE employment was estimated at *ca.* 14,000–15,000 (Ministry of Finance and Economy 2004: 22). POE employment is likely to have increased as in particular the airport and the telecommunications provider PTK have increased employment, while privatisation has reduced the number of SOEs, and hence employment in this sector. Agricultural employment is author's estimates based on the 2008 Agricultural Household survey (Statistical Office of Kosovo 2010), which found that the vast majority of Kosovo's 179,000 agricultural households is smaller than 1.5 ha (126,000), providing employment for an average of one person.
2 POE: publicly owned enterprise.
3 SOE: socially owned enterprise.

have largely failed to create substantial employment. International economic assistance has focussed on SME development, privatisation, and large capital intensive projects, such as support for the development of a new power plant. None of these have contributed substantially to sustainable employment generation, because they focus on capital- rather than labour-intensive industries; and, in the case of most SMEs, because most are small shops that cannot generate any further investment capital.

Remittances fuelled the construction boom in the immediate years after the war, but have mostly been part of the survival strategies of extended, patriarchal households especially in rural Kosovo. While they have undoubtedly alleviated poverty of individual households, and have for decades reduced the political pressures that pervasive unemployment and poverty would otherwise have caused (ESI 2005; Woodward 1995: 342–3) they have also contributed to continued rural underdevelopment (ESI 2005), characterised by large households, substantial gender inequality (both in terms of education and employment), and subsistence farming (World Bank 2009b).

While donors speak about rural underdevelopment as a key challenge to economic development (i.e. European Commission and World Bank 2008; World Bank 2009b), the resources devoted to it by both donors and the Kosovo government tell a different story. Less than 1 per cent of the government budgets in 2009 and 2010 were allocated to agriculture and rural development, and as discussed earlier, donor support for these sectors has been equally sparse. As Kosovo has not attained EU candidate status (unlike Macedonia), it does not qualify for dedicated EU assistance to reform agriculture and the rural economy.

Conclusion

The departure of the Serb state from Kosovo made substantial changes in the political economy of post-war Kosovo inevitable, yet the efforts of UNMIK, KFOR, the EU and other donors have undoubtedly shaped the character of these changes. This is most strongly reflected in the democratic and multi-ethnic political institutions that UNMIK established after 2000, and the decentralisation process which has been at the core of the ICO's political reform agenda. Still, the outcome of over a decade of statebuilding in Kosovo remains decidedly ambiguous, and a far cry from the liberal-democratic transformative visions of external intervenors. Kosovo's statehood remains contested internationally, and the authority of its state institutions continues to be contested internally. Parts of the Kosovo Serb community refuse to recognise and engage with the Kosovar state, and they remain effectively outside the reach of its institutions. In addition, wartime networks associated with the UÇK continue to wield substantial power that undermines the authority of elected officials and the courts, giving the impression of a class of people effectively beyond the reach of the law. Statebuilding outcomes in Kosovo are also ambiguous because of the important continuities in its post-war political economy – continuities both from the 1990s and the war, and continuities from socialist Yugoslavia. The most striking of these continuities are the structural problems of Kosovo's economy, and the persistence of UÇK networks in both the political and economic life of Kosovo.

What explains these outcomes? The current political economy of Kosovo is undoubtedly strongly shaped by historical legacies: not just by the nature of the departure of the presence of the Serbian state from Kosovo; but also by the development of a parallel state and economy in the 1990s following the abolition of its autonomous status; and even older social structures (such as the prominence of extended families) and the particular state–society relations that are associated with that. In addition, it is also shaped by the weakness of the international presence, and by the complex political bargains that UNMIK and its successors have had to make to sustain local support for their statebuilding enterprise.

Importantly, though, outcomes are also a consequence of the priorities of external statebuilding actors in Kosovo – such as UNMIK, KFOR, the EU, and the US – priorities that have either been the consequence of different understandings of the root causes of the conflict, or of wider interests of these external actors and the impact of developments in Kosovo on them, such as concerns about internal EU security issues (in particular migration, drugs, and organised crime). As the analysis highlights, these priorities have clearly influenced the funding and policy priorities of external statebuilders, and have shaped their interactions with local elites. External actors therefore bear some responsibility for the kind of state that has emerged in Kosovo, both by commission and omission. When pointing to the pathologies of the Kosovar state today, international actors need to look at their own policies and priorities as much as at the failings of local institutions and politicians.

Notes

1 SC Res. 1244 of 10 June 1999.
2 Cyprus, Greece, Romania, Slovakia, and Spain.
3 After the declaration of independence and the restructuring of UNMIK, its budget declined to under $49 million in 2009/10.
4 Ramush Haradinaj (2004–5), Agim Ceku (2006–8), and Hashim Thaci (since 2008) were all senior UÇK commanders; Bajram Rexhepi (2002–4) had been a surgeon in the UÇK. Only Bajram Kosumi (2005–6) had not been an active UÇK member. While the UÇK has maintained a strong representation amongst members of parliament especially of the ruling PDK, the 2011 government only contains three former UÇK members, the lowest number of any government since 1999.
5 The Belgrade–Pristina dialogue, which never discussed the status question, was not resumed after the outbreak of violence against Serbs and the international presence in March 2004.
6 EULEX was authorised by a Joint Action of the European Council (Council of the European Union 2008), but the non-recognition of five member states has substantially constrained the Mission. The ICO's authority is not based on a mandate from an established multilateral organisation but on the CSP, which has been rejected by Serbia and most Serbs in Kosovo.
7 Kurti was tried by an international court in Kosovo over public order offences arising from his participation in a demonstration on 10 February 2007, where

UNMIK policemen shot two protesters. His trial was widely criticised by international human rights organisations (Amnesty International 2007) and behind closed doors by the OSCE as politicised and riddled with procedural problems (confidential communication with OSCE official, July 2009).

8 According to the World Bank, 80 per cent of aid to Kosovo was technical assistance, 'but this has not produced lasting capacity within government institutions' (World Bank 2011: 196).

9 The CARDS (Community Assistance for Reconstruction, Development and Stabilisation), IPA (Instrument for Pre-Accession Assistance) and IfS (Instrument for Stability) have been the main EU assistance programmes to South-Eastern European countries.

10 As Kosovo only became a member of the World Bank in June 2009, the World Bank has until 2010 not been among the major donors, providing only $170 million between 1999 and 2007. For 2010 and 2011, it planned IDA financing of $47.5 million (World Bank 2009b).

11 Author's calculations on the basis of figures available at the website of the European Commission Liaison Office in Kosovo, www.delprn.ec.europa.eu/. (calculated April 2011).

12 As Kosovo was only recognised as an ODA recipient by the DAC in 2008/9, USAID assistance figures to Kosovo for 2008 are not separately listed in the US ODA database. This figure excludes the $125 million in debt service support to the Kosovo government from USAID in 2009.

13 Author's calculations from USAID figures from www.usaid.gov/policy/budget/money/ (April 2011).

14 Wittkowsky *et al.* (2006: 53) calculate that UNMIK spent between €66 and €130 million per year on salaries for international and local police officers between 2000 and 2005. Their figures on salaries do not disaggregate spending on international judges and prosecutors by the UN, and on customs officers by the EU. We estimate the latter to be another €5–10 million per year.

15 European Council Joint Action 2009/445/CFSP of 9 June 2009.

16 This estimate is based on the number of personnel dedicated to EULEX's Monitoring, Mentoring, and Assistance (MMA) mandate – *ca.* 400 out of its *ca.* 2,000 international personnel (EULEX 2009: 10), suggesting that *ca.* 20 per cent of its personnel costs (the majority of its budget) go towards capacity building.

17 Interview with EULEX official, 3 July 2009.

18 According to UNHCR (2010: 3), only 21,417 members of minority communities voluntarily returned between 2000 and 2010.

19 Kosovo's constitution guarantees minorities equitable representation in public employment (Article 61); 20 of the 120 seats in the Assembly are reserved for minorities (Article 64); and at least two ministers of the government need to come from minority communities (Article 96).

20 According to the Statistical Office of Kosovo, http://esk.rks-gov.net/eng/ (April 2011).

15 From new dawn to quicksand

The political economy of statebuilding in Afghanistan

Antonio Giustozzi and Niamatullah Ibrahimi

This chapter attempts to examine how international statebuilding efforts in Afghanistan have affected power structures at the national and sub-national level, and specifically why the massive international effort has failed to strengthen the structures of the Afghan state. To that end, the chapter focuses on the patron–client relationship that developed between external intervenors, especially the US, and their local partners. It focuses on two aspects in particular: how external intervention has affected both the selection of the elites inside Afghanistan and the struggles for power among them; and how the statebuilding process has itself been shaped by the interaction of the external intervention with the adaptive behaviour of local elites, constantly developing a variety of strategies and techniques to maximize their own returns and minimize the concessions to the intervening powers. The reason for this choice is that these factors determined, to a large extent, the political course of Afghanistan in subsequent years, relegating other factors to a relatively marginal role.

Among the contemporary examples of statebuilding, the Afghan case is one of two (the other being Iraq) that can be considered special by virtue of the sheer size of international intervention, in particular relative to the size of the pre-intervention economy in Afghanistan. Indeed, the amount of external resources that have been pumped into Afghanistan has exceeded local GDP every year since 2001, in some years by multiples. The impact on Afghan society has, unsurprisingly, been huge. However, this massive expenditure has not translated into a corresponding influence of the intervening powers over political and economic developments in Afghanistan, or even over their Afghan partners. In particular, from 2008 onwards, the relationship between the Kabul ruling elite and its foreign patrons has been increasingly uneasy. Even before that date, it cannot be said that the Afghan partners were delivering much of what was expected from them in terms of state- and institution-building.

The developments following operation Enduring Freedom and the overthrow of the Taliban in late 2001 are best understood in the light of previous developments. The pro-Soviet regime (1978–1992) had been heavily dependent on Soviet aid for its own survival, and the demise of the Soviet Union therefore sealed its fate. None of the regional players that tried to steer

Afghan politics after 1992 could even remotely match Soviet patronage; neither were the US or Western European powers interested in stepping in. Afghan military-political players had to make the best of whatever could be mobilized internally or from regional allies to fund their civil war: smuggling, looting, and illegal money-printing provided most of their revenue. This allowed for the flourishing of war profiteers, who sometimes accumulated substantial fortunes. Despite the individual benefits that could be accrued, the overarching picture is of a country that was cracking under the weight of the war effort and the anarchy that resulted from the inability of the factions to organize the territories they controlled. As the Taliban emerged to challenge the civil war status quo, they were able to mobilize internal and external financial support on the basis of their promise to reopen the highways and unify the country. Their success in seizing control of over 90 per cent of the territory marginalized the war profiteers who were linked to the anti-Taliban factions. The Taliban, however, themselves struggled to raise sufficient funding for anything more than the war effort, a fact which highlights the extent to which the country had become dependent on financial inflows for its viability as a functioning state. We shall never know how the Taliban would have coped with this problem, because the 9/11 attacks resulted in the rapid demise of their regime.

Selecting the post-Taliban ruling elite

This section discusses how a relatively wide coalition, which emerged out of the Bonn Agreement, gradually narrowed down and was increasingly dominated by President Hamid Karzai's circle. It argues that Karzai succeeded in expanding his control of the government through the manipulation of international support, sometimes masking the promotion of cronies and associates as the triumph of technocracy over the warlords and the civil war politicians, sometimes playing 'divide and rule' among other partners in the coalition.

The effect of the Bonn Agreement

The aim of what became known as the Bonn Agreement[1] was to establish a transitional government for Afghanistan. The Taliban were excluded from the table, with the encouragement of Washington, although there were other factors, too. At the time of the conference, the Taliban appeared utterly defeated, there was little incentive to incorporate them in the new political structure; and few believed, in any case, that the Taliban genuinely represented a constituency inside Afghanistan. Amongst the regional powers only Pakistan was mildly advocating the Taliban's inclusion in the settlement. In addition, most of the anti-Taliban factions, in particular the *Jami'at-i Islami*,[2] were resolutely opposed to the involvement of the Taliban in the negotiations. Although there is no evidence of direct American or European encouragement of the harassment of former Taliban in the villages, it seems clear that the security forces of the new regime, bolstered by international support, often indulged in revenge against their old rivals. This attitude contributed greatly to the ignition of the Taliban insurgency from the summer of 2002 onwards (Giustozzi 2008a, 2009a).

The composition of the transitional government

The composition of the new Afghan political elite was initially determined largely by the alliances that the US formed with anti-Taliban groups in 2001. Out of the Bonn discussions emerged an interim coalition government, incorporating the anti-Taliban factions that had been cooperating with the US in the previous months to bring down the Taliban. This coalition was hammered together under the need to quickly exploit the opportunities opened by the fall of the Taliban and by international intervention. Kabul was being occupied once again by the militias of the *Jami'at*, a fact which placed the other 'partners' in the coalition under pressure to rapidly agree to a deal. International sponsorship could counter-balance the military inferiority of the southern factions against the superiority of *Jami'at* forces. Arguably, therefore, the coalition was to an extent formed under duress (Dobbins 2008: 89ff.). Nevertheless, Western diplomats and their Afghan partners seemed unanimous in their assessment of what was necessary for Afghan rehabilitation and there was initial conensus on the road map established in Bonn.

It is not clear how the choice of a president was made, whether it derived from hard pressure placed by Washington on the coalition partners to agree on a candidate to the interim presidency, or from the more general need to form a coalition uniting around the Bonn Agreement. Former US Ambassador to Afghanistan James Dobbins writes that he was presented with Karzai as a *fait accompli*. A member of a leading family within the Popolzai tribe, Hamid Karzai was not a predominant figure within the royalist circles which he belonged to, but exactly for this reason he might have been deemed to be acceptable to the factions opposed to the re-establishment of the monarchy and in particular *Jami'at*.

Offering any objective assessment of the composition of the post-2001 ruling elite is difficult, but one method is to classify ministers in categories according to their social, economic and political backgrounds and to analyse how this has changed over the years that followed.[3] Table 15.1 shows the results. We can identify four main groups within the post-2001 ruling elite:

- warlords, strongmen and civil war politicians (those who had participated in the war as commanders or even as politicians, actively involved in decision-making);
- the *nouveau riche* (businessmen);
- pre-war elites;
- technocrats, not politically aligned to any faction, but with professional credentials.

Table 15.1 Background of Afghan Cabinet ministers from 2001 onwards (% of total cabinet members)

	Civil war participants	Old elite	Technocrats	Businessmen	Total	Share of diaspora returnees in Cabinet
2001	45.2	25.8	22.6	6.5	100.0	29.0
2004	38.6	20.5	34.1	6.8	100.0	43.2
2006	30.0	23.3	43.3	3.3	100.0	50.0
2009	28.6	20.0	42.9	8.6	100.0	45.7

The intelligentsia, weakened by years of war and purges, received few political appointments and remained a marginal influence. The demand for personnel able to manage the reconstruction effort in terms acceptable to the donors was later fulfilled by those returning from exile in the West, some of whom had prestigious intellectual credentials, others rather less (Giustozzi 2004). It is worth considering the returnees as a separate category. These were Afghans residing abroad during the war (or for most of it), who came back after the fall of the Taliban, and it includes individuals from all of the groups indicated above except, of course, the civil war participants. The proportion of the returnees within the ruling elite can be seen as a proxy of foreign influence: as they lacked a base of support within Afghanistan itself, it was often on the insistence of donor countries that they were included in the Cabinet.

While the first group was composed largely of individuals who had either stayed in the country throughout the civil war period or had not been away for long, the second group was more mixed, with a strong presence of civil war profiteers, but also of returnees who had made money whilst abroad. The old, pre-war elites were almost exclusively returnees, as were the large majority of the technocrats. These distinctions within the returnees are important, because their ability to relate to the wider population varied according to their background. The old elites had some residual relationship with local communities in parts of Afghanistan, which the technocrats lacked. The nouveau riche were at least able to buy support among the population, and often had connections with the warlords and the civil war politicians, who could act as their protectors (Giustozzi 2007; see also Stina Torjesen's chapter in this volume).

Shifts in power after 2001

The 2001 interim Cabinet reflected the fact that the Bonn Agreement was, at its heart, a power-sharing agreement and consequently included many factions and saw a strong presence of individuals who took part directly in the civil war. Members of the old elite, technocrats and businessmen were mostly appointed as a result of their links to the factions that negotiated the Bonn Agreement. In subsequent years, the civil war participants gradually lost ground, mostly to the benefit of the technocrats (many of whom were returnees). The power of the old elite also diminished after 2001: its initial influence was due to its strong representation within the so-called 'Rome

Group', the royalist alliance of which Karzai himself was part. Under foreign pressure, Karzai had to gradually make space within the Cabinet for some more technocrats, whom donor countries could trust to be relatively capable of spending their money effectively.

The power struggles that followed the establishment of the interim government in 2001 drove the changes in the composition of the ruling elite. The warlords, the strongmen and the civil war politicians gradually lost ground to cronies of President Karzai and his new allies – businessmen, technocrats and members of the old elite recruited in ad hoc fashion to counterbalance the power of *Jami'at*. In the pre-presidential election Cabinet of 2009, only three of the 28 members (president, vice-presidents and ministers) were civil war participants. The military class nonetheless had a stronger presence in junior positions: among governors in 2008, for example, eight out of 34 had military backgrounds.[4]

Elections and external legitimacy

A key factor in the shift of power after 2001 was the ability of individuals to capitalize on relationships with foreign countries and donors. Some groups and personalities were able to capitalize on their better relations, while others fell out completely with their original external patrons. Groups centred on the warlords and strongmen of the civil wars became increasingly marginalized. By comparison, the returnees enjoyed the advantage of having had greater exposure to Western ways, as well as an ability to communicate directly with Western officials, which the Afghans who had stayed in the country almost always lacked. Language skills, however, were not the determinant factor: the returnees were far from homogeneous as a group in terms of their access to power. Karzai and the small circle around him and his family were able to marginalize any other returnee who dared to confront them: the best-known cases were technocrats such as Ashraf Ghani (Minister of Finance 2002–2004), Ali Ahmad Jalali (Minister of Interior 2003–2005), Hanif Atmar (Minister of Interior 2008–2010, previously Minister of Education and Minister of Rural Reconstruction) and Amrullah Saleh (Head of National Security 2004–2010).

Karzai himself gradually strengthened his position not only through his ability to connect with international figures, but also because of his 'divide and rule' tactics towards his Afghan associates. He succeeded in dividing the various groups of warlords and strongmen from each other and then split each group internally into rival factions. Karzai also drove a wedge between the leadership of these factions and their rank and file. This was achieved through a series of means:

*   the manipulation of official appointments (van Bijlert 2009);
*   the manipulation of the Disarmament, Demobilization and Reintegration (DDR) and Disbandment of Illegal Armed Groups (DIAG) programmes, which forced the political leadership of the factions to distance themselves from their associated military leaders (Giustozzi 2008b);

- the manipulation of the judicial system, over which Karzai had indirect control (Lasseter 2009; Wisner 2008);
- the imposition of 'limited access orders' (favoured access for privileged individuals and groups) in the exploitation of Afghanistan's greatest riches: the drug trade and urban land (Gardizi *et al.* 2010).

Using similar means Karzai and his associates also lured selected local military leaders to their side, in order to weaken the dominant warlords and strongmen (Rashid 2008: 257–8; Giustozzi 2004, 2008c). Initially, American support easily allowed him to win any confrontation, but Karzai was still pushing his adversaries out of the political scene after 2008, as US support for him was widely perceived as waning (see below). Central to his ability to maintain his position in Afghan politics is the legitimacy that he derived from the presidential elections of 2005 and 2009. The elections themselves were hardly an expression of popular support for Karzai's rule: electoral turnout collapsed from 75 per cent in 2004 to 31.4 per cent in 2009;[5] both were accompanied by widespread fraud; and the electorate increasingly mobilized along ethnic lines rather than to support alternative national projects (Crisis Group 2004; NDI 2009; Wilder 2005). What was significant, however, was that both elections were eventually recognized internationally. This granted Karzai legitimacy among external powers, which made it difficult for Washington to abandon support for him even when his plans started to overtly diverge from the US ones. For example, between the end of 2009 and early 2010, when Karzai moved to eliminate from the Cabinet some of the ministers most committed to working with the US and the European powers, the centrality of elections in the legitimation of the international involvement in Afghanistan made it impossible for organizations and governments to withdraw their support for him (Gardizi *et al.* 2010; Thomas 2010; Wittman 2010).

In other words, Karzai and his circle excelled at the manipulation of political processes in Washington and in the international arena, maximizing their own benefit and determining with a fair degree of accuracy how far they would reasonably go without unleashing the reaction of the US. Intervention created a state that could afford to float over society and ignore the need for a stable political settlement; those better able at manipulating external players had an edge over those who had a large constituency inside Afghanistan.

The growing gap between Karzai and the West

In the early years after the overthrow of the Taliban, the key to Karzai's success was his (apparent) pliability to Western demands, in a context where the majority of other political actors seemed to offer at least some resistance. What Karzai's own plans for developing the Afghan state during his tenure as Interim President in 2002–2004 might have been is not known, though he probably inclined towards a traditional patrimonial model of political authority in Afghanistan. Instead, his seeming pliability and readiness to be manipulated was instrumental in winning international endorsement for his election as President. Until 2008 Karzai continued, by and large, to cooperate with the international community, although criticism of his inability to deliver on certain reforms, or of the slow progress being made towards them, could be heard increasingly frequently among foreign officials. During this period Karzai managed to weaken any rival power centre in the provinces, with the exception of the armed opposition of the Taliban. By 2008, the once-mighty *Jami'at* was badly ridden by interpersonal rivalries, usually encouraged by Karzai himself, and represented a barely credible threat or alternative to his power.

During 2008–2009 the main development in Afghan politics was the gradual parting of ways between President Karzai and his external patrons. In Badie's terms, this could be described as a 'populist subterfuge', aimed to bridge the gap between the governing and the governed (2000: 188–9), but it was also underpinned by Karzai's own changing views. Karzai's relationship with Britain, one of the main contributors to ISAF, had been strained since 2006 over British criticism of his policy implementation, but from 2008 he started to assertively argue against NATO military tactics and the civilian casualties deriving from them. At the same time Karzai had a number of clashes with Barack Obama's campaign team during the US presidential elections, which continued after Obama was elected president. For a few weeks, the tension between Washington and Karzai ran so high that the possibility of the US supporting an alternative presidential candidate seemed plausible. However, unconvinced by the alternative candidates, the Obama administration ended up somewhat grudgingly reconfirming its support for Karzai.

Karzai's efforts to distance himself from Washington were the result of several factors. First, he believed that the new Obama administration did not trust him and his management of the government, and would work to replace him. Second, the feeling that the US would eventually leave Afghanistan, and even negotiate with Pakistan and the Taliban behind his back to facilitate this, probably added to his sense of distrust. Finally, Karzai appears to have gradually lost faith in his Western advisers and to have felt that the policies advocated by the international community in Afghanistan were incoherent and ineffective (Hounshell 2010; Filkins 2010; McGurk 2010).

Early in his tenure as Interim President, Karzai might well have considered strengthening the Afghan state and democratic institutions, particularly if a coherent effort of the international community had been pushing him in that direction (Torabi 2009: 422). However, several important developments seem to have contributed to his conviction that institution building was not seriously supported by his external sponsors:

- the image provided by an army of foreign contractors, in some cases obviously exploiting the situation;
- the issuing of reconstruction contracts through processes of dubious transparency;

- the tendency of international partners to encourage backroom negotiations and play 'dirty tricks' against the very process of institution building they were sponsoring in public.[6]

At the root of these developments was, most likely, the lack of political direction from Washington, which led officials on the ground to adopt very short-
term attitudes towards spending the money allocated and how to fix random
problems as they arose.

By 2005 Karzai could be heard regretting having followed the advice of
the 'foreigners' at the expense of his own patrimonial inclinations, for
example, in the removal of Marshal Fahim from his own presidential ticket
and in his later sacking as Defence Minister. Karzai's commitment to statebuilding – never very strong – gradually evaporated, and by 2009 it could be
said to be entirely extinct. Across Afghan society itself, support for statebuilding was always limited; it was mostly advocated by the marginalized intelligentsia and the international community, with competing visions of what the
state should look like. Karzai's own version of the patrimonial model, by contrast, found fertile ground in the country and became the hegemonic
approach to building a political base. Other major political players either
tried to ride Karzai's wave and build their own sub-patrimonial empires in his
shade, or secure alternative sources of funding in opposition to Karzai.
Amongst those who tried the latter approach were the Taliban and Gulbud-
din Hekmatyar's *Hizb-i Islami* (Islamic Party), who secured funding from Pakistan and global jihadist networks, and started to tax the population in
territories they controlled. Others included various anti-Taliban political
groups, which gradually split from the Karzai-led coalition and (allegedly)
secured support from Iran, Turkey and other neighbouring countries (Giustozzi 2007, 2009b; Rashid 2008; RFE/RL 2006; Waldman 2010).

The narrowing and consolidation of Afghanistan's ruling elite

The sociological composition of the post-2001 Cabinets does not, of course,
tell the whole story of change in the post-2001 balance of power. In particular, it does not reflect the emergence of new economic elites, which only
became evident in the 2010 parliamentary elections, at least in areas where
security was relatively good (Foschini 2010). The large inflow of cash into
Afghanistan (in the form of aid and military-related expenditures) was the
result of a counter-insurgency effort that increasingly acquired priority in
Washington. Accelerating rapidly from 2008 onwards, this inflow gave a huge
stimulus to the economy, producing major changes in the composition of the
business class: civil war profiteers were replaced by reconstruction and military contractors, dependent for success on connections with the political elite
and donor countries.

This 'crony capitalism' depended on the fact that access to the main business opportunities was still mostly determined by closeness to the political
elite; in part, the political and the business elites actually overlapped. Some

turf wars were waged over the awarding of contracts particularly in southern Afghanistan, but within a matter of a few years a limited number of individuals at national and local government level emerged as key players in allocating access to contracts. Even illegal trades such as opium became rapidly dependent on the goodwill of groups and individuals within the government, who facilitated specific criminal networks and allowed consolidation of the market in a few oligopolies and regional monopolies. While it could be said that the influence of the nouveau riche had been on the rise during this period, its 'crony' character meant that it remained completely subordinated to political (and military) power (Chatterjee 2009; Giustozzi 2007; Risen 2009; Spilius and Farmer 2009).

While the technocrats and nouveau riche were, in general, privileged in their relationship with external actors (the 'international community'), they had trouble in dealing with the Afghan population and became dependent on the old elite, warlords and civil war politicians. Only the old elite (or rather the portion of it that was well-connected in Washington) was able, to some extent, to maintain relations with both external and internal actors and therefore to emerge as the interface that was badly needed by all parties. This was the key to its success, but also the source of its inability to consolidate the newly found power: it was an interface with a weak power base of its own and acceptable to Afghans and foreigners only by remaining weak. Any effort to create an autonomous power base became highly controversial, as in the heavily rigged 2009 elections (the two main contenders reportedly 'stole' almost two million votes), when what was left of the Bonn coalition came very close to collapsing; in autumn 2009 recruitment into the armed forces dwindled amid fears of an impending civil war (Giustozzi 2009b). The ruling elite increasingly took the shape of a mix of the old elite and the nouveau riche, with technocrats being drafted in ad hoc to help in the day-to-day administration of the country, then disposed of whenever their political ambitions rose too high.

Unfinished elite consolidation

The feeling that Karzai could easily maintain international support is also likely to have contributed to the gradual narrowing of the ruling coalition in Kabul after 2002. It is extremely unlikely that he would have dared to confront the various factions of *Jami'at*, which had temporarily reunified for the 2009 electoral campaign, as well as organize a massive rigging of the presidential elections of that year, if he had not assumed that the UN would have continued to support him. In his efforts to consolidate power, Karzai generally did not rely heavily on armed force, in part because he has no direct control over the army, but also because the police has only very limited capabilities. In 2009 the *Jami'ati* networks still had major influence in both the army and the intelligence and, to a lesser extent, in the police, leaving Karzai with little to counter-balance them. As a result, he actively cultivated the friendship of the UN Special Representative in Kabul, Kai Eide, in order to forestall any challenge to the legitimacy of the elections.

At times, Karzai and his circle have manipulated local factions and war-lords, pitting one against the other and then intervening with the limited forces available to assert the presence of the centre as peacekeeper. However, Karzai did use violence (or the threat of it) in a few cases after 2001: in Herat in 2004, where he intervened to remove the local strongman Ismail Khan from the governorship; and a few deployments in the north to intimidate local factions. At the local level, groups and individuals aligned with Karzai have used armed force to a greater degree to promote their interests, manag-ing most of the time to obtain some support from parts of the international presence. This has been particularly the case in the south, where the practice of 'bad tips' against hostile communities and groups has been most wide-spread: strongmen and their retinues offered military services to foreign mili-taries and received in exchange (mostly unwitting) support in their own feuding with other strongmen and local communities (Daniel 2006; Giustozzi 2009b; Rohde 2004; Stormer 2004).

By contrast, Karzai manoeuvred himself into a position from where he could act arbitrarily (in the terms of the coalition agreements of 2001) but without recourse to violence. Exploiting his international legitimacy, he forced the rivals into a difficult choice between accepting a renegotiation of the terms of their deals with him (which were weighted in Karzai's favour) or openly revolting against a President who was allied with the international community. In the overwhelming majority of cases, Karzai's trick worked, forcing rivals to accept a new settlement in terms more favouable to Karzai, although from 2006–2007 onwards a trickle of local strongmen began taking up arms against the government in the west and north of the country, some-times even establishing relations with the Taliban (Giustozzi 2010a).

The reigning uncertainty over the future alignments in Kabul, deriving as we have seen from Karzai's contested efforts to create an autonomous power base, has had an important impact on political dynamics. Such uncertainty was itself a result of his uncertain control over the army and police, and growing concerns from 2008 onwards that external support might decline. The gradual deterioration of the governing coalition gave strongmen and warlords both inside and outside the coalition, who had maintained control over armed groups, an incentive to focus on their own narrow interests, in the hope of using their political capital to renegotiate the terms of the coali-tion agreement – or at least prevent changes that would prove unfavourable to them. In this context, we have seen examples of genuine mass mobiliza-tion, mostly occurring along ethnic lines, particularly from 2004 onwards. Popular riots and revolts occurred in locations like Sar-i Pul, Shiberghan, Maimana, Kabul and others. Although large groups like the *Jami'at* and *Junbesh* were initially viewed with suspicion by the population because of their role in the civil war and in the brutalities associated with it, these have regained ground as vehicles for expressing popular grievances, despite their own internal divisions. At times, they spent their political capital in support of the government or at least of Karzai, as long as they received political concessions in exchange. The fluidity of the political environment, however,

prevented their influence from being used in ways conducive to the strengthening of the state (Rashid 2008; Giustozzi 2004, 2008c).

One of the priorities of any nascent (or re-nascent) state has to be the
monopolization of large-scale armed force. The unwillingness of ISAF after
2001 to operate more proactively for the consolidation of the central government, and its failure to weaken local and regional strongmen could only
come at the expense of statebuilding in Afghanistan. The risks of short-term
destabilization if ISAF had been more aggressive were real, particularly given
the organization's lack of experience in the field of enforced disarmament.
However, in the long run ISAF's reluctance to take on illegal armed groups
resulted in an Afghan state that in 2010 was still extremely weak and was
faced with a mortal threat from the insurgency. Rather than gradually evapo-
rating, the illegal armed groups that abounded in the country (as distinct
from the insurgents) were expanding in 2009–2010, casting serious doubts
on the ability of the Afghan government to manage security by itself in the
foreseeable future.[7] In 2002, it was believed that by supporting the formation
of national army and police forces, international statebuilders would help the
central government to gradually acquire the ability to confront the local
strongmen in the provinces. However, the demands of coalition-making in
Kabul often allowed the strongmen to infiltrate central government and
largely pre-empt a challenge that could marginalize them, particularly in the
face of weak political leadership in both Kabul and Washington. The Western
powers' weak support for the central government arguably strengthened the
leverage of the local strongmen vis-à-vis the centre, so that even if Karzai had
not drifted away from building strong institutions, institution building would
probably have not worked anyway (Giustozzi 2004, 2009b).

Institutional façades and informal realities: the confrontation and co-optation of informal actors

The desire of Western powers to reshape Afghanistan according to their own
model of what a state should look like, combined with the weak commitment
to follow through, and objective difficulties on the ground, has delivered
contradictory results. International intervention oscillated between, on the
one hand, the temptation to criminalize the Afghan elite (Torabi 2009:
348ff.) for their ruthless accumulation of financial resources and, on the
other, toleration of the most extreme forms of patrimonialism. The short-
term priorities of international actors drove them towards prioritizing the co-
optation of informal networks over confronting them, despite high-sounding
rhetorical statements. The DDR and DIAG programmes are perfect examples
of this. The DDR process was supposed to disarm, disband and demobilize
the anti-Taliban militias formally placed under the control of the Ministry of
Defence in 2002, but ended up simply driving them underground, to add to
the mass of illegal armed groups present in the country. The DIAG had more
modest aims – that is, simply disbanding armed groups and collecting a symbolic number of weapons – but by 2009 even this limited objective had

proved a complete failure in the wake of the rapidly expanding number of illegal armed groups. Few within the international community took the DIAG seriously, a fact that indicates a degree of hypocrisy. In fact, by 2009 the appetite for co-opting those same illegal armed groups in the fight against the insurgency was growing and, in several areas of the country, various experiments took place regarding the formation of more or less openly sponsored anti-Taliban militias. The greater the perception of insecurity, the more the international stakeholders were ready to engage with informal actors and networks and drop any plan to marginalize or eliminate them.[8]

The willingness of international forces to cooperate with informal actors has had implications for the reconstruction of Afghanistan, in that dubious practices have been easily accepted. For example, provincial governors or members of the presidential family have been allowed to obtain contracts in non-competitive ways. In addition, the collaboration with characters well known for their engagement in drugs trafficking has been widespread, particularly in those areas of the country where security was more problematic. From time to time confrontations between international actors and local elites have occurred over individuals linked to the ruling coalition and their involvement in corruption and trafficking, but as a rule international actors have generally backtracked as long as there was no alleged involvement with the insurgency (Giustozzi 2012).

From 2009 onwards the readiness to engage with informal structures such as local communities (tribes, sub-tribes, villages, clusters of villages) has been growing among international stakeholders, as an antidote to the failure to strengthen the government's administrative structures. Thus, international efforts have moved from engagement with the Afghan State in order to strengthen the reach and scope of its institutions (a strategy that largely failed), through attempts to reform the State's institutions (also mostly unsuccessful), to turning their attentions to perceived 'informal' alternatives (informal justice systems, militias, strongmen, etc.) – a process that continues at the time of writing.

The practices of the different international actors, however, have not been consistent in this regard, with some players more reluctant than others to engage with informal actors and others keener to engage informally, while at the same time refusing to openly acknowledge their collaboration. The Netherlands, for example, long refused to deal with some of the most unsavoury characters in Uruzgan, even though the latter were cooperating very closely with the US. Italy and Germany, on the other hand, have been criticized for making under-the-counter deals with armed groups in order to secure their military bases against attacks in western and northern Afghanistan. The debate over the justifiable degree of engagement with informal actors has raged within the UN as well: at a time when the United Nations Assistance Mission in Afghanistan (UNAMA) was most directly involved in pushing through police reform, some officials called for the need to engage with the informal networks that de facto controlled the ministry, arguing that reform would have a chance to succeed only if these networks were on board.

Others, however, were not convinced by the argument, contending that these informal networks were deeply involved in all sorts of criminal activities and corruption and were beyond recovery; they could only be forcefully purged from the system.

The idea of military factions being rewarded with official appointments in the wake of a post-conflict settlement certainly had a great impact on the perceptions of the rest of Afghan society. Although it is very difficult to know for sure what the strategy of the Taliban insurgents might have been, some have argued that their armed activities might, at least initially, have served the purpose of demonstrating that they could not be excluded from the Bonn settlement. The same might be said of the Hekmatyar faction of *Hizb-i Islami* (Giustozzi 2010b), and there is clear evidence that many of the small armed groups that joined the insurgency from 2006 onwards, either independently or linked to the Taliban, were trying to improve their negotiating position with Kabul, hoping to be incorporated (or re-incorporated) in the ruling coalition on better terms (Giustozzi and Reuter 2010).

Informal actors' strategies: confronting and co-opting external actors

A survey of the behaviour of actors in the informal sector in Afghanistan shows that they have tended to react to the perceived challenge of international intervention with a range of strategies, which include:

- testing the resolution of the intervening powers through occasional violence;
- political mobilization (demonstrations, rioting);
- organizing political parties and participation in elections in order to gain political legitimacy;
- negotiating with neighbouring countries and with the armed opposition;
- re-armament;
- the infiltration of government structures;
- cooperating with external statebuilding actors and exploiting their differences (as highlighted above).

Typically, informal actors used a mix of these strategies, sometimes mining roads, sometimes offering their cooperation to Western armies and development agencies, having conveyed a sense of how dangerous it would be for them to be ignored or sidelined. Their participation in the electoral process is a good illustration of how they increasingly played by the rules imposed by the intervening powers, while simultaneously subverting their purpose. Hundreds of informal actors formalized their position through their election to parliament and to the provincial councils from 2005 onwards, then used the parliament as a vehicle for promoting their interests. From the perspective of the intervening powers, this process of formalization presented positive aspects, particularly insofar as it avoided a direct security challenge. However, it was not necessarily conducive to the kind of rapid statebuilding that was the original intention. Moreover, only a minority of informal actors could be formalized this way. In fact, we can speak of a polarization taking place among informal actors after 2001: a minority of well-connected and well-placed groups or individuals benefited greatly from the inflow of money and from their collaboration with both Kabul and the Western powers; the majority were increasingly marginalized. It was not clear at the time of writing whether the wealthy minority of increasingly formalized actors will be able to control the disgruntled majority.

The actual choices made by the local actors have been determined by a variety of factors and considerations, but in general their agenda has been to negotiate a more advantageous position for themselves. Their degree of success in doing this has depended on:

- physical location, with geographically remote actors finding it difficult to reach out to external actors and even to the government;
- connections with the ruling elite;
- control over lucrative trades;
- international connections;
- military power and the social base of support, which in some cases could be rather large;
- the general political-military environment of the region in which they were operating, which determined whether international actors actually needed any local collaboration.

To sum up, the attitude of actors in the informal sector has been driven mostly by pragmatism. Inevitably, local communities such as tribes and villages and their leadership fared worst in this bargaining, because they had the least to offer; remote communities suffered the most because of their marginality. By contrast, warlords and strongmen managed, in some cases, to negotiate quite attractive deals for themselves as guarantors of stability: the best-known examples are those of the governors of Kandahar (and then Nangarhar) Gul Agha Sherzai and of Balkh Atta Mohammed Noor (see also Stina Torjesen's chapter in this volume).

Conclusion

Institution building in a context of weak or non-existent local ownership and in the absence of a solid elite bargain is very difficult or even impossible to achieve; Afghan political actors had little interest in committing themselves to the development of solid institutions in a context where the beneficiaries were, in all likelihood, going to be others. The power struggle in Kabul, which went on without interruption between 2000 and 2010 and which was still unconcluded at the time of writing this chapter, prevented institution building from taking place, although neither the intervening powers nor the UN seemed to have been clearly aware of the problem. Interventions to mediate between factions and personalities within the Afghan ruling coalition were frequent, but had limited effects because they were not going to the heart of the matter: the need to create a political system capable of sorting out differences and tensions without having to rely on external interventions. Indeed, these very interventions might well have prevented Afghan political players from developing their own mechanisms for stabilizing the political system. External actors were divided between the perception of potential gains deriving from a stable political system that was able to function autonomously and the risk that such a political system would take paths that were at odds with Western political interests. Maintaining an Afghan political system dependent on external peacemaking gave leverage to Western powers over the Afghan government. It is easy to understand where the Western wariness which started showing up in 2008 was coming from. The Afghan ruling elite showed a disinclination to deal with a number of issues in the terms demanded by Western governments, such as:

- improving relations with Pakistan and curtailing relations with Iran;
- repressing the drugs trade;
- fighting corruption;
- respecting Afghan Christians.

Local ownership of the political process sounds very good in principle, but in practice it is often at odds with the strategic interests of international sponsors. The fact that international actors did not share the same priorities in their vision for Afghanistan weakened the hand of the international community: while a consensus existed that Christian converts should not be punished according to the Sharia'h, the importance of Afghan friendship with Pakistan or of Afghan enmity with Iran was attributed a different value by different countries. Views about the opportunity to insist on aggressive counternarcotics in the presence of a growing insurgency were also divided, as was the tolerance for corruption and patrimonial practices.

The multinational intervention in Afghanistan struggled from the very beginning to find common ground when it came to designing and implementing its statebuilding practices. In the various sectors of activity, each participating country sought to bring its own model (of policing, of army training, of development funding and so on), but no agency was either able or willing to coordinate the effort and give it some coherence. By 2005 the US increasingly led the statebuilding effort, after it became clear that European commitment to the mission in Afghanistan was limited. However, even the US effort was marred by differences between the Department of Defense and the Department of State, as well as by the inability of the United States Agency for International Development (USAID) to develop a holistic view of its own efforts. The result was that Afghan partners were thrown into confusion over which of the different practices endorsed by the donors were the best ones; moreover, the fact that there were different approaches delegitimized each one in the eyes of the Afghans. Another negative consequence was the fact that Afghan political actors were able to find some room for manoeuvre in the interstices of the multinational intervention framework, reducing the leverage of the international counterparts when negotiating implementation with the Afghans.

The existence of other sources of external intervention beyond the ones endorsed by the UN Security Council (ISAF) further complicates the picture and again widens the playing field of Afghan political actors: Pakistan, Iran, Russia, Turkey and India have all maintained relations with Afghan partners and have pumped money and, in some cases, weapons into the country, maintaining aims often at odds with those of ISAF and the UN. Certainly Afghanistan did not benefit from geopolitical unimportance after 2001; quite the contrary, by 2010 Afghanistan increasingly resembled the DR Congo of the 1990s and early 2000s in having gradually turned into the proxy battlegound of all the regional countries as well as that of the main world powers.

There is no question that the intervening powers had potentially huge leverage over their Afghan partners from 2001 onwards, and that this leverage affected the shape of the developing state – but not in the ways that had been intended. It is also clear that they failed to achieve the level of expected compliance from Afghan elites. Until 2008, although there was little overt opposition, Afghan leaders paid lip service to a process and a set of international demands, while at the same time pursuing divergent agendas. Nevertheless, Karzai complied to an extent with the demand of donors and intervening powers, as the changing composition of the Cabinet shows. A number of concessions were made in terms of developing legislation, setting up institutions, and making appointments in line with the agreed plan to give Afghanistan a central government aligned with Western standards. However, even before Karzai started actively and openly opposing Western demands in 2008, little in terms of substantial advancement towards the stated goal had been achieved. Although Karzai had, on the face of it, appointed technocrats and reformers on a number of occasions, thereby complying with Western pressure, he never conceded much power to them. The turnover rate among the technocrats was also rather high: none of those present in the Cabinet in 2001 were still there in 2009. Those appointees of 2004 who were still there in 2009 were mostly occupying a different ministerial post from the one that they had originally been given. None of them therefore managed to accumulate much power and influence.

By 2009, the elite that had come into power with the Bonn Agreement in 2001 had narrowed to Karzai and his inner circle. It owed its survival in power to two main factors: the international legitimacy gained during the early years of cooperation with the intervening powers, and an alliance with key players in the shadow economy. Virtually every other constituency was opposed to the regime, including the nouveau riche increasingly trying to establish a beachhead for themselves in the political world. Karzai outmanoeuvred his foreign partners by deploying a number of manipulative tricks. Much of what passed for development consisted of façades of change, fuelled by international spending but without much development of productive capacities. A few Potemkin villages of institutionalization remained surrounded by an ocean of patrimonial realities. The clumsy attempts of external actors to instigate reform only succeeded in irritating Karzai, convincing him that a break-up in the relationship was inevitable. Karzai himself, however, was far from assured of his ability to control the situation and future developments. Apart from his shrewd manipulation of both allies and enemies, Karzai had little in the way of firm foundations on which to base his power. In fact, intervention had created a very fluid, shifting environment, which could be aptly described as quicksand.

Notes

1 The Bonn Agreement was stipulated in Bonn, Germany, on 5 December 2001. It envisaged power-sharing among various anti-Taliban factions and a road map for re-establishing an Afghan state through first an interim and then a transitional government. For the text see www.afghangovernment.com/AfghanAgreementBonn.htm.
2 The Islamic Society, an Islamist party which dominated the anti-Taliban coalition.
3 There are obvious limitations to such an approach, not least since it does not weigh the different positions in accordance with their importance. However, any such weighting would ultimately be random, and the importance of a particular position might not only result from its formal powers, but also from the personality and connections of the office holder.
4 Based on a survey of the list of governors in office by the author and collaborators, December 2008.
5 Official figures from the Joint Electoral Management Body. The official turnout in 2009 was 38.7 per cent, but 18.8 per cent of the votes were invalidated by the Electoral Complaint Commission. Presumably a number of fake votes still made it though, particularly in the case of small-scale proxy voting.
6 On corruption in the reconstruction process see Nawa 2006; Rimli and Schmeidl 2007; and SIGAR 2010.
7 Personal communication with UN official, Kabul, April 2010.
8 Personal communication with UN officials, Kabul, 2007–2009; personal communication with European diplomat, October 2009.

16 The political economy of statebuilding in Burundi

Peter Uvin and Leanne Bayer

Burundi consists of three ethnic groups. Broadly speaking, the Hutu comprise 85 per cent of the population, the Tutsi 14 per cent and the Twa 1 per cent. In 1966, only a few years after achieving Independence on 1 July 1962, a small group of Tutsi military officers from one region took power. From this moment onwards until 1993, this small minority controlled the country to the political, social, and economic exclusion of the Hutu majority. An election in 1993 brought a Hutu president to power, but he was killed a few months later in a bloody coup. The resulting crisis led to a civil war, which formally ended in 2005. Following the signing of the Arusha Peace and Reconciliation Agreement in 2000 and the Pretoria Accord in 2002, there was a decisive shift in Burundi's political landscape towards Hutu political enfranchisement. This was, to a large extent, successfully managed and kept on track by the efforts of the international community. Yet international intervention also reproduced and strengthened the neo-patrimonial political economy that had characterized pre-war and wartime Burundi.

This chapter describes the political changes that Burundi has undergone since war broke out in 1993. It seeks to answer the following questions: how did these changes affect Burundi's political economy, and by what means and to what extent did the international community's deep involvement in this period change the distribution of power in the country? To address these questions, the chapter chronologically examines three periods of international involvement in Burundi: during the war and negotiations between 1993 and 2002; the transition period from 2002 to 2005; and the post-election period until the present day.

During the war (1993–2002)

When the war started in 1993, the international community behaved in characteristic fashion: international aid dried up, foreigners left, embassies were scaled down; only the humanitarian presence increased. Within a year, however, the genocide in neighbouring Rwanda had changed the international response to the war in Burundi. The international community made a major commitment to ensure that Burundi, with its almost identical ethnic and historical make-up to Rwanda, would not go down that same road.

Burundi became the subject of what may well be the most complete, sustained, diverse, and cutting-edge practice of conflict resolution interventions that any country – especially a country so politically and economically insignificant as Burundi – has ever seen. It encompassed dialogue, training, radio programmes, mediation, international negotiations, special envoys, workshops, outreach to the diaspora, and sanctions. For more than a decade, Burundi saw it all. Western governments, the United Nations, conflict resolution NGOs and African governments all played key roles in a persistent attempt to end the war by bringing the parties to the negotiating table.[1]

This hard work led to the Arusha Peace and Reconciliation Agreement (APRA), signed in the summer of 2000. The Agreement in itself did not bring an end to the war, however, because the major rebel movements (CNDD-FDD and the FNL)[2] had not been party to the negotiations. The implementation of the APRA only became realistic once the main rebel group, the CNDD-FDD signed a ceasefire and agreed in Pretoria in 2002 to become part of the transition process created by the Arusha agreement.

Criticism of the APRA abounds. Many Burundians believe that the main impact of the internationally supported mediation process was the legitimization of unrepresentative actors, in the form of small and extremist nuisance parties without any far-reaching social basis. Moreover, the APRA led to significant personal enrichment for the lucky few who spent years negotiating this agreement. Any Burundian taxi driver is able to point to the *quartier Arusha*, where new villas have been built supposedly with the *per diem* allowances received through endless years of negotiations. More broadly, the policy of involving all parties, including the violent and extremist ones, in the dialogue is seen by many Burundians as providing legitimacy for the very strategy of using violence and extremism to obtain advantage.

That said, the APRA was a milestone that has shaped the direction the country has taken ever since. Central to the Agreement was a detailed procedure of power-sharing between Hutu and Tutsi, covering all the key positions in the military, government, parliament and even in parastatal enterprises. It was the first document that truly gave significant political power to the Hutu. It was also, without doubt, the first step towards ending a brutal civil war – something all Burundians desired. And it was a testimony of the perseverance of the international community in working for peace in Burundi. This central role is epitomized by the enormous pressure exerted by Nelson Mandela on the Burundian parties present at the negotiations in order to achieve agreement on the APRA. This was about as heavy-handed and activist a position as any mediator could have taken. There is general agreement amongst the negotiators that without Mandela's status, personality and exceptional credibility, the peace agreement would not have been reached (Bentley and Southall 2005).

So, did the intense involvement of the international community change the nature of Burundi's internal power relations? Most people would answer this question in the negative: while significant pressure was exercised to get the parties to agree to the *existence* of the APRA, the actual *content* of the agreement reflects the realities of the situation on the ground. The cards of power in Burundi had already been fundamentally reshuffled on the battlefield even before the conclusion of the negotiations, and the agreement merely reflected this reality. The Tutsi dominated army, backing a Tutsi-dominated regime, could not win the war, and everyone knew it. By the same token, the Hutu rebels were also incapable of winning. While they could control significant parts of the territory, they were not able to capture the capital or to decisively defeat the national army. This was a mutually hurting stalemate, and the content of the APRA reflects this. Yet it could be argued that the fact that an agreement was reached at all, and that it was slowly but steadily implemented (as discussed in the next section), is the consequence of the extensive international involvement. At the very least, then, we can say that the international community *hastened* the transition from the old system of absolute Tutsi dominance to a new system of power-sharing between Hutu and Tutsi.

Outside influence is also reflected in the specific provisions of the peace agreement, especially those affecting the character of Burundi's state institutions. Many of these are common to internationally driven peace settlements across the world: democratic elections, safeguards for free press, judicial reform, a system of transitional justice, and good intentions about development, land reform, and the like. Many of these elements, if implemented, would constitute a major departure from the old system of governance in Burundi and it is therefore unlikely that they would have been inserted into the APRA without international pressure.

In addition to its efforts in resolving the conflict, the international community was involved in Burundi through humanitarian assistance, delivered both by UN agencies and international NGOs (Ould-Abdallah 2000). The effects of this aid were felt predominantly at the micro-political level. In a context of extreme scarcity of resources, the provision of humanitarian assistance enabled local power holders who could control access to this aid to strengthen their power and increase their income. Corruption and abuse of aid resources reached previously unheard-of proportions, and all available evidence suggests that this was beneficial to those with more control over the state, better local networks, and fewer scruples than others.[3] Research also shows profound unhappiness among the people regarding the abuse of humanitarian assistance: this underlies a widespread realization by ordinary Burundians of the way the system abused them, resulting in a palpable desire for change (Uvin 2006: chapter 4).

The war also signalled a dramatic loss of power by the central state. Until just before the war, Burundi was the epitome of a strong, centrally controlled regime. There was only one single political party that could operate legally,[4] and every civil servant, together with anyone with any desire for social mobility, was a member of it. The party was linked to the country's sole women's organization, its only trade union, the single youth organization, and the only newspaper and radio station (Lemarchand 1996). The very first NGO in Burundi was not created until the early 1990s. This total control of society by the state was once and for all destroyed by the war. As the state weakened both militarily and economically, tens of NGOs, radio stations, political parties, and newspapers came into being. While the international community was not responsible for creating these new actors, it did provide significant financial support to many of them, in particular the NGOs and radio stations. In this way, the international community further impacted on the process of transition, away from the old, highly centralized state towards a more fragmented system.

During the transition (2002–2005)

The period of transition, between the signing of the APRA and the first multi-party elections in 2005, saw the formation of the new rules of the game that now characterize Burundian politics. During this period, the international community was highly instrumental in moving a difficult process forward, ensuring that the transition stayed on track, negotiating the reintegration of a hold-out rebel movement (the CNDD-FDD), and ultimately sponsoring and supervising the elections themselves. Its role during these years was also pivotal in managing political competition among the old and emerging new elites.

There have been many small reversals in the implementation of the peace agreement in Burundi in recent years, and a range of issues, such as transitional justice, have not been addressed at all. However, the major trend has been progress on key issues in the APRA. This would not have succeeded if the international community had not coalesced around three common goals in particular: first, the symbolically powerful transfer of power from Tutsi President Buyoya to Hutu President Ndayizeye; second, the process of military integration; and, third, the creation of a power-sharing government.

Throughout the transition period major military, political, economic, and socio-psychological obstacles to the process remained. Many feared the peace process would not hold. The security situation needed to be stabilized. Soldiers and rebels had to lay down their arms: some had to be integrated into the national army and police, and others demobilized and reintegrated into their communities. Rebels who had not signed the agreements had to be brought into the fold. Police and army structures needed to be reformed, both the leadership and the rank and file had to be trained, and their membership had to become more multi-ethnic.

A viable system of guarantees had to be created to prevent renewed ethnic exclusion and destruction. While the initial conflict was clearly rooted in the competition for political power, issues of ethnicity had taken on a life of their own in Burundi in the previous 30 years, and especially during the preceding decade. The social and physical separation between people had grown; a sense of victimization prevailed (the charge of genocide being the trump card on both sides); and fear and distrust along ethnic lines was shared by all. The power-sharing arrangements in the APRA were a response to that, but would require popular support to work.

The reigning Tutsi elites had to be persuaded to withdraw from control of the state, the army, and the economy, and new elites had to be included in these spheres of power. In the immediate post-Arusha phase, this process was managed in part by a temporary expansion of the number of positions available, especially in the realm of the state: a large number of well-paid ministers and parliamentarians allowed most of the competitors for state power to find a safe haven for a few years (Wolpe 2011).

Institutional transformation had to be achieved against a backdrop of unimaginable poverty and the social exclusion of most Burundians. The rural and urban poor, whether Hutu, Tutsi, or Twa, were the ones killed and abused by all sides. They were the people whose land was stolen, whose food, credit, and aid was being skimmed off, whose children were dying from preventable diseases at a rate that was amongst the world's highest. Few of those in power or vying for it, regardless of their ethnicity and party affiliation, were deeply connected to the poor or even particularly concerned about their plight. Thus the risk was real that peace in Burundi would be established on the backs of the poor, the rural dwellers, the urban dispossessed, and the young.

The major obstacle to peace, however, was that many, if not all, of the key warring parties were not part of the negotiations. The FNL and the CNDD-FDD, by far the largest rebel groups, did not participate in the Arusha talks. This was the result of a decision taken early on by the first mediator, President Julius Nyerere of Tanzania (McClintock and Nahimana 2008). While the APRA represented a solution based on power-sharing for Burundi's fractured and deadlocked political system, it nevertheless had very shallow roots in Burundian society, reducing any chance that it would be fully implemented. Most people who mattered in Burundi – the armed movements, the Tutsi political elite, and the major social institutions – did not identify with it and were, indeed, kept at a distance. Most of those who had negotiated and signed in Arusha were unrepresentative nuisance parties without widespread support, often merely promoting themselves. Despite all this, the transition worked: paper became reality. The role of the international community in this process was, if anything, even more significant than in the negotiation of the agreement. The remainder of this section will examine four key steps in this transition from war to peace, from exclusionary to consociational rule (Sullivan 2005), from authoritarianism to democracy, and from the control of the state by the old Tutsi to a new Hutu elite.

The transfer of the presidency

At the time Mandela coaxed major parties to the negotiations to sign the peace agreement there was only a loose framework for the transition. The president of the transitional government had not been identified, and tensions existed between the Hutu and Tutsi blocs. The peaceful handover from President Buyoya (a Tutsi associated with the military dictatorship and minority rule, and the most powerful military and political leader of his generation) to President Ndayizeye (a Hutu from the FRODEBU party)[5] was a watershed moment in the recent history of Burundi for the majority of the population – one which had been negotiated by the international community. Yet, this potent symbol of change did not mark the end of conflict on the ground: hostilities continued throughout the country between the army and the two remaining rebel groups, the CNDD-FDD and the FNL.

The real transition – CNDD-FDD participation in the government

In October 2002 the CNDD-FDD negotiated an agreement with the transitional government, mediated by South African representatives Jacob Zuma and President Thabo Mbeki, which led to a ceasefire and their integration into the transitional government. For the average Burundian, the moment of peace is often characterized as the point when the CNDD-FDD leader Pierre Nkurunziza laid down his gun and took up his post as minister of state, charged with Good Governance and State Inspection.

The international community facilitated the mediation process with the CNDD-FDD and the agreement that emerged from Pretoria once again dramatically shifted the power relationships in Burundi. The transitional government that had been put in place in 2001 provided the two traditional parties (FRODEBU and UPRONA) with an assurance of power. The new agreement brokered in 2003 chipped away at this power and tipped the scales towards the emergence of the CNDD-FDD as most the powerful party in the transitional government. This rebel movement, which at times had consisted of no more than a few hundred fighters, did not hold the presidency, but it did control key ministries, provided 40 per cent of officers in the newly integrated security forces and controlled forces of ex-combatants who still needed to be demobilized and reintegrated, by means of goods and cash payouts. The CNDD-FDD played the international mediation game best, knowing when to use violence and when to engage in talks. As a result, it gained by far the most in the transition period, at the expense of the FNL, which in the following years would find itself marginalized for having manipulated international support with far less skill.

To assist with the implementation of the agreement the South African army took the unusual step of providing personal bodyguards for those rebel leaders who agreed to return to Burundi and engage in the political process. A UN peacekeeping mission, ONUB, was established in June 2004.[6] The presence of ONUB provided some confidence to all participants that the nature of the game was changing from a purely military, zero-sum conflict to a political and negotiated one. In the absence of such strong security and confidence-promoting measures, it is highly unlikely that players would have made the step from war into politics so easily. In other words, the agreement could have remained a dead letter.

Security sector reform: shifting control over the state

During the Arusha negotiations all parties had agreed that the integration of the security forces would be futile while the CNDD-FDD was still waging war. Once the CNDD-FDD became a member of the transitional government, the real work of reintegrating rebels into the military – creating a new civilian police force and demobilizing the combatants – could begin. The international community worked extensively throughout this time on security sector reform in Burundi, and this has remained one of its major preoccupations in the country today.

Military integration and the process of disarmament, demobilization, and reintegration (DDR) consumed the efforts of both the international community and domestic political actors during the transition period. When the military started retreating from the majority of Burundi's territory (with the exception of the FNL areas), Burundians believed that peace had come. After all, to ordinary people the military represented repression and violence. Moving forces back to the barracks and integrating officers and troops of different factions into a new organization was again both highly effective and symbolic. Although the DDR process was supposed to begin immediately after a ceasefire with the CNDD-FDD was brokered in 2003, it took more than a year of negotiations to secure an acceptable and fundable mechanism. During this period, the dedication of the international community towards the peace process in Burundi was evident. Creative funding by the UK's Department for International Development (DFID), for example, kept thousands of combatants fed and sheltered in cantonment sites for months on end while high-level political discussions were slowly moving forward.

The efforts of the international community in managing the establishment of a new security framework for Burundi were pivotal in turning the commitments in the APRA into practice. During the transition period the balance of power shifted from the former powerful Tutsi elite to a new set of actors. The reform of the military and the police, together with the DDR process, moved influence away from powerful army officers first to key FRODEBU and then to CNDD-FDD players. Towards the end of this period, the focus had shifted from the Hutu–Tutsi dichotomy that had dominated politics for decades, towards political competition for power between the leading Hutu parties in the run-up to the elections.

Multi-party elections and the end of transition

The elections of 2005 were a culmination of the process of transferring power through a negotiated transition period to a presumably legitimate government and, again, all major international actors came together as a matter of urgency in order to emphasize their importance. A new constitution had been drafted with the assistance of the international community and all the major political parties agreed on its content. A national referendum early in 2005 saw its passage into law. An independent national electoral commission

(CENI) was established. The international community, operating in a co-ordinated manner through ONUB, worked closely with CENI to devise a new electoral code, the electoral calendar and ballots, and to arrange all of the equipment required to hold the elections. On the designated election days diplomats from the embassies in the capital Bujumbura as well as international election monitors observed the voting and the count, ensuring transparency. The 2005 Burundian elections were therefore a massive international undertaking. And they were a success.

In the run-up to the elections, the real contest for power was between the two dominant Hutu political parties, FRODEBU and CNDD-FDD. Yet all the advantages lay with the CNDD-FDD, which had access to the institutions of the state while still maintaining much of its vertical command structure. Indeed, the CNDD-FDD had militants sited all over the country. Under the APRA, combatants had laid down their weapons and gone into cantonment camps, but the party ordered them out again and placed them in communities in order to mobilize the popular vote. In many regions a shadow CNDD-FDD administration existed in parallel to the official one, often staffed with FRODEBU officials. Even in areas where FRODEBU was officially in power it was a lame duck, as the CNDD-FDD in reality controlled much of the countryside and was awaiting the elections merely to confirm its hegemony. To this end, both the shadow organization and the official party set up informal local networks to manage the electoral process and the transition into legitimate power. Unsurprisingly, the CNDD-FDD did win a landslide victory in 2005. The international community, situated as it was in the capital, was largely unaware of the local CNDD-FDD shadow administrations. Afterwards, these structures dissipated and merged into official political office.

Political outcomes of the transition

In 2000 Tutsi President Buyoya had held on to power through the mediated settlement at Arusha. The military was under his control, as were the key institutions of the state and the economy. Only five years later, the country's president was a Hutu CNDD-FDD former rebel leader, controlling a newly integrated military (with an ongoing DDR process directly under his control), a freshly created police force largely comprising ex-CNDD-FDD rebels, and a new internal security service that reported to him. The political landscape had changed dramatically.

The historical record firmly suggests that this shift in power would not have occurred without the coordinated actions of the international community. All in all, its major and sustained peacebuilding and transitional support work allowed the political situation to change from one dominated by Tutsi interests to one dominated by those of the Hutu, and especially the CNDD-FDD. While it was not the goal as such of the international community to support the CNDD-FDD, this was the de facto consequence of the policies of the different international actors. Because it was the only major rebel group to negotiate a separate deal, the CNDD-FDD received the lion's share of the new positions in the army and especially in the police. As a result of effective negotiation of the demobilization programme, it ended up in charge of this most crucial lever of power. Moreover, the international community did not notice the way the CNDD-FDD created parallel administrations and, through intimidation and control, assured itself of a victory. By allowing this 'strong man' scenario to emerge, the international community supported the ascendency of power of the ruling party through the end of the transition period and afterwards. Indeed, the post-transition period since 2005 has seen the colonization of state institutions by the new ruling party, a reality that has altered the relationship with the international community in Burundi. This is where we turn to now.

After the transition

After the 2005 elections, a number of dynamics occurred simultaneously and rapidly, all of which contributed to a reduction in the de facto power of the international community. First, the high level of coordination among all parties in the international community melted away rapidly once the key objectives of APRA had been achieved: the transition had been successful, elections had been held, and renewed violence had been averted. The peace continued to hold. International actors – regional states, Western donors, and the UN – increasingly pursued different goals and had differing assessments of the situation in Burundi. The international community, therefore, no longer spoke with one voice, and the momentum for further coordinated pressure dissipated.

To an extent, this decline in coordination was a consequence of the move from diplomacy and peacebuilding towards development, which resulted in the arrival of many new actors: NGOs, donors, and consultants working on the development and implementation of development projects. But, equally, it was the consequence of the geopolitical unimportance of Burundi. The lack of strong national interests by any outside power had made coordination around APRA easier, but also meant that once its objectives had been achieved and success could be declared, international involvement became increasingly half-hearted and inconsistent.

At the same time, Burundi was now led by a newly elected and ostensibly power-sharing government, which managed to build on the international legitimacy that it had gained from the elections as well as from its multi-ethnic character. The deference to sovereignty traditionally displayed by the international community began to reassert itself all the more: many international actors now considered their role to be supporting the government in its policies.

Finally, the newly elected government from the beginning assertively confronted the UN, the key institution that had coordinated the transition ultimately to its benefit. Two successive UN heads rolled rapidly: the first, UN Resident Representative Caroline McCaskie, was humiliatingly discarded; the second, acting UN Resident Representative Nureldin Satti, lasted only a few months. By 2006 ONUB had been forcibly downsized to a small political presence. As a result, the UN increasingly retrenched and played it safe. The major donors and regional powers present in Bujumbura either supported the departure of these officials or failed to take a clear stance against it. While the new Burundian leaders might have been largely less-educated rebels, and their state dependent on international aid, they understood how to use state sovereignty strategically in order to neuter the power of the UN. The signal was clear and well understood by all: do not coordinate behind our backs, do not press us for more security sector reform than we are willing to allow, and do not ask critical questions.

The international community's default mode of working through and in support of the government obviously benefits those who control the state, whether in post-war or 'normal' circumstances – the aid relationship tends to support the status quo. In Burundi, this has been even more strikingly so, as donors explicitly set out to create a peace dividend that could be credited to the government in order to solidify the president's power. Massive donations for primary education immediately after the elections, for example, were the result not so much of a shared assessment of its prime importance in Burundi's economic reconstruction and development, but rather of an explicit desire to bolster the government. Other examples include the healthcare policy for children under five, the policy on free childbirth, and the on-going support for DDR, all of which had been critical political promises of the new president. These were prioritized by the international community, at least in good part as an attempt to shore up his legitimacy and thereby strengthen the transition.

As a general point, those who control the state benefit the most from international assistance in that they determine the flow of resources engendered by international aid (as well as by domestic taxation, such as it is). They can allocate the jobs, distribute the resources, favour friendly areas, channel money to politically connected NGOs, exempt allies from taxes, siphon off money for personal enrichment or redistribution, and so on. In Burundi, this has meant that international peace- and statebuilding efforts have supported, even strengthened, the neo-patrimonial system that keeps the current elite in power. The system has been characterized by massive clientelism and corruption, the ever-present wide gap between the city and the countryside[7] and between elites and ordinary people, the continued use of security forces and the justice system for blatantly partisan political goals, and the return to economic policies that benefit the elite in power (Nkurunziza 2009) – in other words, the exact system that prevailed before the war. After hundreds of thousands of lives lost, years of fighting, mass displacement, suffering, and pain – not to mention creative international involvement – what is being rebuilt in Burundi is a neo-patrimonial vertical power structure that perfectly replicates the pre-war order. The only aspect that has changed is the composition of the elites that control power and resources for their own benefit.

However, the international involvement in post-war Burundi has had some countervailing effects. First, in light of a continued fear that violence may break out again, the international community remained concerned with what it considered to be direct threats to sustainable peace. This took two forms in particular: first, it pressurized the government of Burundi into negotiating a ceasefire and military integration with the FNL; and, second, it insisted on the integrity of the next round of elections in 2010. It is especially the latter issue that brought back a coordinated response from the international community. At key moments, such as during debates about the composition of the Electoral Commission (which the government wanted to stack with people beholden to itself), the international community was remarkably consistent and united in its pressure, and was successful: CENI's eventual composition was far more broad based than it otherwise might have been. The international community has therefore made it more difficult for the powers-that-be to reproduce themselves easily or in an uncontested fashion.

In addition, the international community has continued to support civil society, which may not have been very effective as a counter-weight to the government, but has at least been a political nuisance. First, a set of human rights and anti-corruption organizations has emerged that see themselves as fighting a hegemonic and repressive state. Second, while political power has shifted dramatically in Burundi, the social and economic privileges of the past have not yet been undone. Civil society – especially the experienced part, the part capable of writing good proposals and reports to international donors – remains dominated by Tutsi. The government has tried to combat this de facto bias by supporting the creation of new NGOs that are closer to it, and by sending contracts their way. These new NGOs, however, have limited experience and less well-qualified individuals managing them. Their knowledge of the roles and policies of the donors, and hence their influence with them, is weak. Yet, in areas like demobilization, these NGOs have managed to become direct subcontractors and interlocutors to the international community.

That said, the CNDD-FDD has been capable of working around all the constraints engendered by the international community in its quest for fair elections and good governance, in part because of the deep divisions within and the inefficiency of the opposition. All in all, by the time the 2010 elections were over, the CNDD-FDD exercised even stronger control of the machinery of the state, the culmination of a five-year trend. One could argue that all this – the debate, the pressure, the arguments, and the civil society organizations, weak as they are – are practical 'lessons in democracy' for many Burundians, even those ordinary citizens who merely observe the process. The pressures and inducements have obviously not produced the 'real' product (i.e. fair elections or a truly pluralist political system) but they do contribute to creating discourses, popular expectations, and experiences that may, down the road, favour social change.

Conclusion

Our main goal in this chapter was to demonstrate to what extent and in what manner the deep involvement of the international community in peacebuilding in Burundi has affected the political economy and the distribution of power in the country.

The standard impact of the development aid system, and the international community behind it, is the strengthening of executive power, or, more concretely, the power of those people who control the executive (Fritz and Menocal 2007). International aid, then, entrenches local elites. This happens at the expense of the other institutions of state and society. It mostly happens indirectly, as a result of lack of coordination and through a piecemeal, input-based, apolitical approach to development. Local elites, especially those in government, are simply the best placed to benefit from international assistance and involvement; the international community needs to deal with those who are in charge, and overthrowing them as individuals is not, in any case, the aim of intervention. The case of Burundi was no different.

However, there is also a second dynamic. International interventions entrench not only local elites but also local systems of clientelism and, more generally, what de Waal (2008) has called 'the political marketplace'. Thus, the benefit to local elites is the side effect of a deeper dynamic, namely the strengthening of the existing neo-patrimonial political economy. Even with great changes in elites, the system survives amazingly well (see Chabal and Daloz 1999).

That this would also happen in Burundi is not self-evident. After all, the old elite were largely replaced by an entirely new group, many of whom were not only of a different ethnic background but also of a different social class from the ones they fought. The power of the old state declined precipitously during the war. New media and organizations sprang up, and people generally started to think differently, more critically, about the state (Uvin 2006). Why, then, is the new political economy such a perfect copy of the old? In order to analyse this general trend, sociologists and institutional economists have focused on the role of institutions (North 1998; Acemoglu and Robinson 2008; Helmke and Levitsky 2004) and path dependence (Mahoney 2000; Pierson 2000), both highly relevant for understanding the developments in Burundi. Theoretically, then, this comes as little surprise, even though the practitioners and policymakers on the ground did not see it coming.

From the empirical perspective employed in this chapter, it is interesting to tease out how and why the changes that took place during the decade of war failed to produce any lasting result, and reflect on the role of the international community. Part of the answer lies in the politics of accommodation. A power-sharing arrangement, instead of an outright victory, is less likely to lead to a radical departure from the past. The military stalemate almost guaranteed little political change, except for the entry of new faces. But this is not enough: neighbouring Rwanda saw a total destruction of the old power elite and a complete takeover by new elites from abroad, and yet it, too, reconstructed a largely similar pattern of state–society relations to what had preceded. Part of the answer may be that the crucial factor is cognitive: this is how politics in Burundi is done and how competitors for political power have been socialized to work. Indeed, every Burundian who now claims disappointment expected, deep inside, exactly this system to emerge, and in so doing contributed to its emergence.

To this, the political imperatives of a new government can be added. The post-transition government was weak on almost all fronts: militarily threatened by the FNL, by militias of other parties, and by possible dissent within the army; politically challenged by disgruntled elements everywhere (including inside its own party); presiding over one of the world's poorest economies, with few opportunities for economic security and advancement except through the office of the state; and in charge of a state that was little more than an empty shell, a network of personal allegiances rather than a collection of functioning institutions. To establish control and strengthen their position, what else could leaders effectively do but return to the practices that were known to work? They had to return favours to their wartime supporters; co-opt opponents and spoilers, or else intimidate them; weaken organizations that were disloyal to them (whether ministries directed by Tutsi, informal institutions not beholden to them, or the independent media); use the available institutions of the security sector to extend their control (in particular the police, as the army had integrated different armed factions and was also closely followed by the international community). Doing differently in a country without rule of law, without deeply internalized traditions of transparency and bureaucratic autonomy, without assured security in any way, would have seemed suicidal from the perspective of Burundi's new rulers. And in so doing, they of course recreated the system they fought and promised to change.

Additionally, the transition period was one where the international community opened the spigot: large amounts of reconstruction aid arrived, which could be directed and siphoned off to strengthen patronage networks. While the international community regularly complained about corruption and diversion of aid, after the elections its presence was fragmented and weakened, and its voice no longer unified.

Finally there is the impact of sovereignty. While sovereignty may just be a form of politeness, designed to mask profound inequalities of resources and conceptualization between states, it does produce effects. It cannot *ex nihilo* create the power to conceive or fund its own development policies, but it can create a protected space where the international community cannot go: inside party meetings, prison cells, militia meeting places, wedding banquets, and private audiences – in other words, where the real decisions are made. This protected space endows local rulers with the power to resist, subvert, and re-appropriate. There is real power, with real impacts in the formal sphere, even in the international realm. This is well illustrated by the way the UN was rendered toothless through targeted intimidation in a few short months after the 2005 election. From being the core institution in the

Burundian transition, at the heart of every political and policy decision, at the centre of every negotiation table, the UN, in less than a year, was reduced to the usual group of small, squabbling, timid, self-censoring agencies, devoid of any structural or sustained impact. Hypocritical it may be, but sovereignty gets results: first, it usually benefits the group of people who control the government of the country concerned – who 'manage' the sovereignty at the expense of other social forces – and, second, it pushes politics and decisions underground, removed from the donors' prying eyes and interventionist intentions, thus all but assuring that the way politics is done will continue to build from informal, personal, clientelist mechanisms. This is the only place where leaders can make compromises, avert challenges, and implement visions that are not pre-empted by the international community.

Notes

1 For some insights on this, see De Mars *et al.* 1999; Woodrow 2006; Sebudandi and Icoyitungye 2008.
2 *Conseil National de Défense de la Démocratie/Forces de Défense de la Démocratie* – the political and military arms of the largest rebel army, created in 1994; *Forces Nationales de Libération*, the first and oldest rebel movement, formed in 1985 out of an even older radical Hutu movement.
3 Positions of drivers for humanitarian aid, for example, were deeply desirable, not only because they guaranteed salaries in an economy with few formal jobs, but also because they could be parlayed into political and economic benefits for those without scruples.
4 This party was UPRONA, *Union pour le Progrès national*, created in 1961 and heavily associated with the Tutsi military regimes from 1965 to 1993.
5 *Front pour la Démocratie au Burundi*, the first political party formed in 1986, which had won the 1993 elections.
6 *Opération des Nations Unies au Burundi*, established by SC Res. 1545 of 21 May 2004.
7 This is not entirely accurate. The new president is far closer to the people than any previous political leader was or would have wanted to be.

17 The political economy of the Comprehensive Peace Agreement in Sudan

Atta El-Battahani and Peter Woodward

Sudan's Comprehensive Peace Agreement (CPA) of 2005 was a major political event. A country that had started on the road of independence in 1956 as a unitary state with a liberal democracy along Westminster lines had become a place of two dominant armed camps. On one side was the national government, an authoritarian Islamist regime that had seized power through a coup in 1989, and from 1999 was effectively a one-party state under the National Congress Party (NCP). On the other side was a rebel movement in the predominantly non-Arab south that had been fighting from 1983 under the title of Sudan Peoples Liberation Army/Movement (SPLA/SPLM). Yet behind the armed politics lay the influence on both sides of the economy, which both had sought to manipulate as a dimension of conflict in different ways and for different motives. The main thrust of this chapter is to consider the significance of the political economy in the decisions to negotiate peace; the financial and economic aspects of the peace process, and the implementation of those aspects of the CPA since 2005. While it had been intended in the CPA that both parties would work to make unity attractive, in the event that failed to happen and the referendum in the South in January 2011 was overwhelmingly in favour of separation. As a result the questions concerning political economy involve consideration of two separate states from July 2011 onwards. But before these themes can be pursued it is necessary to start with the broader picture of the country's political economy within which developments surrounding the CPA need to be set. The agreement included a referendum for the South in January 2011 that resulted in an overwhelming vote for separation and resulted in the independence of South Sudan on 9 July of that year.

The evolution of Sudan's political economy

As a territorial state roughly corresponding to the country's contemporary borders Sudan is a product initially of nineteenth century imperial ambitions emanating from the Egypt of Mohammed Ali.[1] When his forces advanced up the Nile in the 1820s it was largely with the intention of extracting Sudan's economic resources. Initially the concerns were with manpower for the Egyptian army, and the hopes of finding gold probably in the eastern hills. By the mid-nineteenth century Egypt had penetrated into the south, initially seeking ivory but in time developing a growing commercial slave trade in northern Sudan, Egypt, and the other Ottoman territories; a trade that involved Europeans as well as Egyptians and northern Sudanese (Gray 1961). Though Egyptian rule was ended by the Mahdist revolt in 1885 and British rule from 1898, the legacy of the exploitation of the south, and especially of the slave trade, has lived on.[2]

Britain's motivation in controlling Sudan had more to do with geopolitical strategy in the face of growing European rivalry than its economic expectations for the country. Nevertheless Sudan, like other territories, was required to be revenue earning through the development of an export sector for the imperial state. As it could raise only very limited amounts by taxing the mainly poor population, it depended on the revenues deriving from both exports and imports. In time it was recognized that this would be mainly through cotton, produced largely in the huge Gezira scheme in the centre of the country between the Blue and White Niles and exported chiefly to the cotton mills of Lancashire, England. At its height it was to be the largest agricultural scheme in the world under single management. It dominated the 'modern' sector of the economy for decades and impacted right across the country, drawing in labour not only from the outlying parts of Sudan but from as far afield as Nigeria.[3] At the same time it was creating a 'modern sector' that was essentially 'extraverted' linked less to the growth of a 'national' economy for Sudan than to British imperial economic growth. It was the revenues from the exports and imports from this 'extraverted' economy which provided the core funding of the state. Given the nature of the similarly 'extraverted' origins of the state from the Turco-Egyptian period, the economy was mirroring much of what was developing in the political and social fields as well (Bayart 1993).

While the Gezira scheme lay at the heart of the import–export economy, a number of smaller private schemes were also established along the Nile, and their development contributed to the growth of northern Sudanese commercial life that was already a feature of the river from ancient times. From the time of the Second World War, the growing financial strength and the sectarian ability to mobilize political support of northern Sudan's Sunni Muslim communities gave rise to political parties that were to be the instruments of Britain's overthrow and the inheritors of the imperial state (Niblock 1987). In particular the Umma Party, under the patronage of Sayed Abdelrahman al-Mahdi, drew much of its finance from *Dairat el-Mahdi*, the family's business organization; while the looser Khatmiya sect, led by Sayed Ali al-Mirghani, supported the National Unionist Party. For both parties wealth lay predominantly in the geographically central areas of the country; but they had the means to support their mounting political power with their sectarian support in many rural areas of northern Sudan. However, in those outlying areas of the country there was little comparable economic development or sufficient regional political mobilization to bring about significant change. In the eastern and western regions of northern Sudan, such as Darfur in the extreme west, 'traditional' economic activity was mixed with the growing commercial activities of riverine merchants, known as *jallaba*, and labour migration to the richer centre.[4] This economic imbalance translated into politics as the sectarian based parties used the resources they raised primarily in the central areas of the country to establish patron–client networks in the outlying areas which hindered the growth of more regional representation.

The economic neglect of outlying areas had also been true for the south though in a more extreme form, for from 1930 the British had operated a 'Southern Policy' designed to isolate and 'protect' this non-Muslim region, including trying to reduce the role of northern *jallaba* in the region. There was even an attempt to create an alternative local economy around the Zande scheme in western Equatoria but it was not to last. The legacy of this deliberately classic divide and rule policy in the south was to be an enhancing of the sense of cultural and racial difference. While the north was perceived by Sudan's British rulers as largely inhabited by Arab and Muslim tribes, the south was seen as an area that was characteristically of African origin and whose traditional religions would permit the activities of Christian missionaries who were not allowed to proselytize in the north. While economically the central northern Sudan became the country's backbone, especially the Gezira scheme; the south was in practice largely neglected and seen as geographically remote and with few resources then attractive to the empire. Thus by the end of the Condominium, northern and southern Sudanese were increasingly perceiving themselves as belonging to one or other part of an imperially created and divided country which was the product of first Turco-Egyptian and then British policies.

After independence the inherited political economy largely continued, but with increasing instability and stagnation, partly due to the declining world market returns on the major export crop: raw cotton. The growth of nationalist politics around the links between widespread Islamic sectarianism and the commercial opportunities created by the evolving international economic system intensified party competition to the point of successive unstable coalition governments. But it was less a competition over developmental ideologies than a struggle for the benefits of office, with little thought given to any significant restructuring of the economy. In 1958, the political uncertainty resulted in a military coup led by the army's senior officer, General Abboud. During his regime there was some stabilization and growth in the economy, but essentially on the inherited model and with the acceptance of the sectarian leaders and the commercial sector.

However the outbreak of civil war in the south in the early 1960s encouraged more radical thinking, and in 1964 a popular uprising took place known as the October Revolution: in the face of widespread urban discontent Abboud and his colleagues simply stood aside. Briefly there were hopes for change, but the old parties and squabbling coalition governments returned. Unsurprisingly another coup in 1969 occurred, but this time by more radical middle rank officers like those elsewhere in the Middle East.[5] The new president, Ja'afar al-Nimeiri introduced plans for a state-led transformation of the economy including a widespread programme of nationalization, often hurriedly carried out with little preparation.

Nimeiri survived early challenges, and shifted tack by making peace with the southern rebels in 1972 at Addis Ababa. This achievement went down well in the West and Nimeiri was soon forging new alliances with the US and its newly oil enriched conservative Arab allies: by the end of the decade the regime was seeking a new direction for the country's economy, though still based on agriculture. Sudan was flagged as the new 'bread basket' for the Arab world, and Arab investment backed by Western technology flowed into the country. However, as a result of poor planning, weak infrastructure, and local corruption and inefficiency these projects resulted in little more than large debts.[6] By the late 1970s, Chevron's plans to develop newly found oil-fields in the now peaceful south raised new hopes for economic development. For some years after the peace Nimeiri had been a hero for the south, but his continuing challenges in the north encouraged reconciliation with his former enemies in the Umma Party, and the growing Muslim Brotherhood, though at the price of an Islamist agenda that he finally introduced in 1983, and which was deeply resented in the south. At the same time, he was seeking to undermine the south's own elected regional government to control the new-found oilfields. The combination of national debt and economic woes, Islamization and interference in the south all contributed to the outbreak of renewed civil war in 1983, led by John Garang and the SPLA. The SPLA soon targeted the oilfield around Bentiu (in the process driving out Chevron), and also interrupted the construction of the Jonglei Canal that was perceived as delivering enhanced water supplies to the north and to Egypt. Under the double challenge of Islamism in the north and civil war in the south, Nimeiri's regime finally fell in 1985.

The new 'modern' Islamist movement that emerged in Sudan after the Second World War developed from the influence of Egypt's Muslim Brotherhood, as in a number of other countries in the Middle East. It grew after the October Revolution of 1964, which overthrew the then military regime, under the new dynamic leadership of Hasan al-Turabi. In the name of building a modern Islamic state it challenged the existing sectarian parties, recruiting among the burgeoning student population in particular. Its major political breakthrough came in 1977 when it reached agreement with Nimeiri. Henceforth the movement, trading principles for expediency, entered into many areas of the state, a progress that was helped by the fragmentation of the opposition movement, the wavering of the Umma and Unionist parties on Nimeiri's *sharia* laws, and the return of democracy following Nimeiri's downfall that permitted it to operate as a political party under the new name of the National Islamic Front. In 1989, it staged its own coup and the movement's leader, Omar al-Beshir, has survived in power until the time of writing (El-Affendi 1991; El-Battahani 1996a). The development of the Islamist movement in Sudan was aided by the availability of new sources of finance, in particular the Islamic banking movement, much boosted by the oil price rises of the 1970s. These banks encouraged the small business sector in particular, the growth of which helped to undermine the commercial and financial base of the established sectarian parties. In addition, many educated Sudanese had moved to Saudi Arabia and the Gulf States and they were encouraged to contribute to the movement at home, as well as to the wider Islamist movement across the Middle East.

After the 1989 coup, the movement's efforts to assert control over the economy intensified, not least through the confiscation of properties of the leaders of the traditional parties. Sudan's new leaders also embraced the international trend towards privatization and economic liberalization, to the advantage of themselves and their followers. More foreign capital was also imported as Sudan launched itself as a centre of international Islamism led by its very own *Ingaz* (Salvation) regime. Also welcome were 'brothers in Islam' including Osama bin Laden, who from 1991 to 1996 invested in Sudan's economy as well as growing al-Qaeda. Relationships between the government and businesses came to resemble crony capitalism (as in many parts of Africa and the Middle East), rather than an open and free market. Patronage of this kind created political support from the favoured clients but added to inflation as firms sought to capitalize on market power, increased inequality by excluding the majority from any benefit of privatization, and increased the opportunities for corrupt relationships with officials at all levels (El-Battahani 1996b; Suliman 2007). At the same time, war in the south was linked to the strategy of asserting a new economic dominance: this was done partly through the acquisition of a new cheap labour force from the south displaced northwards by the conflict; and through the re-establishment of control over the oilfields whose exploitation had been checked by the fresh outbreak of rebellion in the south in 1983 but which now came on stream from 1999 (Johnson 2003). It held out the prospect of rentier development for Sudan's economy through the state's direct control over oil revenues which could supplement and expand the still largely 'extraverted' non-oil sectors. It was to be the start of a boom period such as Sudan had never experienced hitherto and from 2005 there was a conglomeration of interests sometimes known as the Sudan Political Islamic Corporate (SPIC), bringing together (despite their political differences) groupings like the Umma Party, DUP, the National Congress Party (former NIF), Muslim Brothers, and new emerging Salafies and new business networks in the oil, communication, and construction sectors.

The political economy of the CPA

Towards peacemaking

Until the late 1990s, the economy itself had remained in poor shape since the failure of the 'bread basket' policy left large debts. Once in power, the Islamist regime had endeavoured to address the situation through neo-liberal policies, but with large inherited debts the situation remained difficult until Asian countries, led by China, moved in to develop Sudan's oil reserves

(Patey 2007). US counter-terrorism sanctions against Sudan meant that the American oil companies previously engaged in Sudan were now excluded from exploitation. Sudan soon became sub-Saharan Africa's third largest oil producer, after Nigeria and Angola, and a major exporter to China in particular, though also of importance for India and Malaysia. The renewed exploitation of Sudan's oil reserves also had significant implications for the civil war in the south.

The civil war and the possibility that northern parties might sacrifice Islamic law for peace had been one of the triggers for the Islamist coup of 1989. It was therefore unsurprising that the new regime made a concerted effort to crush the SPLA in the early 1990s. Equally unsurprisingly, when it failed the SPLA launched new assaults of its own and by 1997 was seriously threatening the regime, now with considerable international encouragement including that of the US (Woodward 2006a). However, it too failed, and in the aftermath it looked ever less likely that either side could achieve a military victory. The recognition of a stalemate eventually contributed to the process leading to the CPA, which itself followed years of intermittent and unsuccessful peace talks, the seriousness of which had always been in doubt.

Deadlock on the battlefield was significant but not sufficient to achieve a peace agreement; economic issues also pushed the NCP and the SPLA towards serious negotiation. While the NCP had established enough control to begin exporting oil in 1999, the situation was still far from stabilized. In 2001 in particular there was fierce fighting in the area of some of the oilfields, and though the government backed its own local ethnic militias, the SPLA remained a real threat to oil production. The SPLA was also allied to growing movements in the eastern Sudan that were increasingly threatening to the pipeline carrying the oil from the distant fields to the terminal on the Red Sea. A peace agreement promised to ease the situation and allow for greater production levels. At the same time, the NCP was under growing pressure from China. The state-run Chinese National Petroleum Corporation (CNPC) was inconvenienced by the conflict in the south but was unlikely to be driven out by it (instead it was selling arms to the NCP government some of which were used by government forces and local militia allies to displace local communities around the oilfields). However China's levels of demand were rising, and in a peaceful Sudan it would find it easier to securely expand its activities. In addition there were those in the NCP who wanted to see a return of the interest of Western majors in oil production, and attract other Western businesses. The US sanctions were not crippling but they were a hindrance, and a peace agreement promised to open the way for the more technologically advanced exploitation of new oilfields in Sudan as well as Western investment in other areas of the by then quite rapidly expanding economy.

As for the SPLA, it was becoming clear that while it could harass oil production in the south and with its allies interrupt flows in eastern Sudan, it was not able to halt oil production. Moreover if production continued to grow in spite of the SPLA's efforts, there was a real danger that over time it would enable the Khartoum government to modernize and enhance its military build-up and finally defeat SPLA forces. A peace agreement could open the way for the SPLA leader, John Garang, to rally the political support of 'marginalized' areas of the north, including Darfur, where the SPLA had attempted an invasion in 1991 to open a new front, but which had been easily crushed by the NCP. Nevertheless, as the situation in Darfur deteriorated in the 1990s the SPLA showed sympathy and helped the revolt of 2003 which, following initial success, soon degenerated into the long running Darfur crisis (Flint and de Waal 2005; Daly 2007). The lesson of the whole CPA process for many in Darfur was that the gun was the route to any regional redress; but the resistance of the NCP to substantial recognition of a new northern claim, coupled with factional divisions in Darfur, prevented agreement in spite of protracted negotiations. The government of South Sudan (GoSS) was to show intermittent concern for Darfur, but the NCP was determined to keep it a 'northern' affair.

Eventually, combined external and internal pressures to put an end to violent conflict in the country, and the momentum for peace generated by negotiations between the NCP and SPLM drove both to sign the CPA, yet for both of them it was a calculated risk. Given the deep-seated mistrust between the two adversaries, leaders of the two conflict parties saw in the agreement a compromise, or at best a truce, to buy time and pursue their goals by other means. Peace negotiations showed major concessions by both sides, but the bottom line for both was not to give an inch when it came to defend the principles on which their legitimacy was based: Islamic sharia for the NCP, and a secular state for the SPLM.

The existence of a referendum in the agreement seemed to favour a non-cooperation strategy on the part of the SPLM to bide time and eventually 'win' the chance of independence; but whether this did put the NCP in a difficult position, since one would presume it did not want to be seen to lose the south, is open to debate. As mentioned above, some observers believed that the NCP never really intended to genuinely work for unity, it was captive of its ideology of building an Islamic state, and many saw in the south an obstacle to that aim, particularly after fighting a lost war in the 1990s. Perhaps both parties were content with separation but for domestic and international reasons did not wish to be seen to be seeking it. Thus, the CPA could be seen as an 'extended ceasefire', with both parties intent on using oil revenues to arm themselves. This is reflected in the original position shared by dominant circles in both NCP and SPLM during the peace negotiations: 'yes to signing the agreement, no to fully complying with it'.

The peace process was not just about the political economy, there were other vital matters too (Woodward 2006b). As well as a 'hurting' deadlock, both parties had political reasons to make peace. Both faced challenges in their own constituencies: the NCP had split in 1999 with its main ideologist and *eminence grise*, Hasan al-Turabi forced out to found his own Islamist party; while there were ethnic and military tensions in the south. Years of failed peace talks between the parties had also meant the growth of mutual understanding and an emerging agenda for negotiation. Another vital factor was the enhanced engagement of the international community. The US had become more involved, especially following intelligence on the presence of a global Islamist movement in Sudan from 2000, and was to become even more concerned after 9/11 (Woodward 2006a). In addition the Christian right was very active on matters pertaining to the war in the south, and President George W. Bush became directly involved in pushing for a peace settlement. The result was major US support for a peace push, with involvement from Britain and Norway (known as the Troika). Regionally there was involvement by the Inter-Governmental Authority for Development (IGAD) whose members all at that time favoured the settlement of Africa's longest running civil war: Kenya, the host for the peace talks, was particularly active. This extensive external involvement led to questions about the role of the US behind IGAD's efforts, and about the degree to which the CPA was actually 'owned' by the Sudanese. However, no matter who ultimately bore the greatest responsibility for the terms of the CPA, the agreement offered potential gains to both parties, and enabled both parties to themselves interpret the provisions of the agreement. In an effort to monitor and indeed influence the implementation of the CPA there was also a Sudanese international Joint Assessment Mission (JAM) under a rotating chairmanship.

The importance of religion to the political identity of both parties was shown in the very first negotiation of the peace process, the Machakos Protocol of 2002. This protocol meant the recognition that northern Sudan would be under Islamic law, but the south would be secular. In addition, in 2011 the south would have a referendum with the right to secede, though both parties also committed themselves to work to make unity attractive. The central and ideologically toughest issues had been settled at the outset. The protocol was followed by a range of other agreements, including the Agreement on Wealth-Sharing of 2004, before the whole CPA package was finally signed in 2005.

Financial and economic aspects of the CPA

Like all the other protocols, wealth-sharing was even on paper a complicated issue. For the SPLA it was an opportunity to start to redress the exploitation of the south that had been going on for over 100 years, and it was particularly keen to break up the control exercised by successive governments in Khartoum, the capital, over the national economy. While not admitting the SPLA's argument in full, the NCP was prepared to recognize regional imbalances and the existence of war-affected areas. As a result, the agreement recognized the need for 'Reconstruction and Development'. This was to be led by the establishment of two reconstruction and development funds, the South Sudan Reconstruction and Development Fund (SSRDF) and the National Reconstruction and Development Fund (NRDF), as well as two Multi-Donor Trust Funds (MDTFs) to handle international assistance. The priorities of the two MDTFs were to fund benchmarked public investment in health, education, and infrastructure; as well as structural changes encouraging private growth in areas such as agro-industries, telecommunications, reconstruction works, waste disposal, and services for international companies in oil and other minerals and timber. New financial arrangements were also to be put in place with a new central bank and a separate Bank of Southern Sudan.

Oil revenues had a central part in the new wealth-sharing arrangements. Seventy-five per cent of the fields under production were in the south and revenues from there were to be shared 50–50 between the new NCP-SPLM dominated Government of National Unity (GNU) and the GoSS. In addition 2 per cent from this allocated revenue was to go to the oil producing federal states themselves in proportion to their levels of output. The oil was to be managed by the National Petroleum Commission (NPC), including southern representatives, to which a Joint Technical Team would report. However existing oil contracts were not to be renegotiated.

While oil was obviously central to the revenues of both the GNU and the GoSS, for millions of Sudan's rural population land had become ever more of an issue. A fast rising population, climate change, and environmental decay have all been putting pressure on what on paper appeared to be Sudan's vast land resources. But the evolving national economy was also creating new pressures. Oil exploitation itself had been accompanied by accusations of population displacement for which there was a growing body of evidence, as well as considerable local environmental damage (Moro 2009). In addition, the growth of commercial agriculture involving national and international capital and spreading along the rain-watered lands east and west of the Blue and White Niles was having a destabilizing impact on local communities, some of whom were being forced into becoming landless agricultural labourers or moving to the growing slums around rapidly expanding towns and cities. In consequence a significant part of the wealth-sharing agreement dealt with the issue of land ownership in a way that sought 'to create a process to resolve conflict on land issues by developing and amending legislation to reflect customary laws and practices, local heritage, and international trends' (Moro 2009). To achieve this, a series of commissions were established: the National Land Commission; the Southern Sudan Land Commission; and the State Land Commissions in each of the federal states. These commissions were established in order to arbitrate claims over lands, and have the power to make recommendations for new or amended legislation to the three levels of government. Clearly these were going to prove complex arrangements in practice and also potentially offered sources of contention. It was not long before all the arrangements were throwing up problems such as those of the state allocation of land to foreign investors in the face of local community claims to traditional collective rights of land use.

For both parties there was an element of calculated risk. For the NCP, its Islamic project was so central to its legitimacy that it appeared prepared to put at risk its dominance of the oil sector with its agreement on a referendum in 2011, since most oil reserves lay in the south. For the SPLM that referendum was its strongest card, but at the same time one which had as its last resort control of an asset that could only be exploited via the long pipeline through the north to the Red Sea. The international community, which had played such a part in all aspects of the CPA, hoped that the recognition of this predicament by both parties to the agreement would bind them together.

Implementation of the financial and economic aspects of the CPA

From the outset, the CPA faced institutional problems. At the national level the NCP was determined to maintain control of the Ministry of Finance, even allowing SPLM nominees to take the Ministry of Foreign Affairs. The Ministry of Finance was at the centre of a web of government spending over which scrutiny and control remained weak, allowing for widespread corruption. While much of this resulted in personal gain (as a pyramid scheme in Darfur, that was headed by two state government officials, and which collapsed in 2010, highlights), it also supported networks of patronage that were at the centre of political control in the central areas of the country, where most of its economic growth was seen. Much of this growth was fuelled by government contracts to its favoured clients. The weak National Audit Chamber has been unable to contain these practices.

Naturally, the counterpart Ministry of Finance of the GoSS in Juba has faced its own problems. As with virtually all the other departments of the new government, there have been organizational problems, such as too few qualified and experienced personnel, and delays in the payment of salaries. There have also been accusations of corruption, some of which have led to dismissals and prosecutions under anti-corruption laws. The establishment of separate banking and currency arrangements for the south was also demanding, with concerns in 2009 that both the new Bank of Southern Sudan and the Nile Commercial Bank, the largest private bank in the region, were running short of cash.

With few sources of revenue other than oil, the GoSS had to await its share of oil revenues which arrived first in Khartoum where monitoring of the wealth sharing provisions was supposed to be provided by the NPC, with its agreed membership drawn equally from the NCP and the SPLM. Though it was established within months of the signing of the CPA its staffing and procedural agreement was delayed with much wrangling until the latter part of 2007. This weakened the authority of the NPC, and undermined the trust between the two parties once it was up and running. Eventually the Minister of Oil and Energy, Awad al-Jaz, was moved but only to swap places with the Minister of Finance, Zubeir Hassan Ahmed. In such circumstances it was no surprise that the SPLM complained regularly about the lack of transparency in the management of the vital oil sector, and in particular that the NPC was not kept fully informed about the revenues from oil sales. Increasingly, the SPLM alleged that the NCP was keeping the bulk of the revenues, and that the GoSS was receiving far less than its due share in spite of the fact that the bulk of the oil derived from the south. Following the elections of 2010, the SPLM did finally take the Ministry of Oil and Energy, in return for giving up the Foreign Ministry, though this made no difference to the allocation of revenues set out in the CPA.

The revenue issue also came under closer scrutiny as oil prices fluctuated. Oil was the main driver behind a period of GDP growth that from 2003–7 was averaging 9 per cent per year, boosting government spending and contributing to the general air of optimism surrounding the CPA. But as the global recession impacted on oil prices revenue dropped sharply, and budget forecasts for 2009 were predicting falls as steep as 44 per cent in national revenues; however, subsequent rises in oil prices once more eased the situation There were not only the questions of the size of the cake and the percentage of oil generated revenues going to the GoSS, but also concern about where the money was being spent. For years, wars in the south and later in Darfur had driven up spending on the military; creating one of the largest military-industrial complexes in Africa that was of great benefit to the ruling elite in Khartoum. The signing of the CPA did not lead to a reduction in government expenditure on armaments, and the agreement itself involved costs for the restructuring and relocation of the Sudan Armed Forces, in effect now a northern rather than a national army. Understandably the SPLM, with memories of the failure of the earlier Addis Ababa agreement to establish a specifically southern force, had insisted that the SPLA would become the army of the GoSS. In consequence the largest item in the GoSS budget was security expenditure, a situation made more critical by the delays in settling the Abyei boundary dispute and the whole north–south border as well as a worsening series of security incidents in the south itself.[7] All the expenditure on the militaries meant that little was available for social development and indeed the budget for defence overall was six times the allocations for health and education combined. That in turn meant that little was provided by way of a 'peace dividend' for people at large especially in the more remote rural areas, contributing to a heightening of scepticism with regard to the CPA as a whole rather than 'making unity attractive' which was stated to be one of the intentions of the agreement.

It was hoped that much of the funding for social development would come from donor support for the CPA. Following its signing in 2005, a donors' conference took place in Oslo by the Sudan Consortium, which was followed by substantial UN pledges. At the same time two multi-donor trust funds were established, one for the country as a whole and the other specifically for the south. The Consortium met again in Oslo in 2008 to review progress and recommit, with pledges of $4.9 billion for socio-economic development and a further $2.2 billion from the UN for humanitarian relief mainly in Darfur and the south. However both the GNU and the GoSS were to voice criticisms over the actual delivery of the monies pledged, and also the failure in practice to deliver the intended outcomes of a variety of 'quick impact programmes'. In total, the financial assistance and the efforts of the international community had little impact on socio-economic development in Sudan.

In part this was due to problems of governmental capacity. In the south, the GoSS had difficulties with recruiting and training staff, in short with creating a state from the wreckage of war; while in the north government was weakest in the poorest areas that were most in need of development. It was also clear that while donors prioritized socio-economic development, for the two parties to the CPA security was the top priority, especially security vis-à-vis each other, whether as deterrence or in the event of a renewal of conflict as many feared. To head off the latter, the parties agreed in the CPA to ask the UN for the deployment of a 10,000 strong peacekeeping force, the UN Mission in Sudan (UNMIS). However, committed to impartiality in its peace-keeping mandate, UNMIS has been unable to prevent incidents such as the major clash of the two armies in the disputed border area of Abyei in 2008.

While Sudan's engagement with the international economy and community were central to the economic aspects of the CPA, for large numbers of people land issues were at least as important. Indeed the eruption of the long festering Darfur crisis in 2003 had much to do with land issues in that region, compounded by national political claims by the main Darfur rebel movements and international involvement by Darfur's neighbours, Chad, the Central African Republic, and Libya (Flint and de Waal 2005). It was a crisis that rapidly gave rise to some two million Internally Displaced People (IDPs). The growth of commercialized agriculture had also had an impact on local economies. Conflicts over land are likely to grow as the NCP has hopes for major land deals involving investors from the Gulf region and East Asia with long term concerns about food security, who once more see Sudan as a potential 'bread basket' (*The Economist* 2009b). In addition the war in the south had also contributed to IDPs and refugees, and in some cases the lands that had been left were to lead to disputes after the coming of peace and with the hopes of many that they would now be in a position to return home. Issues of local land use were also contributing to rising tension in border areas. Abyei attracted the greatest attention but the whole north–south border demarcation holds land use implications. In the face of all these challenges the CPA's land commissions were slow to be established and have had a very limited impact thus far.

Related to agriculture has been the issue of water resources. Before oil emerged as central to the revenues of both the GNU and the GoSS, water had been crucial to the country's agriculturally based economy, and in spite of oil it was widely recognized that agriculture had to remain a top priority. This immediately raised questions once more about the Nile waters which have been central to Sudan's largest schemes; and it is notable that some of the country's major investments of recent years have been in dams in the north. At the same time environmental change has also been important for plans to develop the rain-watered commercial farms across the central belt. In the south there are concerns such as those raised in the late 1970s and early 1980s with regard to the Jonglei Canal, which was itself an early and successful target for the SPLA. The CPA itself did not address issues of water, but below the surface they are recognized by all.

The decision of the south in January 2011 to vote overwhelmingly for independence in the following July brought further concerns about the future development of the economy in both the new countries. In the south concern focused on the overwhelming dependence of the GoSS on oil revenues and the absence of almost any indigenous tax base. At the same time most of the revenues have been spent on salaries and wages and recurrent services such as oil supplies: little has gone on pro-poor spending such as education and health services that have relied heavily on international NGOs which may not be willing or able to continue to operate indefinitely. At the same time the growing numbers of young unemployed in urban areas in particular put pressure on the GoSS to create jobs of its own at a time when prices are rising especially in areas such as housing and cattle trading.

It is expected that oil income for the GoSS will rise since as an independent state it will no longer share revenues with the north, but receive all income from all oil exported from the south and pay rent to the north on its use of the pipelines to the Red Sea. With rent expected to be about 20 per cent of total oil revenue that should swell the coffers of the GoSS, and it is hoped that that will enable the government to spend more on development projects to diversify the economy away from the current reliance on oil. However there are also concerns about the numerous governance problems in the GoSS that will make its management of economic diversification challenging.

The corollary of the south's increase in oil revenues is the sharp reduction in the income of the government in the north, for whom oil revenues at the present constitute over 60 per cent of its income. There are expectations voiced in the government itself of a new era of austerity, which will compound the growing criticism in many quarters of the policy choices in the past that contributed so much to the splitting of the country. All agree that the economy will have a hard time, in the short term at least, and many believe that political repercussions are likely to follow. For the future the government is pinning its hopes on new mineral finds in the north, including gold as well as oil, and attracting Middle Eastern and Asian investors into the agricultural sector.

Conclusion

The intention of the CPA was to restructure Sudan starting with the political system. The national system was to hinge on relations between the NCP and the SPLM in government, but here it was largely a failure. The national presidency in particular failed to become the institution it was intended to be. Possibly it might have worked if John Garang had lived, but his successor Salva Kiir always gave priority to his role as head of the GoSS. This effective separation of the GoSS and the GNU was underlined by the withdrawal of the SPLM candidate shortly before the national presidential election of 2010, allowing Beshir a comfortable victory. As for the parliaments of the national government and the GoSS, they were appointed after the signing of the CPA on the basis of NCP dominance in the former and SPLM dominance in the latter and never seriously challenged executive control in either.

The GoSS effectively became a parallel government for the south, rather than a semi-autonomous regional government. This was underlined by the adoption of the SPLA as the army of the south; as well as developing its own international representation and foreign policy. It was very much an embryonic state with many shortages and teething problems but nevertheless it was becoming more 'state-like', and with it encouraged expectations that it would seek separation in the 2011 referendum while blaming the north for having failed 'to make unity attractive'. The 2011 referendum outcome was the predictable culmination of this policy.

In theory the CPA had offered the prospect of not just the political restructuring of Sudan but also starting to address the inequalities of the political economy that had evolved over some 150 years, and which had contributed significantly to the conflicts the agreement was seeking to halt. The formal record showed some progress with the eventual functioning of the NPC, the establishment of the land commissions, and the donor support. But none of it had gone smoothly (perhaps inevitably) and far from augmenting the NCP–SPLM relations that had grown with the CPA, relations between them had on the whole deteriorated though punctuated by occasional 'summits' to address immediate problems and above all to prevent complete breakdown. Speaking publicly in Sudan in 2008, the former Foreign Minister and SPLM adviser to the presidency, Mansour Khalid, put forward three broad possible outcomes. The first was that the CPA process would continue to run and the country would then remain united under a now oft-repeated formula of 'one country, two systems': effectively moving towards a confederation. On the economic front there would continue to be links around oil, agricultural development in border areas in particular, and water which is an international issue for the Nile basin as a whole. For that to happen, the southern voters in 2011 would have to be convinced that unity was indeed an attractive option, including the implementation of the financial and economic aspects of the CPA discussed above.

The second hope was that in the event of the southerners voting for secession there would be an amicable divorce settlement followed by a soft landing. Economically it would involve new negotiations on oil in particular as part of a process of disconnection. Agreement on oil revenues after separation has proved difficult, and partly as a result there has been talk of a new oil pipeline to Mombasa on the Kenyan coast. In 2010 there was talk of a potential project, perhaps linked to development of the new Ugandan field at Lake Albert, but it will take time, money, and security if it is to be accomplished. There are also signs of the south developing its own business community with economic ties to East Africa and even South Africa.[8] Oil from southern Sudan has been exported to Ethiopia, Kenya, and Eritrea and many businessmen from Kenya and Uganda have pursued opportunities in the south.

The third scenario is that the south separates in an increasingly antagonistic atmosphere which is followed by a hard landing. There have already been clashes in border areas, most notably Abyei, while the negotiation of the border itself remains incomplete and acrimonious. There are fears that this could presage a re-opening of conflict after separation and that the region might see a repetition of the still unresolved Eritrean–Ethiopian conflict. Some in the NCP appear to have been thinking in that direction and seeking to secure sufficient access to oilfields to continue to develop the 'golden triangle' at the centre of the country. The most widely discussed view has been that expressed in a leaked paper in 2005 by the former Minister of Economics and Finance, Abdul Rahman Hamdi (2005). In it he envisaged focusing Sudan's required foreign investment on a central area of the country, which is comparatively homogeneous and predominantly regards itself as Arab and Muslim. Economic growth in this region, especially in commercial agriculture, could develop that would allow for improved services for the local communities. He was explicit in seeing this as political-economy move, since it would be a way to dominate the 2010 elections there, thus furthering the NCP's Islamist agenda. The election outcome, though characterized by a flawed electoral process, followed his prediction. Hamdi's paper was widely criticized for its disregard for the 'marginalized' areas and apparent unconcern at best at the possibility of southern separation. It could be a recipe for continued impoverishment and 'marginalization' of Darfur and the eastern Sudan contributing to further conflicts in the future, as well as a separated South Sudan beginning life as an independent state in most unpropitious circumstances (Young 2007). Leaving aside John Garang's aspirations for a 'New Sudan' it is clear that the secession of South Sudan means a new African country facing the challenges of nation building, economic development, and the consolidation of state institutions. In North Sudan the situation is different: the main challenge is to keep 'northern regions' together under the control of Khartoum. But this is faced by mounting resistance from the Darfur region, the Nuba Mountains, and the Blue Nile, as well as simmering tensions in eastern Sudan. The implications in terms of statebuilding for North Sudan are enormous given the loss of oil revenue, escalating violent conflicts in 'marginalized' regions, and stalled democratic reforms. Whatever happens, the experience of Sudan stands out as a new paradigmatic case for managing complex statebuilding in post-conflict transitions, sending signals and lessons that go beyond Sub-Saharan Africa.

Notes

1 The period is generally known in Sudan as the Turkiyya, standing for Turkish-Egyptian rule since legally, but scarcely in practice, Egypt still remained a part of the Ottoman Empire.

2 Though known officially as the Anglo-Egyptian Condominium, following 're-conquest' in 1898, Britain's control of Egypt, taken by force in 1882, was being extended into Sudan where Britain remained dominant until independence in 1956.

3 Many Nigerians had started out as pilgrims making their way east for pilgrimage in Mecca, and ending up in Sudan.

4 A classic situation developed in Darfur. The Mahdi family had a strong following there and recruited cheap labour for private cotton growing on the White Nile and parachuted in Umma Party (Mahdist-backed) candidates for parliamentary elections.

5 In north-east Africa, 1969 saw not only Nimeiri seize power with radical ideas, but also Qaddafi in Libya, and Siad Barre in Somalia.

6 The major survival from this period is the giant Kenana sugar scheme on the White Nile. It illustrates the relationship between the Sudan government, Western companies, and Arab capital (Cronje *et al.* 1976).

7 There was also a joint force established, the Joint Integrated Units (JIU), but commitment from the two parties was low and progress slow with tensions within those units that were formed.

8 A number of SPLM leaders had had houses and business connections in Kenya and Uganda for years. In 2009 Miller established a brewery in Juba, capital of the south. It is the first brewery in the country since Nimeiri introduced Islamic law in 1983.

18 The political economy of statebuilding in Haiti

Informal resistance to security-first statebuilding

Robert Muggah

Haiti's transition from autocratic to democratic governance from the late twentieth to the early twenty-first century has been marred by chronic violence. The country's public institutions – especially those concerned with the provision of justice and security services – lurched alternately between collapse and crisis (Collier 2011; Muggah 2008). And to the distress of the international donor community, the cumulative efforts of no less than six United Nations peace support missions over the past three decades have yielded few returns.[1] Notwithstanding repeated attempts by foreigners to foment a social contract and reciprocal rights and obligations between the country's elite and its poorer masses, Haitian politics continues to be governed by a zero-sum mentality. Over two decades of externally led statebuilding and tens of billions of dollars later, Haitians are as divided, excluded, and impoverished as they have ever been.

Central to donors' recent efforts in Haiti has been the reconstitution of the authority and capacity of the security and justice sectors. In what can be described as *security-first statebuilding*, United Nations and bilateral donor efforts concentrated on technical service lines – strengthening and modernizing judicial and court systems and personnel, recruiting and training police, rebuilding the penal system, and buttressing border controls and customs between 1990 and 2004. More recently, efforts have focused on neutralizing spoilers and securing urban slums through so-called stability operations. These latter efforts combine aggressive enforcement-led activities targeting gang-influenced areas (known as *bazes*) with development activities and campaigns intended to restore law and order.

A closer inspection of these various generations of security-first statebuilding efforts in Haiti reveals some insights into the causes of continued insecurity. There is little doubt that Haiti's justice and security sectors suffer from acute weaknesses and corruption. Moreover, it is undeniable that certain gangs in urban centres – including the capital Port-au-Prince, but also Gonaives, Cap Haitenne, and Jacmel – have played an important role in shaping the onset, duration, severity, and termination of collective violence. Indeed, gangs and so-called popular organizations (*organisations populaire*) have long been cast as the central villains in undermining political settlements and disrupting the restoration of state functions. And yet, security-first statebuilding embodies a set of potentially short-sighted assumptions amongst foreigners and local elites, including the now widely held position that security is *the* fundamental precondition of meaningful progress on all other fronts. In their rush to address the symptoms of disorder and decay in the security services and the slums, outsiders have unintentionally neglected many of the historic, political, and economic factors that conditioned fragility in Haiti to begin with.

This chapter considers the evolution and outcomes of security-first statebuilding in Haiti. It begins first with a cursory summary of its antecedents, and then examines the range of top-down law and order efforts to contain insecurity during the 1990s and early 2000s, and the more multifaceted stabilization efforts since 2007. The chapter then revisits the characteristics of the 'referent' of these efforts, the so-called gangs, and the violence attributed to them, and examines their resilience and resistance to these efforts through the lens of one prominent neighbourhood of Port-au-Prince, Bel Air. It finds that the limits of security-first statebuilding are perhaps more stark than widely acknowledged, and that a historical and socio-spatial factors loom large.

The antecedents of security-first stabilization

Haiti has been characterized by outsiders as a fragile, failing, or failed state since at least the 1980s, if not well before (Maguire 2009a; Muggah 2008, 2010a; Perito 2009). The country has experienced considerable political, economic, and social volatility over the past two centuries, with more than 30 coups since independence in 1804, and a half dozen United Nations missions since 1991. While geopolitical interference from countries such as the United States, France, and Canada in Haiti has played a significant role in fuelling instability, particularly since the 1990s, certain analysts point to the country's extreme concentration of authority and wealth in the hands of the elite – elected and otherwise – and the progressive neglect of the country's majority rural populations as a source of persistent instability (Maguire 2011, 2009a, 2009b).

For much of Haiti's elite and certain foreign governments, the brutal dictatorships and associated paramilitary rule of Francois 'Papa Doc' Duvalier and his son, Jean-Claude 'Baby Doc' Duvalier from the 1950s to the 1980s afforded a degree of stability even as it denied and suppressed the rights of the majority. Most Haitians, especially those eking out an existence in the country's shantytowns in and around Port-au-Prince and other major cities, were terrorized into submission by the Duvalier dictatorships. The Duvaliers, both father and son, achieved this both through the arming of the so-called *Tontons Macoutes* militia, and by empowering Haiti's armed forces to use indiscriminate killings, torture, and arbitrary detention to enforce their power (Dubois 2012).

Following a popular uprising against Jean-Claude Duvalier in 1986 and his subsequent exile, Haiti experienced a rocky transition to democracy. In the wake of several military coups, and aborted and fraudulent elections, the fire-brand preacher, Jean-Bertrand Aristide, became the country's first democratically elected president after a general election in December 1990, raising expectations of a new epoch of security and progress. The promotion of political participation of the impoverished majority of citizens – a first in the country's history, which won him supporters and critics both at home and abroad – contributed to another coup against Aristide by the country's elites in September 1991, forcing him to flee temporarily to the United States.

Under the threat of a United Nations-authorised and United States-led military intervention, Aristide was able to return and resume office in 1994, as had been agreed in the 1993 Governors' Island Agreement between all Haitian political parties. The first of what would be a long line of United Nations peacekeeping missions was deployed, the UN Mission to Haiti (UNMIH), to support the implementation of the Governors' Island Agreement, assist with the reform and modernization of armed forces, and the establishment of a civilian police force. Many donor governments were confident that with the organization of free and fair elections, Haiti's transition to a more stable order would allow development to ensue (Muggah and Krause 2006).

By far the most far-reaching and controversial reforms advanced by Aristide on his return was the demobilization of the Haitian armed forces by presidential decree in 1994 and the creation of the country's first civilian national police force, the Haitian National Police (HNP) (Dupuy 2005). Haitians (and outsiders) expected that the HNP would effectively control crime and increase safety, especially in the larger cities. During the 1990s, property crime and violence were widespread, in sharp contrast to Haiti's historically low crime rates. Business owners and the wealthy tended to rely on privately hired armed guards – many of whom were frequently implicated in vigilante-style violence – to provide basic security. Notwithstanding considerable investments in capacity development and training of the nascent force (successive United Nations missions supported the strengthening of the police's capacity until 2000 and again from 2004 to the present), the HNP appeared to struggle to contain community-level criminal violence in the first years of its existence (Hayes and Wheatley 1996), particularly as violence became increasingly decentralized.

From first to second generation security-first statebuilding

International donors were increasingly concerned by the apparent expansion of more organized localized 'gang' violence and the implications of contagion terms of both increased migration flows and regional security. A number of international organizations – from the UN to the Organization of American States (OAS) and the International Organization of La Francophonie – signalled a new willingness to strengthen Haiti's security and judicial system from the mid-1990s onwards (Pierre and Fortin 2011). Support ranged from financial assistance and direct budget support to the provision of technical experts in policing, investigation, customs, and corrections reform, and was firmly focused on reforming and strengthening formal state institutions. Donor-supported efforts to promote judicial reform since the mid-1990s focused primarily on the restructuring and revision of judicial procedures, legal codes, and protocols.

One of the stated reasons for the emphasis on reforming the Haitian police force was its apparently low legitimacy amongst ordinary Haitians and concerns of rampant corruption and abuses. During the military dictatorship (1991–94), for example, military police officers had been frequently implicated in the illegal arrest and torture of ordinary citizens (O'Neill 1995). Nevertheless, efforts to clarify, codify, and implement improved criminal and corrections legislation and strengthen police presence during the 1990s yielded few lasting returns. Adding to these challenges, growing instability tested the HNP's ability to fight criminal violence and respond to organized political armed violence committed by groups hostile to Aristide and his transformative policy agendas during the late 1990s. Trafficking in persons, weapons, and drugs, reportedly connected to Haiti's business elite, appeared to be increasing. As tensions mounted between Aristide and certain members of the international donor community, such as the United States and France, former members of the disbanded Haitian armed forces created the so-called 'rebel army', also known as the National Revolutionary Front for the Liberation of Haiti (Muggah 2005). In point of fact, this 'army' was composed of paramilitary thugs active during the 1991–94 military coup years (and before) and had recruited politically motivated gang members into their ranks.

With alleged backing from the United States and support from the national elite, as well as supporters in key positions within the HNP itself, the rebel army proved to be a surprisingly formidable opponent. Heavily armed and with firm supply networks through neighbouring Dominican Republic, the force began launching quiet but effective attacks against border towns and urban centres between 2000 and 2004, with the goal of overthrowing the elected Haitian government. HNP officers struggled to contain escalating violence.[2] By 2004, following successful rebel army attacks in the towns of St. Marc and Gonaïves, the HNP was overcome and scattered. The insurgent army rapidly advanced on the capital. With Aristide swiftly removed from power and with United States marines occupying the National Palace, the insurgents were free to take the capital. One of the insurgents' first actions after entering Port-au-Prince was to march two blocks past the National Palace to the National Penitentiary, where they freed hundreds of convicts (Prengaman 2005).

Despite the controversial circumstances surrounding the rapid establishment of the interim government, the international community stepped in again with the stated goal of restoring law and order and reshaping the fragile security sector. The HNP was purged of 60 per cent of its officers, many of whom fled to other areas of the country or to the Dominican Republic, fearing that remnants of the rebel army might exact revenge. Some 540 members of the rebel army, many of whom had been soldiers in Haiti's demobilized armed forces, were integrated into the 'new' HNP. Few of them, if any, were required to undergo the formal training and graduation from the police academy required of new recruits (Hallward 2008: 128; ICG 2005; Mendelson-Forman 2006).[3]

At the request of the new interim government, the United Nations Security Council established the United Nations Stabilization Mission in Haiti (MINUSTAH) in June 2004.[4] Led by Brazil, Canada, the European Union, and the United States, and involving more than 40 countries, the large-scale deployment of international peacekeepers and police support were focused squarely on stabilizing the country to facilitate a transfer to an elected government. In many respects, the mission was analogous to previous efforts launched by the UN in the mid-1990s (Muggah and Krause 2006). With nearly 9,000 blue helmets and 3,000 international police deployed, the mission had a declared focus on ensuring stability by enhancing HNP capacities, extending the rule of law through improved delivery of justice services, and rebuilding the country's dilapidated judicial system (Muggah 2010a: 451–2). Though upholding an interim government widely viewed by Haitians as illegitimate and repressive, MINUSTAH was nevertheless able to maintain its presence even after the transition to a democratically elected president was made in late 2006.

A departure from previous interventions, however, was the concerted emphasis of international action on stabilizing Port-au-Prince's more restive neighbourhoods – an issue that has remained a priority almost eight years into the mission (Muggah 2010a). The early stirrings of these efforts can be traced to aggressive MINUSTAH peacekeeping interventions between 2004 and 2006 in key urban slums, notably Cité Soleil and Bel Air (Hutson and Kolbe 2006; Hallward 2008). While the early coercive efforts were exceedingly controversial, they are credited with helping reduce acute levels of violence affecting these areas. With a wide range of development activities intensifying from 2007 onwards, bilateral donors such as the United States, Canada, and others sought to reinforce stabilization (and reconstruction) in supposedly at-risk areas of the country. They launched unilateral interventions (in the case of the United States), or supported United Nations and non-governmental-led activities (in the case of Canada). These interventions were expected to enhance the capacity of the Haitian state – especially its law enforcement and justice institutions – and to restore its monopoly over the legitimate use of force.[5]

In the past decade a host of stabilization activities have taken place in Haiti, and the notorious slums of Cité Soleil, Bel Air, and Martissant more specifically. Generally, these efforts were advanced by MINUSTAH peacekeepers with a view to restoring legitimate security and creating the space for wider development activities to proceed. While there were subtle differences in how stabilization is expressed – particularly between the UN, the US, and the 'others' – they all advocated a counter-insurgency strategies to win hearts and minds (Muggah 2010a). Early efforts from 2004–06 were widely criticized by Haitians, urged on as they were by the Haitian police and entailing 'disarm or die' activities that resulted in the accidental shooting and death of dozens of citizens, including children.[6] Some critics claim that muscular coercive operations may have unintentionally dispersed and radicalized the *bazes*, and contributed to new and more insidious forms of violence. Efforts to promote stabilization that recognized the complex local political dynamics in these urban areas, and that engaged in dialogue with the *bazes*, appear to have been marginally more effective (Muggah 2010a). A project by the Brazilian organization Viva Rio in Bel Air, for example, recognized the *bazes* as complex entities with multiple and overlapping local nodes of authority, rather than as simply monolithic criminal elements to be suppressed. It explicitly brought them into a process of negotiation, dialogue, and ultimately auto-regulation through localized peace agreements.[7] Likewise, this project consciously engaged United Nations peacekeepers and the HNP in the process, complementing their activities with training in community relations and outreach, and encouraging a 'softer' problem-solving approach (Moestue and Muggah 2009).

Against a backdrop of MINUSTAH-led security operations, United Nations civilian agencies were busy crafting a reform plan for the HNP with local counterparts in 2006 (United Nations 2006d). In view of the frequency of natural disasters and the legacy of political unrest in Haiti, donors again placed an emphasis on improving HNP capacity to counter floods, fires, and hurricanes throughout the country. In the wake of stability operations and with more forceful engagement from the United Nations Special Envoy, Bill Clinton, by 2009 there was growing confidence among international actors in the potential of the HNP to provide security. And although the United Nations Security Council acknowledged key gaps and challenges, it also cited real improvements.[8]

The impact of the massive January 2010 earthquake on the human and physical infrastructure of the security and justice sectors – and particularly the HNP and the still fragile judicial institutions – was extensive. Hundreds of HNP personnel were killed and injured directly by the earthquake with thousands forced to turn to the care of their families and associated social networks. By United Nations estimates, almost one-quarter of Haiti's police capacity was rendered non-operational. MINUSTAH records show that over 50 buildings used by the HNP were affected, including some 28 facilities suffering 'major damages' such as collapse, and another 27 experiencing 'minor damages'. If these structures are added to the 39 facilities that were already non-operational at the time of the earthquake, almost 40 per cent of HNP capacities could not be used at this stage (Government of Haiti 2010).

In the immediate aftermath of the earthquake, the focus of the United Nations and international donor community was on rapidly ensuring the delivery of life-saving relief, supplies, personnel, and equipment and restoring police communication, coordination, and response capabilities, in particular in anticipation of increased gang violence. International observers were concerned that damage and displacement generated by the earthquake – coupled with the impact of the global fiscal crisis on food prices – could generate a humanitarian disaster and an upswing of crimes against property and violence. In the first six months after the natural disaster, fears that escapees from prisons would perpetrate targeted attacks, extortion, and kidnappings were commonplace among NGOs and international organizations working in Haiti (Muggah 2010a). International aid providers were worried that, if such violence were to occur, it would hamper relief efforts in Haiti and exacerbate instability if such assistance did not successfully reach affected populations. In certain cases, United States officials turned away flights delivering supplies and medical personnel so that planes with US combat troops could land instead.

Throughout this period, MINUSTAH military and police personnel supported domestic efforts alongside United States and Canadian troops. Fears of food riots, fleeing prisoners, and growing disorder were matched with massive investments in restoring public security. The so-called 'security umbrella' generated by this international presence is credited with enhancing humanitarian aid distribution, search and rescue operations, and the gradual return of national police to challenging areas. Meanwhile, a growing number of large, foreign private security companies began to explore opportunities in the country. At the same time, a critical chorus began questioning the ways in which aid had become securitized and worried that it was setting precedents that might undermine longer-term reconstruction.[9]

The limits of security-first statebuilding

The uneven outcomes of security-first statebuilding in Haiti in general and its capital city in particular is partly rooted in the extreme heterogeneity of settings, as well as the historical, political, social, and economic factors shaping urban settlement patterns in Port-au-Prince itself. The capital, not unlike the country as a whole, is marked by both physical and social zones of inclusion and exclusion. Areas that feature populations from lower socio-economic groups – and that are connected with active political and armed groups – are often referred to as 'popular areas'. They are characterized by socio-spatial concentrations of extreme poverty, anarchic urban design, and high levels of intra-communal violence. They have also been been marked for decades by a lack of state services: for their residents, the state for all practical purposes has ceased to exist as a provider of services. Indeed, during the Duvalier years and after, the state while affording a degree of stability, was regarded as predatory. This social distance is in marked contrast to the wealthier areas of Port-au-Prince that displayed – at least prior to the 2010 earthquake and in its aftermath – the exact opposite cluster of characteristics.

Security-first statebuilding efforts in the slums have often been informed by the assumption that the popular areas are effectively 'ungoverned' or 'under-governed spaces'. The policies elicited by these expectations, with their focus on the coercive provision of security, the rule of law, and socio-economic development, have often been inadequately tailored to the realities on the ground. In fact, these popular areas are anything but ungoverned, or devoid of security and order. As is often the case in many poorer informal settlements across the Caribbean and Latin America, security and attendant services in Haiti's slums are simply not provided by institutions of the state.[10]

Whilst the state does not, and has never, provided routine or predictable services to these populations, citizens residing in these areas nevertheless comprise a vast 'political' constituency that responds to national political developments, and takes part in (and at times shapes) wider political dynamics. Most Haitians are acutely aware of the ways in which their rights have been surrendered – particularly those who feel the absence of the police, or disenfranchised youth who have dropped out of school. Persistent economic exclusion and discrimination are widely recognized as a kind of structural violence, and feed a sense of frustration and distress.[11] Crucially, many youth have formed the basis of a critical reservoir of manpower for political propagandists. When manipulated by populist discourses that intensify a binary sense of the 'haves' and 'have nots', the youth of Port-au-Prince have regularly been stirred into a frenzy of outrage and collective violence against the statebuilding efforts of the state elites and the donors supporting them. Such youth, in Haiti as elsewhere, justify violence as a legitimate reaction to redress injustices fuelled by the 'upper classes'.

Resisting statebuilding from below – the case of Bel Air

It is possible to assess some of the complex dynamics of the resistance to statebuilding through an examination of a single neighbourhood, Bel Air. While today one of the Caribbean's (if not the world's) poorest cities, Port-au-Prince is also one of its oldest colonial settlements. And within Port-au-Prince, Bel Air was one of the capital's first official communes, originally established to house and serve the local bourgeoisie. Until the early twentieth century, Bel Air was an influential residential, commercial, and cultural centre, containing the country's most important educational facilities (Lycée Petion), libraries, and artisanal institutions, and located close to the country's principal political and religious institutions.

From the mid-twentieth century onwards, however, Bel Air experienced a period of progressive urban degradation and fragmentation. With the arrival of the Duvaliers and the militarization of the country's political space – including the formation of the *Tonton Macoute* – the neighbourhood underwent a process of demographic and spatial transformation. Led by local intellectuals, artists, and professionals, Bel Air became a wellspring of political resistance to the rise of authoritarianism. As a result, many of its long-term inhabitants were branded enemies of the state, targeted by the Duvaliers, and forced into exile, thrown into prison, or worse. Throughout the 1960s, 1970s, and 1980s, rural migrants were encouraged and in some cases assisted to move into the area in an effort to dilute the potency of the political opposition.

Rural migration into the area continued after the departure of Jean Claude Duvalier and the meteoric rise of President Aristide. The social and economic consequences of rapid in-migration and the neighbourhood's 'de-gentrification' were dramatic. The influx of predominantly rural smallholder farmers and the exodus of wealthier residents reversed the demographic profile of the neighbourhood, and fuelled the building of squatter settlements and new forms of social disorganization. As long-time resident entrepreneurs and private sector actors moved elsewhere, their places in the famous 'iron market' and surrounding area were replaced by informal traders. The creation of sprawling alleys, informal corridors, and intricate private compound spaces offered an environment that suited informal and, is so often the case, criminal activities. Bel Air began to be progressively stigmatized during the closing decades of the twentieth century.

These demographic shifts generated important political repercussions for the wider statebuilding enterprise. They created a social group for whom Jean Betrand Aristide would later agitate under the pro-poor banner. Politically, with the growth of liberation theology and Marxist movements in Port-au-Prince – coalescing into Aristide's Lavalas ('flood') Party in the late 1980s – 'popular organizations' composed of recently migrated youth were in turn radicalized. In the process, Bel Air became a Lavalas stronghold with a sprawling network of community leaders exhibiting strong and enduring relationships to both President Aristide and later president and Aristide associate Rene Preval, a future president (2006–11). Indeed, with President Aristide formerly preaching from the neighbourhood, Bel Air was at the epicentre of repeated outbreaks of intense collective violence in the late 1990s, and after 2004.

External actors have frequently associated such violence in Bel Air and other popular areas after 2004 with 'gangs'. Gangs are themselves implicitly held to encompass a vast number of disparate groups ranging from politicized militia to petty criminals. It is precisely this preoccupation with gangs that has motivated security-first statebuilding efforts – themselves often intent on identifying and neutralizing both the leadership and their rank and file. Considerably less time and effort has been devoted by the United Nations and other security actors to understanding the dynamics of gang formation or, indeed, their shape and character, their dynamic areas of operation, the underlying historical and political factors shaping their resistance to external statebuilding actors, or their role in the wider organization and dynamics of politics and power in Haiti.

Yet in order to understand the dynamics of resistance to security-first statebuilding, it is critical to recognize the forms of violence and roles of armed actors operating within areas like Bel Air. Indeed, since at least 2004 a host of little-known informal actors managed to repulse both United Nations and United States troops on the one hand, and interim government and outside militants on the other. Described alternately as gangs, *mouvman rezistans* (resistance movement), *chiméres*, paramilitaries, and terrorists, these actors presented a major challenge to international and domestic efforts to stabilize so-called ungoverned spaces. From the beginning, outsiders struggled to understand who these actors were – alternately merging them as one, or singling out individuals for neutralization. A narrative ensued that separated the 'bad guys' from the 'good guys' without acknowledging that such individuals were frequently one and the same. The following excerpt from a MINUSTAH report is indicative of the narrow understandings of the 'gang' leader:

> The voodoo priest in Bel-Air, Manasse is described as very skinny, long dread locks, walks with a cane, always wearing glasses and smoking a cigar. Nothing takes place in Bel Air without Manasse's approval. Mannasse is in a band called 'ranran' which is based out of the gang base Cameroon. Manasse drives a white oldsmobile with a red grill cover. Dred Carlos is a gang member in Bel Air with Manasse. Carlo is described as being 70 inches tall, muscular build, and shoulder length dred locks: Carlo rides a green and white Yamaha motorcycle.[12]

It is useful to unpack the informal institutions and actors that alternately provided 'security' or contributed to 'insecurity' in the popular informal settlements. The *bazes*, especially in Bel Air, have their roots in the Lavalas movement, and complemented more spontaneous *comité de vigilance* or neighbourhood watch groups that also served intermittently as pockets of tacit resistance to military dictatorships in the 1970s, 1980s, and 1990s. During the early 1990s, membership in Lavelas armed groups came to constitute a symbol of one's resistance to the military junta and a source of considerable pride and solidarity. After Aristide was reinstated as president in 1994, he quickly consolidated these groups and their affiliates into 'popular organizations'. While most were not violent, some harboured armed members, and worked together with 'ra ra' musical groups and were almost certainly connected to criminal elements. Many of these actors came to form the institutional base of the Lavelas party itself, and, as such, a threat to the very integrity of the state and its elite supporters that opposed Aristide.

In Bel Air, the *bazes* retained a politically literate leadership structure from the Lavalas period, and comparatively coherent armed group structures, using violence mostly to reproduce ostensibly 'political' goals. This contrasted to groups in the equally notorious Cité Soleil or Martissant, where violence while also often politically motivated, adopted a more predatory and economic tenor. Depending on the temporal and spatial setting, the *bazes* have served as the area's political spokespersons and organizers, as predatory actors and neighbourhood toughs, and potential guns for hire for national and municipal politicians in the event mobilization was required. The *bazes* have therefore until today retained an important political role, both instrumentally but also more prosaically in keeping order in neighbourhoods where the state feared to tread.

Armed groups did not emerge spontaneously from the slum, though social and economic disparities and conditions certainly play a role in the susceptibility of youth to recruitment and membership. Instead, political actors and patrons have mobilized armed groups under the guise of popular organizations, explicitly to control specific demographic constituencies and in some cases to forcefully 'get out the vote'. Moreover, during the 1990s, but especially between 2000 and 2004, the state bolstered the status and spatial dominance of armed groups by allowing them dominance in key popular areas. What is more, specific armed groups began to exert diverse forms of control and social orderings in the areas they controlled, in some cases extracting rents and protection money for their 'services'.

As a consequence, Bel Air exhibited a considerable level of resilience when it came to externally driven stabilization efforts. Numbering approximately 90,000 residents, it was the first popular neighbourhood to resist Aristide's (forced) exile to South Africa in 2004, with other communes soon following. Repeated efforts by the HNP to wrest control of the zone from popular organizations were frustrated by the 'baze armée', the armed wing of the *baze*. Public protests, often mobilized by the country's wildly popular ra ra bands, often emerged from Bel Air. Throughout 2004 and 2005, the neighbourhood was considered by many to be impregnable to outside control (Hallward 2008). Although a muscular peacekeeping contingent managed to secure a measure of territory in 2006 and began focused counter-insurgency and 'stabilization' activities soon after, the resilience of its security and service institutions have yet to be fully acknowledged.

The social and spatial morphology of popular areas and the armed groups that inhabit them are critical to understanding the subtle and occasionally violent resistance to statebuilding. On the one hand, these areas concentrate high numbers of chronically impoverished populations who are potentially susceptible to manipulation. A high proportion of disenfranchised youth, coupled with other proximate factors ranging from exposure to intergenerational patterns of violence, the sense of male emasculation brought about by socio-economic exclusion, and the apparent impunity of elites, have meant that these neighbourhoods were ripe for mobilization. It is also worth recalling that many of the popular areas are located close either to national political institutions such as the Presidential Palace (in the case of Bel Air) or important transport arteries (such as Carrefour Feuille and Cité Soleil). Given the weakness of formal security institutions, the ability to mobilize armed groups from Bel Air to protect the president, or groups from Carrefour Feuille and Cité Soleil to block transportation into and out of the city, has been an important source of power in Haitian politics since at least the 1990s.

Conclusion

Notwithstanding decades of investment in justice, police reform, and later stabilization activities targeting gangs, Haiti's security challenges have been particularly resistant to outside efforts to promote stability from above. Part of the reason for this has been a lack of understanding of how instability manifests itself from below, including in neighbourhoods of the country's capital city. The focus of international actors on building capacity and then

forcibly neutralizing gangs side-stepped more intractable issues of urbanization, political resistance, and the social morphology of informal networks
themselves. This approach echoes, in certain ways, the tactics of governments
to tackling security threats elsewhere wherein:

> visible and widely publicized crackdowns on gangs [are pursued] in
> order to avoid taking action on much more tricky issues related to exclu-
> sion, inequality and the lack of job creation. Put another way, it seems
> that gangs have become convenient scapegoats on which to blame [a
> country's] problems and through which those in power attempt to main-
> tain an unequal status quo. At the same time, however, they also simul-
> taneously embody the risks of violent social action that will inevitably
> erupt in the face of attempts to preserve an unjust society.[13]

Stability in popular areas such as Bel Air remains tenuous, even more so since
the catastrophic 2010 earthquake and the disputed election of President Mar-
telly in 2011. While some manifestations of urban violence have receded, a
wide assortment of armed groups remains intact and could be readily reacti-
vated. Moreover, because violence in Bel Air is principally mobilized for political (rather than economic) ends, it is intimately wedded to the ebb and flow
of national-level political dynamics. It is useful to recall that Bel Air never
turned into a criminal stronghold like Cité Soleil. This was partly because of
its deeply entrenched culture of political activism and the persistence of
informal popular organizations, a tradition stretching back decades. Leaders
of the armed *bazes* and of the various political groups have a keen awareness
of the need to maintain their control over community dynamics. Supporters
of security-first stabilization miss these nuances at their peril.

Indeed, rather than acting as predators, they just as often 'protected' their
neighbourhoods from external invasion who might have challenged their
authority. As such, *baze* and political leaders in Bel Air frequently chased out
outsiders, including those who might have intended to use Bel Air as a base
from which to undertake organized crime, including kidnapping. Moreover,
it is also important to recall that strong leaders from within specific *bazes* also
played a crucial role in preventing the regression of armed political mobilization into gang-land violence. Indeed, these actors came to form a leadership
role by promoting informal justice and security for a community only weakly
exposed to state penetration. It could be argued that the contemporary resilience of Bel Air to urban violence is part and parcel of an implicit strategy in
which the control of armed violence is an expression of territorial control by
specific vested interests.

In focusing on the specific trajectories of gang formation and local resistance, this chapter provides a reminder of the danger of ascribing single and
fixed identities and motives to local actors. In Bel Air, as elsewhere, identities
of armed groups are often fluid, with groups displaying complex alliances,
and serving overlapping functions. The idea that the *baze* is criminal neglects
the dynamic and polyarchic identities within them. Coercive and

enforcement-led activities are in danger of ignoring these multiple identities, and the local legitimacy these gangs might enjoy as a consequence of the other functions they exercise.

Notes

1 These include MICIVIH, UNMIH, UNSMIH, UNTMIH, MIPONUH, and since 2004, MINUSTAH.
2 Although UN Security Council Resolution 994 had lifted sanctions on Haiti, unilateral US-led restrictions against arms sales to the government since the early 1990s remained in force, effectively prohibiting the HNP from legally purchasing weapons. The HNP officers who remained committed to upholding the rule of law had little chance of surviving direct armed conflict with the rebel army who had been progressively armed with outside backing (Muggah 2005). In 2006, the United States 'eased', but did not lift, its arms embargo on Haiti. See BBC (2006).
3 By 2008, fewer than 100 of these former soldiers remained in the force, with most retiring, voluntarily moving on to other jobs, or being dismissed for various reasons.
4 SC Res. 1529 of 29 February 2004 and SC Res. 1542 of 30 April 2004.
5 What distinguished these stabilization interventions from earlier efforts to promote security were several characteristics: (i) clearly defined as short-term (two to three years) emphasizing security promotion and police presence (and not necessarily development); (ii) joined-up operations with military and police actors and development agencies to win hearts and minds; and (iii) municipal and neighbourhood-oriented schemes emphasizing 'inclusive' community 'decision-making'.
6 See *New York Times* (2005), Perito (2007), Kolbe and Hutson (2006).
7 Interview with Rubem Cesar Fernando, Director of VivaRio, 4 March 2009.
8 The UN Security Council's report on MINUSTAH, dated 1 September 2009, highlights that 'although the capacity of the National Police is gradually improving, it still lacks the force levels, training, equipment and managerial capacity necessary to respond effectively to these threats without external assistance' (UNSC 2009: para. 21).
9 See Muggah (2010b).
10 See Muggah (2012).
11 See Kolbe *et al.* (2010).
12 MINUSTAH Military Report, June 2004. On file with the author.
13 See Jutersonke *et al.* (2009: 20).

19 Georgia and the political economy of statebuilding

S. Neil MacFarlane

> I would compare their desire to assist us in that tumultuous state-democracy building process with an attempt to build a pyramid from the top … The local traditions, habits, legacies, perceptions/misperceptions were ignored … For them it was a 'project' but it should have been more about Georgia itself.[1]

This chapter examines ways in which external economic engagement has affected the effort to build a sustainable state in Georgia. The project of state-building should be assessed against the state's performance in the delivery of public goods – the enhancement of the security and welfare (quality of life) of citizens. To be able to perform adequately on these measures, a state needs at least three things. The first is robust and responsive public institutions that understand what it is they are supposed to be doing, are organized to deliver, and are populated by people who are competent and generally honest. The second is a stable flow of resources, which translates into effective mechanisms for the extraction of revenue and for ensuring that revenue is used to promote the public good. The third is an economic base from which necessary resources can be extracted.

It is plausible that states with non-democratic or hybrid political structures and processes could deliver respectably in terms of these metrics. China and Singapore come to mind. But democratic systems are likely to perform better, because they are more accountable to those paying for the provision of, and consuming, public goods, and because democratic systems are generally more transparent in their operations.

The notion of international economic engagement has a number of boundary problems. For example, support for political change (as in Georgia in 2003) may have significant consequences for economic policy after change has occurred. Capacity building is often intended to have economic effects, and often does. Humanitarian action (as, for example, with international efforts to address displacement) relieves governments of a share of this burden of post-conflict assistance, allowing local resources to be focused on recovery. Military assistance may also have indirect economic effects. These can be positive in the sense that external assistance may allow a recipient government to divert local resources to developmental purposes. They can also be negative, as the growth of military establishments may create longer term burdens for the recipient, who must eventually pay to maintain the larger sector.

The chapter begins with a section on the background to post-conflict state-building in Georgia. Here it is worth noting that Georgia's conflicts were never resolved, and the effort to build the state has been complicated by this lack of resolution. A description of the nature and dimensions of international engagement in the country's efforts to build a sustainable and effective state follows. It then turns to a discussion of the extent to which the project has succeeded, and concludes with an effort to explain the results.

The summary argument is as follows. Georgia benefited from comparatively impressive flows of economic assistance, particularly since the 'Rose Revolution' in 2003. This assistance was relatively successful in facilitating higher rates of growth and in the creation of a more effective state. There are, however, questions about the sustainability of this achievement. The record is less positive on measures of democratic transition, for example media freedom, fairness in elections, and judicial independence and impartiality. Uneven success is in part the result of the approaches taken by international actors in their programming in Georgia. It also reflects the continuing hostility of Georgia's near neighbour, Russia. Finally, it reflects certain deeply rooted patterns in Georgian society and in state–society relations.

The focus here is on international engagement in statebuilding. Little is said about the engagement of international actors to resolve durably the country's two protracted internal conflicts. This choice of emphasis reflects the modesty of international resources committed to the direct pursuit of peace compared to the investment in the building of the state, and the evident ineffectiveness of international efforts concerning conflict resolution at micro- or macro-levels. In 2008, fifteen years of pursuit of a sustainable peace collapsed in renewal of the conflicts, the invasion of the country by Russia, the partial dismemberment of Georgia, and the further ethnic cleansing of the two separatist enclaves – Abkhazia and South Ossetia. Turning the issue around, however, the approach of international actors to building the Georgian state may have increased the probability of conflict recidivism. In this respect, international actors may share some of the responsibility for the unfortunate outcome in 2008.

It should be stressed that rigorous evaluation of the effect of international engagement would require knowing what would have occurred in its absence. That is not possible; assessment of impact is necessarily inferential.

Background

At independence, Georgia faced multiple local grievances and conflicts that attracted the protracted and often unconstructive intervention of Russia. Georgia re-emerged into independent statehood in 1991. One aspect of its move towards independence was the outbreak of a small conflict in South Ossetia in early 1990. This conflict ended in a ceasefire agreement mediated

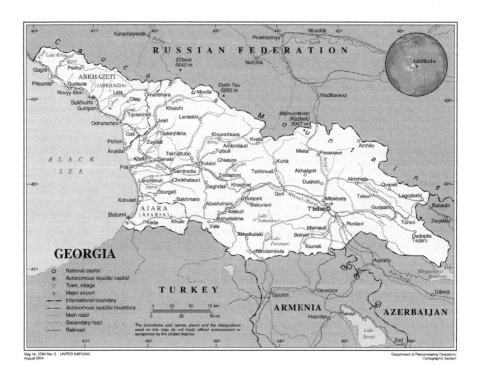

Map 19.1 Map of Georgia (source: United Nations).

by the Russian Federation in June 1992. The agreement left most of the region under secessionist administration, although Georgia retained control of a number of ethnically Georgian villages inside the enclave. Between 1992 and 2007, the ceasefire was monitored by a joint peacekeeping force and political matters were addressed in a joint control commission, the CSCE/OSCE having observer status.

Frustrations over the conduct of the Osset conflict and over the accelerating economic collapse provoked an insurrection in Tbilisi and the ouster of the elected president, Zviad Gamsakhurdia. In March of 1992, Eduard Shevardnadze returned to Georgia to take a leadership role. Gamsakhurdia and his supporters retreated into Mingrelia (western Georgia), where they revolted against the new government. Georgian efforts to suppress this revolt eventually drew the government into conflict with the regional authorities in Abkhazia, who were moving towards their own declaration of sovereignty.

In 1993, Abkhaz forces, assisted by volunteers from the North Caucasus and receiving Russian military assistance, took the offensive, ultimately driving the Georgians (civilian and military) out of the region.[2] Russia negotiated a ceasefire, which defined a security zone between Abkhaz and Georgian forces that peacekeepers were to police. Russia's peacekeeping deployment was recognized by the United Nations in 1994.[3] The UN strengthened its own observer force (UNOMIG) with a mandate to observe the Russians. Georgia settled into a situation in which two of its regions remained outside central government control, effectively protected by Russian or Russian dominated peacekeeping forces.

The story of statebuilding in Georgia is also complicated by the challenges of transition from being a dependent part of the Soviet state and command economy to independence. When the USSR unravelled, economic relations with Russia collapsed, and the Georgian economy evaporated.

Although Georgia stabilized its currency and returned to modest growth by 1995, as the years passed the Shevardnadze government performed increasingly poorly in implementing adopted reforms. In the judgement of the World Bank:

> By 2003, reform momentum sputtered to a halt, and Georgia was a near failed state. Political power was increasingly fragmented, corruption and crime were rampant, there were massive arrears in pension payments and teachers' salaries, and infrastructure was in a state of near collapse, with most of the country without power and the road network increasingly deteriorated.
>
> (World Bank 2009b: 1)

In short, in their efforts to contribute to the building of the Georgian state, international agencies were faced with a daunting agenda of post-communist political and economic transition, and addressing the consequences of multiple conflicts, while engaging with an increasingly dysfunctional state partner.

Economic stagnation, governmental ineffectiveness, and corruption produced the 'Rose Revolution' in November 2003, in which the Shevardnadze government was overthrown and replaced by a coalition led by Mikheil Saakashvili. Saakashvili rapidly consolidated his authority through presidential and parliamentary elections and through constitutional amendments to strengthen the presidency. He also reduced petty corruption significantly, and substantially improved revenue collection, while clearing pension and salary arrears. The rate of growth accelerated, hitting a peak of 12.3 per cent in 2007 (World Bank 2010).

President Saakashvili was committed to restoring control over all of Georgia's territory. Georgian efforts to push this agenda in South Ossetia in 2004–2005 began a dramatic worsening of Georgia's relations with Russia. This process culminated in Georgian attacks on South Ossetia in August 2008, Russia's invasion of Georgia, and Russia's detachment and recognition of South Ossetia and Abkhazia (MacFarlane 2010). Although Georgia received a very large package of post-war assistance in 2008–2010, the global economic crisis and a 25 per cent decline in remittances, coupled with shaken investor confidence and a year-on-year drop of 60 per cent in foreign direct investment in the first three quarters of 2009, produced a GDP contraction of 4 per cent in that year (Antidze 2010).

The role of international actors

The role of international actors in statebuilding after conflict in Georgia has comprised, among other things, rehabilitation, macroeconomic stabilization, reconstruction and infrastructural modernization, support for law and order, the effort to create viable Georgian military and border forces, capacity building in state institutions, efforts to support displaced persons, and efforts to promote conflict resolution and conflict prevention.

One should begin by noting the diversity of approaches to the problem of statebuilding by the various international actors. Some agencies focus quite narrowly on particular sectors (for example, the IMF in macroeconomic stabilization and currency support). Some (UNHCR) are primarily humanitarian. Some (i.e. the World Bank) primarily address economic development; others lean towards capacity building in public institutions (the EU's TACIS programme), going beyond the specifically economic to security, law, education, civil society promotion, environmental programming, and conflict resolution. Some agencies limit themselves to national programming; others (the EU) also conduct regional programming in the Caucasus as a whole and extending further into Central Asia. Some focus on the state sector (i.e. the IMF, the World Bank); some mix state sector with NGO support (i.e. USAID, the EU), some work primarily with the private sector (i.e. the EBRD).

Some donors do not explicitly relate assistance to broader international objectives, some do. In this latter context, for example, US defence assistance has been linked to the war on terror and to Georgia's participation in the wars in Iraq and Afghanistan. In the case of the EU, statebuilding assistance in the last decade has been linked to Union neighbourhood objectives: 'It is in the European interest that countries on our borders are well-governed … Our task is to promote a ring of well governed countries to the East of the European Union' (European Commission (EC) 2003: 7–8).

Diversity in approaches is accompanied by diversity of actors. Some are national, some regional, and some multilateral. Many major players are linked one way or another to states or groups of states; some are non-governmental. This plethora of actors and functions immediately raises significant issues of coordination, an issue the chapter returns to below.

Although this discussion covers the twenty-two years since independence, the emphasis is on 2000–2010 for two reasons: first, the data are better; and second, it was after the 2003 revolution that the major efforts to build the state were undertaken. This analysis focuses on three questions: how much have these agencies invested in Georgia's project; what are the substantive foci of their engagement; and how has this investment varied across the period?

The major international players in economic engagement with statebuilding in Georgia have been the international financial institutions (IFIs), the European Union (EU), the EBRD, and, at the state level, the United States (US). Most began to focus on statebuilding and economic development after 1994, when the humanitarian situation had stabilized.

The Russian Federation has also provided substantial assistance, much of which has focused on maintaining and building state structures, but to the separatist regions of South Ossetia and Abkhazia. In other words, Georgia has been a case of competitive statebuilding. Russian policy undermines statebuilding in Georgia by impeding the restoration of territorial integrity, and also by encouraging a diversion of resources and political attention in Georgia away from the many other developmental tasks facing the country.

In the 2000s, official bilateral development assistance ranged from $169 million (2000) to $382 million (2007) and $888 million (2008) (OECD 2010a). The jump in 2008 reflects the early phase of a post-war reconstruction package of $4.5 billion,[4] which, if completely disbursed, will amount to about $1000 per person. Georgia has clearly received a higher level of ODA *per capita* than many developing states, including those in post-conflict situations.[5] These figures understate the full flow of assistance, because some elements of economic engagement do not fall clearly into the World Bank's and the OECD DAC's classification.

Looking at the data longitudinally, support was relatively modest in the late 1990s, and then declined in 2000–2003. This reflected international disillusionment with the Shevardnadze government. In at least one case, the IMF, the agency gave up entirely and suspended programming, 'the international financial institutions having lost hope in the ability of Georgia to return to the path of economic reform' (Papava 2009: 45). IMF withdrawal in turn resulted in significant reduction in World Bank activity. The reduction in allocations for Georgia was in a way an application of conditionality: international agencies were providing resources to assist Georgia in meeting reform objectives. When the government ceased moving in the desired direction, the aid was cut. Reduction in foreign assistance and the evident loss of international confidence that it implied contributed to the preconditions of the 2003 Rose Revolution.

As a result of the revolution, external assistance grew substantially. For example, EBRD loan volume grew from around €40 million to approximately €160 million between 2004 and 2005 (EBRD 2010), and EU grants rose from €22 million in 2002–2003 to €71 million in 2006 (EC 2007b: Annex 3, p. 33), while the IMF resumed programming under the Poverty Reduction and Growth Facility. The change reflected substantial improvement in state performance on the budget and also the seriousness with which the government attacked petty corruption by government officials.

There were occasional disagreements, as with IMF concerns over extra-budgetary state accounts in 2004–2005 (Papava 2009: 46, 47), but, on the whole, there has been little evidence of serious efforts to apply conditionality.

After the 2004 accession round, the EU reorganized its assistance to neighbouring countries in the east and south through the European Neighbourhood Policy (ENP). Earlier Partnership and Cooperation Agreements were supplemented by ENP Action Plans. The purpose was to allow partner countries to develop their relations with the EU, moving from cooperation towards greater integration, and from capacity building (as under TACIS) to broader support for political and economic reform, but without the presumption of eventual accession.

The war in 2008 occasioned further substantial increases in international economic assistance to Georgia. The EU and the World Bank co-sponsored a donors' conference which produced pledges of $4.5 billion, of which the United States promised $1 billion, and the European Community some €483 million, with EU member states putting in another €131 million. Much of this assistance was humanitarian (i.e. shelter and sustenance for displaced persons), for infrastructure, and, in the case of the reopening of an IMF lending facility, for currency and macroeconomic support.

In 2009, the EU's ENP was in turn supplemented by the Eastern Partnership (EAP), involving six post-Soviet states, including Georgia. The partnership adds €300 million in new funds, the remainder of the €600 million being financed out of the ENP Instrument. The policy as applied to Georgia has clear statebuilding implications. The first priority of Georgia's EAP Action Plan is the strengthening of judicial policy and institutions, as well as further progress on democratic reform and the protection of human rights. Moreover, success in eventual negotiation on deep free trade will require substantial strengthening of regulatory structures (such as those concerning monopolies, the labour code, and food safety standards). The EU has made clear that progress in integration depends on performance with regard to fair elections and judicial independence.[6]

Before turning to assessment of results, some mention of military assistance is appropriate, since, as suggested in the introduction, it is indirectly relevant to the issue of international economic engagement. Security is a precondition for development. In principle, external support of military programmes permits reallocation of local funds that would otherwise be used for defence into developmental activities. Alternatively, external support of particular defence budget lines (i.e. training and logistics) may allow redirection of national resources to armaments, affecting the probability of renewal of conflict.

The US has been the major provider of military assistance to Georgia since 1994. The longitudinal data show very modest beginnings and an early focus on training and capacity building. The second period (1997–2001) was one of marked growth, particularly in financial support, and sales and donations of non-lethal equipment. The third period (2001–2006) was dominated by the war on terror and Georgia's contributions to that endeavour. Here too, the emphasis was on training, capacity building, and logistics, and on counterinsurgency (especially the Georgia Train and Equip Program (GTEP)). In general, the US was reluctant to enhance Georgia's capacity for conventional ground operations, given the risk that this capacity would be used unilaterally against Georgia's separatist enclaves and also owing to concern over Russian sensitivities.

Finally, the general level of US military assistance programming in Georgia fell sharply in 2006–2008, notably in the area of commercial and foreign

military sales. Presumably this reflects the tapering off of the need for technical assistance (GTEP, for example, was wound down in 2006), and the completion of various procurement programmes. It may also have reflected
concerns about the intentions of the Georgian government in view of Georgian challenges to separatist authorities in South Ossetia in 2004. There has
been no reversal of the downward trend since the August 2008 war, and the
United States has repeatedly refused Georgian requests for what the Georgians term defensive weaponry (Just Anti-Corruption 2010).[7]

Independent analysis shows that US military assistance grew very
rapidly indeed from 2001–2007 (CDI 2007). It is not clear, however, that
there was any significant displacement of national budgetary resources
towards development, since on-budget defence spending also grew extremely
rapidly after the Rose Revolution. On the other hand, it is plausible that
sizeable US assistance to cover administrative, infrastructural, and logistical
elements allowed the Georgian government to focus its resources on
weapons acquisition from third parties. The lead-up to the August 2008 war
displays a marked military buildup with purchases from Ukraine and the
Czech Republic leading the way (Pukhov 2010: 139–141). In the lead-up to
the war in 2008, the Georgians also reportedly bought considerable quantities of weaponry and associated equipment from Israel (Just Anti-Corruption
2010).

Summary

Several general points arise. There is wide interest among donors in the
project of statebuilding. Their programming also displays a preference for
democratic governance. Most combine development assistance programming
with governance assistance. However, there is little clear evidence of the
implementation of democratic conditionalities. Conditionality per se has
been weak. Perhaps the most that can be said here is that there was a clear
reduction in the flow of economic assistance in the period 2000–2005,
reflecting concerns over the apparent failure of governance and associated
exacerbation of corruption during the later Shevardnadze years. Not only
was funding reduced, but the direction shifted away from government and
towards NGOs out of which the revolutionaries came. Moreover, international support of civil society organizations including finance, capacity building, and the sharing of experience considerably enhanced the capacity of the
opposition to organize an effective challenge to the Shevardnadze government after its rigging of parliamentary elections in 2003. In this respect,
international actors played a role in the arrival of the Rose Revolution in late
2003.

Equally clear is both the gradual acceleration of international actors'
engagement with the statebuilding project after the Saakashvili government
had consolidated its authority in elections in 2004; and a shift in the direction of funding from civil society to the state. This reflects an enthusiasm
well-articulated in the EC Country Strategy Paper for 2007–2013:

Following the events which led to the 'Rose Revolution' at the end of 2003, and the rise to power of President Saakashvili, Georgia is pursuing an agenda of ambitious political and economic reforms in order to fight endemic corruption and build a modern state based on democracy, the rule of law, good governance and market economic principles.

(EC 2006: 8)

The uncritical quality of international (in particular American) engagement in Georgia may have encouraged Saakashvili to believe that he would be backed if he came to a confrontation with the Russians over South Ossetia and Abkhazia (Cooley and Mitchell 2009). The substantial flows of international assistance during the period facilitated the greater concentration of public resources on defence and weapons acquisition. The period of increased international assistance was also that of the most rapid increase in defence spending of any former Soviet republic (from 0.7 per cent of GNP in 2003 to 8.1 per cent in 2008). As one commentator put it, by 2007, defence spending accounted for 30 per cent of the state budget, 'an absurdly high percentage for any country' (Boonstra 2010: 9).

Results

For reasons already stated, there doesn't seem to be much point in considering the consequences of international engagement in the effort to re-establish the state's control over its sovereign territory. Instead, the focus here is on two issues: economic development and governance, and democratization and the rule of law.

The economy and economic governance

A quick glance at Table 19.1 confirms dramatic improvement on key macro-economic indicators.

Table 19.1 Georgia: major economic indicators

	2000	*2005*	*2007*	*2008*	*2009*
GDP (US$ billion)	3.06	6.41	10.18	12.79	10.74
GDP growth	1.8	9.6	12.3	2.3	–4
Public revenue/GDP	10.4	18.1	24	25.7	–
Inflation	4.7	7.9	9.7	10	1.7
FDI (US$ million)	131	453	1,750	1,564	764
External debt	1.64/	1.9/	2.29/	3.38/	–
(US$ billion)*	1.27	1.49	1.54	2.22	

Source: World Bank 2010.

Note
* The first figure is total external debt, the second is public and publicly guaranteed debt.

GDP has quadrupled (albeit from a low base) since 2000. Given that the population is declining, this growth translates into very sizeable increases in per capita income, and in average monthly earnings (up 9 per cent per year over 2003–2006). Economic growth was impressively high in 2005–2007 before a substantial drop in 2008 related to the war and also to the emerging global economic crisis.

Georgia's currency was stabilized in the late 1990s with assistance from the IMF and the World Bank and remained so until the war. After a sudden depreciation in late 2008, the currency has been more or less steady against the dollar. Inflation was low in the late 1990s, but crept upwards with the rapid growth of the mid-2000s. After a drop in the year after the war, it has resumed its upward trend, in part because of the large influx of foreign reconstruction funding. The rise to 14 per cent in 2010 also reflects increases in global food prices. Despite the upward trend, inflation remained many orders of magnitude below its peak at the height of Georgia's crisis in 1994. Foreign direct investment, negligible in the 1990s and the early years of the 2000s, grew rapidly in 2004–2008. However, it has slumped since the war and does not show signs of early recovery.[8] The tax share of GDP has risen from very low levels, providing the state with substantial additional resources to finance its activities.

Concerning economic governance, a recent World Bank report summarizes:

> Since 2003, Georgia has implemented an impressive array of reforms. These reforms are reflected in the pronounced political, social and economic transformations following the 'Rose Revolution' at the end of 2003. The processes since the start of reforms can be qualified as unique in terms of the speed of reforms, degree of innovations, and extent of institutional restructuring. The reforms are recognized to have noticeably improved the institutional environment, provided a basis for sustained economic growth and human capital accumulation, and increased multifold foreign direct investments.
>
> (World Bank 2009b)

A similar conclusion might be drawn from Georgia's rise through the ranks of the Global Doing Business Index to twelfth globally. However, as shall be suggested later, this development may be explained more through the government's targeting of easier metrics in the index to boost their position (World Bank 2010).[9] One key element of these reforms has been considerable improvement in Georgia's performance in the area of corruption since 2003. Petty corruption has largely disappeared, to the relief of the population as a whole.[10] Georgia's *Corruption Perception Index* score has risen from 2.4 (on a scale of 9) in 2002 to 4.1 in 2009, and it has moved from a ranking of 85 to a ranking of 66 during the same period (Transparency International 2009).

However, the aggregate data on the economy and economic governance obscure a more complex reality. One element of concern is public finance.

From 2004 to 2007, the government made significant progress in controlling overall public sector debt, which dropped from 40 to 22 per cent of GDP, before the ratio began to rise again in 2008. On the other hand, private foreign debt grew rapidly as a result of rising capital inflows from abroad. In 2009, combined public and private external debt exceeded 58 per cent of GDP (IMF 2011b: 27).

The war and the global economic crisis have changed the financial dynamics considerably. The state budget deficit rose to 9.7 per cent of GDP, and the government is working to take the deficit below 3 per cent by 2013. The IMF expected the public debt to GDP ratio to peak at 62 per cent of GDP in 2011, dropping to 48 per cent by the end of their projection (2016). The government has forestalled a repayment crunch in 2013 by floating a second Eurobond issue to pay off an issue maturing in 2013, as well as some additional foreign liabilities. That merely kicks the problem down the road. In the meantime, after several years of steady growth, remittance income has declined in 2009.

The IMF has consistently taken the view that the most important way to reduce external vulnerability is rapid public sector deficit reduction (IMF 2009b: 18). That is easier said than done. Sluggish or negative growth makes revenue enhancement difficult. If anecdotal reports are true, government agencies are putting increasing pressure on local businessmen to increase their contribution to state revenue. This is unlikely to encourage entrepreneurship and may engender capital flight. Cutting government spending also has a depressive effect on GDP. If flows of foreign (particularly US) assistance decline as the post-war aid package comes to an end, pressure against the Georgian lari may intensify. Likely depreciation will in turn affect the inflation rate, particularly on food and utilities. Second, examination of poverty and employment issues suggests numerous persisting problems. There is a 43 per cent rural–urban income gap: 60 per cent of the poor are rural. While agricultural employment accounts for 60 per cent of total employment, most of that is subsistence farming, involving a group with a disproportionately high incidence of poverty. Youth are particularly badly affected. Rapid increases in average wages have tended to be in sectors employing relatively few people. Unsurprisingly, Georgia has a reasonably high Gini coefficient at around 40.4 (UNDP 2008b: 34). In other words, rapid growth has not been equitable growth and there exists a comparatively high and stagnating incidence of poverty (23.7 per cent in 2007, with an expected rise to 27.1 per cent) (World Bank 2009b). The UNDP estimates that a quarter of the population lives below the $2/day poverty line and notes general agreement that there has been no significant reduction in poverty or extreme poverty rates, despite rapid growth (UNDP 2008b: 2, 34). Accelerating inflation and notably exploding food prices, are likely to exacerbate these trends.[11] As noted earlier, it is plausible that the post-war infusion of aid has also contributed to the rise, given its effect on price levels.

Concerning employment, it appears that the share of the population employed has declined over the past ten years, despite a declining population. There has been a decrease in total employment and increase in the numbers of unemployed (reflecting the substantial downsizing of the public sector and the failure of alternative sources of employment to emerge). IMF mandates and targets to reduce public sector spending are a contributing factor here.

As noted, social transfers improved as the government began to pay pension and other entitlements regularly and to clear substantial arrears. But they remain at levels that are inadequate to meet basic needs (EC 2007a: 15–16). More generally, although the UNDP HDI for Georgia advanced fairly rapidly from a low point in 1995 to 2000, improvement slowed in 2000–2005 (a period shared by Shevardnadze and Saakashvili as presidents), and slowed further in 2005–2010. That suggests that the improvements at the macroeconomic level are being weakly translated into improvement in the population's quality of life (UNDP 2010b).[12] Continuing economic and social hardship are one reason that Georgia's population is declining at about 1 per cent a year.

There has been significant progress in the economic dimension of statebuilding, but the coming to term of post-war stabilization and reconstruction assistance, the evolving debt structure of the country, continuing high poverty rates, weak performance on employment, and the inadequacy of social transfers, raise real questions about how durable the project is. Such doubts are enhanced by increases in the lari price of essential commodities, and the effect of wider economic slowdown on remittances, a key source of foreign currency and a central (informal) element of the social safety net.[13] The potential for persisting poverty and high unemployment to provoke social unrest was evident in the December 2007 protests in Tbilisi (UNDP 2008b: 1). Social issues were also a contributing factor in the confrontation between the police and opposition demonstrators in late May 2011, in which a number of people were killed. The government was widely criticized for excessive use of force after both incidents.

Democracy, the rule of law, human rights, and civil society

In the second dimension of statebuilding, results are less encouraging. Examination of Freedom House[14] indices from 1999/2000 to 2009 suggests decline on four indices (electoral process, independent media, governance, judicial framework and independence) and on the aggregate (democracy) score. Georgia is performing at the same level on civil society and on corruption.[15] In no category was Georgia performing better in 2009 that in 1999–2000. The 2010 report showed no improvement on the aggregate score.

The most prominent example of undemocratic behaviour is the violent police suppression of the December 2007 opposition demonstrations in front of Parliament, followed by the declaration of emergency rule (the president arguing that the demonstrations were 'masterminded by Russia'), and the curbing of media freedom, culminating in the sacking of the principal opposition television outlet, *Imedi* (Human Rights Watch 2007), followed by its seizure. Ownership subsequently shifted offshore; it is widely believed that the station is now controlled by people close to the government. Lack of transparency of ownership of media, coupled with the difficulty that opposition groups encounter in obtaining nationwide broadcast licences remain a bone of contention within Georgia, but also with international organizations.

Legal and judicial reform has been a consistent mantra of external aid agencies since Georgia's independence. Programmes have focused on due process, the rights of detainees, judicial independence, the training of judges, and assistance in the drafting of relevant amendments to relevant codes and procedures. The analyses of all major players (the EU, the Council of Europe, USAID, and the State Department) suggest that significant weaknesses remain. Particular concerns include arbitrary detention, the rarity of bail and the frequency of the use of plea bargaining without appropriate engagement by judges, the abuse of detainees, the undue influence of the procuracy, the extraordinary rate of conviction (over 99 per cent), and lack of transparency of judicial process. A recent UN delegation summed up well:

> The United Nations Working Group on Arbitrary Detention urged the Government of Georgia to address problems such as the excessive use of detention in court cases, the use of harsh sentences as punishments, the diminished rights of persons charged with administrative offences and the non-existent use of bail. The independence of the judiciary was also questioned by the group of independent experts, particularly in relation to plea bargains … 'The fact that about 90% of the cases that go through the court resort to plea bargain arrangements with minimal intervention from judges is alarming'.
>
> (UNHCHR 2011)

An analyst resident in Georgia put the matter of judicial independence more succinctly: 'The least independent sector of politics is the courts. In cases that are remotely political, there are *no* decisions that go against the government' (Fairbanks 2010: 147).

This was written prior to the adoption of a constitutional reform, one component of which is a probationary period of three years for new judges. That raises further questions about judicial independence.

Putting all this together produces an ironic result, given external actors' hopes that the Rose Revolution and its leader would move Georgia towards a more complete democratic transition. The result seems to have been movement in the opposite direction, creating, in statebuilding terms, a hybrid. Georgia has made progress in economic reform and governance. In contrast, in political terms, it is less free than it was.

That produces another irony: whereas international actors did exercise a degree of conditionality to influence or to rid Georgia of Mr. Saakashvili's predecessor, they have largely failed to exercise governance conditionality over the current government, while providing it with substantial means to continue and to consolidate the quasi-authoritarian project. In this respect, international partners might be said to be complicit in the hybridization of the Georgian state.

After the war, international organizations and friendly states and institutions have become more vocal on the issue of democratic transition. This has produced further constitutional reform shifting power away from the presidency and towards the Parliament and the prime minister. These amendments, however, will not take effect until after the next presidential election, generating speculation that Saakashvili, who cannot run for a further presidential term, may emulate his nemesis, Vladimir Putin, and take up the post of prime minister.

In addition, the local elections of May 2010 were deemed to be a considerable improvement on previous ones. The government in November 2010 embarked on discussion of reform of the electoral system in response the opposition claims that the existing system resulted in the under-representation of opposition sentiment in Parliament. It is not yet clear where this second wave of democratization will end. But it does appear that the government has become more sensitive to the democratic and legal objectives of its international partners.

Summary

In short, Georgia under Saakashvili performs reasonably well on the economic and order dimensions of statebuilding, although there remain important weaknesses, and there is reason to question just how durable this improvement will be. The state performs less well on transparency and accountability metrics. To the extent that statebuilding in post-conflict societies is seen to be linked to the building of durable peace, efforts in this area have been an abject failure.

Taking all of this together, the international statebuilding endeavour in Georgia appears to have had the following consequences.

- First, informal application of conditionalities (the decline in assistance to the government and the assistance provided to non-governmental political actors) facilitated the (unconstitutional) transition from Shevardnadze to Saakashvili in 2003.
- Second, the very active engagement with the Saakashvili government has had a role in the generation of a more effective state – one that exerts much greater control over its economy, and is able to extract significant resources from the population and to apply those resources to the purposes of the state.
- Third, the lack of political conditionality (de facto) on this substantial assistance has assisted the Saakashvili government in consolidating a political system that is less free than Georgia was in 2000.
- Fourth, the uncritical embrace of President Saakashvili in the years leading up to the August 2008 war may have contributed to the resumption of hostilities.

Conclusion

The record of international engagement in statebuilding in Georgia is decidedly mixed. Why is this so? To some extent it is a product of the usual
difficulties of coordination encountered by international agencies seeking to
redesign post-conflict societies and states. Different actors have different priorities. Some embrace political objectives, some eschew them. Mandates
overlap. Recipient state agencies are overwhelmed with competing and sometimes redundant interventions. Noise obscures signals. Donor agencies can
be played off one against the other.[16]

A second possibility is the weak application of conditionalities. On the economic side, this was because, on the whole, the government embraced the
logic of free markets and economic openness; conditionalities were unneces-
sary as the government was already on board and performed well on metrics
that mattered to major funding agencies. On the political side, the weakness
of conditionality appears to have resulted from a suspension of critical
analysis on the part of partner governments and organizations.

Post-2003 Georgia defined itself as a success in the development of democratic politics preferred by Western donors. This group, particularly the
United States under the George W. Bush administration, embraced Georgia
as a poster child of successful transition, a 'beacon of liberty'. This embrace
was encouraged by Georgia's unreserved embrace of wider US foreign and
security policy priorities (including the substantial deployment of Georgian
forces to Iraq and in Afghanistan). Georgia consistently ranks as one of the
top per capita contributors of forces to these operations, as well as being very
cooperative on matters of trans-shipment of supplies to coalition forces in
Afghanistan. Georgia, just like Afghanistan, highlights that once the narrative
of successful democratization had been bought, it was difficult to abandon
(see also Antonio Giustozzi and Niamatullah Ibrahimi's chapter in this
volume), isolating the government and local elites from pressure and criticism. This effect was complemented by the care that the Georgian government took to cultivate allies within the US Congress and analytical
community. Performance on rule of law, human rights, and media metrics
was weaker than might have been hoped for, in part because international
actors did not impose costs for non-compliance.[17]

A third element of an explanation concerns a deep contradiction in international engagement. Western actors may have thought that they were trying
to build a viable, effective, and territorial integral democratic state in
Georgia. Russia did not share this objective. Russian policy fairly steadily cut
across the statebuilding project. Russia sought a Georgia that was compliant.
Failing that, it sought a Georgia that was weak and divided. Since it could not
get the former, it invested in the latter, by impeding the conflict resolution
process, and by providing increasing financial and other support to Georgia's
breakaway regions. Georgia's economic recovery was undermined by the
Russian trade embargo. The considerable investment that Georgia has made
in defence and security, wise or not, was in some sense a response to this

pressure and diverted resources from more productive use. In 2008, Russia invaded Georgia in the apparent hope of unseating the Saakashvili government. There is an important lesson here: statebuilding efforts that fail to take proper account of the regional context in which these efforts occur may be self-defeating.

Leaving aside the factors mentioned above, the outcome of international engagement in statebuilding in Georgia, as elsewhere in the region, is strongly affected by historical legacy, social practices, and ingrained popular and elite assumptions about politics and the state. First, concerning legacy, Georgia had no recent experience of independent statehood. It had no experience of the liberal economy and had had little exposure to international models prior to independence. In other words, in bureaucratic/administrative and political terms, it was starting from a very low point. Second, and recalling Joel Migdal's work on statebuilding in the Third World, state–society relations in post-colonial societies tend to be complex and dialectical: 'Focusing merely on the direct impact of states on societies ... would give us only a partial view of the relations between peoples and states and would miss important aspects of why some states are more capable than others' (Migdal 1988: xiii–xiv). This appears to apply to Georgia and the other states of the Caucasus. There is broad consensus in the recent literature (King 2008: 203; Swietochowski 1995: 211; Suny 1993: 113–120) that, in the Soviet era, strong traditional kinship, patronage, and village-based networks were strengthened, rather than destroyed by Soviet modernization. These networks were forms of protection and livelihood in the face of an abusive, distant, and unaccountable state: 'The local, traditional sociocultural systems of the pre-revolutionary period, segmented and small in scale, were resistant to forced change and provided havens from Soviet interventions' (Suny 1993: 115).

King (2008: 203) argues that large scale urbanization transported these village-based networks into the urban landscape, the social structures of the urban population 'arranged according to traditional hierarchies and values that privileged personal loyalty over duty to the society as a whole'. Finally, much of the politics of the Soviet era concerned the distribution of the resources of the state through the patronage networks of those who controlled state resources. At independence, Georgia was left with a society that had little if any concept of state legitimacy and ample reason to perceive the state as at best irrelevant, and, at worst, parasitic and dangerous. Elites, meanwhile, were accustomed to seeing state structures as a means for personal and group gains. There is no evidence (yet) that international statebuilding efforts have affected these deeply rooted socio-cultural patterns. This is not surprising. If they were strong enough to survive the application of Soviet rule, then one would expect them to be resilient in the face of much less intrusive and coercive international engagement in the post-Soviet era. Indeed these networks seem to have been quite successful in influencing the flow of international resources for their own ends.

The intersection of international efforts at statebuilding with this difficult local context has been troubled. Shevardnadze took power in 1992 on the backs of his Soviet-era patronage network. As King puts it, his political party 'became a mechanism for capturing the state rather than transforming it' (2008: 229). When Shevardnadze was overthrown by a younger member of his own patronage network, it appeared that the way was clear for the emergence of a democratic and liberal order. But, with time, the same pattern appears to be reasserting itself. One patronage network captured the state from another. In this game, the essence is control of the state in order to channel resources. It is about ownership not stewardship. That the traditional pattern reappeared reflects not only the durability of deeply rooted social practices, but also the diffidence of international actors in resisting this process, and, possibly, an insufficient understanding of how Georgian politics, state, and society work.

Notes

1 A comment from a former senior Georgian government official and diplomat, in response to a request for his view of the impact of international actors on state-building in post-conflict Georgia, 2 December 2009.
2 For a useful assessment of the war, see HRW (1995).
3 SC Res. 937 of 21 July 1994.
4 See European Commission/World Bank (2008b).
5 For example, per capita ODA is considerably lower across the period in Afghanistan and Sierra Leone (see http://data.worldbank.org/indicator).
6 See, for example, the remarks of Gunnar Weigand, the EU's chief negotiator on Georgia's EAP Association Agreement, as reported in Civil.ge (2011). Successful conclusion of the Association Agreement is a precondition for movement towards deeper free trade.
7 In June 2010, US Assistant Secretary of State Philip Gordon noted that, although the US had no military embargo on Georgia, the US government felt that the sale of military equipment to Georgia might complicate the American effort to reduce tensions in the region. As reported in Civil.ge (2010).
8 Mitchell (2010) reports that FDI fell to $272 million for the first six months of 2010.
9 Interviews in Tbilisi, November 2010. If one looks at the disaggregated metrics, for example, one finds that Georgia ranks eighth in starting a business, seventh in dealing with construction permits, and second in ease of registering property. On the other hand, it ranks sixty-first in paying taxes, and 105th in closing a business (World Bank 2010).
10 However, many observers take the view that improvement has been less evident at higher levels of government, where the political leadership uses its tight hold on power to secure control over key economic assets (Fairbanks 2010).
11 In 2011 and 2012, inflation dropped significantly as a result of decline in world food prices. In mid-2012, global food prices began to rise rapidly again. The prospect, given Georgia's considerable dependence on food imports, is a return to high inflation rates. That trend will be exacerbated by government funding decisions in the lead-up to the October 2012 parliamentary elections.
12 The trend shows a rise of 0.38 in the first period, 0.36 in the second, and 0.17 in the third.
13 Remittance income ($695 million) was 182 per cent of ODA ($382 million) in 2007.
14 The use of Freedom House data was somewhat controversial. But the Georgia

report is written by a senior RFE/RL analyst with over twenty years' experience with the country, and with a reputation for lack of bias. The data conform to numerous other sources (HRW, USSD, Reporters without Borders, etc.). They are also broadly consistent with my own interviews and experience in the country, both recently and over the past twenty years.

15 This finding is less encouraging than the Transparency International data discussed earlier. The discrepancy reflects methodological differences. Whereas Transparency International focuses on business perceptions, Freedom House supplements this metric with analysis of 'the business interests of top policy makers, laws on financial disclosure and conflict of interest, and the efficacy of anti-corruption initiatives' (Freedom House 2010: 12).

16 For a good discussion of these issues in Georgia, see Boonstra (2010: 2, 7).

17 For a similar view, see Boonstra (2010: 9) and in particular his remark about the 'backfiring' of reform due to the failure of donors to define clear benchmarks.

20 How the EU and the US stopped a war and nobody noticed

The containment of the Macedonian conflict and EU soft power

Kristof Bender

Looking back a decade after its conclusion, and after a string of statebuilding and peacebuilding failures (most notably in Afghanistan and Iraq), the 2001 conflict in Macedonia looks like a model case of effective foreign intervention. Of some 115,000 refugees and internally displaced persons (UNHCR 2001), most refugees and all but 621 displaced persons had returned by 2009 (EC 2010a: 22). The rebel group that started the conflict has disarmed and now pursues its goals through the political process. The country has remained peaceful and all the major provisions of an ambitious peace agreement can be considered to have been fully implemented. The grievances of the Albanian minority have been addressed head on, substantially transforming the character of the state and its relationship with its Albanian population. In 2005, just over four years after the conflict had ended, Macedonia was granted official candidate status by the EU.

Nevertheless, Macedonia has not made it into the state- and peacebuilding literature as an outstanding success story, not least because the conflict appeared so minor compared to the wars in Bosnia, Rwanda or Somalia that cost hundreds of thousands of lives.[1] In Macedonia fewer than 250 people were killed during the seven-month period of violence.[2] However, one can also turn the argument around by saying that it is exactly the fact that a full-scale war (which could have claimed many more victims) was avoided that shows how successful the intervention in Macedonia was. Judging by previous events in Macedonia's history or the other Yugoslav wars of the 1990s, a major conflict was far from an implausible prospect. When the Ohrid Agreement was signed on 13 August 2001, the danger of escalation seemed very real, as the few days before and after the accord were the most lethal of the whole period, leaving more than 20 people dead (Popetrevski and Latifi 2002: 55–57; Jovanovski and Dulovi 2002: 60–61). A month after the agreement was signed, *The Economist* (2001) forecast:

> Any peace will be artificial. Having created a politically modified Macedonia, the West is going to have to police it – or leave it to fresh violence, not just between the two main communities, maybe, but between the moderates and hardliners of the Slavic one.

Six months later, Alice Ackermann argued that 'there is a succinct threat and fear that the peace accord already holds the seeds of another war' (2002: 80). The question this raises is why, instead of fresh violence, the last decade has witnessed the comprehensive and successful implementation of a demanding peace agreement.

This chapter addresses this question in five steps. First, it examines the political economy of the conflict in Macedonia, and argues that there were much stronger structural reasons behind the conflict between ethnic Macedonians and Albanians than there were, for example, between Bosniaks, Croats and Serbs in Bosnia and Herzegovina. Second, it analyses the role of international actors in containing the conflict and facilitating a peace agreement that would substantially transform the Macedonian state. The third section looks at the impressive track record of the Ohrid Agreement, while the fourth examines what could have gone wrong with the implementation of the agreement and why it did not. The concluding section analyses why the ethnic Macedonian leadership went along with the implementation of the agreement, even though it imposed a very high political price, consisting not only of practical losses for its constituency, but also of acknowledging that Macedonia was a multi-ethnic country and not a nation state. It highlights the role of EU soft power, in particular the provision of a credible vision for a stable and prosperous future for the country – a goal shared by both communities.

The political economy of Macedonia's conflict

Ethnic Macedonians and Albanians are not only divided by culture, language and religion, but also by social, economic and demographic patterns. These latter inter-ethnic divisions run much deeper in Macedonia than in the parts of former Yugoslavia that descended into terrible wars in the first half of the 1990s, such as Bosnia and Herzegovina (where the communist system had carefully tried to avoid discrimination based on ethnicity). These divisions are also a rather recent development within Macedonian society.

In her extraordinary study of families in 300 Balkan villages in the 1930s, the anthropologist Vera Erlich found that traditional multiple-family households, or *zadrugas*,[3] having all but disappeared in most of the rural Balkans, could – at the time of her studies – still be found in Macedonia (and Kosovo).

> The basic principle of the *zadruga* was that the male members never leave the common home. Sons and their descendants remain within it, and only daughters leave it on marriage to become members of the *zadrugas* of their husbands. The *zadruga* was governed by a hierarchical system, every member having a definite rank within it. Rank was determined by age and sex, the sex criterion being stronger than the age criterion: all males were superior to any of the womenfolk.
>
> (Erlich 1966: 32)

Interestingly, as Ulf Brunnbauer points out, Erlich could not observe any significant differences between Muslim Albanian and Orthodox Slav families. This changed only after the Second World War. Until then Macedonia's economy and society had remained almost entirely rural. In 1940 there were only 110 industrial enterprises in the country, 'most of which were small and were effectively only mechanized workshops' (Brunnbauer 2004: 580). Under the new communist regime, urbanisation and industrialisation, which had already led to the disappearance of the multi-family household in other parts of the Balkans, were now spreading into Macedonia, although they predominantly affected the Orthodox Slavic population. As Brunnbauer (2004: 583) observed,

> Once communist power was established, the Albanians, and the Muslim communities in general, felt increasingly alienated from the state, for example, because of its anti-religious agenda, its ethnic Macedonian outlook, the strong Serbian influence, and its radical attempts to change the role of women. They also regarded urbanization and industrialization as threats to their cultural traditions, and saw their moral values threatened by the ruling ideology.

This resulted in clearly diverging patterns of migration and economic activity during the second half of the twentieth century. Ethnic Macedonians tended to leave the harsh life in the remote countryside behind to take up newly created jobs in industry and public administration in provincial towns or the capital Skopje. Ethnic Albanians, however, tended to remain in the rural areas, making a living from agriculture and small private enterprise (tolerated by Yugoslav communism). In the ethnically mixed region of Kičevo in Western Macedonia, for example, the population of all 45 ethnic Macedonian villages declined between 1948 and 1994, in 29 of them by more than three-quarters. By contrast, 18 of the 24 ethnic Albanian villages in the region experienced population growth, six of them more than doubling in size (Bender *et al.* 2004: 120). Most of Macedonia's Albanians who decided to migrate did not move to Macedonian towns, but went to look for work abroad. The different economic trajectories consolidated over time and there is some literal truth to Robert Hislope's assertion that the culture of Albanians in Macedonia remained 'in many aspects pre-industrial' (Hislope 2003: 135). In 1986, Albanians, while accounting for over 20 per cent of the population, filled only 7 per cent of jobs in the social sector (Milosavlevski and Tomovski 1997: 313). The end of communism and Macedonia's birth as an independent state in 1991 – the only one of the former Yugoslav republics to separate peacefully at the time – would have provided an opportunity for providing interethnic co-existence with a new foundation. However, two major developments prohibited this.

First, the collapse of communism and the disintegration of socialist Yugoslavia had major repercussions on the economic worlds of both ethnic Macedonians and Albanians, and brought them into increasing competition for shrinking resources. Ethnic Macedonians, the primary beneficiaries of four decades of socialist industrial development, were suddenly left exposed to the rapidly declining fortunes of the region's socialist-era state companies. The disappearance of the formerly secure Yugoslav market and the inability to compete with Western producers quickly turned many of these companies into huge loss-makers, unable to pay their workers. The Albanian population had been excluded from the public sector in socialist times and forced to rely on alternative economic strategies such as labour migration abroad and small-scale trade. They therefore emerged better equipped to survive the collapse of the socialist economy. However, as the opportunities for work migration increasingly narrowed during the 1990s due to constraints on EU labour markets and newly introduced visa regimes, the economic situation of the ethnic Albanians also worsened. They increasingly sought employment on the Macedonian labour market, which was already contracting due to massive layoffs in the (formerly) socially owned industries. Each community tended to misinterpret the fortunes of the other: many ethnic Albanians still perceived ethnic Macedonians as privileged by well-paid state jobs and networks of patronage; many ethnic Macedonians saw the ethnic Albanians as backward, prone to crime and their new-found wealth as the fruits of illicit activity (Bender *et al.* 2004: 107).

The second factor that prohibited the addressing of the legacy of communist inter-ethnic relations was the deliberate effort of the leadership during the 1990s to build a nation state for ethnic Macedonians, disregarding the third of the population that was formed by various minorities. National tensions in Macedonia had already increased during the 1980s, but on a smaller scale than in neighbouring Kosovo. The Macedonian authorities reacted by limiting the number of Albanian language classes in schools, dismissing ethnic Albanian civil servants and refusing to register certain Albanian names with nationalist connotations, such as Relindja, meaning 'rebirth', or Flamur, meaning 'flag' (Poulton 1995: 127–130; see also Neofotistos 2004: 61; Sidiropoulos 1999: 142). In 1989 the constitution of the Socialist Republic of Macedonia was changed so that it became 'the national state of the Macedonian nation' rather than 'the state of the Macedonian people and the Albanian and Turkish minorities' as before (Daskalovski 2004: 62). After independence in late 1991, the new constitution stuck to the formulation 'the national state of the Macedonian people', though it added 'providing for the full equality of citizens and permanent coexistence of the Macedonian people with Albanians, Turks, Roma and other nationalities'. Article 19 of the constitution singled out the Macedonian Orthodox Church to be mentioned by name, while all other faiths were subsumed under 'other religious communities and groups'.

Most ethnic Albanians boycotted the independence referendum held on 8 September 1991. In January 1992 a separate, clandestine referendum on the independence of Western Macedonia was organised by Albanian leaders, producing an overwhelming 90 per cent in support. While this was not followed by any moves to declare independence, on 31 March 1992 around

40,000 Albanians demonstrated in Skopje, calling for Macedonia to remain unrecognised until the state granted greater autonomy to regions and villages where Albanians constituted the majority of the population (Ministry of Internal Affairs 2001: 314).

The desire to remodel Macedonia as a nation state led to further steps that alienated Macedonia's Albanians. In December 1992, parliament passed a new citizenship law, which included a 15-year residency requirement in order to be eligible for Macedonian citizenship. This measure was heavily criticised and strongly resented by the Albanian community, as a sizeable number had moved to Macedonia from other parts of Yugoslavia (mostly Kosovo) only in the 1980s and thus did not qualify. In 1994 a private Albanian-language university was established in the West Macedonian town of Tetovo. State authorities quickly moved to close it down, but it continued to operate without being recognised by Macedonian state institutions (Daskalovski 2004: 57–58). Discriminatory practices could also be observed in budgetary allocations for local infrastructures. In the Kičevo area in Western Macedonia, for example, the two rural Albanian municipalities, which accounted for 37 per cent of the population, received only 14 per cent of the funds spent there by the national water and canalisation programme between 1997 and 2001, while the two rural ethnic Macedonian municipalities, representing only 10 per cent of the total population, received 48 per cent of these funds (Bender *et al.* 2004: 128–133).[4]

The 1990s were also not without security incidents. These included violent clashes between Albanians and police in Skopje in November 1992, which left four people dead and 36 injured (Ministry of Internal Affairs 2001: 315), the seizure of illegally stored weapons, and the arrest of several Albanian politicians following accusations that they were creating an 'All-Albanian Army'. In 1997 the Albanian mayors of Gostivar and Tetovo defied a constitutional court ruling banning the display of flags of other countries in public. In an effort to de-escalate the situation, parliament passed a law allowing minorities to fly their national flags on certain state holidays, but the mayors still refused to remove the Albanian and Turkish flags. When special police forces were sent to take down the flags in Gostivar, they clashed with a hostile crowd, resulting in the deaths of three protestors and the arrest of 312 people, including the mayor (ibid.: 319–320). Additionally, 1998 and 1999 witnessed a number of small explosions aimed at police stations (Rusi 2002: 21).

However, after initial worries about Macedonia's stability in the early part of the 1990s, few among the ethnic Macedonian elite and foreign observers perceived general Albanian grievances or these violent incidents as a major concern. From the early 1990s, every government had included an Albanian party as a coalition partner and, when compared with Croatia, Bosnia and Kosovo, the minority situation was indeed much better. In addition, most ethnic Macedonians apparently did not think there was a problem with the country's Albanians. According to a United Nations Development Programme (UNDP) poll at the eve of the outbreak of the conflict, only 37.6 per cent of respondents saw 'ethnic problems' as one of the 'most important problems confronting the nation'. Eight other issues scored higher: unemployment (70.4 per cent), low salaries (61.7 per cent), poverty (59.2 per cent), high prices (50.2 per cent), crime (48.7 per cent), corruption (46.9 per cent), health (40.9 per cent) and instability in the region (38.3 per cent) (Hislope 2003: 137).

However, another UNDP study conducted three months earlier reveals that 93.4 per cent of Albanians said they did not have enough rights (ibid.: 134). As Zhidas Daskalovski, an ethnic Macedonian political scientist, points out: 'The government did not act upon Linz's and Stepan's recommendation that to consolidate democracy in a plural society requires the state attention to the needs of national minorities' (2004: 64). This also meant that Macedonia's Albanians did not identify with an independent Macedonia to any great extent. Arben Xhaferi, the leader of the Democratic Party of Albanians (DPA) at the time, told Robert Hislope in an interview in December 2000 that 'Albanians did not vote for the constitution, so we don't feel the need to be loyal to the state' (Hislope 2003: 139). For Daskalovski, this 'stateness problem ... with a major segment of the population challenging the very foundations of the state', has been the fundamental issue for Macedonia's failure to consolidate democracy (2004: 52).

The Macedonian government had repeatedly announced that it would address the concerns of its Albanian citizens, but could point to few results even after a decade of ethnic Albanian participation in government. This allowed for the emergence of new actors willing to pursue their interests outside the political process. The Kosovo Liberation Army in neighbouring Kosovo had shown the effectiveness of violence to advance their agenda, by managing to draw NATO into the conflict. It is against this background that the first serious acts of violence erupted in January 2001.

Armed conflict and containment

There is little doubt that the conflict in Macedonia could have turned into a full-scale war, as had happened in other parts of the former Yugoslavia in the previous decade. Both sides had access to an ample supply of weapons: the ethnic Albanian rebels could rely on supplies from Kosovo; ethnic Macedonian leaders controlled the army and the police. In addition, according to *The Economist* (2001), Interior Minister Ljube Boškovski had distributed about 10,000 Kalashnikov rifles to civilians and police reservists in the spring of 2001. Leaders on both sides could have recurred to a rich heritage of grievances, stereotypes and emotionally laden pieces of historical fabric to fuel violence. In addition, there were individuals from the ethnic Albanian and Macedonian population willing to escalate and to undermine the peace process. But it did not happen: the conflict was successfully contained. Fighting stopped after less than seven months, claiming fewer than 250 lives in total. International actors played a crucial role in this, as this section illustrates. A constraining role was also played by the International Criminal Tribunal for the Former Yugoslavia (ICTY) in The Hague. With a number of

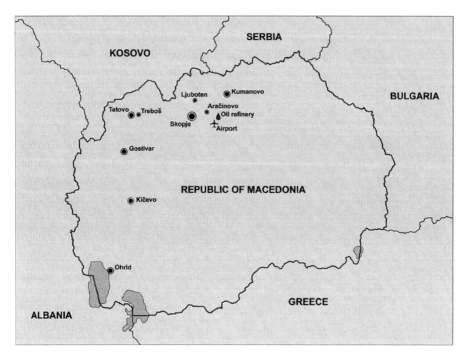

Map 20.1 Map of Macedonia.

high-level indictments and arrests since 1999 – including of that of Slobodan Milošević – the ICTY started to show that perpetrators of war crimes could not count on impunity.

When fighting broke out between the National Liberation Army (NLA) and the government in early 2001,[5] hardly anyone took the NLA seriously. 'They are not many, but you know how difficult it is to fight radicals. We will not allow them to provoke a conflict', a spokesman for the Macedonian Army told the *New York Times* (Gall 2001). Mendu Thaçi, Vice President of the DPA, demanded that the Macedonian forces 'deal swiftly and harshly with groups which they, like their Macedonian counterparts in government, regarded as criminals and extremists' (Ordanoski 2002: 39). On 20 March, the DPA issued a joint statement with the Party for Democratic Prosperity (PDP), the other important ethnic Albanian party at the time, calling on the NLA to lay down their arms (Rusi 2002: 25). NATO sent an emergency team and deployed more tanks and troops along the Kosovo border, with increased helicopter support to prevent illegal border crossings. NATO Secretary General George Robertson condemned the actions against Macedonian security forces and EU foreign policy chief Javier Solana urged all ethnic Albanians to 'distance themselves from these acts of violence, to isolate the extremists' (Balalovska *et al.* 2002: 21).

In mid-March military activities resumed, this time around Tetovo (ibid.: 20). The Macedonian army gave an ultimatum and then started shelling (largely empty) villages around Tetovo. The following five months saw major fighting, though mostly concentrated in one location at a time, and separated by periods without much military activity. Most affected were the areas around Tetovo, west of Kumanovo, and Aračinovo.

As Christopher Chivvis points out, from early on the EU and the US pursued a twin-track policy: while they backed the Macedonian government and condemned NLA violence, the same diplomats pressed the ethnic Macedonian and Albanian political parties to come to an agreement on Albanian political rights. This was a difficult balancing act as it 'implicitly recognised the legitimacy of the NLA's demands while maintaining that the group represented an extremist fringe' (Chivvis 2008: 145). By early May, Solana and Robertson were engaged in intense shuttle diplomacy. On 8 May, during a visit by Solana, a deal was struck to establish a government of national unity, which would include all major ethnic Macedonian and Albanian parties (ibid.: 145). Macedonian President Boris Trajkovski initiated a dialogue with the four main political parties, but did not make much progress. While the Albanians played for time, hoping for international engagement and mediation, ethnic Macedonian leaders still sought a resolution of the crisis through victory on the battlefield.

The NLA rebels were not involved in any direct talks with the government. Robert Frowick, a US diplomat sent as the personal representative of the Chairman-in-Office of the Organisation for Security and Co-operation in Europe (OSCE), set about to change this. In late May he facilitated a joint meeting of the party leaders of the DPA and PDP, Arben Xhaferi and Imer Imeri, with the leader of the NLA, Ali Ahmeti, in the Kosovar town of Prizren. The resulting so-called Prizren Declaration caused a public outcry among ethnic Macedonians and strong condemnation from the ethnic Macedonian leadership and foreign representatives alike. Frowick was asked to leave the country. However, as Iso Rusi points out, the agreement 'linked the real strength and influence of the NLA with the formal legitimacy of the DPA and PDP, gained at parliamentary elections in 1998'. The declaration amounted to 'a mandate from the NLA for the political parties to represent Albanians from Macedonia in any negotiations mediated by representatives of the international community' (Rusi 2002: 26).

In June the conflict entered its most dramatic phase. On 8 June the NLA took Aračinovo near Skopje, bringing not only the capital but also the airport and Macedonia's only oil refinery within easy reach. As Macedonian troops unsuccessfully tried to drive the rebels back, Solana negotiated a ceasefire. On 25 June, amidst massive protests from the ethnic Macedonians which accused NATO of collaborating with 'the terrorists', five NATO buses shuttled some 400 fully armed NLA fighters out of Aračinovo to NLA-held territory (Balalovska *et al.* 2002: 33).

Pressure for a political settlement mounted. By the end of June the EU and the US appointed mediators to Macedonia: former French Defence Minister François Léotard and James Pardew of the US State Department. The earlier talks initiated by President Trajkovski, though unsuccessful, had made clear what had to be addressed: decentralisation, fair and appropriate representation of minorities in the public administration, the status of the Albanian language at state level and the organisation of the police. Talks resumed in early July. While a basic understanding about decentralisation and a greater number of state jobs for minorities could be reached quickly, the issues of the status of the Albanian language and minority representation in the police posed major problems (Popetrevski and Latifi 2002: 51).

Faced with deadlock, the talks were moved out of Skopje on 28 July to a lake resort close to the town of Ohrid. The NLA was not directly involved, but remained in constant touch with the Albanian political parties (ibid.: 52). On 1 August the stalemate surrounding the language question was broken by a compromise solution worked out by Léotard, Pardew and former OSCE High Commissioner on National Minorities, Max van der Stoel (ibid.: 53). Four days later, Solana brokered a deal regarding the police, whereby local com-manders would be chosen by the municipal council from a shortlist provided by the interior ministry (ibid.: 54). After the sequencing of disarmament and constitutional changes were worked out, the agreement was initialled on 9 August (despite increased violence on the battlefield) and signed on 13 August in Skopje by the leaders of the four biggest political parties.

The Ohrid Framework Agreement of 2001, as it is officially called, does not read like a classic peace accord. While the cessation of hostilities, disar-mament of the Albanian rebels and a general amnesty were among its key provisions, most of the agreement concerned increased rights for the Alban-ian minority – rights that would require substantial changes in key state institutions:

- enhanced competences at local government level, including finances and the redrawing of municipal boundaries;
- non-discrimination and equitable representation of minorities in the state administration;
- special parliamentary procedures to ensure that minorities could not be out-voted on a number of issues they deemed important;
- education and language use, including state-funded university-level edu-cation in Albanian;
- the use of national emblems of minorities (such as flags) at the local level.

The track record of the Ohrid Agreement

While reaching a peace agreement can be difficult enough, the main chal-lenges frequently lie in its implementation. When one or more signatories see their interests threatened, there is often little that prevents the peace process from falling apart, as seen in the Democratic Republic of Congo, Angola or Rwanda (del Castillo 2008: 10). With this in mind, reviewing the implementation of the individual measures of the Ohrid Agreement makes for impressive reading.

Cessation of hostilities, amnesty and disarmament

NATO's operation 'Essential Harvest' collected 3,875 voluntarily delivered weapons, including two tanks and two transporters, 17 air defence systems, 483 machine guns and 161 mortars (Jovanovski and Dulovi 2002: 68). All NLA fighters were granted amnesty. The number of violent incidents, still high in the weeks after the agreement was signed, declined dramatically. Macedonia has now been peaceful for nearly a decade.

Decentralisation

The competencies of municipalities, which hitherto had been very restricted, were considerably extended, as were their financial resources. Major newly acquired municipal responsibilities included the establishment, financing and administration of primary and secondary schools; the execution of social welfare and child protection activities; local economic development; culture and sports. Competencies for urban planning, environment protection and health care were enhanced (Republic of Macedonia 1995: art. 17; 2002: art. 22). The number of municipalities was reduced to 84, largely rectifying previous alterations, which had been perceived at the time by ethnic Albanians as gerrymandering. (In 1996 the number had expanded from 34 to 123, cutting off Albanian-inhabited rural hinterland from urban centres.) A referendum instigated by opponents of these new municipal boundaries in 2004 failed due to a low turnout of only 26 per cent (van Hal 2005). While smaller municipalities in particular still struggle with the implementation and financing of the new competences, the new laws have addressed the long-standing concerns of the Albanian community, which now has considerably more freedom in organising its affairs.

Equitable representation of minorities in state institutions

Within two years, from December 2002 to December 2004, the number of Albanian staff paid from the state budget increased from 8,164 to 10,294, representing a rise from 11.65 to 14.54 per cent. The share of ethnic Macedonians decreased from 83.27 to 80.31 per cent over the same period (Republic of Macedonia 2005: 396). Widening Albanian participation in the police and the armed forces was particularly difficult and sensitive. Nevertheless, the number of ethnic Albanians in the police force increased from 350 in 2001 to 1,659 in 2004, a rise from 3.6 to 13.31 per cent of the total, while the share of ethnic Macedonians declined from 92 to 82 per cent (ibid.: 403–404). The number of Albanians in the Macedonian army, subject to additional pressure to reform by aspirations for NATO membership, rose from 129 in 2001 to 796 in 2004, that is, from 2.25 to 10.18 per cent of the total staff (ibid.: 406–407).

A case study of the Kičevo area conducted by the European Stability Initiative (2006) found that the number of Albanians employed in the state administration had considerably increased. While in 2002 Albanians held only three leading positions in the Kičevo area, by 2005 they held 20 (including the director of the hospital, the director of the biggest primary school, two police station commanders and the heads of six branch offices of government ministries). The number of Albanian policemen had virtually doubled to 85 (out of a total of around 350). Similarly, the number of Albanian staff in schools and the hospital had increased considerably (ibid.: 9). These changes were representative of state-wide developments: by December 2009, the overall number of civil servants from the non-majority ethnic communities in Macedonia had reached 29 per cent (EC 2010a: 21).

Parliamentary safeguards

The Ohrid Agreement provides for a double-majority principle in the parliament on issues that affect minorities (the so-called 'Badinter majority'), such as laws relating to culture, language, education, personal documentation and the use of national symbols. This principle requires that whenever such laws are put to a vote, there should be both a majority of all MPs and a majority of all minority MPs. An Inter-Community Relations Committee has been set up to address any disputes regarding these issues. The agreement also grants minorities the power of veto over the election of one-third of the Constitutional Court judges, three of the seven members of the Judicial Council and the Ombudsman.

University education

A new South East European University, operating in Albanian, Macedonian and English, was officially inaugurated on 20 November 2001 in Tetovo. In addition, the formerly illegal Albanian University of Tetovo was formally recognised by a new law adopted on 20 January 2004 (Czaplinski 2008: 265, 270). The number of Albanians enrolled in recognised institutions of tertiary education increased from 2,285 in 2000/01 to 9,540 in 2004/05. The respective share in the total number of students increased from 5.7 to 15.5 per cent (Republic of Macedonia 2005: 402).

Language use and symbols

Under the Ohrid Agreement, Macedonian remains the country's official language, but any other language spoken by at least 20 per cent of the population has been declared an official language that can be used for personal documents, civil and criminal proceedings, by municipal institutions and in communication between citizens and the central government. Albanian MPs can also use Albanian in the parliament. A law passed in 2005 allows for the Albanian flag to be flown on public buildings in municipalities with an Albanian majority. According to a constitutional court ruling in 2007, the Albanian flag can only be flown on certain holidays, but this has been largely ignored, both by Albanian mayors (who still fly the Albanian flag on a daily basis) and by central government institutions (who tolerate it).

Importantly, those who had previously taken up arms acknowledge the successful implementation of the agreement. Speaking on the seventh anniversary of the signing of the Ohrid Agreement, former rebel leader Ali Ahmeti stated:

> I think the greatest triumph for the Macedonian and Albanian nations is that with [the] Ohrid agreement all feel Macedonia as their state and loyal to it. I think matters are going properly and much good work has been done.
>
> (Alsat 2008)

What could have gone wrong – and why it did not

When looking back at the successful implementation of the Ohrid Agreement, it is tempting to underestimate the difficulties that had to be overcome. An examination of the political dynamics of the weeks after the signing of the agreement makes clear that things could have turned out very differently.

The signing of the agreement and the first phase of implementation took place against the backdrop of a considerable level of violence, which raised serious questions about its viability. After the death of five armed Albanians at the hands of a special unit of the Ministry of Interior on 7 August, nine reservists of the Macedonian army were killed in an ambush on the Skopje–Tetovo highway the following day. Despite public protests, the agreement was initialled the following day. On 10 August, an anti-tank mine killed seven members of Macedonia's security forces, triggering reprisals against the village of Ljuboten (Popetrevski and Latifi 2002: 55–57). Despite the signing of the agreement, there were almost daily incidences of violence, 'marking the bloodiest week since the beginning of the Macedonian-Albanian conflict' (Jovanovski and Dulovi 2002: 60–62).

Another worrying development was the formation in July and August 2001 of a special police unit called the 'Lions', which came directly under the command of the hard-line Interior Minister Ljube Boškovski. The Lions performed very few military activities (they were established when the conflict was almost over), but were 'a one-party formation that VRMO-DMMNE was preparing for "peace time" activities' (Ordanoski 2002: 44f.). As *The Economist* observed in September 2001:

> In provincial towns they and those like them are extorting money from businesses, buying off local police and other officials, and chasing out of town those who might support President Boris Trajkovski and others trying to build peace. When NATO goes home, it is suspected, Mr Boskovski will strike against ethnic Albanians and moderates in his own community alike.

In the light of lingering mistrust between the communities, the activities of informal actors such as the Lions, 'anti-peace accord sentiments' and 'widespread rumours of a new "spring offensive" by rebel forces', Alice Ackermann warned half a year after the agreement was signed that '[t]he post-peace agreement environment remains politically, economically and militarily precarious' and that 'Macedonia remains on the razor's edge' (2002: 74, 80).

Achieving signatures on the Ohrid Agreement was a key contribution of the international community but not its only one. A combination of diplomatic engagement, the limited but crucial presence of foreign troops and the provision of financial aid were central to implementing the accord and keeping all relevant actors involved in the peace process, in particular during the fragile first weeks and months after its signing.

The Ohrid Agreement linked the disarmament and disbanding of the NLA to sweeping constitutional changes, and was divided into three phases. First, a draft proposal for the required constitutional changes was to be submitted to parliament once the NLA had delivered the first third of its weapons for decommissioning; the exact amendments were to be determined after a further third was handed over; and, finally, once all weapons had been surrendered, the constitutional changes were to be adopted (Jovanovski and Dulovi 2002: 60).

Several events threatened to derail the agreement. First, Prime Minister Ljubčo Georgievski of the governing VMRO-DPMNE[6] announced that he would grant a free vote to his party's 46 MPs on the constitutional amendments (ibid.: 60), putting the required two-thirds majority in doubt. Second, a major row broke out over how many weapons were to be collected from the NLA insurgents, whose numbers were estimated by domestic and international military analysts at 2,000–3,000 fighters (Ordanoski 2002: 38). Proposed figures for the weaponry ranged from 2,000 by NATO Secretary General George Robertson to 85,000 by Interior Minister Ljube Boškovski (Jovanovski and Dulovi 2002: 61). On 22 August, NATO agreed to deploy a 3,500-strong force for 'Operation Essential Harvest' to collect weapons. This mission was frequently ridiculed by Macedonian journalists and politicians, some of whom who suggested that the operation should be called 'Museum Harvest', as the weapons collected were so old (*Irish Times* 2001). Nevertheless, the deployment of NATO troops was an important constraint on further major violent confrontations.

Third, when NATO announced on 29 August that the first third of weapons (1,400 pieces) had been collected, displaced ethnic Macedonians from the Tetovo area prevented MPs from attending parliament and discussing the constitutional changes. Prime Minister Georgievski promptly stated that all ethnic Macedonian displaced persons had to be able to return to their homes before the amendments could be discussed, and the President of the parliament announced he would postpone the session indefinitely. Only after criticism from the opposition Social Democratic Union of Macedonia (SDSM) and pressure by Léotard and Pardew did the session continue. After Javier Solana had met personally with all 46 VMRO MPs, an overall majority of 91 out of 120 (including all except seven of the VMRO MPs) supported the start of procedures for constitutional change (Jovanovski and Dulovi 2002: 65).

The second phase passed without much fuss. Then another stumbling block appeared, with two small parliamentary parties calling for a referendum on the constitutional changes. Prime Minister Georgievski jumped at the opportunity to score some points among nationalist voters, but soon climbed down, leaving the initiative without its most powerful advocate. On 25 September Robertson declared that 3,875 weapons had been handed over by the former rebels (ibid.: 68). Operation 'Essential Harvest' formally ended on 27 September; it was replaced by a smaller NATO force, mandated to protect OSCE and EU observers ('Operation Amber Fox') but, in actuality, 'intervening whenever the NATO command would deem it necessary to prevent clashes between Macedonian security forces and ethnic Albanian extremists or other forms of violence' (Balalovska *et al.* 2002: 61). Former NLA commander Ali Ahmeti announced that the NLA had disbanded.

Two more hurdles were left: the preamble of the constitution and the question of amnesty for former NLA fighters. According to the agreement, no particular ethnic group was to be mentioned in the new preamble, but this was very difficult for ethnic Macedonians to accept. Seeing the threat of stalemate, Solana proposed that 'Macedonian people' be reinserted, but that at the same time Macedonia would also be defined as the state of Albanians, Turks, Serbs, Vlachs, Roma and the people who live there. While this solution was criticised as clumsy and strange, it was eventually accepted by all parties (ibid.: 66–71).

The issue of amnesty was resolved by George Robertson on 7 November in a marathon session with ethnic Macedonian and Albanian leaders, which involved a pledge from the government to exchange letters with NATO, stating that the prosecution of any Albanian fighter would be left to or approved by the UN tribunal. The 224 rebels for whom the Interior Ministry had prepared indictments were to be pardoned, if not subject to the UN tribunal's investigations (ibid.: 68).[7]

Hardliners, led by Interior Minister Boškovski, continued in their efforts to derail the process by disregarding a carefully developed plan for the redeployment of police to areas formerly controlled by the NLA. After news reports about a mass grave near Treboš, Boškovski sent special units to the village on 11 November, arresting a number of former NLA fighters. The units were then ambushed, leaving three policemen dead, several injured and dozens of civilians as hostages (Ackermann 2002: 75). Instead of hampering the peace process, however, the incident led the PDP to reconsider its opposition to the preamble, paving the way for parliament to finally adopt the constitutional changes on 16 November, with 90 votes in favour (ten more than the required two-thirds majority). Police redeployment was successfully completed, although it took a few weeks longer than expected.

The last formal piece of the puzzle was put in place on 24 January 2002, when the Macedonian parliament passed (again by a two-thirds majority) a new law on local government, paving the way for the convening of a donors' conference that had already been postponed four times. This raised €309 million, of which €104 million came from the EC and €102 million from EU member states. A further €274 million was announced for other development assistance in 2002, including €135 million from the EC and EU member states (European Commission/World Bank 2002). More than half of the available funds, therefore, was provided by the EU and its member states, and these made an important contribution to finance reconstruction and the first phases of the implementation of the agreement.

After the turbulence of the initial months subsided, during which frequent visits were made by Solana and Robertson, a small team surrounding the EU Special Representative continued to play a key role, mediating between the parties when differences on practical questions relating to the implementation of the agreement arose (Ackermann 2002: 76). On 1 November 2005 this body merged with the EC Delegation.

The NATO force, whose presence had been repeatedly extended, eventually handed over on 31 March 2003 to 'Operation Concordia', the first ever EU military mission, which lasted until December 2003. It was succeeded by an EU police mission ('Proxima'), which continued until December 2005.

As Balalovska *et al.* (2002: 56) point out, the role of EU and NATO representatives in the process was essential:

> What emerges distinctly from an examination of the political debate and controversies that accompanied the parliamentary ratification process is the active participation in that process of EU and NATO representatives, who shuttled between Brussels and Skopje almost daily and were in Skopje at each and every turning point, mediating, suggesting solutions, reminding Macedonians of their obligations to implement the Ohrid deal and encouraging Albanians to show flexibility when needed, resorting to praise (or blackmail) to force decisions, making direct appeals to Macedonia's public opinion through press conferences and interviews when they thought that political leaders were reluctant to follow their advice.

The role of EU soft power

The implementation of the Ohrid Agreement involved extremely hard political choices for the ethnic Macedonian leaders, as it entailed losses for their political constituencies on three fronts. First, it was clear that any adjustment towards a more equitable representation of Albanians in the public administration would mean a loss in job opportunities and fewer actual jobs for ethnic Macedonians. Second, the strengthening of local government institutions meant a reduction of effective power in central government (which was and still is dominated by ethnic Macedonians); the special parliamentary procedure with a veto for minorities on certain issues further constrained the power of the majority. And third, the agreement entailed symbolic losses for the ethnic Macedonians, such as allowing the display of Albanian and other flags on (certain) public buildings and the use of the Albanian language in parliament. In essence, the implementation of the agreement meant conceding that Macedonia was a multi-ethnic country rather than an ethnic Macedonian nation state. This was a huge pill to swallow, particularly against the background of the identity-building project of the 1990s.

So why did the ethnic Macedonian leadership go along with it? The first key factor was one that had nothing to do with EU (or US) influence: the country happened to be endowed with reasonable political leaders on all sides, who showed the ability and vision to bring back Macedonia from the brink by taking brave political decisions. These included President Boris Trajkovski, who emerged as a non-partisan broker, earning the respect of many Albanians. Also the leadership of the Social Democrats – having stared into the abyss – sensed that compromise and increased rights for Macedonia's Albanians was the only way to save the country. Similarly, rebel-leader-turned-politician Ali Ahmeti embraced a multi-ethnic vision of Macedonia (rather than pushing for unachievable goals such as regional autonomy like others in the Albanian community).

The second major factor was the provision by the EU of a credible vision for a stable and (relatively) prosperous future within the EU. When the Social Democrats won the September 2002 elections, they formed a government with the Democratic Union for Integration (DUI), which had been established by Ahmeti less than four months previously (humorously referred to as the 'guns 'n' roses' coalition (van Hal 2005: 41)). Although the DUI took the large majority of the ethnic Albanian vote, it was hugely unpopular among ethnic Macedonians as it comprised former insurgents. The ethnic Macedonian parties could have – while formally adhering to the Ohrid Agreement – ignored or delayed the difficult and painful measures when it came to implementation, but both the SDSM and subsequent VMRO-led governments maintained their commitment to its principles.

Graciana del Castillo maintains that, after a conflict, 'for the transition to succeed, people need to identify peace with personal benefits that outweigh the short-term costs that they inevitably will have to bear' (2008: 232). In the case of Macedonia, the EU provided this through a vision for the moderates to embrace. A crucial step in this regard was the signing of a so-called Stabilisation and Association Agreement (SAA) with the EU in April 2001. Though it was widely belittled as a desperate effort by the EU at the height of the crisis to stop the fighting (which it did not), it showed that the prospect of EU membership was serious. In the words of Zoran Ilievski and Dane Taleski (2009: 357), it 'was one of the crucial incentives for the peaceful resolution of the crisis'.

Moreover, they also assert that 'the EU's "carrot" for securing the compromises entailed in the [Ohrid Framework Agreement] was the prospect of EU membership for Macedonia' (ibid.: 360). Armend Reka comes to the same conclusion: 'The carrot of EU and NATO membership was an important incentive that brought the 2001 conflict to an end and facilitated the implementation of the Ohrid Agreement' (2008: 67). This view is also shared by former Deputy Prime Minister for European Integration, Radmila Šekerinska, a key protagonist at the time, who told the European Stability Initiative (2010):

> When politicians and experts read the Ohrid Agreement, they said: 'Oh my god, this would be difficult to implement even in a richer, stronger and more mature country. And it is difficult to do it in a few years.' So they said: 'Ok, if you do this, then you'll show that Macedonia can actually progress in the future.' And we took it for granted and we said: 'OK, if it's the Ohrid Agreement [that counts] then so be it.' We were aware that Macedonia would not be a perfect candidate country in a few years, but the Ohrid Agreement was the big argument in our favour because it became clear in 2005 that Macedonia has implemented the most difficult parts of the Ohrid Agreement against all odds and against all predictions.

Another important element of the EU's approach was continuous financial assistance by the EU which – among other benefits – helped to lower the implementation costs of some aspects of the agreement, for example through direct budget support and various institution-building assistance.

Crucially, the prospect of EU membership also united ethnic Macedonians and ethnic Albanians in a joint vision for the future. As Reka points out, 'Macedonia's EU membership aspirations are a crucial factor in the interethnic equation' (2008: 67). The government's efforts were not left unrewarded. In March 2004, less than three years after the conflict ended, Macedonia formally applied for EU membership and in December 2005 received the status of an official 'candidate country' (at the time of writing in early 2011 a privilege held by only four other countries: Croatia, Iceland, Montenegro and Turkey).

It is the combination of these two major factors – a credible vision provided by the EU and a Macedonian leadership that embraced that vision – that explains Macedonia's success.

In October 2009 the EC proposed to launch membership negotiations with Macedonia. This step could have triggered the strongest soft power tools of the EU, as shown by the last EU enlargement round, which has transformed the former communist states of Eastern Europe to an extent unmatched by any other development programme. It would have started the last chapter of consolidation and stabilisation of Macedonia as a democratic and multi-ethnic market economy. However, Greece blocked the start of EU membership negotiations (after it already blocked Macedonia's accession to NATO in 2008). Greece does not dispute that Macedonia has met the required criteria, but maintains that the term 'Macedonia' refers to the historical Kingdom of Macedon and that its use in a neighbouring country's name would usurp an essential part of exclusively 'Greek' culture and heritage. Greece also contends that the use of the name 'Macedonia' implies territorial ambitions on the northern Greek province that bears the same name.

This does not mean that Macedonia will now disintegrate or revert to violence. But in the longer term, if this issue is not resolved, EU membership will cease to be a credible prospect, removing reform incentives and the joint vision held by ethnic Macedonians and ethnic Albanians of how their state can develop to the satisfaction of all its citizens.

Notes

1 The number of victims in Bosnia lies probably below this figure. According to latest figures compiled by the Research and Documentation Centre in Sarajevo during the war in Bosnia and Herzegovina 97,207 people, including soldiers and civilians, were killed or went missing (Research and Documentation Centre, www.idc.org. ba).
2 Most likely the total is considerably lower, but there are no official figures available for Albanian fighter casualties. According to the Macedonian Ministry of Internal Affairs, by 10 August 2001 70 Macedonian soldiers and ten civilians had been killed (Ministry of Internal Affairs 2001: 8).
3 Also called 'Balkan patriarchal families', 'Balkan family households' or 'communal joint families'.
4 The remainder went to the urban (and ethnically mixed) municipality of Kičevo.
5 While most analysts date the outbreak of the conflict to a clash between masked NLA gunmen and the security forces in the village of Tanuševci on 16 February 2001, the NLA had already released a statement in the aftermath of an attack on a police station in Tearce on 22 January, announcing that it would fight the Macedonian government until constitutional changes strengthened Albanian rights and transformed Macedonia into a 'Macedonian-Albanian – or Albanian-Macedonian – state' (Rusi 2002: 20).
6 Internal Macedonian Revolutionary Organisation – Democratic Party for Macedonian Unity, a rightist mainstream party that derived its name from the Internal Macedonian Revolutionary Organisation, a rebel movement established in the late nineteenth century.
7 Ironically, the only two people from Macedonia who had to stand trial at the ICTY in The Hague were former Interior Minister Boškovski and Police commander Jovan Tarculovski. While Boškovski was acquitted, the first-instance ruling for Tarculovski was a 12-year prison sentence.

Bibliography

3C Conference Report (2009), *Improving Results in Fragile and Conflict Situations*, 19–20 March, Geneva: Centre on Conflict, Development and Peacebuilding, Graduate Institute of International and Development Studies.

Acemoglu, D. and J. Robinson (2008), *The Role of Institutions in Growth and Development*, Commission on Growth and Development Working Paper 10, Washington DC: World Bank.

Ackermann, A. (2002), 'Macedonia in a post-peace agreement environment: A role for conflict prevention and reconciliation', *International Spectator*, 37/1, 71–82.

Adams, D. (2004), 'Taint of drugs reaching Haiti's upper echelons', *St. Petersburg Times*, 3 April.

AF-P (Agence France-Presse) (2003), 'UN forms anti-corruption unit in Kosovo', 5 November.

African Development Bank (2008), *Conflict Resolution, Peace and Reconstruction in Africa*, Oxford: Oxford University Press.

African Union (2002), *Protocol Relating to the Establishment of Peace and Security Council of African Union*, Addis Ababa: African Union.

African Union (2007), *Post-Conflict Reconstruction and Development Policy*, Addis Ababa: African Union.

African Union (2008), 'Tenth ordinary session of the assembly', Assembly/AU/Dec.177(x), 31 January to 2 February.

African Union (2009), 'Draft report of the panel of the wise on strengthening the role of the AU in the prevention, management and resolution of election-related disputes and violent conflict in Africa', 191st Meeting of the Peace and Security Council, PSC/PR/2(CXCI), Addis Ababa, 5 June.

African Union (2010), 'Multidisciplinary mission for evaluation of post-conflict reconstruction and development needs in DRC and Burundi: Major conclusions and recommendations', 230th Meeting of the Peace and Security Council, PSC/PR/2(CCXXX), 27 May.

al-Jezairy, Z. (2009), *The Devil you Don't Know: Going Back to Iraq*, London: Saqi.

al-Khafaji, I. (2000), 'The myth of Iraqi exceptionalism', *Middle East Policy*, 7/4, 62–91.

Alao, A. and C. Ero (2001), 'Cut short for taking short cuts: The Lomé peace agreement on Sierra Leone', *Civil Wars*, 4/3, 117–134.

Alden, C., D. Large and R. Soares de Oliveira (eds) (2008), *China Returns to Africa: A Continent and a Rising Power Embrace*, London and New York: Hurst Publishers and Columbia University Press.

Aldonas, G.D. (2011), *Analysis of Section 1504 of the Wall Street Reform and Consumer Protection Act*, Washington, DC: American Petroleum Institute.

Allawi, A.A. (2007), *The Occupation of Iraq: Winning the War, Losing the Peace*, New Haven, CT: Yale University Press.

Alsat (2008), 'DUI leader Ahmeti says Ohrid agreement toward implementation', 14 August, available at www.alsat.tv, accessed 29 October 2010

Alvarez-Plata, P. and T. Brück (2007), 'Postwar debts: Time for a new approach', in J.K. Boyce and M. O'Donnell (eds), *Peace and the Public Purse: Economic Policies for Postwar Statebuilding*, Boulder, CO, and London: Lynne Rienner, 245–270.

Amnesty International (2007), 'Kosovo (Serbia): Albin Kurti – A Politically Motivated Prosecution', London, 10 December.

Amorim Neto, O. and M. Costa Lobo (2010), 'Between constitutional diffusion and local politics: Semi-presidentialism in Portuguese-speaking countries', Paper presented at the APSA 2010 Annual Meeting, available at http://papers.ssrn.com/sol3/papers.cfm?abstract_id=1644026, accessed 15 February 2012.

Anastasakis, O., J. Bastian and M. Watson (eds) (2011), *From Crisis to Recovery: Sustainable Growth in South East Europe*, Oxford: South East European Studies at Oxford.

Andersen, R. (2000), 'How multilateral development assistance triggered the conflict in Rwanda', *Third World Quarterly*, 21/3, 441–456.

Anderson, L. (1987), 'The state in the Middle East and North Africa', *Comparative Politics*, 20/1, 1–18.

Andreas, P. (ed.) (2004), 'The clandestine political economy of the Western Balkans', *Problems of Post-Communism*, 51/3, 3–9.

Aning, K. (2007), *Africa: Confronting Complex Threats*, New York: International Peace Institute.

Aning, K. and A.S. Bah (2009), *ECOWAS and Conflict Prevention in West Africa: Confronting the Triple Threats*, New York: Center on International Cooperation.

Aning, K. and E. Birikorang (2010), 'The African Union and civil society organizations: Defining an emerging relationship?' in W. Feichtinger, U. Werther-Pietsch and G. Barnet (eds), *Coordinated, Complementary and Coherent Action in Fragile Situations: The Vienna 3C Conference*, Vienna: National Defence Academy, 106–111.

Aning, K. and E. Lartey (2010), 'Establishing the future state of the peacebuilding commission: Perspectives on Africa', Working Paper, the Future of the Peacebuilding Architecture Project, Oslo and Ottawa: CIPS and NUPI.

Antic, Z. (1981), 'Economic Development of Kosovo under Discussion', RAD Background Report 320 (Yugoslavia), Radio Free Europe Research, 20 November.

Antidze, M. (2010), 'IMF sees signs of Georgia recovery, more to be done', *Georgian Daily*, 11 February.

Aronson, D. (2011), 'How Congress devastated Congo', *New York Times*, 7 August.

Ashdown, P. (2004), 'Identifying common themes and key factors in post-conflict reconstruction processes', in Conference report 27–28 October, *Beyond Cold Peace: Strategies for Economic Reconstruction and Post-Conflict Management*, Berlin: Federal Foreign Office, 39–40.

Ashton, A. (2008), 'With Iraqi parliament approving pact, Maliki's stature grows', *McClatchy Newspapers*, 27 November, available at www.mcclatchydc.com/251/story/56610.html, accessed 27 June 2012.

Assembleia Constituinte (2001), Comissão de Sistematização e Harmonização (2001), 'Texto Base e Recomendações', Dili.

Aucoin, L. and M. Brandt (2010), 'East Timor constitutional passage to independence', in L.E. Miller (ed.), *Framing the State in Times of Transition: Case Studies in Constitution Making*, Washington, DC: USIP Press, 245–274.

Autesserre, S. (2009), *The Trouble with the Congo: Local Violence and the Failure of International Peacebuilding*, Cambridge: Cambridge University Press.

Aziz, T.A. (2002), 'Fighting corruption in Asia and the Pacific', *Singapore Institute of International Affairs Reader*, 2/1, 21–28.

Bach, D.C. (2006), *Regional Governance and State Reconstruction in Africa*, Kyoto: Asian Center for Peace and Development Studies.

Badie, B. (2000), *The Imported State*, Stanford, CA: Stanford University Press.

Bafilemba, F. (2011), 'To the editor: A conflict over "conflict minerals"', *New York Times*, 10 August.

Bain, W. (2003), *Between Anarchy and Society: Trusteeship and the Obligations of Power*, Oxford: Oxford University Press.

Balalovska K., A. Silj and M. Zucconi (2002), *Minority Politics in Southeast Europe: Crisis in Macedonia*, Ethnobarometer Working Paper Series 6, Rome: Ethnobarometer.

Baram, A. (1998), *Between Impediment and Advantage: Saddam's Iraq*, Washington, DC: United States Institute of Peace Special Report.

Baran, D. (2003), 'Saddam Hussein's armourers', *Eurozine*, 30 September, available at www.eurozine.com/articles/2003-09-30-baran-en.html, accessed 18 December 2011.

Barbedo de Magalhães, A. (2006), *Timor-Leste, As Crises e Os Protagonistas*, Porto: IASI.

Barkan, Joel D. (1995), 'Elections in agrarian societies', *Journal of Democracy*, 6/4, 106–116.

Barnett, M. and C. Zürcher (2009), 'The peacebuilder's contract: How external state-building reinforces weak statehood', in R. Paris and T. Sisk (eds), *The Dilemmas of State Building: Confronting the Contradictions of Post-War Peace Operations*, Abingdon: Routledge, 23–52.

Barron, P. (2010), 'CDD in post-conflict and conflict-affected areas: Experiences from East Asia', Background Paper for the World Development Report 2011, available at http://wdr2011.worldbank.org/input-papers, accessed 10 July 2012.

Bauer, A., R. Hasan, R. Magsombol and G. Wan (2008), *The World Bank's New Poverty Data: Implications for the Asian Development Bank*, ADB Sustainable Development Working Paper Series No. 2, Metro Manila, Philippines: Asian Development Bank.

Bauer, S. (2009), 'Iraq's new death squad', *The Nation*, 22 June, available at www.thenation.com/doc/20090622, accessed 18 December 2011.

Bayart, J.-F. (1993), *The State in Africa: The Politics of the Belly*, London: Longman.

Bayart, J.-F., S. Ellis and B. Hibou (1999), *The Criminalization of the State in Africa*, Oxford: James Currey.

BBC (2006), 'US eases arms embargo on Haiti', *BBC News*, 11 October.

Beattie, A. (2003), '"Surprise" revamp for Iraq's economy', *Financial Times*, 22 September.

Beblawi, H. (1990), 'The rentier state in the Arab world', in Giacomo Luciani (ed.), *The Arab State*, London: Routledge, 85–94.

Belloni, R. (2011), 'Part of the problem or part of the solution? Civil society and corruption in post-conflict states', in C.S Cheng and D. Zaum (eds), *Corruption and Post-Conflict Peacebuilding: Selling the Peace?* London: Routledge, 218–236.

Bender K., M. Cox and G. Knaus (2004), 'The political economy of interethnic relations: Ahmeti's village or the Macedonian case', in A. Mungiu-Pippidi and I. Krastev (eds), *Nationalism after Communism: Lessons Learned*, Budapest and New York: Central European University Press, 101–146.

Benner, T. and R. Soares de Oliveira (2010), 'The good/bad nexus in global energy governance', in A. Goldthau and J.M. Witte (eds), *Global Energy Governance: The New Rules of the Game*, Washington, DC: Brookings Institution Press, 287–314.

Benner, T. and J.M. Witte (2006), 'Rules for global players? Governing multinational corporations in developing countries', *Internationale Politik – Global Edition*, Fall, 56–61.

Bentley, K.A. and R. Southall (2005), *An African Peace Process: Mandela, South Africa and Burundi*, Cape Town: HSRC Press.

Berdal, M. (2008), 'The UN Peacebuilding Commission: The rise and fall of a good idea', in M. Pugh, N. Cooper and M. Turner (eds), *Critical Perspectives on War-transformed Economies*, Basingstoke: Palgrave, 356–372.

Berdal, M. (2009), *Building Peace after War*, London: Routledge.

Berdal, M. and D. Keen (1997), 'Violence and economic agendas in civil wars: Some policy implications', *Millennium: Journal of International Studies*, 26/3, 795–818.

Berdal, M. and M. Leifer (2007), 'Cambodia', in M. Berdal and S. Economides (eds), *United Nations Interventionism, 1991–2004*, Cambridge: Cambridge University Press, 32–63.

Berdal, M. and N. Mousavizadeh (2010), 'Investing for peace: The private sector and the challenges of peacebuilding', *Survival*, 52/2, 37–58.

Bergamaschi, I. (2009), 'Assess, influence, govern. Data and PRSP politics in Mali: the matrix', Paper presented at the Annual Conference of the International Studies Association, New York, February.

Bermúdez-Lugo, O. (2009), *2009 Minerals Yearbook: The Mineral Industries of Liberia and Sierra Leone*, Washington, DC: US Dept of the Interior and US Geological Survey.

Bieber, F. (2010), 'Constitutional reform in Bosnia and Herzegovina: Preparing for EU accession', Policy Brief April 2010, European Policy Centre, Brussels.

Bird, G. and P. Mosley (2006), 'Should the IMF discontinue its long-term lending role in developing countries?' in G. Ranis, J.R. Vreeland and S. Kosack (eds), *Globalization and the Nation State: The Impact of the IMF and the World Bank*, London and New York: Routledge, 378–403.

Blair, T. (2003), *Speech to the Extractive Industries Transparency Initiative (EITI) London Conference 17 June 2003*, London: Office of the Prime Minister.

Block, F. (2001), 'Introduction', in K. Polanyi, *The Great Transformation: The Political and Economic Origins of Our Time*, Boston, MA: Houghton Mifflin, xviii–xxxviii.

Boege, V., A. Brown, K. Clements and A. Nolan (2009), 'Building peace and political community in hybrid political orders', *International Peacekeeping*, 16/5, 599–615.

Bojicic-Dzelilovic, V. (2002), 'World Bank, NGOs and the private sector in post-war reconstruction', in E. Newman and A. Schnabel (eds), *Recovering from Civil Conflict: Reconciliation, Peace, and Development*, London and Portland, OR: Frank Cass, 81–98.

Bolkovac, K. and C. Lynn (2011), *The Whistleblower: Sex Trafficking, Military Contracts and One Woman's Fight for Justice*, Basingstoke: Palgrave Macmillan.

Boon, K.E. (2007), '"Open for business": International financial institutions, post-conflict economic reform, and the rule of law', *International Law and Politics*, 39, 513–581.

Boone, P., H. Gazdar and A. Hussain (1997), 'Sanctions against Iraq: Costs of failure', Paper presented at 'Frustrated Development: the Iraqi Economy in War and in Peace' conference at the University of Exeter, Centre for Gulf Studies in collaboration with the Iraqi Economic Forum.

Boonstra, J. (2010), *Assessing Democracy Assistance: Georgia*, Madrid: FRIDE.

Boucher, A.J., W.J. Durch, M. Midyette, S. Rose and J. Terry (2007), *Mapping and Fighting Corruption in War-Torn States*, Washington, DC: Henry L. Stimson Center.

Bourdieu, P. (1986), 'The forms of capital', in J.G. Richardson (ed.), *Handbook of Theory and Research for the Sociology of Education*, New York: Greenwood Press, 241–258.

Bourdieu, P. and L.J.D. Wacquant (1992), *An Invitation to Reflexive Sociology*, Cambridge: Polity.

Boyce, J.K. (2002), *Investing in Peace: Aid and Conditionality after Civil Wars*, Adelphi Paper 351, Oxford: Oxford University Press.

Bremer, L.P. with M. McConnell (2006), *My Year in Iraq: The Struggle to Build a Future of Hope*, New York: Simon & Schuster.

Broodryk, A. and H. Solomon (2010), 'From war economies to peace economies in Africa', *South African Journal of Military Studies*, 3/1, 1–24.

Brown, C. (2009), 'Democracy's friend or foe? The effects of recent IMF conditional lending in Latin America', *International Political Science Review*, 30/4, 431–457.

Brunnbauer, U. (2004), 'Fertility, families and ethnic conflict: Macedonians and Albanians in the Republic of Macedonia, 1944–2002', *Nationalities Papers*, 32/3, 565–598.

Bryden, A., T. Donais and H. Hänggi (2005), *Shaping a Security Governance Agenda in Post-Conflict Peacebuilding*, Geneva: Centre for the Democratic Control of Armed Forces.

Bryden, A., B. N'Diaye and F. Olonisakin (2005), *Security Sector Governance in West Africa: Turning Principles to Practice*, Geneva: Centre for the Democratic Control of the Armed Forces.

Bull, C.G. (2008), *No Entry Without Strategy: Building the Rule of Law under UN Transitional Administration*, Tokyo: United Nations University Press.

Burnside, C. and D. Dollar (1997), *Aid, Policies and Growth*, World Bank Policy Research Working Paper 1777, Washington, DC: World Bank.

Burnside, C. and D. Dollar (2004), *Aid, Policies and Growth: Revisiting the Evidence*, World Bank Policy Research Working Paper 3251, Washington, DC: World Bank.

Bush, G.W. (2005), *Inaugural Address*, Washington, DC, 20 January.

Call, C.T. (ed.) (2007), *Constructing Justice and Security after War*, Washington, DC: USIP.

Call, C.T. (2008a), 'Ending wars, building states', in Charles T. Call with Vanessa Wyeth (eds), *Building States to Build Peace*, Boulder, CO: Lynne Rienner, 1–22.

Call, C.T. and W. Stanley (2002), 'Civilian security', in Stephen John Stedman, Donald Rothchild and Elizabeth Cousens (eds), *Ending Civil Wars: The Implementation of Peace Agreements*, Boulder, CO, and London: Lynne Rienner, 303–326.

Call, C.T. with V. Wyeth (eds) (2008b), *Building States to Build Peace*, Boulder, CO: Lynne Rienner.

Cammack, P. (2007), *Forget the Transnational State*, Papers in the Politics of Global Competitiveness 3, Manchester: Manchester Metropolitan University.

Caplan, R. (2005), *International Governance of War-Torn Territories*, Oxford: Oxford University Press.

Caplan, R. (2010), *The ICJ's Advisory Opinion on Kosovo*, USIP Peace Brief 55, Washington, DC, 17 September.

Carnagey, N.L., C.A. Anderson and B.J. Bushman (2007), 'The effect of video game violence on physiological desensitization to real-life violence', *Journal of Experimental Social Psychology*, 43/4, 684.

Carnahan, M., W. Durch and S. Gilmore (2006), *Economic Impact of Peacekeeping: Final Report*, New York: United Nations Department of Peacekeeping Operations.

Carothers, T. (2006), 'The rule of law revival', in Thomas Carothers (ed.), *Promoting the Rule of Law Abroad: In Search for Knowledge*, Washington, DC: Carnegie Endowment for International Peace, 3–13.

CAVR (Comissão de Acolhimento, Verdade e Reconciliação) (2005), *Chega! Final Report of the Commission for Reception, Truth and Reconciliation*, Dili: CAVR.

CDI (Center for Defense Information) (2007), *Georgia*, Washington, DC: CDI.

Central Intelligence Agency (2010), *World Fact Book*, available at www.cia.gov/library/publications/the-world-factbook/geos/iz.html, accessed 15 February 2012.

Chabal, P. and J.P. Daloz (1999), *Africa Works*, Bloomington, IN: Indiana University Press.

Chand, S. and R. Coffman (2008), *How soon can Donors Exit from Post-Conflict States?* Center for Global Development Working Paper 141, Washington, DC: Center for Global Development.

Chandler, D. (2006), *Empire in Denial: The Politics of State-Building*, London: Pluto.

Chandler, D. (2010), *International Statebuilding: The Rise of Post-Liberal Governance*, London: Routledge.

Chandrasekaran, R. (2007), *Imperial Life in the Emerald City: Inside Baghdad's Green Zone*, London: Bloomsbury.

Chang, H.-J. (2007), *Bad Samaritans: The Guilty Secrets of Rich Nations and their Threat to Global Prosperity*, London: Random House.

Chatterjee, P. (2009), 'An inside look at nepotism and corruption in Karzai's Afghanistan', *TomDespatch*, 18 November.

Cheng, C. (2011), 'Extralegal groups, natural resources, and statebuilding in post-conflict Liberia', D.Phil. dissertation, University of Oxford.

Cheng, C.S. and D. Zaum (eds) (2011a), *Post-Conflict Peacebuilding and Corruption: Selling the Peace?* London: Routledge.

Cheng, C.S. and D. Zaum (2011b), 'Selling the peace? Corruption and post-conflict peacebuilding', in C.S Cheng and D. Zaum (eds), *Post-Conflict Peacebuilding and Corruption: Selling the Peace?* London: Routledge, 1–26.

Chesterman, S. (2005), 'Imposed constitutions, imposed constitutionalism, and ownership', *Connecticut Law Review*, 37/4, 947–954.

Chivvis, C. (2008), 'The making of Macedonia', *Survival*, 50/2, 141–162.

Civil.ge (2010), 'US official: "We have no arms embargo on Georgia"', 10 June, available at www.civil.ge, accessed 16 February 2012.

Civil.ge (2011), 'EU chief negotiator speaks of association agreement talks with Georgia', 18 May, available at www.civil.ge, accessed 16 February 2012.

Clark, H. (2000), *Civil Resistance in Kosovo*, London: Pluto Press.

Claude, Inis L. (1966), 'Collective legitimization as a political function of the United Nations', *International Organization*, 20/3, 367–379.

Claude, Inis L. (1984), *Swords into Plowshares*, 4th edn, New York: McGraw-Hill.

Claude, Inis L. (1996), 'Peace and security: Prospective roles for the two United Nations', *Global Governance*, 3/2, 289–298.

Cleary, P. (2007), *Shakedown: Australia's Grab for Timor Oil*, Crows Nest, Australia: Allen & Unwin.

Cliffe, S. (2000), 'The joint assessment mission and reconstruction in East Timor', in J. Fox and D. Soares Babo (eds), *Out of the Ashes: The Destruction and Reconstruction of East Timor*, Adelaide, Australia: Crawford Press, 237–243.

CNRT (1999), *Diagrama Para Transição Em Timor*, Dili, 15 September.

CNRT (2000a), *Outcomes of the CNRT National Congress 21–30 August 2000*, Dili.

CNRT (2000b), *Processo Global até à Declaração da Independência de Timor Leste*, Dili, 20 November.

CNRT (2001), *Declaração Final, Encontro de Quadros do CNRT*, Balide, Dili, 17 January.

Comissão de Inquérito Independente para as F-FDTL (2004), *Relatório*, Dili.

Cockayne, J. and A. Lupel (eds) (2011), *Peace Operations and Organized Crime: Enemies or Allies*, London: Routledge.

Cole, J. (2009), 'Iraqi parliament passes electoral law', available at www.juancole. com/, accessed 9 November 2009.

Cole J. (2010), 'Iraq: National unity government or return to sectarianism?' available at www.juancole.com/, accessed 27 March 2010.

Colletta, N. and R. Muggah (2010), 'Context matters: Interim stabilization and second generation disarmament, demobilization and reintegration', *Conflict, Security and Development*, 9/4, 425–453.

Collier, D., L. Elliot, H. Hegre, A. Hoeffler, M. Reynal-Querol and N. Sambanis (2003), *Breaking the Conflict Trap: Civil War and Development Policy*, Washington, DC: World Bank.

Collier, P. (1996), 'The role of the African state in building agencies of restraint', in Mats Lundahl and Benno J. Ndulu (eds), *New Directions in Development Economics: Growth, Environmental Concerns, and Government in the 1990s*, London and New York: Routledge, 282–298.

Collier, Paul (2011), 'Haiti's rise from the rubble', *Foreign Affairs*, September.

Collier, P. and A. Hoeffler (2004), 'Greed and grievance in civil wars', *Oxford Economic Papers*, 56/4, 563–595.

Cook, N. (2007), *Liberia's Post-war Recovery: Key Issues and Developments*, Washington, DC: Congressional Research Service.

Cooley, A. and L. Mitchell (2009), 'No way to treat our friends: Recasting recent U.S.– Georgia relations', *Washington Quarterly*, 32/1, 27–41.

Cooley, A. and J. Ron (2002), 'The NGO scramble: Organizational insecurity and the political economy of transnational action', *International Security*, 27/1, 5–39.

Cooper, N. (2007), 'On the crisis of the liberal peace', *Conflict Security and Development*, 7/4, 605–616.

Cooper, N., M. Turner and M. Pugh (2011), 'The end of history and the last liberal peacebuilder: A reply to Roland Paris', *Review of International Studies*, 37/4, 1995–2007.

Cordesman, A.H. with A. Mausner and L. Derby (2010), *Iraq and the United States: Creating a Strategic Partnership*, Washington, DC: Centre for Strategic and International Studies.

Corpora, C.A. (2004), 'The untouchables: Former Yugoslavia's clandestine political economy', *Problems of Post-Communism*, 51/3: 61–68.

Council of Europe (2003), 'Evaluation report on Bosnia and Herzegovina', Strasbourg, 11 July.

Council of the European Union (2005), 'A strategy for the external dimension of JHA: Global freedom, security, and justice', Brussels, 11 November.

Council of the European Union (2008), 'Council joint action 2008/124/CSFP on the European Union rule of law mission in Kosovo, EULEX Kosovo', Brussels, 4 February.

Cousens, E.M., C. Kumar and K. Wermester (eds) (2000), *Peacebuilding as Politics: Cultivating Peace in Fragile Societies*, Boulder, CO: Lynne Rienner.

Cramer, C. (2006), *Civil War is Not a Stupid Thing: Accounting for Violence in Developing Countries*, London: Hurst.

Crawford, G. (2006), 'The World Bank and good governance: Rethinking the state or consolidating neo-liberalism?' in A. Paloni and M. Zanardi (eds), *The IMF, World Bank and Policy Reform*, Abingdon: Routledge, 115–141.

Crisis Group (2004), *Afghanistan: From Presidential to Parliamentary Elections*, Kabul/Brussels: Crisis Group.

Cronje, S., M. Ling and A. Cronje (1976), *LONHRO: Portrait of a Multinational*, Harmondsworth: Penguin.

CSDG (Conflict, Security and Development Group) (2003), *A Review of Peace Operations: A Case for Change*, London: King's College London.

Ćulafić, Z. (2002), 'Customs in Kosovo', UNMIK on Air, 4 February, available at www.unmikonline.org/radio/scripts/Englsh/february04/021604.htm, accessed 17 December 2011.

Curtis, D. (2005), 'Memo on research findings (post-conflict governance)', Paper presented to Workshop on Post-Conflict State Building: The Academic Research, New York: Graduate Center, City University of New York, November.

Curtis, D. (2007), 'Transitional governance in the Democratic Republic of Congo (DRC), and Burundi', in K. Guttieri and J. Piombo (eds), *Interim Governments: Institutional Bridges to Peace and Democracy?* Washington, DC: United States Institute of Peace, 171–194.

Czaplinski M. (2008), 'Conflict prevention and the issue of Higher Education in the mother tongue: The case of the Republic of Macedonia', *Security and Human Rights*, 19/4, 260–272.

da Silva, K.C. (2007), 'A Bíblia como Constituição ou a Constituição como Bíblia? Projetos para a construção do Estado-Nação em Timor-Leste', *Horizontes Antropológicos*, 13/27, 213–235.

da Silva, K.C. (2008), 'A cooperação internacional como dádiva: Algumas aproximações', *Mana*, 14/1, 141–171.

Dagher, S. (2009), 'Iraqi report on corruption cites prosecutors' barriers', *New York Times*, 6 May, available at www.nytimes.com/2009/05/06/world/middleeast/06iraq.html, accessed 10 July 2012.

Daly, M. (2007), *Darfur's Sorrow: A History of Destruction and Genocide*, Cambridge: Cambridge University Press.

Daniel, S. (2006), 'Afghanistan: "Résister aux talibans? A quoi bon!"', *Le Nouvel Observateur*, 10 August.

Daskalovski, Z. (2004), 'Democratic consolidation and the "stateness" problem: The case of Macedonia', *Ethnopolitics*, 3/2, 52–66.

Dawisha, A. and L. Diamond (2006), 'Iraq's year of voting dangerously', *Journal of Democracy*, 17/2, 89–103.

De Coning, C. (2008), 'The coherence dilemma in peacebuilding and post-conflict reconstruction system', *African Journal of Conflict Resolution*, 8/3, 85–110.

De Mars, W., P.D. Gaffney, R. Vayrynen and J. Leatherman (1999), *Breaking Cycles of Violence: Conflict Prevention in Intrastate Crises*, West Hartford, CT: Kumarian Press.

de Mello, S.V. (2000), 'Near verbatim transcript of address of the Special Representative of the Secretary-General, Sergio Vieira de Mello, at the 1st CNRT Congress', 21 August, Dili.

de Mello, S.V. (2001), 'UNTAET: Lessons to learn for future United Nations peace operations', Presentation to the Oxford University European Affairs Society, 26 October.

de Mello, S.V. (2002), 'UNTAET: Debriefing and lessons for the future', UNITAR-IPA-JIIA Conference, Tokyo, 16–18 September.

De Soto, Á. and G. del Castillo (1994), 'Obstacles to peacebuilding', *Foreign Policy*, 94, 69–83.

de Waal, A. (2009), 'Missions without end? Peacekeeping in the African political marketplace', *International Affairs*, 85/1, 99–113.

del Castillo, G. (2008), *Rebuilding War-Torn States: The Challenge of Post-Conflict Economic Reconstruction*, Oxford and New York: Oxford University Press.

Department of Defense (2009), 'Measuring stability and security in Iraq; June 2009', Report to Congress in accordance with the Department of Defense Supplemental Appropriations Act 2008, (Section 9204, Public Law 110–252).

DFID (2008), *UK Assessment and Proposed Support in the Rule of Law Sector in Kosovo*, London: Department for International Development.

Diamond, L. (1997), 'Introduction: In search of consolidation', in Larry Diamond, Marc F. Plattner, Yun-han Chu and Hung-mao Tien (eds), *Consolidating the Third Wave Democracies: Themes and Perspectives*, Baltimore, MD, and London: Johns Hopkins University Press: xii–l.

Diamond, L. (1999), *Developing Democracy: Towards Consolidation*, Baltimore, MD: Johns Hopkins University Press.

Diamond, L. (2005), *Squandered Victory: The American Occupation and the Bungled Effort to Bring Democracy to Iraq*, New York: Times Books.

Diamond, L. (2006), 'What civil war looks like: Slide rules', *New Republic*, 13 March.

Diario Nacional (2011), 'Prof. Jeffry Sachs, Osan Mina rai tenki investe ba Desenvolvimentu', 13 July.

Divjak, B. and M. Pugh (2011), 'The political economy of corruption in Bosnia and Herzegovina', in C.S. Cheng and D. Zaum (eds), *Corruption and Post-Conflict Peacebuilding: Selling the Peace?* London: Routledge, 99–113.

Dobbins, J. (2008), *After the Taliban: Nation-building in Afghanistan*, Washington, DC: Potomac Books.

Dobbins, J., K. Crane, S.G. Jones, A. Rathmell, B. Steele and R. Teltschik (2005a), *The UN's Role in Nation-Building: From the Congo to Iraq*, Santa Monica, CA: Rand Corporation.

Dobbins, J., J.G. McGinn, K. Crane, S. Jones, R. Lal, A. Rathmell, R. Swanger and A. Timilsina (2005b), *America's Role in Nation-Building: From Germany to Iraq*, Santa Monica, CA: Rand Corporation.

Dobbins, J., S.G. Jones, B. Runkle and S. Mohandas (2009), *Occupying Iraq: A History of the Coalition Provisional Authority*, Santa Monica, CA: Rand Corporation.

Dodge, T. (2005), 'Iraq transitions: From regime change to state collapse', *Third World Quarterly*, 26/4, 699–715.

Dodge, T. (2006), 'The Sardinian, the Texan and the Tikriti: Gramsci, the comparative autonomy of the Middle Eastern state and regime change in Iraq', *International Politics*, 43/4, 453–473.

Dodge, T. (2008), 'Iraq and the next American president', *Survival: Global Politics and Strategy*, 50/5, 37–60.

Dodge, T. (2010a), 'Iraq's perilous political carve-up', available at www.iiss.org/whats-new/iiss-voices/?blogpost=91, accessed 12 December 2011.

Dodge, T. (2010b), 'The failure of sanctions and the evolution of international policy towards Iraq; 1990–2003', *Contemporary Arab Affairs*, 3/1, 83–91.

Donais, T. (2004), 'Policing Human Security: The International Police Task Force and Peacebuilding in Bosnia' *Human Security Fellowship Research Paper*, Canadian Consortium on Human Security.

Downs, A. (1957), *An Economic Theory of Democracy*, New York: Harper and Row.

Doyle, M. and N. Sambanis (2006), *Making War and Building Peace: United Nations Peace Operations*, Princeton, NJ: Princeton University Press.

Dubois, L. (2012), *Haiti: The Aftershocks of History*, New York: Metropolitan Books.

Duchene, F. (1972), 'Europe's role in world peace', in R. Mayne (ed.), *Europe Tomorrow: Sixteen European Look Ahead*, London: Fontana, 32–47.

Duffield, M. (2007), *Security, Development and Unending War, Governing the World of Peoples*, Cambridge: Polity.

Dupuy, A. (2005), 'From Jean-Bertrand Aristide to Gerard Latortue: The unending crisis of democratization in Haiti', *Journal of Latin American and Caribbean Anthropology*, 10/1, 186–205.

Durch, W.J. (1993), 'The UN operation in the Congo: 1960–64', in W.J. Durch (ed.), *The Evolution of UN Peacekeeping: Case Studies and Comparative Analysis*, Basingstoke: Macmillan, 315–352.

Duverger, M. (1954), *Political Parties: Their Organization and Activity in the Modern State*, New York: Wiley.

Dwan, R. and L. Bailey (2006), *Liberia's Governance and Economic Management Assistance Programme (GEMAP): A Joint Review by the Department of Peacekeeping Operations' Peacekeeping Best Practices Section and the World Bank's Fragile States Group*, New York: UN DPKO.

East Timor Joint Assessment Mission (1999a), *Annex 1: Summary*, Washington, DC: World Bank.

East Timor Joint Assessment Mission (1999b), *Macro-Economics Background Paper*, Washington, DC: World Bank.

East Timor Joint Assessment Mission (1999c), *Governance Background Paper*, Washington, DC: World Bank.

EBRD (2010), *Georgia: Overview*, available at www.ebrd.com/pages/country/georgia.shtml, accessed 12 December 2011.

Economides, S. and J. Ker-Lindsay (2010), 'Forging EU foreign policy unity from diversity: The "unique case" of the Kosovo status talks', *European Foreign Affairs Review*, 15/4, 495–510.

Economist (2001), 'Macedonia: No outside police? No peace. Violence will surely break out again if no outside force stays to prevent it', London, 13 September.

Economist (2009a), 'Kosovo and media freedom: No criticism, please', London, 2 July.

Economist (2009b), 'Sudan: Political economy of the Comprehensive Peace Agreement', London, 11 July.

Economist (2011a), 'A lobster pot of troubles', London, 4 June.

Economist (2011b), 'The Queensway syndicate and the Africa trade', London, 13 August.

ECOWAS (1991), *Brief Declaration of ECOWAS Political Principles*, Lagos: Executive Secretariat of ECOWAS.

ECOWAS (2001), *Protocol on Democracy and Good Governance: Supplementary to the Protocol Relating to the Mechanism for Conflict Prevention, Management, Resolution, Peacekeeping and Security*, A/Sp1/12/01, Abuja: ECOWAS Commission.

ECOWAS (2008), *ECOWAS Conflict Prevention Framework, Regulation*/MSC/REG.1/01/08, Abuja: ECOWAS Commission.

ECOWAS (2009), '16th EU-ECOWAS ministerial troika meeting communiqué', Abuja, 11 November.

ECOWAS Commission (2010), 'Extra-ordinary session of the authority of heads of state and government, final communiqué', Abuja, 20 September.

ECOWAS Commission (2011), '39th ordinary session of the authority of heads of state and government, final communiqué', Abuja, 23–24 March.

Edwards, B. and I. Watson (2003), 'Confrontation between warlords in Afghanistan', *Morning Edition*, National Public Radio, 5 November.

Eide, K. (2005), 'A comprehensive review of the situation in Kosovo', UN doc. S/2005/635, 7 October.

Eigen, P. (2007), 'Fighting corruption in a global economy: Transparency initiatives in the oil and gas industry', *Houston Journal of International Law*, 29/2, 327–354.

EITI (2011), 'EITI fact sheet', available at http://eiti.org/files/2011-05-03_English_FactSheet.pdf, accessed 20 July 2011.

El-Affendi, A. (1991), *Turabi's Revolution: Islam and Power in Sudan*, London: Grey Seal.

El-Battahani, A. (1996a), *Economic Transformation and Political Islam in Sudan, 1975–1989*, Working Paper 5/96, University of Helsinki: Institute of Development Studies.

El-Battahani, A. (1996b), *The Social and Political Impact of Economic Liberalization and Social Welfare in Sudan*, Working Paper 6/96, University of Helsinki: Institute of Development Studies.

Elkins, Z., T. Ginsberg and J. Melton (2008), 'Baghdad, Tokyo, Kabul...: Constitution making in occupied states', *William and Mary Law Review*, 49/4, 1139–1179.

Elliott, D.J. (2010), 'Iraq Order of Battle', http://home.comcast.net/~djyae/site/?/page/Iraq_Order_of_Battle/, accessed 17 February 2012.

Ellis, S. (1999), *The Mask of Anarchy*, London: Hurst and Co.

Ellis, S. (2005), 'How to rebuild Africa', *Foreign Affairs*, 84/5, 135–148.

Elster, J., C. Offe and U. Klaus Preuss (1998), *Institutional Design in Post-Communist Societies: Rebuilding the Ship at Sea*, Cambridge: Cambridge University Press.

Erlich, V.St. (1966), *Family in Transition: A Study of 300 Yugoslav Villages*, Princeton, NJ: Princeton University Press.

Emerson, M. (2009), *Recalibrating EU Policy Towards the Western Balkans*, CEPS Policy Paper 175, Brussels: Centre for European Policy Studies.

ESI (European Stability Initiative) (1999), *Reshaping International Priorities in Bosnia and Herzegovina: Part I, Bosnian Power Structures*, Brussels/Sarajevo/Berlin: ESI.

ESI (European Stability Initiative) (2000), *Reshaping International Priorities in Bosnia and Herzegovina: Part II: International Power in Bosnia and Herzegovina*, Brussels/Sarajevo/Berlin: ESI.

ESI (European Stability Initiative) (2002), *De-industrialisation and its Consequences: A Kosovo Story*, Prishtina/Berlin: ESI.

ESI (European Stability Initiative) (2004), *The Lausanne Principle: Multiethnicity, Territory and the Future of Kosovo's Serbs*, Prishtina: ESI.

ESI (European Stability Initiative) (2005), *The Helsinki Moment: European Member-State Building in the Balkans*, Brussels/Sarajevo/Berlin: ESI.

ESI (European Stability Initiative) (2006), *Kicevo: A Case Study of Ohrid Agreement Implementation*, Berlin: ESI.

ESI (European Stability Initiative) (2009), *Cutting the Lifeline: Migration, Families, and the Future of Kosovo*, Berlin: ESI.

ESI (European Stability Initiative) (2010), *Radmila Sekerinska: Earning EU Candidate Status for Macedonia*, Berlin: ESI.

Etzioni, A. (2004), 'A self-restrained approach to nation-building by foreign powers', *International Affairs*, 80/1, 1–17.

EULEX (2009), *EULEX Programme Report June 2009*, Prishtina: EULEX.

European Commission (2003), *A Secure Europe in a Better World: European Security Strategy*, Brussels: EU.

European Commission (2004), *The Stabilisation and Association Processes for South-East Europe: Third Annual Report*, Brussels: EU.

European Commission (2006), *European Neighbourhood Policy: EU-Georgia Action Plan*, Brussels: EC.

European Commission (2007a), *Multi-Annual Indicative Planning Document for Kosovo (under UNSCR 1244), 2007–2009*, Brussels: EC.

European Commission (2007b), *European Neighbourhood Partnership Instrument (Georgia): Country Strategy Paper, 2007–13*, Brussels: EC

European Commission (2009), *Kosovo under UNSCR 1244/99 Progress Report*, Brussels: EC.

European Commission (2010a), *The Former Yugoslav Republic of Macedonia 2010 Progress Report*, COM(2010)660, 9 November.

European Commission (2010b), *Kosovo 2010 Progress Report*, Brussels, 9 November.

European Commission/World Bank (2002), 'FRY Macedonia: Donors' meeting', Brussels, 12 March.

European Commission/World Bank (2008a), 'Kosovo: Donors' conference prospectus', Brussels, 11 July.

European Commission/World Bank (2008b), 'Georgia: Donors' conference', Brussels, 22 October.

European Council (1993), 'Presidency conclusions', Copenhagen, 21–22 June.

European Council (2003), 'A secure Europe in a better world', Brussels, 12 December.

European Council (2005), 'EUJUST LEX/Iraq', available at www.consilium.europa.eu/eeas/security-defence/eu-operations/eujust-lex.aspx?lang=en, accessed 12 December 2011.

Fadel, L. and K. DeYoung (2010), 'Ayad Allawi's bloc wins most seats in Iraqi parliamentary elections', *Washington Post*, 27 March.

Fairbanks, C. (2010), 'Georgia's Soviet legacy', *Journal of Democracy*, 21/1, 144–151.

Fakiolas, F.T. and N. Tzifakis (2008), 'Transformation or accession? Reflecting on the EU's strategy towards the Western Balkans', *European Foreign Affairs Review*, 13/3, 377–398.

Faraj, S. (2010), 'Iraq election officials bar nearly 500 candidates from poll', *Associated French Press*, 15 January.

Farer, T.J. (1999), *Transnational Crime in the Americas: An Inter-American Dialogue Book*, New York: Routledge.

Fearon, J. and D. Laitin (2004), 'Neotrusteeship and the problem of weak states', *International Security*, 28/4, 5–43.

Fearon, J., M. Humphreys and J.M. Weinstein (2009), *Development Assistance, Institution Building, and Social Cohesion after Civil War: Evidence from a Field Experiment in Liberia*, Working Paper 194 (December), Washington: Center on Global Development.

Feijó, R. (2006), *Timor: Paisagem Tropical com Gente Dentro: Ensaios de Análise Política sobre a Construção da Democracia Timorense*, Lisbon: Campo da Comunicação.

Feldman, N. (2004), *What We Owe Iraq: War and the Ethics of Nation Building*, Princeton, NJ: Princeton University Press.

Feldman, N. (2005), 'Imposed constitutionalism', *Connecticut Law Review*, 37/4, 857–890.

Fifield, A. and A. England (2009), 'Fall in revenues threatens Iraq security plans', *Financial Times*, 25 March.

Filkins, D. (2010), 'Karzai is said to doubt west can defeat Taliban', *New York Times*, 11 June.

Firger, D. (2010), 'Transparency and the natural resource curse: Examining the new extraterritorial information forcing rules in the Dodd-Frank Wall Street Reform Act of 2010', *Georgetown Journal of International Law*, 41, 1043–1096.

Fjelde, H. and I. De Soysa (2009), 'Coercion, co-optation, or cooperation? State capacity and the risk of civil war, 1961–2004', *Conflict Management and Peace Science*, 26/1, 5–25.

Flint, J. and A. de Waal (2005), *Darfur: A Short History of a Long War*, London: Zed Books.

Flores, T.E. and I. Nooruddin (2009a), 'Financing the peace: Evaluating World Bank post-conflict assistance programs', *Review of International Organization*, 4/1, 1–27.

Flores, T.E. and I. Nooruddin (2009b), 'Voting for peace: Do post-conflict elections help recovery?' manuscript, George Mason University and Ohio State University.

Fonseca, J. (2001), 'Komentar tentang Proses Konstitusi dan Pemilihan', National Council Public Hearings, 20 January.

Forna, A. (2009), 'Tourism will not be a quick fix for Sierra Leone', *Guardian*, 13 May.

Foschini F. (2010), '2010 elections (35): How the west was won', *Afghan Analyst Network*.

Foucault, M. (2004 [2010]), *The Birth of Biopolitics: Lectures at the College de France, 1978–1979*, Basingstoke: Palgrave Macmillan.

Freedom House (2010), *Nations in Transit 2010*, Washington, DC: Freedom House.

Freedman, L. and E. Karsh (1993), *The Gulf Conflict: 1990–1991*, London: Faber & Faber.

Fretilin (1998), *Documentos Aprovados na Conferência Extraordinária da Fretilin, em Sydney 14–20 August 1998, Manual e Programas Políticos*, Dili.

Fretilin (2000), *Conferência Geral de Quadros*, Dili, 15–20 May.

Fretilin Central Committee (2006), *Análise da situação e Perspectivas*, Dili, 29 October.

Fretilin.Media (2010), 'Bancada Fretilin Nia Intervensaun Iha Enseramentu Debate Generalidade Orsamentu Recifikativu 2010', 25 June.

Fritz, V. and A.R. Menocal (2007), 'Developmental states in the new millennium: Concepts and challenges for a new aid agenda', *Development Policy Review*, 25/5, 531–552.

Fukuda-Parr, S., M. Ashwill, E. Chiappa and C. Messineo (2008), 'The conflict-development nexus: A survey of armed conflicts in Sub-Saharan Africa 1980–2006', *Journal of Peacebuilding and Development*, 4/1, 6–19.

Fuller, E. (2009), 'Georgia', in Freedom House, *Nations in Transit 2009*, New York: Freedom House, 211.

Galbraith, P.W (2001), 'Statement of Peter Galbraith, Cabinet Minister, Political Affairs and Timor Sea, Standing Committee on Political Affairs, Public Hearings on the Political Transition Calendar', 20 January.

Gall, C. (2001), 'For Kosovars, battle moves to the border of Macedonia', *New York Times*, 25 February.

Gardizi, M., K. Hussmann and Y. Torabi (2010), *Corrupting the State or State-Crafted Corruption? Exploring the Nexus between Corruption and Subnational Governance*, Kabul: AREU.

Gatehouse, G. (2010), '"No fraud found" as Iraq election recount ends', *BBC News*, 14 May, available at http://news.bbc.co.uk/2/hi/middle_east/8684071.stm accessed 17 February 2012.

Ghani, A. and C. Lockhart (2008), *Fixing Failed States*, New York: Oxford University Press.

Ghani, A., C. Lockhart, N. Nehan and B. Massoud (2007), 'The budget as the linchpin of the state: Lessons from Afghanistan', in J.K. Boyce and M. O'Donnell (eds), *Peace and the Public Purse: Economic Policies for Postwar Statebuilding*, Boulder, CO, and London: Lynne Rienner, 153–184.

Gharekhan, Chinmaya R. (2006), *The Horseshoe Table: An Inside View of the UN Security Council*, New York: Longman.

Giegerich, B. (2008), *European Military Crisis Management: Connecting Ambition and Reality*, Adelphi Paper 397, London: Routledge for IISS.

Gillies, A. (2010), 'Reputational concerns and the emergence of oil sector transparency as an international norm', *International Studies Quarterly*, 54/1, 103–126.

Gillies, A. and P. Dykstra (2011), 'International campaigns for extractive industry transparency in post-conflict settings', in C. Cheng and D. Zaum (eds), *Corruption and Post-Conflict Peacebuilding: Selling the Peace*, Abingdon: Routledge, 239–258.

Gilpin, R. (1987), *The Political Economy of International Relations*, Princeton, NJ: Princeton University Press.

Giustozzi, A. (2004), *Good State vs. Bad Warlords? A Critique of State-building Strategies in Afghanistan*, Crisis States Programme, Working Paper 51, LSE, London.

Giustozzi, A. (2007), 'War and peace economies of Afghanistan's strongmen', *International Peacekeeping*, 14/1, 75–89.

Giustozzi, A. (2008a), *Koran, Kalashnikov, and Laptop: The Neo-Taliban Insurgency in Afghanistan*, London: Hurst.

Giustozzi, A. (2008b), 'Bureaucratic façade and political realities of disarmament and demobilisation in Afghanistan', *Conflict, Security and Development*, 8/2, 169–192.

Giustozzi, A. (2008c), 'Afghanistan: Political parties or militia fronts?' in Jacob de Zeeuw (ed.), *From Soldiers to Politicians: Transforming Rebel Movements after Civil War*, Boulder, CO: Lynne Rienner, 179–202.

Giustozzi, A. (ed.) (2009a), *Decoding the New Taliban: Insights from the Afghan Field*, London: Hurst.

Giustozzi, A. (2009b), *Empires of Mud: Wars and Warlords of Afghanistan*, London: Hurst.

Giustozzi, A. (2009c), 'The Afghan national army unwarranted hope?' *RUSI Journal*, 154, 36–42.

Giustozzi, A. (2010a), *The Taliban beyond the Pashuns*, Waterloo, Ontario: CIGI.

Giustozzi, A. (2010b), *Negotiating with the Taliban: Issues and Prospects*, New York: Century Foundation.

Giustozzi, A. (2012), 'Auxiliary irregular forces in Afghanistan: 1978–2008', in M. Innes (ed.), *Making Sense of Proxy Warfare: States, Surrogates, and the Use of Force*, Washington, DC: Potomac Books, 89–109.

Giustozzi, A. and Christoph Reuter (2010), *The Northern Front: The Afghan Insurgency Spreading beyond the Pashtuns*, Kabul: Afghan Analyst Network.

Glanz, A. and R. Mohammed (2008), 'Premier of Iraq is quietly firing fraud monitors', *New York Times*, 18 November.

Global Infrastructure Holding Limited (2005), 'Petitioners' answering affidavit to respondents' returns', 30 May.

Global Witness (2006), *Heavy Mittal? A State within a State: The Inequitable Mineral Development Agreement between the Government of Liberia and Mittal Steel Holdings NV*, London: Global Witness.

Global Witness (2009), *Natural Resource Exploitation and Human Rights in the Democratic Republic of Congo, 1993 to 2003*, Global Witness Briefing Paper, London: Global Witness.

Global Witness (2010), 'U.S. passes landmark reforms on resource transparency', Press Release, 15 July, available at www.globalwitness.org/sites/default/files/pdfs/reformbill.pdf accessed 14 September 2011.

Global Witness (2011), *Oil Revenues in Angola: Much More Information but not Enough Transparency*, London: Global Witness.

Gluck, J. (2009), 'Iraq's constitutional review committee delivers its final report to parliament', available at www.comparativeconstitutions.org, accessed 17 February 2012.

Goldberg, S. (2003), 'Everywhere and nowhere, Saddam retains his grip on Baghdad's imagination', *Guardian*, 9 October.

Goodhand, J. (2004), 'Afghanistan in Central Asia', in Michael Pugh and Neil Cooper (eds), *War Economies in a Regional Context: Challenges of Transformation*, Boulder, CO: Lynne Rienner, 45–89.

Goodhand, J. (2011), 'Corruption or consolidating the peace? The drugs economy and post-conflict peacebuilding in Afghanistan', in C. Cheng and D. Zaum (eds), *Post-Conflict Peacebuilding and Corruption: Selling the Peace*, London: Routledge, 144–161.

Goodhand, J. and M. Sedra (2010), 'Who owns the peace? Aid, reconstruction, and peacebuilding in Afghanistan', *Disasters*, 34, Issue Supplement s1, S78–S102.

Gordon, M. (2004), '"Catastrophic success": The strategy to secure Iraq did not foresee a 2nd war', *New York Times*, 19 October.

Gordy, E. (2004), 'Serbia after Djindjic: War crimes, organized crime, and trust in public institutions', *Problems of Post-Communism*, 51/3, 10–17.

Goulding, M. (1997), 'Practical measures to enhance the UN's effectiveness in the field of peace and security', Report to the Secretary-General, UN, 30 June.

Government of Haiti (2010), 'Haiti earthquake PDNA: Assessment of damage, losses, general and sectoral needs', Annex to the Action Plan for National Recovery and Development of Haiti, Port-au-Prince: GoH.

Government of Kosovo (2008), 'Medium-term expenditure framework 2009–2011', Prishtina, 12 June.

Graham-Brown, S. (1999), *Sanctioning Saddam: The Politics of Intervention in Iraq*, London: I.B. Tauris.

Gray, R. (1961), *A History of the Southern Sudan, 1839–1889*, London: Oxford University Press.

Grindle, M. (2004), 'Good enough governance: Poverty reduction and reform in developing countries', *Governance: An International Journal of Policy, Administration and Institutions*, 17/4, 525–548.

Guardian (2006), 'Corruption: The "second insurgency" costing US$4bn a year', 2 December, 16–17.

Guardian (2007), 'How the US sent $12bn in cash to Iraq: And watched it vanish', 8 February, 1–2.

Guardian (2011), 'Report identifies Hashim Thaci as "big fish" in organised crime', 24 January, 19.

Gusmão, X. (1988), 'Reajustamento Estrutural da Resistência e Proposta de Paz', in X. Gusmão (1994), *Timor Leste: Um Povo, Uma Pátria*, Lisbon: Edições Colibri.

Gusmão, X. (1989), 'Timor Leste: Algema de Lágrimas in', in X. Gusmão (1994), *Timor Leste: Um Povo, Uma Pátria*, Lisbon: Edições Colibri.

Gusmão, X. (2000), 'Kay Rala Xanana Gusmão, president of the CNRT/CN, New Year's message', 31 December, available at members.pcug.org.au/~wildwood/Jan-NewYear.htm, accessed 12 December 2011.

Gusmão, X. (2002), 'First Speech to the national parliament: Considering a policy of national reconciliation', 21 October, in X. Gusmão (2005), *Timor Lives! Speeches of Freedom and Independence*, Alexandria, Australia: Longueville Books.

Gusmão, X. (2011), 'A Transição de Timor-Leste do Conflito para a Estabilidade', Speech at DFID, London, 7 March

Habib, M. and L. Zurawicki (2002), 'Corruption and foreign direct investment', *Journal of International Business Studies*, 33/2, 291–307.

Haggard, S. and R. Kaufman (1995), *The Political Economy of Democratic Transitions*, Princeton, NJ: Princeton University Press.

Hallward, P. (2008), *Damming the Flood: Haiti, Aristide, and the Politics of Containment*, London: Verso Press.

Hamdi, A. (2005), 'Future foreign investment in Sudan', trans. Mohammed al-Tom, *Sudan Studies Association Newsletter*, 24, 1.

Hameiri, S. (2009), 'Capacity and its fallacies: International state building as state transformation', *Millennium-Journal of International Studies*, 38/1, 55–81.

Hanjan, R.M. (2002), 'Policy transfer within the United Nations transitional administration in East Timor: Local democratic institutions (the case of community empowerment project)', M.A. Thesis, Institute of Administration and Organization, University of Bergen.

Haq, A. (2010), 'Speech by the Special Representative of the Secretary-General for Timor-Leste and Head of UNMIT, Ms Ameerah Haq, Timor-Leste Development Partners Meeting 2010', 7 April.

Harley, G.W. (1941), *Notes on the Poro in Liberia*, Cambridge, MA: Museum Press.

Harris-White, B. (2003), *India Working: Essays on Society and Economy*, Cambridge: Cambridge University Press.

Hartzell, C. and M. Hoddie with M. Bauer (2010), 'Economic liberalization via IMF structural adjustment: Sowing the seeds of civil war?' *International Organization*, 64/2, 339–356.

Hayes, M. and G. Wheatley (1996), *Interagency and Political-Military Implications of Peace Operations: Haiti – A Case Study*, Washington, DC: National Defense University.

Heilbrunn, J.R. (2011), 'Post-conflict reconstruction, legitimacy, and anti-corruption commissions', in C. Cheng and D. Zaum (eds), *Corruption and Statebuilding: Selling the Peace*, London: Routledge, 201–217.

Helander, B. (2005), 'Who needs a state? Civilians, security and social services in North-East Somalia', in Paul Richards (ed.), *No Peace, No War: An Anthropology of Contemporary Armed Conflicts*, Oxford: James Curry, 193–202.

Hellman, J., G. Jones and D. Kaufmann (2000), *Seize the State, Seize the Day: State Capture, Corruption and Influence in Transition*, Washington, DC: World Bank.

Helmke, G. and S. Levitsky (2004), 'Informal institutions and comparative politics', *Perspective on Politics*, 2/4, 725–740.

Herbst, J. (1997), 'Responding to state failure in Africa', *International Security*, 21/3, 120–144.

Hicks, D. (1983), 'Unachieved syncretism: The local-level political system in Portuguese Timor, 1966–1967', *Anthropos*, 78/1–2, 17–40.

Hill, J.N.C. (2009), 'Challenging the failed state thesis: IMF and World Bank intervention and the Algerian civil war', *Civil Wars*, 11/1, 39–56.

Hislope, R. (2003), 'Between a bad peace and a good war: Insights and lessons from the almost-war in Macedonia', *Ethnic and Racial Studies*, 26/1, 129–151.

Hohe, T. (2004), 'Delivering feudal democracy in East Timor', in Edward Newman and Roland Rich (eds), *The UN Role in Promoting Democracy: Between Ideals and Reality*, Tokyo: United Nations University Press, 302–319.

Hohe, T. (2005), 'Developing local governance', in G. Junne and W. Verkoren (eds), *Post-conflict Development Meeting New Challenges*, Boulder, CO, and London: Lynne Rienner, 59–72.

Holsti K. (1996), *The State, War, and the State of War*, Cambridge: Cambridge University Press.

Hood, L. (2006), 'Security sector reform in East Timor, 1999–2004', *International Peacekeeping*, 13/1, 60–77.

Hope, K.R. (2010), 'Liberia's Governance and Economic Management Assistance Program (GEMAP): An impact review and analytical assessment of a donor policy intervention for democratic state-building in a post-conflict state', *South African Journal of International Affairs*, 17/2, 243–263.

Hope, C. and K. Cunningham (2011), 'WikiLeaks: Julian Assange could start publishing leaked details of Swiss bank tax accounts in two weeks', *Daily Telegraph*, 17 January.

Horowitz, D.L. (1985), *Ethnic Groups in Conflict*, Berkeley, CA: University of California Press.

Horowitz, D.L. (2002), 'Constitutional design: Proposals versus processes', in Andrew Reynolds (ed.), *The Architecture of Democracy: Constitutional Design, Conflict Management, and Democracy*, Oxford: Oxford University Press, 15–36.

Hounshell, B. (2010), 'The stressful relationship', *Foreign Policy*, 10 May.

Huesmann, L.R. and L. Kirwil (2007), 'Why observing violence increases the risk of violent behavior by the observer', in D.J. Flannery, A.T. Vazsonyi and I.D. Waldman (eds.), *The Cambridge Handbook of Violent Behavior and Aggression*, New York: Cambridge University Press: 545–570.

HRW (Human Rights Watch) (1995), *Georgia/Abkhazia: Violation of the Laws of War and Russia's Role in the Conflict*, New York: HRW.

HRW (Human Rights Watch) (2007), *Crossing the Line: Georgia's Violent Dispersal of Protestors and Raid on Imedi Television*, New York: HRW.

HRW (Human Rights Watch) (2010), *Transparency and Accountability in Angola: An Update*, New York: HRW.

Hutson, R. and A. Kolbe (2006), 'Human rights abuses and other criminal violations in Port-au-Prince, Haiti: A random survey of households', *Lancet*, 368/9538, 864–873.

Huyse, L. (2008), 'Introduction: Tradition-based approaches in peacemaking, transitional justice and reconciliation policies', in L. Huyse, and M. Salter (eds), *Traditional Justice and Reconciliation after Violent Conflict: Learning from African Experiences*, Stockholm: International Institute for Democracy and Electoral Assistance, 1–22.

ICG (International Crisis Group) (2002), *Implementing Equality: The 'Constituent Peoples' Decision in Bosnia and Herzegovina*, Sarajevo: ICG.

ICG (International Crisis Group) (2003), *Governing Iraq*, Baghdad: ICG.

ICG (International Crisis Group) (2004), *Rebuilding Liberia*, Brussels: ICG.

ICG (International Crisis Group) (2005), 'Spoiling Security in Haiti', Latin America/Caribbean Report No. 1, May.

ICG (International Crisis Group) (2008), *Kosovo's Fragile Transition*, Brussels/Prishtina: ICG.

ICG (International Crisis Group) (2009a), *Iraq's Provincial Elections: The Stakes*, No. 82 (January), Baghdad: ICG.

ICG (International Crisis Group) (2009b), *Serb Integration in Kosovo: Taking the Plunge*, Prishtina: ICG.

ICG (International Crisis Group) (2010a), *Loose Ends: Iraq's Security Forces between US Drawdown and Withdrawal*, Baghdad: ICG.

ICG (International Crisis Group) (2010b), 'Timor-Leste: Time for the UN to step back', Dili/Brussels, 15 December.

ICG (International Crisis Group) (2010c), *The Rule of Law in Independent Kosovo*, Brussels: ICG.

Ignatius, D. (2009), 'Behind the carnage in Baghdad', *Washington Post*, 25 August.

IISS (International Institute for Strategic Studies) (1999), 'Divided Macedonia: The next Balkan conflict?' *Strategic Comments*, 5/5, 1–2.

IISS (International Institute for Strategic Studies) (2009a), *The Military Balance*, London: IISS.

IISS (International Institute for Strategic Studies) (2009b), 'Iraq's provincial elections', *Strategic Comments*, 15/2, 1–2.

Ilievski Z. and D. Taleski (2009), 'Was the EU's role in conflict management in Macedonia a success?' *Ethnopolitics*, 8/3–4, 355–367.

IMF (International Monetary Fund) (2008), *Democratic Republic of Timor-Leste: 2008 Article IV Consultation*, Washington, DC: IMF.

IMF (International Monetary Fund) (2009a), 'Republic of Kosovo: IMF staff visit concluding statement', Prishtina, 24 June.

IMF (International Monetary Fund) (2009b), *Georgia: Third Review under the Standby Arrangement*, IMF Country Report 09–267, Washington, DC: IMF.

IMF (International Monetary Fund) (2011a), *Democratic Republic of Timor-Leste: 2010 Article IV Consultation*, Washington, DC: IMF.

IMF (International Monetary Fund) (2011b), *Georgia: Staff Report for the 2011 Article IV Consultation*, IMF Country Report 11/87, Washington, DC: IMF.

Innercity Press (2010), 'As UN quietly re-starts military help in Congo, says not with Zimulinda', 4 March, available at www.innercitypress.com/drc1leo030410.html, accessed 17 February 2012.

Irish Times (2001), 'NATO chief inspects arms collection mission', 29 August.

Islami, N. (2002), 'Mayor to lift lid on Kosovo corruption', Institute of War and Peace Reporting, BCR No. 332, 19 April.

Jabar, F.A. (2003), 'Sheikhs and ideologues: Deconstruction and reconstruction of tribes under patrimonial totalitarianism in Iraq; 1968–1998', in F.A. Jabar and H. Dawod (eds), *Tribes and Power: Nationalism and Ethnicity in the Middle East*, London: Saqi, 69–109.

Jabri, V. (2010), 'War, government, politics: A critical response to the hegemony of the liberal peace', in Oliver P. Richmond (ed.), *Palgrave Advances in Peacebuilding: Critical Development and Approaches*, Basingstoke: Palgrave Macmillan, 41–57.

Jahn, B. (2007), 'The tragedy of liberal diplomacy: Democratization, intervention, state-building, Part I and II', *Journal of Intervention and Statebuilding*, 1/1, 87–106, and 1/2, 211–229.

Jarstad, A. (2008), 'Power-sharing: Former enemies in joint government', in Anna K. Jarstad and Timothy D. Sisk (eds), *From War to Democracy: Dilemmas of Peacebuilding*, Cambridge: Cambridge University Press, 105–133.

Jasarević, L. (2006), 'Everyday work: Subsistence economy, social belonging and moralities of exchange at a Bosnian (black), market', in X. Bougarel, E. Helms and G. Duijzings (eds), *The New Bosnian Mosaic: Identities, Memories and Moral Claims in a Post-War Society*, Aldershot: Ashgate, 273–294.

Jean, F. and J.-C. Rufin (eds) (1996), *Économie des Guerres Civiles*, Paris: Hachette, Collection Pluriel.

Johnson, D. (2003), *The Root Causes of Sudan's Civil Wars*, Oxford: James Currey.

Johnson-Sirleaf, E. (2006), 'Inaugural Address', available at www.emansion.gov.lr/doc/inaugural_add_1.pdf, accessed 8 August 2011.

Johnston, M. (2010), 'First, do no harm – then build trust: Anti-corruption strategies in fragile situations', *World Development Report 2011 Background Paper*, available at http://wdr2011.worldbank.org/sites/default/files/pdfs/WDR%20Background%20 Paper%20-%20Johnston_0.pdf, accessed 12 March 2012.

Jones, B.G. (ed.) (2006), *Decolonising International Relations*, Lanham, MD: Rowman & Littlefield.

Jones, S., J. Wilson, A. Rathmell and K. Jack Riley (2005), *Establishing Law and Order after Conflict*, Santa Monica, CA: RAND Corporation.

Jovanovski, V. and L. Dulovi (2002), 'A new battlefield: The struggle to ratify the Ohrid Agreement', in Institute for War and Peace Reporting (IWPR), *Ohrid and Beyond: A Cross-ethnic Investigation into the Macedonian Crisis*, London: IWPR, 59–72.

Judah, T. (2002), *Kosovo: War and Revenge*, 2nd edn, New Haven, CT: Yale University Press.

Juhasz, A. (2004), 'The hand-over that wasn't: How the occupation of Iraq continues', *LeftTurn Magazine* (September/October), available at www.leftturn.org, accessed 17 February 2012.

Just Anti-Corruption (2010), 'Saakashvili protegé helped lead Georgia to war with Russia', 1 November.

Jutersonke, O., R. Muggah and D. Rodgers (2009), 'Gangs, urban violence and security interventions in Central America', *Security Dialogue*, 40/4–5, 373–397.

Kahler, M. (2008), 'Aid and state-building', Paper presented to the Workshop on Economic Aid Policy and Statebuilding, CUNY: The Graduate Center, 3–4 April.

Kang, S. (1999), 'IFIs' conditionality revisited at power dimension: A strategic bargaining model of IMF's conditions to loans to development countries', Paper presented to the Annual Conference of the International Studies Association, Washington, DC, 16–21 February.

Karl, T.L. (2007), 'Ensuring fairness: The case for a transparent fiscal social contract', in M. Humphreys, J. Sachs and J. Stiglitz (eds), *Escaping the Resource Curse*, New York: Columbia University Press, 256–285.

Keefer, P. (2005), *Programmatic Parties: Where Do They Come From and Do They Matter?* Washington, DC: World Bank working paper.

Keen, D. (1998), *The Economic Functions of Violence in Civil Wars*, Adelphi Paper 320, Oxford: Oxford University Press.

Keen, D. (2000), 'Incentives and disincentives for violence', in M. Berdal and D.M. Malone (eds), *Greed and Grievance: Economic Agendas in Civil Wars*, Boulder, CO: Lynne Rienner, 19–42.

Keen, D. and A. Adebajo (2007), 'Sierra Leone', in M. Berdal and S. Economides (eds), *United Nations Interventionism, 1991–2004*, Cambridge: Cambridge University Press, 246–273.

Kent, L. (2010), 'The politics of remembrance and victims' rights', in M. Leach, N. Canas Mendes, A.B. da Silva, A. da Costa Ximenes and B. Broughton (eds), *Hatene kona ba/Compreender/Understanding/Mengerti Timor-Leste*, Dili: Timor-Leste Studies Association, 190–195.

Keohane, R.O. (2003), 'Political authority after intervention: Gradations in sovereignty', in J.L. Holzgrefe and R.O. Keohane (eds), *Humanitarian Intervention: Ethical, Legal, and Political Dilemmas*, Cambridge: Cambridge University Press, 275–298.

Khalid, M. (ed.) (1987), *John Garang Speaks*, London: KPI.

Khan, M. (2010), 'Post-Oslo state-building strategies and their limitations', Yusif A. Sayigh Development Lecture 2010, Palestine Economic Policy Research Institute (MAS), Ramallah, 1 December (author's copy).

Khare, A. (2009), 'Peace building, state building and nation building in Timor-Leste', speech given at IRI/East West Center, 13 February.

Killick, T. (1998), *Aid and the Political Economy of Policy Change*, London: Routledge.

King, C. (2008), *The Ghost of Freedom*, Oxford: Oxford University Press.

King, I. and W. Mason (2006), *Peace at any Price: How the World Failed Kosovo*, London: Hurst.

Klein, N. (2007), *Shock Doctrine: The Rise of Disaster Capitalism*, New York: Metropolitan Books.

Kleinfeld Belton, R. (2005), *Competing Definitions of the Rule of Law: Implications for Practitioners*, Carnegie Papers No. 55.

Knack, S. (2002), 'World Bank approach: Second generation of indicators', as summarized in the report of the workshop on 'Measuring Democracy and Good Governance', Munich, Carl Duisberg Gesellschaft (CDG Munich), 21–23 January.

Kolbe, A. and R. Hutson (2006), 'Human rights abuse and other criminal violations in Port-au-Prince, Haiti: A random survey of households', *Lancet* 368/9538, 864–873.

Kolbe, A. and R. Muggah (2010), 'Surveying Haiti's post-quake needs: A quantitative approach', *Humanitarian Exchange*, 48, available at www.odihpn.org/report. asp?id=3131, accessed 10 July 2012.

Kolbe, A. and R. Muggah (2011a), 'Securing the state: Haiti before and after the earthquake', in *Small Arms Survey 2011: States of Security*, Cambridge: Cambridge University Press, 229–260.

Kolbe, Athena and Robert Muggah (2011b), 'Haiti: Why an accurate death toll matters', *Los Angeles Times*, 12 July, available at http://articles.latimes.com/2011/jul/12/opinion/la-oe-muggah-haiti-count-20110712, accessed 10 July 2012.

Kolbe, A., R.A. Huston, S. Harry, E. Trzcinski, B. Miles, N. Levitz, M. Puccio, L. James, J.R. Noel and R. Muggah (2010), 'Mortality, crime and access to basic needs before and after the Haiti earthquake: A random survey of Port-au-Prince households', *Medicine, Conflict and Survival*, 26/4, 281–297.

Korski, D. and Gowan, R. (2009), *Can the EU Rebuild Failing States? A Review of Europe's Civilian Capacities*, London: European Council on Foreign Relations.

Kosovar Stability Initiative (2008), *Image Matters: Deconstructing Kosovo's Image Problem*, Prishtina: IKS.

Kosovar Stability Initiative (2010), *Untying the Knot: The Political Economy of Corruption and Accountability in Kosovo*, Prishtina: IKS.

Kramer, A. (2011), 'In rebuilding Iraq's oil industry, U.S. subcontractors hold sway', *New York Times*, 16 June.

Kramer, H. and V. Dzihic (eds) (2005), *Die Kosovo Bilanz: Scheitert die international Gemeinschaft?* Vienna: Lit Verlag.

Krasner, S. (1999), *Sovereignty: Organised Hypocrisy*, Princeton, NJ: Princeton University Press.

Krastev, I. (2002), 'A moral economy of anti-corruption sentiments in Eastern Europe', in Y. Elkana, I. Krastev, E. Macamo and S. Randeria (eds), *Unravelling Ties: From Social Cohesion to New Practices of Connectedness*, Chicago, IL: University of Chicago Press, 99–116.

Krastev, I. (2007), 'The strange death of the liberal consensus', *Journal of Democracy*, 18/4, 56–63.

Kumar, K. (ed.) (1998), *Postconflict Elections, Democratization, and International Assistance*, Boulder, CO: Lynne Reiner.

Kwaje, S. (2005), *The Comprehensive Peace Agreement: A Summary Booklet*, Juba: Ministry for Information and Broadcasting.

Lamamra, R. (2009), 'Towards an AU policy on security sector reform', *African Executive*, 25, available at www.africanexecutive.com, accessed 17 February 2012.

Lar, J.T. (2009), *The ECOWAS SSR Agenda in West Africa: Looking Beyond Normative Frameworks*, KAIPTC Occasional Paper No. 24, Accra: Kofi Annan International Peacekeeping Training Centre.

Large, D. (ed.) (2005), *Corruption in Post-War Reconstruction: Confronting the Vicious Circle*, Beirut: Lebanese Transparency Association for TIRI.

Lasseter, T. (2009), 'Afghan drug trade thrives with help, and neglect, of officials', *McClatchy Newspapers*, 10 May.

Latal, S. (2010), 'Bosnia faces critical challenges in 2010', *Balkan Insight*, 21 January.

Lavenda, R. and E. Schultz (2007), 'Secret societies in Western Africa', *Supplemental Chapter Materials to Anthropology: What Does It Mean To Be Human?* available at www.oup.com/us/companion.websites/9780195189766/student_resources/Supp_chap_mats/Chapt07/Secret_Soc_West_Africa/?view=usa, accessed 12 March 2012.

Le Billon, P. (2011), 'Corrupting peace? Corruption, peacebuilding, and reconstruction', in C.S Cheng and D. Zaum (eds), *Corruption and Post-Conflict Peacebuilding: Selling the Peace?* London: Routledge, 62–79.

Le Billon, P. and C. de Freitas (2011), 'Resources for peace', Peacebuild Workshop on 'Natural resource conflicts and conflict transformation', Ottawa.

Lemarchand, R. (1996), *Burundi: Ethnic Conflict and Genocide*, Washington, DC: Woodrow Wilson Center.

Linklater, A. (2005), 'A European civilising process', in C. Hilland and M. Smith (eds), *International Relations and the European Union*, Oxford: Oxford University Press, 367–387.

Linz, J. and A. Stepan (1996), *Problems of Democratic Transition and Consolidation: Southern Europe, South America, and Post-Communist Europe*, Baltimore, MD: Johns Hopkins University Press.

Lister, S. (2005), *Caught in Confusion: Local Governance Structures in Afghanistan*, Kabul: Afghanistan Research and Evaluation Unit.

Looney, R. (2011), 'Reconstruction and peace building under extreme adversity: The problem of pervasive corruption in Iraq', in C.S Cheng and D. Zaum (eds), *Corruption and Post-Conflict Peacebuilding: Selling the Peace?* London: Routledge, 162–179.

Luciani, G. (1990), 'Allocation vs. production states: A theoretical framework', in G. Luciani (ed.), *The Arab State*, London: University of California Press: 68–84.

Lugar, R.G. (2008), 'Letter of transmittal', in U.S.F.R. Committee, *The Petroleum and Poverty Paradox: Assessing U.S. and International Community Efforts to Fight the Resource Curse*, Washington, DC: US Government Printing Office, v.

Lund, M. (2001), 'A toolbox for responding to conflict and building peace', in L. Reychler and T. Paffenholz (eds), *Peacebuilding: A Field Guide*, Boulder, CO: Lynne Rienner, 16–20.

Lusa (2009a), 'Nos últimos anos foi preciso comprar a paz', 27 August.

Lusa (2009b), 'MNE afirma que tiveram que comprar a paz', 15 January.

Lyons, T. (2005), *Demilitarizing Politics: Elections on the Uncertain Road to Peace*, Boulder, CO: Lynne Rienner.

McCarthy, R. (2003), 'Foreign firms to bid in huge Iraqi sale', *Guardian*, 22 September.

McClintock, E.A. and T. Nahimana (2008), 'Managing the tension between inclusionary and exclusionary processes: Building peace in Burundi', *International Negotiation*, 13/1, 73–91.

MacFarlane, S.N. (1998), 'On the front lines in the near abroad: The OSCE and the CIS in Georgia's civil wars', in Thomas G. Weiss (ed.), *Beyond UN Subcontracting: Task-Sharing with Regional Security Arrangements and Service Providing NGOs*, Basingstoke: Macmillan, 115–136.

MacFarlane, S.N. (2010), 'Colliding state building projects and regional insecurity in the former Soviet space: Georgia, Russia, and the conflict in South Ossetia', *Comparative Social Research*, 27, 103–126.

MacGinty, R. (2008), 'Indigenous peacemaking versus the liberal peace', *Cooperation and Conflict*, 43/2, 139–163.

MacGinty, R. (2011), *International Peacebuilding and Local Resistance: Hybrid Forms of Peace*, Basingstoke: Palgrave Macmillan.

McGurk, Brett H. (2010), 'Karzai's visit: Rebranding the partnership', *Council on Foreign Relations*, 10 May.

MacWilliam, A. (2005), 'Houses of resistance in East Timor: Structuring sociality in the new nation', *Anthropological Forum*, 15/1, 27–44.

Maguire, R. (2009a), *Transcending the Past to Build Haiti's Future*, Peace Brief, Washington, DC: United States Institute for Peace.

Maguire, R. (2009b), *What Role for the United Nations in Haiti?* Peace Brief, Washington, DC: United States Institute for Peace.

Maguire, R. (2011), *The Challenge of Keeping Haitians Safe*, Peace Brief 96, Washington, DC: United States Institute for Peace.

Mahoney, J. (2000), 'Path dependence in historical sociology', *Theory and Society*, 29/4, 507–548.

Malcolm, N. (1998), *Kosovo: A Short History*, Basingstoke: Macmillan.

Mallaby, S. (2004), *The World's Banker: A Story of Failed States, Financial Crises, and the Wealth and Poverty of Nations*, New York: Penguin Press.

Malloch-Brown, M. (2011), *The Unfinished Global Revolution*, London: Allan Lane.

Mampilly, Z. (2011), 'The nexus of militarization and corruption in post-conflict Sri Lanka', in C.S Cheng and D. Zaum (eds), *Corruption and Post-Conflict Peacebuilding: Selling the Peace?* London: Routledge, 180–198.

Mani, R. (2002), *Beyond Retribution: Seeking Justice in the Shadows of War*, London: Polity.

Mann, M. (1984), 'The autonomous power of the state: Its origins, mechanisms, and results', *European Journal of Sociology*, 25/2, 185–213.

Mann, M. (1986), *The Sources of Social Power: Volume 1, A History of Power from the Beginning to AD 1760*, Cambridge: Cambridge University Press.

Manners, I. (2002), 'Normative power Europe: A contradiction in terms?' *Journal of Common Market Studies*, 40/2, 235–258.

Manson, K. (2010), 'Payments don't add up in Congo's resources report', *Reuters*, 22 March.

Marr, P. (2000), 'Comments', *Middle East Policy*, 7/4.

Marr, P. (2006), *Who are Iraq's New Leaders? What do they Want?* Washington, DC: United States Institute of Peace Special Report.

Marzouk, L. (2009), 'Assassin claims intelligence link to Kosovo murders', *Balkan Insight*, 30 November.

Marzouk, L. and P. Collaku (2010), 'Kosova minister's friends flourish from road bonanza', *Prishtina Insight*, 8 April.

Mattelaer, A. (2010), *The Strategic Planning of EU Military Operations: The Case of EUFOR TCHAD/RCA*, Working Paper No. 5/2008, Brussels: Institute for European Studies.

Mattoso, J. (2005), *A Dignidade: Konis Santana e a Resistência Timorense*, Lisbon: Temas e Debates.

Mendelson-Forman, J. (2006), 'Security sector reform in Haiti', *International Peacekeeping*, 13/1, 14–27.

Menkhaus, K. (2010), 'State failure and ungoverned space', in M. Berdal and A. Wennmann (eds), *Ending Wars, Consolidating Peace: Economic Perspectives*, Abingdon: Routledge for the IISS, 171–188.

Michailof, S., M. Kostner and D. Xavier (2002), *Post-Conflict Recovery in Africa: An Agenda for the Africa Region*, Washington, DC: World Bank.

Migdal, J. (1988), *Strong Societies, Weak States*, Princeton, NJ: Princeton University Press.

Mihaljek, D. (1993), 'Intergovernmental fiscal relations in Yugoslavia, 1972–90', in V. Tanzi (ed.), *Transition to Market: Studies in Fiscal Reform*, Washington, DC: IMF, 177–201.

Millennium Project (2005), *Investing in Development: A Practical Plan to Achieve the Millennium Development Goals, Overview Report*, New York: United Nations.

Milosavlevski, S. and M. Tomovski (1997), *Albanians in the Republic of Macedonia 1945–1995: Legislative, Political Documentation, Statistics*, Skopje: NIP 'Studentski Zbor'.

Ministère des Finances de la RDC (2011), 'Programme de Gouvernance Economique: Matrice d'Actions', available at www.globalwitness.org/sites/default/files/library/La%20Gouvernance%20Economique%20-%20Matrice%20des%20actions%20-%2030mars2011.pdf, accessed 2 August 2011.

Ministry of Finance and Economy (2004), *Macroeconomic Monitor Kosovo: January 2004*, Prishtina: MFE.

Ministry of Internal Affairs of the Republic of Macedonia (2001), *White Book. Terrorism of the So-Called NLA*, Skopje: Ministry of Internal Affairs of the Republic of Macedonia.

Mitchell, L. (2010), 'Georgia's paradoxes', *Faster Times*, 9 November, available at http://thefastertimes.com/, accessed 10 July 2012.

Moestue, H. and R. Muggah (2009) Social Integration, Ergo, Stabilisation: assessing Viva Rio's security and development programme. Geneva: Small Arms Survey and Viva Rio.

Moestue, H. and R. Muggah (2010), *Social Integration, Ergo, Stabilization: Viva Rio in Port-au-Prince*, Rio de Janeiro/Geneva: Viva Rio and Small Arms Survey.

Mohammed, A. (2008), 'Iraqi forces battle for control of oil city', *Reuters*, 26 March.

Moodie, E. (2010), *El Salvador in the Aftermath of Peace: Crime, Uncertainty, and the Transition to Democracy*, Philadelphia, PA: University of Pennsylvania Press.

Moro, L. (2009), 'Oil development induced displacement in the Sudan', *Durham Middle East Papers*, University of Durham, Centre for Middle Eastern and Islamic Studies.

Morrow, J. (2005), *Iraq's Constitutional Process II: An Opportunity Lost*, USIP Special Report 155.

Morrow, J. and R. White (2002), 'The United Nations in transitional East Timor: International standards and the reality of governance', *Australian Year Book of International Law*, 22, 1–46.

Moxham, B. (2005), 'The World Bank's land of kiosks: Community driven development in Timor-Leste', *Development in Practice*, 15/3–4, 522–528.

Muggah, R. (2005), *Securing Haiti's Transition: Reviewing Human Insecurity and the Prospects for Disarmament, Demobilization, and Reintegration*, Occasional Paper 14, Geneva: Small Arms Survey.

Muggah, R. (2008), 'The perils of changing donor priorities in fragile states: The case of Haiti', in Jennifer Welsh and Ngaire Woods (eds), *Exporting Good Governance: Temptations and Challenges in Canada's Aid Program*, Waterloo: Wilfrid Laurier University Press, 169–202.

Muggah, R. (2009), 'Du vin nouveau dans de vieilles bouteilles? L'analyse de l'impasse de la gouvernance en Haïti', *Telescope*, available at www.enap.ca/OBSERVATOIRE/docs/Telescope/Volumes12-15/Telv15n2_muggah.pdf, accessed 10 July 2012.

Muggah, R. (2010a), 'The effects of stabilisation on humanitarian action in Haiti', *Disasters*, 34/3, 444–463.

Muggah, R. (2010b), 'Dealing with Haiti's gangs', *Ottawa Citizen*, 31 January, available at http://www2.canada.com/ottawacitizen/story.html?id=9497e7a4-c3c2-4552-9167-664bc712129d&p=3, accessed 10 July 2012.

Muggah, R. (2012), *The Urban Dilemma: Urbanization, Poverty and Violence*, London: Department for International Development and the International Development Research Centre.

Muggah, R. and K. Krause (2006), 'A true measure of success? The discourse and practice of human security in Haiti', *Whitehead Journal of Diplomacy and International Relations*, 57/2, 153–181.

Mukhopadhyay, D. (2009a), *Warlords as Bureaucrats: The Afghan Experience*, Washington, DC: Carnegie Endowment for International Peace.

Mukhopadhyay, D. (2009b), 'Disguised warlordism and combatanthood in Balkh: The persistence of informal power in the formal Afghan state', *Conflict, Security and Development*, 9/4, 535–564.

Mulbah, G.S. (2005), Affidavit by George Mulbah, Assistant Minister of Labour for Trade Union Affairs at the Ministry of Labour, 25 May.

Murithi, T. (2006), 'Towards a symbiotic partnership: The UN Peacebuilding Commission and the evolving African Union/NEPAD post-conflict reconstruction framework', in A. Adekeye and H. Scanlon (eds), *A Dialogue of the Death: Essays on Africa and the United Nations*, Johannesburg: Jacana, 250–251.

Musah, A. (2009), *West Africa: Governance and Security in a Changing Region*, New York: International Peace Institute.

Myint-U, Thant (1978), *View from the UN*, Garden City, NY: Doubleday & Co.

Myint-U, Thant and A. Scott (2007), *The UN Secretariat: A Brief History*, New York: IPA.

Naím, M. (2000), 'Washington consensus or Washington confusion?' *Foreign Policy*, 118, 87–103.

Nakaya, S. (2008), 'Paradox of peacebuilding aid: Post-conflict exclusion and violence in Tajikistan and beyond', Ph.D. dissertation, Department of Political Science, Graduate Center, City University of New York.

Nakaya, S. (2009), 'Ownership in post-conflict state building' *Policy Memo*, City University of New York.

Narten, J. (2009), 'Assessing Kosovo's postwar democratization: Between external imposition and local self-government', *Taiwan Journal of Democracy*, 5/1, 127–162.

National Statistics Directorate (2005), *Census of Population and Housing 2004, Atlas*, available at www.dne.mof.gov.tl, accessed 17 February 2012.

National Statistics Directorate (2010a), *Population and Housing Census 2010: Preliminary Results*, available at www.dne.mof.gov.tl, accessed 17 February 2012.

National Statistics Directorate (2010b), *Timor Leste Demographic and Health Survey 2009–10*, Dili

Nawa, F. (2006), *Afghanistan Inc.*, San Francisco, CA: Corpwatch.

Naylor, R.T. (1999), *Patriots and Profiteers: On Economic Warfare, Embargo Busting and State-Sponsored Crime*, Toronto: McClelland & Stewart.

NDI (2009), *The 2009 Presidential and Provincial Council Elections in Afghanistan*, Washington, DC: National Democratic Institute.

Neofotistos, V. (2004), 'Beyond stereotypes: Violence and the porousness of ethnic boundaries in the Republic of Macedonia', *History and Anthropology*, 15/1, 1–36.

Neupert, R. and S. Lopes (2006), 'The demographic component of the crisis in Timor-Leste, political demography: Ethnic, national and religious dimensions', Association for the Study of Ethnicity and Nationalism, London School of Economics, 29–30 September.

New York Times (2005), 'Up to 25 die in police raid on Haiti slums', 5 June.

Niblock, T. (1987), *Class and Power in Sudan: The Dynamics of Sudanese Politics, 1898–1985*, London: Macmillan.

Niblock, T. (2001), *'Pariah States' and Sanctions in the Middle East: Iraq, Libya, Sudan*, Boulder, CO: Lynne Rienner.

Niner, S. (ed.) (2000), *To Resist is to Win: The Autobiography of Xanana Gusmão with Selected Letters and Speeches*, Melbourne: Aurora/David Lovell Publishing.

Niner, S. (2009), *Xanana: Leader of the Struggle for Independent Timor-Leste*, Melbourne: Australian Scholarly Publishing.

Nixon, H. (2008), *Subnational Statebuilding in Afghanistan*, Kabul: Afghanistan Research and Evaluation Unit.

Nkurunziza, J.D. (2009), *Inequality and Post-Conflict Fiscal Policies in Burundi*, Oxford: Centre for Research on Inequality, Human Security and Ethnicity (CRISE).

NORAD (2007), *Review of Development Cooperation in Timor-Leste*, Oslo: NORAD.

North, D. (1998), 'Understanding economic change', in J.M. Nelson, C. Tilly and L. Walker (eds), *Transforming Post-Communist Political Economies*, Washington, DC: National Academies Press, 11–18.

Nooruddin, I. and J.W. Simmons (2006), 'The politics of hard choices: IMF programs and government spending', *International Organization*, 60/4, 1001–1033.

Norris, P. (2004), *Electoral Engineering: Voting Rules and Political Behavior*, Cambridge: Cambridge University Press.

Noutcheva, G. (2007), *Fake, Partial and Imposed Compliance: The Limits of the EU's Normative Power in the Western Balkans*, CEPS Working Document No. 274. Brussels: Centre for European Policy Studies.

Nwauche, S.E. (2009), 'Regional economic communities and human rights in West Africa and the African Arabic Countries', in A. Bösl and J. Diescho (eds), *Human Rights in Africa: Legal Perspectives on their Protection and Promotion*, Windhoek: Konrad-Adenauer-Stiftung, 320–330.

O'Donnell, M. (2005), 'UN peacekeeping and the World Bank: Perceptions of senior managers in the field', External Study for United Nations Department of Peacekeeping Operations.

O'Donnell, M. (2008), 'Corruption: A rule of law agenda?' in A. Hurwitz with R. Huang (eds), *Civil War and the Rule of Law*, Boulder, CO: Lynne Rienner, 225–259.

O'Hanlon, M.E. and I. Livingston (2009), 'Iraq Index, tracking variables of reconstruction and security in post-Saddam Iraq', 20 November, available at www.brookings.edu/~/media/Files/Centers/Saban/Iraq%20Index/index.pdf, accessed 15 February 2012.

O'Neill, W. (1995), 'Human rights monitoring vs. political expediency: The experience of the OAS/U.N. mission in Haiti', *Harvard Human Rights Journal*, 8, 101–128.

O'Neill, W. (2002), *Kosovo: Unfinished Peace*, Boulder, CO: Lynne Rienner.

Obwona, M. and M. Guloba (2009), 'Poverty reduction strategies during post-conflict recovery in Africa', *Journal of African Economies*, 18 (supplement 1), i77–i98.

Ocampo, J.A., S. Spiegel and J.E. Stiglitz (2008), 'Introduction', in J.A. Ocampo and J.E. Stiglitz (eds), *Capital Market Liberalization and Development*, Oxford: Oxford University Press, 1–47.

OECD (Organisation for Economic Cooperation and Development) (2010a), 'Table 25: ODA receipts and selected indicators for developing countries and territories', available at www.oecd.org/document/9/0.3343,en_2649_34447_1893129_1_1_1_1, 00.html, accessed 12 February 2012.

OECD (Organisation for Economic Cooperation and Development) (2010b), *Development Aid: Net Official Development Assistance*, Paris: OEDC/DAC, available at http://dx.doi.org/10.1787/20743866-2010-table1 accessed 12 February 2012.

OECD/DAC (2008), *Concepts and Dilemmas of State Building in Fragile Situations: From Fragility to Resilience*, Paris: OECD Publishing.

OECD/DAC (2011), *Supporting Statebuilding in Situations of Conflict and Fragility*, DAC Guidelines and Reference Series, Paris: OECD Publishing.

Olonisakin, F. (2011), 'ECOWAS and West African conflicts: The dynamics of conflict and peace-building in West Africa', in T. Jaye, D. Garuba and S. Amadi (eds), *ECOWAS and the Dynamics of Conflict and Peacebuilding*, Dakar: CODESRIA, 11–26.

Orakhelashvili, A. (2008), 'Statehood, recognition, and the United Nations system: A unilateral declaration of independence in Kosovo', *Max Planck Yearbook of International Law*, 12, 1–44.

Ordanoski, S. (2002), 'Lions and tigers: The militarisation of the Macedonian right', in Institute for War and Peace Reporting (IWPR), *Ohrid and Beyond: A Cross-ethnic Investigation into the Macedonian Crisis*, London: IWPR, 35–48.

Orford, A. and J. Beard (1998), 'Critique and comment: Making the state safe for the market: The World Bank's World Development Report 1997', *Melbourne University Law Review*, 22, 195–216.

OSCE (Organization for Security and Co-operation in Europe) (2003), *Parallel Structures in Kosovo*, October, Prishtina: OSCE.

OSCE (Organization for Security and Co-operation in Europe) (2007), *Parallel Structures in Kosovo, 2006–2007*, Prishtina: OSCE.

OSCE (Organization for Security and Co-operation in Europe) (2009), *Legal System Monitoring Section Monthly Report: June 2009*, 1 September, Prishtina: OSCE.

Ottaway, M. (2002), 'Rebuilding state institutions in collapsed states', *Development and Change*, 33/5, 1001–1023.

Ottaway, M. (2005), 'Tyranny's full tank', *New York Times*, 31 March.

Ould-Abdallah, A. (2000), *Burundi on the Brink 1993–95*, Washington, DC: United States Institute of Peace.

Owen, J.M. (2002), 'The foreign imposition of domestic institutions', *International Organization*, 56/2, 375–409.

Özbudun, E. (1987), 'Institutionalizing competitive elections in developing countries', in Myron Weiner and Ergun Özbudun (eds), *Competitive Elections in Developing Countries*, Durham, NC: Duke University Press, 393–421.

Packer, G. (2005), *Assassins' Gate: America in Iraq*, New York: Farrar, Straus and Giroux.

Palairet, M. (1992), 'Ramiz Sadiku: A case study in the industrialisation of Kosovo', *Soviet Studies*, 44/5, 897–912.

Papava, V. (2009), 'The "rosy" mistakes of the IMF and World Bank in Georgia', *Problems of Economic Transition*, 52/7, 44–56.

Papava, V. (2010), 'Georgia's hollow revolution', *Harvard International Review, Web-feature*, available at http://hir.harvard.edu/georgia-s-hollow-revolution, accessed 17 February 2012.

Paris, R. (2004), *At War's End: Building Peace after Civil Conflict*, New York: Cambridge University Press.

Paris, R. (2010), 'Saving liberal peacebuilding', *Review of International Studies*, 36/2, 337–365.

Paris, R. and T.D. Sisk (2009), 'Introduction: Understanding the contradictions of postwar statebuilding', in R. Paris and T.D. Sisk (eds), *The Dilemmas of Statebuilding: Confronting the Contradictions of Postwar Peace Operations*, London: Routledge, 1–20.

Parker, N. and C. Ahmed (2010), 'Maliki seeks recount in Iraq elections', *Los Angeles Times*, 22 March.

Patey, L. (2007), 'State rules: Oil companies and armed conflict in Sudan', *Third World Quarterly*, 28/5, 997–1016.

Patrick, S. (2011), *Weak Links: Fragile States, Global Threats, and International Security*, New York: Oxford University Press.

Paterson, A. (2005), *Understanding Markets in Afghanistan: A Study of the Market for Petroleum Fuels*, Kabul: Afghanistan Research and Evaluation Unit.

Paterson, A. (2006), *Going to Market: Trade and Traders on Six Afghan Sectors*, Kabul: Afghanistan Research and Evaluation Unit.

PBS Frontline (2004), 'Interview with Walter Slocombe', in 'Rumsfeld's War', 17 March, available at www.pbs.org/wgbh/pages/frontline/shows/pentagon/interviews/slocombe.html, accessed 17 February 2012.

Perito, R. (2007), *Haiti: Hope for the Future, USIP Special Report*, Washington, DC: United States Institute for Peace.

Perito, R. (2009), *Haiti after the Storms: Weather and Conflict*, Peace Brief, Washington, DC: United States Institute for Peace.

Persson, T. and G. Tabellini (2005), *The Economic Effects of Constitutions*, Cambridge, MA: MIT Press.

Phillips, D.L. (2005), *Losing Iraq: Inside the Post-war Reconstruction Fiasco*, Boulder, CO: Westview Press.

Phillips, D.L. (2010), 'The Balkans' underbelly', *World Policy Journal*, 27/3, 93–99.

Philp, M. (2011), 'Conceptualising corruption in peacebuilding contexts', in C.S Cheng and D. Zaum (eds), *Corruption and Post-Conflict Peacebuilding: Selling the Peace?* London: Routledge, 29–45.

Pierre, I.-F. and I. Fortin (2011), 'La réforme de la Police Nationale et la constructions democratique en Haïti', *Canadian Journal of Development Studies*, 32/1, 64–78.

Pierson, P. (2000), 'Increasing returns, path dependence, and the study of politics', *American Political Science Review*, 94/2, 251–267.

Pierson, P. (2004), *Politics in Time: History, Institutions, and Social Analysis*, Princeton, NJ: Princeton University Press.

Pinto, J.T. (2009), 'Reforming the security sector: Facing challenges, achieving progress in Timor Leste', *Tempo Semanal*, 18 August.

Pires, E. and M. Francino (2007), 'National ownership and international trusteeship: The case of Timor-Leste', in J.K. Boyce and M. O'Donnell (eds), *Peace and the Public Purse: Economic Policies for Postwar Statebuilding*, Boulder, CO, and London: Lynne Rienner, 119–152.

Planning Commission (2002), *East Timor National Development Plan*, Dili.

Polanyi, K. (2001), *The Great Transformation: The Political and Economic Origins of our Time*, Boston, MA: Houghton Mifflin.

Pollack, K.M. (2009), 'The battle for Baghdad', *National Interest*, September/October.

Ponzio, R. (2011), *Democratic Peacebuilding: Aiding Afghanistan and other Fragile States*, Oxford: Oxford University Press.

Popetrevski, V. and V. Latifi (2002), 'The Ohrid Framework Agreement negotiations', in Institute for War and Peace Reporting (IWPR), *Ohrid and Beyond: A Cross-ethnic Investigation into the Macedonian Crisis*, London: IWPR, 49–57.

Pouligny, B. (1999), 'Peacekeepers and local social actors: The need for dynamic, cross-cultural analysis', *Global Governance*, 5/4, 403–424.

Poulton, H. (1995), *Who are the Macedonians?* London: Hurst.

Power, S. (2008), *Chasing the Flame: Sergio Vieira de Mello and the Fight to Save the World*, New York: Penguin.

Prengaman, P. (2005), 'Scores of prisoners at large in Haiti after prison attack', *Associated Press*, 21 February.

Pridham, G. (2008), 'Change and continuity in the European Union's political conditionality: Aims, approach and priorities', *Democratization*, 14/3, 446–471.

Privatization Agency of Kosovo (2009), *Work Report August 2008–August 2009*, Pristina: Privatisation Agency of Kosovo.

Pugh, M. (2002), 'Postwar political economy in Bosnia and Herzegovina: The spoils of peace', *Global Governance*, 8/4, 467–482.

Pugh, M. (2004), 'Rubbing salt into war wounds: Shadow economies and peacebuilding in Bosnia and Kosovo', *Problems of Post-Communism*, 51/3, 53–60.

Pugh, M. (2006), 'Crime and capitalism in Kosovo's transformation', in Tonny Brems Knudsen and Carsten Bagge Lausten (eds), *Kosovo Between War and Peace*, London: Routledge, 116–134.

Pugh, M. (2008), 'Employment, labour rights and social resistance', in M. Pugh, N. Cooper and M. Turner (eds), *Whose Peace? Critical Perspectives on the Political Economy of Peacebuilding*, Basingstoke: Palgrave, 139–156.

Pugh, M., N. Cooper with J. Goodhand (2004), *War Economies in a Regional Context: Challenges of Transformation*, Boulder, CO: Lynne Rienner.

Pugh, M., N. Cooper and M. Turner (eds) (2008), *Whose Peace? Critical Perspectives on the Political Economy of Peacebuilding*, Basingstoke: Palgrave.

Pugh, M. and B. Divjak (2011), 'The political economy of corruption in Bosnia and Herzegovina', in C.S. Cheng and D. Zaum (eds), *Corruption and Post-Conflict Peacebuilding: Selling the Peace?* London: Routledge, 99–113.

Pukhov, R. (ed.) (2010), *The Tanks of August*, Moscow: Center for Analysis of Strategies and Technologies.

Putnam, R.D., R. Leonardi and R. Nanetti (1993), *Making Democracy Work: Civic Traditions in Modern Italy*, Princeton, NJ: Princeton University Press.

Radin, B.A. (2007), 'Performance measurement and global governance: The experience of the World Bank', *Global Governance*, 13/1, 25–33.

Rajagopal, B. (2008), 'Invoking the rule of law: International discourses', in A. Hurwitz with R. Huang (eds), *Civil War and the Rule of Law*, Boulder, CO: Lynne Rienner, 47–67.

Ramos-Horta, J. (1996), 'Nobel lecture', Oslo, 10 December.

Ramos-Horta, J. (2001), 'Presentation to Standing Committee on Political Hearings', in ETTA, *Report on the Transitional Calendar*, Dili, 22 February.

Rashid, A. (2008), *Descent into Chaos*, London: Viking.

Ray, Aswini K. (2011), 'India and the challenge of the new protectorates', in J. Mayall and R. Soares de Oliveira (eds), *The New Protectorates: International Tutelage and the Making of Liberal States*, London: C. Hurst & Co, 105–120.

RDTL (República Democrática de Timor-Leste) (2006a), 'Speech by the Prime Minister, Mari Alkatiri, at the opening session of the Timor-Leste development partners meeting', Dili, 4 April.

RDTL (República Democrática de Timor-Leste) (2006b), *Combating Poverty as a National Cause: Promoting Balanced Development and Poverty Reduction*, Dili: RDTL.

RDTL (República Democrática de Timor-Leste) (2006c), *Relatório da Comissão de Notáveis Sobre o Caso "'Peticionários'*, Dili: RDTL.

RDTL (República Democrática de Timor-Leste) (2007), Ministry of Finance, 'General Budget of the State 2008', Budget Paper No. 1, Dili.

RDTL (República Democrática de Timor-Leste) (2009), Address by His Excellency the Prime Minister Kay Rala Xanana Gusmão on the Occasion of the Opening Session of the Timor-Leste Development Partners Meeting, Dili, 2–4 April.

Rees, E. (2004), *Under Pressure: Falintil-Forças de Defesa de Timor-Leste, Three Decades of Defence Force Development in Timor-Leste, 1975–2004*, Geneva, DCAF.

Reid, A. (2010), *Imperial Alchemy: Nationalism and Political Identity in Southeast Asia*, Cambridge, Cambridge University Press.

Reilly, B. (2004), 'Elections in post-conflict societies', in E. Newman and R. Rich (eds), *The UN Role in Promoting Democracy: Between Ideals and Reality*, Tokyo: United Nations University Press, 113–134.

Reilly, B. (2006), *Democracy and Diversity: Political Engineering in the Asia-Pacific*, Oxford: Oxford University Press.

Reilly, B. (2008), 'Post-conflict elections: Uncertain turning points of transition?' in Anna K. Jarstad and Timothy D. Sisk (eds), *From War to Democracy: Dilemmas of Peacebuilding*, Cambridge: Cambridge University Press, 157–181.

Reilly, B. (2010), 'Centripetalism', in Karl Cordell and Stefan Wolff (eds), *The Routledge Handbook of Ethnic Conflict*, London: Routledge, 288–299.

Reilly, B. and P. Nordlund (eds) (2008), *Political Parties in Conflict-Prone Societies: Regulation, Engineering and Democratic Development*, Tokyo: United Nations University Press.

Reilly, C. (2009), 'Iraq's once-envied health care system lost to war, corruption', *McClatchy Newspapers*, 17 May, available at www.mcclatchydc.com/227/story/68193. html, accessed 17 February 2012.

Reka, A. (2008), 'The Ohrid Agreement: The travails of inter-ethnic relations in Macedonia', *Human Rights Review*, 9/1, 55–69.

Reno, W. (1995), *Corruption and State Politics in Sierra Leone*, Cambridge: Cambridge University Press.

Reno, W. (1998), *Warlord Politics and African States*, Boulder, CO: Lynne Rienner.

Reno, W. (2011a), 'Understanding criminality in West African conflicts', in J. Cockayne and A. Lupel (eds), *Peace Operations and Organized Crime: Enemies or Allies*, London: Routledge, 68–83.

Reno, W. (2011b), 'Anti-corruption efforts in Liberia: Are they aimed at the right targets?' in C.S. Cheng and D. Zaum (eds), *Corruption and Post-Conflict Peacebuilding: Selling the Peace?* London: Routledge, 126–143.

Republic of Macedonia (1995), 'Zakon za lokalnata samouprava' [Law on Local Self-Government], Official Gazette, 52/1995.

Republic of Macedonia (2002), 'Zakon za lokalnata samouprava' [Law on Local Self-Government], Official Gazette, 5/2002.

Republic of Macedonia (2005), 'Answers to the EC questionnaire: Political criteria', Skopje, 14 February.

Reynolds, A. (ed.) (2002), *The Architecture of Democracy: Constitutional Design, Conflict Management, and Democracy*, Oxford: Oxford University Press.

Reynolds, A., B. Reilly and A. Ellis (2005), *Electoral System Design: The New International IDEA Handbook*, Stockholm: International IDEA.

RFE/RL (2006), 'Interview: Afghan President Karzai talks to RFE/RL', *Radio Free Europe/Radio Liberty*, 6 April.

Richards, P. (ed.) (2005), *No Peace, No War: An Anthropology of Contemporary Armed Conflicts*, Oxford: James Curry.

Richmond, O. (2005), *The Transformation of Peace*, Basingstoke: Palgrave Macmillan.

Richmond, O. (2009), 'Becoming liberal, unbecoming liberalism: Liberal-local hybridity via the everyday as a response to the paradoxes of liberal peacebuilding', *Journal of Intervention and Statebuilding*, 3/3, 324–344.

Richmond, O. (2011), *A Post-Liberal Peace*, Abingdon: Routledge.

Rimli, L. and S. Schmeidl (2007), *Private Security Companies and Local Populations: An Exploratory Study of Afghanistan and Angola*, Bern: Swisspeace.

Risen, J. (2009), 'Another Karzai forges Afghan business empire', *New York Times*, 5 March.

Roberts, A. (2003), 'Order/justice issues at the UN', in Rosemary Foot, J.L. Gaddis and A. Hurrell (eds), *Order and Justice in International Relations*, Oxford: Oxford University Press, 49–79.

Robertson, C. (2008), 'Iraq private sector falters: Rolls of government soar', *New York Times*, 10 August.

Rohde, D. (2004), 'G.I.'s in Afghanistan on hunt, but now for hearts and minds', *New York Times*, 30 March.

Rose-Ackerman, S. (2011), 'Corruption and government', in C.S. Cheng and D. Zaum (eds), *Corruption and Post-Conflict Peacebuilding: Selling the Peace?* London: Routledge, 46–61.

Rose-Ackerman, S. and T. Søreide (2012), *International Handbook on the Economics of Corruption, Volume Two*, Cheltenham: Edward Elgar.

Rosen, N. (2010), 'Iraq's fragile peace rests on its own forces', *Nation*, 10 September, available at http://thenational.ae/apps/pbcs.dll/article?AID=/20100910/REVIEW/709099998/1008, accessed 17 February 2012.

Ross, M.L. (2001), 'Does oil hinder democracy?' *World Politics*, 53/3, 325–361.

Ross, M.L. (2004), 'How do natural resources influence civil war? Evidence from thirteen Cases', *International Organization*, 58/1, 35–67.

Ross, M.L. (2008), 'Blood barrels', *Foreign Affairs*, 83/3, 2–9.

Rotberg, R.I. (ed.) (2004), *When States Fail: Causes and Consequences*, Princeton, NJ: Princeton University Press.

Rotberg, R.I. (ed.) (2009), *Corruption, Global Security, and World Order*, Washington, DC: Brookings Institution Press.

Rubin, B.R. (2005), 'Constructing sovereignty for security', *Survival*, 47/4, 93–106.

Rusi, I. (2002), 'From army to party: The politics of the NLA', in Institute for War and Peace Reporting (IWPR), *Ohrid and Beyond: A Cross-ethnic Investigation into the Macedonian Crisis*, London: IWPR, 19–34.

Russett, B. (1993), *Grasping the Democratic Peace*, Princeton, NJ: Princeton University Press.

Sadiku, M. (2001), 'The impact of corruption on Kosovo's economy', survey conducted by the Riinvest Institute for Development Research, Priština, December.

Sampson, S. (2005), 'Integrity warriors: Global morality and the anticorruption movement in the Balkans', in C. Shore and D. Haller (eds), *Understanding Corruption*, London: Routledge, 103–130.

Sampson, S. (2010), 'The anti-corruption industry: From movement to institution', *Global Crime*, 11/2, 261–278.

Schimmenfennig, F. (2007), 'European regional organizations, political conditionality and democratic transformation in Eastern Europe', *East European Politics and Societies*, 21/1, 126–141.

Schwalbe, M. (2007), *Rigging the Game: How Inequality is Reproduced in Everyday Life*, Oxford: Oxford University Press.

Shaxson, N. (2011), *Treasure Islands: Tax Havens and the Men Who Stole the World*, London: Bodley Head.

Seattle Times news services (2008), 'Fighting leaves crucial truce with Iraq militia in shambles', *Seattle Times*, 26 March.

Sebastián, S. (2011), *Breaking the Impasse: Constitutional Reform in* Bosnia, FRIDE Briefing Paper No 69.

Sebudandi, C. and J. Kavabuha Icoyitungye (2008), *The Cumulative Impacts of Peacebuilding in Burundi: Strengths and Weaknesses of a Process*, Cambridge, MA: Center for Development Action.

Selowsky, M. (1998), 'We did not neglect institutional development: Interview with World Bank's ECA Chief Economist Marcelo Selowsky', *Transition*, 9/5, 1–4.

Senor, D. and W. Slocombe (2005), 'Too few good men', *New York Times*, 17 November.

Shadid, A. and N. Bakri (2009), 'In sign of times, alliances shift ahead of Iraqi elections', *Washington Post*, 30 September.

Sherman, J. (2009), *Strengthening Security Sector Governance in West Africa*, New York: Center on International Cooperation.

Shoesmith, D. (2003), 'Timor-Leste: Divided leadership in a semi-presidential system', *Asian Survey*, 43/2, 231–252.

Sidiropoulos, E. (1999), 'Minority protection in the former Yugoslav republic of Macedonia: Will it preserve the state?' *Cambridge Review of International Affairs*, 12/2, 139–152.

SIGAR (2010), *Quarterly Report to Congress*, Washington, DC, 30 January.

SIGIR (2010), *Quarterly Report to the United States Congress*, Washington, DC, 30 October.

Skocpol, T. (1985), 'Bringing the state back in: Strategies of analysis in current research', in P. Evans, D. Rueschemeyer and T. Skocpol (eds), *Bringing the State Back In*, Cambridge: Cambridge University Press, 3–43.

Smith, D.J. (2006), *A Culture of Corruption: Everyday Deception and Popular Discontent in Nigeria*, Princeton, NJ: Princeton University Press.

Soares de Oliveira, R. (2011), 'Illiberal peacebuilding in Angola', *Journal of Modern African Studies*, 49/2, 287–314.

Sogge, D. (2002), *Give and Take: What's the Matter with Foreign Aid?* London and New York: Zed Books.

SoSCM (Secretary of State for the Council of Ministers) (2011a) 'Government of Timor-Leste welcomes 2011 with resolve and support of the people', Dili, 3 January.

SoSCM (Secretary of State for the Council of Ministers) (2011b), 'Timor-Leste predicted to be one of the top ten fastest growing economies for 2011', Dili, 20 January.

Sousa-Santos, J.K.L. (2009), ' "The last resistance generation": The reintegration and transformation of freedom fighters to civilians in Timor-Leste', Paper presented at conference on Nation-Building in Urban and Rural Timor-Leste, RMIT University, Dili, 8–10 July.

Spector, B.I., S. Winbourne and L.D. Beck (2003), 'Corruption in Kosovo: Observations and implications for USAID', USAID and Management Systems International, Washington, DC.

Spillius, A. and B. Farmer (2009), 'Karzai Inc: Has Afghanistan's leader turned the country into a family business? *Daily Telegraph*, 7 August.

Statistical Office of Kosovo (2009), *Structural Business Survey 2005, 2006, and 2007*, Pristina: SOK.

Statistical Office of Kosovo (2010), *Agricultural Household Survey 2008*, Pristina: SOK.

Stearns, J. (2011), 'Opinion: US policy on Congo conflict minerals well-intentioned, but misguided', *Christian Science Monitor*, 4 August.

Stedman, S.J., D. Rothchild and E.M. Cousens (eds) (2002), *Ending Civil Wars: The Implementation of Peace Agreements*, Boulder, CO, and London: Lynne Rienner, for the International Peace Academy.

Steele, J. (2003), 'De Mello knew sovereignty, not security, is the issue: Britain should persuade the US to give the UN a larger role in Iraq', *Guardian*, 21 August.

Steele, J. (2008), 'Iraqi army readies for showdown with Kurds', *Guardian*, 3 September.

Steven, S. and R. Smits (2010), *Aiming High, Reaching Low: Four Fundamentals for Gender Responsive State-building*, CRU Policy Brief No. 13, Clingendael Conflict Research Unit, March 2010.

Stewart, F. and M. Wang (2006), 'Do PRSPs empower poor countries and disempower the World Bank, or is it the other way round?' in G. Ranis, J.R. Vreeland and S. Kosack (eds), *Globalization and the Nation State: The Impact of the IMF and the World Bank*, London and New York: Routledge, 290–322.

Stiglitz J. (2001), 'Foreword', in K. Polanyi, *The Great Transformation: The Political and Economic Origins of our Time*, Boston, MA: Houghton Mifflin, vii–xvii.

Storey, A. (2001), 'Structural adjustment, state power and genocide: The World Bank and Rwanda', Paper presented at a conference on 'The Global Constitution of "Failed States": Consequences of a New Imperialism?' Sussex, 18–20 April.

Stormer, C. (2004), 'Winning hearts, minds and firefights in Uruzgan', *Asia Times*, 6 August.

Strazzari, F. (2008), '*L'Oeuvre au Noir*: The shadow economy of Kosovo's independence', *International Peacekeeping*, 15/2, 155–170.

Stubbs, P. (2001), '"Social sector" or the diminution of social policy? Regulating welfare regimes in contemporary Bosnia-Herzegovina', in Z. Papic (ed.), *International Support Policies to SEE Countries: Lessons (Not), Learned in Bosnia-Herzegovina*, Sarajevo: Fond Otvoreno Drustvo Bosne i Hercegovine, 95–110.

Suara Timor Lorosa'e (2007), 'Alkatiri: Timor Lalika Buka Uma Lisan', 7 May.

Suhrke, A. and J. Buckmaster (2006), 'Aid, growth and peace: A comparative analysis', *Conflict Security and Development*, 6/2, 227–263.

Suliman, O. (2007), *Current Privatization Policy in Sudan*, Policy Brief 52, Ann Arbor: William Davidson Institute, University of Michigan.

Sullivan, D. (2005), 'The missing pillars: A look at the failure of peace in Burundi through the lens of Arend Lijphart's consociational theory', *Journal of Modern African Studies*, 43/1, 75–95.

Suny, R.G. (1993), *The Revenge of the Past: Nationalism, Revolution and the Collapse of the Soviet Union*, Stanford, CA: Stanford University Press.

Suskind, R. (2004), *The Price of Loyalty: George W. Bush, the White House, and the Education of Paul O'Neill*, New York: Simon & Shuster.

Swietochowski, T. (1995), *Russia and Azerbaijan: A Borderland in Transition*, New York: Columbia University Press.

Szeftel, M. (2000), 'Between governance and underdevelopment: Accumulation and Africa's catastrophic corruption', *Review of African Political Economy*, 27/84, 287–306.

Tadesse, M. (2010), *The African Union and Security Sector Reform: A Review of the Post Conflict Reconstruction and Development (PCRD), Policy*, Addis Ababa: Friedrich-Ebert-Stiftung.

Tansey, O. (2008), 'Debate: Reply and response to Jahn's "tragedy of liberal diplomacy"', *Journal of Intervention and Statebuilding*, 2/1, 87–98.

Tansey, O. (2009), *Regime-building: Democratization and International Administration*, Oxford: Oxford University Press.

Tansey, O. and D. Zaum (2009), 'Muddling through in Kosovo', *Survival*, 51/1, 13–20.

Taylor, R. (ed.) (2009), *Consociational Theory*, London and New York: Routledge.

Thomas, G. (2010), 'Karzai visit stabilizes shaky relationship, differences remain', *Voice of America*, 14 May.

Tilly, C. (1975), *The Formation of National States in Western Europe*, Princeton, NJ: Princeton University Press.

Tilly, C. (1985), 'War making and state making as organized crime', in Peter B. Evans, Dietrich Rueschemeyer and Theda Skocpol (eds), *Bringing the State Back In*, Cambridge: Cambridge University Press, 169–187.

Timor Post (2010), 'Fretilin: AMP Compra a Paz com Dólares', 10 August.

Tocci, N. (2008), 'The European Union as a normative foreign policy actor', in N. Tocci (ed.), *Who is a Normative Foreign Policy Actor? The European Union and its Global Partners*, Brussels: Centre for European Policy Studies, 24–75.

Tolbert, D. with A. Solomon (2006), 'United Nations reform and supporting the rule of law in post-conflict societies', *Harvard Human Rights Journal*, 19, 18–62.

Tomaš, R. (2010), *Kriza I Siva Ekonomija u Bosni I Hercegovini* [Crisis and Grey Economy in Bosnia and Herzegovina], Sarajevo: Friedrich Ebert Stiftung BiH.

Torabi, Y. (2009), 'State-, nation- et peace-building comme processus de transactions: l'interaction des intervenants et des acteurs locaux sur le théâtre de l'intervention en Afghanistan, 2001–08', Ph.D. Thesis, Institut d'Etudes Politiques de Paris.

Transparency International (2007), *National Integrity System Study: Bosnia and Herzegovina, 2007*, Berlin: Transparency International.

Transparency International (2008a), 'Corruption perceptions index', available at www.transparency.org/publications/publications/annual_reports/, accessed 17 February 2012.

Transparency International (2008b), *Promoting Revenue Transparency: 2008 Report on Revenue Transparency of Oil and Gas Companies*, Berlin: Transparency International.

Transparency International (2009), 'Corruption perception index', available at www.transparency.org/publications/publications/annual_reports/ accessed 17 February 2012.

Traube, E.G. (2007), 'Unpaid wages: Local narratives and the imagination of the nation', *Asia Pacific Journal of Anthropology*, 8/1, 9–25.

Treisman, D. (1999), *After the Deluge: Regional Crises and Political Consolidation in Russia*, Ann Arbor, MI: University of Michigan Press.

Trimberger, A.K. (1978), *Revolutions from Above: Military Bureaucrats and Development in Japan, Turkey, Egypt and Peru*, New Brunswick: Transaction Press.

Tripp, C. (2000), *A History of Iraq*, Cambridge: Cambridge University Press.

Tripp, C. (2002), 'What lurks in the shadows?' *Times Higher Education Supplement*, 18 October.

Tripp, C. (2002–2003), 'After Saddam', *Survival*, 44/4, 22–37.

Turner, M. (2004), 'Poll planning on track but no room for hitches', *Financial Times*, 14 October.

Turner, M. (2009), 'The power of "shock and awe": The Palestinian Authority and the road to reform', *International Peacekeeping*, 16/4, 562–577

UN Millenium Project (2005), *Investing in Development: A Practical Plan to Achieve the Millennium Development Goals*, London: Earthscan.

UN Peacekeeping fact sheet, available at www.un.org/en/peacekeeping/resources/statistics/factsheet.shtml, accessed 31 Oktober 2011.

UNDGO/WB (Development Group Office and World Bank) (2006), 'PCNA Review: Phase One Timor-Leste Joint Assessment Mission (JAM), Comparison Case Study', Dili, October.

UNDP (1970), *Study of the Capacity of the UN Development System*, New York: UNDP.

UNDP (2005), *Institutional Arrangements to Combat Corruption: A Comparative Study*, Bangkok: UNDP.

UNDP (2008a), *Post-Conflict Economic Recovery: Enabling Local Ingenuity*, New York: Bureau for Crisis Prevention and Recovery.

UNDP (2008b), *Georgia Human Development Report: The Reforms and Beyond*, Tbilisi: UNDP.

UNDP (2009), *Preliminary Corruption Perceptions Results*, Pristina: UNDP.

UNDP (2010a), *Early Warning Report Kosovo April–June 2010*, Pristina: UNDP.

UNDP (2010b), 'World wide trends in the human development index, 1979–2010', available at http://hdr.undp.org/en/data/trends/, accessed 17 December 2012.

UNDP (2011), *Timor-Leste Human Development Report 2011, Managing Natural Resources for Human Development: Developing the Non-Oil Economy to Achieve the MDGs*, Dili, UNDP.

UNHCHR (2011), *Harsh Sentencing, Prosecutor's Role and Low Acquittal Rate raise Concerns about Arbitrary Detention in Georgia*, Geneva: UNHCHR, 24 June.

UNHCR (2001), *UNHCR Country Operations Plan 2002: fYR of Macedonia*, 1 December, available at www.unhcr.org/refworld/docid/3c639d00a.html, accessed 12 January 2011.

UNHCR (2010), 'OCM Pristina: Statistical overview', Pristina, September.

United Nations (1970), 'Study of the capacity of the UN development system', UN Doc. DP/5 (Jackson Report), March.

United Nations (1993), 'Report of the Joint Inspection Unit on staffing of the United Nations peacekeeping and related missions (Civilian Component)', UN Doc. JIU/REP/93/6, September.

United Nations (1994), 'Report of the Secretary-General on improving the capacity of the United Nations for peacekeeping', UN Doc. A/48/403-S26450, 14 March.

United Nations (1996), 'An agenda for democratization', Letter dated 17 December 1996 from the Secretary-General to the President of the General Assembly, UN Doc. A/51/761, 20 December.

United Nations (1999), Security Council Resolution 1244, UN Doc. S/RES/1244, 10 June.

United Nations (2000), 'Report of the panel on UN peace operations (Brahimi Panel)', UN Doc. A/55/305-S/2000/809, 21 August.

United Nations (2001), 'Report of the Secretary-General on Afghanistan', UN Doc. A/65/873-S/2011/381, 23 June.

United Nations (2004a), 'Secretary-General's report on the situation in Guinea Bissau and activities of the UN peace building support office in Guinea Bissau', UN. Doc. S/2004/969, 15 December.

United Nations (2004b), 'The political transition in Iraq: Report of the fact-finding mission', UN Doc. S/2004/140, 23 February.

United Nations (2005a), General Assembly Resolution, UN Doc. A/RES/59/286/Add.1, 27 May.

United Nations (2005b), General Assembly Resolution, UN Doc. A/RES/59/286, 29 April.

United Nations (2006a), 'Secretary-General's report on the situation in Guinea Bissau and activities of the UN peace building support office in Guinea Bissau', UN Doc. S/2006/487, 6 July.

United Nations (2006b), 'Report of the United Nations independent special commission of inquiry on Timor-Leste,' Geneva, 2 October.

United Nations (2006c), 'Delivering as one: Report of the Secretary-General's high level panel on UN system-wide coherence', UN Doc. A/61/583, 9 November.

United Nations (2006d), 'Haitian national police reform plan', UN Doc. S/2006/726, 12 September.

United Nations (2007), 'Comprehensive Proposal for the Kosovo Status Settlement,' UN Doc. S/2007/168/Add.1 of 26 Mar. 2007.

United Nations (2008), General Assembly Resolution, UN Doc. 63/263, 24 December.

United Nations (2009a), *United Nations Policy for Post Conflict Employment Creation, Income Generation and Reintegration*, New York: UN.

United Nations (2009b), 'Report of the Secretary-General on the United Nations stabilization mission in Haiti', UN Doc. S/2009/439, 12 September.

United Nations (2010a), Security Council Resolution, UN Doc. S/RES/1959, 16 December.

United Nations (2010b), 'Results-based budgeting framework for the UN integrated peacebuilding office in Sierra Leone', UN Doc. A/65/328, Add.3, 10 October.

United Nations (2011a), 'Report of the Secretary-General on strengthening the capacity of the United Nations to manage and sustain peacekeeping operations', UN Doc. A/65/624, 10 May.

United Nations (2011b), General Assembly Document, A/66/347, 8 September.

United Nations (2011c), 'Civilian capacity in the aftermath of conflict: Independent report of the senior advisory group', UN Doc. A/65/747-S/2011/85, 22 February.

United Nations Country Team (2001), 'Building blocks for a nation: Common country assessment for East Timor', Dili, November.

United Nations News Centre (2010), 'Timor-Leste's economy at "turning point", says top UN envoy', 7 April.

United Nations Office of the Special Advisor on Africa (2007), 'The emerging role of the AU and ECOWAS in conflict prevention and peacebuilding', Background Paper, 28 December.

United States Government (2002), 'The national security strategy of the United States of America', Washington, DC, September.

United States Institute for Peace (2009), *Guiding Principles for Stabilization and Reconstruction*, Washington, DC: USIP.

UNMIK (2003), 'Standards for Kosovo', Pristina, 10 December.

UNODC (2008), *Crime and its Impact on the Balkans and Affected Countries*, Vienna: UNODC.

UNSC (2009), 'Report of the Secretary-General on the United Nations Stabilisation Mission in Haiti', S/2009/439, 1 September.

UNTAET (2000), 'CivPol briefing', 10 March.

UNTAET (2001), *Working Paper No. 1 on Preparatory Constitutional Issues in East Timor 2001, The Appropriateness of a Constitutional Assembly to Draft a Constitution: Criteria for Choice*, Dili: UNTAET.

USAID (2002), *A Guide to Economic Growth in Post-conflict Countries*, Washington, DC: USAID.

USAID (2009), *Foreign Operations Appropriated Assistance: Georgia*, Washington, DC: USAID, 20 January.

Utas, M. (ed.) (2012), *African Conflicts and Informal Power: Big Men and Networks*, London: Zed Books.

Uvin, P. (1998), *Aiding Violence: The Development Enterprise in Rwanda*, West Hartford, CT: Kumarian Press.

Uvin, P. (2006), *Life after Violence*, London, Zed Books.

van Bijlert, M. (2009), *Between Discipline and Discretion: Policies Surrounding Senior Subnational Appointments*, Kabul: AREU.

van de Walle, N. (2001), *African Economies and the Politics of Permanent Crisis*, New York: Cambridge University Press.

van Hal, A. (2005), 'Back to the future: The referendum of November 7th in Macedonia', *Helsinki Monitor*, 16/1, 36–52.

van ser Gaage, N. (1999), 'Iraq: The pride and the pain', *New Internationalist*, 316.

Vershbow, A. (2009), 'Comment on *Johnson's Russia List* (#44-JRL 2009–149)', available at www.cdi.org/Russia/Johnson/2009-149-44.cfm, accessed 19 February 2012.

Visser, R. (2009), 'No longer supreme: After local elections, ISCI becomes a 10 per cent party south of Baghdad', 5 February, available at www.historiae.org/ISCI.asp, accessed 19 February 2012.

Von Billerbeck, S.B.K. (2011), 'Aiding the state or aiding corruption? Aid and corruption in post-conflict countries', in C.S. Cheng and D. Zaum (eds), *Corruption and Post-Conflict Peacebuilding: Selling the Peace?* London: Routledge, 80–96.

Waldman, M. (2010), *The Sun in the Sky*, London: Crisis States Research Centre.

Weingast, B.R. and D.A. Wittman (2006), 'The reach of political economy', in B.R. Weingast and D. Wittman (eds), *The Oxford Handbook of Political Economy*, Oxford: Oxford University Press, 3–25.

Weller, M. (2008), 'The Vienna negotiations on the final status for Kosovo', *International Affairs*, 84/4, 659–681.

Weller, M. (2009), *Contested Statehood: Kosovo's Struggle for Independence*, Oxford: Oxford University Press.

Wennmann, A. (2011), 'Breaking the conflict trap? Addressing the resource curse in peace processes', *Global Governance: A Review of Multilateralism and International Organizations*, 17/2, 265–279.

Whalan, J. (2010), 'The power of friends: The regional assistance mission to Solomon Islands', *Journal of Peace Research*, 47/5, 627–637.

White House (2002), 'The national security strategy of the United States of America', Washington, DC, September.

Whitfield, L. and A. Fraser (2009), 'Negotiating aid', in L. Whitfield (ed.), *The Politics of Aid: African Strategies for Dealing with Donors*, Oxford: Oxford University Press.

Wilder, A. (2005), *A House Divided? Analysing the 2005 Afghan Elections*, Kabul: AREU.

Williams, P. (2004), 'Peace operations and the international financial institutions: Insights from Rwanda and Sierra Leone', *International Peacekeeping*, 11/1, 103–123.

Williams, P. (2009a), 'Organized crime and corruption in Iraq', *International Peacekeeping*, 16/1, 115–135.

Williams, T. (2009b), 'U.S. fears Iraqis will not keep up rebuilt projects', *New York Times*, 21 November.

Willie, M.K. (2004), Letter to the LIMINCO Board of Directors from the Deputy Minister for Operations and Chairman of the Inter-Ministerial Mineral Technical Committee, Monrovia, 14 October.

Wisner, D. (2008), 'Is time ripe for transitional justice in Afghanistan?' *al Naklah: The Fletcher School Online Journal for Southwest Asia and Islamic Civilization*, Fall, 1–12.

Wittkowsky, A., E. Bajraktari, A. Martinatto, O. Nikšić, P. Oldham and G. Thwaites (2006), *UNMIK's Impact on the Kosovo Economy: Spending Effects 1999–2006 and the Possible Consequences of Downsizing*, Pristina: UNMIK European Union Pillar.

Wittman, G.H. (2010), 'No Kumbaya in Kabul', *American Spectator*, 23 June.

Wolf, S. (2010), 'Assessing Eastern Europe's anti-corruption performance: Views from the Council of Europe, OECD and Transparency International', *Global Crime*, 11/2, 99–121.

Wolff, S. and K. Cordell (2010), 'Power-sharing', in K. Cordell and S. Wolff (eds), *The Routledge Handbook of Ethnic Conflict*, London and New York: Routledge, 300–310.

Wolpe, H. (2011), 'Making peace after genocide: Anatomy of the Burundi peace process', *Peaceworks* No. 70, Washington, DC: United States Institute of Peace.

Woodrow, P. (2006), *NGO Participation in Conflict Prevention in Burundi*, Cambridge, MA: Center for Development Action.

Woods, N. (2003), 'Iraq must buy time before turning to a free market: Life in post-cold war Russia should deter the coalition's haste for reform', *The Times*, 8 October.

Woods, N. (2006), *The Globalizers: The IMF, the World Bank, and their Borrowers*, Ithaca, NY: Cornell University Press.

Woodward, B. (2006), *State of Denial*, New York: Simon & Schuster.

Woodward, P. (2006a), *US Foreign Policy and the Horn of Africa*, Aldershot: Ashgate.

Woodward, P. (2006b), 'Peacemaking in Sudan', in O. Furley and R. May (eds), *Ending Africa's Wars: Progressing to Peace*, Aldershot: Ashgate, 169–180.

Woodward, S.L. (1995), *Socialist Unemployment: The Political Economy of Yugoslavia 1945 – 1990*, Princeton, NJ: Princeton University Press.

Woodward, S.L. (2002), *On War and Peacebuilding: Unfinished Legacy of the 1990s*, New York: Social Science Research Council.

Woodward, S.L. (2007), 'Does Kosovo's status matter? On the international management of statehood', *Südosteuropa*, 55/1, 1–25.

Woodward, S.L. (2011), 'The Bosnian paradox: On the causes of postwar inequality and barriers to its recognition and reduction', in A. Langer, F. Stewart and R. Venugopal (eds), *Horizontal Inequalities and Post-Conflict Development: Laying the Foundations for Durable Peace*, Basingstoke: Palgrave Macmillan, 131–157.

World Bank (1989), *Articles of Agreement* (as amended effective 16 February 1989), Washington, DC: World Bank.

World Bank (1997), *World Development Report 1997: The State in a Changing World*, New York: Oxford University Press for the World Bank.

World Bank (1998), *The World Bank's Experience with Post-Conflict Reconstruction*, Washington, DC: World Bank Operations Evaluation Department.

World Bank (2008), *Poverty in a Young Nation*, Washington, DC: World Bank.

World Bank (2009a), *A 2009 Update of Poverty Incidence in Timor-Leste using the Survey-to-Survey Imputation Method*, Washington, DC: World Bank.

World Bank (2009b), *Georgia: Poverty Assessment, April 2009*, Washington, DC: World Bank.

World Bank (2010), 'Economy rankings', available at www.doingbusiness.org/rankings, accessed 19 February 2012.

World Bank (2011), *World Development Report 2011: Conflict, Security, and Development*, Washington, DC: World Bank.

World Economic Forum (2010), *The Global Competitiveness Report, 2010–2011*, Geneva: World Economic Forum.

Wunch, N. and J. Rappold (2010), *Western Balkans: EU Enlargement in Crisis*, DGAP Analyse No. 6, Berlin: Deutsche Gesellschaft für Auswaertige Politik.

Xharra, J. (2009), 'Kosovo: Journalist under fire', *Balkan Investigative Reporting Network*, 4 June.

Yabi, G.O. (2010), *The Role of ECOWAS in Managing Political Crisis and Conflict: The Cases of Guinea and Guinea-Bissau*, Abuja: Friedrich-Ebert-Stiftung.

Young, J. (2007), *Emerging North-South Tensions and Prospects for a Return to War*, Geneva: Small Arms Survey.

Zakhilwal, O. and J.M. Thomas (2008), 'Afghanistan: What kind of peace? The role of rural development in peacebuilding', in S. Baranyi (ed.), *The Paradoxes of Peacebuilding Post-9/11*, Vancouver: University of British Columbia Press, 147–178.

Zartmann, W. (ed.) (1995), *Collapsed States: The Disintegration and Restoration of Legitimate Authority*, Boulder, CO: Lynne Rienner.

Zaum, D. (2007), *The Sovereignty Paradox: The Norms and Politics of International Statebuilding*, Oxford: Oxford University Press.

Zaum, D. (2011), 'The new protectorates: Statebuilding and legitimacy', in James Mayall and Ricardo Soares de Oliveira (eds), *The New Protectorates: International Tutelage and the Making of Liberal States*, London: C. Hurst & Co, 281–295.

Zaum, D. (2012a), 'Beyond the liberal peace?' *Global Governance*, 18/1, 121–132.

Zaum, D. (2012b), 'Statebuilding and governance: The conundrums of legitimacy and local ownership', in Devon Curtis and Gwinyayi Dzinesa (eds), *Peacebuilding, Power, and Politics in Africa*, Athens: Ohio University Press, 80–101.

Index

26999672R00230

Printed in Great Britain
by Amazon